In this well-e̶ Simon Baughen expertly covers the whole spectrum of English shipping law, placing the highly specialised rules of shipping in a commercial context and relating them to the general principles of contract and tort law. The book's accessible narrative and useful glossary of key terms will especially benefit students new to shipping law or from non-law backgrounds.

In-depth commentary on judicial decisions and well-balanced coverage and analysis of recent and key cases, such as *The New Flamenco*, *The Ocean Victory* and *The Kos*, provide an up-to-date reference for all students on Shipping Law courses. The comprehensive overview of topics also ensures that the book is ably suited to course use, including discussion of such areas as:

- Bills of lading
- Charterparties
- Salvage
- Marine Pollution
- Arbitration
- Accidents and collisions

Fully updated throughout, this sixth edition provides an invaluable source of reference and will be of use to both students and to those in practice.

Simon Baughen is Professor of Shipping Law at Swansea University. Previously Reader at the University of Bristol Law School, he studied law at Oxford and spent a number of years practising maritime law.

Shipping Law

SIXTH EDITION

Simon Baughen

Routledge
Taylor & Francis Group

LONDON AND NEW YORK

Sixth edition published 2015
by Routledge
2 Park Square, Milton Park, Abingdon, Oxon OX14 4RN

and by Routledge
711 Third Avenue, New York, NY 10017

Routledge is an imprint of the Taylor & Francis Group, an informa business

First published by Cavendish Publishing Limited 1998
Fifth edition published by Routledge 2012

British Library Cataloguing in Publication Data
A catalogue record for this book is available from the British Library

Library of Congress Cataloging-in-Publication Data
Baughen, Simon, author.
  Shipping law / Simon Baughen.—Sixth edition.
     pages cm
  Includes index.
  ISBN 978-0-415-71218-7 (hbk)—ISBN 978-0-415-71219-4 (pbk)—
  ISBN 978-1-315-88421-9 (ebk)   1. Maritime law—Great Britain.   I. Title.
  KD1819.B38 2015
  343.4109'6—dc23   2014035778

ISBN: 978-0-415-71218-7 (hbk)
ISBN: 978-0-415-71219-4 (pbk)
ISBN: 978-1-315-88421-9 (ebk)

Typeset in Joanna
by RefineCatch Limited, Bungay, Suffolk

Printed and bound by CPI Group (UK) Ltd, Croydon, CR0 4YY

Outline Contents

Detailed Contents

Preface to the Sixth Edition

Since the publication of the fifth edition in 2011 the world of maritime law has seen a number of significant developments. The 2007 Nairobi International Convention on the Removal of Wrecks, which the UK has ratified, will come into effect on 14 April 2015. However, the 2010 HNS Convention is still to come into force and progress on the 2009 Rotterdam Rules is moving at a snail's pace with only three ratifications to date.

The situation within the EU has continued to be dominated by developments in the saga of the 'Italian torpedo', where a party to an English arbitration agreement runs off to commence litigation in the courts of another EU Member State, in breach of their contractual undertaking. Following the ECJ's decision in 2009 in *The Front Comor* – Case C-185/07; [2009] 1 AC 1138 – it is no longer possible to obtain an anti-suit injunction from the English courts in respect of the foreign proceedings. However, if an arbitral award is obtained and turned into a judgment under s.66 of the Arbitration Act 1996 and this happens before a judgment is given under the foreign proceedings, it may be possible to block enforcement of the foreign judgment at least in England by reference to art. 34 (3) of the Judgment Regulation. In *West Tankers Inc v Allianz SpA*, the shipowners obtained a final arbitration award in England declaring that they were under no liability to the insurers in respect of the collision and the Court of Appeal, [2012] 1 Lloyd's Rep. 398, upheld the decision of Field J that the award should be converted into a judgment. Such a pre-emptive strike was successfully launched in *The London Steam-Ship Owners' Mutual Insurance Association Ltd v The Kingdom of Spain, The French State (The Prestige)* [2013] EWHC 3188 (Comm); [2014] 1 Lloyd's Rep. 309, where Spain and France brought criminal proceedings in Spain against the master of the *Prestige* in respect of the oil spill off the coast of Galicia in 2002. Attached to these proceedings was a claim for civil compensation to which the vessel's P&I Club were joined and which claimed compensation far in excess of the shipowner's limitation figure under the 1992 CLC. The Club commenced arbitration against France and Spain and obtained an award declaring that their liability would be subject to the terms of the shipowner's insurance with the Club, including the 'pay and be paid' clause. In October 2014 Hamblen J held that the award could be converted into a judgment.

There have been two other significant developments in the EU. First, the Judgments Regulation has been amended with effect from January 2015 and will be known as the Recast Regulation. It applies to legal proceedings instituted on or after 10 January 2015. This has entailed some renumbering of the articles of the Regulation and the admission of new provisions which should limit the future scope of 'torpedo' actions. Article 31(2) of the Recast Regulation now provides that where an EU Member State court, in favour of which an exclusive jurisdiction clause exists, is seized then any other EU Member State court shall stay its proceedings and this is reinforced by Recital 22. Recital 12 emphasises the free-standing nature of the process and states that a court's decision that an arbitration clause is void does not preclude its award on the substance being enforced under the Regulation and so reverses the decision in *The Wadi Sudr*, [2010] 1 Lloyd's Rep 193. Secondly Directive 2013/30 on safety of offshore oil and gas operations has extended the ambit of the provisions of the Environmental Liability Directive 2004/35 so that the ambit of damage to surface water covers all EU waters including the exclusive economic zone (about 370 km from the coast) and the continental shelf where the coastal member states exercise jurisdiction, with a transposition deadline of 19 July 2015.

There have been several important developments in shipping law in cases before the courts of England and Wales. In *The Kos*, [2012] 2 A.C. 164, the Supreme Court considered the relationship between shipowners and time charterers following a withdrawal when cargo remained on the vessel and had to be discharged. It overturned the decision of the Court of Appeal and held that the shipowners could claim the time and costs of the discharge operations from the charterers by way of a claim for indemnity and by reference to the law of bailment. The tenor of the judgments makes it likely that such a claim would also be successful in the event that the shipowners complete voyages under 'freight prepaid' bills of lading following withdrawal of the vessel. This runs contrary to what had generally assumed to be the position following Lord Denning MR's *dicta* to the contrary in [1982] 1 Lloyd's Rep 232, 237. It has generally been a profitable few years for shipowners in their relationships with time charterers. In *The Astra* [2013] 2 Lloyd's Rep. 69 Flaux J held that following a withdrawal the shipowners could claim damages for losses sustained as a result of having to refix their vessel at a lower rate than that in the withdrawn charter, classifying the obligation to pay hire as a condition. Again this runs contrary to the general assumption, based on Lord Diplock's *dicta* in *The Afovos* [1983] 1 WLR 195 that the obligation to pay hire is an innominate term and not a condition. Further changes have been seen in the Court of Appeal's decision in *The Lehmann Timber* [2013] 2 Lloyd's Rep 541 whereby the costs to the shipowner of exercising a lien on cargo are recoverable from charterers. There have also been two important decisions on the calculation of damages following charterer's repudiation of a charterparty. In *The Glory Wealth* [2013] EWHC 3153 (Comm); [2014] 2 W.L.R. 1405, the compensatory principle referred to in *The Golden Victory* was applied in a case of an accepted repudiation which did not involve a right of cancellation that would have been exercised had the contract not been repudiated. In *The New Flamenco* [2014] EWHC 1547 (Comm) Popplewell J held that in assessing owners' damages no account was to be taken in the benefit to owners of being able to sell the vessel in 2007 following the repudiation as this was not a benefit legally caused by charterer's breach. The area of charterer's liability in respect of unsafe ports has also been the subject of judicial enquiry with the finding in *The Ocean Victory* [2014] 1 Lloyd's Rep. 59 that the insurance provisions of cl.12 of Barecon 1989 did not provide a complete code to deal with insured losses and that the demise charterers accordingly remained liable under the safe port warranty.

In the field of cargo claims, there has been the decision in *The EEMS Solar* [2013] 2 Lloyd's Rep 487 (QB) holding that the principle in *The Jordan II* applies where a bill of lading incorporates the terms of a charter providing that charterers are to load, stow and discharge, but which makes no reference to shippers and/or receivers. Section 2(1) of COGSA 1992 has received very recent judicial attention in *The Erin Schulte* which involved a bank to whom bills of lading had been indorsed pursuant to a letter of credit and which then refused to pay out under the credit, while retaining the bills. In doing so it held the bills on account of the shippers and the Court of Appeal within the last month, [2014] EWCA Civ 1382, has overruled the first instance decision referred to in Chapter 2 of this edition, and held that there was no completion of delivery by indorsement and that while the bank had the bills but were not paying under the credit they were not the lawful holder of the bills. When the bank did eventually relent, by which time the cargo had been discharged, they then became the lawful holder under the provisions of the Act relating to spent bills.

This edition takes account of the law as of 1 November 2014.

Simon Baughen
November 2014

Acknowledgements

I would like to thank the following people who have read and commented on sections of this book. Their help has been very much appreciated. Any errors that remain are, of course, my own:

- Professor Jonathan Hill of the School of Law, University of Bristol;
- Professor Gerard McMeel of the School of Law, University of Bristol;
- Joanne Moody;
- Alison Shaw-Lloyd;
- Juan Carlos Ortiz Camacho.

Thanks also to Professor Francis Rose, George Arghyrakis, Natalie Campbell and Dr Raid Al-Zude.

Thanks to Philip Hinks for assisting in the updating of Chapters 18 and 19 for the fourth edition.

I would also like to acknowledge the debt that I owe to all those to whom I have taught this subject over the years: your questions about 'obvious' points have greatly assisted my understanding of the subject.

Table of Cases

Table of Statutes

Table of Statutory Instruments

Table of International Conventions

Abbreviations

BIFA	British International Freight Association
BIMCO	Baltic and International Maritime Council
Bolero	Bills of Lading in Europe
cif	cost, insurance, freight
CJEU	Court of Justice of the European Union
CLC	International Convention on Civil Liability for Oil Pollution Damage 1969
CMI	Comité Maritime International
CMR	UN Convention Relative au Contrat de Transport International de Marchandises par Route
COGSA	Carriage of Goods by Sea Act
COTIF	Convention Internationale sur le Transport de Marchandises par Chemin de Fer
CPR	Civil Procedure Rules
ECJ	European Court of Justice
EDI	electronic document interchange
EFTA	European Free Trade Association
ETA	estimated time of arrival
FCL	full container load
F, D & D	freight, defence and demurrage
fiost	free in, out, stowed and trimmed
fob	free on board
grt	gross register tonnage
HNS	Hazardous and Noxious Substances
ICA	Inter-Club Agreement
ICC	International Chamber of Commerce
IMO	International Maritime Organisation
ISU	International Salvage Union
LANBY	large automatic navigation buoy
LCL	less than container load
LLMC	Convention on Limitation of Liability for Maritime Claims
LMAA	London Maritime Arbitration Association
LOF	Lloyd's Open Form
LSSA	Lloyd's Standard Salvation and Arbitration clauses
MTO	multimodal transport operator
NODISP	no disposal
NOR	notice of readiness
NVOC	non-vehicle-owning carrier
NYPE	New York Produce Exchange
OBO	oil, bulk, ore carriers
OLSA	Ocean Liner Service Agreement
OPOL	Offshore Pollution Liability Agreement
PD	Practice Direction

P&I	protection and indemnity
Ro-ro	roll-on, roll-off
RSC	Rules of the Supreme Court
SCOPIC	Special Compensation P&I Clause
SDR	Special Drawing Right
SMS	safety management system
STOPIA	Small Tanker Oil Pollution Indemnification Agreement
TEU	twenty foot or equivalent units
TOPIA	Tanker Oil Pollution Indemnification Agreement
UNCITRAL	United Nations Commission on International Trade Law
UNCTAD	United Nations Commission on Trade and Development
wccon	whether customs cleared or not
wibon	whether in berth or not
wifpon	whether in free pratique or not
wipon	whether in port or not

Glossary

A

Actual authority. The authority that an agent actually has, either expressly or impliedly, so as to bind its principal.

Apparent authority. The authority that an agent appears to have to third parties, which will bind its principal in the absence of actual authority.

Approach voyage. The preliminary voyage made from the vessel's discharging port under a previous charterparty to the loading port or berth under a voyage charter.

Arrest. Judicial detention of a vessel pending provision of security for a maritime claim. The procedure is also used to serve *in rem* proceedings on a vessel.

Arrived ship. A ship that has arrived at the geographical position from which notice of readiness can be given under a voyage charter.

Attornment. The acknowledgment by a bailee in actual possession of goods of a transfer of constructive possession from the bailor to a third party.

B

Bail bond. Formal security provided to secure a vessel's release from arrest. Security may also be provided by the provision of a letter of undertaking from the shipowner's P&I Club.

Bailment. Obligations in respect of goods that arise out of the transfer of possession in them from a bailor to a bailee, such as a carrier or warehouseman. The bailee will be strictly liable for loss or damage to the goods that occurs while they are in its custody unless it can prove that it took reasonable care of them.

Bareboat charter. *See* Demise charterparty.

Berth charterparty. A voyage charter where the vessel becomes 'arrived' on reaching the loading or discharging berth.

Bill of lading. A receipt issued by or on behalf of the shipowner in respect of goods loaded on board its ship. As well as being a receipt, the bill of lading may also act as a contract and a document of title. In issuing a bill of lading, the shipowner undertakes to the consignor to deliver the goods only on presentation of an original bill of lading relating to those goods. This undertaking is transferable to subsequent holders of the bill of lading without any further involvement of the shipowner. The use of the words 'to order' or 'to assigns' indicates the transferability of this undertaking, which is what gives the document its character as a document of title.

- *Bearer bill of lading.* A bill of lading that does not identify a consignee, but is merely marked 'to order'. When a bearer bill is transferred to a third party, constructive possession can be transferred without the need for indorsement of the bill.
- *Charterer's bill of lading.* A bill of lading issued by a charterer rather than a shipowner. Any implied or statutory contract that arises under this document will be with the charterer, rather than the shipowner.
- *Charterparty bill of lading.* A bill of lading that incorporates the terms of a charterparty.
- *Claused bill of lading.* A bill of lading that contains adverse remarks as to the apparent order and condition of the goods to which it refers, or a bill of lading that contains qualifications as to the weight or quantity of the goods loaded thereunder.
- *Clean bill of lading.* A bill of lading that notes the loading of goods in apparent good order and condition.
- *Combined transport bill of lading.* A bill of lading issued for carriage that will involve more than one mode of transport, for example, road and sea carriage.

- *Freight forwarder's bill of lading.* A bill of lading whereby the contractual carrier will be a freight forwarder, notwithstanding that this party will play no physical role in the actual carriage of the goods.
- *Freight prepaid bill of lading.* A bill of lading marked in this manner will generally prevent the carrier from claiming freight from the bill of lading holder or from exercising a lien over its cargo.
- *Liner bill of lading.* A bill of lading under which the carrier is responsible for loading, stowing and discharging the cargo.
- *Ocean bill of lading.* A bill of lading under which the carrier's responsibilities for the cargo start with its loading and end with its discharge.
- *Order bill of lading.* A bill of lading that names a consignee, for example, 'to X or order'. The bill of lading must be indorsed by the consignee, by signing the reverse of the bill, when it transfers the document to a third party.
- *Received for shipment bill of lading.* A bill of lading that records receipt of the goods by the carrier at a time prior to that at which they are loaded onto the carrying vessel.
- *Shipowner's bill of lading.* A bill of lading under which the shipowner is the contractual carrier.
- *Shipped bill of lading.* A bill of lading that records receipt of the goods by the carrier at the time that they are loaded onto the carrying vessel.
- *Spent bill of lading.* A bill of lading that can no longer be used to transfer constructive possession in the goods that it represents, for example, where the person entitled to possession of those goods receives the bill of lading after it has actually taken delivery of the goods.
- *Straight bill of lading.* A bill of lading that names a consignee, but is not a document of title due to the absence of words such as 'to order'. Such a document is very similar to a waybill, save that delivery still has to be made against production of an original bill of lading.
- *Through bill of lading.* A bill of lading that is issued when the carriage will involve transshipment. Depending on the terms of the bill, the initial carrier may continue to be liable after transshipment.

Breach of warranty of authority. An agent's liability to a third party in respect of losses suffered by that party as a result of the agent's not having the authority that it claimed to bind its principal.

Brussels Convention 1968. An international convention regulating jurisdiction and enforcement of judgments in the courts of EC Member States, which has been incorporated into the law of the UK.

Bunkers. Fuel oil and diesel oil used in the running of a vessel.

C

Carrier. The party contractually liable under a bill of lading for the carriage of the goods referred to therein.

Carrying voyage. The voyage, under a voyage charterparty, that starts with the completion of loading and ends when the vessel becomes an 'arrived ship' at the port or berth of discharge.

Cesser clause. A clause in a voyage charterparty under which the charterer's liability ceases at some stage before completion of discharge, for example, on completion of loading.

Charterparty. A contract for the carriage of goods for a particular voyage (voyage charter), or a contract for the use of the vessel for a set period of time (time charter), or a contract that is a hybrid of these two forms (trip charter). If the charterer provides its own crew, the charter is a bareboat or demise charter.

CIF (cost, insurance, freight) contract. A sale contract under which the seller arranges and pays for the carriage of the goods and their insurance whilst in transit. The seller will assign its insurance policy to the buyer and this will form one of the documents, along with the bill of lading, against which it will receive payment of the purchase price.

CLC Convention. An international convention regarding civil liability for maritime oil pollution. There are two versions: the 1969 and the 1992 Conventions. The UK applies the latter.

CMI. The Comité Maritime International is a private organisation of national maritime law associations, which was established in 1897 in Antwerp as a committee of the International Law Association. It has been responsible for the adoption of a great number of international maritime conventions, such as the Hague Rules and the 1952 Collision and Arrest Conventions. It has also drafted various sets of rules for voluntary adoption, such as the York Antwerp Rules on General Average and the 1990 Uniform Rules for Waybills and for Electronic Documentation.

CMR. An international convention regulating international contracts for the carriage of goods by road.

Common carrier. The status of a shipowner who carries goods in the absence of any express contract. A shipowner who deviates will be demoted to this status.

Consignee. The person named in the bill of lading, or waybill, as the person to whom delivery of the goods loaded thereunder is to be made.

Consignor. The person entitled to possession of goods at the time that they are loaded onto a ship. The bill of lading should be issued to this party even if another party has made the contract of carriage with the shipowner, for example, an fob buyer.

Constructive possession. The right to take delivery of goods at the discharge port from a carrier who is currently in actual possession of them.

Conversion. The tort of wrongful interference with possessory rights in chattels. A carrier will be liable in conversion if it delivers goods to a party who does not have possessory title to them.

D

Deadfreight. Compensation due from a charterer for failing to load the minimum quantity of cargo specified in the charter. The shortfall in cargo loaded will give rise to a liability assessed at the freight rate.

Delivery order. An instruction by the bill of lading holder to the shipowner as to delivery of bulk cargo to a third party who has bought part of the cargo referred to in the bill of lading. Where the shipowner or its agent 'attorns', by agreeing to follow the instructions, the delivery order is a 'ship's delivery order'. Otherwise, it is a 'merchant's delivery order'.

Demise charterparty. A charterparty under which the charterer appoints its own crew. Where there is a demise charter, cargo claims must generally be made against the demise charterer, rather than the shipowner. There are specific statutory provisions to permit the arrest of vessels on demise charter in respect of maritime claims against the demise charterer.

Demise clause. A clause that identifies the contractual carrier under a bill of lading.

Demurrage. A liquidated damages clause in a voyage charterparty for all time used in loading or discharging cargo from the vessel after the expiry of laytime.

Despatch. Compensation payable to a charterer under a voyage charterparty in the event that loading or discharge finishes before the expiry of laytime, usually assessed at half the demurrage rate.

Detention. Liability of a charterer in respect of delays occurring prior to the commencement of laytime, for example, for failure to nominate a load port within a reasonable time.

Deviation. Failure of a carrying vessel to keep to the usual, direct geographical route between the ports of loading and discharge.

Disponent owner. A charterer who subcharters the vessel. Under the subcharterparty, the charterer will assume the rights and obligations of a shipowner, as regards the subcharterer.

Documentary credit. *See* Letter of credit.

Document of title. A document by which the holder acquires constructive possession in the goods to which it refers.

E

Endorsement. *See* Indorsement.

F

Fob (free on board) contract. A sale contract under which the buyer is responsible for paying for and arranging the carriage of the goods and the seller is obliged to get the goods to the quayside so as to enable them to be loaded onto the vessel nominated by the buyer.

Forum non conveniens. A ground for staying proceedings on the basis that another forum is the appropriate forum in which to bring those proceedings.

Free in/free out. A clause that allocates responsibility for loading and discharge to the charterer or bill of lading holder.

Freezing order. An order of the court preventing the defendant from removing some or all of its assets from the jurisdiction (formerly known as a 'Mareva injunction').

Freight. Payment made under a voyage charter for use of the vessel, either by way of a lump sum or calculated by reference to the quantity of cargo loaded. Depending on the terms of the charter, it may either be paid in advance, on completion of loading, or on 'right and true delivery' at the port of discharge.

Freight forwarder. A party acting as agent for shippers for the purpose of arranging carriage of goods for them. Sometimes, this party will contract with a shipper to carry the goods, as principal, and not merely to arrange carriage.

G

General average. A mode of apportioning extraordinary sacrifices and expenditure that are incurred on a voyage for the benefit of all concerned, among the shipowner, the cargo owners and the charterers according to the value of their interests in the voyage.

H

Hague, Hague-Visby Rules, Hamburg Rules. Mandatory codes governing the contractual terms applicable to bill of lading contracts. The UK currently applies the Hague-Visby Rules, which have the 'force of law' under the **Carriage of Goods by Sea Act 1971**.

Himalaya clause. A clause that extends to independent contractors, servants and agents of the carrier the benefits of exceptions and limitations available to a carrier under a bill of lading.

Hire. Daily rate of payment under a time charter by the charterer for the use of the vessel. Usually paid in advance in monthly or semi-monthly instalments.

HNS Convention 1996. An international convention, which is not yet in force, regulating civil liability for pollution arising out of the sea carriage of hazardous and noxious substances.

Hull and machinery cover. Insurance cover taken out by shipowners to cover loss or damage sustained by their vessels.

I

Identity of carrier clause. *See* Demise clause.

IMO. The International Maritime Organization (until 1982, the Inter-governmental Maritime Consultative Organization) is a specialised agency of the United Nations that has been responsible for the preparation and implementation of many important international conventions on maritime conventions, such as the 1974 Safety of Life at Sea Convention (SOLAS), and the CLC and Fund Conventions, and subsequent Protocols that deal with compensation for loss or damage due to oil pollution at sea.

Implied contract. A contract that is inferred from the conduct of the carrier and the consignor on loading or the carrier and the receiver on discharge.

Indemnity. A promise, express or implied, by one party to pay costs incurred by another party as a consequence of acting on its instructions. Examples include: the time charterer's obligation to indemnify the shipowner in respect of losses sustained as a consequence of following its orders as to the employment of the vessel; the receiver's indemnity to the shipowner as to the losses that it may incur in agreeing to deliver without presentation of an original bill of lading; and the shipper's indemnity to the shipowner in respect of losses that it may sustain by reason of issuing a 'clean' bill of lading for damaged cargo. This last indemnity is generally unenforceable.

Indorsement. The transfer of an 'order' bill by the consignee to a third party. Physical delivery is insufficient to effect a transfer of constructive possession. The consignee must also 'indorse' the bill of lading by signing it, usually on the reverse. The third party is known as the 'indorsee' (or endorsee).

In personam. Legal proceedings that are brought against an individual, for example, the registered owner of a ship. Where the defendant is based outside the jurisdiction of the English High Court, leave of the court must generally be obtained to serve proceedings.

In rem. Legal proceedings that are brought against the ship itself, with service generally being effected by the arrest procedure. After proceedings are served, the action takes on many of the characteristics of an *in personam* action against the registered owner, or demise charterer, of the vessel.

L

Laytime. The contractual time allowed to a voyage charterer within which the vessel is to be loaded and discharged.

Letter of credit. The financing of an international sale contract whereby payment is made to the seller by a bank on presentation of various documents, the most important of which will be the bill of lading. The seller will be paid either by its own bank (the correspondent bank) or by the buyer's bank (the issuing bank).

Liberty clause. A clause authorising the carrier to deviate in specified circumstances.

Lien. Either a right to retain possession of cargo to secure outstanding claims due to the carrier (a lien on cargo) or the right of the carrier to intercept subfreights due to the charterer from its subcharterer (a lien on subfreights). *See, also*, Maritime lien and Statutory lien.

Limitation. A mechanism for capping the carrier's overall responsibility for certain maritime claims. 'Package limitation' does this by fixing a maximum amount per package for which the carrier can be liable. The Hague, Hague-Visby and Hamburg Rules all contain different package limitation provisions. 'Tonnage limitation' fixes the overall maximum liability of the carrier for all maritime claims arising out of a single incident, by reference to a sum related to the tonnage of the vessel. There are two international tonnage limitation conventions, the 1957 and the 1976 Conventions, the provisions of which vary substantially. The UK is a signatory to the 1976 Convention.

Lis alibi pendens. A ground for staying proceedings on the basis that the same or related proceedings have already been commenced in a court in another jurisdiction.

LOF (Lloyd's Open Form). A standard form of salvage contract that is in widespread use. Key features are the agreement that disputes be arbitrated and the admission that the salved vessel/cargo was in a position of danger. The most recent version is LOF 2011.

M

Mareva injunction. *See* Freezing order.

Maritime lien. A maritime claim, recognised at common law as justifying arrest of a vessel and one that remains valid despite changes in ownership of the vessel that gave rise to the claim.

Master. The captain of a vessel.

Multimodal transport. Carriage that involves more than one mode of transport, for example, road and air.

N

Notice of readiness (NOR). The notice that the master must give to the charterer's agents when the vessel becomes an 'arrived ship' under a voyage charterparty.

O

Off-hire. A provision in a time charter for the suspension of hire.

OLSA. Ocean Liner Service Agreement. *See* Volume Contract.

Ostensible authority. *See* Apparent authority.

P

P&I Clubs. Shipowners' mutual insurance associations to cover shipowners' liabilities for breaches of contracts of carriage, for torts committed by shipowners (for example, collisions) and for pollution liability. They are of great practical importance in shipping law. They also offer F, D & D (freight, defence and demurrage) cover, to indemnify members in respect of legal costs involved in connection with disputes under charterparties.

Port charterparty. A voyage charterparty where the vessel becomes an 'arrived ship' on reaching the usual waiting anchorage within the legal and commercial limits of the port of loading or discharge.

Q

Quantum meruit. A reasonable sum awarded for services generating an implied right to remuneration.

Quasi-deviation. Unauthorised stowage of cargo on deck.

R

Receiver. The party taking delivery of goods on discharge, usually on presenting the bill of lading to the vessel's captain (or master).

Res judicata. A ground for dismissing proceedings on the basis that a foreign judgment has been given in respect of the same proceedings.

Risk. The time at which the seller's responsibility for delivery of the goods crystallises. Under cif and fob contracts, risk will pass on the loading of the goods on to the vessel. However, property in those goods will usually pass later when payment is made against production of the shipping documents.

S

Salvage. Compensation awarded for the successful rescue of ships or cargo in danger at sea. The law of salvage is now governed by the Salvage Convention 1989, which has been incorporated into the law of the UK.

Shipper. Generally, the person who makes the initial contract of carriage with the carrier. However, it may also be used to refer to the consignor. This person may not always have made the initial contract of carriage, as is the case with most fob contracts.

Sister ship arrest. Arrest procedure available against a ship the registered owner of which would also be the person liable *in personam* in respect of a statutory lien in respect of another ship.

Statutory lien. A maritime claim justifying arrest of a vessel and which ceases to be valid if ownership of the vessel that gave rise to the claim is transferred to a third party before a writ is issued. These claims are derived from the 1952 Arrest Convention and are listed in s 20(2) of the **Supreme Court Act 1981**.

Stevedore. A docker.

Sub-bailment on terms. The doctrine that entitles a sub-bailee to rely on the terms of its sub-bailment when sued in bailment.

Supercession. The termination of the shipper's original contract of carriage and its replacement with another contract of carriage with another party, for example, where the shipper's initial contract with a time charterer is replaced by a contract with the shipowner on the issue of a shipowner's bill of lading.

T

Tackle to tackle. The period between the start of loading and the completion of discharge for which a carrier is responsible for the cargo under an ocean bill of lading; also known as the 'alongside' rule.

Time bar. The time set by statute or by contract for commencement of suit, failing which the claim will be barred. The most important statutory time bar is the 12-month time bar contained in the Hague-Visby Rules in relation to claims against carriers under bills of lading. A two-year time bar applies to salvage and collision claims.

Trip charter. A voyage charter that uses the format of a time charter.

U

UCP 500. A set of standard contractual terms regulating letters of credit. It has no statutory effect, but is in widespread use.

UNCITRAL. The United Nations Commission on International Trade Law was established in

1966, with the aim of harmonising and unifying international trade law. It was responsible for the 1978 Hamburg Rules and the 1991 Convention of the Liability of Operators of Transport Terminals in International Trade. It is currently drafting an instrument on carriage of goods.

V

Volume contract. A contract of carriage that provides for the carriage of a specified quantity of goods in a series of shipments during an agreed period of time. Also known as an Ocean Liner Service Agreement (OLSA).

W

War risks cover. Additional hull and machinery cover that is taken out to maintain this cover when the vessel enters areas that are excluded from cover by virtue of war risks associated with trading in those areas.

Waybill. A non-negotiable receipt under which delivery is made to the named consignee upon proof being provided of their identity. Unlike a 'straight' bill of lading, the consignee named in a waybill need not present any document to obtain delivery.

Withdrawal. The option given to a shipowner to terminate a time charter in the event that an instalment of hire is not paid in full or is not paid promptly.

Y

York Antwerp Rules. A set of rules regulating general average. They have no statutory force, but are widely used. The most recent version was published in 2004, although earlier versions, such as the 1974 and 1994 versions, may still be used.

Part 1

Dry Shipping

Chapter 1

The Commercial Background

Chapter Contents

A shipowner's business principally consists of satisfying the demands made by parties to contracts of sale that are located in different countries. The structure of these international sale contracts has had a profound influence on the contracts of carriage made by sellers and buyers to fulfil their commitments towards each other. Therefore, it is helpful to examine this underlying sales structure before going on to consider the nature of the carriage contracts that it generates.

International sales of goods

International sales of goods differ from domestic sales in two important respects.[1] First, there is the inconvenience of having payment on delivery when buyer and seller are in different countries. Secondly, there is a commercial need to be able to sell and resell certain types of cargo while in transit. Some oil cargoes, for example, may be sold and resold over 100 times while in transit. The **1980 United Nations Convention on Contracts for the International Sale of Goods** (the 'CISG') provides a comprehensive international code for commercial sales of goods and came into force on 1 January 1988. However, it has not been ratified by the UK, which regulates sales of goods through the **Sale of Goods Act 1979**.

The two most common types of international sales contract are the fob and the cif contract. Under the fob (free on board) contract, the buyer pays for and arranges carriage and the seller's duty is to load the goods onto a vessel nominated by the buyer. In contrast, under a cif (cost, insurance, freight) contract, it is the seller who pays for and arranges carriage, as well as takes out a policy of insurance on the goods, which will be assigned to the buyer. There are a number of variants,[2] but these are the two most significant contractual forms.

Both contracts' forms display two distinctive characteristics.

Payment against documents

With a sale against documents, the parties contract that payment will be made by the seller tendering various documents to the buyer in return for the contract price. These will include the invoice for the goods and, with a cif contract, the insurance policy covering the goods. However, the most important document that must be tendered under a fob or a cif contract is the bill of lading. This is a multipurpose document, which serves as a receipt, a document conferring constructive possession in the sale goods during the period of their carriage, a document of title and a potentially transferable contract of carriage. These functions will shortly be examined in more detail.

As will be explained below, possession of the bill of lading will confer on its holder constructive possession of the goods during their carriage. This is because the shipowner, who has actual possession, will only deliver the goods to a party presenting a bill of lading that covers them. Therefore, the seller knows that, by retaining the bill of lading, it will also retain control over the sale goods until the buyer pays the contract price. In turn, the buyer will feel secure in paying against this document, because possession of the bill of lading will enable it to take delivery of the goods described therein. If the buyer wishes to resell the goods while they are afloat, it can do so by making a sub-sale, which also provides for payment against transfer of documents relating to the goods, as opposed to payment against actual delivery of the goods. Under these types of contract, the seller will owe a dual obligation to the buyer. The first obligation relates to delivery of the goods themselves; the second relates to transfer to the buyer of documentation relating to the goods.

---

1 For further details, see Atiyah, P, *The Sale of Goods*, 9th edn, 1995, London: Pitman.
2 Such as the c & f contract, which is a cif contract without the insurance element.

The financing role of banks

Cif and fob sales are usually mediated through banks that finance the sales under 'letters of credit'. The buyer will instruct its bank to open a letter of credit in favour of the seller. This will usually be on the terms of UCP 600, a purely voluntary set of rules, which are generally used by banks when opening a letter of credit.[3] The seller will tender the documents specified by the letter of credit to the buyer's bank, which will pay the price in exchange for the documents on being satisfied that the documents conform with the description set out in the terms of the letter of credit. Alternatively, the buyer's bank, 'the issuing bank', may arrange for payment to be made by another bank in the seller's country, 'the correspondent bank'. The seller will then present the documents to the 'correspondent' bank, which will, in turn, pass the documents on to, and receive payment from, the 'issuing' bank.

The buyer's bank will be entitled to retain the documents until the buyer makes reimbursement of the sale price, which has been advanced by the bank. If the buyer needs the bill of lading to resell the goods, the bank may release it in return for a 'trust receipt' under which the buyer declares itself trustee of the goods for the bank. On sale of the goods, the buyer will hold the proceeds of sale on trust for the buyer. This proprietary remedy remains available to the bank so long as the sale proceeds remain traceable in equity. Although the indorsement of the bill of lading to the buyer's bank may transfer property in the goods to the buyer, the bank, as pledgee of those goods, will have the possession of the bill of lading and consequently constructive possession in the goods that it represents. If the buyer defaults, the bank will be able to realise its security by taking delivery of the goods and selling them.

Transfer of risk on loading

The seller's obligation to deliver goods of the contract specifications will crystallise not when the goods are actually delivered to the buyer, but when they are loaded onto the carrying vessel. Thereafter, the 'risk' in the goods will be with the buyer, even though constructive possession of, and property in, the goods will very probably remain with the seller pending payment by the buyer.[4] The transfer of risk on loading means that, vis-à-vis the seller, the buyer accepts the risk of loss or damage to the goods while in transit. So long as the goods match the contract description at the time of loading, the seller will be entitled to its price and will not be liable to the buyer if the goods are damaged between loading and their eventual physical delivery to the buyer. The contract description will specify not only the type, quantity and condition of goods being sold, but also a period of time within which they must be loaded.

For a buyer or a bank financing the purchase through a letter of credit, the transfer of risk on loading will only be acceptable if two conditions are met. First, there must exist some reliable documentary evidence to show that the seller has met its delivery obligations by loading goods of the contract description on board the vessel. Secondly, there must exist a reliable mechanism for recovering loss or damage sustained during transit from the carrier, in the absence of any recourse against the seller. As we shall see, the bill of lading satisfies both of these requirements.

---

3 UCP 600 became available for incorporation into letters of credit from 1 July 2007. A useful guide to UCP 600 can be found at <http://www.kantakji.com/fiqh/Files/Economics/5538.pdf> (accessed 11 April 2011). See, further, De Battista, C, 'The new UCP 600 – changes to the tender of the seller's shipping documents under letters of credit' [2007] JBL 329 and Ulph, J, 'The UCP 600: documentary credits in the 21st century' [2007] JBL 355–77. For a detailed examination of the types of shipping document acceptable to the banks under the previous version of UCP, UCP 500, see De Battista, C, 'Banks and the carriage of goods by sea: secure transport documents and the UCP 500' (1994) 9 Butterworths Journal of International Banking and Finance Law 329.

4 Under fob and cif contracts, the parties intend that risk should pass on loading, and this intention will displace the presumption in s 20 of the Sale of Goods Act 1979 that risk passes with property.

The four functions of the bill of lading

We shall now examine in more detail how the four functions of the bill of lading interrelate to satisfy the expectations of buyers and sellers in sales where risk passes on loading and payment is made against delivery of documents rather than delivery of the goods themselves.

Receipt

The bill of lading will state the condition and quantity of the goods when they are transferred into the custody of the carrier. It will also state the date on which they were loaded, and will identify the carrying vessel as well as the ports of loading and discharge. It will usually be prepared by the consignor, the party who is the current owner of the goods to be loaded onto the vessel. In doing so, it will rely on the 'mate's receipts', which are the ship's records of the cargo loaded and presented to an agent of the carrier, such as the captain of the vessel (the ship's 'master'), for signature. It is common for bills of lading to be issued in sets of three originals. Once the bills of lading have been signed, they will be issued to the party handing over custody of the goods to the carrier. This party is usually the current owner of the goods in question and is referred to as the 'shipper' or the 'consignor'. The carrier will usually be the shipowner, but this is not always the case. The carrier may, in fact, have chartered or subchartered the vessel.

The sale contract and, where applicable, the letter of credit, will usually require that the bills of lading tendered for payment to the buyer or the bank constitute what are called 'shipped', 'clean' bills of lading.

Where the goods are transferred into the custody of the carrier when loaded onto the vessel, the bill of lading will be a 'shipped' bill of lading. A 'shipped' bill will enable a buyer to whom risk passes on loading to check whether the goods at the time of loading match up to the description in the contract of sale. In contrast, where the goods are transferred into the carrier's custody at an earlier stage – for example, on delivery to the carrier's warehouse at the port of loading – the bill of lading will be a 'received for shipment' bill of lading. Such a bill can be turned into a 'shipped' bill if it is subsequently marked by the carrier or its agent to that effect.

A 'clean' bill of lading is one that contains an acknowledgment by the person on whose behalf the bills were signed that the goods described therein were loaded in 'apparent good order and condition'. If the bill of lading contains adverse comments as regards the condition of the goods on loading, it is called a 'claused' bill of lading.

Document transferring constructive possession

The bill of lading will have on its face a space identifying the party to whom delivery of the goods is to be made when the vessel reaches its port of discharge. This party is known as the 'consignee', although it obtains no contractual rights to take delivery merely by reason of being designated as such.[5] The consignor, as the original contracting party, retains the right to give new delivery instructions to the carrier, so long as it is still in possession of the bill of lading.[6] Furthermore, a bill of lading will not simply identify a party as the consignee. If X is the named consignee, the bill of lading will not instruct the shipowner simply to deliver to X, but rather to make delivery to 'the order of X or assigns' (an 'order' bill). Alternatively, the delivery instructions may be left blank without naming a consignee, or may simply state 'to order' or 'to order or assigns' (a 'bearer' bill).

---

5 However, a party named as consignee may obtain possessory rights over the goods specified in the bill of lading if the consignor designated it as consignee with the intention of completing a sale or a pledge to it. See *Kum v Wah Tat Bank Ltd* [1971] 1 Lloyd's Rep 439, PC.

6 *Mitchell v Ede* (1840) 11 Ad & El 888.

Such wording constitutes an undertaking by the carrier to the consignor that the cargo will be delivered to the person presenting an original bill of lading, whether that person be the named consignee or a subsequent holder of the bill of lading.[7] The unique characteristic of the bill of lading is that this initial delivery undertaking is transferable to subsequent holders of the document without the need for any further involvement of the carrier, so transferring constructive possession to the new holder of the document. Where a 'bearer' bill is involved, constructive possession can be transferred by simple physical transfer. However, where an 'order' bill is involved, something more is required. It must also be 'indorsed' by the named consignee signing the reverse of the bill. Two types of indorsement are possible: a special indorsement, which identifies the indorsee; and an indorsement in blank, which does not. After an indorsement in blank, the bill of lading can subsequently be transferred in the same manner as a bearer bill. In contrast, where any other type of document is involved, constructive possession can be transferred only if the party who gave the delivery undertaking expressly acknowledges that it will now honour that undertaking in favour of a third party. This process is known as 'attornment'. The bill of lading is, however, the only document under which, at common law, constructive possession can be transferred without an attornment.[8] The transfer of constructive possession will occur automatically on transfer of the bill of lading provided that such is the intention of the transferor. However, a bill of lading that only designates a consignee and lacks the additional wording 'to order' or 'to order or assigns' is known as a 'straight' bill. Such a bill can be used to effect only a single transfer of possession, from the consignor to the consignee.[9]

Constructive possession will entitle the holder of the bill of lading to claim the goods from the carrier, as bailee, at the port of discharge and to sue the carrier in conversion if the goods have been delivered to someone else. Such a misdelivery claim can also be made in contract, provided that, as will generally be the case, the bill of lading constitutes a contract between its holder and the carrier. The carrier who delivers to a party who cannot produce an original bill of lading runs the risk of being sued for misdelivery, even if s/he delivers to the named consignee[10] or to the owner of the goods.[11] In both situations, a bill of lading may well have been pledged to a bank by way of security for an advance and the bank will have constructive possession by virtue of holding an original bill of lading. Possessory rights, therefore, prevail over proprietary ones.

Given that bills of lading are frequently issued in sets of three or more originals, the carrier can never be sure that the person presenting the bill of lading actually possesses the best right to possess the goods.[12] However, if that risk materialises, the carrier will have a good defence to a misdelivery claim, whether in conversion or in contract, by virtue of having made delivery against production of an original bill of lading, provided that it had no notice of any want of title in the party presenting that bill.[13] A bill of lading is 'spent' once its transfer can no longer transfer constructive possession in the goods to which it refers.[14] This will happen when the party entitled to possession of the goods takes delivery of them on discharge prior to receiving an original bill of lading.

---

7 In addition, the carrier must also take reasonable steps to verify the identity of the consignee or indorsee who is presenting the bill to claim delivery. See Gaskell, Asariotis and Baatz in *Bills of Lading: Law and Practice*, 2000, London: LLP, at 14.22.
8 *Barber v Meyerstein* (1866) LR 2 CP 38; *Official Assignee of Madras v Mercantile Bank of India Ltd* [1935] AC 53, PC, 59. Indorsement of a bill of lading will therefore satisfy the requirements of s 29(4) of the Sale of Goods Act 1979 regarding the seller's delivery obligations when the goods are in the hands of a third party at the time of sale. However, 'attornment' is still required for establishing title to sue in bailment where the bill of lading holder is not the original bailor. This is discussed in more detail below: Chapter 2, pp 48–9.
9 *The Rafaela S* [2005] UKHL 11; [2005] 2 AC 423; affirming [2002] EWCA Civ 694; [2003] 2 Lloyd's Rep 113, CA.
10 *The Stettin* (1889) 14 PD 142.
11 As in *The Jag Shakti* [1986] AC 337.
12 The holder of the first assignment for value obtains a priority over those who obtain possession of the other bills. *Barber v Meyerstein* (1869–70) LR 4 HL 317.
13 *Glyn Mills Currie & Co v The East and West India Dock Co* (1882) 7 App Cas 591, HL.
14 *East West Corp v DKBS 1912* [2003] EWCA Civ 174; [2003] 1 Lloyd's Rep 239, applying *dicta* of Willes J in *Barber v Meyerstein* (1866) LR 2 CP 38, 53.

Document of title

Since *Lickbarrow v Mason*[15] in 1791, the courts have recognised the custom of merchants that the indorsement of a bill of lading could transfer not only possessory rights, but also rights of ownership in the goods described therein, if that was the intention of the parties when indorsing the bill of lading. The seller is not obliged to transfer property in the goods when they are delivered either to the buyer or to a carrier for delivery to the buyer. By s 19(1) of the **Sale of Goods Act 1979**, the seller is entitled to contract on the basis that it reserves a right of disposal over the goods in these situations until some condition, usually payment of the price, is satisfied. Where the bill of lading makes the goods deliverable to the order of the seller or its agent, s 19(2) provides a presumption that such a right of disposal has been reserved. If the bill of lading makes the goods deliverable to the order of the buyer, the statutory presumption does not apply. Nonetheless, the fact that the parties contract on the basis of a payment against documents will show their intent that the seller should still have this right of disposal.

The bill of lading is the only document of title recognised at common law.[16] However, it is not a fully negotiable document, in that the indorser cannot pass by indorsement any rights in the goods greater than those that s/he already has.[17]

A potentially transferable carriage contract

The bill of lading also serves a contractual function. It frequently evidences the terms of the initial contract of carriage. The **Carriage of Goods by Sea Act 1992**, replacing the **Bills of Lading Act 1855**, provides a statutory exception to the doctrine of privity of contract, allowing this initial contract to be passed down the chain of sellers, banks and buyers that may come into existence before the ultimate discharge of the goods. In most instances, the effect of the Act will be to ensure that contractual rights of suit are vested in the person with possessory rights over the goods described in the bill of lading.

The parties to this initial contract will be the 'carrier', usually the shipowner, and the 'shipper'. The meaning of the latter term depends upon the context in which it arises. When the courts have considered the parties to the initial contract, they have used the term to refer to the party who contracts with the carrier. That party will often be a different person from the 'consignor', to whom the bill of lading must be issued on completion of loading. However, in other contexts, the term 'shipper' has been used to mean 'consignor'.[18] The contracts of carriage made on or before loading will now be examined in more detail.

Contracts of carriage

The two main types of contract in use for the carriage of goods by sea are the bill of lading and the charterparty.

The bill of lading

The bill of lading not only provides information as to the goods loaded, it also contains contractual terms. These are usually to be found on the reverse of the document. Sometimes, the bill of lading

---

15 [1794] 5 TR 683.
16 *Official Assignee of Madras v Mercantile Bank of India Ltd* [1935] AC 53, PC.
17 Subject to the exceptions provided by s 24 of the Sale of Goods Act 1979 and by the Factors Act 1889 relating to dispositions by a mercantile agent (s 2), a seller in possession (s 8) and a buyer in possession (s 9).
18 The context of the discussion in Chapter 3 of the evidential effects of the bill of lading requires 'shipper' to refer to the consignor.

may expressly incorporate terms from another document, a charterparty, by the use of words of incorporation on its front. Charterparty terms will form no part of the bill of lading contract in the absence of such words of incorporation. The charterparty and the bill of lading remain two distinct contracts. This is equally true when the terms of a charterparty are expressly incorporated into the bill of lading.

If the shipper wishes to use only a part of the vessel, it will usually contract on the basis of the contractual terms contained in the bill of lading. The actual contract will be made informally when the shipper books space on the vessel. The initial contract may be made purely orally or may be committed to a short document, a 'booking note'. Unlike a charterparty, this initial contract is not definitive of the contractual terms. These will be fleshed out by the terms of the carrier's usual bill of lading, which will be issued when the goods are eventually loaded. This may happen expressly, as in *Armour & Co Ltd v Walford*,[19] or impliedly, as in *Pyrene Co Ltd v Scindia Navigation Co Ltd*.[20] The terms of the expected bill of lading will form part of the contract from its inception, even if no bill of lading is ever issued.

Bill of lading contracts with the shipper are subject to statutory intervention in three respects. First, the **Carriage of Goods by Sea Act 1971** provides that an international Convention, the Hague-Visby Rules, shall have the force of law as regards such terms of these contracts as concern the carriage of the goods, depending, *inter alia*, on the country in which the bill of lading is issued.[21] All bills of lading issued in the UK are subject to the Hague-Visby Rules. Secondly, the **Carriage of Goods by Sea Act 1992**[22] effects a statutory transfer of this initial contract to a party who subsequently becomes a 'lawful holder' of the bill of lading. Thirdly, both the **Carriage of Goods by Sea Act 1971** and the **Carriage of Goods by Sea Act 1992** entitle third-party holders of the bill of lading to rely on the truth of certain evidential statements contained in the bill of lading, notwithstanding that the carrier may possess the evidence necessary to refute them.

The voyage charterparty

If the whole or a substantial part of the vessel is to be used, as would be the case with bulk cargoes, then a *charterparty* is more likely to be used. This is a formal written contract, definitive of the terms of the contract between the parties. Where the vessel is required for just a single voyage, a *voyage charter* will generally be used. The charterer will pay *freight* to the carrier as its carrying charge. It will also undertake to load and discharge the vessel within a set period of time. This is known as *laytime*. If it exceeds this period, it will become liable to pay liquidated damages to the shipowner. This is known as *demurrage*. Voyage charters generally involve the use of the whole vessel, but can involve the use of only part of its cargo-carrying capacity. A variant of the voyage charter is the 'slot charter' of dry cargo ships adapted for the carriage of container boxes in twenty-foot or equivalent units (TEUs) in 'slots' or 'cells'. Instead of chartering the whole or part of a specific vessel, a container operator will book a set number of TEUs on sailings by ships of a particular operator.

Charterparties are subject to none of the statutory provisions that affect bills of lading. A bill of lading will still be issued, but in the hands of the charterer it will generally have no contractual significance. This is so whether or not the charterer receives the bill of lading when it is issued[23] or,

---

19 [1921] 3 KB 473.
20 [1954] 2 QB 402.
21 Many countries are still signatories to an earlier convention, the Hague Rules. The differences between the two conventions are discussed in detail in Chapter 5. A new convention, on international carriage of goods wholly or partly by sea, has recently been concluded by UNCITRAL and has been open for signing since September 2009. It will be known as 'The Rotterdam Rules' and is discussed in Chapter 6.
22 Replacing the Bills of Lading Act 1855.
23 *Rodoconachi, Sons and Co v Milburn Bros* (1886) 18 QBD 67, CA.

subsequently, on indorsement.[24] However, in the hands of parties other than the charterer, the bill of lading is likely to constitute a contract with the carrier by virtue of the statutory assignment effected by the **Carriage of Goods by Sea Act 1992**. The Act will still operate even if the bill of lading temporarily loses its contractual status when it passes through the hands of a charterer. Therefore, whether or not the shipper initially contracts on the basis of a charterparty, the buyer at the end of the sale chain who actually takes delivery of the goods will generally obtain a statutory right of action against the carrier for transit loss or damage. Such an action will be contractual on the terms of the bill of lading and will probably be subject to the provisions of the Hague-Visby Rules.

Contracts for the use of the vessel – time charters

Charterparties may also be defined not by relation to a particular voyage but by relation to a particular period of time. Such charters are called *time charters*, and *hire* rather than *freight* will be paid to the shipowner. Delays during the charter will be governed by an *off-hire* clause rather than by *laytime* and *demurrage* provisions. An important commercial feature of most time charters is that it will be the time charterer, and not the shipowner, who makes the express contracts with the shippers[25] whose goods are to be carried on the ship. Time charters have traditionally been regarded as contracts for the use of a vessel rather than contracts for the carriage of goods. This reflects the wider choice that such contracts extend to the charterer in relation to the cargoes that may be carried and the available voyage destinations. To a limited extent, the distinction is reflected in the law. For example, bills of lading and voyage charters, but not time charters, are excluded from the operation of the **Law Reform (Frustrated Contracts) Act 1943**. However, in many other areas, such as the operation of the **Carriage of Goods by Sea Acts 1971 and 1992**, the key division is between bills of lading and charterparties, whether voyage or time. The conceptual divide between the two types of charterparty has been further eroded by the emergence of a hybrid, the 'trip' charter, which is essentially a voyage charter, but one that adapts the contractual format of the time charter.

In both voyage and time charters, the crew will generally be employed by the shipowner. However, a time charterer may sometimes contract on the basis that it provides its own crew. Such a charter is known as a *demise charter*. Unlike an ordinary charterer, the demise charterer obtains a possessory interest in the chartered vessel.

Modifications to the traditional carriage contract model

The traditional view of the initial carriage contract is that it is an express contract between the shipper and the carrier for sea carriage and that a bill of lading will be issued in respect of the goods carried. This view needs to be modified in the following respects to take in developments in commercial practice over the years.

Use of documents other than the bill of lading

With changing patterns of international trade, other documents have emerged to duplicate many of the functions of the bill of lading.

---

24 *The President of India v Metcalfe Shipping Co Ltd (The Dunelmia)* [1970] 1 QB 289, CA.
25 Such parties will be shippers *vis-à-vis* the time charterer and consignors *vis-à-vis* the shipowner.

The sea waybill

In many trades, such as the container trade, it is not expected that the goods will be resold while afloat. The use of the bill of lading can cause problems if the goods reach the port of discharge before the bill of lading comes into the hands of the buyer. It will only be able to persuade the shipowner to deliver if it provides a suitable guarantee to indemnify the shipowner against any misdelivery claims. Apart from the inconvenience caused by arranging such guarantees, there will also be some cost involved for the buyer if the shipowner insists on a bank providing the guarantee.

These problems can be avoided by using a sea waybill. This is a non-negotiable form of bill of lading where delivery is to be made to the named consignee without any need for production of the original waybill. Although the sea waybill is or evidences a contract between the carrier and the consignor, the **Carriage of Goods by Sea Act 1992** now gives the named consignee in a waybill a right to sue the carrier in contract on the terms contained in the waybill. The sea waybill therefore has a contractual and an evidential effect, but is not capable of transferring either title or constructive possession to the goods described therein. For these reasons, the sea waybill is not well adapted to use in letters of credit. If a bank is named as consignee, it takes the risk that the carrier may accept instructions from the consignor to deliver to a new consignee. This can be avoided if the bank is named as consignor, but in doing so, it exposes itself to any liabilities to the shipowner that may be outstanding under the contract of carriage evidenced by the waybill. Notwithstanding these problems, the use of the sea waybills in letters of credit is recognised by Art 21 of UCP 600.

However, the position is different where a similar document, the straight bill of lading, is issued. The carrier must now deliver against production of the document by the consignee. This is the result of the House of Lords' reasoning in *The Rafaela S*,[26] which led it to conclude that such a document amounts to a 'bill of lading' for the purposes of the Hague-Visby Rules. The difference in delivery obligations makes critical the correct classification of a document as a bill of lading or a sea waybill. The principal way of distinguishing between the two types of document is by reference to the way in which the document is titled.

The delivery order

Where bulk cargo is sold, the seller may wish to divide a consignment among several buyers. As there is only one consignment, only one bill of lading can be issued. A new document needs to be generated to replicate the possessory function of the bill of lading. That document is the delivery order, an instruction by the shipper to the shipowner to deliver so many tons out of the whole bill of lading consignment to a named consignee or to the holder of the delivery order. Once the shipowner agrees to carry out the instructions and 'attorns' to the delivery order through its signature or that of its agent, such as the master, the delivery order becomes a 'ship's delivery order'. The 'attornment' constitutes an undertaking by the shipowner to the holder of the delivery order that it will deliver to it the goods covered by the delivery order against presentation of that document. This undertaking will replace the prior undertaking given on issue of the bill of lading to deliver against presentation of that document. Without such attornment, the delivery order is no more than a 'merchant's delivery order', which gives the holder no right to claim delivery from the shipowner.[27]

Only a 'ship's delivery order' can transfer constructive possession to the holder. For this reason, only ship's delivery orders are an acceptable substitute for bills of lading where part of a bulk cargo is sold under a contract of sale that provides for payment against documents. By virtue of the **Carriage of Goods by Sea Act 1992**, the holder of a ship's delivery order will have a contractual

---

26 [2005] UKHL 11; [2005] 2 AC 423; [2002] EWCA Civ 694; [2003] 2 Lloyd's Rep 113.
27 Moreover, such a document will not satisfy the requirements of s 29(4) of the Sale of Goods Act 1979, which deals with the seller's delivery obligations when a third party is in possession of the goods at the time of the sale.

right to sue the carrier on the terms of the original bill of lading contract in respect of loss or damage to the goods covered by the delivery order.

Combined transport bills of lading

This type of bill of lading is used in contracts of carriage on a combined transport basis – that is, carriage from an inland point in one country to an inland point in another country. Such a contract will be multimodal, in that it will involve not only carriage by sea, but also carriage by at least one other form of transport, usually road. The bill of lading will usually be a 'received for shipment' bill of lading rather than a 'shipped' bill of lading.

If a combined transport bill of lading is issued by a non-vehicle-owning carrier (NVOC), such as a freight forwarder,[28] then there is some doubt as to whether such a document can transfer either ownership in or constructive possession of the goods described therein. Such a bill of lading would therefore be akin to a 'straight' bill of lading – that is, a non-negotiable document that, unlike a waybill, must still be presented to obtain delivery from the carrier. A holder of such a bill of lading who is not the original shipper probably obtains a contractual right of action against the carrier by virtue of the provisions of the **Carriage of Goods by Sea Act 1992** concerning sea waybills.

Implied contracts

The traditional model of carriage contracts assumes direct contractual dealings between shippers and shipowners. Yet, in the following situations, there are no such direct dealings. The first is where the shipowner has time chartered its vessel for a period of, say, 12 months. During that period, it will be the time charterer and not the shipowner who enters into direct contractual relations with the consignors whose goods are to be carried on the ship. The second is where there is a fob contract, under which the buyer makes the contract of carriage. The shippers in the first instance and the seller in the second are both tacitly assumed to be contractually linked with the shipowner on the terms of the bill of lading, despite the absence of any direct contract between them. Such contracts, therefore, must be implied contracts.

Expansion of the contractual service from pure sea carriage

The law of carriage of goods by sea developed at a time when the relevant contract of carriage would involve a single sea voyage, with the carrier undertaking responsibility for the goods from the moment at which they were loaded onto its vessel to the moment of their discharge.[29] This is known as the 'tackle to tackle' or 'alongside' rule: it is also the period covered by the Hague and Hague-Visby Rules. However, even under traditional ocean bills of lading, the carrier's period of responsibility usually extends beyond these termini, in that the cargo owner will usually take delivery at the port of discharge after the completion of discharge. For example, after discharge, the goods may be stored in the warehouse of a terminal operator or customs agent appointed by the carrier. The receiver will then obtain delivery of the goods from that party on presentation of the bill of lading. The carrier's responsibility as bailee will continue until this point, notwithstanding that the goods are no longer on the vessel but have been transferred into the custody of an independent contractor engaged by the carrier.

The carrier's responsibility as bailee will also start before the start of the 'tackle to tackle' period if the carrier, or its agent, receives the goods prior to the commencement of loading. Bills of lading invariably contain 'period of responsibility' or 'before and after' clauses determining the extent of

---

28 Freight forwarders usually act solely as agents in arranging contracts of carriage, rather like travel agents.
29 Bills of lading issued for such a voyage are termed 'ocean' bills of lading.

the carrier's responsibility, if any, for the goods during these periods. Article VII of the Hague and Hague-Visby Rules specifically preserves the carrier's right to rely on such clauses.

It is now, also, quite common for the period of contractual responsibility to extend beyond one sea voyage. One example is where the initial sea carrier can complete only part of the contractual voyage and needs to trans-ship the goods onto the vessel of another carrier, which will take the goods on to the port of discharge. Another example is where the carrier takes over the goods at an inland depot and contracts to deliver the goods at another point inland in the country of destination. Such a contract will necessarily involve a mode of transport other than sea transport and is 'multimodal'.

These expanded carriage contracts are of two basic types. Under the first type, the initial carrier undertakes to act as principal as regards that part of the contract that it will perform personally and will contract with the other carriers as the shipper's agent. Under such contracts, a 'through' bill of lading will be issued, which will contain a clause permitting trans-shipment and will provide that the carrier's liability shall cease once the goods are no longer in its custody.

In contrast, under the second type of contract, the carrier contracts as principal as regards the entire contractual service, even though it may, in fact, use subcontractors to perform parts of the contract. Such subcontractors will have a contract only with the carrier and not with the shipper. The bill of lading issued in this case will be a 'combined transport' bill of lading. It may be issued by a person, such as a freight forwarder, who is neither the owner nor the charterer of a vessel, in which case it will be a 'received for shipment' bill of lading. This will not affect its contractual status, but may rob the document of any proprietary or possessory status.[30] Such documents may have achieved negotiable status by virtue of a trade custom or usage, as was held to be the case with mate's receipts in Singapore in *Kum v Wah Tat Bank Ltd*.[31] The matter is still uncertain, given the decision in *Diamond Alkali Export Corp v Fl Bourgeois*[32] that 'received for shipment' bills of lading are not good tender under a cif contract.[33] However, the fact that such bills have, to some extent, become acceptable documents under a letter of credit subject to UCP 600 is likely to be cogent evidence that they have achieved negotiable status by virtue of a trade custom or usage.

Containerisation

The expansion of contracts of carriage beyond the geographical limits of the traditional ocean bill of lading has gone hand in hand with the use of containers for the carriage of most non-bulk cargoes. The containers used may be those of the shipper, but are more likely to be supplied by the carrier. If the shipper can fill an entire container, the carrier will deliver one to its premises. The shipper will then pack, or 'stuff', the container, which will then be taken to the container depot by either the shipper or the carrier, ready for loading onto the carrying vessel. A contract on this basis is known as 'full container load' (FCL).[34] The equivalent operation at the end of the carriage will involve delivery of the full container to the consignee, who will unpack it, and then return the empty container to the carrier at the container terminal. Such a contract will be FCL/ FCL. If the shipper can use only part of a container, it will take its goods to the container terminal, where they will be packed by the carrier into a container along with goods dispatched by other shippers in a similar position. A contract on this basis is known as

---

30 A further problem is that, under classic cif law, a bill of lading is unacceptable if it fails to provide the necessary 'continuous documentary cover'. See *Hamsson v Hamel and Horley* [1922] 2 AC 36, HL.

31 [1971] 1 Lloyd's Rep 439.

32 [1921] 3 KB 443.

33 In contrast, in *The Marlborough Hill* [1921] AC 444, PC, a 'received for shipment' bill of lading was held to amount to a 'bill of lading' for the purposes of s 6 of the Admiralty Court Act 1861.

34 This contract will be 'FCL door' where the carrier takes the packed container back to the container depot and 'FCL depot' where this done by the shipper.

'less than container load' (LCL).[35] The equivalent operation at the end of the carriage will involve the consignee taking delivery of its goods after they have been unpacked from the container at the container terminal by the carrier's agent. Such a contract will be LCL/LCL. The arrangements for unpacking the container may, however, differ from those governing its stuffing. For example, where the shipper packs a single container for goods to be delivered to more than one consignee, the contract will be FCL/LCL.

The contract will also need to specify the movement of the container – that is, the place of its receipt by and delivery from the carrier. Where these operations take place at the premises of the shipper and consignee, respectively, the contract will be on 'house to house', or 'door to door', terms: this is the form usually adopted when the contract is on an FCL/FCL basis. However, where the contract provides for pure sea carriage, it will be on 'pier to pier', or 'port to port', terms. A further variant is where the contract provides for receipt or delivery at a container depot. These options may be combined with FCL and LCL terms to meet the contractual needs of the parties to the contract of carriage.

Most contracts of carriage involving containers will involve some element of combined transport. Most use the sea waybill as the contractual document. However, some still use the bill of lading, although it is extremely rare for containerised goods to be sold and resold while in transit.

The use of containers causes considerable evidential problems to cargo claimants in proving that the goods packed inside the container were damaged during the custody of the carrier. If the shipper loads them into the container, which is then sealed, the carrier will have no means of verifying what is inside the container. Accordingly, when it issues the bill of lading or sea waybill, it will protect itself by qualifying any statement as to the contents of the container with words such as 'said to contain'. The effect of these words is to oblige the cargo claimant to prove by independent evidence exactly what was in the container at the time that the carrier took it over and the condition in which it then was. In many cases, this will prove to be an insurmountable evidential burden.

The cargo claim enquiry

Having sketched in the general background, we can now move on to consider in detail the subject of the first part of this book: the process of recovering from carriers for loss or damage to goods, which occurred during their custody. In assessing the merits of such a claim, the following questions have to be answered.

Does the claimant have title to sue the defendant?

'Title to sue' means the claimant's right to sue the defendant in respect of what it has lost by reason of the defaults of the carrier or its subcontractors during the carriage of the goods. The claimant will generally be the buyer taking delivery at the end of a chain of sale contracts under which risk passes on shipment. However, the claimant might also be the original shipper or a bank that has made a payment in respect of the goods under a letter of credit. The principal types of loss will be: damage to cargo; non-delivery of cargo; misdelivery of cargo; and late delivery of cargo. If the claimant has insured the goods and has been indemnified by its insurer, then the action may be brought in its name by the insurers under the process of subrogation. The shipowner's liability in respect of cargo claims will generally be covered by liability insurance, known as 'P&I' (protection and indemnity) insurance. Shipowners will not be covered in respect of claims arising out of

---

35 This is known as 'LCL depot'. Where the carrier collects the goods from the shipper and takes them to the container terminal to be loaded into a container with goods from other shippers, the contract is one of 'LCL door'.

deviation, misdelivery or the issuing of a 'clean' bill of lading for goods that were damaged prior to loading.

Claims may be brought contractually or non-contractually in negligence, bailment, conversion or deceit. It will generally be preferable for any action to be brought in contract for the following reasons. First, the position as regards jurisdiction and choice of law is likely to be simplified as the result of express contractual clauses. Secondly, there are no restrictions on recovery of economic loss in contract of the type that have limited the scope of the action in negligence. The defendant will usually be the shipowner because of the possibility of obtaining security for the claim by way of the arrest procedure. Arrest is a form of judicial detention available against the carrying vessel or a sister ship in most jurisdictions throughout the world. Once a vessel is arrested, it will be unable to leave the port until security for the claim has been provided, failing which, it will be subject to judicial sale. The defendant may also be a charterer or a freight forwarder who has contracted as a carrier or a subcontractor, such as a firm of stevedores that has been engaged by the carrier to load or discharge the vessel. If an inaccurate bill of lading is signed, the defendant could also be the party who actually signed the bill of lading.

There may, indeed, be an advantage to the claimant directing its claim at the carrier's subcontractors, rather than at the carrier itself. The claim will be non-contractual and therefore outside the scope of the Hague or Hague-Visby Rules. This means that a claim involving physical harm to cargo will be recoverable in full. The subcontractor will be unable to rely on provisions of the Rules, such as package limitation, that would have been available to the carrier had the claim been directed at it under the bill of lading. Such non-contractual actions tend to undermine the aim of the Rules in providing a uniform framework for the treatment of cargo claims. This has, in response, prompted a remarkable degree of judicial ingenuity and creativity directed at reining back such claims into the ambit of the Rules. This will be examined in detail at the end of Chapter 2.

In the event of the claimant obtaining a judgment against a shipowner, which it is unable to satisfy due to its insolvency, the **Third Parties (Rights against Insurers) Act 1930** allows the claimant to assume the rights of the shipowner as against its liability insurer. However, any direct action against the insurer will be frustrated by the fact that the rules of all of the P&I Clubs make it a precondition of any indemnity that the assured shall have first settled the claim or satisfied any judgment itself. Obviously, an insolvent assured is in no position to do so and in *Firma C-Trade v Newcastle P&I Association (The Fanti and The Padre Island)*,[36] the House of Lords held that the third party had no right against the P&I Club under the 1930 Act, as its rights could be no greater than those enjoyed by the assured under the terms of the liability insurance.[37] To avoid these problems, the claimant should seek, at the earliest opportunity, to obtain security for its claim by use of the arrest procedure.

The P&I Clubs also offer legal expenses cover, 'defence' or 'F, D & D' (freight, defence and demurrage) cover. Both types of insurance are often taken out by charterers as well. The vessel itself will be insured against loss or damage, so-called 'hull and machinery' insurance. If the vessel is trading in an area subject to hostilities, this cover will cease and a separate 'war risks' policy will need to be obtained.

If the claimant does have title to sue, can it bring an action against the defendant in the English courts?

English lawyers will become involved with cargo claims when the substantive dispute is heard in the English courts or in English arbitration. Additionally, recourse will be had to the English courts to obtain security where the substantive dispute is proceeding in a foreign court or by way of

---

36 [1991] 2 AC 1.
37 The Third Parties (Rights of Insurers) Act 2010 received the royal assent on 25 March 2010 but is not yet in force. Section 9(5) of the 2010 Act abrogates the effect of 'pay first' clauses but s 9(6) preserves the effect of such clauses as regards contracts of marine insurance, except where the liability of the insured is a liability in respect of death or personal injury.

arbitration. The jurisdictional and procedural rules involved will be considered in detail in Part 2 of this book. These issues are as important as the merits of the claim itself. It is no good having an excellent claim if one's client is ultimately unable to turn that claim into an enforceable judgment.

Has the loss or damage occurred during the period for which the carrier was responsible for the goods?

The claimant will first need to prove when the defendant's period of responsibility for the goods began and what was the condition of the goods at that time. In establishing the condition and quantity of the goods at the start of the defendant's period of responsibility, the claimant will be able to rely on the common law and statutory rules that govern the effect of statements in shipping documents, such as bills of lading. These rules are examined in detail in Chapter 3.

The claimant will then need to prove when the defendant's period of responsibility ceased and what was the condition of the goods at that time. This is largely a question of fact, but where a claim in contract is made, it will also involve questions of construction as to the period of the defendant's responsibility for the goods. Unlike an action in tort, this period will not necessarily coincide with the period in which the goods are in the physical custody of the defendant. This is the case with combined transport bills of lading.

If loss is established during the relevant period, what is the defendant's responsibility for it?

If the action is brought in tort, this will be a pure question of fact revolving around whether or not the defendant took reasonable care of the goods while they were in its custody. If the action is brought in contract, the terms of the contract of carriage need to be considered, as these may afford a defence to the defendant. These terms may be express, implied or statutory. The **Carriage of Goods by Sea Act 1971** implements the Hague-Visby Rules and provides that they are to have the force of law. The Hague-Visby Rules apply to every bill of lading relating to the carriage of goods between ports in two different States if: (a) the bill of lading is issued in a contracting State, or (b) the carriage is from a port in a contracting State, or (c) the contract contained in or evidenced by the bill of lading provides that these Rules or legislation of any State giving effect to them are to govern the contract, in respect of the following contracts of carriage.[38] The 1971 Act also provides for the application of the Hague-Visby Rules to waybills 'if the contract contained in or evidenced by it is a contract for the carriage of goods by sea which expressly provides that the Rules are to govern the contract as if the receipt were a bill of lading'.[39] The application of the Hague-Visby Rules is considered in detail in Chapter 5.

If the defendant is responsible for the loss, how will damages be assessed?

The answer to this question involves the application of the principles relating to remoteness of damage, which are discussed in Chapter 13. Different rules apply depending on whether the claim is made in tort or in contract. In addition, contractual claims may be reduced by virtue of limitation provisions in the contract. Where the contract is subject to the Hague-Visby Rules, the carrier will be entitled to rely on the package and gross weight limitation provisions contained in Art IV(5)(a).

---

38 Article X.
39 Section 1(6)(b). However, where the Act applies to waybills the second sentences of Art III(4) and Art III(7) are omitted.

Chapter 2

Title to Sue

Chapter Contents

In this chapter, we will examine the means by which the claimant can establish a route of recovery against the defendant in respect of loss or damage to goods in transit.

The claimant will be the party who has ended up bearing that loss or damage. It will usually be a buyer at the end of a chain of sale contracts. It may, however, be a seller if the buyer has defaulted or if the terms of the sale contract vary the usual transfer of risk on loading. It may also be a bank that has financed a purchase under a letter of credit and which has been unable to obtain reimbursement from the buyer.

The defendant will usually be the shipowner, but could be a charterer or an independent contractor, such as a firm of stevedores engaged to load or unload the vessel. The defendant could also be a person who is neither a shipowner nor a charterer of a vessel, as would be the case where a freight forwarder contracts as principal to a multimodal contract of carriage.

The right of action will usually be contractual. If parallel actions exist in tort and bailment, recovery under such actions will generally be limited by the terms of the applicable contract.[1] Accordingly, actions in bailment and tort will only be of relevance when the claimant has no contractual right of action against the defendant.

This chapter begins by examining the express contracts of carriage made between shippers and carriers at the time that the goods are loaded onto the carrying vessel. It will proceed to show how such express contracts are supplemented by implied contracts, before considering the process by which the contracts created at the time of loading are assigned by statute to third parties during the course of the carrying voyage. It will conclude by considering actions in bailment and tort.

Express contracts on loading

A contract for the sale of goods, whereby risk passes on loading but property and possession pass when the bill of lading is transferred in exchange for the price, will leave the buyer without recourse against the seller if the goods are lost or damaged on the voyage, for the seller will have performed its obligations. It will need some means of recovering this loss from the party during whose custody the loss occurred. For reasons that will be explained later in the chapter, the preferred route for such recovery is a contractual one. Our analysis of contractual recovery will start with an examination of the express contracts of carriage that are made on or shortly before the loading of the goods onto the carrying vessel.

Under both cif (cost, insurance, freight) and fob (free on board) contracts, someone has to conclude a carriage contract if the buyer is eventually to receive the goods. With a cif contract, this party is generally the seller; with a fob contract, this party is generally the buyer.[2] On the assumption that the relevant party under the sale contract ('the shipper') deals directly with the shipowner, the resulting contract may be on one of three basic forms: the charterparty, the bill of lading or the waybill.

The voyage charterparty

If a large quantity of goods is to be shipped, involving the use of the whole or a substantial part of the carrying space of the vessel, the relevant contract will usually be a charterparty.

---

1 This is the effect of *Pyrene Co Ltd v Scindia Navigation Co Ltd* [1954] 2 QB 402, at common law, and of Art IV(1) *bis* of the Hague-Visby Rules.

2 It is, however, quite feasible that, for reasons of commercial convenience, the fob seller makes the contract of carriage as agent for the buyer.

This will be a written document, signed by both parties, and negotiated by brokers before the goods are loaded. The contract itself will usually come into existence before the signing of the charter itself, once agreement is reached at the end of negotiations between the brokers. However, there can be no contract if such an agreement is expressed to be 'subject to details'.[3]

The charterparty will contain an exhaustive list of terms to cover the loading, carriage and discharge of the goods, as well as provisions for the payment of freight and demurrage. It will also provide for the payment of commissions to each set of brokers. Shippers who charter directly from shipowners usually use a voyage charter form, although the time charter format may be adapted for use with a single voyage. Such a hybrid is known as a trip charter.

The contract of carriage embodied in the charterparty will undoubtedly contemplate the issue of a bill or bills of lading to cover the cargo to be loaded. However, it is unlikely that the parties will intend such a bill of lading to have any status between the contracting parties other than that of a receipt. No such intention was found in *Rodoconachi, Sons & Co v Milburn Bros*,[4] where the bill was issued to the charterer as the original shipper. Nor was it found in *The President of India v Metcalfe Shipping Co Ltd*,[5] where the charterer received the bill of lading as indorsee and the parties' intention that the bills of lading should not amount to a variation was further underlined by a clause in the charter providing that bills of lading were to be issued 'without prejudice to the terms of this charter'. It is likely that the same decision would have been reached even without the presence of this clause in the charter.[6] It is important to note that this rule applies only where there is a charterparty between the claimant and the party who has issued the bill of lading. If a shipowner's bill has been issued and the claimant has a charterparty with an intermediate charterer (or 'disponent owner'), then it will have no contractual link with the shipowner. In such a situation, the claimant can proceed against the shipowner in contract only by showing that it is a lawful holder of a bill of lading and has thereby acquired a statutory right of action against the shipowner under the terms of the bill of lading, by virtue of s 2(1) of the **Carriage of Goods by Sea Act 1992**.

In some instances, however, the charterer may need to base its claim on the bill of lading rather than the charterparty, in which case the terms of the former will govern its claim. An example is *Calcutta SS Co Ltd v Andrew Weir & Co*,[7] where the charterers lent money to the bill of lading holder who indorsed the bill to them as security. The goods were delivered in a damaged condition and it was held that, as the claim arose under the bill of lading and not the charterparty, it was governed by the terms of the bill of lading.[8]

The changing contractual status of the bill of lading

This example is based on the facts of *President of India v Metcalfe Shipping Co Ltd*, but with the buyer effecting a sub-sale to the second buyer. Express contracts are shown by solid lines, implied and statutory contracts by dotted lines.

---

3   *The Junior K* [1988] 2 Lloyd's Rep 583.
4   (1886) 18 QBD 67, CA.
5   [1970] 1 QB 289, CA.
6   This was the view of the Court of Appeal in *The El Amria and The El Mina* [1982] 2 Lloyd's Rep 28, especially *per* Donaldson LJ, at 31.
7   [1910] 1 KB 759.
8   An action for breach of contract under the charter would, presumably, have resulted in the award of no more than nominal damages, because the charterer had suffered no loss in its capacity as charterer.

Stage 1: Issue of bill of lading

There are two express sale contracts, and one express carriage contract under the charterparty made between the buyer and the shipowner. There is also an implied contract between the shipowner and the seller on the terms of the bill of lading.

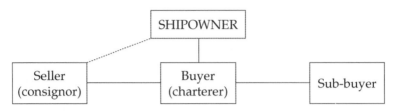

Stage 2: Indorsement of bill of lading to buyer

The bill of lading in the hands of the buyer loses its contractual status.

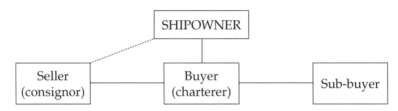

Stage 3: Indorsement of bill of lading to sub-buyer

The contractual status of the bill of lading now revives in the hands of the sub-buyer. By virtue of s 2(1) of the **Carriage of Goods by Sea Act 1992**, it constitutes a statutory contract with the ship-owner. Section 2(5) will now divest the seller of its contractual rights under the bill of lading, although its liabilities thereunder remain in force by virtue of s 3(3).

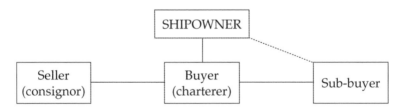

The bill of lading[9]

With smaller shipments, a more informal mode of contracting is adopted. The shipper will book space with the shipowner through its agents and it is at this stage that the actual contract of carriage is usually made. If the parties are not *ad idem* on important terms of the contract by the time of shipment, no express contract will come into being. This happened in *The Barranduna and the Tarrago*,[10] and consequently, the shipper was unable to maintain an action for shut-out cargo. The only contract with the carrier was one implied from the actions of the parties in loading the cargo onto the

---

9 In this chapter, 'bill of lading' will, unless the contrary is indicated, refer to the standard 'shipped', 'ocean' bill of lading. Non-standard bills of lading, such as 'received for shipment', 'through' and 'combined transport' bills of lading are discussed in Chapter 7.

10 [1985] 2 Lloyd's Rep 419, PC.

vessel. Consequently, the carrier's contractual obligations related only to the cargo actually loaded and not to the additional cargo that the shipper wanted to be carried.

The initial contract of carriage can also be made through a freight forwarder, who acts as agent for the shipper in arranging a contract of carriage, fulfilling a role similar to that of a travel agent. Occasionally, the freight forwarder may contract as principal and undertake to carry the goods, not merely to arrange their carriage. This will generally be the case where the forwarder, rather than charging a commission based on the total freight cost, makes an all-in charge.[11] The freight forwarder may also incur a personal liability to the carrier for freight where it contracts in its own name, even though the bill of lading subsequently names its customer as the shipper.[12] In the London freight market, there is a clear usage that forwarding agents who act for a shipper whose name is not disclosed incur personal liability for freight unless the carrier is given notice that the forwarder acts as agent only.[13] In addition, the forwarder will become personally liable if it accepts a freight quotation in which it is named as the customer.[14] In Australia, it has been suggested that a freight forwarder who undertakes a personal liability may also act in a dual capacity as agent for the shipper when it books space on the ship.[15]

Unlike the position with a charterparty, the terms of the initial contract concluded before loading will either expressly, as in *Armour & Co v Walford*,[16] or impliedly, as in *Pyrene Co Ltd v Scindia Navigation Co Ltd*,[17] be subject to the terms of the bill of lading that will be issued once the goods have been loaded onto the carrying ship. Moreover, in the latter case, the terms of the anticipated bill of lading were held to govern the contract from its inception, even though a bill of lading was never actually issued. A fire tender was damaged during the start of the loading process before it had crossed the ship's rail. Accordingly, because it was never carried by the vessel on its voyage, no bill of lading was ever issued in respect of it. Notwithstanding this, Devlin J held that because the contract of carriage made when the fob buyers booked space with the shipowners anticipated the issue of a bill of lading, the terms of such anticipated bill of lading covered the whole performance of the contract by the shipowners and not just that part of the performance that was done after a bill of lading was actually issued.[18]

If the original express contract contemplates that the terms of the eventual bill of lading will govern it, what then is the position if its terms conflict with those in the original contract? The issue first arose in *Leduc v Ward*,[19] in the context of a claim against a shipowner brought by an indorsee of the bill of lading. The shipowner had committed a deviation to Glasgow that was not justified by the wording of the liberty clause contained in the bill of lading. The shipowner argued that the original shipper had known that the ship would first call at Glasgow and that the indorsee was thereby bound by this oral expansion of the scope of the liberty clause in the bill of lading. The Court of Appeal found for the indorsee, primarily on the ground of the wording of s 1 of the **Bills of Lading Act 1855**, which referred to the transfer to the indorsee of 'all rights of suit . . . as if the contract contained in the bill of lading had been made with himself' (emphasis added).

The issue next arose, in a rather different context, in *The Ardennes*.[20] The claim was now being made by the original shipper, rather than by a third party relying on the **Bills of Lading Act 1855**. In addition, it was now the shipper, rather than the shipowner, who sought to rely on what had been said before the issue of the bill of lading. The shipowner's agent had given an oral promise to

11 *Aqualon (UK) Ltd v Vallana Shipping Corp* [1994] 1 Lloyd's Rep 669.
12 *Lidgett v Perrin* (1862) 2 F & F 763.
13 *Anglo-Overseas Transport v Titan Industrial Corp (UK)* [1959] 2 Lloyd's Rep 152.
14 *Cory Bros Shipping Ltd v Baldan Ltd* [1997] 2 Lloyd's Rep 58, QB. See, also, *Coli v Merzario* [2002] 2 Lloyd's Rep 608, CLCC.
15 *Carrington Slipways Pty Ltd v Patrick Operations Pty Ltd (The Cape Cormorin)* (1991) 24 NSWLR 745, Sup Ct (NSW).
16 [1921] 3 KB 473.
17 [1954] 2 QB 402.
18 See, also, *Mayhew Foods Ltd v Overseas Containers Ltd* [1984] 1 Lloyd's Rep 317, QB.
19 (1888) 20 QBD 475, CA.
20 *SS Ardennes (Cargo Owners) v SS Ardennes (Owners)* [1951] 1 KB 55.

the shipper that the cargo of mandarin oranges loaded at Cartagena in Spain would be carried directly to London. In fact, after leaving Cartagena, the ship first proceeded to Antwerp. The ship, accordingly, arrived later at London than should have been the case. By the time of her arrival, the shipper had suffered a double economic loss in that not only had the price of oranges fallen, but also the rate of import duty had increased.

When the shipper sought to reclaim these losses, the shipowner's response was to refer to a liberty clause on the reverse of the bill of lading under which the deviation to Antwerp would be justified. Looking solely at the terms of the bill of lading itself, it was clear that there would have been no breach of contract by the shipowner. However, what of the oral undertaking that had been given before the bill had been issued? The shipowner argued that the issue of the bill had reduced the contract to writing and, therefore, the parol evidence rule meant that the contract was not subject to the prior oral undertaking. Lord Goddard CJ rejected this argument, stating that:

> . . . a bill of lading is not in itself the contract between the shipowner and the shipper of goods, although it has been said to be excellent evidence of its terms . . . The contract has come into existence before the bill of lading is signed; the latter is signed by one party only, and handed by him to the shipper usually after the goods have been put on board. No doubt if the shipper finds that the bill contains terms with which he is not content, or does not contain some terms for which he has stipulated, he might, if there were time, demand his goods back; but he is not, in my opinion, for that reason, prevented from giving evidence that there was in fact a contract entered into before the bill of lading was signed different from that which is found in the bill of lading, or containing some additional term . . .

A problem with this reasoning is that, in *Leduc v Ward*, Lord Esher MR clearly stated that, once the contract had been reduced to writing by the issue of the bill of lading, 'parol evidence to alter or qualify such writing is not admissible, and the writing is the only evidence of the contract'.[21] This reasoning would apply to any claim under a bill of lading, whether brought by the original shipper or by a third party. However, the parol evidence rule can be circumvented by classifying the oral undertaking as a separate contract collateral to the written contract contained in the bill of lading.[22] The result in *The Ardennes* may still, therefore, be justified on this basis and, indeed, Lord Goddard CJ gave as an additional ground for his decision the fact that 'the representation that the ship would sail direct to London would amount to a warranty . . . a promise that the shipowner would not avail himself of a liberty which would otherwise be open to him'.

To deal with the problem of inconsistent terms, many bills of lading contain a clause by which the terms of the previous contract are expressly superseded by the terms of the bill of lading. Such a clause may also provide for a supersession of the carrier on issue of the bill of lading, for example, the replacement of a time charterer by a shipowner. Logically, however, such a clause should appear in the prior contract that is to be superseded by the issue of the bill of lading, rather than in the bill of lading itself. As regards the other party to the bill of lading contract, the shipper, the courts have proved generally unwilling to find that this party is other than the party identified as shipper or consignor in the bill itself.

In conclusion, the effect of the decisions in *Leduc v Ward* and *The Ardennes*, as well as of those referred to in the previous section on the voyage charterparty, is as follows.

(a)   When a claim is made by a third-party holder of a bill of lading whose rights of suit derive from the **Carriage of Goods by Sea Act 1992**, the bill of lading will be the statutory contract.

---

21 *Leduc v Ward* (1888) 20 QBD 475, 480. See, also, De Battista, C, 'The bill of lading as the contract of carriage: a re-assessment of *Leduc v Ward*' (1982) 45 MLR 652.

22 A technique also adopted by the Court of Appeal in *Evans (J) & Sons (Portsmouth) Ltd v Andrea Merzario* [1976] 1 WLR 1078.

(b)   When a claim is made under the bill of lading by a party whose rights derive from its being the original shipper, then the terms of the bill of lading may be displaced by clear evidence of contrary terms previously agreed with the carrier.

(c)   The bill of lading will have no contractual effect in the hands of a person who has concluded a charterparty with the party that has issued the bill of lading.

Sea waybills

Sea waybills are non-negotiable bills of lading. They may be used instead of bills of lading if the seller and buyer do not want the buyer to have the facility of reselling the goods while in transit. The contractual status of such documents on loading will be exactly the same as that described above in relation to the bill of lading. The only difference lies in the shipowner's obligations of delivery. With a bill of lading, the shipowner must deliver against production of an original bill of lading. With a sea waybill, all that is required is that the shipowner deliver the goods to the consignee named in the waybill on receiving satisfactory proof of its identity. The consignee is not further obliged to produce an original waybill.

This works to the advantage of the consignee in that it simplifies the process of obtaining delivery of the cargo. However, this factor may also work to the disadvantage of the consignee in that, until the moment of delivery, the consignor retains the right to give new delivery instructions to the carrier. This right also exists under a bill of lading, but is lost once the bill leaves the possession of the consignor. Once the consignee named in the bill of lading takes possession of the bill, it will, therefore, have the security of knowing that it will be entitled to take delivery of the goods no matter what contrary directions the consignor may subsequently purport to give the carrier. To replicate this security in a sea waybill, which is not subject to physical transfer to the consignee, recourse is often had to a specific contractual term, called the 'NODISP' (no disposal) clause. This clause contains an undertaking by the shipper not to change the identity of the named consignee. However, there is nothing to stop the carrier and the shipper varying the contract by agreeing to disregard such a clause. The position is unaffected by the **Contracts (Rights of Third Parties) Act 1999**, as s 6(5) precludes its operation in respect of the granting of contractual rights to third parties under documents covered by the **Carriage of Goods by Sea Act (COGSA) 1992**.

In addition, there are the 1990 CMI Rules, which were drafted for voluntary incorporation into sea waybills. The Rules attempt to equate the position of a consignee named in a waybill with that of the holder of a bill of lading. Clause 3 deals with the rights of suit of the consignee and the carrier vis-à-vis each other by stating that shipper contracts both as principal and as agent for consignee. This has lost much of its significance, given the provisions of **COGSA 1992** relating to sea waybills. Clause 4 deals with the terms of the contract by applying the International Convention or national law, which either apply, or would have applied, compulsorily had the contract of carriage been covered by a bill of lading or similar document of title. Clause 5 deals with the evidential effects of statements in the sea waybill. It provides that, in the absence of any reservation, these statements will have prima facie effect as between the carrier and the shipper, and conclusive effect as between the carrier and the consignee.

Clause 6 specifies that the right of control resides with the shipper, who may change the identity of the consignee at any time up to that at which the consignee claims delivery. This right is subject to two provisos. First, the shipper must give reasonable notice of this change to the carrier. Secondly, the shipper must indemnify the carrier in respect of any additional expense caused thereby. The shipper is also given an option to transfer the right of control to the consignee. This must be exercised no later than the receipt of the goods by the carrier and must be noted on the sea waybill. Clause 7 provides for delivery to be made by the carrier to the consignee on production of proper identification. This obligation is not strict, but only requires the carrier to take reasonable care.

Straight bills

These are bills of lading that name a consignee, but lack the additional wording such as 'to order', which is necessary to achieve the negotiability that is characteristic of an ordinary bill of lading. The straight bill of lading shares some similarities with the sea waybill in that neither document is transferable like an ordinary bill of lading. However, until recently, the nature of the carrier's delivery obligations under the straight bill was uncertain. One view was that the carrier was simply required to deliver to the named consignee on being provided with satisfactory proof of its identity.[23] The other view was that the carrier should also require presentation of the straight bill before delivering the cargo to the named consignee.[24] The House of Lords, in *The Rafaela S*,[25] has now endorsed the second of these two views. What was at issue was whether such a document amounted to a bill of lading for the purposes of the Hague-Visby Rules. The House of Lords affirmed the finding of the Court of Appeal that this was, indeed, the case because the consignee could not obtain delivery without presentation of the document. The document was still transferable, albeit only once, from consignor to consignee.

Although the straight bill in question contained an express provision on its face requiring it to be surrendered in exchange for delivery of cargo, Rix LJ, *obiter*, was strongly of the view that the delivery obligation would have been the same even without such a clause. The House of Lords was of the same view. It is likely that the straight bill will now be regarded as a document of title whereby transfer of the document to the named consignee will transfer constructive possession without an attornment from the carrier.[26] However, a purported indorsement by the consignee of a straight bill will pass neither possessory nor proprietary rights.[27]

Electronic documentation

Developments in computer cryptography have made it possible to substitute the paper bill of lading or waybill with an electronic equivalent. Instead of the bill of lading being transferred by physical indorsement, it is generated by computer and transferred by the transmission of an electronic message by the sender, using a private digital key, to a recipient who decrypts it using a public digital key. This system of generating paperless documents is known as *electronic document interchange* (EDI). The first attempt to apply such an electronic system to bills of lading was the SEADOCS scheme in the mid-1980s. This was followed by the CMI Rules 1990, under which transmission was made through the carrier, who would issue a new private key to each indorsee. However, this system was regarded as insecure and many traders were unhappy at the important role played by the carrier in the process of indorsement, a process that had not involved them at all when a paper bill of lading was used.

The most recent project involving electronic bills of lading is the *Bolero* ('Bills of Lading in Europe') project. The transmission of data is routed through a centralised online registry, using a system of private and public digital keys for senders and recipients, respectively. This is operated by the Bolero Users Association, a club to which all its users belong, be they carriers, shippers, consignees or banks. All of its members agree to abide by its rules. Two registries are operated. The first receives and passes on the parties' messages, thereby acting as a register of who is currently entitled to the goods covered by an electronic bill of lading. The second is a register of the public

---

23 See Treitel and Reynolds, *Carver on Bills of Lading*, 2001, London: Sweet & Maxwell, pp 6–7, and Gaskell, Asariotis and Baatz, *Bills of Lading: Law and Practice*, 2000, London: LLP, 14.24, and the decision of the Hong Kong court in *The Brij* [2001] 1 Lloyd's Rep 431.
24 See the decision of the Singapore Court of Appeal in *Voss Peer v APL* [2002] 2 Lloyd's Rep 707.
25 [2005] UKHL 11; [2005] 2 AC 423; [2002] EWCA Civ 694; [2003] 2 Lloyd's Rep 113.
26 But see Treitel, G, 'The legal status of straight bills of lading' (2003) 119 LQR 608.
27 *The River Ngada* [2002] LMLN, 13 September, QB.

keys used to decrypt the messages sent by the club's members. The registry authenticates these keys by adding its own electronic signature.

Under Bolero, a 'holder to order' will be designated when the cargo is loaded. If it wishes to take delivery of the cargo itself, then, prior to discharge, it will notify this to the Bolero Registry and it will no longer have the capacity to designate a new 'holder to order'. This is the electronic equivalent of the surrender of a paper bill to the carrier's agent, save that the surrender is being made prior to delivery. The Bolero Registry will advise the carrier of this and delivery will be made to the former 'holder to order' on production of satisfactory proof of identity. In this respect, the delivery process has some similarities with that applicable to paper sea waybills. More commonly, the initial 'holder to order' will wish to sell or pledge the goods. The Bolero Rules enable it to replicate the transfer of constructive possession that follows the indorsement and transfer of a paper bill of lading by advising the Bolero Registry that another Bolero member is to replace it as the 'holder to order'. Alternatively, it can designate another Bolero member as the pledgee holder. In doing so, the 'holder to order' loses its rights to designate a new 'holder to order', for the pledgee is now given the right to designate itself as such. It also loses the right to take delivery of the cargo by the electronic surrender of the bill for which Bolero provides. If the pledgee holder needs to enforce its pledge, it is given the right to designate itself as the new 'holder to order'. Eventually, the end buyer will be designated as the 'holder to order' and will obtain delivery after it has notified the Bolero Registry of the surrender of the electronic bill of lading. The Bolero system can proceed electronically in this manner only as between Bolero members. When the intent is to sell or pledge the cargo to a non-member, the Bolero Rules provide that a paper bill of lading must be issued, so ruling out any further use of an electronic bill.

Although the project appears to offer an effective and secure alternative to the paper bill of lading, promising great savings in time and money, there are still a number of legal obstacles that need to be addressed before an electronic bill of lading can be regarded as the functional equivalent of its paper counterpart. The fundamental obstacle is the fact that the essence of a paper bill of lading is that it is a signed document. Section 7 of the **Electronic Communications Act 2000** now provides for the recognition of electronic signatures in legal proceedings. However, an electronic bill of lading is still unlikely to be regarded as the functional equivalent of a paper bill of lading because it is not in documentary form.[28]

To some extent, these obstacles can be removed by express contractual provisions in the sale contract requiring both parties to treat the electronic bill of lading as though it were a paper bill. In particular, the parties could expressly provide for the transfer of property in the goods represented by the electronic bill of lading by the transfer of the appropriate electronic messages. Although such arrangements would fall outside the protection afforded to bill of lading holders by s 24 of the **Sale of Goods Act 1979**, it would be open to the parties to achieve similar results by an appropriately worded clause in the sale contract.

Further problems arise when one comes to analyse the relationship between the carrier and the persons entitled to the cargo under the electronic bill of lading. Although the Secretary of State has power to extend the provisions of **COGSA 1992** to electronic bills of lading, that power has yet to be exercised. Furthermore, no equivalent power is contained in the **Carriage of Goods by Sea Act 1971** allowing for a similar extension of the provisions of the Hague-Visby Rules. It would, therefore, seem very difficult for an electronic bill of lading issued in the UK to replicate the functions of its paper equivalent, which would be subject to the provisions of both these statutes.

However, even under current law, these problems are not insuperable. The involvement of the carrier, under the CMI Rules, or its agent, under Bolero, in the indorsement process, would probably constitute an attornment by the carrier for the purposes of an action in bailment. This would

---

28 The definition of writing in the Interpretation Act 1978 includes 'other modes of representing or reproducing words in a visible form' – this would not cover an electronic message, which is not, in itself, visible.

be good enough to give the transferee of an electronic bill of lading title to sue, but would not be sufficient to subject it to liability for freight under the electronic bill of lading. Furthermore, where a charterer is the original shipper, the bailment will be on the terms of the charter and not the electronic bill of lading.[29]

For these reasons, a contractual solution on the terms of the electronic bill of lading is much to be preferred. One possible solution would be to use the doctrine of implied contract. However, given the uncertainties associated with this doctrine following the Court of Appeal's decision in *The Aramis*,[30] an alternative solution needs to be found.[31] The solution adopted by the Bolero Rules is to provide for a novation of the contract, with each change of the party designated as 'holder to order'. Novation replaces the contract between the previous 'holder to order' and the carrier with a new contract, on identical terms, between the new 'holder to order' and the carrier.[32] The continuing liability of the original holder to order is preserved, although it is difficult to see how this is possible, given the mechanism of novation adopted by the Bolero Rules. Another important feature of the Bolero Rules is that contracts of carriage that fall within their ambit are made subject to the Hague-Visby Rules by means of a clause paramount.

It should be noted that the provisions of the **Contracts (Rights of Third Parties) Act 1999** cannot assist here, as s 6(5) specifically excludes from the Act's ambit contracts for the carriage of goods by sea, which are defined in s 6(6)(b) as those 'contained in or evidenced by a bill of lading, sea waybill or corresponding electronic transaction . . .'. Section 6(7)(b) goes on to define a 'corresponding electronic transaction' as 'a transaction within s 1(5) of [COGSA 1992] which corresponds to the issue, indorsement, delivery or transfer of a bill of lading, sea waybill or ship's delivery order'. Accordingly, electronic bills of lading fall outside the **Contracts (Rights of Third Parties) Act 1999**, even though the Secretary of State has yet to exercise its power under s 1(5) to make provision for the application of **COGSA 1992** to electronic documentation.

Implied contracts on loading

The express contracts created on loading bring only the shipper into direct contractual relations with the carrier. But what of the seller under a fob contract, the buyer under a cif contract, and sub-buyers under both fob and cif contracts? None of these will have any express contract of carriage with the carrier. Moreover, if the vessel is time chartered, nor will the shipper itself, for it will have booked space directly with the time charterer.

Nonetheless, the courts have proceeded on the tacit assumption[33] that, where goods have been loaded on board a vessel,[34] the bill of lading issued to the consignor in respect of those goods will also constitute a contract between the consignor itself and the party issuing the bill of lading, even in the absence of any prior express contractual dealings between the two parties. This contract is not express and can arise only by implication.[35] There are two advantages to finding a contract between the consignor and the shipowner. First, as pointed out by the arbitrator, Robert Clyde, in *The Dunelmia*,[36] the consignor will be able to give instructions to the shipowner to deliver the cargo

---

29 *The Gudermes* [1993] 1 Lloyd's Rep 311, CA.

30 [1989] 1 Lloyd's Rep 213. The doctrine of implied contract is discussed further below and at p 36.

31 For further consideration of these issues, see Faber, D, 'Electronic bills of lading' (1996) LMCLQ 232.

32 Where there is a pledgee holder, novation will not occur until it has availed itself of its right to designate itself as the 'holder to order'.

33 For example, Lord Denning in *The President of India v Metcalfe Shipping Co Ltd* [1970] 1 QB 289, 304A, identified four contracts, the third of which was between the shipowner and the consignor to whom it had issued the bill of lading.

34 However, the issuing of a bill of lading for goods that are never, in fact, loaded onto the vessel cannot amount to a contract. Such a bill of lading was held to be a 'nullity' in *Heskell v Continental Express Ltd* (1950) 83 LlL Rep 438, KB.

35 See Baughen, S, 'The legal status of the non-contracting shipper' [2000] IJSL 21.

36 [1970] 1 QB 289, at [18] of the award.

to its order at the port of discharge. Secondly, the relationship between these parties will be subject to the provisions of the Hague and Hague-Visby Rules.

It is likely that such an implied contract comes into existence before the issue of the bill of lading, once the shipowner starts to load the consignor's goods. In *Pyrene Co Ltd v Scindia Navigation Co Ltd*,[37] a fire tender was damaged during loading. As this occurred before it had crossed the ship's rail, risk had not passed to the fob buyer. The seller sued the shipowner in tort for £966 in respect of damage to the fire tender. Devlin J held that the seller was bound by the terms of the contract of carriage concluded by the buyer when it booked space with the shipowner. One of these terms limited the shipowner's liability to £200 per package. Devlin J justified his decision on two grounds, one of which was on the basis of an implied contract arising out of the conduct of the seller and the shipowner during the loading of the goods.[38]

This assumption is carried forward into the situation in which the shipper contracts not with the shipowner, but with a person who has chartered the vessel from the shipowner. The assumption is further bolstered by including a 'demise' clause in the bill of lading stating that the bill of lading shall take effect as a contract between the shipowner and the consignor.

The contractual status of a bill of lading with such a clause in the hands of a consignor was accepted without question in *The Berkshire*[39] and *The Jalamohan*.[40] The latter provides quite a useful illustration of the complex shifting of contracts that occurs at common law when goods are loaded onto a time-chartered vessel.

The vessel was time chartered to Express, which was part of the Afea Group. The consignor concluded a fixture note with Afea, Hong Kong. It contained no demise clause, but cl 10 stated that it was subject to the terms of 'carrier's usual bill of lading'. A bill of lading was issued on an Afea Lines form. On the reverse was a demise clause. The shipowners wanted to claim freight from the consignor, Express having defaulted on its hire payments. The bill of lading was marked 'freight prepaid', so the shipowners argued that it did not constitute a contract between themselves and the consignors, thereby leaving them free to pursue a claim for *quantum meruit* freight.[41] The bill of lading was held to amount to a contract between the shipowners and the consignors.[42] The consignors were thereby protected from any contractual liability to pay freight to the shipowners by the 'freight prepaid' statement on the face of the bill.

It is probable that a bill of lading signed on behalf of the shipowner would have had a similar contractual status, even without the inclusion of a 'demise' clause. However, such a clause might prove significant if these assumed contracts between shipowners and shippers contracting with time charterers ever receive the judicial scrutiny that they deserve. They are clearly not express contracts. They can only be implied contracts, and as such, will be subject to the restrictive approach adopted by the Court of Appeal in *The Aramis*[43] to implied contracts arising out of the conduct of the parties on *discharge*. The fatal obstacle to the implication of such a contract will be the absence of an intention to create legal relations. A demise clause might overcome this obstacle, but without it no contract could be implied on loading consistent with the principles applied by the Court of Appeal to the implication of contracts on discharge. These are discussed in more detail at p 36.

Another consequence of the finding in *The Jalamohan* that the bill of lading was a contract between the shipowner and the consignor was that, once the bill was issued, the effect of cl 10 of

---

37 [1954] 2 KB 402.
38 Devlin J primarily based his decision on a refined application of the principles of agency. This aspect of the decision is considered in detail below, p 52.
39 [1974] 1 Lloyd's Rep 185, QB.
40 [1988] 1 Lloyd's Rep 443, QB. However, this position was not accepted in the Canadian decision in *The Roseline* [1987] 1 Lloyd's Rep 18, where the bill of lading made the cargo deliverable to a person other than the consignor.
41 This is a restitutionary claim for payment for services rendered at the request of the consignor and is based on the current market rate.
42 By virtue of the demise clause in the bill of lading.
43 [1989] 1 Lloyd's Rep 213.

the fixture note was that Afea now dropped out of the picture. Thenceforth, the consignor's only contract was with the shipowners on the terms of the bill of lading. This is a somewhat strange conclusion, as there was nothing in either the fixture note or the bill of lading to provide for the termination of contractual relations between Afea and the consignor once a shipowner's bill had been issued. The conclusion is probably premised on the assumption that one cannot have two contractual carriers at the same time in respect of one sea carriage. Although there is no logical reason for such a premise, the contractual disappearance of the time charterer after the issue of a shipowner's bill of lading was accepted without question by Clarke J in *The Ines*.[44]

Where freight is to be paid to the time charterer on delivery, such supersession could prove most inconvenient. The time charterer's remedy is either to issue a 'charterer's bill' or to issue a 'shipowner's bill' that incorporates the terms of the contract with the consignor. Payment of the outstanding freight to the time charterer will discharge the consignor's obligation to pay freight that appears from the bill to be owed to the shipowner. For payment purposes, the charterer will be regarded as the agent of the shipowner.[45]

However, the underlying assumption in the above cases, that a consignor could be made contractually liable for bill of lading freight, has been challenged by the decision of the Court of Appeal in *Cho Yang Shipping Co Ltd v Coral (UK) Ltd*.[46] Three separate carriage contracts were made at different freight rates. The party that had contracted directly with the shipowner defaulted, and the shipowner attempted to claim bill of lading freight from the actual shipper of the goods with which it had had no direct contractual dealings. The shipowner's claim failed on the grounds that the parties to the three carriage contracts had all contracted solely as principals and therefore the shipowner could claim freight only from the party with which it had made an express contract of carriage. This finding was supported by the fact that the bill of lading was claused 'freight prepaid', which indicated that the consignor had never undertaken any liability for freight. However, it is likely that the result would have been the same even in the absence of this wording.

The contractual network where goods are shipped under a time charter

Before issue of a 'shipowner's bill of lading':

Shipowner

↓

Time charterer

↓

Consignor

After issue of a 'shipowner's bill of lading':

Shipowner   Shipowner

↓   ↓

Time charterer   Consignor

The consignor's express contract with the time charterer has been replaced by an implied contract with the shipowner.

44 [1995] 2 Lloyd's Rep 144, QB.
45 *Wehner v Dene SS Co* [1905] 2 KB 92 and also *The Indian Reliance* [1997] 1 Lloyd's Rep 52, QB.
46 [1997] 2 Lloyd's Rep 641.

Shipowner's bill or charterer's bill?

The bill of lading will only amount to an implied contract with the consignor if it is signed by the shipowner or its agents, in which case it will constitute a 'shipowner's bill of lading'. When indorsed, any statutory contract with the holder of the bill of lading, under s 2 of **COGSA 1992**, will be with the shipowner. If a 'shipowner's bill of lading' is issued, the claimant will be able to arrest the vessel to secure its claim. This procedure is dealt with in more detail in Chapter 19.

On the other hand, if it is signed by the charterer or its agents, it will constitute a 'charterer's bill of lading' and the only possible implied contract can be with the charterer. When indorsed, any statutory contract will be between the charterer and the holder of the bill of lading.

English law has proceeded on the assumption that only one party can assume responsibility as carrier under the bill of lading. It is therefore critical that the carrier is correctly identified; otherwise, proceedings will be commenced against the wrong party. The problem will be compounded by the fact that, by the time it is realised that a mistake has been made, it is likely that the one-year limit for bringing claims under the Hague and Hague-Visby Rules will have passed and it will therefore be too late to proceed against the correct party. Various factors must be considered in deciding whether a bill of lading is a shipowner's bill or a charterer's bill.

The most important facts to ascertain are who signed the bill and in what capacity they signed it. Bills of lading signed by the charterer or its servants or agents will amount to charterer's bills.[47] Bills of lading by the servants or agents of the shipowner, such as the master of the vessel, will amount to shipowner's bills, unless the ship is on demise charter, when the charterer will appoint its own crew, including the master.[48]

Terms of the charter that purport to give a dual authority to the captain will not bind the bill of lading holder. In *Manchester Trust Ltd v Furness Withy & Co Ltd*,[49] the charter, which was not a demise charter, provided that, for the purposes of signing bills of lading, the master was to be regarded as the servant of the charterer. Such a provision was held only to affect the position between owners and charterers, and did not prevent a bill signed by the master from constituting a shipowner's bill of lading in the hands of a shipper with no notice of the charter clause.

If the bill of lading is signed by the charterer or its servants or agents, it will still, as a general rule, amount to a shipowner's bill if they sign 'on behalf' of the master. Such a signature can bind the shipowner if the signer has been given actual authority under the charterparty to do so. Even if they do not have express actual authority to sign the bills of lading themselves, the charterers will have implied actual authority to do so if the charter expressly authorises them to require the master to sign bills of lading as presented by the charterer. In *The Vikfrost*,[50] this implied authority extended not only to the subcharterer, but also to its loading agents. Their signature for the master therefore meant that the bill became a shipowner's bill.

A problem arises where the charterers exceed the limits of their actual authority under the charterparty. For example, the charter might provide that the master is to sign bills of lading in accordance with the mate's receipts. Suppose that the charterers, on behalf of the master, sign bills of lading that are not in accordance with the mate's receipts: the bills of lading will only bind the shipowner if the person signing them had ostensible authority to do so. For there to be ostensible authority, the shipowner must have done something to represent that the person signing bills of

47 *Samuel v West Hartlepool SN Co* (1906) 11 Com Cas 115.
48 *Baumwoll Manufactur Von Carl Scheibler v Furness* [1893] AC 8.
49 [1895] 2 QB 539. It should be noted that the bill of lading merely stated 'freight as per charterparty'. Had the bill of lading, instead, incorporated 'all terms and conditions of the charterparty', the clause in question would have been incorporated into the bill of lading and become one of its terms. In such circumstances, a different decision might very well have been reached.
50 [1980] 1 Lloyd's Rep 560.

lading was authorised to do so. This representation clearly exists where the master himself signs the bill, but it is less clear whether it also exists where the charterer, or its agent, signs on behalf of the master.[51] Sheen J, in *The Nea Tyhi*,[52] found that there was ostensible authority in such a situation, quoting with approval the following passage from Wilford: 'Owners who time charter their ship and put them on charterers' berths without taking positive steps to indicate to the contrary may well be taken to have held out the charterers and their agents as having authority to make bill of lading contracts on their behalf.'[53] In contrast, Rix J, in *The Hector*,[54] took a contrary view, albeit *obiter*, as his decision was based on the fact that the bill of lading was clearly, on its face, a charterer's document.[55] However, a charterer will have no implied or ostensible authority to issue a second set of bills of lading, and, where it does so, such bills do not constitute a contract with the shipowner.[56]

Exceptionally, the bill can still be a charterer's bill, even if the charterer signs on behalf of the master. This will occur where the charterer intends to sign so as to bind the charterer and not the shipowner. This happened in *The Okehampton*,[57] where the charterer's agent signed the bill above the printed words 'el capitan' on its front. It also happened in *Elder Dempster & Co Ltd v Paterson Zochonis & Co Ltd*,[58] where Elder Dempster Lines, which was a shipowner in its own right, chartered in additional tonnage and used its own forms of bill of lading. The mere use of charterers' forms of bills of lading does not, however, point to their constituting charterer's bills even if signed for the master. In *The Rewia*,[59] it was stressed that what mattered was the intention with which the bills of lading had been signed. If the charterparty authorised the charterers to sign on behalf of the master, and so bind the shipowners, no enquiry would be made into the signer's actual intention: it would be presumed that they were signing on behalf of the shipowners. The *Elder Dempster* case was distinguished on the grounds that the charterers there were also shipowners in their own right.

Identity of carrier clauses

To avoid uncertainty as to whether a bill is a charterer's or a shipowner's document, bills of lading frequently contain a clause defining who is to be regarded as the 'carrier' under it. One such clause is the 'demise clause', which developed as a means of channelling cargo claims away from charterers to shipowners at a time when charterers lacked the right to limit claims against them. Such a clause might, typically, read as follows:

> If the ship is not owned or demise chartered by demise to the company or line by whom this bill of lading is issued (as may be the case notwithstanding anything which appears to the contrary) the bills of lading shall take effect as a contract with the Owner or demise charterer, as the case may be, as principal made through the agency of the said company or line who act as agents only and shall be under no personal liability whatsoever in respect thereof.

---

51 See *Carver on Bills of Lading*, *op cit* fn 23, at 4.033.
52 [1982] 1 Lloyd's Rep 606.
53 Wilford, Coghlin and Kimball, *Time Charters*, 5th edn, 2003, London: LLP, at 21.67.
54 [1998] 2 Lloyd's Rep 287.
55 Rix J, at 299, was attracted to the possibility that had the bill of lading, on its face, appeared to have been a shipowner's document, the shipper would have had a contract with the shipowner, independent of the bill of lading. However, as the bill was a charterer's bill on its face, the point did not need to be determined.
56 *The Atlas* [1996] 1 Lloyd's Rep 642, QB.
57 [1913] P 173.
58 [1923] 1 KB 420.
59 [1991] 2 Lloyd's Rep 325, CA.

The clause presents problems for the bill of lading holder who wishes to ascertain the identity of the contractual carrier, as it does not specify whether or not the party who has issued the bill is, in fact, the owner of the vessel or its demise charterer. A clearer clause is the 'identity of carrier' clause, which might, typically, read as follows:

> The contract evidenced by this bill of lading is between the Merchant and the Owner of the vessel named herein and it is, therefore, agreed that the said shipowner alone shall be liable for any damage or loss due to any breach or nonperformance of any obligation arising out of the contract of carriage.

Such clauses have been recognised by the English courts since the decision of Brandon J in The Berkshire, which involved a demise clause that turned what would have been a charterer's bill into a shipowner's bill. Until recently, the terms of such clauses were thought to be conclusive of this issue, irrespective of the manner in which the bill had been signed, as happened in The Venezuela,[60] where the bill was signed by the subcharterers' agents on behalf of the master. Ordinarily, this would have resulted in its being a shipowner's bill of lading. However, on the facts, it was held to amount to a contract with the subcharterers, by virtue of a clause in the bill of lading defining the carrier in this way. This might seem a somewhat unusual clause but for the fact that the subcharterers were shipowners in their own right who had chartered in the vessel for a voyage and were using their own form of bill of lading.[61] The decision must, however, now be reconsidered in light of the decision of the House of Lords in The Starsin,[62] which is discussed below.

Problems can arise when the identity of the carrier clause on the rear of the bill of lading conflicts with contradictory statements on the front of the bill as to the identity of the contractual carrier. In The Hector,[63] Rix J was faced with three conflicting elements in the bill of lading. The form of signature on the front of the bill and the demise clause on the reverse pointed towards a shipowner's bill of lading. As against this, there was a clear typed statement on the front of the bill that identified the charterer as the carrier and it was to this that Rix J accorded primacy in holding the bill to be a charterer's document. The position is more difficult when the statement on the front of the bill is less clear-cut. This is illustrated by two first-instance decisions in which the same form of bill of lading was considered. The bill of lading was on the form of the charterer, CPC, and the attestation clause on the front stated that the bill was signed 'by agents for CPC' or 'by agents for CPC as carrier'. Two printed clauses on the reverse of the bill made it clear that the bill of lading was a shipowner's bill. In The Flecha,[64] Moore-Bick J found that the attestation clause was, on its own, not enough to show that CPC was contracting as carrier contrary to the terms on the rear of the bill and held that the bill was a shipowner's bill. However, Colman J, in The Starsin,[65] found that there was no ambiguity in the attestation clause and held that the bill was a charterer's bill.

The Court of Appeal then overruled the decision of Colman J in The Starsin[66] and found that the bill of lading was a shipowner's bill. The majority placed great significance on the wording of cl 35, the 'demise clause' – in particular, the following words: '(as may be the case notwithstanding anything that may appear to the contrary)'. Chadwick LJ stated that there was a difference between a bill of lading that included only an identity of carrier clause and one that included such a clause

---

60 [1980] 1 Lloyd's Rep 393, QB.
61 See, also, The Ines [1995] 2 Lloyd's Rep 144, QB, and The Jalamohan [1988] 1 Lloyd's Rep 443, QB, where bills of lading that would probably have been regarded as 'charterer's bills' from the form in which they were signed were construed as 'shipowner's bills' due, inter alia, to the presence of an 'identity of carrier' clause.
62 [2003] UKHL 12; [2003] 1 Lloyd's Rep 571.
63 [1998] 2 Lloyd's Rep 287, QB, noted (1999) LMCLQ 1.
64 [1999] 1 Lloyd's Rep 612, QB.
65 [2000] 1 Lloyd's Rep 85, QB.
66 [2001] 1 Lloyd's Rep 437, CA.

as well as a demise clause. In the latter situation, 'the proper approach . . . is to construe the two clauses together on the basis that one is not intended to be a mere repetition of the other'. Rix LJ, dissenting, took the view that the form of signature was decisive and that the words of cl 35 in parentheses did not act as a paramount clause. Commercial certainty was more likely to be promoted by focusing on the form of signature on the face of the bill rather than on demise clauses in tiny print on its reverse.

These views received the universal approval of the House of Lords, which reversed the decision of the Court of Appeal and held the bills of lading to be charterer's bills.[67] The decision was strongly influenced by the view that commercial people, as opposed to lawyers, would expect the identity of the carrier to be revealed in the material on the front of the bills – an assumption that was reflected in the provisions of Art 23(a) of UCP 500. The decision leaves it unclear, however, whether a demise or identity of carrier clause on the reverse of the bill can ever prevail over the form of signature on the front. It must be recalled that the attestation clause in question in The Starsin had been specifically written onto the front of the bill of lading. Therefore, as Lord Millett pointed out, it should clearly prevail over a standard printed term. It is possible that the result might have been different had the attestation clause also appeared in a standard printed form. However, the views expressed by Lords Bingham, Steyn and Hoffmann make it clear that the significant factor was the fact that the attestation clause was on the front of the bill. It is worth noting that, in The Hector, the conflict was between a typed identity of carrier clause and a printed attestation clause, both of which were to be found on the face of the bill. The typed clause was held to prevail and there is nothing in the judgments in The Starsin to throw doubt on the correctness of this decision. The material on the reverse of the bill may still, however, be significant where there are conflicting indications on the front of the bill that are both of the same order – that is, both are typed, or both are printed.[68]

Shipowner's position when a charterer's bill is issued

The position between shipper and shipowner must also be considered when a charterer's bill is issued. Their relation is probably one of bailor and bailee, on the terms of the charterer's bill of lading, as suggested by Lord Sumner in the Elder Dempster case.[69] The shipowner would be obliged to deliver the cargo against production of an original charterer's bill of lading in accordance with the terms of the head bailment to the charterers. Its liability for cargo claims would be in bailment, limited by the terms of the bill of lading. Alternatively, the shipowner may be regarded as a sub-bailee of the charterer, in which case it would be entitled to rely on the terms of the sub-bailment under the charterparty.[70] If a charterer's bill is issued, the ship may still be arrested in respect of any non-contractual claim that may be brought against it by the cargo owner. However, the effect of the rather complex rules of English law governing such claims entails that, in many instances, the cargo owner will have no title to sue in either bailment or negligence, and therefore there will be no claim in respect of which the ship can be arrested.[71]

This analysis would preclude any recovery of freight by the shipowner from the bill of lading holder. For freight to become due, there would need to be a parallel contract implied between shipowner and shipper. This is unlikely, given the assumption of the courts that there cannot be two

---

67 [2003] UKHL 12; [2003] 1 Lloyd's Rep 571.
68 As in Carewins Development (China) Ltd v Bright Fortune Shipping Ltd (Hong Kong CA; CACV 328/2006 and CACV 329/2006), where the material on the reverse of the bill of lading was used to clarify the effect of the attestation clause on the front.
69 [1924] AC 522.
70 Per Lord Hobhouse of Woodborough in The Starsin [2003] EWCA Civ 174; [2003] 1 Lloyd's Rep 239, at [131].
71 See, most recently, The Starsin [2003] UKHL 12; [2003] 1 Lloyd's Rep 571, in which charterer's bills were issued and all but one of the claimants failed to establish a claim in either bailment or negligence against the shipowner.

contractual carriers for the same sea voyage, as shown in *The Jalamohan*.[72] However, the shipowner's argument in that case was premised on the existence of a right to freight on a *quantum meruit* basis under a common carrier contract, assuming that the bills of lading were 'charterer's bills'. This premise was not attacked in the judgment, so the position remains open. In contrast, in New Zealand, it was held in *The AES Express*[73] that, in such a situation, the shipowner has no right to freight, and furthermore must perform the voyage stipulated in the time charterer's bill of lading. The second part of this decision is open to criticism in that, if there is no contract between the parties and therefore no right to claim freight, their relationship must be based on bailment. A bailee will have a duty to take reasonable care of the goods whilst in its custody, but will not be obliged to carry them on a voyage stipulated in a contract to which it is not a party.[74]

Third-party rights under the initial carriage contract at common law and in equity

The contracts implied on loading will still not assist the cif buyer or any sub-buyers under a fob contract. Only the shipper will have an express or implied contract with the shipowner. Two principles of English law preclude the end buyer from suing on the coat tails of the shipper's contract with the shipowner. The first is the doctrine of privity of contract, whereby only the parties to a contract may sue on it. If A makes a contract with B, only A and B may sue on it, notwithstanding that performance of the contract may entail a benefit being conferred on C. The second, related, principle is that damages for breach of contract are assessed by relation only to the loss suffered by a party to that contract. The loss suffered by a third party, such as C in the above example, is not recoverable, and if B itself suffers no loss, it will be unable to recover more than nominal damages. However, there are the following ways in which a third party may be able to seek recourse from the carrier, directly or indirectly, by using the law of contract.

Agency

In contracts for carriage by road, there is a presumption that the seller makes the carriage contract as undisclosed principal for the buyer where property in the goods has already passed to the buyer.[75] This presumption cannot apply to contracts for the carriage of goods by sea where, as is usually the case, the consignee will not obtain property in the goods until payment has been made against documents at some stage during the voyage. Accordingly, where the contract of carriage is concluded by a fob seller, rather than by the buyer, the bill of lading has still been held to evidence a contract between the seller, as shipper, and the carrier.[76] The buyer will only be able to obtain rights of suit under the bill of lading by the operation of statute. This judicial reluctance to depart from the presumption that the carrier has contracted with the party named as consignor in the bill has recently been evidenced by *Evergreen Marine Corp v Aldgate Warehouse*,[77] in which Moore-Bick J held that a party named as 'notify' party did not become liable under the bill if it never took possession of the document. An importer had concluded a freight agreement with a liner operator whose

---

72 [1988] 1 Lloyd's Rep 443, QB.
73 [1990] 20 NSWLR 57, Sup Ct (NZ).
74 *The Hector* [1998] 2 Lloyd's Rep 287, QB, noted (1999) LMCLQ 1.
75 *Mullinson v Carver* (1843) LT (OS) 59. The position is the same even if the consignor has agreed to pay the freight. See *King v Meredith* (1811) 2 Camp 639.
76 *The El Amria and The El Mina* [1982] 2 Lloyd's Rep 28, CA. See, also, *Fortis Bank SA/NV v Indian Overseas Bank* 17 March 2011 [2011] EWHC 538 (Comm); [2011] 2 Lloyd's Rep 190, where it was held that the requirement in the letter of credit that the bank be named as consignee did not mean it had authorised the consignor to contract with the carrier on its behalf.
77 [2003] EWHC 667 (Comm); [2003] 2 Lloyd's Rep 597, QB.

services it regularly used. Bills of lading were issued naming the exporting manufacturer as shipper. These were subsequently rejected as containing the wrong shipment date. The liner operator was held to have no claim for freight or demurrage against the importer. The freight agreement determined freight rates that would be applicable in the event that the importer became liable once it had become the lawful holder of the bill of lading. If this never happened, the importer could not be held liable, as it was not a party to the initial contract of carriage contained or evidenced by the bill of lading. The position is, of course, different where the bill of lading specifically states that one party is acting on behalf of another as shipper.[78]

Accordingly, agency is of very little use in granting rights of suit to parties who do not appear to be party to the original contract for the sea carriage of the goods. *Dicta* of Mustill LJ in *The Kapetan Markos NL*[79] suggest that, where a bill of lading is issued to a consignor who does not own the goods and who will take no further part in their transportation, it might take effect as a contract between the carrier and the consignor as agent for the undisclosed principal, a buyer to whom property in the goods has already passed. However, such situations are likely to be rare. It is worth noting that the agency argument does not appear to have been advanced in the context of claims by shippers against second carriers where the goods have been trans-shipped. In *The Pioneer Container*,[80] the claim against the second carriers was made by virtue of their status as sub-bailees. There was no suggestion that the bill of lading issued to the first carrier on trans-shipment should have been regarded as a contract with the goods' owner, the shipper, through the agency of the first carrier.

A more sophisticated use of agency can be seen in the use of 'partial agency' in 'Himalaya' clauses, which are used to extend the benefit of contractual exceptions to subcontractors of the carrier. Such a clause operates by the carrier contracting as principal in respect of the whole contract of carriage, and also as agent in respect of another party, but only in respect of those parts of the contract that involve that party. The Himalaya clause will be discussed in more detail at pp 52–6, in the section on claims in tort.

The Contracts (Rights of Third Parties) Act 1999

The common law doctrine of privity of contract has been radically altered by the **Contracts (Rights of Third Parties) Act 1999**, which came into effect on 11 May 2000. An appropriately worded clause in the contract can now enable third parties to obtain rights thereunder. Section 1(1) allows a third party to enforce a term of the contract in its own right in two situations. The first, in s 1(1)(a), is where the contract expressly provides that it may. The second, in s 1(1)(b), is where the term purports to confer a benefit on the third party, but this will not apply 'if on a proper construction of the contract it appears that the parties did not intend the term to be enforceable by the third party'. Section 1(3) requires the third party to be expressly identified in the contract 'by name, as a member of a class or as answering a particular description but need not be in existence when the contract is entered into'. In *Nisshin Shipping Co Ltd v Cleaves & Co Ltd*,[81] a broker was held to be entitled to sue for commission due to him under a clause in a charterparty, pursuant to s 1(1)(b). The broker's claim was subject to the arbitration clause in the charter, even though the clause referred only to disputes between the shipowner and the charterer. In *The Laemthong Glory (No. 2)*,[82] it was held that a shipowner was entitled to rely on a letter of indemnity given by receivers to charterers, on back-to-back terms to an indemnity given from charterers to the shipowner, pursuant to s 1(1)(b).

---

78 As in *The Andros and Xingcheng* [1987] 1 WLR 1213.
79 [1987] 2 Lloyd's Rep 321, 329.
80 [1994] 2 AC 324.
81 [2003] EWHC 2602 (Comm); [2004] 1 Lloyd's Rep 38, noted [2005] S&TLI, 5(1), 7.
82 [2005] EWCA Civ 519; [2005] 1 Lloyd's Rep 688.

The Act, however, does not provide for third parties to become subject to the obligations imposed under a contract. More importantly, for our purposes, the effect of s 6(5) prevents third parties from obtaining positive rights of suit under contracts of carriage that are subject to the operation of **COGSA 1992**. This limitation on the ambit of the 1999 Act is intended to avoid the uncertainty that would apply were there two parallel statutory means for third parties to acquire rights of suit under contracts for carriage of goods by sea. The limitation also prevents the divesting provisions of s 2(5) of **COGSA 1992** from being undermined by express clauses in the bill of lading giving rights of suit to a third party.

Two points should, however, be noted. First, the limitation mentioned above does not prevent a clause in a contract of carriage that is subject to **COGSA 1992** from conferring on a third party the right to rely on exclusion and limitation clauses contained in the contract of carriage. Secondly, not every contract for the carriage of goods by sea is subject to the operation of **COGSA 1992**. The voyage charterparty is an obvious example of such a contract. It would, therefore, now be possible to confer positive rights of suit under such a contract on a third party, provided that the clause satisfied the requirements of s 1 of the 1999 Act.

Trust

If the shipper is found to have contracted as trustee for a third party, not only will it be able to recover damages for that party's loss, but the third party will also obtain a right to sue on the shipper's contract. Such a trust is very unlikely to exist in the light of the Court of Appeal's decision in *Re Schebsman*,[83] where it held that there must be clear evidence of an intention by the original contracting party to hold its contractual rights on trust for the third party.

Suit by the shipper

In 1839, in *Dunlop v Lambert*,[84] the House of Lords recognised a limited exception to the general principle of contract law that damages cannot be recovered in respect of a loss suffered by a third party. It held that a consignor could claim substantial damages under a bill of lading contract in respect of damage sustained by the consignee's goods, if it was in the contemplation of the parties that the ownership of the goods might change during the performance of the carriage. Such damages would be held on trust for the consignee who has suffered the loss. A similar, but separate, rule applies to entitle a party who has not suffered the loss to recover substantial damages on the basis either that they had possessory rights over the goods at the time of the breach[85] or that they were the owner of the goods at this time.[86] In both instances, the damages recovered are held on trust for the party that has actually suffered the loss.

Although *Dunlop v Lambert* is still good law and underpinned the decision of the House of Lords in *Linden Gardens Trust Ltd v Lenesta Sludge Disposals Ltd*,[87] it is of very little relevance to shipping law. In *The Albazero*,[88] the House of Lords held that the case did not cover a situation in which there was a contractual nexus between the consignee buyer and the shipowner. On the facts, such a nexus had been created by the operation of the **Bills of Lading Act 1855**. The buyer allowed these contractual

---

83 [1944] Ch 83.
84 (1839) 6 Cl & F 600.
85 *The Winkfield* [1902] P 42.
86 *The Sanix Ace* [1987] 1 Lloyd's Rep 465, QB. The goods owner is entitled to full recovery in such circumstances whether the claim be made in contract or in negligence.
87 [1994] 1 AC 85. The facts of the case concerned the construction industry.
88 [1977] AC 774.

rights to become time-barred, and therefore persuaded its seller, an associated company, to sue for breach of the charterparty. However, the charterer's recovery was limited to nominal damages. *Dunlop v Lambert* will probably continue to be of relevance only in respect of claims by charterers on behalf of a third party who has not obtained independent contractual rights of action under **COGSA 1992**.[89] Such situations are likely to be rare.

Assignment

The seller could expressly assign to the buyer its contractual rights under the bill of lading. To perfect the assignment, which could be either legal[90] or equitable, notice would have to be given to the shipowner. This would make it a cumbersome process with strings of sub-sales. It should also be noted that, under English law, an assignment can only transfer rights, not duties. However, in certain situations, this solution might still be appropriate. In *The Aliakmon*,[91] while the goods were still afloat, their sale was converted from one on c & f (cost, freight) terms[92] to one *ex-warehouse*, but one under which risk still passed on loading. This was due to the inability of the buyers to pay for the goods at that stage. One of the ways in which they could have protected themselves would have been to have taken such an assignment when the contract was renegotiated. The assignment will be valid provided that the assignee has a legitimate commercial interest in the goods in question. In *The Kelo*,[93] Staughton J held that the assignee would have such an interest even where it sought to enforce the assigned rights as agent for a third party. Rights of action in respect of torts resulting in property damage are probably assignable as well, as long as there is no assignment of a bare right of action.[94]

Implied contract

In *Brandt v Liverpool Brazil & River Plate SN Co*,[95] a bank, which had financed the purchase of goods under a letter of credit, took delivery of the goods, which were discharged in a damaged condition. The Court of Appeal held that the bank obtained title to sue the carrier under the bill of lading by virtue of an implied contract arising out of the conduct of the parties on discharge. Its presentation of the bill of lading was an offer to the shipowner to contract on the terms of that document, which was accepted when the shipowner agreed to deliver the goods.

This doctrine developed as the principal way in which the courts were able to fill the gaps in the **Bills of Lading Act 1855**. With the passing of **COGSA 1992**, this device is largely otiose. It should briefly be noted that its utility has been severely restricted by the Court of Appeal's decisions in *The Aramis*[96] and *The Gudermes*.[97] Mere delivery of the goods without some payment to the shipowner from the party taking delivery will, in the absence of some unusual degree of cooperation between the parties to facilitate delivery,[98] be insufficient to justify the implication of such a

---

89 A statutory version of *Dunlop v Lambert*, in respect of claims by the 'lawful holder' of a bill of lading for loss sustained by a third party, is provided by s 2(4) of the Act. The section does not, however, cover claims under a charterparty, which is why *Dunlop v Lambert* will continue to be relevant to such claims.

90 Subject to the requirements of s 136 of the Law of Property Act 1925.

91 [1986] 1 AC 785.

92 I.e. a cif contract without the insurance element.

93 [1985] 1 Lloyd's Rep 557, QB.

94 Per Lord Roskill in *Trendtex Trading Corp v Credit Suisse* [1982] AC 679, HL 703, in which his Lordship posited the following two-stage test: first, 'the assignee must show that he has a genuine commercial interest in the enforcement of the claim of another'; secondly, the assignee must not fall foul of the law of champerty.

95 [1924] 1 KB 575.

96 [1989] 1 Lloyd's Rep 213.

97 [1993] 1 Lloyd's Rep 311.

98 Such as was found on the unusual facts of *The Captain Gregos* (No. 2) [1990] 2 Lloyd's Rep 395, CA. The case is also noteworthy in that the implied contract was on the terms of the bill of lading even though delivery had been made without presentation of the bill.

contract. Furthermore, such cooperation must be willing cooperation and not such as is imposed upon the parties by the exigencies of the situation.[99]

Statutory transfer – the Carriage of Goods by Sea Act 1992

The first legislative attempt to address the problems of title to sue for transit loss faced by cargo owners, other than the original shipper, was the **Bills of Lading Act 1855**. Section 1 effected a statutory assignment of the contract contained in the bill of lading to the consignee named in the bill or to the indorsee, provided that property in the goods had passed to them by reason of the consignment or indorsement, respectively. Both the benefits of this contract, the right to sue the issuer of the bill, and its burdens, the liability for any freight or demurrage due to the carrier under the bill, would follow the bill of lading as it passed down the chain of buyers until it ended up with the buyer who used it to take delivery of the goods.[100]

However, neither the naming of a consignee nor the indorsement of the bill was, of itself, sufficient to effect this statutory assignment. The Act stipulated that the assignment would occur only when the property in the goods passed 'upon or by reason of' the consignment of the goods or the indorsement of the bill of lading. This property link had the effect of excluding four categories of claimant who needed to establish a contractual means of recovering transit loss from the shipowner: (a) pledgees of the bill of lading, such as banks financing sales through letters of credit;[101] (b) buyers of part of an unascertained bulk of cargo;[102] (c) buyers under sale contracts where the indorsement or transfer of the bill of lading was not critical to the passing of property;[103] (d) holders of documents other than bills of lading, such as delivery orders and waybills.[104]

The position of such parties was particularly critical, as frequently they would also be unable to establish a right of action in tort or bailment as an alternative means of recovery against the carrier. The doctrine of implied contract was widely used after *Brandt v Liverpool Brazil & River Plate SN Co*[105] to fill in some of these gaps, but in the light of its restricted application by the Court of Appeal in *The Aramis*,[106] it became clear that statutory reform was essential.

The Carriage of Goods by Sea Act 1992

In 1991, the Law Commission produced Report No. 196, *Rights of Suit in Respect of Carriage of Goods by Sea*, and its draft Bill became enacted, without amendment, as the **Carriage of Goods by Sea Act**

---

99 As in *The Gudermes* [1993] 1 Lloyd's Rep 311, where the parties arranged for trans-shipment of a cargo of oil that had not been heated to a sufficient degree to allow it to be discharged directly from the ship into the receiver's pipeline.

100 Section 2 expressly provided that the original shipper would continue to be liable for freight due under the bill.

101 In *Sewell v Burdick* (1884) 10 App Cas 74, the House of Lords confirmed that such an indorsement only passed 'special property' in the goods (that is, a security interest) and not the 'general property' (that is, ownership itself) necessary to satisfy the definition of 'property' in the Act.

102 The effect of s. 16 of the Sale of Goods Act 1979 was to prevent the buyers from obtaining ownership in the goods until they had become ascertained on discharge. In these circumstances, whatever the parties' intentions, the transfer of the bill of lading was insufficient to transfer property in the goods. That could be effected only when they became separated into different parcels on delivery. The position of such purchasers has been substantially improved by the Sale of Goods Act 1995. The Act adds a new s 20(A) to the Sale of Goods Act 1979, under which the buyer of goods from part of an identified bulk becomes a tenant in common of the appropriate proportion of that bulk after payment of the purchase price. The buyer is thereby protected in the event of the seller becoming insolvent in the interval between payment and delivery.

103 As in *The Delfini* [1990] 1 Lloyd's Rep 252 (CA), where the bill of lading was indorsed some time after the goods had been delivered to the buyer. The Court of Appeal held that as property had passed to the buyer, at the very latest by the time the goods were delivered to it, the subsequent indorsement of the bill of lading failed to satisfy the property link required by the Act.

104 The Act applied only to bills of lading and it was also unclear whether it applied to 'received for shipment' bills. Cf the divergent judicial views on the status of such bills expressed in *Diamond Alkali Export Corp v Fl Bourgeois* [1921] 3 KB 443 and *The Marlborough Hill* [1921] AC 444.

105 [1924] 1 KB 575.

106 [1989] 1 Lloyd's Rep 213.

1992. COGSA 1992 came into force in respect of bills of lading, waybills and ship's delivery orders dated on or after 16 September 1992. It abolishes the property link required by the **Bills of Lading Act 1855**. It also provides for a separate statutory transfer of contractual rights and duties under contracts contained in, or evidenced by, the above documents.[107]

Transfer of contractual rights

Bills of lading

The statutory transfer of rights under the bill of lading contract now depends on the claimant establishing that it is the 'lawful holder' of the bill of lading at the time that it commences suit. Section 2(1) provides that the lawful holder 'shall have transferred to and vested in it all rights of suit under the contract of carriage as if it had been a party to that contract'. Section 5(1) defines 'contract of carriage' as 'the contract contained in or evidenced by that bill of lading'. The effect of these provisions will be that the contractual rights, acquired under s 2(1), will be subject to all of the terms of the bill of lading.[108]

It is worth contrasting the wording used in **COGSA 1992** with that used in the **Bills of Lading Act 1855**, which referred to 'the contract contained in the bill of lading'. It is therefore possible that, in a case like *The Ardennes*,[109] the entire contract of carriage, including the parol terms, might be transferred to the 'lawful holder' of the bill of lading. This would not prejudice a third party where the parol terms were to its advantage. However, the third party would suffer a prejudice if the parol agreement were to the benefit of the carrier, as was the case in *Leduc v Ward*.[110] It is likely, however, that, in such a situation, the shipowner would be estopped from relying on any term that does not appear in the bill of lading as against a third party with no notice of the parol terms of the initial contract of carriage.[111] In *The Michael S*,[112] it was held that if the shipper and the shipowner had agreed to incorporate the charterparty bill of lading clause in the bill of lading, that agreement would not affect the lawful holder of the bill of lading.

When a bill of lading is indorsed or transferred so that the third party qualifies as a 'lawful holder', the effect of s 2(5) is that the previous holder will cease to be a 'lawful holder' and will lose any rights of suit conferred by s 2(1). This provision also operates so as to divest the original shipper, the consignor, of any of his express or implied contractual rights under the bill of lading, once it has transferred or indorsed the bill and rights of suit have been transferred to that third party pursuant to s 2(1). In *East West Corp v DKBS 1912*,[113] Thomas J held that s 2(5) did not apply as regards a 'straight' bill of lading. He also held that, when a bill of lading is involved, s 2(5) divests not only contractual rights, but also rights that may exist by way of bailment.[114] This part of the decision was overruled by the Court of Appeal,[115] which held that the shippers retained rights of suit in bailment notwithstanding that contractual rights of suit had passed under s 2(1) of **COGSA 1992** to their agents, as named consignee, to whom the bills had been physically transferred.[116]

---

107 For a good review of the Act, see Reynolds, FMB, 'The Carriage of Goods by Sea Act 1992' (1993) LMCLQ 436.
108 Including any jurisdiction clause: *The Kribi* [2001] 1 Lloyd's Rep 76, QB.
109 [1951] 1 KB 55.
110 (1888) 20 QBD 475, CA.
111 *Carver on Bills of Lading*, op cit fn 23, at 5022, takes the view that the modified wording of s 5(1) does not effect any change in the law as it was under the Bills of Lading Act 1855. Gaskell, *Bills of Lading: Law and Practice*, op cit fn 23, at 2.24, is of the same opinion.
112 [2001] All ER (D) 325 (QB).
113 [2002] 2 Lloyd's Rep 535.
114 However, the claimant was entitled to sue in negligence. Although there had been no damage to the goods, the shipowner's misdelivery had damaged the shipper's proprietary interest therein.
115 [2003] EWCA Civ 174; [2003] 1 Lloyd's Rep 239.
116 Such transfer had not, however, transferred legal possession. Even if it had, the shippers retained a reversionary interest sufficient to allow them to sue in bailment.

The aim of s 2(5) is to prevent the carrier from being faced with actions from different parties in respect of the same loss. This aim has not entirely been achieved, for these provisions only divest rights of suit from parties whose title to sue is based on the bill of lading in some way. They have no effect on claims that may be made against the shipowner by a charterer. Where a charterer owns the goods at the time of breach, as was the case in *The Sanix Ace*,[117] it will be entitled to recover substantial damages, in either contract or tort, from the shipowner in respect of loss or damage to the goods, notwithstanding that risk in the goods may have been transferred to a third-party buyer.[118] In *The Sanix Ace*, the third party had no rights of suit under the **Bills of Lading Act 1855**. However, the effect of **COGSA 1992** is that most such third parties would acquire statutory rights of suit against the shipowner, leaving open the possibility that the shipowner could face two separate actions against it in respect of the same loss, with each claimant being entitled to recover substantial damages. A shipowner faced with such a dilemma should interplead, although this may be problematic where the bill of lading and the charterparty contain differing provisions as to jurisdiction and/or arbitration.[119]

What is a bill of lading under the Act?

The Act provides no positive definition of a 'bill of lading'. Instead, s 1(2)(a) provides that references in the Act to a bill of lading 'do not include references to a document which is incapable of transfer either by indorsement or, as a bearer bill, by delivery without indorsement'. It is, therefore, clear that 'straight' bills fall outside the provisions of the Act that refer to 'bills of lading'. Such documents, however, almost certainly fall within the provisions of the Act relating to sea waybills.[120] By virtue of s 1(2)(b), 'received for shipment' bills fall within the provisions of the Act that relate to bills of lading.[121] Section 5(4) expressly applies the Act to situations in which goods cease to exist after the issue of the document (that is, a bill of lading, waybill or ship's delivery order) or cannot be identified 'whether because they are mixed with other goods or for any other reason'.[122]

Holder

Section 5(2) of **COGSA 1992** defines a holder of the bill of lading to cover three categories of person. First, there is '(a) a person with possession of the bill who, by virtue of being the person identified in the bill, is the consignee of the goods to which the bill relates . . .'. Such a bill of lading will be an 'order' bill. The consignee will transfer the bill by indorsement. This may be a special indorsement in favour of a designated party, in which case that party will need to make a further indorsement when it transfers the bill. The indorsement may also be a general indorsement (or an 'indorsement in blank'), which does not specify a designated party, in which case the bill of lading after indorsement will be treated as a bearer bill and further transfers will not require indorsement. A bank holding such a bill by way of security will need the cooperation of the consignee in indorsing the bill to it if it is to acquire rights of suit under the Act. This cooperation may not always be forthcoming and, for this reason, banks generally require a 'bearer' bill to be submitted under a

---

117 [1987] 1 Lloyd's Rep 465, QB.

118 This principle, which was also applied in *The Fjord Wind* [1999] 1 Lloyd's Rep 307, 337, QB, aff'd [2000] 2 Lloyd's Rep 191, CA, is distinct from that applied in *Dunlop v Lambert* (1839) 6 Cl & F 600. It is therefore not affected by the limitations on that principle effected in *The Albazero* [1977] AC 774.

119 This problem could also occur under a waybill, as the Act does not divest the consignor of its rights thereunder. However, interpleader would be a straightforward matter, as both parties would be claiming against the carrier under the same document.

120 These are defined by s 1(3) as 'any document which is not a bill of lading but: (a) is such a receipt for goods as contains or evidences a contract for the carriage of goods by sea; and (b) identifies the person to whom delivery of the goods is to be made by the carrier in accordance with the contract'.

121 Provided, of course, that they are not straight bills, which fall foul of s 1(2)(a).

122 Section 5(4)(b) of COGSA 1992.

letter of credit.[123] When the bill of lading is transferred to the named consignee, that party will become a lawful holder, even though it is acting as the agent for another party.[124]

Secondly, there is '(b) a person with possession of the bill as a result of the completion, by delivery of the bill, of any indorsement of the bill or, in the case of a bearer bill, of any other transfer of the bill . . .'. Where the third party is the indorsee of an order bill or the transferee of a bearer bill, the fact that it physically possesses the bill of lading will not necessarily mean that it satisfies the definition of a 'lawful holder' contained in s 5(2)(b) of **COGSA 1992**. Unless it possesses the intent to accept delivery of the bill, there will be no completion of delivery as required by s 5(2)(b).[125] In *The Erin Schulte*,[126] a bank to whom a bill of lading was indorsed pursuant to a letter of credit was held to be a 'lawful holder' even though the bank held the documents presented to the order of the presenter until there had been a compliant presentation. The bank had initially rejected the documents as non-compliant but retained them and subsequently accepted their validity and paid out under the letter of credit, by which time the cargo had been delivered. Accordingly, the bank was a lawful holder and had a contractual right to sue in respect of the mis-delivery of the goods. There may be cases where the holder of an order bill of lading is not entitled to endorse it, in which case any such endorsement will be invalid and incapable of constituting any subsequent transferee of the bill of lading a 'holder' for the purposes of section 5(2)(b) of the **COGSA 1992**. This was the case in *The Dolphina*,[127] where the purported indorsement was fraudulent, the indorser having previously taken delivery on providing an indemnity in which it had undertaken to surrender the bill of lading when it came into its possession.

Thirdly, there is '(c) a person with possession of the bill as a result of any transaction by virtue of which he would have become a holder falling within paragraph (a) or (b) above had not the transaction been effected at a time when possession of the bill no longer gave a right (as against the carrier) to possession of the goods to which the bill relates . . .'. This covers persons who have become the holders of a 'spent' bill, but would have fallen within either of the two previous categories had they obtained possession of the bill at a time when possession of the bill gave a right to possession of the goods to which the bill relates, as against the carrier. The scope of this category was considered in *The Ythan*.[128] Aikens J held that a transfer of the bill of lading after the cargo was lost following an explosion on board the vessel did not render the transferee a 'lawful holder'. The bill of lading had been forwarded to the buyer's insurance agent for the purpose of settling a claim under the buyer's policy. Although the broker held the bills on behalf of the buyer, the transaction was one that would not have occurred had the cargo not been lost.

A bill will not become 'spent' if delivery is made by the carrier to a party not entitled to possession of the goods. This was to prove significant in *East West Corp v DKBS 1912*.[129] The sellers were issued bills of lading that named their Chilean bank as consignee. The bank was to act under their directions at all times as regards the bills. Notwithstanding this, the bank, as named consignee, obtained rights of suit under s 2(1) as the 'lawful holder' of the bills. In consequence, s 2(5) divested the sellers of their rights of suit under the bills. The bank then transferred the bills back to the sellers, but failed to indorse them. The sellers argued that they were now the lawful holder under s 5(2)(c), because, if the goods had not been delivered, then under their arrangement with the bank the bills would have been endorsed back to them to enable them to take delivery of them. However, this argument had no prospect of success because this provision applied only

---

123 A bank to which such a bill is transferred by way of pledge will become the lawful holder thereby. See *Motis Exports (No. 2)* (2001) Admlty Ct, 2 February; [2001] WL 239695.
124 *East West Corp v DKBS 1912* [2003] EWCA Civ 174; [2003] 1 Lloyd's Rep 239.
125 *The Aegean Sea* [1998] 2 Lloyd's Rep 39, QB.
126 [2013] EWHC 808 (Comm); [2013] 2 Lloyd's Rep. 338. Subsequently overruled; see Preface.
127 [2012] 1 Lloyd's Rep 304 H Ct Sing.
128 [2005] EWHC 2399 (Comm); [2006] 1 Lloyd's Rep 457, noted (2006) S & TI, 5(4), 14.
129 [2003] EWCA Civ 174; [2003] 1 Lloyd's Rep 239.

where bills were spent. This was not the case here, as delivery had not been made to the party entitled to possession of the cargo: the sellers. As a result, the sellers' action against the shipowner could only be brought non-contractually.

Section 5(2) provides that holders in either of these categories will be regarded as 'lawful holders' whenever they 'become the holder of the bill of lading in good faith'. The reference to 'good faith' would prevent a party from qualifying as a 'lawful holder' where they were aware of any defect in title in the person who transferred the bill of lading to them.

A shipper that loses its rights of suit under s 2(5) may reacquire them if it, in turn, becomes a 'lawful holder'. Thus, in *Motis Exports (No 2)*,[130] the shipper lost its rights as the initial holder of a bearer bill when it transferred the bill to its bank by way of pledge. However, when its sale to the buyer collapsed and the bank returned the bill to it, the shipper then obtained contractual rights under the bill of lading as a lawful holder, as defined in s 5(2)(b). It was still held to be acting in 'good faith' notwithstanding that, by this time, it may well have become aware of the fact that the goods had been misdelivered against presentation of a forged bill of lading. Even if such awareness had been relevant to this issue, it was clear that none had existed at the relevant time, which was when the bank and the shipper had concluded their contract.

'Spent' bills of lading

When a person becomes the lawful holder of a 'spent' bill of lading, s 2(2) provides that rights of suit shall only be transferred in the following two instances. The first is where a person becomes holder 'by virtue of a transaction effected in pursuance of any contractual or other arrangements made before the time when such a right to possession ceased to attach to possession of the bill'. Under this provision, the holder of such a 'spent' bill will have to establish when arrangements for transfer of the bill of lading were finalised. If the arrangements were made before discharge, the contract will transfer to the indorsee even if the actual transfer occurs after discharge, as was the case on the facts in *The Delfini*.[131] The relevant time is not that of the *transfer* of the bill itself, but that of the *arrangements* made for that transfer. If the arrangements for the transfer of the bill are made after discharge, the Act will not apply. As can be seen in *The David Agmashembeli*,[132] it may not always be easy to determine when such arrangements were made. The master had claused the bill of lading, which had led to its rejection under the letter of credit. The seller then took delivery of the cargo by presenting to the shipowner an original bill of lading marked 'accomplished'. The sale contract was then varied so as to reduce the price and to provide for delivery of the goods from the seller rather than from the vessel. Payment of the varied price was made under letter of credit. The transfer of the bill first to the bank and then to the buyer did not entail that the buyer became a 'lawful holder' under s 2(2)(a), as the arrangement was made under the varied sale contract at a time after delivery had been made by the ship to the seller. By that time, the bills of lading had ceased to give their holder possessory rights in the cargo.[133] The second instance, which is provided for under s 2(2)(b), is where a person becomes holder 'as a result of the rejection to that person by another person of goods or documents delivered to the other person in pursuance of such arrangements'.

---

130 (2001) Admlty Ct, 2 February; [2001] WL 239695.
131 [1990] 1 Lloyd's Rep 252, CA.
132 [2002] EWHC 104 (Admlty); [2003] 1 Lloyd's Rep 95, QB.
133 In *The Ythan* [2005] EWHC 2399 (Comm); [2006] 1 Lloyd's Rep 457, Aikens J was of the view, *obiter*, that s 2(2)(a) would not apply where the bills of lading had been transferred to the buyer's insurance broker to facilitate a claim being made on the policy following the destruction of the cargo on board the vessel. The proximate cause of the transfer of the bills to the broker was the actual or contemplated compromise settlement of the insurance claim. This occurred after the right to possession had ceased to attach to the bills, with the loss of the cargo. Applying this test, Teare J, in *Pace Shipping Co Ltd v Churchgate Nigeria Ltd* [2009] EWHC 1975 (Comm); [2010] 1 Lloyd's Rep 183, was of the view, *obiter*, that arbitrators were entitled to infer that the contract of sale had been the cause of the transfer or delivery of the bill of lading even though there may have been no contractual entitlement at the time the endorsement was made.

Bills of lading in the hands of a charterer

The Act says nothing about the position of the charterer holder of a bill of lading. Accordingly, the current case law will continue to apply and the bill of lading will have no contractual significance in the hands of a charterer. This gives rise to a theoretical problem, which also existed with the **Bills of Lading Act 1855**. Section 2(1) states that the lawful holder, '(by virtue of becoming the holder of the bill . . . [shall] have transferred to and vested in him all rights of suit under the contract of carriage as if he had been a party to that contract)'.

Section 5(1)(a) defines 'contract of carriage' as 'the contract contained in or evidenced by that bill . . .'. However, where the shipper is a charterer, the initial contract of carriage will be contained in the charterparty, not the bill of lading, which is a mere receipt. The intention behind the Act, which is to transfer contractual rights in the bill of lading and not the charterparty, will be frustrated by the fact that, in the charterer's hands, the bill of lading will be a mere receipt. There will therefore be no contractual rights capable of transfer on indorsement of the bill. The purpose of the Act can be fulfilled only if a bill of lading in a charterer's hands is deemed to be a contractual document, but solely for the purposes of vesting contractual rights of suit in the hands of a holder other than the original charterer.[134] The Act also leaves untouched the current law relating to whether a bill of lading constitutes a 'shipowner's' or a 'charterer's' bill.

Recovery of third-party losses under the Act

The Act makes establishing title to sue very easy for most cargo owners. However, a practical problem may arise where the bill of lading gets stuck in a chain of banks and is not in the physical possession of the end buyer at the time that the one-year Hague/Hague-Visby time limit is about to expire. The end buyer will be unable to establish title to sue if the courts take a literal approach to the definition of 'lawful holder'.

A partial remedy is provided by s 2(4), which allows the person with statutory rights of suit under s 2(1) (thereby excluding the original consignor) to exercise those rights on behalf of 'a person with any interest or right in or in relation to goods to which the document relates' who has sustained 'loss or damage in consequence of a breach of the contract of carriage'.[135] The provision refers to 'any document to which this Act applies' and therefore applies equally to waybills and ship's delivery orders. The words 'interest or right' would appear to cover situations in which the bill of lading is in the possession of an agent or where the goods were still at the risk of the third party at the time of the breach. So, for example, this provision would assist a cif seller under an 'outturn' contract whereby it has agreed with the buyer to bear the risk of outturn shortages. However, s 2(4) imposes no duty on the lawful holder of the bill of lading to make such a claim on behalf of the third party.[136] Finally, one should note that s 2(4) contains the proviso that the rights are to be exercised for the third party 'to the same extent as they could have been exercised if they had been vested in the person for whose benefit they are exercised', which seems designed to cover the situation in which the third party is the original shipper and the original contract of carriage contains additional parol terms as in *The Ardennes*.

---

134 The problem of a transfer of a bill from a charterer under the Bills of Lading Act 1855 was briefly dealt with by an *obiter dictum* of Lord Atkin in *Hain SS Co Ltd v Tate & Lyle* (1936) 41 Comm Cas 350, 356, to the effect that the provisions of the Act ensured that a new contract sprung up in such circumstances.

135 The lawful holder of a bill of lading who makes a claim under s 2(4) is not making a separate claim on behalf of the party that has suffered loss but is pursuing his own cause of action. However, such a claimant should particularise the third party's losses for which he is claiming. *Pace Shipping Ltd v Churchgate Nigeria Ltd* [2010] EWHC 2828 (Comm); [2011] 1 All ER (Comm) 939; [2011] 1 Lloyd's Rep 537.

136 For this reason, a seller under a cif contract on 'outturn' terms is better protected by a contractual stipulation obliging the buyer to effect an assignment to it of its contractual rights under the bill of lading so far as they relate to non-delivery claims.

Delivery orders

A similar mechanism for transfer of suit applies to ship's delivery orders.[137] The delivery order is defined in s 1(4) as a document that is neither a bill of lading nor a sea waybill and which contains 'an undertaking by the carrier to a person identified in the document to deliver the goods to which the document relates to that person'.[138] The person so identified obtains rights of suit under s 2(1)(c) by reason of being so identified, rather than by being the holder of the document. Section 5(3) provides that the reference to identification in s 1(4)(b) includes references to that person's 'being identified by a description which allows for the identity of the person in question to be varied'. This is designed to cover a delivery order that directs delivery to 'X or order'. When X, then, designates Y as the person to whom the goods covered in the order should now be delivered, the effect of this provision is to allow Y to obtain rights of suit under s 2(1)(c). Rights of suit will pass only if the undertaking is given by the 'carrier'. The Act does not define this term, but, presumably, it refers to the contractual carrier under the bill of lading. It is arguable that it could also refer to a non-contractual carrier who actually performs the carriage as a bailee. A shipowner will be such a party where cargo is carried under a charterer's bill. Such a construction would bring a delivery order containing an undertaking by the shipowner within s 1(4). However, where a shipowner's bill is issued, an undertaking by the charterer would not fall within this construction, as any bailment to the charterer would cease when the goods entered the shipowner's custody.[139]

The rights conferred by s 2(1)(c) are rights of suit under the contract of carriage pursuant to which the undertaking was given. This is defined in s 5(1) as 'the contract under or for the purposes of which the undertaking contained in the order is given'. This definition contains no reference to the contract being contained in, or evidenced by, a bill of lading or sea waybill. Such rights are subject to the terms of the order and, by s 2(3)(b), are expressed to relate only to that part of the contract of carriage that relates to the goods described in the delivery order. Section 2(5) divests parties who have previously acquired rights of suit under the delivery order of those rights of suit when they are transferred to a new party. However, this divestment operates without prejudice to any rights deriving from a document other than a delivery order and so will not divest the current holder of the bill of lading, whether the original consignor or a subsequent 'lawful holder', of its rights of suit.

Waybills

Unlike the previous two documents, delivery is not made against production of the document, but on proof of the identity of the consignee named in the waybill. The transfer of suit under s 2(1)(c), therefore, is not to holders of such documents but to the 'person entitled to delivery'. This may not always be the named consignee, as the shipper, prior to delivery, may instruct the carrier to deliver to someone else. Section 1(3) defines a waybill as:

> . . . any document which is not a bill of lading but—
> (a) is such a receipt for goods as contains or evidences a contract for the carriage of goods by sea; and
> (b) identifies the person to whom delivery of the goods is to be made by the carrier in accord-ance with that contract.

This definition is probably wide enough to embrace 'straight' bills of lading, including bills, such as some combined transport bills, that are intended to be negotiable but the negotiability of which is in doubt as a matter of law.

---

137 Defined in s 1(4) of COGSA 1992.
138 Subheading (b). Heading (a) provides that the undertaking is 'given for the purposes of a contract for the carriage by sea of the goods to which the document relates, or of goods which include those goods'.
139 *The Ines* [1995] 2 Lloyd's Rep 144, QB.

Unlike the position with a bill of lading, s 2(5) does not operate so as to divest the original contracting party under a waybill of its rights of suit thereunder. Because of this, the distinction between a bill of lading and a waybill can sometimes be critical, as in *The Chitral*,[140] where a bill of lading was marked 'if order state notify party'. As no notify party was named, the bill was non-negotiable and treated as a sea waybill, with the result that the original consignor was still able to sue on it.

Transfer of contractual liabilities

The original bill of lading holder will be liable for freight and demurrage in accordance with the terms of the bill of lading. He will also be liable, as a matter of law, for general average contributions and for damage suffered as a result of the loading of dangerous cargo. The shipper may also be under an implied obligation to load the vessel within a reasonable time, and the receiver under a similar obligation in respect of discharge.[141] However, he will not be liable in respect of any damage suffered by the shipowner in respect of the unsafety of the loading or discharging port.[142] The transfer of these contractual liabilities is dealt with separately under s 3. These will not automatically pass to those who obtain rights of suit under s 2(1). Section 3(1) provides that the person obtaining rights of suit under s 2(1) will be liable only if: (a) it 'takes or demands delivery of any of the goods to which the document relates',[143] or (b) 'makes a claim under the contract of carriage against the carrier in respect of those goods'.[144] The 'carrier' is not defined in the Act and must refer to the contractual carrier under the bill of lading. Where a charterer's bill is issued, problems arise, in that delivery will be effected by the shipowner, not the charterer. However, if the shipowner is regarded as the charterer's agent for this purpose, then there should be no problem in the operation of s 3(1) so as to transfer liabilities under a charterer's bill. Section 3(1)(c) also provides for the holder of a 'spent' bill of lading to become liable, retrospectively, to the time at which it took or demanded delivery of the goods covered in the document. Section 3(2) expressly provides that, where delivery is taken under a delivery order, its holder shall not be under any liability in respect of goods not covered by the order. When the section operates, it will transfer all liabilities under the bill of lading, even those accruing prior to the transfer of the bill.

However, a problem arises with intermediate holders of a bill of lading who satisfy the requirements of s 3(1), for the section contains no provision equivalent to s 2(5) to divest them of liability. This situation is unlikely to arise often in practice. However, it did arise in *The Berge Sisar*,[145] where the intermediate holder requested samples prior to delivery, on the basis of which it rejected the cargo and resold it to the party that eventually took delivery at another port. The intermediate holder subsequently came into possession of the bill of lading, which it then indorsed to its buyer. Lord Hobhouse, who gave the principal judgment of the House of Lords, held that there had been no 'demand' made by the intermediate holder, because, at the time that it requested the samples, it did not have possession of the bill and therefore had no authority to make any demand for delivery of the shipowner – a point not argued before the Court of Appeal. Therefore, liability under s 3(1)(c) never arose in the first place and Lord Hobhouse was of the view that it was likely that liability thereunder would only arise where there had been actual delivery of the cargo to the defendant.

---

140 [2000] 1 Lloyd's Rep 529, QB.
141 *The Spiros C* [2000] 2 Lloyd's Rep 550, CA.
142 *The Aegean Sea* [1998] 2 Lloyd's Rep 39, QB.
143 In *The Aegean Sea* [1998] 2 Lloyd's Rep 39, QB, Thomas J held that (a) any 'delivery' had to be made by the carrier and therefore did not cover a delivery of some salved oil after a spill pursuant to orders of the local authority and (b) that an agreement to provide an indemnity in return for delivery of the cargo without production of a bill of lading did not constitute a 'demand for delivery'. In *The Berge Sisar* [2001] 2 WLR 1118, HL, it was held that there will be no 'demand for delivery' when a receiver requests samples of the cargo from the carrier before it can be decided whether the vessel can be allowed to discharge its cargo into the terminal.
144 A 'claim' will not be made when a cargo owner threatens to arrest the vessel to obtain security, per Aikens J, *obiter*, *The Ythan* [2005] EWHC 2399 (Comm); [2006] 1 Lloyd's Rep 457.
145 [2001] 2 WLR 1118, HL; [1998] 2 Lloyd's Rep 475, CA, noted (1999) LMCLQ 161 and [2000] JBL 196.

His Lordship was also of the view that, in any event, **COGSA 1992** was founded on a principle of mutuality that justified the preservation of the decision in *Smurthwaite v Wilkins*,[146] which had formed the basis of the decision of the Court of Appeal. A logical consequence of this principle of mutuality, whereby statutory burdens must coexist with statutory benefits, is that an intermediate party will always be divested of liability when s 2(5) operates so as to divest it of rights of suit, even though the party who subsequently becomes a 'lawful holder' may not necessarily incur liability under s 3(1) in its turn.

A bank that chooses not to take delivery of goods under a pledged bill will still be protected, as in *Sewell v Burdick*,[147] from any suit against it in respect of sums due to the carrier under the bill. Notwithstanding the transfer of liabilities to a third party under this section, s 3(3) expressly provides for the continuance of all of the original shipper's liabilities under the contract, unlike s 2 of the **Bills of Lading Act 1855**, which referred only to its liability for freight.

Claimants outside the Carriage of Goods by Sea Act 1992

There will still be some claimants who fall outside the Act. Principally, these are as follows:

(a) a claimant who has taken delivery of the goods without production of a bill of lading and has yet to receive the bill of lading;[148]

(b) a claimant who is not the 'lawful holder' of the bill of lading, but nonetheless has suffered loss because some part of the risk of transit damage has been allocated to it under the sale contract. For example, under a cif outturn contract, the seller must reimburse the buyer in respect of any short delivery. The seller will bear the risk of this loss, but the bill of lading will have passed to the buyer;

(c) a claimant who is the 'lawful holder' of a charterer's or freight forwarder's bill of lading, but who wants to sue the shipowner;

(d) a claimant whose goods have been trans-shipped and damaged after trans-shipment where the terms of the initial bill of lading relieve the carrier of liability for any damage to the goods sustained after trans-shipment;

(e) a claimant under an electronic bill of lading who is not a party to the original contract of carriage; and

(f) a claimant under a combined transport bill of lading who is not a party to the original contract of carriage.[149]

In these situations, if the claimant cannot persuade the 'lawful holder' to sue on its behalf under s 2(4), which would be possible only in the first two instances given above, the claimant will need to have recourse to some alternative mode of recovering its losses. One possibility is the doctrine of implied contract, which has the advantage of subjecting the claim to the Hague or Hague-Visby Rules, as the contract will be on the terms of the bill of lading. However, the restrictions imposed on this doctrine by the Court of Appeal in *The Aramis* and *The Gudermes*[150] make it likely that few claimants will be able to rely on this device. Instead, they will be forced to sue the shipowner non-contractually in tort or bailment. The claimant may also wish to sue the shipowner, or its contractors,

---

146 (1862) 11 CB (NS) 842.
147 (1884) 10 App Cas 74.
148 It is likely that a claimant must acquire physical possession of an original bill of lading before it can qualify as a lawful holder. See *dicta* of Rix J in *The Giovanna* [1999] 1 Lloyd's Rep 867, 873–4.
149 Due to the uncertainty as to whether such a document falls within COGSA 1992, an issue that is discussed in more detail in Chapter 7.
150 [1989] 1 Lloyd's Rep 213 and [1993] 1 Lloyd's Rep 311.

in tort, to avoid contractual limitation clauses that might otherwise have limited its recovery under a contractual action.[151] In dealing with non-contractual actions against the shipowner, the courts should bear in mind two objectives. First, claimants with no contractual nexus with the shipowner should still be able to obtain compensation from the shipowner in respect of loss or damage that occurs while the goods are in its custody. Secondly, claimants who do have a contractual nexus with the shipowner should not be allowed to undermine the uniform operation of the Hague or Hague-Visby Rules by choosing to direct their action at third parties engaged by the shipowner in the performance of its contractual duties.

Non-contractual actions

Bailment

Bailment involves the transfer of legal possession in goods when their owner, the bailor, hands them over to the safe keeping of a party such as a carrier or warehouseman, the bailee. Physical possession need not be transferred. In *Spectra International plc v Hayesoak Ltd*,[152] a freight forwarder became a bailee by virtue of its authority to make arrangements to place the goods into a bonded warehouse prior to customs clearance and then to arrange for their delivery to an inland destination.[153] The bailee may, in turn, pass on possession to another party, the sub-bailee. By virtue of the bailment, the bailee owes a duty of care to the bailor in respect of the goods while they are in its custody. This duty will be subject to the terms on which the bailee accepts custody of the goods, which are usually, but not invariably, to be found in a contract between the bailor and bailee. Such a bailment is known as a 'bailment on terms'. Accordingly, bailment as a cause of action against the carrier will be superfluous when the shipper has a contract of carriage with the carrier. However, if the shipper is divested of its contractual rights under the bill of lading by s 2(5) of **COGSA 1992**, it will still retain its rights of suit in bailment, provided that possession has not wholly passed to the new holder of the bill of lading.[154]

However, there are two situations in which the shipper will need to base its action against the carrier on the bailment. The first is where it contracts directly with the charterer,[155] receives a charterer's bill of lading, and wishes to sue the shipowner. In the *Elder Dempster* case,[156] the shipowner was successful in relying on terms in a charterer's bill protecting the shipowner. The most convincing explanation for this decision is that offered by Lord Sumner, who regarded the situation as a bailment to the shipowner on the terms of the charterer's bill of lading. However, the courts have subsequently proved unwilling to allow shipowners to rely on the doctrine of bailment of terms, at least where they seek to rely on a jurisdiction clause in a charterer's bill of lading. This was the result in *The Forum Craftsman*,[157] where the Court of Appeal pointed to the undesirability of subjecting a third party to a jurisdiction clause in a contract to which it was not a party. The Privy Council came to the same decision, but by different reasoning, in *The Mahkutai*, where it held that, if the charterer's bill of lading contained a 'Himalaya' clause, any bailment on terms would be coextensive

---

151 For an excellent analysis of this problem, see Wilson, J, 'A flexible contract of carriage: the third dimension?' (1996) LMCLQ 187. See, also, Girvin, S, 'The Law Commission's Draft Contracts (Rights of Third Parties) Bill and the Carriage of Goods by Sea' (1997) LMCLQ 541; Baughen, S, 'Bailment's continuing role in cargo claims' (1999) LMCLQ 393; and Baughen, S, 'Charterers' bills and shipowners' liabilities: a black hole for cargo claimants?' [2004] JIML 248.
152 [1997] 1 Lloyd's Rep 153, Central London County Court.
153 Cf *The Ines* [1995] 2 Lloyd's Rep 144, QB, where a time charterer's status as bailee was held to cease once it had procured the issue of a shipowner's bill of lading.
154 *East West Corp v DKBS 1912* [2003] EWCA Civ 174; [2003] 1 Lloyd's Rep 239, CA.
155 Or a freight forwarder for a combined transport bill of lading.
156 [1923] 1 KB 420.
157 [1985] 1 Lloyd's Rep 291, CA.

with the terms on which it could rely by virtue of that clause. As the Himalaya clause did not entitle the shipowner to rely on the jurisdiction clause in the bill of lading, that clause could not form part of the terms of the bailment to the shipowner.[158]

The second is where the bill of lading permits trans-shipment, damage occurs after trans-shipment and the shipper wishes to recover against the second shipowner. The potential defendant will now be liable as a sub-bailee, not only to the head bailee, the first carrier, but also to the bailor, the shipper, provided that it was aware when it received the goods that they were not owned by the bailee.[159] It may, however, be able to rely, by way of a defence, on the terms of its contract with the head bailee. This is the doctrine of 'sub-bailment on terms' and was successfully pleaded in *The Pioneer Container*,[160] where goods were trans-shipped and damaged on the second sea voyage. The second carrier, as sub-bailee, was liable to the original shipper, but was entitled to rely on the jurisdiction and choice of law clause in the bill of lading that it had issued to the first carrier on trans-shipment. This was because the bill of lading issued by the first carrier to the shipper permitted trans-shipment 'on any terms whatsoever'. The apparent inconsistency as regards the treatment of jurisdiction clauses by the Privy Council in *The Pioneer Container* with *The Mahkutai* disappears once it is recalled that, in a sub-bailment on terms, the shipowner is relying on a jurisdiction clause in its own contract, whereas in a bailment on terms, it is seeking to rely on such a clause that appears in a contract to which it is not a party. An alternative and, perhaps, a preferable analysis of the shipowner's position, when a charterer's bill is issued, is to regard the shipowner as a sub-bailee who has taken possession of the goods on the terms of the charterparty, rather than as a head bailee relying on the terms of the charterer's bill of lading.

Consent

An important element in the Privy Council's judgment was its insistence that the sub-bailee's ability to rely on the terms of its own contract with the bailee was dependent on the bailor having consented to a sub-bailment on such terms.[161] On the facts, there was express consent to the terms of the sub-bailment by virtue of a term in the head bill of lading giving the carrier liberty to trans-ship on any terms whatsoever. The second carrier was, therefore, entitled to rely on a jurisdiction clause in the bill of lading that it had issued to the first carrier.[162] Consent might also be implied. The courts are likely to imply consent when the sub-bailee's terms are in widespread use.[163] Furthermore, in *Sonicare International Ltd v East Anglia Freight Terminal Ltd*,[164] it was held that the bailor might still have impliedly consented to such terms even though they were more onerous, as regards the bailor, than those imposed by the head bailment.[165] The terms of a sub-bailment in the UK will be subject to the

---

158 [1996] AC 650, noted (1997) LMCLQ 1. This part of the Privy Council's reasoning is suspect, given that it felt it unnecessary to decide the issue of whether a shipowner could rely on a 'Himalaya' clause worded so as to protect 'subcontractors'.

159 In such a situation, the sub-bailee may still be liable in negligence, as in *Awad v Pillai* [1982] RTR 266, CA.

160 [1994] 2 AC 324, PC, noted (1995) LMCLQ 183.

161 In this, it preferred the view of the Court of Appeal in *Morris v CW Martin & Sons Ltd* [1966] 1 QB 716 to that of Donaldson J in *Johnson Matthey & Co Ltd v Constantine Terminals Ltd* [1976] 2 Lloyd's Rep 215, QB, who was of the view that the doctrine could be invoked even in the absence of consent by the bailor.

162 See, also, *Jarl Tra AB v Convoys Ltd* [2003] EWHC 1488; [2003] 2 Lloyd's Rep 459, QB, where the shipper was held to have consented to a clause in the terminal operator's contract with the carrier, which entitled it to lien cargoes for sums due to it from the carrier by virtue of a similar clause in the bill of lading.

163 An example of implied consent is provided by *Spectra International plc v Hayesoak Ltd* [1997] 1 Lloyd's Rep 153, Central London County Court, where the bailor consented to the freight forwarder sub-bailing on terms usually current in the trade, such as the Road Haulage Association (RHA) terms used by domestic road hauliers.

164 [1997] 2 Lloyd's Rep 48, County Court.

165 A further factor influencing the court in its finding was the fact that the head bailor remained liable under its bill of lading for events occurring after trans-shipment.

Unfair Contract Terms Act 1977, which subject exceptions and limitations clauses to a test of reasonableness.[166]

In the absence of consent, whether express or implied, the doctrine may be invoked under the principles of ostensible authority. This would require the bailor to have made some representation to the sub-bailee that it consents to a sub-bailment on the terms of its contract with the head bailee. An example might be where a shipper and carrier orally agree that there shall be no trans-shipment, yet the shipper accepts a bill of lading that contains a liberty to trans-ship and the carrier then goes ahead and trans-ships.

Attornment and successors in title

A problem that has not yet been satisfactorily resolved by the courts is the extent to which a successor in title to the original bailor can sue in bailment, or whether they must sue in negligence. An action in bailment has the advantage that the burden of proof is the opposite of that pertaining to negligence, in that it is for the bailee to prove that it took reasonable care of the goods. In addition, a bailee is liable if the goods are stolen while they are in his custody, unlike the position in negligence.[167] On the other hand, an action in negligence has the advantage that recovery will not be limited by the terms of any contract between the bailee and the sub-bailee.

The basic rule is that a successor in title to the original bailor may sue in bailment only if the bailee, or sub-bailee, attorns to it, by explicitly recognising it as the bailor.[168] If there is an attornment, it appears to have a retrospective effect, allowing the successor in title to sue the bailee in respect of loss or damage that was caused while the original bailor still retained constructive possession of the goods.[169]

The naming of a party as consignee in the bill of lading, as with the financing bank in *The Future Express*,[170] will not, by itself, amount to an attornment. However, in *Sonicare International Ltd v East Anglia Freight Terminal Ltd*,[171] it was held that the need for an attornment might be dispensed with if the bailment is on the terms of the bill of lading and the benefit of that contract is assigned to the successor in title. An attornment will also be unnecessary if an apparent third party is actually the original bailor. Usually, the consignor will be the bailor, but this will not be the case where a party has been named as consignee with the intent that a sale or pledge shall be completed on the delivery of the goods to the carrier.[172] The consignee will now be the original bailor and will, therefore, not need to rely on an attornment.[173] Where, as in *The Future Express*,[174] a party is named as consignee with the intent that a pledge to it shall be completed at some stage *after* the loading of the goods onto the vessel, that party will not be the original bailor and will need to establish an attornment in its favour if it is to proceed against the carrier in conversion or in bailment.

---

166 In *Singer Co (UK) Ltd v Tees and Hartlepool Port Authority* [1988] 2 Lloyd's Law Rep 164 (QB), the Port Authority's standard terms and conditions contained an exception providing that they would be under no loss except for injury or damage arising from the proven negligence of their servants or agents, as well as a clause limiting their liability to $800 per tonne. Both clauses were held to be reasonable.

167 *Johnson Matthey & Co Ltd v Constantine Terminals Ltd* [1976] 2 Lloyd's Rep 215, QB.

168 See dicta of Lord Brandon in *The Aliakmon* [1986] 1 AC 785, 815. However, although the point was not in issue, the wording of the Privy Council's judgment in *The Pioneer Container* [1994] 2 AC 324 suggests that the sub-bailee owes its duty directly to whomsoever is owner at the time of trans-shipment and does not simply assume the duties owed by the head bailee. See, also, Lord Hobhouse of Woodborough in *The Starsin* [2003] EWCA Civ 174; [2003] 1 Lloyd's Rep 239, at [136].

169 See *The Gudermes* [1993] 1 Lloyd's Rep 311 and see, also, *Sonicare International Ltd v East Anglia Freight Terminal Ltd* [1997] 2 Lloyd's Rep 48, Central London County Court, where no objection was taken to the fact that the breach may have preceded the attornment. But cf *Motis Exports (No 2)* (2001) Admlty Ct, 2 February; [2001] WL 239695, where Moore Bick J held there was a good arguable case that a claimant might only be able to sue in conversion if it could show that it had the immediate right to possession of the goods at the time of their misdelivery.

170 [1993] 2 Lloyd's Rep 542, CA.

171 [1997] 2 Lloyd's Rep 48, County Court.

172 As happened in *Kum v Wah Tat Bank Ltd* [1971] 1 Lloyd's Rep 439, PC, where the consignee was named in the mate's receipt.

173 The consignee's possessory right to take delivery of the goods will not be affected by any contractual right the consignor may still possess to give different delivery instructions to the carrier.

174 [1993] 2 Lloyd's Rep 542, CA.

Even if the bailee does attorn to the new owner, it will not necessarily be on the terms of the bill of lading. In *The Gudermes*,[175] a cargo of oil was loaded under a charterparty with the consignor to whom the bill of lading was issued. Ownership in the cargo then passed to the buyer, Mitsui. The temperature of the oil meant that it could not be discharged into the receiver's pipeline at Ravenna and had to be trans-shipped into another vessel. Prior to trans-shipment, the shipowners negotiated directly with the new owners, Mitsui, regarding the problem. This constituted the attornment, but it was not on the terms of the bill of lading but on the terms of the original bailment by the charterers. This was on the terms of the charterparty, which, unlike the bill of lading, contained no terms relating to the temperature at which the oil was to be carried.

Negligence

An action against the shipowner will be possible in negligence under the principles set out by the House of Lords in *Donoghue v Stevenson*.[176] The major drawback to the action stems from the decision of the House of Lords in *The Aliakmon*[177] that, in relation to goods, a general duty of care is owed only to a party who is either the owner of those goods or entitled to immediate possession of them. In *The Starsin*,[178] it was confirmed that the time at which this is established is not the time of breach, but the time at which the first significant damage to the goods occurs. The case involved negligent stowage, which led to condensation damage. Even though the damage was progressive, rights of suit in negligence crystallised only once: at the time that the first significant damage occurred. The effect was that only one of the claimants was able to bring itself within the rule in *The Aliakmon*.[179]

The advantages of bailment as an action, especially as regards the reversal of the burden of proof, mean that the claimant will generally have recourse to negligence only when it is suing a defendant who is not a bailee and with whom it has no contract, or when the claimant is a successor in title to the bailor and there has been no attornment in its favour by the bailee or sub-bailee. The content of the duty of care in negligence is unaffected by the terms of any contract of carriage,[180] and this is a major difference to the position in bailment. In *The Starsin*,[181] the shipowners were held to owe a duty to ensure the cargo was properly stowed notwithstanding that no such duty existed under the time charter, under which it was the charterer who had undertaken to load, stow and discharge.[182] We shall now examine the requirements that the claimant must show that it either owned, or had the immediate right to possession of, the goods at the time that they were lost or damaged.[183]

---

175 [1993] 1 Lloyd's Rep 311, CA.
176 [1932] AC 562.
177 [1986] 1 AC 785.
178 [2003] UKHL 12; [2003] 1 Lloyd's Rep 571.
179 It is unclear whether the original shippers would have been able to sue the shipowner in negligence or bailment, notwithstanding the fact that they would have ceased to own the goods at the time of bringing proceedings. *The Sanix Ace* [1987] 1 Lloyd's Rep 465 suggests that the shippers could still proceed non-contractually, holding any damages on trust for their successors in title, but is distinguishable on the facts in that ownership of the goods never passed to the buyers.
180 Per Lord Brandon in *The Aliakmon* [1986] 1 AC 785, 818.
181 [2001] 1 Lloyd's Rep 437, at [100].
182 This fact would have afforded the shipowner a complete defence had it been sued as a sub-bailee, rather than a head bailee, for then it would have been able to rely on the terms of the sub-bailment embodied in the time charter.
183 A claimant may, however, choose to proceed exclusively in negligence to escape the effect of his claim being subject to the terms of the bailment or sub-bailment. The law is currently unclear as to whether a general duty of care in negligence arises when the defendant owes the claimant a duty in bailment. See *Johnson Matthey & Co Ltd v Constantine Terminals Ltd* [1976] 2 Lloyd's Rep 215, 220.

Ownership

Ownership of the goods at the time of damage will depend upon the terms of the underlying sale contract.[184] In most cif and fob sales, the parties will intend to pass property in the goods when payment is made against documents.[185] A problem arises where there are multiple purchasers of undivided bulk cargo, as the goods allocated to each purchaser will be unascertained until the bulk is divided among them on discharge. The solution adopted by s 16 of the **Sale of Goods Act 1979** was to preclude the passing of property until discharge, even if that was what the parties intended.[186] This could lead to inconvenient results if the seller became insolvent in the interval between payment of the price and the ascertainment of the purchaser's share on discharge. A different solution has been adopted by s 1(3) of the **Sale of Goods Act 1995**, which adds a new s 20(A) and (B) to the **Sale of Goods Act 1979**, under which the buyer of goods from part of an identified bulk will obtain ownership rights in that bulk as a tenant in common once the price has been paid.

Possession

Actual or constructive possession of the goods at the time of damage will also suffice to found a suit in negligence. This can be established by possession of the bill of lading[187] or of a 'ship's delivery order'.[188] The shipowner will also have possession of the goods while they are being carried; so, too, will the charterer when a charterer's bill of lading is issued.[189]

Pure economic loss

Even if the claimant can establish a right to sue in negligence, its position will generally be less favourable than it would be under an action in contract. Liability in contract is usually strict and covers nonfeasance and misfeasance. In tort, it is based on a duty to take reasonable care and only covers misfeasance. Most importantly, there is generally no recovery for pure economic loss in tort. Following *Murphy v Brentwood District Council*,[190] 'pure economic loss' has been very widely defined.

A good example is provided by *The Gudermes*,[191] where, *obiter*, Hirst J was of the view that transshipment costs incurred as a result of the shipowner's failure to heat a cargo of oil so that it was in a condition in which it could be discharged into the receiver's pipeline were not recoverable in tort, but could be recovered in contract. A more liberal approach was taken in *The Orjula*,[192] where loss suffered by shipowners as a result of chemicals leaking from drums requiring the re-stowing of the drums and the cleaning of the deck was categorised as pure economic loss in the context of a claim against the suppliers of the drums. However, there was an arguable case that the costs might be recoverable if the shipowners could show that they had been incurred in removing from circulation a positive source of danger in the form of leaking drums of chemicals.

---

184 It must be stressed that, following the coming into force of COGSA 1992, this inquiry is completely redundant with regard to the establishment of contractual rights of suit.

185 Although the parties may have other reasons than securing the price to delay the passing of property until the bill of lading is indorsed. So, in *The Albazero* [1977] AC 774, where the buyer and seller were associated companies and the sale was on credit terms, it was nonetheless held that they had intended to pass property on indorsement, as this would make it easier for the buyers to give orders relating to discharge directly to the shipowner.

186 Subject to the doctrine of exhaustion applied in *The Elafi* [1982] 1 All ER 208. After the penultimate discharging port, all of the other bulk consignees had taken delivery of their cargo. Therefore, the plaintiff owned the totality of cargo left on board and was able to sue in respect of damage sustained to it during discharge.

187 But not if the holder possesses the document purely as an agent for another, as in *The Aliakmon* [1986] 1 AC 785.

188 If a merchant's delivery order is issued, the claimant will have no immediate right to possession of the goods and will therefore be unable to sue in negligence. See *Margarine Union GmbH v Cambay Prince SS Co* [1969] 1 QB 219.

189 As in *The Okehampton* [1913] P 173. Following a collision, the charterers were able to sue the colliding vessel for the freight that they had lost by reason of the loss of the goods being carried.

190 [1991] 1 AC 398, HL.

191 [1991] 1 Lloyd's Rep 456.

192 [1995] 2 Lloyd's Rep 395, CA.

Protecting subcontractors from unlimited liability in negligence

Where the defendant's liability in negligence is based on an act that would also constitute a breach of contract with the claimant, the claimant's recovery in negligence will be subject to the exceptions and limitations on which the defendant could rely had it been sued in contract.[193] On the other hand, where there is no contract between the claimant and the defendant, the claimant will be able to recover its losses in full, notwithstanding that recovery would have been limited by contractual exceptions and limitations had it chosen to sue the carrier in contract. This will be the case where the cargo claimant chooses to sue the stevedoring firm that damaged the goods during discharge, rather than to sue the carrier under the bill of lading. This is good news for cargo claimants, but seriously undermines the uniform application of the Hague and Hague-Visby Rules.[194] For this reason, the courts have, wherever possible, sought to find ways whereby such recovery can be brought within the limits of these Rules. We will now consider four possible ways by which this result might be achieved.

Article IV *bis* of the Hague-Visby Rules

First, the Hague-Visby Rules, but not the Hague Rules, contain the following provision in Art IV *bis*.

(1)   The defences and limits of liability provided for in these Rules shall apply in any action against the carrier in respect of loss or damage to goods covered by a contract of carriage whether the action be founded in contract or tort.

(2)   If such an action is brought against a servant or agent of the carrier (such servant or agent not being an independent contractor), such servant or agent shall be entitled to avail himself of the defences and limits of liability which the carrier is entitled to invoke under these Rules.

This provision has a very limited effect. Subsection (1) operates when the claimant has parallel claims against the carrier in tort and in contract, under the bill of lading, but has no effect when the claimant's only claim against the carrier lies in tort.[195] Subsection (2) is limited to 'servants and agents' of the carrier and therefore cannot cover independent contractors.[196] To be properly effective, this provision needs to be revised, so that it covers any third party that performs services for which the carrier is responsible under the Hague-Visby Rules.

No duty of care

Secondly, the courts could simply deny the existence of a duty of care, and so exclude recovery altogether. An example is the explicit reference to policy grounds by the House of Lords in *Marc Rich & Co AG v Bishop Rock Marine Co Ltd (The Nicholas H)*.[197] Their Lordships, Lord Lloyd of Berwick dissenting, held that a classification society did not owe a duty of care to cargo owners when its surveyor decided whether or not to pass the vessel as fit to resume its voyage.[198] The claim was brought against the classification society after the shipowner had settled the claim up to the maximum amount for which it was liable under the applicable tonnage limitation convention. Lord Steyn, who gave the majority judgment, was strongly influenced by the disruptive effects of allowing cargo claimants to recover more in tort from third parties, in respect of the same loss, than they

---

193 At common law, see *Pyrene Co Ltd v Scindia Navigation Co* [1954] 2 QB 402, and *Tai Hing Cotton Mill Ltd v Liu Chong Hing Bank* [1986] AC 80, HL. Article IV(1) *bis* of the Hague-Visby Rules has similar effect in relation to contracts covered by the Rules.

194 In contrast, an action in bailment will generally be subject to the terms of the bailment or sub-bailment, which will generally incorporate the Rules.

195 *The Captain Gregos* [1990] 1 Lloyd's Rep 310, CA.

196 The specific exclusion of 'independent contractors' is, therefore, otiose. Moreover, servants and agents receive no protection from this provision in respect of services performed outside the termini of the Rules, i.e. before loading and after discharge.

197 [1995] 3 WLR 227.

198 Cf *Johnson Matthey & Co Ltd v Constantine Terminals Ltd* [1976] 2 Lloyd's Rep 215 and *Norwich City Council v Harvey* [1989] 1 WLR 828.

could recover in contract from the carrier. His Lordship drew attention to the fact that existing insurance practices were based on the assumption that cargo claims would be channelled through a mandatory convention, such as the Hague Rules, as well as through one of the two international tonnage limitation conventions. To allow claims to circumvent these channels would lead to the imposition of an extra layer of insurance cover, which would lead to an increase in shipping costs. His Lordship also took the view that the public status of classification societies also militated against the imposition of a duty of care.[199] However, a weakness of this approach is that it does not simply confine a claim to the accepted channels; rather, it rules it out altogether, which would lead to harsh results where the contractual claim, for whatever reason, could not be enforced against the carrier.

A variant of this technique would be to limit the duty by the doctrine of *volenti non fit injuria*. This possibility was canvassed, unsuccessfully, by Lord Denning in *Midland Silicones Ltd v Scruttons Ltd*,[200] which is discussed in more detail below.

Agency and the 'Himalaya' clause

Thirdly, the courts could find a contract between the claimant and the defendant, which would be subject to the terms of the Hague and Hague-Visby Rules. The action can still proceed in tort, but recovery will be limited to that permitted by the terms of the contract between the parties.[201] However, the measure of damages will still be governed by tortious principles. The technique of inventing a contractual relationship between the parties first surfaced in *Pyrene Co Ltd v Scindia Navigation Co Ltd*,[202] where the seller sued the shipowner in tort for the damage and the shipowner successfully argued that it was able to rely on the terms of its carriage contract with the buyer by way of defence. Devlin J held that the contract of carriage between the buyer and shipowner was also a tripartite contract involving the seller as regards that part of the contractual performance, the loading of the goods, in which the seller's cooperation was essential.

Although this result could be reached by implying a contract on the terms of the anticipated bill of lading, Devlin J preferred to base his decision on a sophisticated modification of the principles of agency. He found that the buyer had contracted in a dual capacity. It had contracted as principal as regards the entirety of the contract, and also as agent for the seller as regards that part, the loading operations, that would require the seller's involvement. In doing so, he was strongly influenced by the doctrine of 'vicarious immunity' under which 'agents' (including independent contractors) could rely on the contractual defences available to their 'principals'. This doctrine was then said to be the basis of the decision of the House of Lords in the *Elder Dempster* case.[203]

The 'partial agency' technique gained impetus as cargo owners sought to make unlimited recovery in negligence from the contractors employed by the shipowners who had actually damaged the cargo. In particular, these actions were directed at stevedores,[204] which, as commercial undertakings rather than private individuals such as the vessel's crew, are far more likely to have sufficient assets to make them worth suing. As a matter of strict contractual theory, it is difficult to see how the relationship between stevedoring companies and cargo owners could be governed by any contract, whether express or implied. However, the strong policy reasons for channelling such claims into the law of contract have led to considerable judicial ingenuity in overcoming the

---

199 A similar approach was adopted by the Court of Appeal in *Reeman v Department of Transport* [1997] 2 Lloyd's Rep 648, when it held that the Department of Transport owed no duty of care in preparing a certificate that a fishing boat complied with its regulations as to seaworthiness.

200 [1962] AC 446.

201 *Pyrene Co Ltd v Scindia Navigation Co Ltd* [1954] 2 QB 402. The technique will have erratic results where the initial contract with the carrier is a charterparty and, therefore, outside the scope of the mandatory regimes.

202 [1954] 2 QB 402.

203 [1924] AC 522. The actual *ratio* of the case is, however, extremely elusive.

204 Otherwise known as dockers. The word 'stevedore' derives from the Spanish *estivar*, meaning 'to stow'.

difficulties that English contract law places in the path of arguing that a party can take advantage of provisions in a contract to which it is not a party.

The strict contractual approach was evidenced in *Midland Silicones Ltd v Scruttons Ltd*,[205] where the House of Lords laid to rest the doctrine of 'vicarious immunity'. Cargo owners sued the stevedores in tort for negligently damaging their cargo on discharging the vessel. The stevedores attempted to argue that they could rely on bill of lading exceptions in favour of 'the carrier' – in particular, the package limitation – by way of defence. The House of Lords rejected their argument and limited *Elder Dempster* to its own facts. Viscount Simmonds sought to explain it as rule-specific to bailment, whereby the shipowner was a bailee of the goods on the terms of the charterer's bill of lading. However, when stevedores load and unload the vessel, they do not constitute bailees.[206] This explanation of *Elder Dempster* is similar to the concept of *volenti non fit injuria* to which Lord Denning alluded before holding that the use of the word 'carrier' precluded its application to a claim against a stevedore.[207]

Nor would a straightforward application of agency principles assist the stevedores. The doctrine of undisclosed principal could not be invoked, because it would have the effect of joining them to the entire contract of carriage.[208] Any agency would have to be solely in respect of that part of the bill of lading contract with which the stevedores were concerned. Such a partial agency could be achieved provided that the exceptions clause was drafted to satisfy four conditions set out by Lord Reid. First, the bill of lading must make it clear that the stevedore is intended to be protected by the limitation clause. This was fatal to the bill of lading under consideration by their Lordships, which protected only the 'carrier'. Secondly, the bill of lading must make it clear that the carrier is also contracting as agent for the stevedore. Thirdly, the carrier must have the stevedore's authority to make such a contract on its behalf. If the stevedore has not given such authority to the carrier, it may, however, subsequently ratify the contract. Fourthly, the stevedore must have provided consideration.

Lord Reid's suggestions were taken to heart by those responsible for drafting bills of lading and a clause emerged that satisfied the first two of the four preconditions. Such a clause is known as a 'Himalaya' clause[209] and its validity was confirmed in *New Zealand Shipping Co Ltd v AM Satterthwaite (The Eurymedon)*,[210] where the Privy Council, by a majority, held that it had the desired effect of allowing the stevedores to rely on the Hague Rules package limitation in the bill of lading. The other two conditions were also satisfied: the third because the stevedoring company and the carrier were associated companies;[211] and the fourth by an extension of the principle of *Scotson v Pegg*[212] to unilateral contracts.

Even the Himalaya clause was not without its problems. The majority of the Privy Council construed it as a unilateral promise that matured into a contract when the stevedores performed their part of the bargain and started to unload the ship.[213] However, Viscount Dilhorne, for the

---

205 [1962] AC 446.

206 Although they do when they store the goods after discharge and thereby act as warehousemen. See *Gilchrist Watt and Sanderson Pty Ltd v York Products Ltd* [1970] 1 WLR 1262, PC.

207 Lord Denning also based his decision on the basis that the bailor's claim against the stevedore in tort was limited by the terms of the contract between the bailee, the shipowner and its sub-bailee, the stevedore. Under this contract, the stevedore's liability was to be subject to the maximum limits specified by the Hague Rules. The problem with this analysis is that Lord Denning was the only one of their Lordships prepared to find a relationship of bailment on the facts.

208 This is the point made by Diplock J in *Midland Silicones Ltd v Scruttons Ltd* [1959] 2 QB 171, 185.

209 After the name of the ship in *Adler v Dickson* [1955] 1 QB 158, in a case that involved an unsuccessful attempt to argue that contractual terms could be relied on by a non-party.

210 [1975] AC 154, PC.

211 On this point, see *The Suleyman Stalkiy* [1976] 2 Lloyd's Rep 609, Can Ct.

212 (1861) 6 H & N 295. Performance of a pre-existing contractual duty owed to a third party was held to amount to sufficient consideration.

213 Lord Goff doubted this analysis in *The Mahkutai* [1996] AC 650 and stressed the importance of not being overly technical in the approach to this problem.

minority, held that the clause was not worded as an offer to be taken up by performance by the stevedore, but as a concluded contract with the stevedore. It plainly could not be such a contract when the bill was issued, because nothing in it suggested that the stevedore could sue the consignee for its fees or that the consignee could compel the stevedore to perform its contract with the carrier. Nonetheless, the majority had no difficulty in holding that this wording had a dual capacity. As regards the carrier, it represented a concluded contract. As regards the stevedore, it represented an offer that was accepted by the shipper on acceptance of the bill of lading. Where the claim was made by an indorsee of the bill of lading in respect of stevedore negligence on discharge, the parties were linked by an implied contract, on the basis of *Brandt v Liverpool Brazil & River Plate SN Co*,[214] on the terms of the bill of lading.[215]

The Privy Council again upheld the validity of a Himalaya clause in *Salmond & Spraggon Ltd (Australia) Pty Ltd v Joint Cargo Services Pty Ltd (The New York Star)*.[216] It also held that the clause protected the stevedores in respect of activities that took place outside the 'tackle to tackle' period to which the Hague and Hague-Visby Rules apply.[217] The stevedores who had misdelivered the cargo were therefore able to rely on a clause in the bill of lading exempting the carrier in the event of misdelivery. As the stevedores' default occurred while the carrier was still contractually responsible for the goods, they were able to rely on this clause in the same way as the carrier could have, had it been sued instead of them. However, the clause will not protect a subcontractor whose default occurs outside the carrier's contractual period of responsibility. In *Raymond Burke v Mersey Docks and Harbour Board*,[218] goods were handed over into the custody of the terminal operator prior to loading. While waiting to be loaded, they were damaged by negligent handling of goods being discharged from another vessel. Leggatt J held that the carrier's contractual responsibility would not begin until loading of the goods in question had begun. As the goods were damaged prior to this point, it followed that the Himalaya clause in the carrier's standard form of bill of lading could not protect them. On the facts, it was significant that the carrier had dealt with the shipper in a twofold capacity: it had acted as a freight forwarder in arranging for the goods to be taken to the port terminal, but it would only start to act as a carrier under a 'port to port' bill once loading began.

The subcontractor will also lose the protection of the Himalaya clause if it has dealt directly with the shipper on its own terms. This happened in *The Rigoletto*,[219] where the terminal operator handed the shipper a receipt when it took custody of its goods. When sued by the shipper, the terminal operator could rely on the terms of the receipt through the doctrine of bailment, or sub-bailment on terms. It could not, however, elect to rely on the terms of a Himalaya clause in the carrier's bill of lading. Where, however, there is no such direct dealing between the parties, the sub-bailee will be entitled to choose between the protection offered by its own terms under the sub-bailment or that offered under the head bailment by virtue of the Himalaya clause.

The subcontractor may also find that it cannot rely on bill of lading terms that would be rendered void, as regards the contractual carrier, by virtue of the operation of Art III(8). In *The Starsin*,[220] once the House of Lords found the cargo to have been carried under charterer's bills of lading, the issue arose as to what defences the shipowner could raise to the cargo owner's tort claim against them of the negligent stowage of the cargo. As regards the one claimant that was able to establish title to sue, the shipowners relied on the Himalaya clause in the bill of lading that purported

---

214 [1924] 1 KB 575.
215 The limitations on this doctrine by the Court of Appeal in *The Aramis* [1989] 1 Lloyd's Rep 213 are unlikely to affect the validity of such clauses because the nature of their wording makes it clear that the parties do intend to create a legal relationship with each other.
216 [1981] 1 WLR 138, PC.
217 See also *The Antwerpen* [1994] 1 Lloyd's Rep 213, Sup Ct (NSW) Court of Appeal.
218 [1986] 1 Lloyd's Rep 155, QB.
219 [2000] 2 Lloyd's Rep 532, CA.
220 [2003] UKHL 12, [2003] 1 Lloyd's Rep 571.

to confer a complete immunity on the carrier's subcontractors. The House of Lords held that the clause was an exceptions clause, rather than a circular indemnity clause, and that the shipowners fell within its ambit because they qualified as a 'subcontractor'. However, for a Himalaya clause to be effective, it must be worded so as to be parasitic on the contract of carriage contained or evidenced in the bill of lading. The references to the bill of lading in its wording made it necessary to construe the bill itself. Clause 2 incorporated the Hague Rules, which were stated to be 'BASIS OF CONTRACT'. This rendered it necessary to consider the effect of Art III(8). By a 4:1 majority, their Lordships held that the Himalaya clause amounted to a contract of carriage and so fell within the ambit of the Article, notwithstanding that the shipowners never undertook to perform any of the carrier's obligations under the Rules. What entitled the shipowners to the protection of the Himalaya clause was the fact they had in fact actually performed the carriage of the goods and that they had become a party to the contract of carriage by the words in the clause to the effect that sub-contractors 'be deemed to be parties to the contract contained in or evidenced by this bill of lading'. Lord Hobhouse explained: 'The purpose of the additional use of these express words is to procure that transferees of the bill of lading shall be bound as well as the shipper . . . Clause 5 deliberately makes the contract between such persons and the shipper part of the bill of lading contract so as to obtain the benefit of it against other persons besides the shipper. Were it not for the inclusion of these words in the clause the shipowners would not have been able to rely upon it as against any of the claimants in this litigation'.[221] The general exemption in the clause was therefore rendered void by Art III(8). The result would probably have been otherwise had a stevedore attempted to rely on the general exemption, as the services it performed would not be those of carriage of the goods and therefore the contract created by the Himalaya clause would not amount to a contract of carriage within Art III(8). While there is much to be said for the dissenting views of Lord Steyn that there cannot be a 'contract of carriage' when the shipowner does not undertake the obligations of a carrier, the decision is welcome on pragmatic grounds. These were identified by Lord Hoffmann, who pointed out that, had the clause been upheld, a claimant would be unable to arrest a vessel in respect of cargo claims arising under carriage under a charterer's bill. The decision means that, in such circumstances, the vessel may still be arrested in respect of a claim against the shipowner brought in negligence. The effect of the clause will be to ensure that the shipowner is entitled to the same exceptions and limitations that would apply if the charterer were being sued, but not to afford them a greater protection than that available to the charterer.

A further limitation on the clause was revealed in *The Mahkutai*,[222] where the Privy Council held that it does not entitle third parties to claim the benefit of clauses in the bill of lading that are for the mutual benefit of the contracting parties, such as choice of law and jurisdiction clauses. This is in marked contrast to its position relating to such clauses in the context of the doctrine of sub-bailment on terms as seen in *The Pioneer Container*. The Privy Council found it unnecessary to make any finding on the second issue before it – namely, whether a shipowner could rely on a Himalaya clause in a charterer's bill of lading the exceptions and limitations of which were extended to 'subcontractors'.[223] The House of Lords, in *The Starsin*, has now confirmed that this term does, indeed, cover a shipowner who is performing the carriage called for under a charterer's bill.

---

221 These words were also present in the 'Himalaya' clauses in *The Eurymedon* and *The New York Star* but are not present in the 'Himalaya' provisions in many standard forms of bills of lading. Absent such wording, it would seem that the subcontractor would be unable to rely on the protection of the clause when sued by a cargo owner who was not the original shipper under the bill of lading. However, it is likely that such a clause would now be effective against a claim by the lawful holder of the bill of lading as it would fall under s 1(1) of the Contracts (Rights of Third Parties) Act 1999.

222 [1996] AC 650.

223 Although its decision on the bailment point assumed that the shipowner could rely on the clause. However, its decision in *The Pioneer Container* [1994] 2 AC 324 on sub-bailment disregarded a Himalaya clause in the first bill of lading.

A similar result can now be achieved with a more straightforwardly drafted clause by reliance on the provisions of the **Contracts (Rights of Third Parties) Act 1999**, which applies to contracts entered into on or after 11 May 2000. Although the effect of s 6(5)–(7) is that the Act does not apply to contracts for the carriage of goods by sea that are subject to **COGSA 1992**, s 6(5) also goes on to state 'except that a third party may by virtue of that section [s 1] avail itself of an exclusion or limitation of liability in such a contract'. Section 1 will therefore make effective an exclusion or limitation clause in favour of a third party if there is either an express term to that effect in the contract, or if the contract purports to confer that benefit on the third party. Section 1(3) provides that the third party need not be identified by name, nor need they be in existence at the time the contract is made. It will be enough that they are a member of a class or answer to a particular description. Stevedores and other subcontractors can now be protected by much simpler wording by virtue of s 1 and, although the third party's security is potentially threatened by the provisions on variation and cancellation contained in s 2, this is unlikely to be a problem in practice. However, the Act does not make it possible to draft a clause entitling the third party to rely on a jurisdiction clause. For this reason, there may still be some merits in relying on a version of the Himalaya clause that is drafted specifically to include this type of clause so as to get around the decision of the Privy Council in *The Mahkutai*.

The 'circular indemnity' clause

Another clause used by carriers to protect their subcontractors is the 'circular indemnity' clause. This consists of an undertaking by the bill of lading holder not to sue the carrier's servants, agents and subcontractors, or else not to bring an action against them on terms more favourable than those available against the carrier. The bill of lading holder further agrees to indemnify the carrier against all consequences of breaking its undertaking not to sue such third parties. The validity of the clause was upheld in *The Elbe Maru*,[224] where the carrier under a combined transport bill of lading obtained a perpetual stay of an action in tort brought by the cargo owner, in breach of the undertaking, against the subcontracted road carrier.

The circular indemnity clause will have the effect of giving the carrier's sub-contractors a blanket immunity from suit. In *The Marielle Bolten*,[225] the carrier sought an injunction to restrain proceedings in Brazil by the bill of lading holder against its subcontractors. The bill of lading contained a clause consisting of a circular indemnity clause and a 'Himalaya' clause for the benefit of the carrier's servants, agents and subcontractors. The bill of lading holders argued that the Himalaya clause made the subcontractors a party to the bill of lading, which was subject to the Hague Rules, and that Art III(8) therefore rendered null and void the circular indemnity clause as it would have the effect of giving the carrier's subcontractors a blanket exemption from liability. The argument was rejected and the injunction granted. The mere fact that the third parties entitled to the protection of a 'Himalaya' clause had performed 'carriage functions' did not make them a party to the contract of carriage evidenced by the bill of lading which was governed by the Hague Rules. In contrast, in *The Starsin* the Himalaya clause had provided that the carrier's subcontractors should be deemed to be parties to the bill of lading. Nor could the clause be struck out because it had the indirect effect of circumventing the Hague Rules. The third parties here had performed services incidental to the carriage but had not actually performed the actual carriage or been constituted as the carrier under the Hague Rules.

However, the clause's utility is seriously weakened by the following factors. First, the clause gives a remedy to the carrier, but does not directly prevent the subcontractor from being liable in tort. The covenant not to sue in the first part of the clause has been held to inure only for the benefit

---

224 [1978] 1 Lloyd's Rep 206.
225 [2009] EWHC 2552 (Comm), [2010] 1 Lloyd's Rep 648.

of the contractual carrier.[226] Even where the carrier, the subcontractor and the claimant are all before the court, it is unlikely that the subcontractor will have any success in raising a plea to dismiss the tort action against it on the ground of 'circuity of action'. Unless it files a cross-claim against the carrier, the court will be unable to decide to what extent the subcontractor is entitled to a contractual indemnity from the carrier in the event that it is sued by a cargo owner.[227] Secondly, the carrier will not automatically be able to stay the proceedings against the third party. In *The Elbe Maru*, Ackner J stressed[228] that a stay would be granted only if the carrier had a real financial interest in having the action stayed.[229] Thirdly, the carrier will not be able to obtain a stay where there is a triable issue that the subcontractor performed its services after the termination of the carrier's contract with the cargo owner.[230]

Other torts

Our discussion of non-contractual actions has, up to now, focused on claims in bailment or negligence for recovery of loss or damage to the cargo. However, two other types of claim are possible. The first arises out of the issue of a bill of lading that contains inaccurate statements. This will give rise to a potential liability either in deceit or for negligent misstatement. Such claims will be considered in more detail in the following chapter. The second arises out of the delivery of cargo without production of a bill of lading.[231]

When a carrier issues a bill of lading, it undertakes to deliver the goods to the person entitled to their possession, on presentation of an original bill of lading. If this undertaking is broken, it will give rise to a liability both for breach of contract and in conversion. The right to sue in conversion is based on the claimant having the immediate right to possession of the cargo, through possession of the bill of lading. In most cases, it will also have a parallel right to sue in contract under the bill of lading. A suit in conversion will be subject to the exceptions and limitations contained in this contract, although damages will be assessed on a tortious, rather than a contractual, basis. The House of Lords, in *Kuwait Airways Corp v Iraqi Airways Co (Nos 4 and 5)*,[232] held that, in an action for conversion, the claimant will be able to claim both the value of the goods converted and any consequential loss. The value of the property will be the value of the property to the claimant.[233] This may exceed the value of the property that would be awarded in an action for breach of contract.[234] A claim for consequential loss will be subject to the usual tortious principles governing remoteness of damage. However, Lord Nicholls of Birkenhead stated that, where the conversion was deliberate, consequential loss would be awarded on the basis applicable to a claim in deceit, which did not require the loss to have been reasonably foreseeable at the time of the breach.

The carrier will remain vicariously liable for the defaults of any subcontractor, such as a terminal operator, by whom the misdelivery is actually effected. The position is less clear where the

---

226 *The Marielle Bolten* [2009] EWHC 2552 (Comm), [2010] 1 Lloyd's Rep 648.
227 See *PS Chellaram v China Ocean Shipping Co* [1989] 1 Lloyd's Rep 413, Sup Ct (NSW).
228 [1978] 1 Lloyd's Rep 206, 210.
229 In *The Marielle Bolten* [2009] EWHC 2552 (Comm), [2010] 1 Lloyd's Rep 648, the carrier had sufficient interest in having the clause enforced through an anti-suit injunction against proceedings in Brazil against the protected subcontractors.
230 As in *The Chevalier Roze* [1983] 2 Lloyd's Rep 438.
231 See Todd, P, 'The bill of lading and delivery: the common law actions' [2006] LMCLQ 539.
232 [2002] UKHL 19, [2002] 2 AC 883.
233 The proper measure of damages is the full market value of the cargo at the time and place of conversion, it being irrelevant that the claimant might have to account to another party for part of the amount recovered. *The Jag Shakti* [1986] AC 337, PC.
234 In *The MSC Amsterdam* [2007] EWCA Civ 794; [2007] 2 Lloyd's Rep 622, the conversion led to the detention of a container of copper by the Chinese authorities that was still continuing at the time that the claim was heard in England. The value of the copper was assessed at the date of the judgment and not at the date of the conversion. During this interval, the value of the cargo had substantially appreciated. Cf *The Arpad* [1934] P 189, where the goods were valued without reference to their price under a sub-sale by the plaintiff.

bailment is non-contractual. The Court of Appeal in *East West Corp v DKBS 1912*[235] was of the view that the carrier might not be liable in conversion where the misdelivery was effected by terminal operators at the port of discharge, acting as independent contractors. It did not decide the point, but held that the carrier would be liable in bailment. The carrier, as bailee, on parting with physical possession to a sub-bailee, continues to owe two duties to the bailor. First, it must take reasonable steps to ensure that the sub-bailee is subject to the fundamental obligations of the head bailment, such as the obligation to deliver the cargo only on presentation of the bill of lading. Secondly, it must ensure that the sub-bailee is reasonably competent. On the facts, these duties had been breached.[236] However, the issue as regards conversion is still undecided and it is possible that the bailee's duties might be regarded as being non-delegable, so as to make it vicariously liable for the defaults of the sub-bailee. The courts are more likely to come to such a conclusion where the bailment was initially contractual in nature, as in the *East West* case.

A misdelivery will occur whenever cargo is delivered other than against production of a bill of lading. This will be the case notwithstanding that the person taking delivery is the owner of the goods,[237] the named consignee,[238] or even the person entitled to possession of the goods.[239] As delivery will generally take place after discharge, the carrier's obligation needs to be examined in light of the status of the party that actually takes possession of the cargo after it leaves the ship's holds. Prior to delivery, the goods may be stored by a party acting as the carrier's agent. In this case, the carrier owes a non-delegable duty to ensure that such agent only releases the cargo to a party that presents an original bill of lading.[240] Any misdelivery will occur not at the moment of discharge, but at the time that the agent relinquishes possession of the cargo. On the other hand, it is possible that the party discharging the cargo will be acting as agent for another party, such as the receiver. This will happen where the cargo is carried on 'free out' terms, as in *The Sormovskiy 3068*.[241] In this situation, the carrier will lose control over the delivery process once the cargo starts to be discharged. It must therefore insist that an original bill of lading be presented before discharge begins.

Where cargo is misdelivered, the carrier will have a defence if delivery was made against an original bill of lading, provided that the carrier had no notice that the party presenting the bill was not entitled to possession of the goods referred to therein.[242] This defence, however, requires presentation of a genuine bill and is not available when delivery is made against a forged bill of lading, notwithstanding that the carrier had no reasonable means of knowing this.[243] It must also be questionable whether this defence would apply to the practice whereby an original bill of lading is handed to the master at the start of the voyage to hand back to the receiver at the port of discharge, so enabling the receiver to present an original bill of lading. However, where the custom of the port permits delivery without presentation of the bill of lading, or where the law at the port of discharge prevents the carrier from insisting that delivery be made on presentation of the bill of

---

235 [2003] EWCA Civ 174, [2003] 1 Lloyd's Rep 239, noted [2003] LMCLQ 413.
236 At first instance, the case was decided on the basis that the carrier was liable under the general duty of care in negligence, although this overlooks the problem that the claim would be one for pure economic loss.
237 *The Jag Shakti* [1986] AC 337.
238 *The Stettin* (1889) 14 PD 142.
239 Although, in this latter situation, it is difficult to see how damages could be other than nominal.
240 This may not be the case where the bailment is non-contractual, which will make it difficult to recover in conversion, as the intent of the agent will not be regarded as that of the carrier. However, the bailee may still be liable in respect of its own wrong if it has failed to contract with the sub-bailee on terms obliging it to deliver only against presentation of an original bill of lading. See *EastWest Corp v DKBS 1912* [2003] EWCA Civ 174, [2003] 1 Lloyd's Rep 239.
241 [1994] 2 Lloyd's Rep 266. The receiver was, however, held not to be acting as agent for the party entitled to possession of the goods.
242 *Glyn Mills Currie & Co v The East andWest India Dock Co* (1882) 7 App Cas 591.
243 *Motis Exports Ltd v AF 1912* [2000] 1 Lloyd's Rep 211, CA, noted (1999) LMCLQ 449.

lading, it is probable that the carrier will incur no liability if it delivers to a party who does not present an original bill of lading.[244]

The carrier's delivery obligation may also be qualified by the terms of any exceptions in the bills of lading, particularly those contained in a 'before and after' clause. It must be recalled that Art VII of the Hague and Hague-Visby Rules maintains the carrier's freedom of contract as regards clauses that deal with events that occur before loading and after discharge. It used to be the case that misdelivery was classified as a fundamental breach[245] so as to debar the shipowner from relying on such provisions, but after *Photo-Production Ltd v Securicor Transport Ltd*,[246] this is no longer the law. Exceptions and limitations clauses are now capable of being applied to misdelivery claims, but the courts have adopted a very restrictive approach to interpretation. The clause needs to identify clearly that it covers such claims. Thus, in *The Sormovskiy 3068*,[247] a clause protecting the shipowner in the event of 'loss or damage' to the goods occurring after discharge was held not to cover a misdelivery claim. This was because, on the facts, the misdelivery occurred at the time of discharge. Nor will such a clause cover a misdelivery when the misdelivery occurs after discharge.[248]

Very specific wording is therefore required if a clause is to relieve a carrier from liability for misdelivery.[249] Finally, one must consider whether or not the carrier's delivery obligations are affected by a clause in the charterparty that gives the charterer the right to require the shipowner to deliver the cargo without production of a bill of lading in return for an indemnity. Such a clause will only be capable of affecting the bill of lading holder if the terms of the charter are incorporated into the bill of lading. This happened in *The Sormovskiy 3068*, but, even so, Clarke J held that the incorporated clause did not affect the basic obligation of the shipowner to make delivery only on presentation of an original bill of lading. Indeed, the reference to the charterer's indemnity in the clause confirmed the fact that the shipowner's delivery obligation under the bill of lading was unaffected. This is the case even where the charterparty clause requires the owner to deliver without production of a bill of lading in return for an indemnity.[250]

244 See, in this respect, Art 10(2) of the Rome Convention, as implemented by the Contracts (Applicable Law) Act 1990. This provides: 'In relation to the manner of performance [of the contract] and the steps to be taken in the event of defective performance regard shall be had to the law of the country in which performance takes place.'
245 *Sze Hai Tong Bank Ltd v Rambler Cycle Co Ltd* [1959] AC 576.
246 [1980] AC 827, HL.
247 [1994] 2 Lloyd's Rep 266, QB.
248 Such wording has been held to cover only physical loss or damage to the cargo. See *Motis Exports Ltd v AF 1912* [2000] 1 Lloyd's Rep 211, CA; *East West Corp v DKBS 1912* [2003] EWCA Civ 174; [2003] 1 Lloyd's Rep 239. It is unclear whether or not these words would cover theft.
249 In *The Antwerpen* [1994] 1 Lloyd's Rep 213, Sup Ct (Aus), a clause exempting the carrier in respect of loss or damage after discharge was held to have this effect by virtue of additional wording that provided that it should have effect even in the event that there had been a fundamental breach of the contract. It seems strange that the clause should have this effect by reference to a defunct doctrine of contract law.
250 *The Aegean Sea* [1998] 2 Lloyd's Rep 39 (QB); *The Dolphina* [2012] 1 Lloyd's Rep 304 H.Ct Sing.

Chapter 3

Proving Loss or Damage in Transit

Once a claimant has established title to sue its defendant in an English forum, it must next establish that the loss or damage complained of occurred during a period for which the defendant was responsible for the goods. At common law, the carrier's period of responsibility under an 'ocean' bill of lading extends from the time at which the goods cross the ship's rail on loading, to the time at which they cross it on discharge. This is known as the 'tackle to tackle' or 'alongside' rule. This period is frequently extended, either contractually or by custom of the port, to include the whole of the operations of loading and discharge. The period of responsibility will be the same whether the action is brought in contract, bailment or tort.

It is to this period of responsibility that the Hague-Visby Rules attach with the force of law. However, the carrier's contractual responsibility, and also its parallel responsibility as a bailee, extends to the time at which it makes delivery of the goods to the person entitled to their possession. The carrier will remain responsible for the goods notwithstanding that they are no longer on the carrying vessel but have been transferred into the custody of a subcontractor engaged by the carrier, such as a terminal operator. Thus, in *Sze Hai Tong v Rambler Cycle Co*,[1] the carrier was liable both in breach of contract and in conversion when its agent at the port of discharge wrongfully released the cargo to a party without production of the bill of lading.

There will, therefore, be two periods of responsibility for the sea carrier. The first is that covered by the Hague-Visby Rules, from the start of loading to the completion of discharge. The second is the period from the completion of discharge to the delivery of the cargo to the bill of lading holder. In practice, the focus tends to be on the former period when claims are made under the bill of lading in respect of loss or damage to the cargo. This is because the bill of lading will almost certainly contain a wide-ranging exemption clause in favour of the carrier in respect of loss or damage arising before loading or after discharge. Such clauses do not fall foul of Art III(8) of the Hague-Visby Rules and, indeed, the carrier's freedom to include such stipulations in the bill of lading is specifically sanctioned by Art VII.[2]

The claimant will be able to establish a prima facie case of breach, either of the contract or of the bailment represented thereby, on proving that the goods delivered were not of the same condition and/or quantity as the goods loaded. To do this, the claimant will need to establish two things. First, it must prove the condition and/or quantity of the goods at the start of this period. Secondly, it must prove the condition and/or quantity of the goods at the end of this period. This second requirement will usually be satisfied by reference to a report by a firm of cargo surveyors instructed to attend the discharge of the cargo. Evidence of the condition of the goods at the time of discharge will trump later evidence as to their condition at the time of delivery. This is because the carrier will almost certainly be able to rely on a 'before and after' clause in the bill of lading to escape liability in respect of loss or damage that occurs in the second period of responsibility that arises in the gap between discharge and delivery. However, the claimant may not need to provide independent evidence of the condition of the goods on loading. Instead, it will generally be able to rely on the statements contained in the bill of lading. The most important of these statements will be those relating to the type of goods loaded, their apparent order and condition on loading, the quantity of goods loaded and the date on which they were loaded. These statements are classified as representations, rather than terms of the bill of lading contract.[3]

---

1 [1959] AC 576, PC.
2 However, this second period of responsibility will assume great importance in respect of claims for misdelivery, as references to 'loss or damage' in 'before and after' clauses have been held not to cover such a breach by the carrier.
3 Statements as to the identity of the carrying vessel, the port of loading and that of discharge do, however, constitute terms of the bill of lading contract.

Before considering the evidential effect of such representations, the nature of the loss suffered by the claimant needs to be analysed in some detail. If the claimant is the original shipper,[4] its complaint will be that goods loaded in apparent good order and condition were either discharged in a damaged condition or not discharged at all. Its claim will be pleaded as a breach of the contract of carriage. If the bill of lading is inaccurate, that will give the shipper no additional cause for complaint. As the original shipper, it had a first-hand opportunity to check the accuracy of the bill of lading for itself when it received it. Indeed, any inaccuracy in the bill is likely to have occurred at the instigation of the shipper, who wishes to conceal the fact that the goods loaded do not match the description set out in the contract of sale. For example, the sale contract may call for a May shipment. If the goods are actually loaded on 1 June, it will be in the interest of the shipper to persuade the carrier to sign a bill of lading dated 31 May so as to enable the shipper to tender to its buyer a document in apparent conformity with the terms of the contract of sale.

In contrast, the indorsee or transferee of a bill of lading has no independent means of checking the condition of the goods on loading. It is wholly reliant on the accuracy of the statements in the bill of lading. If those statements are accurate, it will want to rely on the bill of lading as evidence of the condition of the goods on loading and so support a claim for breach of contract against the carrier if the goods are discharged in a damaged condition. If, on the other hand, the statements in the bill of lading are inaccurate, its real loss is somewhat different. What has been lost is the opportunity to reject the documents and the goods that it would have had if an accurate, and non-contractual, bill of lading had been tendered by the shipper.[5]

In many situations, this loss can be adequately recouped by bringing an action for breach of the contract of carriage, proceeding on the assumption that the bill of lading was accurate. Therefore, if goods were damaged prior to loading, but described in the bill of lading as having been loaded in apparent good order and condition, the buyer can recoup from the carrier the losses that it has suffered by reason of the difference in value between sound goods and damaged goods. It will do this by alleging that the loss took place in transit and therefore constituted a breach of carriage. The truth is that there was no breach of contract, because the goods were damaged prior to loading, but if the carrier is prevented from proving this fact, it will be unable to escape liability.

This chapter will primarily be concerned with the rules of law that have developed to enable an indorsee to recover its losses on the basis of a presumed breach of the contract of carriage. However, not all losses suffered by the indorsee can be recovered contractually. There may be no contract with the carrier, or no breach of contract, or contractual damages may be inadequate, such as where the market for the sale goods falls between the date of the contract and the payment against documents. In these situations, the claimant may need to proceed in tort against the carrier, or to proceed against the party who actually signed the inaccurate bill of lading. These additional possibilities will be considered later in the chapter.

The evidential hierarchy of bill of lading statements

A bill of lading can either be *conclusive* evidence, prima facie evidence, or *no* evidence of the truth of the statements it contains.

If it is *conclusive* evidence, the carrier cannot dispute the truth of the statements it has made therein, even if, in fact, it possesses the evidence needed to contradict them. So, if goods are loaded

---

4   In this chapter, 'shipper' will be taken to mean 'consignor', as this is the sense in which the phrase has been used in this particular area of shipping law.

5   *Kwei Tek Chao v British Traders and Shippers Ltd* [1954] 2 QB 459. The buyer's loss of its right under the sale contract to reject the goods or the documents is of particular significance in a falling market.

in a damaged condition but a 'clean' bill of lading is issued, the carrier will be unable to adduce evidence of this fact. The damage will be presumed to have occurred after loading and the carrier will therefore be liable for it.

If it is prima facie evidence, it can be contradicted by independent evidence to the contrary adduced by the defendant. So, on the example given above, the carrier would escape liability if it could provide evidence that, contrary to what is said in the bill of lading, the goods were already damaged prior to loading. However, if it lacks such evidence, the statements in the bill of lading will be taken to be true, and the carrier will be liable for the loss.

If it is of no evidential value, the claimant must prove the necessary facts relating to the goods on loading by independent evidence. So, on the example given above, it is now the claimant on whom the evidential burden falls. Unless it can prove the condition of the goods on loading by evidence independent of the bill of lading, it will be unable to prove that the loss occurred during the carrier's custody and the carrier will escape liability.

A statement in a bill of lading will fall into this third category if the bill is 'claused', in the sense that it qualifies a statement in the bill of lading. For example, bills of lading for bulk cargoes frequently contain a printed clause stating 'weight unknown, particulars supplied by shipper'. The effect of such a clause is that the claimant must prove the quantity loaded by independent means and cannot rely on the figure inserted in the bill of lading. A bill of lading is also referred to as 'claused' when it notes defects in the condition of the goods on loading. This type of 'clausing' has a different effect, in that it amounts to an unqualified statement as to the condition of the goods on loading, albeit in a defective, rather than a sound, condition.

Bill of lading statements and contractual actions against the carrier

The common law position

If the action is brought by a shipper, the bill of lading will either be prima facie evidence, or no evidence if 'claused'. It will never be conclusive evidence.[6] If the action is brought by the indorsee, the equitable doctrine of estoppel will generally mean that statements in the bill of lading become conclusive evidence. However, some statements in the bill of lading may still have only prima facie effect, even when the action is brought by an indorsee. A 'claused' bill of lading will oblige the shipper and indorsee to support their claim by independent evidence of those statements in the bill that are qualified in this way.

Conclusive evidence

Estoppel

The elements of an estoppel are: a representation of existing fact by the party being sued (the carrier) or its agent, which is intended to be relied on and is, in fact, relied on by a third party to its detriment. The effect of the estoppel is that the carrier is estopped from adducing evidence to prove that it was not in breach, because the goods were already damaged when loading commenced. The damage will therefore be treated as having occurred during the period of the carrier's responsibility for the goods under the bill of lading contract. The bill of lading holder's action for breach of the contract of carriage will therefore succeed, even if the truth is that there never was such a breach.

---

6   Unless there is an express contractual term to that effect.

In establishing an estoppel against the carrier, it will be critical to establish on whose behalf the person who actually signed the bill of lading was acting. The same principles will apply as govern the issue of whether a bill of lading is a shipowner's or a charterer's bill. The most likely person to sign the bill is the master, who is usually the shipowner's agent for the purposes of signing bills of lading; his signature will therefore be treated as that of the shipowner, who will be treated as having made the representation necessary to establish an estoppel.

Even if the statement is made by a person acting on behalf of the carrier, an estoppel will not necessarily be established. To do this, the buyer must show that it relied on the accuracy of the statement to its detriment. Problems may arise when the terms of the buyer's sale contract would have obliged it to accept a properly claused bill of lading. If that is the case, what has it lost by accepting a 'clean' bill? In *The Skarp*,[7] the shipowners were not estopped because the bill of lading holders would have been obliged to accept properly claused bills under their sale contract. In contrast, in *The Dona Mari*,[8] it was found as a fact that, had the bills been claused, the indorsee would not have paid its seller or presented any bill of lading to it, even if by so doing the indorsee became liable to its seller under its sale contract. This was sufficient to establish the element of detrimental reliance necessary in an estoppel. The key question is what the indorsee would have done, in *fact*, had a claused bill been issued, rather than what it would have been entitled to do, in *law*.

Apparent order and condition

The most important statement in the bill of lading is that relating to the condition of the goods on loading. A bill of lading is 'clean' if it states that the goods were in 'apparent good order and condition' when loaded. It will be 'claused' if it makes adverse remarks about the condition of the goods on loading. The common law estoppel covers unqualified statements as to the apparent order and condition of the goods on loading.[9]

The dividing line between condition (the external aspect of the goods) and quality (their internal nature) can often be quite fine. The distinction is important, as statements as to the quality of the goods loaded have only prima facie effect. 'Apparent good order and condition' was defined by Sir R Phillimore in *The Peter der Grosse*[10] as meaning that 'apparently, and so far as meets the eye, and externally, they were placed in good order on board this ship'.[11] The application of the test is well illustrated by the decision of the Court of Appeal in *Silver v Ocean SS Co.*[12] The bill of lading acknowledged the shipment of a consignment of cans of frozen eggs in apparently good order and condition. This statement estopped the shipowner from arguing that the eggs were insufficiently packed, by reason of the particular nature and shape of the cans, or from proving that the cans were seriously gashed on shipment. However, the shipowner was allowed to prove that the cans were punctured with pinholes. This was the type of defect that a master loading the goods would not reasonably be expected to detect. Similarly, in *The Athelviscount*, the estoppel was not established in respect of a cargo of kerosene loaded by being pumped through pipe-lines on shore into the ship's pipe-lines and thence into her tanks, as no reasonable examination could have disclosed to the master the existence of the defect complained of.[13]

---

7 [1935] P 134.
8 [1973] 2 Lloyd's Rep 366.
9 *Cia Nav Vasconcada v Churchill & Sim* [1906] 1 KB 237. Previously, in *The Peter der Grosse* (1875) 1 PD 414, the statement in the bill of lading as to the apparent order and condition of the goods had been treated as having prima facie effect only.
10 (1875) 1 PD 414, 420.
11 Applying this test when a bill of lading is issued in relation to a shipper-stuffed container leads to the conclusion that the wording 'apparent order and condition' relates only to the container and not the goods within it. See *The TNT Express* [1992] 2 Lloyd's Rep 636, Sup Ct (NSW).
12 [1930] 1 KB 416.
13 (1934) 48 Ll L Rep 164. Branson J held that the defect, the discoloration of the cargo, was a defect of quality, not of condition.

Leading marks

The common law estoppel also applies in relation to statements as to leading marks. These are marks that go to the identity of the goods carried rather than to their identification. This distinction was drawn by the Court of Appeal in *Parsons v New Zealand Shipping*,[14] where 608 carcasses of frozen lamb were stated to be shipped, marked 'Sun Brand 622x'. Only 507 were, in fact, so marked, but 101 were marked 'Sun Brand 522x'.

The price of lamb having fallen, the indorsees refused delivery of the carcasses marked 522x and sued for non-delivery. It was held that, as the 522x carcasses had the same character and value as those marked 622x, the shipowners were entitled to establish as against the indorsees of the bill of lading that these were the same carcasses as those marked 622x. Had the marks gone to the identity of the goods, the plaintiffs would have been able to rely on the statutory estoppel contained in s 3 of the **Bills of Lading Act 1855**.[15]

However, the numbers merely recorded the date of freezing for the shipper's own convenience and, *per* Kennedy J:

> . . . the meat as a commercial article is absolutely unaffected in its character or value, whether it is marked 522 or 622.

The combined result of the decision and that in *Cox, Patterson & Co v Bruce & Co*,[16] discussed below, is that quality marks and identification marks have only prima facie effect, while leading marks have conclusive effect. In practice, the distinction between leading marks and quality marks may prove to be a fine one.

Prima facie evidence

Not every statement in the bill of lading will trigger the estoppel. Some matters are plainly not within the scope of the judgment of the master or other person signing the bill of lading. Therefore, the buyer should not expect such statements to be more than the mere reiteration of information from the shipper. For this reason, the Court of Appeal in *Cox, Patterson & Co v Bruce & Co*[17] held that the shipowner was entitled to adduce evidence to prove the inaccuracy of statements in the bill of lading as to marks that indicated the quality of 500 bales of jute. It was held that the master had no duty to put in quality marks at all, but only leading marks.[18]

In contrast, a statement as to the quantity of cargo loaded would appear to be one within the knowledge of the master upon which the buyer can reasonably be expected to rely. However, the common law estoppel does not apply to such statements, because of the finding in *Grant v Norway*[19] that the master has no authority to sign a bill of lading in respect of goods that are never loaded on board the ship. The decision is out of line with the general principles relating to ostensible authority subsequently established by the House of Lords in *Lloyd v Grace, Smith & Co*,[20] but has never been overruled. Strictly speaking, the decision only covers a situation in which none of the cargo referred to in the bill of lading has been loaded, but in *Thorman v Burt*,[21] it was also applied when some cargo was loaded, but the bill of lading overstated its quantity. However, the courts have refused to extend the decision beyond statements relating to the quantity loaded. Thus, in

---

14 [1900] 1 QB 714; [1901] 1 KB 237.
15 The decision is based on the assumption that the signature of the shipowners' agent will bind the shipowners for the purposes of the estoppel in s 3 of the Bills of Lading Act 1855, contrary to *Thorman v Burt* (1886) 54 LT 349, CA.
16 (1886) 18 QBD 147.
17 Ibid.
18 Such a statement will still be prima facie evidence of the shipment of goods bearing those marks. See *Compagnia Importadora de Arroces Collette y Kamp SA v P & O Steam Navigation Co* (1927) 28 Ll L Rep 63.
19 (1851) 10 CB 665.
20 [1912] AC 716. However, the House of Lords in that case did not overrule *Grant v Norway*.
21 (1886) 54 LT 349.

The Nea Tyhi,[22] Sheen J rejected the shipowner's argument that a bill of lading, signed by the charterer's agent 'for the master', did not constitute a shipowner's bill because the agent had no authority to sign a bill of lading that falsely stated that goods loaded on deck had been stowed below deck.

Statements in the bill of lading as to quantity loaded will still amount to prima facie evidence of the facts thereby stated.[23] Therefore, if the shipowner can adduce evidence that a lesser quantity was loaded than that stated on the bill of lading, this will enable it successfully to defend an action for short loading brought against it by the buyer. The burden of proof in such a case was set out by Lord Shand in *Smith and Co v Bedouin SN Co* as follows:[24]

> Proof must be met by counter-proof, and that counter-proof will be insufficient if it be not strong enough to displace the consistent and clear evidence of the acts of the shipowners' own servants or employees. It will not be sufficient to shew that fraud may have been committed, or to suggest that the tallymen may have made errors or mistakes, in order to meet a case of positive proof on the other side. It must be shewn that there was in fact a short shipment – that is, the evidence must be sufficient to lead to the inference not merely that the goods may possibly not have been shipped, but that in point of fact they were not shipped . . .

No evidential effect – 'claused' bills of lading

Where the statement in the bill of lading is qualified, the bill of lading will amount to a 'claused' bill of lading. Such clausing is common with regard to statements as to quality or value, which the carrier's servants have no independent means of verifying, but which will have prima facie effect if unqualified. This is also the case with regard to statements as to the weight of bulk cargoes that are loaded, or as to the contents of shipper-stuffed containers that are loaded. In these instances, it is usual to clause the bill of lading with phrases such as 'weight unknown' and 'said to contain', respectively.

The validity of these types of clause was upheld in *New Chinese Antimony Co Ltd v Ocean SS Co*,[25] where the bill of lading statement as to the weight of a cargo loaded in bulk was claused 'said to be' or 'weight unknown'.[26] The statements as to quantity loaded ceased to have any evidential value whatsoever. The plaintiff therefore was required to prove the quantity loaded by independent evidence.[27]

In some situations, the claimant may be able to prove this inferentially. In *Attorney General of Ceylon v Scindia SN Co Ltd*,[28] the Privy Council held that the words 'weight unknown' did not qualify the statement as to the number of bags of rice loaded, which therefore constituted prima facie evidence of the number of bags loaded. The plaintiff, however, still needed to establish the weight of the short-landed bags by independent evidence. It was able to do this by reference to the average weight of the bags delivered, as it was a reasonable inference that the missing bags would have weighed the same.

This type of clausing will not detract from the evidential effect of the statement that the goods were loaded in apparent good order and condition. In *The Peter der Grosse*,[29] the clausing of a bill of lading 'weight, contents and value unknown' was held not to qualify the effect of the statement that

---

22 [1982] 1 Lloyd's Rep 606.
23 *Smith and Co v Bedouin SN Co* [1896] AC 70.
24 Ibid, at 78–9.
25 [1917] 2 KB 664.
26 A printed clause stating 'weight unknown' will be equally effective without the addition of the typed rider 'said to be'. See *The Atlas* [1996] 1 Lloyd's Rep 642, QB.
27 But the clause may fail to protect a shipowner where it should have been clear to him that the weight figures supplied by the shipper could not have been accurate. See *The Sirina* [1988] 2 Lloyd's Rep 613, QB, 615.
28 [1962] AC 60, PC.
29 (1875) 1 PD 414.

the goods were loaded in 'good order'. The combined effect of the two statements was that the master stated that the outside of the packages seemed in order, but admitted nothing as to their contents.

However, suitable wording can derogate from a statement as to 'apparent good order and condition', but it must be placed on the front of the bill of lading where it will be drawn to the attention of the indorsee. In *The Skarp*,[30] timber was shipped already damaged. The master's addition of a qualification on the *reverse* of the bill was not enough to contradict the effect of the front of the bill, which was 'clean'. In contrast, in *Canadian and Dominion Sugar Co Ltd v Canadian National (West Indies) SS Co*,[31] the front of a 'received for shipment' bill was stamped 'signed under guarantee to produce ship's clean receipt'. This was another case of pre-shipment damage. The ship's receipt stated 'many bags stained, torn and resewn'. The shipowner was not estopped from proving pre-shipment damage.

With cargoes of steel, metal and timber, a standard clause has been used on the front of the bill of lading qualifying what is meant by the statement that the cargo is loaded in apparent good order and condition. This is the 'Retla' clause, the validity of which was recognised by the 9th Circuit in the US in *Tokyo Marine & Fire Ins Co Ltd v Retla SS Co*.[32] The clause states:

> . . . the term 'apparent good order and condition' when used in this bill of lading with reference to iron, steel or metal products does not mean that the goods, when received, were free of visible rust or moisture. If the shipper so requests, a substitute bill of lading will be issued omitting the above definition and setting forth any notations as to rust or moisture which may appear on the mates' or tally clerks' receipts.

The 9th Circuit held that the effect of the clause was there was no affirmative representation by the owners that the pipe was free of rust or moisture when it was received by the carrier, and that all surface rust of whatever degree was excluded from the representation of apparent good order and condition. The English courts considered the effect of the clause in *The Saga Explorer*.[33] Simon J held that the 'Retla' clause did not apply to all rust, of whatever severity, but only to minor or superficial rust that would be present on any steel cargo. The clause was not a contradiction of the representation as to the cargo's good order and condition but was a qualification that there was an appearance of rust and moisture of a type which may be expected to appear on any cargo of steel: superficial oxidisation caused by atmospheric conditions. The clause did not cover the level of rust on the cargo noted by the loading port survey report which was appended to the mate's receipts. Accordingly, there had been a fraudulent misrepresentation by the carrier in issuing a clean bill.

Shipper's indemnities

A shipper who knows that a 'clean' bill is required under its sale contract will be tempted to put great pressure on the shipowner to issue such a bill, even where there has been pre-shipment damage. It will frequently offer to indemnify the shipowner for any liability it incurs by not issuing a 'claused' bill of lading. However, such an indemnity is of no value, unless issued in response to a genuine dispute between the shipper and the carrier as to the condition of the goods on loading. In *Brown Jenkinson & Co Ltd v Percy-Dalton (London) Ltd*,[34] a shipowner was debarred from suing under such an indemnity, as it constituted a fraud on subsequent indorsees of the bill of lading and was

---

30 [1935] P 134.
31 [1947] AC 46.
32 [1970] 2 Lloyd's Rep 91 (9th Cir).
33 [2012] EWHC 3124 (Comm); [2013] 1 Lloyd's Rep. 401.
34 [1957] 2 QB 621.

therefore unenforceable as an illegal contract. Moreover, such pre-loading damage will generally fall outside the scope of the shipowner's P&I cover.

Statutory modifications under the Hague and Hague-Visby Rules

Article III(3) – shipper's right to demand an 'unclaused' bill of lading

This Article appears in both the Hague and Hague-Visby Rules and entitles the shipper[35] to demand a bill of lading, which states:

(a) The leading marks necessary for identification of the goods as the same are furnished in writing by the shipper before the loading of the goods starts, provided such marks are stamped or otherwise shown clearly upon the goods if uncovered, or on the cases or coverings in which such goods are contained, in such a manner as should ordinarily remain legible until the end of the voyage.

(b) Either the number of packages or pieces, or the quantity, or weight, as the case may be, furnished in writing by the shipper.

(c) The apparent order and condition of the goods.

The Article contains a proviso that:

. . . no carrier, master or agent of the carrier shall be bound to state or show in the bill of lading any marks, number, quantity, or weight which he has reasonable ground for suspecting not accurately to represent the goods actually received, or which he has had no reasonable means of checking.

The proviso gives the carrier no right to refuse to state the apparent order and condition of the goods loaded.[36] The bill of lading must contain an unqualified statement as to apparent order and condition, whether it be clean or claused. However, the shipowner will be potentially liable in damages if the master wrongfully clauses the bill. This happened in *The David Agmashembeli*,[37] where the master claused the bill, incorrectly stating that the cargo was contaminated. However, the bill of lading holder was unable to recover damages for this breach because, on the facts, the master could still have claused the bill on the ground of the cargo's discoloration. A charterer who is also the shipper is probably entitled to rely on this Article by virtue of Art V, which provides that 'the provisions of the Rules shall not be applicable to charterparties, but if bills of lading are issued in the case of a ship under a charter party they shall comply with the terms of these Rules . . .'.[38]

The Rules themselves are silent as to the validity of qualifying statements such as 'said to contain' or 'weight unknown'. In *The Esmeralda 1*,[39] an Australian court held that the clausing 'said to contain', which appeared on a bill of lading in respect of the contents of a shipper-stuffed container, did not conflict with the Hague Rules. The decision is not surprising because, on the facts, the proviso to Art III(3) would have entitled the carrier to refuse a demand by the shipper for an unqualified statement as to the contents of the container.

---

35 'Shipper' here must mean consignor, rather than the party who makes the contract of carriage with the carrier, for otherwise, a fob buyer would be entitled to demand the bill of lading on shipment.

36 Although where containers are loaded under a bill claused 'said to contain', the statement as to apparent order and condition will relate to the container and not the goods inside it.

37 [2002] EWHC 104 (Admlty); [2003] 1 Lloyd's Rep 92, QB.

38 See Treitel and Reynolds, *Carver on Bills of Lading*, 2001, London: Sweet & Maxwell, pp 9–262. However, Scrutton, *Charterparties and Bills of Lading*, 20th edn, 1996, London: Sweet & Maxwell, p 456, takes the contrary view.

39 [1988] 1 Lloyd's Rep 206, Sup Ct (NSW).

On the other hand, if the qualifying statement is not justified by the proviso, there is a strong argument that it must be regarded as being 'null and void' under Art III(8). However, this was not the position taken in *The Atlas*.[40] A bill of lading subject to the Hague Rules acknowledged the shipment of 1,380 bundles of steel billets weighing 12,038.20 tons. It contained a printed clause to the effect that 'weight . . . number . . . quantity unknown'. Longmore J held that the clausing deprived the statements as to quantity and weight of any evidential status.[41] The provisions of Art III(4) were only triggered if the shipper actually demanded, and obtained, an unqualified bill of lading pursuant to Art III(3). As this had not happened, there could be no conflict between the clausing and the provisions of the Hague Rules. The rather unsatisfactory effect of the decision is that the indorsee's right to rely on the provisions of Art III(4) in the Hague Rules, or its modified equivalent in the Hague-Visby Rules, will depend entirely on the shipper's exercising its right to demand an unqualified bill of lading pursuant to Art III(3). This reasoning was followed in *The Mata K*[42] by Clarke J, who also observed that, if a demand was made and not complied with, the clause would still not fall foul of Art III(8). This view assumes that the words 'loss or damage in connection with the goods in this article' apply only to breaches of Art III(1) and (2).

Article III(5) of the Hague and Hague-Visby Rules gives the carrier an indemnity from the shipper in respect of 'the marks, number, quantity and weight as furnished by him'. The purpose of the provision is to compensate the carrier for its obligation to issue a bill of lading stating those particulars imposed by Art III(3). However, the indemnity does not extend to statements as to the apparent order and condition of the goods that the carrier is also obliged to note on the bill of lading by virtue of Art III(3)(c).

Article III(4) – conclusive effect of statements listed in Art III(3)

Article III(4) of the Hague-Visby Rules provides that:[43]

> . . . such a bill of lading shall be prima facie evidence of the receipt by the carrier of the goods as described in accordance with paras (a), (b) and (c). However, proof to the contrary shall not be admissible when the bill of lading has been transferred to a third party acting in good faith.

This provision largely remedies the mischief of *Grant v Norway*. Statements as to quantity loaded fall within Art III(3)(b), and the carrier will no longer be entitled to admit proof to the contrary when the claimant is a third party, acting in good faith, who holds a bill of lading to which the Rules apply. The statutory estoppel also extends to leading marks 'necessary for the identification of the goods', which, at common law, had only prima facie effect.[44] The shipper's position is governed by the common law position that statements in the bill of lading have only prima facie effect. Furthermore, not every third-party holder of a bill of lading will be entitled to rely on Art III(4), for Art V of the Hague and Hague-Visby Rules provides that the Rules do not apply to charterparties. In addition, in the charterer's hands, the bill of lading will not amount to a 'contract of carriage', as defined by Art I(b) of the Rules, in that it will not regulate the relations between the shipowner and the charterer. Therefore, a charterer who obtains a bill of lading by indorsement, as occurred in *The President of India Lines v Metcalfe Shipping Co Ltd*,[45] will not qualify as a 'third party' under this provision.

---

40 [1996] 1 Lloyd's Rep 642, QB.
41 The fact that the weight had been typed onto the bill and the qualifying clause was printed did not alter the position.
42 [1998] 2 Lloyd's Rep 614.
43 The equivalent provision in the Hague Rules provided only that the statements set out in Art III(3)(a)–(c) had prima facie effect. However, this did not have the effect of excluding the common law estoppel. See *Silver v Ocean SS Co* [1930] 1 KB 416.
44 However, the words 'necessary for the identification of the goods' may indicate that Art III(3) refers only to marks that go to the commercial identity of the goods.
45 [1970] 1 QB 289.

Where the Rules apply to a waybill voluntarily, neither Art III(3) or (4) will apply, as they are worded to apply solely to 'bills of lading'. However, where the Rules apply mandatorily by virtue of s 1(6)(b) of the **Carriage of Goods by Sea Act (COGSA) 1971**, they will be modified as necessary, except for the second sentence of Art III(4) and for Art III(7). In both instances, an express conclusive evidence clause is therefore required if the rule in *Grant v Norway* is to be disapplied as regards a third party suing under the waybill.

Section 4 of the Carriage of Goods by Sea Act 1992

This provision replaces s 3[46] of the **Bills of Lading Act 1855** and provides that:

A bill of lading which:

(a) represents goods to have been shipped on board a vessel or to have been received for shipment on board a vessel; and

(b) has been signed by the master of the vessel or by the person who was not the master but had the express, implied or apparent authority of the carrier to sign bills of lading,

shall in favour of a person who has become the lawful holder of the bill, be conclusive evidence against the carrier of the shipment of the goods, or, as the case may be, of their receipt for shipment.

This provision will prevent a shipowner who is sued for breach of a bill of lading contract that is not subject to the Hague-Visby Rules from relying on *Grant v Norway* so as to adduce evidence that less cargo was actually loaded than that stated on the bill of lading.[47] Section 4 will also enable a claimant to obtain rights of suit under s 2(1) as a 'lawful holder' of a bill of lading even where no goods have been loaded and the bill is therefore a nullity. The carrier in such a situation will wish to argue that s 2(1) cannot apply to a document that is not, in fact, a bill of lading although it gives every outward appearance of being so. Section 4 will prevent the carrier from denying the fact of shipment recorded in the document and will therefore estop it from arguing that the bill is a mere nullity.[48]

As the words 'representing goods to have been shipped' are exactly the same as those to be found in s 3 of the **Bills of Lading Act 1855** considered by the Court of Appeal in *Parsons v New Zealand Shipping*, it is probable that s 4 also applies to statements in the bill of lading relating to marks that go to the commercial identity of the cargo carried.

Although s 4 is not expressly limited to third parties, its provisions apply only in favour 'of a person who has become the lawful holder of the bill'. Furthermore, s 5(5) of **COGSA 1992** provides that its provision 'shall have effect without prejudice to the application, in relation to any case, of the Rules [the Hague-Visby Rules] which for the time being have the force of law by virtue of s 1 of the Carriage of Goods by Sea Act 1971'. As Art III(4) of the Hague-Visby Rules does not affect the position between the carrier and the original shipper, neither will s 4. Therefore, the statements in the bill of lading as to the quantity loaded are still only of

---

46 This provided that: 'Every bill of lading in the hands of a consignee or endorsee for valuable consideration representing goods to have been shipped on board a vessel shall be conclusive evidence of such shipment as against the master or other person signing the same, notwithstanding such goods or some part thereof may not have been so shipped . . .'. The section was of little use, given that the estoppel operated only as against the master or other person who had signed the bill.

47 Unlike Art III(3) of the Hague-Visby Rules, s 4 contains no reference to a bill of lading signed by the carrier itself. This is because the mischief of *Grant v Norway* would not apply to such a bill of lading, as no issue of agency would be involved.

48 This analysis assumes that the initial burden of proof on a claimant who wishes to rely on s 2(1) obliges the claimant to do no more than establish that it has become the lawful holder of a document that gives the outward appearance of a bill of lading issued on behalf of the carrier.

prima facie effect when the carrier is sued by the original shipper.[49] The same applies to bills of lading that are indorsed or transferred to a charterer, given the exclusion of charterparties from the Rules effected by Art V.

However, *Grant v Norway* is still good law as regards contractual actions against carriers under documents other than bills of lading, particularly sea waybills and delivery orders.[50] It is also still good law as regards claims in tort against the carrier arising out of the false statement made by its servant or agent.

Tort actions against the carrier

False statements in the bill of lading can also give rise to a right to sue the carrier under the tort of deceit. This avenue will be useful if the doctrine of estoppel cannot be used to establish a breach of contract by the carrier, as was the case in *The Saudi Crown*.[51] There, the bill of lading bore the incorrect date, but there was no breach of contract by the shipowner in that the goods themselves had been carried safely. However, the buyers suffered a loss of their right to reject the goods under the sale contract and suffered an economic loss due to a fall in the market for the goods. Had the bill of lading been correctly dated, they would have realised that it was a non-contractual tender, being outside the loading dates in the sale contract, and rejected it. They were, however, able to recover their loss by an action in deceit against the shipowner, who was held vicariously liable for the wrongful action of the master in signing the incorrectly dated bill of lading.

Alternatively, actions would be possible for negligent misstatement under *Hedley Byrne & Co Ltd v Heller & Partners*,[52] subject to proof of the necessary 'proximity'[53] between the person signing the bill of lading and the person relying on it or under s 2(1) of the **Misrepresentation Act 1967**. The latter would be preferable, not only because of the reversal of the burden of proof effected by the Act, but also because of the decision of the Court of Appeal in *Royscot Trust Ltd v Rogerson*[54] that damages are to be assessed in the same way as in an action for deceit, in which all direct loss, whether foreseeable or not, is recoverable.[55] However, Scrutton argues[56] that the words of s 2(1) of the **Misrepresentation Act 1967**, 'enters into a contract',[57] are not apt to cover the statutory *assign-ment* of a contract that is effected under **COGSA 1992**.[58]

A claimant who suffers loss when it takes up such a bill of lading will still be expected to mitigate its losses. However, the innocent party will not be expected to take unreasonable steps to mitigate its loss, as can be seen in *Standard Chartered Bank v Pakistan National Shipping*

---

49 By parity of reasoning, it could be argued that s 4 should not protect third parties who claim under bills of lading to which the Hague-Visby Rules do not apply. However, the protection of such persons does not directly prejudice the Hague-Visby Rules and, furthermore, such a construction would strip s 4 of any effect whatsoever.

50 Or as regards claims under bills of lading dated before 16 September 1992 and which were not subject to the Hague-Visby Rules.

51 [1986] 1 Lloyd's Rep 261. Furthermore, the fact that the master has signed an antedated bill of lading does not invalidate its effect as a contract of carriage. See *Alimport v Soubert Shipping Co Ltd* [2000] 2 Lloyd's Rep 447, QB.

52 [1964] AC 465.

53 Following the decision of the House of Lords in *Caparo Industries plc v Dickman* [1990] 2 AC 605, it has become far more difficult to establish the necessary 'proximity'. However, it is submitted that it is likely that the courts would nonetheless be prepared to find it between the person signing the bill of lading and subsequent holders of that document.

54 [1991] 3 All ER 294.

55 These direct losses are not limited to losses under the carriage contract, but include losses sustained under the sale contract covered by the bill of lading, as in *The Saudi Crown* [1986] 1 Lloyd's Rep 261. A degree of expectation loss can be recovered in an action for deceit as in *Bank Berlin v Makris* (1999) Lloyd's Alert Service 40, QB, where a bank recovered damages for the profits that it would otherwise have made on funds advanced on a loan that had been procured by deception.

56 Op cit Scrutton fn 38, p 117.

57 The equivalent requirement for deceit is wider. The representee merely needs to show that it acted in reliance on the false statement.

58 These words would, however, cover the first 'lawful holder' to take an indorsement of a bill of lading from a charterer, in whose hands the bill would have had no contractual significance.

Corp (No 3),[59] where a bank suffered loss when it paid under a letter of credit, under which the seller had tendered a falsely dated bill of lading. The bank was held to owe no duty to try to sell either the documents or the goods once it found out about the fraud. As there was no ready market for either the documents or the goods, the bank had, therefore, not failed to mitigate its losses. Furthermore, in *Standard Chartered v PNSC (No 2)*,[60] the House of Lords held that the bank was not prevented from claiming by the fact that it was partly responsible for its loss, in that it could have rejected the documents, which were tendered outside the period stipulated in the letter of credit. So long as the false representation as to the date of shipment induced them to pay out under the letter of credit, they were able to maintain an action in deceit not only against the seller, but also against the director of the seller that had actually made the representation.

A difficult question arises as to whether recovery under either of these actions would be limited by reference to the terms of the bill of lading. The answer is probably that it would not. The loss sustained is not strictly 'loss or damage *to goods*' and would therefore fall outside Art IV*bis*(1) of the Hague-Visby Rules. Nor would recovery be so limited at common law, as the cause of action arises from facts that would not sustain an action for breach of contract. Furthermore, the provisions of the Rules on which the carrier is most likely to seek to rely – namely, the time bar under Art III(6) and the package limitation under Art IV(5) – are, by their own wording, not apt to cover the type of claim that is likely to be brought in this situation.

Vicarious liability and *Grant v Norway*

In all of the actions discussed above, the carrier would need to be made vicariously liable for the wrongdoing of the party who actually signed the bill of lading. *Grant v Norway* will probably still be relevant to tort actions against the shipowner, as the person signing the bill will not be regarded as the servant or agent of the carrier in the event that the bill of lading overstates the quantity of cargo loaded on the vessel or inaccurately notes the quality marks of the goods loaded. In such situations, an action would have to be brought against the signer of the bill of lading personally.

Actions against the person who actually signed the bill of lading

Where *Grant v Norway* applies, the claimant will lose the benefit of the common law estoppel against the shipowner because of the lack of authority of the person who signed the bill of lading. However, the claimant will be able to proceed against that person in an action for breach of warranty of authority. Damages will be assessed on the basis of the loss suffered due to the fact that the person signing the bill of lading lacked the authority to bind the carrier.[61]

The drawbacks of this type of action were exposed in *Heskell v Continental Express Ltd*.[62] The seller wanted to ship goods from Manchester to Teheran. It engaged a freight forwarder to arrange the carriage of the goods. The freight forwarder booked space for the goods through Strick Lines, the shipowner's agents, but never sent the goods from its warehouse to that of the shipowner. The problem was compounded when Strick Lines issued a bill of lading for the goods, even though, far from being loaded on the vessel, they were still languishing in the freight forwarder's warehouse.

---

59 [1999] 1 Lloyd's Rep 747, QB.
60 [2003] 1 Lloyd's Rep 227, HL.
61 Such an action is of no practical use if the person signing the bill of lading, such as a master, lacks the wherewithal to satisfy any judgment.
62 (1950) 83 Ll L Rep 438.

The sellers faced a claim from their buyer for breach of contract, involving loss of profit of £1,392, which they settled. Fourteen months later, they eventually recovered their goods from the freight forwarder's warehouse, by which time their market value had fallen by £175.

The sellers sought to recover the sum that they had paid to their buyers for breach of the contract of sale. Their problem was in finding a party to sue. There was no express contract with the shipowners, because under the rules of the Port of Manchester at the time, bookings of space did not attain contractual effect until the goods had been received into the shipowners' warehouse. The mere issue of a bill of lading could not constitute a contract. If the goods were never loaded, the bill of lading was a mere 'nullity'. As the law then stood, there was no possibility of suing either Strick Lines or the shipowner for negligent misstatement in issuing a bill of lading falsely recording the loading of the goods at Manchester.

However, they were able to sue Strick Lines for breach of warranty of authority by signing the bill of lading. The problem that the sellers faced was that they could not show that they had suffered loss by reason of the false warranty of authority. Even if the shipowners had expressly authorised Strick Lines to sign the false bill of lading, the sellers would still have been no better off: they would still have had neither a contractual nor a tortious action against the shipowners. In the end, the sellers had to be content with recovery of £175 from the freight forwarders for breach of contract in failing to send the goods down to the shipowners' warehouse.[63]

Had there been a contract with the shipowners, damages might well have been recovered from the person signing the bill of lading. This would be on the basis that the lack of warranted authority had allowed the shipowners to rely on *Grant v Norway* and that what had been lost thereby was the chance of a successful action against the shipowners for non-delivery. Indeed, this was the result reached by Mocatta J in *V/O Rasnoimport v Guthrie*,[64] when he awarded damages against freight forwarders who had signed a bill of lading that overstated the quantity loaded. The fact that some cargo had been loaded under the bill of lading meant that the plaintiff had a contractual action against the shipowners. However, the defendant's lack of warranted authority entailed that the shipowners would have been able to defend any such action by proof of the actual quantity loaded. If the defendant had had the shipowners' authority to issue the bill of lading in this form, the shipowners would have been estopped from adducing such evidence. Damages therefore represented the loss that the plaintiff had suffered by not being able to make a successful recovery against the shipowners under the bill of lading contract.

Were the facts of *Heskell* to recur today, an action for negligent misrepresentation would be possible, at least as against the ship's agents. In assessing damages, the court would have to ask what the seller had lost by relying on the statement in the bill of lading. The answer would be that it had acted so as to expose itself to liability towards its buyer under the sale contract. This is a more straightforward question than the one that has to be posed in an action for breach of warranty of authority and would have resulted in the award of at least some damages against the ship's agents, limited only by principles of remoteness. However, *Grant v Norway* would still operate to prevent the shipowners from being vicariously liable for the negligent misstatement of the person signing the bill of lading. The statutory provisions as to the conclusive effect of statements in the bill of lading do not affect this issue.

---

63 The damages paid out by the sellers to their buyers were too remote to be recoverable from the freight forwarders.
64 [1966] 1 Lloyd's Rep 1. Mocatta J also held that s 3 of the Bills of Lading Act 1855 provides a statutory estoppel in such a situation, but does not actually create a cause of action against the person signing.

Chapter 4

The Terms of the Bill of Lading Contract

Chapter Contents

Once the claimant has established that the loss or damage to the goods took place during the period for which the defendant undertook responsibility for their safety, it will then need to establish that the defendant is liable for such loss or damage. In most instances, such proof will raise a prima facie case as to liability that the defendant will then need to rebut.

Common law liability of sea carriers

If the action is brought in bailment, the defendant will be liable unless it can prove that the loss or damage was not caused by any failure on its part to take reasonable care of the goods while they were in its custody. If the action is brought in negligence, the claimant must prove that the loss was caused by the defendant's failure to take reasonable care of the goods. However, in many instances, the doctrine of *res ipsa loquitur* will operate, in which case the burden of proof equates with that under bailment. The defendant will now have to establish that it did, in fact, take reasonable care of the goods.

If the action is brought in contract, the position is less clear. At common law, land carriers could be either common carriers or carriers for reward. A common carrier was one who undertook to carry the goods of any person willing to pay their charges. Its liability was strict and was subject to only four defences: Act of God; act of the Queen's enemies; inherent vice of the cargo; and fault of the consignor.

All other carriers by land were carriers for reward. Their duty was that of a bailee for reward. Unlike a common carrier, they could escape liability by proving that the loss or damage was not caused by their negligence. With sea carriers, it is unclear whether or not the distinction between common carriers and carriers for reward holds good. Brett J, in *Liver Alkali Co v Johnson*,[1] was of the view that all carriers by sea were subject to the liabilities of a common carrier, even if they were not, in fact, common carriers. In contrast, the Court of Appeal held, in *Nugent v Smith*,[2] that a carrier who was not a common carrier owed the duties of a bailee and could escape liability by disproving negligence. However, when the common law position was reviewed by the Privy Council in *Paterson SS Ltd v Canadian Co-operative Wheat Producers*,[3] Lord Wright made no distinction between common and other carriers in thus stating the obligation of a carrier of goods by sea or water: 'At common law, he was called an insurer, that is he was absolutely responsible for delivering in like order and condition at the destination the goods bailed to him for carriage.'

Exceptions clauses and implied obligations

To avoid the rigours of the common law position, carriers started to include widely worded exceptions clauses in their bills of lading. The courts' reaction was to narrow down the apparent effect of these clauses. They did this by holding that an exceptions clause would not protect the carrier in respect of breaches of certain obligations that are implied into every contract of carriage of goods by sea and into every charterparty, in addition to the absolute obligations of a common carrier. To protect itself against liability for breach of an implied obligation, the carrier would have to word its exceptions clause so that it specifically covered loss due to breach of the implied obligation. There are three such obligations:

---

1   (1874) LR 9 Ex 338. The Court of Appeal was also of the view that, even if the carrier had been a common carrier, on the facts it would have come within the defence of Act of God.
2   (1876) 1 CPD 423.
3   [1934] AC 538.

(a)   to provide a seaworthy vessel at the start of the voyage;
(b)   to take reasonable care of the goods during the voyage, which must be prosecuted with reasonable dispatch, and also during the process of loading and unloading;
(c)   not to deviate from the contractual voyage.

These obligations are implied not only into contracts under bills of lading and waybills, but also into voyage and time charterparties.[4]

In *The Glendarroch*,[5] a cargo of cement was rendered a total loss due to wet damage following the stranding of the ship in Cardigan Bay. The shipowners relied on an exception of 'perils of the sea'. Initially, Sir FH Jeune held that, to bring themselves within the exception, they also needed to prove that the loss had happened without negligence on their part. The Court of Appeal reversed this decision and ordered a new trial. It held that once a defendant had brought itself within the wording of a contractual exception, it would escape liability unless the plaintiff could prove that the loss was caused by its negligence or by the unseaworthiness of the vessel. However, it was the view of Lord Sumner in *FC Bradley & Sons Ltd v Federal Navigation Ltd*,[6] that a much stricter burden was imposed on a defendant who sought to rely on an exceptions clause:

> Accordingly, in strict law, on proof being given of the actual condition of the apples on shipment and of their damaged condition on arrival, the burden of proof passed from the consignees to the shipowners to prove some excepted peril which relieved them from liability, and, further, *as a condition of being allowed the benefit of that exception, to prove seaworthiness at Hobart, the port of shipment, and to negative negligence or misconduct of the master, officers and crew* ... [emphasis added]

This formulation applies what might be called 'bailment reasoning' to the issue of the construction of contractual exceptions. It will be recalled that, in bailment, the bailor will recover on proof that the goods were lost or damaged in the custody of the bailee. The bailee will escape liability only if it can, in turn, prove that it had taken reasonable care of the goods entrusted to it. However, although a contract for the carriage of goods is undoubtedly a contract of bailment, this principle does not easily operate in the context of a bailment that is modified by contractual terms. Lord Sumner's approach would entail that the bailee would have to prove an absence of negligence, irrespective of whether the contract contained exceptions clauses. If this is the case, one might ask why such clauses had been included in the contract in the first place.

In contrast, the reasoning in *The Glendarroch* starts from the premise that the carrier's core obligation under a contract of carriage is the absolute liability of a common carrier. It then follows that the defendant's only means of escaping liability is by reliance on an exceptions clause. If it brings itself within such a clause, then it can only be denied this protection if the claimant can show a breach of one of the secondary obligations that are implied into a contract of carriage. Unlike the position with the core common carrier obligation, breach of such an obligation will not be established merely on proof that the loss or damage took place while the goods were in the carrier's custody. This approach has been more generally accepted by the English courts than the bailment approach, both at common law and as regards the application of the Hague Rules.[7]

Applying the principle in *The Glendarroch*, where the defendant can show that the loss falls within an excepted peril, such as fire, it will prima facie escape liability for the loss. However, if the claimant can then establish that the cause of the fire was due to the unseaworthiness of the vessel,

---

4   As regards time charters, there is uncertainty as to the time at which the first of these obligations crystallises. See p 197.
5   [1894] P 226.
6   (1927) 27 Ll L Rep 395, 396.
7   These cases are discussed in the following chapter.

the defendant will be unable to rely on the exceptions clause. Only an exceptions clause specifically protecting it in the event of loss due to unseaworthiness will suffice to protect the defendant in this situation. Moreover, with the obligation not to deviate, the defendant will lose its right to rely on an exceptions clause, even if the claimant cannot prove that the deviation has any causal connection with the loss it has suffered.

As the majority of cargo claims arise under bills of lading that are subject to the mandatory operation of the Hague Rules or the Hague-Visby Rules, it might be thought that the common law rules are of little importance. However, they are still of relevance for two reasons. First, cargo claims may be made under contracts such as charterparties and sea waybills that are outside the mandatory ambit of the Hague or Hague-Visby Rules. Secondly, the uncertainties of the common law rules have coloured the interpretation of the Hague and Hague-Visby Rules themselves.[8]

In conclusion, the defendant's liability for cargo loss or damage that the claimant has proved took place during the period for which the defendant was in charge of the goods will be assessed by reference to the common law rules, as modified by the terms of the contract of carriage. First, the express terms need to be considered. These may contain exceptions clauses and may also contain clauses defining the obligations of the parties as regards performance of the contract. For example, a 'free in' bill of lading will oblige the shipper, and not the carrier, to load the cargo onto the vessel. The shipowner would not then be liable for damage to the goods by stevedores during loading, as any breach of the contract would be a breach by the shipper.

Secondly, if the defendant can show that the loss falls within the wording of an exceptions clause, the claimant will then need to prove that the loss was caused by a breach of one of the implied terms of the contract so as to disentitle the defendant from relying on an exceptions clause.

Thirdly, the parties must consider any statutory terms of the contract that flow from the operation of the Hague and Hague-Visby Rules. When these Rules have mandatory effect, the common law rules will be of no direct relevance.

Finally, it should be noted that the terms of the contract of carriage are not solely relevant to cargo claims against the carrier. They will also govern claims made by carriers against shippers and indorsees. These claims may be for freight, for demurrage or for damage to the vessel caused by the loading of dangerous cargo.

Express terms

The bill of lading may contain express contractual terms that will usually be found on the reverse. These will be interpreted under normal contractual principles of construction (which are dealt with at p 79) *except* that, to the extent that any clause is inconsistent with the Hague or Hague-Visby Rules, it will be void, under Art III(8), where those Rules have mandatory effect. However, the Rules only govern the performance of a bill of lading contract between loading and discharge and therefore any contractual performance outside these termini will be governed by general contractual principles of construction, subject to the possible application of the **Unfair Contract Terms Act 1977**.

The bill of lading may also incorporate the provisions of the relevant charterparty.[9] If the charter is not identified, and the date in the incorporating words is left blank, the head charter will be incorporated, provided that it is a voyage charter.[10] If it is a time charter, the subcharter will be

---

8 Especially as regards whether a carrier must positively disprove negligence if it is to rely on the defences given to it under Art IV(2) of the Rules.

9 For the effect of charterparty bills of lading on cif and fob contracts, see *Siat v Tradax* [1978] 2 Lloyd's Rep 470, especially 492; [1980] 1 Lloyd's Rep 453.

10 *The San Nicholas* [1976] 1 Lloyd's Rep 8; *The Sevonia Team* [1983] 2 Lloyd's Rep 640.

incorporated.[11] If the bill of lading is to incorporate the terms of a charterparty, that charterparty must have been concluded, and reduced to writing, before the bill is issued. The Court of Appeal in *The Epsilon Rosa*[12] held that these conditions were satisfied even though there was no signed charterparty in existence, only a recap telex. However, it is not possible to incorporate a charterparty that has not been reduced to writing at all.[13] It must be remembered that a bill of lading that incorporates the terms of a charter is still a separate contract from that charter. Charterparty terms will be of no relevance to a bill of lading contract if the bill of lading does not expressly incorporate them.

Incorporation of charter terms into a bill of lading raises two problems of construction. First, will every charter clause be read into the bill of lading? Secondly, how will the courts construe charterparty clauses in a bill of lading context if, for example, the charter only refers to the obligations of 'the charterer'?

The effect of general incorporation clauses

If a general incorporation clause is used, for example, 'incorporating all terms and conditions of the charter dated . . .', only those primary clauses germane to the actual carriage of the goods will be incorporated.[14] Arbitration and jurisdiction clauses will not be incorporated into the bill of lading unless specifically incorporated.[15] Alternatively, they will be incorporated if the wording of the charterparty arbitration clause expressly refers to disputes under the bill of lading.[16] The position is unaffected by the addition of the words 'whatsoever' to the general words of incorporation.[17] The incorporation of the terms and conditions of a charterparty will, however, bring in a charterparty choice of law clause in the absence of an express choice of law clause in the bill of lading.[18]

Construing a charter clause in a bill of lading context

A clause may be incorporated because it is directly germane to the shipment of the goods, yet fail to have any effect because the charter wording does not cover a bill of lading context. The courts will generally only manipulate the charterparty language to make sense of it in a bill of lading context if the clause would otherwise be meaningless. In *Adamastos Shipping Co Ltd v Anglo-Saxon Petroleum Co Ltd*,[19] a charter incorporated the terms of the **US Carriage of Goods by Sea Act of 1936**. Without manipulating the wording of the Act so that 'this bill of lading' could read 'this charterparty', the clause would have been devoid of meaning.[20] However, in *The Miramar*,[21] the House of Lords refused to manipulate the wording of a charter demurrage clause brought into the bill of lading by words of general incorporation. The charter clause referred to an obligation on 'the charterer' to pay demurrage and was given its literal meaning. Its incorporation into the bill of lading was not

---

11 *The SLS Everest* [1981] 2 Lloyd's Rep 389.
12 [2002] EWHC 762 (Comm); [2003] 2 Lloyd's Rep 509.
13 *The Heidberg* [1994] 2 Lloyd's Rep 287, QB.
14 *Hogarth Shipping Co Ltd v Blyth, Greene, Jourdain & Co Ltd* [1917] 2 KB 534, especially 551.
15 *TW Thomas & Co Ltd v Portsea Steamship Co Ltd* [1912] AC 1. *The Varenna* [1983] 3 All ER 645. However, in *The Merak* [1965] P 223, the Court of Appeal held that the words 'all terms, conditions, *clauses*, and exceptions . . .' would be apt to incorporate a suitably drafted arbitration clause.
16 The use of neutral wording, such as a reference to disputes under 'this contract', will be insufficient for this purpose. See *The Federal Bulker* [1989] 1 Lloyd's Rep 103.
17 *Siboti v BP France* [2003] EWHC 1278 (Comm); [2003] 2 Lloyd's Rep 364, QB.
18 *The Njegos* [1936] P 90, and if necessary its wording will be manipulated so that the reference to 'this charterparty' becomes 'this charterparty and bill of lading' – as in *The Dolphina* [2012] 1 Lloyd's Rep 304, H Ct Sing.
19 [1959] AC 133, HL.
20 See, alsoo, *The Happy Ranger* [2002] EWCA Civ 694; [2002] 2 Lloyd's Rep 357. The paramount clause included a provision that, in trades to which the Hague-Visby Rules applied compulsorily, the provisions of the relevant legislation would be incorporated into the bill of lading. The Court of Appeal, by a majority, held that this provision would apply only if the contract of carriage fell within Art X of the Hague-Visby Rules, which, on the facts, it did.
21 *The Miramar* [1984] AC 676.

meaningless, even though it referred to the obligations of a third party, the charterer. The bill of lading holder was therefore not liable for demurrage.[22]

The position may be different where the demurrage clause in the charter does not specify who is to pay demurrage but, instead, provides simply for 'demurrage to be paid'.[23] Lord Diplock doubted whether the nineteenth-century cases supporting this conclusion would be decided the same way today.[24] His Lordship was clearly unhappy with the idea of liability for demurrage claims being transferred to bill of lading holders in any circumstances, particularly in the light of the practical problems that could arise where a number of bills of lading incorporated the demurrage provisions of a single voyage charter. Notwithstanding his Lordship's misgivings, the old cases were not overruled and, in *The Spiros C*,[25] were assumed still to be good law. In this case, the laytime provisions of the charter were neutrally worded, but the demurrage provisions referred to 'the charterer'. For this reason, the incorporated charter provisions could impose no liability on the bill of lading holder. The Court of Appeal further held that, while the shipper in such circumstances might well be under an implied obligation to load within a reasonable time, it would be under no such obligation as regards discharge.

However, the courts are more willing to manipulate the language of a clause that is specifically incorporated by the words of incorporation on the bill of lading. In *The Nerano*,[26] the bill of lading specifically incorporated the arbitration clause in the charter, and its language was manipulated so as to make it applicable to disputes between the shipowner and the bill of lading holder.[27] Similarly, in *The Channel Ranger*[28] a bill of lading that specifically incorporated an English 'law and arbitration' clause in a charterparty was read as referring to a clause in the charterparty that conferred jurisdiction on the English court.

Construing exceptions clauses

The general principles of contract law will govern the construction of such clauses. The burden of proving that the loss comes within the clause will fall on the party seeking to rely on the clause. After the decision of the House of Lords in *Photo Production Ltd v Securicor Transport Ltd*,[29] which abolished the doctrine of 'fundamental breach', the courts will give full effect to the clear meaning of a clause. Where the meaning of the clause is unclear or ambiguous, the courts will resolve the uncertainty by the use of canons of construction such as the *ejusdem generis* rule[30] or the 'four corners' rule.[31] On occasion, these canons of construction have been used to limit clauses the wording of which is neither ambiguous nor uncertain. In *The Chanda*,[32] Hirst J held that, as a matter of construction, the carrier could not rely on the exceptions and limitations in the Hague Rules when the loss was caused by an unauthorised mode of performing the contract, by carrying the cargo on deck. The Court of Appeal has now overruled the decision in

---

22 A further example of the courts' reluctance to manipulate the wording of a clause is provided by *The Filikos* [1983] 1 Lloyd's Rep 9, where the Court of Appeal held that 'shipper' in Art IV(2)(i) of the Hague Rules did not include a charterer who was not the consignor.
23 *Gray v Carr* (1871) LR 6 QB 522. See, also, *The Constanza M* [1980] 1 Lloyd's Rep 505, QB, where the words 'freight to be paid' were held to have similar effect in imposing on a bill of lading holder the freight obligations contained in the charter.
24 *The Miramar* [1984] AC 676, 686.
25 [2000] 2 Lloyd's Rep 550, CA.
26 [1994] 2 Lloyd's Rep 50, QB; aff'd [1996] 1 Lloyd's Rep 1 (CA).
27 By this reasoning, the court would manipulate the wording of a charterparty freight clause where the bill was marked 'freight as per charterparty'. It is, however, less clear whether it would be prepared to do so with a clause 'demurrage as per charterparty', given the observations of Lord Diplock in *The Miramar* [1984] AC 676, 686.
28 [2013] EWHC 3081 (Comm); [2014] 1 Lloyd's Rep. 337.
29 [1980] AC 827.
30 General words in a clause given a restrictive meaning by reference back to preceding specific words in a clause.
31 By not applying the clause when performance is radically different from that contemplated by the contract, as in *The Cap Palos* [1921] P 458.
32 [1989] 2 Lloyd's Rep 494.

The Kapitan Petko Voivoda.[33] Where two clauses in the contract are inconsistent with each other, typed clauses will generally prevail over printed ones, and clauses on the front of the bill will prevail over those on the reverse of the document. The following clauses are the most usual to be found in contracts of carriage and have received the following judicial interpretation.

Perils of the sea

A peril of the sea is a fortuitous occurrence that is characteristic of carriage by sea, rather than by other modes of transport. Lopes LJ, in *Hamilton, Fraser & Co v Pandorff & Co*, stated that such a peril must constitute 'a sea damage, occurring at sea and nobody's fault'.[34] This definition must be read in the light of two qualifications. First, the exception will cover events that are characteristic of sea carriage, even though they occur in port before the ship starts on her voyage. Thus, in *The Stranna*,[35] the exception was held to cover loss of deck cargo that fell overboard when the vessel listed while loading. Secondly, as was held by the Court of Appeal in *The Glendarroch*,[36] the defendant can bring itself within the exception without being also required to prove an absence of negligence. An entry of seawater into a vessel will still be a 'fortuity' even if the reason for the entry is due to the negligence of the crew or the unseaworthiness of the vessel. While such reasoning may be appropriate in considering the phrase in the context of a policy of marine insurance, where negligence will not vitiate the cover, it may be doubted whether it should be applied in the context of an exceptions clause in a contract of carriage.[37]

However, notwithstanding the apparent width of the clause, the protection that it offers will often be illusory. The carrier will be faced with the argument that the ingress of seawater that constitutes the 'peril of the sea' is only partly causative of the loss; the loss will have been caused concurrently by either the negligence of the crew or a defect in the vessel's structure that permitted the ingress of seawater. The burden will then fall on the carrier, as the party relying on the exception, either to prove exactly how much of the loss was caused solely by the exception of 'peril of the sea' or to prove that the concurrent cause also fell within the wording of another exception. This reasoning was adopted by Hobhouse J in *The Torenia*[38] to prevent reliance on this exception when cargo was damaged by the ship sinking on the voyage. The most likely cause of the sinking was a defect in the ship's structure, which the shipowner was unable to prove fell within the wording of any of the other exceptions in Art IV(2) of the Hague Rules.

The following causes have been held to fall within the exception: a collision,[39] even if it does not take place in bad weather;[40] grounding of a vessel in the river approach to a port;[41] entry of water into a hold as a result of a rat gnawing a lead pipe;[42] and damage resulting from action designed to prevent a peril of the sea.[43]

---

33 [2003] EWCA Civ 451; [2003] 2 Lloyd's Rep 1.
34 (1885) 16 QBD 629, 635, approved by Lord Bramwell (1887) 12 App Cas 518, 526.
35 [1938] P 69, CA.
36 [1894] P 226.
37 Cf *Hollier v Rambler Motors* [1972] 2 QB 71, CA, where the bailee was unable to rely on a fire exception once it had failed to discharge the burden of proving that the fire had not been caused by its negligence.
38 [1983] 2 Lloyd's Rep 210.
39 *The Xantho* (1887) 12 App Cas 503, HL.
40 In *The Bunga Seroja* [1994] 1 Lloyd's Rep 455, Sup Ct (NSW), Admlty Div, aff'd [1999] 1 Lloyd's Rep 513, an 'expectable' storm was held to be capable of amounting to a 'peril of the sea', provided that the carrier could prove an element of fortuity in the loss.
41 *The Theodegmon* [1990] 1 Lloyd's Rep 52, QB. However, the carrier lost the benefit of the exception once the plaintiff established that the cause of the grounding was the unseaworthiness of the vessel on sailing from the port.
42 *Hamilton, Fraser & Co v Pandorff & Co* (1887) 12 App Cas 518, HL. Lord Bramwell, at 527, was also of the opinion that wind and waves are perils of the sea, but not fire and lightning.
43 *Canada Rice Mills Ltd v Union Maritime and General Insurance Co Ltd* [1941] AC 55, PC. The exception covered damage to a cargo of rice, which overheated through lack of ventilation due to closure of the cowl ventilators and hatches during bad weather.

Act of God

Loss that is the result of a direct, violent, sudden and irresistible act of nature will be regarded as due to an Act of God provided that the carrier can prove that it has taken all reasonable steps to ensure the safety of the goods.[44]

Negligence

Exceptions clauses will not cover negligence unless they specifically refer to it, or unless the wording of the clause could cover negligence and there is no other realistic liability to which it could refer.[45] Thus, 'errors of navigation' has been held not to cover negligent navigational errors.[46] However, a limitation clause the language of which is capable of referring to negligence, even though it does not specifically refer to negligence, will be valid, even if the clause could cover other liabilities.[47]

Implied terms

Seaworthiness

What is seaworthiness?

The vessel must be in such a state at the start of the voyage that it can perform the contract voyage in safety, both as regards the vessel itself and the particular cargo to be carried on the voyage.

Unsafety as regards the vessel

Although the obligation (often described as the 'warranty' of seaworthiness) is absolute in nature, the courts apply a relative standard. The shipowner's duty is to make *this ship* fit for *this cargo* on *this voyage*. Thus, in *Burges v Wickham*,[48] the use of a river steamer for an ocean voyage was held not of itself to make the vessel unseaworthy. Although the vessel might be unsuitable for the voyage contemplated, if there was nothing further that the owners could do to make her fit for that voyage, then the implied warranty under the policy of insurance would not be broken. Blackburn J stated:

> . . . but the assured do not in any case warrant the prudence of the adventure – that is for the underwriters to consider when fixing the premium.

Unseaworthiness can arise from defects affecting the safety of the vessel or those affecting the safety of the cargo. The former must usually be proved to exist at the time of sailing. Examples of unseaworthiness are: a leaky hull;[49] defective propellers;[50] and a crankshaft with a flaw in a weld.[51] A vessel may be unseaworthy in a non-physical sense if she lacks documentation required by the law of the vessel's flag or by the laws, regulations or lawful administrative practices of governmental or local authorities at the vessel's ports of call.[52] However, lack of the 'blue card', required by the International Transport Workers' Federation (ITF) to indicate that the crew's contracts of employment meet the standards required by the union, does not render the vessel unseaworthy.[53]

---

44 *Nugent v Smith* (1876) 1 CPD 423, CA.
45 *Canada Steamships Line Ltd v The King* [1952] 1 Lloyd's Rep 1; *The Raphael* [1982] 2 Lloyd's Rep 42.
46 *The Emmanuel C* [1983] 1 Lloyd's Rep 310, QB. The Hague and Hague-Visby Rules contain a similar exception in Art IV(2)(a), which specifically covers 'neglect or default' by the master or crew in 'the navigation or management' of the vessel.
47 *Ailsa Craig Fishing Co Ltd v Malvern Fishing Co Ltd and Securicor (Scotland) Ltd* [1983] 1 WLR 964, HL.
48 (1863) 3 B & S 669.
49 *Lyon v Mells* (1804) 5 East 428.
50 *Snia v Suzuki* (1924) 29 Com Cas 284.
51 *The Glenfruin* (1885) 10 PD 103.
52 For example, in *Ciampa and Ors v British India SN Co* [1915] 2 KB 774, one of the reasons for the vessel's unseaworthiness was that she lacked any document certifying a 'clean bill of health' after her call at Mombasa at a time when that port was in the grip of an outbreak of plague.
53 *The Derby* [1985] 2 Lloyd's Rep 325, CA.

Unsafety as regards the cargo carried

The vessel must also be able to carry the cargo safely on the contract voyage. Uncargoworthiness will amount to unseaworthiness, even though the vessel itself might well be able to complete the contract voyage in safety. Examples of uncargoworthiness are: defective cargo gears;[54] leaky hatch covers;[55] and a defective bullion room in which to store a cargo of gold sovereigns.[56]

Cargoworthiness is relative to the cargo carried. A vessel may be able to carry one cargo safely but not another, depending on the characteristics of the goods to be carried. Thus, in *Tattersall v National SS Co*,[57] a vessel was unseaworthy for the carriage of livestock because the holds had not been disinfected after discharging a previous cargo of cattle that were infected with foot-and-mouth disease. The warranty extends beyond the vessel itself to the equipment on board necessary for the safe carriage of the cargo. In *The Maori King (Owners) v Hughes*,[58] a cargo of frozen mutton was damaged during the voyage due to the breakdown of the vessel's refrigeration unit. The shipowners were unable to rely on an exceptions clause protecting them in the event of 'failure or breakdown of machinery, insulation and other appliances'. Such a clause did not protect them in respect of their breach of the implied obligation to have the refrigeration unit working properly at the start of the voyage so as to make the vessel cargoworthy.

Similarly, in *Stanton v Richardson*,[59] the shipowner was held to have breached the implied obligation when its pumps were unable to cover a cargo of wet sugar tendered by the charterer. Although the vessel's pumps could cope with dry sugar, the shipowner had still broken the warranty because the charter gave the charterer an option to load wet sugar. At first sight, this decision appears inconsistent with *Burges v Wickham*.[60] However, a salient feature of that case was that the assured had made full disclosure to the underwriters of the characteristics of the vessel prior to the issue of the policy. In *Stanton v Richardson*, in contrast, the charterer would be entitled to assume that the vessel had the equipment necessary to carry the wet sugar safely by reason of the option given to it in the charterparty to carry that specific cargo.

The vessel must usually be cargoworthy when the cargo is loaded, rather than when the vessel sails. If the vessel becomes uncargoworthy after this point, this will not necessarily amount to a breach of the implied warranty. That will depend on whether the cause of the subsequent uncargoworthiness was latent at the time of loading. This was the case in *Ciampa and Ors v British SN Co*,[61] where a cargo of lemons was loaded from Naples for Marseilles. Prior to loading at Naples, the vessel had been at Mombasa, where there had been an outbreak of plague. Because of this, the port authorities required the vessel to be fumigated prior to discharge. The lemons were damaged during the fumigation process. The damage was held to result from a breach of the implied warranty because, at the time that the lemons were loaded at Naples, it was inevitable that they would have to be fumigated at Marseilles.

In contrast, in *Elder Dempster & Co Ltd v Paterson Zochonis & Co Ltd*,[62] damage to a cargo of barrels of palm oil when subsequently overstowed with a heavy cargo of palm kernels was held not to be due to any breach of the implied warranty. At the time that the palm oil was loaded, the vessel was suitable for its safe carriage and there was no inevitability that it would become unsafe during the voyage. The shipowners could have taken on less palm kernel cargo and avoided overstowing it on top of the barrels of palm oil, although such a possibility was commercially unlikely as it would

---

54 *Hang Fung v Mullion* [1966] 1 Lloyd's Rep 511. The vessel was still unseaworthy despite the fact that the charterers were obliged to load the vessel. In loading the vessel, they were to be allowed the use of the vessel's cargo gear.
55 *The Gundulic* [1981] 2 Lloyd's Rep 418.
56 *Queensland National Bank v Peninsular and Oriental SN Co* [1898] 1 QB 567, CA.
57 (1884) 12 QBD 297.
58 [1895] 2 QB 550, CA.
59 (1874) LR 9 CP 390.
60 (1863) 3 B & S 669.
61 [1915] 2 KB 774, KBD.
62 [1924] AC 522, HL.

reduce the carrying capacity, and therefore the profitability, of the vessel. If, however, contractual commitments had already been entered into in respect of carriage of the palm kernel cargo from the second port at the time that the palm oil was loaded at the first port, it is likely that the vessel would have been unseaworthy as regards the palm oil.

Burden of proof

The burden of proving unseaworthiness is generally accepted to fall on the claimant. In certain situations, the court may be prepared to infer unseaworthiness, so throwing the burden of proof back onto the defendant. In The Torenia,[63] Hobhouse J held that such an inference was raised by the sinking of the vessel in weather conditions of the sort that were to be expected at some stage during the voyage.[64] So, too, in Fiumana Societa di Navigazione v Bunge & Co Ltd,[65] where Wright J held that the breaking out of fires in four different bunker spaces raised the inference that the cause of the fire must have been due to a defect in the bunkers taken on board at Rotterdam for a round trip to Argentina. This defect therefore rendered the vessel unseaworthy at the start of her loading in the River Plate.

Absolute nature of the duty

At common law, the duty is absolute. Once the standard is set, failure to meet it constitutes a breach of contract. It is no defence to say that the shipowner took reasonable steps to attain the standard. In Petrofina SA of Brussels v Compagnia Italiana Trasporto Olii Minerali of Genoa,[66] a cargo of benzine was discoloured due to failure to clean the vessel's tanks properly prior to loading. The shipowners were liable for breach of the implied warranty notwithstanding that there was found to be no want of due diligence on their part and that the tanks had been inspected to the satisfaction of the charterer's surveyor, as expressly required by the charterparty. This position is modified by the Hague and Hague-Visby Rules, which have mandatory application to most bill of lading contracts, to one of due diligence.

Exceptions clauses will not cover losses due to unseaworthiness unless the clause itself explicitly states this.[67] This is a stricter canon of construction than that applied to the question of whether negligence is covered by an exception. It is, therefore, of critical importance whether or not the claimant can prove that a loss has been caused by unseaworthiness, rather than by some other breach of contract that may be covered by an exceptions clause.

The 'doctrine of stages'

The duty of seaworthiness operates at different points in the contract of carriage and is not a continuous obligation throughout the voyage. This is known as the 'doctrine of stages'. The most usual stages are the commencement of loading of cargo and the sailing of the vessel. A deficiency in the ship's condition at the loading stage may not amount to a breach of the duty of seaworthiness, provided that it is remedied by the sailing stage. For example, a ship may be unable to sail safely without adequate charts, but this deficiency will not impair her ability safely to load the cargo.

Further stages may exist, depending on the circumstances of the voyage. For long voyages, the vessel will need to bunker at an intermediate port. The provision of proper bunkers is part of the

---

63 [1983] 2 Lloyd's Rep 210.
64 A similar inference was raised in The Theodegmon [1990] 1 Lloyd's Rep 52, QB, from the fact that the vessel's steering gear broke down so soon after leaving the port of loading.
65 [1930] 2 KB 47.
66 (1937) 53 TLR 650, CA.
67 Steel v State Line SS Co (1877) 3 App Cas 72, HL (Sc). In The ChristelVinnen [1924] P 208, CA, a clause protecting the shipowner in the event of 'damage occasioned by latent defect in the hull . . . even when occasioned by the negligence of the servants of the shipowner' was held not to cover latent defects in existence at the time of sailing.

duty of seaworthiness. In these circumstances, it will crystallise not only on sailing, but also on rebunkering en route. In *The Vortigern*,[68] the vessel rebunkered with insufficient coal and, as a consequence, had to have recourse to the plaintiff's cargo of copra as fuel. The contract contained a clause excepting the negligence of the master and crew. However, the shipowners were unable to rely on it because they had broken the absolute warranty of seaworthiness that had reattached as regards the provision of bunkers at the intermediate fuelling port.[69]

Causation

Cargo may be damaged by multiple causes. If unseaworthiness is *a* cause, then the shipowner will be liable, provided that the loss is not too remote.[70] This can be illustrated by *McFadden v Blue Star Line*.[71] The vessel's ballast tank was being filled with seawater and the crew attempted to close the seacock, but did not do so effectively. The continued water pressure eventually forced a defective valve chest, and water flowed through the valve chest and through the open sluice door into the hold containing the plaintiff's cargo of cotton, which was damaged. Two of the causes, the failure to close the seacock and the failure to close the sluice door, took place after the goods were on board. These two causes fell in the interval between the loading and sailing stages, and did not therefore constitute a breach of the warranty of seaworthiness. These two causes were therefore covered by an exceptions clause covering accidents of navigation even when occurring by negligence.[72] However, the warranty was breached by the third cause, the defective valve chest, which had been defective at the start of loading. That breach was a cause of the damage and therefore the shipowner was liable in full for the damage to the cotton.

Similar principles apply where the damage is caused by the unseaworthiness and made worse by negligence of the crew. In *The Christel Vinnen*,[73] a cargo of maize was damaged by ingress of water due to a leak in a rivet hole from which the rivet had dropped out. Much less damage would have been done had the crew been ordinarily careful in taking soundings, which would have alerted them to the leak at a much earlier stage. Nonetheless, the shipowner was liable for the cargo damage in full, as the initial unseaworthiness of the vessel was still *a* cause of the entire damage.

However, if there are two *distinct* instances of cargo damage, one of which is caused by unseaworthiness, the other not, the shipowner will be able to rely on an exceptions clause in respect of that damage not caused by unseaworthiness.[74] In *The Europa*,[75] the vessel struck the dock wall when entering the dock at Liverpool. This caused a pipe to fracture, which allowed water to flow into the tween-decks and damage the cargo stowed there. Some scupper holes in the tween-deck were imperfectly plugged. This allowed the water to leak down and damage the cargo stowed below in the lower hold. The shipowners were able to rely on an exception in the event of 'collisions' as regards the damaged sugar in the tween-deck, but not as regards that in the lower hold. The failure to plug the scupper holes amounted to initial unseaworthiness and was a cause of the damage to the sugar stowed in the lower hold, but had no causative link with the damage to the sugar in the tween-decks themselves.[76]

---

68 [1899] P 140, CA.
69 Another example of a stage occurred in *Reed v Page* [1927] 1 KB 743, CA, where a barge took on 14 per cent more cargo than her proper load, thereby becoming unseaworthy at the stage of waiting in the river for a tug.
70 The contractual principles relating to remoteness of damage are considered in Chapter 13 at pp 256–9.
71 [1905] 1 KB 697.
72 They could only have amounted to breaches of the implied warranty at the time that the vessel sailed, and then only if they could not have been easily remedied after sailing.
73 [1924] P 208, CA.
74 The burden of proving that there are, in fact, two distinct heads of loss will fall on the shipowner.
75 [1908] P 84.
76 See, also, *The Torepo* [2002] EWHC 1481 (Admlty); [2002] 2 Lloyd's Rep 535, where a discrepancy in the charts was held not to have been causative of a grounding caused by pilot error when navigating the vessel through the Patagonian channels. A separate allegation that the error was caused by a failure to provide proper rest periods for the two pilots was not substantiated and, even if it had been, it would have not amounted to unseaworthiness, but would have been merely an instance of negligence.

A related problem arises when the unseaworthiness is a contributing cause along with fault on the part of the claimant. In *Vinmar International v Theresa Navigation SA (The Atrice)*,[77] a contamination claim arose out of the shipowners' failure to clean or purge the vessel's tanks of a previous cargo. The shipowners argued that most of the loss was caused by the claimant's decision to continue loading. Tomlinson J held that the claimant's conduct could only be regarded as having broken the chain of causation if it could be regarded as the sole cause of the loss. The claimant's decision had involved the taking of a very considerable risk, but it had to be borne in mind that they had been put in this difficult position by the admitted wrongdoing of the shipowners.

Crew negligence or unseaworthiness?

The incompetence of the crew can sometimes go beyond negligence and amount to unseaworthiness. In *Hong Kong Fir Shipping Co Ltd v Kawasaki Kisen Kaisha Ltd*,[78] the vessel's diesel engines and other machinery were in reasonably good order when the vessel was delivered to the time charterers. However, by reason of their age, the engines needed to be maintained by an experienced, competent, careful and adequate engine room staff. In fact, the engine room staff was incompetent, with a chief engineer addicted to drink, thereby rendering the vessel unseaworthy.

Moreover, an otherwise competent crew can be rendered incompetent by lack of knowledge. In *Standard Oil Co of New York v Clan Line Steamers Ltd*,[79] the shipowners failed to pass on to the master instructions from the manufacturers of the vessel that the vessel had to retain water ballast when loaded with a full homogeneous cargo. The master ordered the crew to empty the vessel's ballast tanks, with the result that she keeled over and sank in calm seas. The damage was held to be attributable to the unseaworthiness of the vessel at the start of her voyage. So too, in *The Star Sea*,[80] it was held, in the context of s 39(5) of the **Marine Insurance Act 1906**, that the shipowner's failure to ensure that the master was familiar with the operation of the vessel's CO_2 system for extinguishing fires amounted to unseaworthiness at the start of the voyage.

On the other side of the line, one finds damage caused by the negligence of an otherwise competent crew. This will not, of itself, breach the implied warranty, provided that the negligence is remediable after the vessel has sailed. In *Steel v State Line Steamship Co*,[81] a cargo of wheat was damaged by an ingress of water through a porthole, about a foot above the water line, which had been insufficiently tightened. As the jury had made no finding on the issue of seaworthiness, the House of Lords remitted the case for a new trial. Lord Blackburn nonetheless gave his views on the issue. The vessel would clearly have been unseaworthy on the following hypothesis:

> If, for example, this port was left unfastened, so that when any ordinary weather came on, and the sea washed so high as the port, it would be sure to give way and the water come in, unless something more was done – if in the inside the wheat had been piled up so high against it and covered it, so that no one would ever see whether it had been so left or not, and so that if it had been found out or thought of, it would have required a great deal of time and trouble (time above all) to remove the cargo to get at it and fasten it . . .

---

77 [2001] 2 Lloyd's Rep 1.
78 [1962] 2 QB 26, CA. Crew incompetence also amounted to unseaworthiness in *Adamastos Shipping Co Ltd v Anglo-Saxon Petroleum Co Ltd* [1959] AC 133. However, the charter there incorporated the Hague Rules, and the shipowners were able to escape liability by proving that they had taken due diligence in engaging the crew.
79 [1924] AC 100, HL (Sc).
80 [1995] 1 Lloyd's Rep 651, QB; aff'd on this point [1997] 1 Lloyd's Rep 360, CA.
81 (1877) 3 App Cas 72, HL.

However, the vessel would not have been unseaworthy on the alternative hypothesis that:

> . . . if this port had been, as a port in the cabin or some other place would often be, open, and when they were sailing out under the lee of the shore remaining open, but quite capable of being shut at a moment's notice as soon as the sea became in the slightest degree rough, and in case a regular storm came on capable of being closed with a dead light . . . that thing could be set right in a few minutes, and there is always some warning before a storm comes on . . . If they did not put it right after such a warning, that would be negligence on the part of the crew, and not unseaworthiness of the vessel. But between these two extremes, which seem to me to be self-evident cases as to what they would be, there may be a great deal of difficulty in ascertaining how it was here . . . [82]

A subsequent case that fits Lord Blackburn's second hypothesis is *International Packers London Ltd v Ocean Steam Ship Co Ltd*.[83] Forty-eight hours after the vessel sailed from Melbourne, a storm blew up and stripped the tarpaulins from the hatch covers, which led to an ingress of water that damaged the cargo. The vessel had locking bars to secure the tarpaulins, but these were not in place at the time of the incident. This was due to crew negligence, not unseaworthiness. When the vessel sailed from Melbourne, the weather forecast gave no indication that the locking bars needed to be fitted at that stage.

In many instances, what appears to be crew negligence will, in fact, be the result of a failure to provide proper management systems, which will constitute unseaworthiness. In *The Eurasian Dream*,[84] severe damage was caused when a fire broke out on a car-carrier due to the stevedores simultaneously refuelling and jump-starting cars. The third officer should have supervised them and prevented this dangerous practice. Furthermore, the crew's lack of training in firefighting procedures meant that they were unable to contain the fire that took over the vessel and rendered it a constructive total loss. The crew's inability in this respect was caused by many factors, including an absence of walkie-talkies to enable them to communicate with each other during the firefighting. In addition, there was also a clear failure on the part of the shipowners to set up a proper system to ensure that the crew were able to deal with such emergencies. The shipowners had provided voluminous safety documentation, which would have taken the master two or three weeks to digest. What was needed was information on safety procedures that were related to the specific vessel.

The International Safety Management Code (the ISM Code) was introduced into SOLAS[85] as a new Chapter IX in November 1993, and came into force as regards passenger ships and tankers from 1 July 1998. On 1 July 2002, it came into force as regards cargo ships and mobile drilling units of 500 gross tonnage and above. The Code establishes safety management objectives and requires a safety management system (SMS) to be established by the 'company' (the shipowner or any person who assumed responsibility for operating the ship, such as a manager or demise charterer). The company is required to set up and operate a policy for achieving the objectives of the Code and must 'designate a person or persons ashore having direct access to the highest level of management'. SMS procedures should be documented in a safety management manual, a copy of which is to be kept on board the vessel.

The general implementation of the ISM Code is likely to alter the legal boundary between unseaworthiness and crew negligence. In future, it will be more difficult to defend cargo claims on the basis of the defences provided by Art IV(2)(a) of the Hague Rules as 'neglect or default of the master or crew in the navigation and management of the vessel' will, in many cases, result from a

---

82 (1877) 3 App Cas 72, HL, 90–1.
83 [1955] 2 Lloyd's Rep 218.
84 [2002] EWHC 118 (Comm); [2002] 1 Lloyd's Rep 719, QB.
85 The 1974 Convention on Safety of Life at Sea.

failure by the 'company' to comply with its obligations under the ISM Code, in which case it is likely that a court will find that the shipowner was in breach of its obligation under Art III(1) to provide a seaworthy ship. The same is likely to happen as regards the 'fire' exception under subheading (b).

Unseaworthiness or bad stowage?

The issue of whether cargo was damaged by bad stowage or unseaworthiness will be particularly important in two situations. First, there is the context of the application of exceptions clauses. Secondly, the charterer may have undertaken the obligation of stowage in which resultant losses will fall to its account and not that of the shipowner.

The manner in which the cargo is loaded will not necessarily amount to unseaworthiness. It will do so if it affects the ship's safety, as in *Kopitoff v Wilson*,[86] where the stowage was so bad that the cargo broke loose and pierced the vessel's holds. The vessel's safety was also endangered in *Ingram & Royle Ltd v Services Maritimes du Tréport Ltd*[87] and *Smith, Hogg & Co v Black Sea and Baltic General Insurance Co*.[88] However, if it only affects the cargo's safety, it does not breach the warranty of seaworthiness.[89] The sequence in which cargo was loaded may be critical. In *The Thorsa*,[90] a cargo of chocolate was tainted by cheese loaded next to it. The chocolate was loaded before the cheese; therefore, at the time of loading, the vessel was in a fit state to carry that cargo. However, the same would not have been true had the cheese been loaded first and the chocolate then loaded next to it. Loading chocolate adjacent to cheese would inevitably have led to its becoming tainted. However, if chocolate is loaded first, its tainting can be prevented by the shipowner deciding not to load a subsequent cargo of cheese adjacent to it.[91]

The distinction between unseaworthiness and bad stowage has lost much of its importance with the implementation of the Hague Rules. Stowage is one of the duties listed in Art III(2) and therefore any express exception relieving the carrier of liability for bad stowage will be rendered void by Art III(8). The distinction will, however, remain important under a 'free in' bill of lading under which the carrier undertakes no obligation to stow, this being undertaken by the shipper. Following the decision of the House of Lords in *The Jordan II*,[92] the carrier will incur no liability under the bill of lading in respect of bad stowage. This remains the case even though the claimant is the receiver and has, therefore, not undertaken responsibility for this task. However, if the stowage were such as to imperil the safety of the vessel, the carrier would then be in breach of its obligation under Art III(1).

The consequences of unseaworthiness

Unlike deviation, unseaworthiness behaves like any other contractual breach. It gives rise to a right to damages, but not to any automatic right to terminate the contract. The innocent party will have that right only if the consequences of the breach are so serious as to frustrate the commercial

---

86 (1876) 1 QBD 377.
87 [1914] 1 KB 541, CA. Cases of metallic sodium, which was saturated with petrol, were stowed on deck with inadequate protection. The vessel encountered the ordinary rough weather of the English Channel, which caused heavy seas to come over the deck. This contact caused the sodium to explode and ignite, leading to fires breaking out in the hold and the engine room. This, in turn, caused the vessel to split in two and sink.
88 [1940] AC 997. Excessive deck cargo was loaded, which caused the vessel to list during the voyage and turn on her beam ends while bunkering.
89 *Elder Dempster & Co Ltd v Paterson Zochonis & Co Ltd* [1924] AC 522, HL, where Lord Sumner considered that the case of unseaworthiness might have been sustainable on the alternative ground, not advanced at the trial, that the vessel was unseaworthy due to the incompetence of the captain and mate, 'who were without experience of such a cargo and knew their business no better than to overload the puncheons till they inevitably collapsed'.
90 [1916] P 257, CA.
91 Even though this is commercially unlikely, if it means that the cargo of cheese would otherwise have to be shut out. See, also, in this respect, *Elder Dempster & Co Ltd v Paterson Zochonis & Co Ltd* [1924] AC 522, HL.
92 [2004] UKHL 49; [2005] 1 Lloyd's Rep 57.

purposes of the contract. The 'warranty' of seaworthiness is, therefore, strictly speaking, a misnomer. The Court of Appeal recognised this in *Hong Kong Fir Shipping Co Ltd v Kawasaki Kisen Kaisha Ltd*,[93] where it classified the obligation as an 'innominate term'. In assessing whether the right to terminate arises, the courts will chiefly be guided by comparing the delay caused by remedying the unseaworthiness with the total contractual period. This is likely to be the sole criterion adopted when considering the right to terminate a time charter for unseaworthiness.[94] However, with a voyage charter, a trip charter, or a bill of lading contract, it is probable that the courts will also consider the effect of any delay on the goods that are to be carried under the contract. The right to repudiate may arise before the goods are loaded,[95] during the charter,[96] or before the charter commences.[97]

Breach of the implied warranty does not extinguish the shipowner's own contractual rights, such as the right to a lien on freight;[98] nor does it disentitle it to rely on exceptions clauses when the loss is not caused by unseaworthiness.[99]

The obligation to take reasonable care of the cargo

Even if the vessel is seaworthy, the carrier must also take reasonable care of the cargo while it is in its custody. This includes an obligation to prosecute the contractual voyage with reasonable dispatch.[100] At common law, the period of the carrier's responsibility extends from the time at which the goods cross the ship's rail on loading to the time at which they cross back over it on discharge.[101] The shipowner must not only bear the cost of the operations between these points, including that of stowage, but will also become liable for any cargo damage caused during the resulting operations.

These operations are usually performed by independent stevedoring companies, over which the carrier will have no practical control. Nonetheless, if the goods are damaged by such contractors, the shipowner will be liable under the bill of lading contract.[102] The employees of the stevedoring company will be regarded as the servants of the carrier, which will be vicariously liable for their negligence.[103] If the bill of lading provides for loading and/or discharge to be performed by the shipper and/or receiver, the shipowner will not be liable if the goods are damaged during the loading and discharge operations. Such a bill of lading is known as a 'free in/free out' bill of lading. These terms may appear in the bill of lading itself, or be incorporated by a reference to a charter. This happened in *The Jordan II*.[104] The charter allocated responsibility for loading, trimming and discharging to 'charterer/shipper/receiver'. The Court of Appeal held that 'trimming' was to be construed (or, arguably, manipulated) to cover 'stowage' because of the reference to stowage in the separate clause that provided who was to pay for these activities. The result was that the shipper would

---

93 [1962] 2 QB 26, CA.
94 *Hong Kong Fir Shipping Co Ltd v Kawasaki Kisen Kaisha Ltd* [1962] 2 QB 26, CA. A delay of some 20 weeks at the beginning of a two-year time charter, when the vessel was not on a cargo-carrying voyage, was there held not to be so serious as to entitle the charterers to terminate the charter.
95 *Stanton v Richardson* (1872) LR 7 CP 421; (1874) LR 9 CP 390.
96 *Snia v Suzuki* (1924) 29 Com Cas 284.
97 *Jackson v Union Marine Insurance Co Ltd* (1874) LR 10 CP 125.
98 *Kish v Charles Taylor, Sons & Co* [1912] AC 604, HL.
99 *The Europa* [1908] P 84.
100 This obligation is considered in more detail in Chapter 9 at pp 208–10.
101 See dicta of Lord Esher MR on this point in *Harris v Best, Ryley and Co* (1892) 68 LT 76, 77, although the shipowner is usually responsible for the entirety of the loading and discharging operations, either by custom of the port, or by virtue of express provisions in the bill of lading.
102 Where the shipowner's liability for loading and discharge is based on the position at common law, it would, presumably, not be liable for damage to the goods caused by the stevedores on the shore side of the ship's rail. This would be consistent with *Transoceanica Societa v Skipton* [1923] 1 KB 31, where additional discharging costs were apportioned between the parties on this basis.
103 *RF Brown & Co Ltd v T & J Harrison* (1927) 43 TLR 633.
104 [2003] EWCA Civ 144; [2003] 2 Lloyd's Rep 87, CA; aff'd [2004] UKHL 49; [2005] 1 Lloyd's Rep 57.

be responsible for loading and stowing, the receiver for discharge, and the shipowner for none of these activities.

Consequently, the shipowner would not be liable to the receiver in respect of a claim arising out of damage to the goods due to negligent stowage, for which the shipper had undertaken responsibility. The same would apply, *mutatis mutandis*, in respect of a claim by the shipper in respect of damage to the goods during discharge. However, where the bill provides for the carrier to arrange and pay for the stevedoring operations (what is known as a 'liner bill of lading'), a clause that purports to make the bill of lading holder responsible for these operations will constitute an exceptions clause and, as such, will be rendered void by Art III(8) of the Hague or Hague-Visby Rules.[105] Furthermore, a shipper is not affected by any terms of the charterparty, of which it has no notice, which shift responsibility for loading or discharge onto the charterers.[106]

The obligation to proceed on the contract voyage without deviating

What is deviation?

Scrutton defines deviation thus: 'In the absence of express stipulations to the contrary, the owner of a vessel . . . impliedly undertakes to proceed in that ship by a usual and reasonable route without unjustifiable departure from that route and without unreasonable delay'.[107] Deviation is not just straying from the route, but may also include a deliberate reduction of speed along the route. In *Scaramanga v Stamp*,[108] a vessel was held to have deviated when she gave a tow to another vessel because, although she kept to the route, her speed was deliberately reduced thereby.

Not every straying from the route will constitute deviation. Some deviations may be justified, as where they are made to save life or the cargo carried,[109] but not for the purpose of salving another vessel. They will also be justified if there is a usual commercial practice to bunker at a particular port off the route, as in *Reardon-Smith v Black Sea Line*,[110] on a voyage from Poti to the USA, with a deviation to bunker at Constantza.

Stowage of cargo on deck that is not authorised by any liberty in the contract is a breach of contract that is regarded as a 'quasi-deviation'. Where loss results from breach of this obligation, the shipowner will be unable to rely on any exceptions or limitations in the contract of carriage.[111] However, the breach will not have this effect when it is not the cause of the loss. In this respect, 'quasi-deviation' is more akin to unseaworthiness than to deviation.

'Liberty' clauses

A deviation may also be justified by the terms of a specific clause in the bill of lading or charterparty giving the shipowner a 'liberty' to call at additional ports during the voyage. However, the courts have tended to construe these narrowly. In *Glynn v Margetson*,[112] the bill of lading contained a clause giving the carrier:

> . . . liberty to proceed to and stay at any port or ports in any station in the Mediterranean, Levant, Black Sea or Adriatic or on the coast of Africa, Spain, Portugal, France, Great Britain and Ireland, for the purpose of delivering coals, cargo or passengers or for any other purpose whatsoever.

---

105 *The Lucky Wave* [1985] 1 Lloyd's Rep 80, QB.
106 *Sandemann v Scurr* (1866) LR 2 QB 86.
107 Scrutton, *Charterparties and Bills of Lading*, 20th edn, 1996, London: Sweet & Maxwell, p 256.
108 (1880) 5 CPD 295, CA.
109 But see Lord Porter's dictum in *Monarch SS Co Ltd v A/B Karlshamns Oljefabriker* [1949] AC 196, 212, that a shipowner who has to put into a port of refuge after knowingly sending an unseaworthy ship out to sea will have committed a deviation.
110 [1939] AC 562, HL.
111 *The Chanda* [1989] 2 Lloyd's Rep 494, QB.
112 [1893] AC 351, HL.

On a voyage from Malaga to Liverpool, the shipowner deviated from the direct route to a port on the east coast of Spain. The delay caused damage to the cargo of oranges. It was held that the liberty clause was restricted to ports in the course of the voyage and therefore did not cover this particular deviation.[113]

An even more extreme example of the courts' willingness to cut back the apparent width of the language used in the clause can be seen in *Connolly Shaw Ltd v A/S Det Nordenfjelske D/S*,[114] where a clause gave liberty:

> . . . to proceed to or return to and stay at any ports or places whatsoever (although in a contrary direction to or out of or beyond the route of the said port of delivery) once or oftener in any order, backwards or forwards, for loading or discharging cargo . . . or for any purpose whatsoever, whether in relation to her homeward voyage, or to her outward voyage, or to an intermediate voyage and all such ports, places and sailing shall be deemed included within the intended voyage of the said ports.

Although the clause covered the particular deviation, Branson J held that he would have been prepared to disregard those parts of it that conflicted with the main purpose of the contract – namely, the safe carriage of a perishable cargo.

The Hague and Hague-Visby Rules both provide, in Art IV(4), a liberty for the carrier to make 'reasonable' deviations.[115] This term is wider than the common law concept of a justified deviation in that, in deciding what is 'reasonable', regard can be had to the interests of the shipowner as well as those of the cargo. In *Stag Line Ltd v Foscolo Mango and Co Ltd*,[116] a deviation to take on replacement crew was 'reasonable', although not the subsequent route taken out of the port, which sacrificed safety for speed.

The deviation may be reasonable even if planned before the issue of the bill of lading as in *The Al Taha*.[117] On her approach voyage, the vessel suffered heavy weather damage and also damage to a boom. The shipowners decided to repair the damage at the load port, Portsmouth, US, and to send the boom away to Boston for repairs. Owing to bad weather conditions, delay was expected in transporting the boom by road to Portsmouth and, therefore, before sailing to Izmir, the discharge port, and before issue of a bill of lading, the shipowners sailed to Boston to pick up the boom. While leaving Boston, the vessel became stranded due to pilot negligence and general average was declared. The deviation was held to be 'reasonable' within Art IV(4).

The consequences of deviation

The 'pure' doctrine

A breach of the implied obligation not to deviate has consequences for the shipowner, which are far more serious than those attendant on any other breach of contract. A deviation automatically debars the shipowner from relying on any term of the contract; whether as a defence, such as an exceptions clause, or as a positive right, such as a right to claim freight or demurrage. This is the case whether or not the deviation has any causative effect on the damage complained of. In *Thorley v Orchis*,[118] cargo was damaged by stevedores during discharge. There was no link between damage and deviation, yet the shipowner was held not to be entitled to rely on a bill of lading clause

---

113 See, also, *Leduc v Ward* (1888) 20 QBD 475, CA.
114 (1934) 49 Ll L Rep 183.
115 The Article also allows deviations 'in saving or attempting to save life or property at sea'.
116 [1932] AC 328.
117 [1990] 2 Lloyd's Rep 117.
118 [1907] 1 KB 660, CA.

excepting liability for damage caused by stevedore negligence. The Court of Appeal justified this result by reasoning that performance of the voyage in the contemplated manner – that is, without deviation – was a condition precedent of the carrier's right to rely on the contract of carriage. The harshness of the rule is illustrated in even more extreme fashion by *International Guano en Superphospaten-Werken v Robert MacAndrew & Co Ltd*,[119] where the shipowners were not entitled to rely on a bill of lading exceptions clause in respect of damage occurring *prior* to the deviation. The justification for the severity of the rule was said to be the fact that, as deviation vitiated the cargo owner's goods' insurance, the carrier should assume the mantle of insurer. However, this reason explains neither the retrospective effect of a deviation – for the goods' insurance remains in force until the moment of deviation – nor its effect on the carrier's positive rights.[120] Furthermore, where a deviation is notified in advance to the cargo owner, the insurance cover may be maintained under a 'held covered' clause on payment of an additional premium.

Once there has been a deviation, the shipowner is reduced to the status of a common carrier. The only defences to a claim for cargo damage are Act of God, acts of the King's enemies, inherent vice of the cargo[121] and fault of the consignor. However, even these defences will be lost if the damage takes place during the course of a deviation. In *James Morrison & Co Ltd v Shaw, Savill and Albion Co Ltd*,[122] a vessel was sunk by a U-boat off the coast of France in the First World War, *while deviating* from her voyage. The shipowner was unable to rely on the common carrier exception of acts of the King's enemies.

As a common carrier, the shipowner will be entitled to *quantum meruit* freight, a reasonable sum based on the current market rate. The same will apply with demurrage. In *United States Shipping Board v Bunge y Born Limitada Sociedad*,[123] the shipowner, due to a deviation, was unable to rely on the demurrage clause in the bill of lading. It would be entitled to demurrage on a *quantum meruit* basis, but only if the vessel did not discharge within a reasonable time, but this was not proved on the facts.

The modified doctrine

The severity of the rule has been justified by reference to the fact that, from the moment of deviation, the cargo insurance ceases to have effect. It is therefore reasonable that, from that point on, the shipowner take over the mantle of the goods insurer. However, this rationale has been eroded by the practice of extending the cover by payment of an additional premium for deviation, and, in any case, does not justify the shipowner having to step into the insurer's shoes for events *before* the deviation when the policy is still in force.

In *Hain SS Co Ltd v Tate & Lyle Ltd*,[124] the House of Lords sought to restrict the severity of the rule to events occurring after the deviation. It regarded a deviation as a breach of a condition entitling the innocent contracting party to treat the contract as at an end thenceforth.[125] That party could elect to keep the contract alive, as the charterers were held to have done, by ordering the vessel to load at the next charter load port after they had become aware of the deviation. However, the bill of lading holders had not waived the deviation merely by taking delivery of the cargo on presentation of the bill of lading. Therefore, the shipowners' claim for bill of lading freight failed as, from the moment of deviation onwards, the bill of lading contract ceased to regulate relations between the shipowners and the cargo owners. It was replaced by a contract on common carrier terms.

---

119 [1909] 2 KB 360, KB.
120 In *Balian & Sons v Joly, Victoria & Co* (1890) 6 TLR 35, the Court of Appeal had previously confined itself to stating that the doctrine only removed the carrier's rights to rely on exceptions and limitations conferred by the contract of carriage.
121 This defence was successfully relied on in *International Guano en Superphospaten-Werken v MacAndrew & Co Ltd* [1909] 2 KB 360.
122 [1916] 2 KB 783, CA.
123 [1925] 42 TLR 73.
124 (1936) 41 Com Cas 350.
125 This analysis, though persuasive, is strictly *obiter*. It has been followed in *Thiess Bros (Queensland) Pty Ltd v Australian Steamships Pty Ltd* [1955] 1 Lloyd's Rep 459, Sup Ct (NSW), where a claim for loading freight that had accrued before the deviation was successful.

Quantum meruit freight was not awarded, as the terms of the charter contained no cesser clause[126] and therefore allowed the shipowners to claim the outstanding freight from the charterers.

The approach of the House of Lords has had the beneficial effect of restricting the effect of the doctrine to post-deviation events. However, the attempt to assimilate the doctrine with the ordinary contractual rules on discharge by breach is unconvincing. The position with repudiatory breaches in the general law of contract is that the innocent party must make a positive election to end the contract.[127] This was confirmed by the Court of Appeal in *STC v Golodetz*.[128] If an election is made, the contract ends from the date of the election, not from the date of the breach. If none is made within a reasonable time, the contract continues. With deviation, the House of Lords in *Hain* reversed the rule. The contract is presumed to end from the moment of breach unless resurrected by a positive election by the innocent party. Moreover, in the case of a bill of lading holder, it is difficult to see what conduct might ever suffice to constitute such an election.

Deviation and the Hague and Hague-Visby Rules

In *Stag Line Ltd v Foscolo Mango and Co Ltd*,[129] the Court of Appeal held that the doctrine of deviation subsists even where the Hague Rules apply. It gave short shrift to the argument that the Rules provided a self-contained code governing breaches by the shipowner. Such an argument might have more success, at least as regards cargo claims, where the Hague-Visby Rules are concerned. In *The Antares*,[130] the Court of Appeal, dealing with a case of 'quasi-deviation', an unauthorised stowage of cargo on deck, held that the Hague-Visby Rules time limit could be relied on by the shipowner. It reasoned that, because the **Carriage of Goods by Sea Act 1971**, unlike the **Carriage of Goods by Sea Act 1924**, provided that the Rules were to have the 'force of law', the Rules could be construed only by a consideration of their own language, without reference to any judicial canons of construing contractual clauses. In contrast, in *The Chanda*,[131] the package limitation in the Hague Rules was construed by reference to the 'four corners' rule so that the carrier could not rely on it when the claim arose out of unauthorised stowage on deck. The Court of Appeal subsequently overruled the decision in *The Kapitan Petko Voivoda*.[132]

Therefore, by analogy, it could be argued that the common law doctrine of deviation should be disregarded in deciding whether or not a shipowner who has deviated can rely on a defence of exception provided by the Hague-Visby Rules. The answer to this question should be decided solely by reference to the language of the Rules themselves, which say nothing about the carrier losing the benefit of their exceptions and limitations in the event of a deviation. Even without accepting that the reference to the Hague-Visby Rules having 'the force of law' has such an effect, it is likely that the time bar and package limitation provisions will now be available to a carrier, notwithstanding that there has been a deviation that falls outside the liberty afforded by Art IV(4). This is because of two changes that the Hague-Visby Rules have made in respect of these provisions. The first is the inclusion of the word 'whatsoever' into Art III(6). The second is the inclusion of a new provision, Art IV(5)(e), which removes the right to limit where there has been wilful default on the part of the carrier or ship. On the other hand, if the consequences of deviation derive not from the construction of clauses in the contract, but from the termination of the contract itself, the Rules will cease to be relevant once the bill of lading contract has been superseded by a contract on common carrier terms.[133]

---

126 A 'cesser' clause is found in many voyage charters and provides for the charterer's liability under the charter to cease once the cargo has been loaded. For liabilities arising after that point, the shipowner must proceed against the bill of lading holder.

127 Occasionally, an election can be made by inactivity, as in *The Santa Clara* [1996] AC 800, where the House of Lords held that the innocent party had elected to terminate once it took no further steps to continue performance of the contract.

128 [1989] 2 Lloyd's Rep 277.

129 [1931] 2 KB 48.

130 [1987] 1 Lloyd's Rep 424.

131 [1989] 2 Lloyd's Rep 494, QB.

132 [2003] EWCA Civ 451; [2003] 2 Lloyd's Rep 1.

133 For further discussion of this issue, see Baughen, S, 'Does deviation still matter?' (1991) LMCLQ 70.

Chapter 5

Statutory Terms of the Bill of Lading Contract

Chapter Contents

The Hague and Hague-Visby Rules

Unrestricted freedom of contract allows parties with a dominant market position to impose their terms and conditions on parties in a weaker position. Before the First World War, shipowners occupied this position of dominance. They used this position to impose on shippers bills of lading containing very widely drafted exclusion clauses. After the First World War, the international community recognised the need to redress this imbalance. The result was the **Brussels Convention** of 1924, which gave birth to the Hague Rules.

The Hague Rules attempted to impose uniformity into contractual terms relating to the carriage of goods under bills of lading. In doing so, a balance was struck between the interests of maritime nations and of trading nations. This was done by providing in Art III a bedrock minimum of contractual obligations on the part of the carrier. Article IV provided a corresponding maximum of contractual defences and exceptions available to the carrier. Article III(8) prevented contracting out by providing that any clause that attempted to go below the minimum duties or the maximum defences set out in the Rules should be 'null and void and of no effect'.[1] However, Art VII maintained the parties' freedom of contract as regards any contractual duties occurring before loading or after discharge.

One of the signatories to the Convention was the UK, which brought the Rules into domestic law by the **Carriage of Goods by Sea Act (COGSA) 1924**.[2] The Act provided that bills of lading covering shipments out of Great Britain should be required to contain a statement that the contract incorporated the Rules. The Rules were subsequently amended as the Hague-Visby Rules, although not all parties to the Hague Rules have adopted them. The Hague-Visby Rules became part of domestic law by **COGSA 1971**, which came into effect on 23 June 1977. The Act went further than its predecessor in providing that the Rules should have 'the force of law' in respect of bills covered by the Act. Moreover, the Act extended the categories of bills of lading contracts to which the Rules would apply. The Rules will be examined in two parts. First, the ambit of their mandatory application will be considered, and then, the operation of the Rules themselves.

The ambit of the Rules

The Rules can apply either mandatorily, in which case they will have 'the force of law', or voluntarily, through incorporation by what is known as a 'clause paramount'. Article III(8) will only apply to the former category.[3] Therefore, a clause in conflict with the Rules may prevail over the Rules if they have been voluntarily incorporated. In The Strathnewton,[4] a time charter was subject to the Inter-Club Agreement. By virtue of a clause paramount, it was also subject to the Hague Rules. It was held that the one-year time limit under the Rules did not apply to claims by charterers against owners for indemnity under the Inter-Club Agreement.[5] It is therefore critical to establish whether or not the Rules apply to any given contract mandatorily or voluntarily. If the Rules do apply mandatorily, there is no question of their application being qualified by the provisions of the **Unfair Contract Terms Act 1977**, as s 29(1)(a) of that Act permits reliance on contractual terms

---

1 Although Art V allows the carrier to agree to increase its liabilities and decrease its defences.
2 One notable absentee from the list of signatories to the latter conventions is the USA, which operates a similar statutory regime of its own to bills of lading under the Harter Act of 1893 and the Carriage of Goods by Sea Act of 1936, based on the Hague Rules.
3 However, s 1(6) provides that the Rules shall have the 'force of law' when incorporated into bills of lading. This would cover bills of lading that would otherwise be outside COGSA 1971, such as bills issued in non-Contracting States.
4 [1983] 1 Lloyd's Rep 219, CA.
5 See, also, The European Enterprise [1989] 2 Lloyd's Rep 185, QB, where a contractual package limitation in a sea waybill prevailed over that provided by the Hague-Visby Rules, which had been expressly incorporated.

'authorised or required by the express terms or necessary implication of an enactment'. Furthermore, Sched 1 to the Act excludes the operation of ss 2(2) and (3), 3, 4 and 7 to charter-parties or contracts for the carriage of goods by sea or by hovercraft, except in favour of a person dealing as a consumer.[6]

Mandatory application

Section 1(2) of **COGSA 1971** provides that:

> The provisions of the Rules as set out in the Schedule to this Act, shall have the force of law.

Application to bills of lading

With one limited exception,[7] the Rules apply only where the contractual document is a 'bill of lading or similar document of title' within the following definition in Art I(b):

> 'Contract of carriage' applies only to contracts of carriage covered by a bill of lading or any similar document of title, in so far as such document relates to the carriage of goods by sea . . .

This definition is reinforced by s 1(4) of **COGSA 1971**, which provides that:

> . . . nothing in this section shall be taken as applying anything in the Rules to any contract for the carriage of goods by sea, unless the contract expressly or by implication provides for the issue of a bill of lading or any similar document of title.

In *The Happy Ranger*,[8] the Court of Appeal held that the words 'covered by a bill of lading' in Art I(b) required only that the contract of carriage contemplated the issue of a bill of lading. There was no additional requirement that the bill of lading should contain the terms of the contract between the parties. As the contract of carriage contemplated the issue of a bill of lading and was not a charter-party (which would be taken outside the Rules by Art V), it was therefore subject to the Rules.

The definition given by Art I(b) includes bills of lading issued under or pursuant to a charter-party, but only from 'the moment at which such bill of lading or similar document of title regulates the relations between the carrier and the holder of the same'. Therefore, bills of lading will not attract the operation of the Rules, while *in the hands of the charterer*.

The reference to 'any similar document of title' is probably intended to cover bills of lading other than 'shipped' bills of lading to fall within the Rules, provided that they are negotiable documents. This conclusion is supported by the provisions of Art III(7) relating to the surrender of any previous document of title (such as a 'received for shipment' bill) in exchange for a shipped bill of lading. However, if such a bill of lading is not a document of title at common law, it cannot qualify as a 'similar document of title' for the purposes of Art I(b). If, on the other hand, such a bill is a document of title at common law, then it will qualify as a 'bill of lading' under Art I(b).[9] It is there-fore likely that the reference to a 'similar document of title' adds nothing to Art I(b).

Following the decision of the House of Lords in *The Rafaela S*,[10] it is now clear that a straight bill of lading constitutes a bill of lading under Art I(b) of the Hague and Hague-Visby Rules. This

---

6 Section 2(1), however, remains effective as regards these contracts.
7 In s 1(6)(b), relating to waybills that incorporate the Rules.
8 [2002] EWCA Civ 694; [2002] 2 Lloyd's Rep 357.
9 In *The Rafaela S* [2005] UKHL 11; [2005] 2 AC 423, Lord Rodger of Earlsferry, at [77], was of the view that had a straight bill of lading not qualified as a 'bill of lading' under Art 1(b), it would have fallen under the Rules as a 'similar document of title'.
10 [2005] UKHL 11; [2005] 2 AC 423, noted [2005] LMCLQ 273–80; affirming the decision of the Court of Appeal [2002] EWCA Civ 694; [2003] 2 Lloyd's Rep 113.

conclusion followed from their Lordships' finding that, where a straight bill has been issued, the carrier's delivery obligation equates to that pertaining under a negotiable bill, rather than a sea waybill: it must only deliver against presentation by the consignee of the original bill.

Bills of lading subject to the Rules

Article X of the Hague-Visby Rules provides that the Rules shall apply to:

> . . . every bill of lading[11] relating to the carriage of goods between ports in two different States if:
>
> (a)   the bill of lading is issued in a Contracting State;
> OR
> (b)   the carriage is from a port in a Contracting State;
> OR
> (c)   the contract of carriage, contained in or evidenced by the bill of lading, provides that these Rules or the legislation of any State giving effect to them are to govern the contract, whatever may be the nationality of the ship, the carrier, the shipper, the consignee or any other interested person.

These three categories will now be examined in more detail.

Case (a) is self-evident. All that the claimant needs to know is whether the bill of lading was issued in a Contracting State. This will usually be the place of shipment.

Case (b) will cover instances in which the bill of lading is issued in a different state from the state of the port of loading.[12] In *Mayhew Foods Ltd v Overseas Containers Ltd*,[13] the contract was to carry goods from Shoreham in Sussex to Jeddah. The bill of lading was not issued until the goods were trans-shipped at Le Havre. It was held that the Hague-Visby Rules governed the entire voyage from Sussex and not just from Le Havre, as the parties had contracted on the basis that a bill would be issued at some stage.[14] The bill was issued in France, a Contracting State,[15] and the contract provided for carriage from a Contracting State, the UK; therefore, once the bill was issued, the Hague-Visby Rules applied and attached to the whole contract of carriage from Shoreham to Jeddah, including the period of storage at Le Havre pending trans-shipment.

The primacy attached to the parties' contractual intention as regards the issue of the bill of lading can also be seen in *The Anders Maersk*,[16] which is, in many ways, a mirror image of *Mayhew Foods Ltd v Overseas Containers Ltd*. A bill of lading was issued for a voyage from Baltimore to Shanghai, incorporating the provisions of the **US Carriage of Goods by Sea Act of 1936**, with a liberty to trans-ship that was exercised in Hong Kong. The goods were damaged on the Hong Kong to Shanghai leg of the voyage. The cargo owners sued the original carrier, which had issued the bill of lading in Baltimore, but argued that as the goods had been trans-shipped in Hong Kong, which applied an appropriately modified version of **COGSA 1971**, their claim should be subject to the package limit contained in the Hague-Visby Rules, rather than the lower one contained in the **US Carriage of Goods by Sea Act of 1936**. The cargo owners' claim was rejected. 'Shipment in Hong Kong' in s 1(3) of the modified **COGSA 1971** did not cover 'trans-shipment' and the reference to a bill of lading in s 1(4) must

---

11   'Bill of lading' probably impliedly includes 'any similar document of title'. These documents are expressly referred to in Art 1(b).
12   The reference to a 'bill of lading' in the opening words of Art X means that case (b) does not cover every carriage from a port in a Contracting State, but only those that are to be covered, at some stage, by a bill of lading. It will be particularly relevant when trans-shipment or combined transport operations are involved.
13   [1984] 1 Lloyd's Rep 317.
14   So applying the reasoning of Devlin J in *Pyrene Co Ltd v Scindia Navigation Co Ltd* [1954] 2 QB 402, that the Rules apply to contracts of carriage and not just to those parts that are covered by a bill of lading.
15   There is, however, nothing in the language of Art X(b) to suggest that the position would be any different where the bill of lading is issued in a non-Contracting State, provided that carriage is from a Contracting State.
16   [1986] 1 Lloyd's Rep 483, High Ct (Hong Kong).

refer back to the original contract voyage contemplated by the parties, which was one from Baltimore to Shanghai. In identifying the port of shipment for the purposes of the Hague-Visby Rules, the key question where trans-shipment is involved is whether the contract contemplates two separate voyages or a single voyage with a liberty to trans-ship en route. In *The Rafaela S*,[17] the bill of lading contemplated a voyage from Durban to Felixstowe, but also provided that Boston was the final destination and the place at which freight would be paid. The bill of lading did not entitle the shipowners to make a single shipment from Durban to Boston with a liberty to trans-ship, but clearly contemplated that two separate voyages would be involved. The Court of Appeal, therefore, held that, as regards the second leg of the carriage, it was Felixstowe that constituted the port of shipment so as to trigger the application of the Hague-Visby Rules as regards this part of the performance of the contract.

The position might well be different if the contract of carriage not only contains a liberty to trans-ship, but also makes it clear that the carriage will be performed by trans-shipment. Therefore, in *Captain v Far Eastern Shipping Co*,[18] it was held that the Hague Rules ceased to apply while the goods were in storage awaiting trans-shipment. The carrier was therefore not entitled to rely on the Hague Rules package limitation in respect of damage to the goods during this period. At the time that the contract was made, it had been made clear to the cargo owner that the voyage would definitely involve trans-shipment.

An interesting issue may arise if, in circumstances similar to those in *Pyrene Co Ltd v Scindia Navigation Co Ltd*,[19] no bill of lading is ever issued. If a bill of lading is contemplated that would have been subject to the Hague-Visby Rules, then the parties would be taken to have contracted on the basis that the Rules govern the entire contract of carriage. However, what would be uncertain is whether the Rules would apply by 'force of law' so as to displace any inconsistent terms in the bill of lading, such as a package limitation that is more favourable to the carrier than that permitted by the Rules. The opening words of Art X refer to 'every bill of lading relating to the carriage of goods between ports in two different States . . .'. Read literally, none of the three situations referred to in the Article could cover a situation in which a bill of lading was never, in fact, issued.

Where goods are damaged after completion of loading, as in *Mayhew Foods Ltd v Overseas Containers Ltd*,[20] the problem could be solved by the shipper exercising its right under Art III(3) to demand a 'shipped' bill of lading. This solution would not be applicable in a situation such as *Pyrene Co Ltd v Scindia Navigation Co Ltd*,[21] where the goods are damaged during the loading process before they cross the ship's rail. As a matter of contract, the effect of this decision is that the contract of carriage would be 'covered' by a bill of lading *ab initio*, notwithstanding that no bill of lading was ever issued. However, for the Rules to have *mandatory* effect, the wording of Art X would still require a bill of lading to have been issued.[22] The problem can probably be solved at a contractual level by finding that, as the parties anticipated the issue of a bill of lading, they intended the Rules to have mandatory effect over their contract of carriage. If a bill were never issued, their contractual intention would be that the Rules would, nonetheless, govern their contract 'as if' they had the force of law, thereby ensuring that full effect was given to Art III(8).

---

17 [2002] EWCA Civ 694; [2003] 2 Lloyd's Rep 113.
18 [1979] 1 Lloyd's Rep 595.
19 [1954] 2 QB 402.
20 [1984] 1 Lloyd's Rep 317.
21 [1954] 2 QB 402.
22 The position is not changed by the reference in s 1(4) of COGSA 1971 as follows, 'unless the contract expressly or by implication provides for the issue of a bill of lading or similar document of title'. The section merely excludes certain categories of carriage contracts from the operation of the Rules. It does not positively state which contracts fall within the ambit of the Rules.

Case (c) covers bills of lading that would otherwise fall outside the Hague-Visby Rules, where the parties expressly provide that the bill of lading shall be subject either to the Rules themselves or to the legislation of any state giving effect to the Rules. Therefore, a bill of lading that expressly incorporated either the Hague-Visby Rules themselves or **COGSA 1971** would be within this category.[23] A clause incorporating the Hague-Visby Rules 'if compulsorily applicable' does not come within Art X(c) unless the Rules are compulsorily applicable under either the applicable law of the contract or of the place in which suit is commenced against the carrier.[24]

However, what of a bill of lading that contains a submission to the jurisdiction of the English High Court, but contains no express reference either to **COGSA 1971** or to the Rules? In *The Komninos S*,[25] the Court of Appeal considered whether a bill of lading was covered by case (c) merely by virtue of the fact that it provided that all disputes were to be referred to 'the British courts'. The case involved a carriage of steel coils from Greece to Italy. At the relevant date, Greece was not a Contracting State, so neither Art X(a) nor (b) applied. The plaintiff argued that the jurisdiction clause amounted to a submission to the jurisdiction of the English High Court. By implication, the relevant law should be English law. Therefore, the bill of lading was one that provided that the legislation of the UK giving effect to the Rules should govern the contract. The Court of Appeal accepted the first two of these propositions, but rejected the final one. It is possible that a different result may be reached where a bill of lading *expressly* provides for English law to govern the contract.

The three cases covered by Art X are supplemented by two provisions in the Act itself.

(a) Section 1(3) extends these provisions to *any* voyage from a UK port, so as to cover internal UK voyages. The provision is, however, 'without prejudice' to s 1(2), which refers to 'the provisions of these Rules . . .'. Therefore, s 1(3) will apply only where a bill of lading is, or is expected to be, issued.

(c) Section 1(6)(a), without prejudice to Art X(c) above, provides that the Rules shall have 'the force of law' in relation to 'any bill of lading if the contract contained in it or evidenced by it expressly provides that the Rules shall govern the contract'. It is difficult to see what, if anything, this provision adds to Art X(c).

Bills of lading outside the Hague-Visby Rules

The **Carriage of Goods by Sea Act 1971** does not impose the Hague-Visby Rules on every bill of lading likely to generate a cargo claim that will be heard in an English forum, such as bills of lading that fall outside Art X or s 1(3) or (6)(a) of **COGSA 1971**. It is important to note that the state of *loading* is crucial to the operation of the Rules, not that of discharge. Therefore, shipments *to* the UK from non-Convention States will not involve the Hague-Visby Rules. It is likely that such bills of lading will be subject to the Hague Rules or their equivalent.[26] Following *The Komninos S*,[27] such bills of lading will not fall under Art X(c) simply because they contain a clause submitting any disputes to the jurisdiction of the English High Court or to arbitration in England. Where a bill of lading is issued in a state the legislation of which requires the Hague Rules to be incorporated into it, the English courts will take no account of such legislation unless the issuing of a bill of lading without such a statement is illegal under the law of the state where the goods are loaded, in which case the shipowner will be treated as a common carrier. This means that if the bill of lading fails to

---

23 The majority of the Court of Appeal in *The Happy Ranger* [2002] EWCA Civ 694; [2002] 2 Lloyd's Rep 357 held that Art X(c) could apply only where the contract was covered by a bill of lading within Art 1(b). Rix LJ, dissenting, held that the issue of contractual incorporation of the Hague-Visby Rules should depend solely on the terms of the incorporating contract.
24 *The MSC Amsterdam* [2007] EWCA Civ 794; [2007] 2 Lloyd's Rep 622.
25 [1991] 1 Lloyd's Rep 370.
26 As with the US Carriage of Goods by Sea Act of 1936.
27 [1991] 1 Lloyd's Rep 370.

THE AMBIT OF THE RULES

incorporate the Hague Rules, the English courts will give effect to its express terms.[28] If the Hague Rules are incorporated, the English courts, as a matter of contractual construction, will generally accord them precedence over other conflicting printed terms of the bill of lading.[29]

Disputes may now appear in an English forum that involve the Hamburg Rules, following their coming into force on 1 November 1992. These Rules, which are far more onerous to the carrier than either the Hague or Hague-Visby Rules, will apply whenever the cargo is loaded or discharged in a state that is a signatory to the Hamburg Rules. The position is complicated somewhat by the fact that many of the signatory states are not currently applying the Hamburg Rules. The Hamburg Rules, and their potential to conflict with the Hague-Visby Rules, are discussed at p 136.

Use of documents other than bills of lading

As discussed above, the definition of 'contract of carriage' in Art I(b) leads to the conclusion that the Rules apply only to bills of lading or 'similar documents of title'. A sea waybill, not being a document of title, would, therefore, appear to be outside the ambit of the Rules. Nonetheless, there are provisions in both the Rules and the Act that suggest that the Rules might nonetheless apply to such documents. These will now be considered in turn.

First, there is s 1(3), which provides that the Rules shall have the force of law, 'in relation to and in connection with the carriage of goods by sea in ships where the port of shipment is a port in the United Kingdom ...'. However, this provision is expressed to be 'without prejudice' to s 1(2), which, in turn, refers back to 'the provisions of the Rules'. Article I(b) defines 'contract of carriage' so as to cover contracts covered by 'a bill of lading or *similar document of title*' (emphasis added). Furthermore, s 1(4) goes on to state:

> Subject to sub-s (6) below,[30] nothing in this section shall be taken as applying anything in the Rules to any contract for the carriage of goods by sea, unless the contract expressly or by implication provides for the issue of a bill of lading or any *similar document of title*. [emphasis added]

Secondly, there is Art II, on which Tetley relies.[31] This provides:

> Subject to the provisions of Art VI, under every contract of carriage of goods by sea the carrier, in relation to the loading, handling, stowage, carriage, care and discharge of such goods, shall be subject to the responsibilities and liabilities, and entitled to the rights and immunities hereinafter set forth.

Although the Article refers to '*every* contract of carriage of goods by sea', these words have to be read in the light of the definition given in Art I(b).

Thirdly, there is Art VI, which expressly deals with the issue of loading documents other than bills of lading. Freedom of contract is preserved provided that no bill of lading is issued and the contractual terms are embodied in 'a receipt which shall be a non-negotiable document and shall be marked as such'. However, the Article contains a proviso that it shall not apply to:

> ... ordinary commercial shipment made in the ordinary course of trade, but only to other shipments where the character or condition of the property to be carried or the circumstances, terms and conditions under which the carriage is to be performed are such as reasonably to justify a special agreement.

---

28 *Vita Food Products Inc v Unius Shipping Co Ltd* [1939] AC 277, PC, dissenting from *The Torni* [1932] P 78, CA.
29 *Ocean SS Co v Queensland State Wheat Board* [1941] 1 KB 402, CA. See, also, *Finagra UK (Ltd) v OT Africa Line Ltd* [1998] 2 Lloyd's Rep 622, QB.
30 Which deals with non-negotiable receipts.
31 Tetley, *Marine Cargo Claims*, 3rd edn, 1988, Montreal: International Shipping Publications, BLAIS, pp 11, 944–50.

Tetley[32] argues that the effect of the proviso is to prevent the carrier avoiding the Rules by issuing a sea waybill.[33] However, such an interpretation goes against the clear wording of s 1(4) of the Act. It also goes against the decision of the Court of Session, in *Harland & Wolff Ltd v Burns & Laird Lines Ltd*,[34] that the identical Article in the Hague Rules applied only to shipments where it would be customary to issue a bill of lading, but the parties had complete freedom to contract on the basis that the contractual document should not be a bill of lading. In the latter situation, the shipper would have no right to demand a bill of lading under Art III(3), as the Rules did not apply to the contract of carriage in question.

It is therefore unlikely that the Rules, by their own wording, apply to any document other than a bill of lading. After *The Rafaela S*,[35] this will include a straight bill of lading. However, s 1(6)(b) of **COGSA 1971** provides that the Rules shall have the force of law in relation to 'any receipt which is a non-negotiable document marked such if the contract contained therein or evidenced by it is a contract for the carriage of goods by sea which expressly provides that the Rules are to govern the contract as if the receipt were a bill of lading . . .'.[36] Thus, sea waybills will be brought within the mandatory ambit of the Hague-Visby Rules provided, first, that they are marked as being non-negotiable and, secondly, that the correct wording of incorporation is used.

There are conflicting first-instance decisions on the wording that is required to have this effect. A general incorporation sufficed in *The Vechscroon*,[37] but not in *The European Enterprise*,[38] where Steyn J held that the clause paramount in the waybill must also contain the additional words, 'as if this receipt were a bill of lading', which are referred to at the end of the section itself. The advantage of this approach is that it gives the parties the choice of incorporating the Hague-Visby Rules on either a voluntary or a mandatory basis. Steyn J was of the view that the words of s 1(6)(b) 'were no doubt designed to bring clearly to the mind of the parties what documents will attract the statutory regime ordinarily reserved for bills of lading'. Another ground for the decision was that the reference to 'the Rules' in the section required the Rules to be incorporated in their entirety. This condition was not satisfied where the incorporation clause in the sea waybill in question specifically excluded particular provisions of the Rules.

Scope of contractual services subject to the Rules

Article I(e) defines 'carriage of goods' so as to cover 'the period from the time when the goods are loaded on to the time they are discharged from the ship'. This definition entails that the Rules have mandatory effect on a 'tackle to tackle' basis from the start of loading[39] to the conclusion of discharge. In *The Arawa*,[40] Brandon J held that where the vessel discharged into lighters, the sea carriage terminated for the purposes of the applicability of the Hague Rules.[41] However, exceptionally, the Rules have been held to cover part of the contract that does not involve carriage by sea, such as the period of onshore storage pending trans-shipment in *Mayhew Foods Ltd v Overseas*

---

32 Ibid.
33 A view shared by Carver, *Carriage by Sea*, 13th edn, 1982, London: Stevens, Vol 1, pp 495–7. However, the contrary view is now taken by Treitel and Reynolds, *Carver on Bills of Lading*, 2001, London: Sweet & Maxwell, at 9.265.
34 (1931) 40 Ll L Rep 286.
35 [2002] EWCA Civ 604; [2003] 2 Lloyd's Rep 113; aff'd [2005] UKHL 11; [2005] 2 AC 423.
36 This position is subject to 'any necessary modifications'. In particular, it provides for the omission both of the conclusive evidence provisions contained in the second sentence of Art III(4) and of the provisions, contained in Art III(7), for turning a 'received for shipment' bill into a 'shipped' bill.
37 [1982] 1 Lloyd's Rep 301, QB.
38 [1989] 2 Lloyd's Rep 185.
39 In *Pyrene Co Ltd v Scindia Navigation Co Ltd* [1954] 2 QB 402, Devlin J held that 'loading' covers the entire operation of loading and not just that part that is performed once the goods cross the ship's rail.
40 [1977] 2 Lloyd's Rep 416.
41 But discharge into lighters will not be complete until all of the goods scheduled for lightering have been discharged. If the claimant's goods have been discharged into the lighter, the Rules will continue to apply while other goods are being discharged. See *Goodwin, Ferreira & Co v Lamport & Holt Ltd* (1929) 34 Ll L Rep 192.

Containers Ltd.[42] This will be the case where the parties have not specifically agreed a trans-shipment, but where the carrier has nonetheless arranged to trans-ship pursuant to a liberty clause in the contract.

It is, of course, always open to the parties to extend the operation of the Rules to other contractual operations by express contractual provision.[43] Such a provision is quite common in bills of lading and sea waybills, for, even with 'port to port' carriage, it is likely that the carrier's responsibility for the goods will extend beyond the 'tackle to tackle' period.[44] Express contractual clauses that govern the performance of that part of the contract that falls outside the Rules will be regulated by the **Unfair Contracts Terms Act 1977**.[45] Schedule 1(2)(c) provides that s 2(1) will apply to any contract for the carriage of goods by ship or hovercraft. However, ss 2(2), 3, 4 and 7 do not extend to any such contract except in favour of a person dealing as consumer. Furthermore, many disputes that come before the English courts may fall outside this section by virtue of s 27, which excludes sections 2 to 7 and 16 to 21 of the Act when English law is the proper law of the contract, solely by virtue of a choice of law clause in the contract.

Voluntary incorporation

The Rules are frequently incorporated into documents other than bills of lading, such as charter-parties or waybills, by virtue of a clause called a 'clause paramount'.[46] In such a situation, they will not have the force of law,[47] and their provisions may therefore be displaced by contrary clauses elsewhere in the contract, subject to general principles of contractual construction, whereby typed clauses will usually prevail over printed ones in the event of inconsistency between them.

Contracting out

Article V allows the carrier to surrender any of its rights or immunities or to increase its obligations and responsibilities, 'provided such surrender or increase shall be embodied in the bill of lading issued to the shipper'. However, any direct attempt by the carrier to *improve* on its position under the Rules by inserting contrary provisions in the bill of lading will fall foul of Art III(8), which provides:

> Any clause, covenant, or agreement in a contract of carriage relieving the carrier or the ship from liability for loss or damage to, or in connection with, goods arising from negligence, fault or failure in the duties and obligations provided in this article or lessening such liability otherwise than as provided in these Rules, shall be null and void and of no effect . . .

The Article has effect only when the Rules apply mandatorily to a particular contract.[48] Where the Hague Rules apply mandatorily in the country of shipment and have been expressly incorporated into the bill of lading, the English courts have also given effect to Art III(8), even though, under English law, neither the Hague nor the Hague-Visby Rules have mandatory effect over such a bill of lading.[49] However, the fact that the Hague Rules apply mandatorily in the country of loading should

---

42 [1984] 1 Lloyd's Rep 317.
43 This may be implied when the bill of lading expressly incorporates the Rules, unless there are express clauses rebutting this implication, as was the case in *The MSC Amsterdam* [2007] EWCA Civ 794; [2007] 2 Lloyd's Rep 622.
44 This is because delivery of the goods will generally be effected at a time after the completion of discharge.
45 Unless the contract is for 'combined transport', in which case part of its performance may be regulated by another mandatory convention applicable to the further mode of carriage, such as the CMR for international road transport.
46 The linguistic problems raised by such a clause are considered in Chapter 9.
47 Subject to s 1(6)(b) of COGSA 1971 in relation to waybills.
48 See Baughen, S, 'Article III rule 8: a killer provision?' (2002) S & TLI, 3(3), 14.
49 See, e.g., *The River Gurara* [1996] 2 Lloyd's Rep 53, QB, 63.

be of no consequence when construing the terms of a bill of lading that is subject to English law.[50] Accordingly, where there is a conflict between the provisions of the Hague Rules, incorporated under a clause paramount, any conflict between their provisions and express terms of the contract should be resolved by reference to the ordinary contractual principles of construction without reference to Art III(8). Rix J adopted this approach in *Finagra UK (Ltd) v OT Africa Ltd*,[51] but nonetheless found, as a matter of construction of the complex clauses involved, that the one-year time bar under Art III(6) prevailed over an express time bar of nine months. This approach, however, leaves open the possibility that a provision in the incorporated Hague Rules will be trumped by a contrary express clause in the bill of lading – as happened in *The Tasman Discoverer*,[52] where a specific package limitation in the contract prevailed over that applicable under the Hague Rules.

However, there are indirect ways in which attempts have been made to avoid the effect of the Rules.

Jurisdiction and choice of law clauses

Article X of the Hague Rules required any bill of lading issued in a Contracting State to contain an express clause incorporating the Rules. This provision was not enacted into English law. Instead, **COGSA 1924** applied the provisions of the Hague Rules to outward shipments from the UK. Under English law, the sanction for non-compliance would be the reduction of the carrier to the status of a common carrier. However, there was nothing in the Rules to prevent the carrier issuing a bill of lading without the necessary incorporation provision and then adding a clause referring disputes to the jurisdiction of another non-Convention country.

This gap in the Rules was revealed, in *Vita Food Products Inc v Unius Shipping Co Ltd*,[53] to extend even to a clause giving jurisdiction to another Convention country. A bill of lading issued in Newfoundland failed to contain the necessary statement that the Rules applied. The bill of lading contained an English choice of law clause. Under English law, **COGSA 1924** applied. However, that Act only applied to shipments out of Great Britain. Therefore, the failure of a bill of lading issued in Newfoundland to contain a statement that the Hague Rules applied was not contrary to English law. The terms of the bill of lading were therefore upheld.

In contrast, **COGSA 1971** provides that the Hague-Visby Rules are to have the 'force of law'. The effect of this wording was considered by the House of Lords in *The Hollandia* (sub nom *The Morviken*).[54] The plaintiff was claiming in respect of a shipment from Scotland under a bill of lading submitting to Dutch jurisdiction. At the time of the action, Holland was still applying the Hague Rules, the package limitation of which was more favourable to the shipowner than that allowed under the Hague-Visby Rules. By virtue of s 1(3) of **COGSA 1971**, the Hague-Visby Rules governed the shipment from Scotland. The House of Lords refused to stay the action in the English courts on the grounds of the Dutch jurisdiction clause. To uphold the clause and grant a stay would effectively be to contradict s 1(3) of **COGSA 1971**, which provides that the Hague-Visby Rules shall have 'the force of law' in respect of all bill of lading shipments out of the UK. There are powerful *dicta* in the case that the result would have been the same if the bill of lading had contained a choice of law clause where the chosen law did not apply the Hague-Visby Rules.

However, jurisdiction and choice of law clauses will be upheld, provided that the court is satisfied that the Hague-Visby Rules will govern any claim under the bill of lading. In *The Benarty*,[55] cargo claims against a charterer arose under bills of lading from ports in European countries, most of

---

50 Article 7(1) of the 1990 Rome Convention covers this situation, but is not in force in the UK.
51 [1998] 2 Lloyd's Rep 622, QB.
52 [2002] 1 Lloyd's Rep 528, NZ Ct.
53 [1939] AC 277.
54 [1983] 1 AC 565.
55 [1985] QB 325, CA.

which were signatories to the Hague-Visby Rules, to Indonesia, which was not. The bills contained terms incorporating the Hague Rules and providing for Indonesian law and jurisdiction. The jurisdiction clause was upheld on the charterer undertaking not to take any point more favourable to it than would be the case under the Hague-Visby Rules. The charterer wished to have the case heard in Indonesia to take advantage of more generous limitation provisions based on the vessel's tonnage. Article VIII of the Hague-Visby Rules provides: 'The provisions of these Rules shall not affect the rights and obligations of the carrier under any statute for the time being in force relating to the limitation of the liability of owners of seagoing vessels.' The Court of Appeal construed 'statute' so as to include limitation statutes in countries other than the UK and the shipowner was therefore entitled to rely on the relevant provisions of the Indonesian Civil Code.

Deck cargo and livestock

Article I(c) excludes from the definition of 'goods', 'live animals and cargo which by the contract of carriage is stated as being carried on deck and is so carried'. For the Rules not to apply, it is not enough that the cargo may be carried on deck and is carried on deck. The bill of lading must also state that it is carried on deck. In *Aktiebolaget Svenska Tractor v Maritime Agencies (Southampton) Ltd*,[56] it was held that a clause in the bill of lading giving liberty to carry on deck did not amount to a statement that the goods were carried on deck. The Hague Rules, therefore, continued to apply to the bill of lading, although the liberty clause meant that the carrier was not in breach by loading goods on deck. If the Rules cease to apply in this way, any clause in the bill of lading excepting the shipowner's liability in relation to the carriage of deck cargo will be valid (for the construction of clauses such as 'at shipper's risk', see the discussion at pp 200–2 of similar clauses that appear in charterparties).

Where the Hague-Visby Rules have the force of law under s 1(6), through their express incorporation into the contract of carriage contained in or evidenced by the bill of lading or non-negotiable receipt of **COGSA 1971**, s 1(7) disapplies the exclusion contained in Art I(c) in relation to deck cargo and live animals. In *The BBC Greenland*,[57] cargo was carried on deck and was stated in the bill of lading to be carried on deck. The carriage was from Italy so the Hague-Visby Rules applied by virtue of Art X(a). The bill of lading also provided that in trades where the Hague-Visby Rules applied compulsorily, the provisions of the respective legislation were to be considered incorporated in the bill of lading. It was held that s 1(7) did not apply because the Hague-Visby Rules did not apply compulsorily, as the cargo was deck cargo.

Where the bill of lading gives the carrier no liberty to carry the goods on deck, the goods must be carried under deck. A failure to do so will not only be a breach, it will also be a very serious breach of the kind known as a 'quasi-deviation'. Does such a breach remove the carrier's entitlement to rely on the exceptions and limitations contained in the Rules? The answer to this question used to depend on whether or not the Hague-Visby Rules applied to the contract with 'the force of law'. In *The Antares*,[58] the Court of Appeal held that the carrier could rely on the one-year time bar, as nothing in its language suggested that it did not apply when there had been a very serious breach of contract. This reasoning would apply equally to the limitation provisions of Art IV(5), particularly as the Hague-Visby Rules have added Art IV(5)(e), which provides for the carrier to lose its right to limit when it has been guilty of wilful default. Linguistically, there is also nothing in the exceptions in Art IV(2) to suggest that they are not available when the carrier has committed a very serious breach of its obligations under Art III(2), even though Art IV(2) does not provide that the exceptions shall apply 'in any event'.

56 [1953] 2 QB 285.
57 [2011] EWHC 3106 (Comm); [2012] 1 Lloyd's Rep 230.
58 [1987] 1 Lloyd's Rep 424.

Until recently, the position was different where the Hague Rules applied. Under English law, these can now apply only by virtue of contractual incorporation, notwithstanding that this is made mandatory by the law of the state of loading. Hirst J, in *The Chanda*,[59] held that, as a matter of construction, the protection of the Rules could only be claimed by a carrier when it was performing the carriage in an authorised manner. Therefore, where the goods had been damaged as a result of their unauthorised stowage on deck, the carrier could not rely on the Hague Rules package limit.[60] A similar decision was reached in Australia in *The Pembroke*.[61] However, the Court of Appeal in *The Kapitan Petko Voivoda*[62] has now overruled *The Chanda* in holding that the carrier remains entitled to rely on the Hague Rules package limitation notwithstanding that the goods have been damaged due to unauthorised deck stowage. The Court of Appeal drew attention to the words 'in any event' in the package limitation, which Hirst J had failed to consider in *The Chanda*. However, its decision was not based solely on this ground, but rather on the wider ground that the applicability of exceptions or limitations should depend upon a construction of their language and not be influenced by the seriousness of the breach. It is unlikely, however, as a matter of construction, that any of the exceptions in Art IV(2) would exonerate the carrier in the event that cargo was damaged due to its carriage on deck. The carrier would have to show that the cargo would still have been damaged due to the excepted peril even if it had been carried below deck.

'Obligations' and 'exceptions' clauses

In *Pyrene Co Ltd v Scindia Navigation Co Ltd*, Devlin J was faced with the question of deciding when the Hague Rules started to apply during the process of loading a ship. He rejected the idea that the Rules applied only from the moment at which the goods had actually been loaded onto the vessel. In considering the meaning of 'loading' in Art III(2), he stated:[63]

> The phrase 'shall properly and carefully load' may mean that the carrier shall load and that he shall do it properly and carefully: or that he shall do whatever loading he does properly and carefully. The former interpretation perhaps fits the language more closely, but the latter may be more consistent with the object of the Rules . . . It is difficult to believe that the Rules were intended to impose a universal rigidity in this respect, or to deny freedom of contract to the carrier. The carrier is practically bound to play some part in the loading and discharging, so that both operations are naturally included in those covered by the contract of carriage. But I see no reason why the Rules should not leave the parties free to determine by their own contract the part which each has to play. On this view the whole contract of carriage is subject to the Rules, but the extent to which loading and discharging are brought within the carrier's obligations is left to the parties themselves to decide.

This reasoning allows the parties freedom of contract in respect of the allocation of responsibilities under a bill of lading contract, as opposed to the standard to which those responsibilities must be performed. It was adopted by a majority of the House of Lords in *Renton (GH) & Co Ltd v Palmyra Trading Corp of Panama*.[64] In that case, a bill of lading clause permitted delivery at an alternative port in the event of a strike. Three of the bills provided for delivery at London and a fourth for delivery at Hull. As both ports were strike-bound, the shipowners delivered at Hamburg, as permitted by the terms of the clause. The shipowners made no arrangements to trans-ship the cargo to the discharge port

---

59 [1989] 2 Lloyd's Rep 494.
60 Hirst J distinguished *The Antares* [1987] 1 Lloyd's Rep 424 on the grounds, first, that it involved the Hague-Visby Rules, and secondly, that it involved the time bar and not the package limit.
61 [1995] 2 Lloyd's Rep 290.
62 [2003] EWCA Civ 451; [2003] 2 Lloyd's Rep 1.
63 [1954] 2 QB 402, 417–18.
64 [1957] AC 149.

specified on the front of the bill of lading once the strike had ended. The plaintiffs argued that the strike clause offended Art III(8) and that the discharge at Hamburg did not amount to a 'reasonable deviation' under Art IV(4). The House of Lords held that the clause defined the voyage that the shipowner had agreed to undertake and was therefore not repugnant to the Hague Rules. There was therefore no need for the carrier to rely on Art IV(4) to justify its deviation. However, the application of this distinction between obligations and exceptions clauses can give rise to problems, as a consideration of the following three types of clause will demonstrate.[65]

First, there are trans-shipment clauses. These usually contain a liberty to trans-ship, coupled with a clause stating that the carrier's period of responsibility shall cease once the goods have left its possession. The liberty itself will not be caught by Art III(8), as held by Branson J in *Marcelino Gonzales Y Compania S en C v James Nourse Ltd*.[66] Here, goods were damaged following discharge into lighters. The carrier was successfully able to avoid liability by showing that such discharge fell within a liberty to trans-ship and that it was therefore entitled to rely on the exceptions contained in the bill of lading. The classification of the second part of a trans-shipment clause, however, is unclear. By its wording, it would seem to define the scope of the carrier's contractual undertaking contractually in exactly the same way as the strike clause in *Renton (GH) & Co Ltd v Palmyra Trading Corp of Panama*.[67] On the other hand, it could be argued that it is more in the nature of an exceptions clause if the liberty to trans-ship can be invoked wholly for the commercial convenience of the carrier. In contrast, the strike clause in *Renton v Palmyra* was directed at a specific problem arising through the actions of a party over which neither the carrier nor the cargo owner had any control. Dicta in *Holland Colombo Trading Society v Alawdeen*[68] suggest that such a clause may be caught by Art III(8). However, the decision predates *Renton v Palmyra* and the dicta make no reference to the critical distinction between obligations and exceptions clauses. If such a clause is, in truth, an obligations clause, the carrier may find that it is subject to a restrictive construction, such as that adopted by Brandon J in *The Berkshire*.[69]

Secondly, there are 'identity of carrier' and 'demise' clauses. Since *The Berkshire*, the courts have upheld these to the extent of allowing the claimant to sue the party named as carrier by the clause. It is still an open question as to whether the clause exonerates the party who would, in the absence of the clause, be held to be the carrier. However, given the use of the word 'carrier' in the singular in the Rules themselves, it is likely that the English courts would hold that there could be only one carrier under the Rules, and that it should be the party defined in the clause and no other.

Thirdly, there are 'free in' and 'free out' clauses. These allocate responsibility for loading and stowing, and discharge to the shipper and receiver, respectively. The House of Lords, in *The Jordan II*,[70] has confirmed that such clauses constitute valid obligations clauses, which are, therefore, outside the scope of Art III(8). A cargo of steel was carried from India to Spain under a bill of lading that incorporated the terms of a Stemmor ore charter. Clause 3, the freight clause, provided that the charter was on fiost ('free in, out, stowed and trimmed') terms, while cl 17 provided that 'Shipper, charterer, receiver'[71] were to load, trim and discharge the cargo. Read together, these clauses relieved the shipowner not only of the costs of these operations, but also of the responsibility for them. Although cl 17 made no reference to stowage, when read in conjunction with cl 3 it was clear that the carrier was also undertaking no responsibility in respect

---

65 See Baughen, S, 'Defining the ambit of Article III(8) of the Hague Rules: obligations and exceptions clauses' [2003] JIML 115.
66 [1936] 1 KB 565.
67 [1957] AC 149.
68 [1954] 2 Lloyd's Rep 45.
69 [1974] 1 Lloyd's Rep 185.
70 [2004] UKHL 49; [2005] 1 Lloyd's Rep 57, noted [2005] LMCLQ 153.
71 The specific reference to the 'shipper' and 'receiver' meant that there were no linguistic problems in construing the clause in its bill of lading context of the sort seen in *The Miramar* [1984] AC 676.

of this operation. The effect of the clauses, once incorporated into the bill of lading, was that the shipper undertook to load and stow the ship, and the receiver undertook to discharge her.

But what would be the position where a claim was made by the receiver in respect of damage sustained by the cargo during the operations of loading and stowing and by the shipper in respect of damage sustained during discharging? At first instance, Nigel Teare QC accepted the shipowner's argument that, although the ship would remain liable to the receiver, it would be able to rely by way of defence on Art IV(2)(i).[72] Before the Court of Appeal, the shipowner argued, for the first time, that the effect of cll 3 and 17 was that it had undertaken no responsibility at all for any of these operations under the bill of lading contract. Therefore, it could not be in breach of that contract if the goods were damaged during any of those operations. The Court of Appeal held that this was indeed the position.[73] The problem with this result is that the receiver is left with no contractual recourse against either the shipowner or the shipper in respect of damage sustained during loading or stowing.[74] Although the shipper and receiver are both linked contractually with the carrier, no such nexus exists as between themselves. From the receiver's point of view, the shipper is as much a third party as was the time charterer in *The Coral*,[75] where the Court of Appeal held that there was a good arguable case that a shipowner would not be liable for loss due to bad stowage where the bill of lading incorporated the terms of a time charter under which the time charterer undertook responsibility for stowage. The House of Lords affirmed the decisions of the lower courts.[76] Their Lordships saw no reason to depart from the views of Devlin J expressed in *Pyrene v Scindia*, which had been endorsed by the House in *Renton v Palmyra*. Lord Steyn described Devlin J's view in terms that a shipowner retained contractual freedom to provide by clear words in the bill of lading that it was not undertaking responsibility for some of the operations listed in Art III(2). This would appear to validate a clause whereby responsibility for an operation was transferred to a third party to the bill of lading – for example, a charterer – and would probably also legitimate clauses that provided for the shipowner's responsibility to cease following a transshipment of cargo pursuant to a liberty in the bill of lading. However, the shipowner would not be entitled to provide that it did not undertake some of the obligations imposed on it under Art III(1).[77]

A difficult question arises when the bad stowage is such as to make the vessel unseaworthy at the start of the voyage. In *The Jordan II*, Lord Steyn stated:

> For example, it is obvious that the obligation to make the ship seaworthy under article III, r. 1, is a fundamental obligation which the owner cannot transfer to another. The Rules impose an inescapable personal obligation: *Riverstone Meat Co Pty Ltd v Lancashire Shipping Co Ltd* [1961] AC 807. On the other hand, article III, r. 2, provides for functions some of which (although very important) are of a less fundamental order e.g. loading, stowage and discharge of the cargo.

This would suggest that the shipowner could still be liable under art IV.1 where damage results from the way in which the cargo is loaded or stowed which makes the vessel unseaworthy. This argument was raised in *The EEMS Solar* and dismissed by Jervis Kay QC, who held that there was a significant distinction between unseaworthiness arising from the state of the vessel and unseaworthiness arising from the manner of her loading. The shipowner would not be liable for damage

---

72 [2002] EWHC 1268 (Comm); [2002] 2 All ER (Comm) 364. In the converse situation, where the shipper brought the claim and the goods had been damaged on discharge, the ship would also be liable but would have a defence under Art IV(2)(q).
73 [2003] EWCA Civ 144; [2003] 2 Lloyd's Rep 87, CA, noted [2004] LMCLQ 129.
74 The same applies, *mutatis mutandis*, as regards the shipper's claim in respect of damage sustained during discharging.
75 [1993] 1 Lloyd's Rep 1.
76 [2004] UKHL 49; [2005] 1 Lloyd's Rep 57.
77 A point overlooked by Morison J in *Compania Sud American Vapores v MS ER Hamburg Schiffahrtsgesellschaft mbH & Co KG* [2006] EWHC 483 (Comm); [2006] 2 Lloyd's Rep 66, noted [2007] LMCLQ 1.

arising from improper stowage which rendered the vessel unseaworthy unless the bad stowage leading to the damage could be shown to have arisen from a significant intervention by the shipowners or their master. The evidence showed that the cargo damage was caused by cargo movement during the voyage due to an absence of locking coils, so rendering the cargo stow inadequate to meet the foreseeable weather conditions on the voyage. The shipowners had provided the stevedores with a stowage plan that did not provide for locking coils but this did not constitute an intervention by the master in the stowage as the stevedores had ignored the plan and followed their own devices. Had the damage been caused by the unseaworthiness of the vessel herself or had there been a significant intervention in the stowage by the master, the owners would have been liable.

Third-party reliance on the Rules

Article IVbis was introduced by the Hague-Visby Rules to regulate actions in tort that were brought either against the carrier itself or against its servants or agents. Subheading (1) provides:

> The defences and limits of liability provided for in these Rules shall apply in any action against the carrier in respect of loss or damage to goods covered by a contract of carriage whether the action can be founded in contract or tort.

It might be thought that the effect of this provision was to apply the Rules to pure tort claims arising out of carriage under a Hague-Visby bill of lading. However, in *The Captain Gregos*,[78] the Court of Appeal held that this provision applies to a tort claim against the carrier only where the plaintiff also has a parallel contractual action against the carrier that is subject to the Rules.

Article IVbis(2) provides: 'If such an action is brought against a servant or agent[79] of the carrier (not being an independent contractor), such servant or agent shall be entitled to avail himself of the defences and limits of liability which the carrier is entitled to invoke under these Rules.' However, independent contractors are specifically excluded from the ambit of this provision. Independent contractors, such as stevedoring companies, can therefore take advantage of the provisions of the Rules only by means of a 'Himalaya' clause, or else by a similar clause drafted to take advantage of the **Contracts (Rights of Third Parties) Act 1999**.[80]

The content of the Rules

The carrier's duties under Art III

The Rules impose two duties on the carrier as regards care of the cargo under the bill of lading contract.[81] The first, contained in Art III(1), is a modified duty of seaworthiness. The second, contained in Art III(2), is a duty 'properly and carefully' to load, handle, stow, carry, keep, care for, and discharge the goods carried. Each duty contains its own corresponding exceptions in Art IV(1) and Art IV(2), respectively.

---

78 [1990] 1 Lloyd's Rep 310.
79 The reference to agents can initially be confusing, as agency is the device by which 'Himalaya' clauses are validated. However, for this to happen, it is the *shipowner* that must act as the agent for the stevedore in concluding the bill of lading contract. Thus the stevedore, for certain purposes, stands as the shipowner's *principal*.
80 The 1991 UN Convention on the Liability of Operators of Transport Terminals in International Trade sets out a regime of liability, exceptions and limitations for terminal operators, but is not yet in force.
81 They also impose obligations as regards the form of the bill of lading to which the shipper is entitled. These are discussed in Chapter 3.

If goods are lost or damaged, it is of the utmost importance to ascertain which of these two duties was breached. This is because the exceptions provided in Art IV(2) can only be relied on for breaches of Art III(2) and not of Art III(1).[82] So, in *Maxine Footwear Co Ltd v Canadian Govt Merchant Marine Ltd*,[83] a ship in port caught fire, after loading had begun, due to crew negligence in thawing out scuppers with a blowtorch. The loss was held to be due to the shipowners' breach of their obligations under Art III(1), which meant that they could no longer rely on the exception in Art IV(2)(b) of 'Fire, unless caused by the actual fault or privity of the carrier'. Had the ship already sailed when the fire broke out, the shipowners could have relied on this exception. The breach would, by then, have ceased to be one relating to seaworthiness and have been transformed into a breach of Art III(2).

Article III(1)

Article III(1) provides that:

> The carrier shall be bound before and at the beginning of the voyage to exercise due diligence to:
>
> (a)   make the ship seaworthy;
> (b)   properly man, equip and supply the ship;
> (c)   make the holds, refrigerating and cool chambers, and all other parts of the ship in which goods are carried, fit and safe for their reception, carriage and preservation.

Article III(1) modifies the common law obligation of seaworthiness in two respects. First, the carrier is only bound to exercise 'due diligence' in making the ship seaworthy. Secondly, the doctrine of stages is modified. The onus of proving unseaworthiness is generally accepted to be on the cargo owner, as is the case at common law.[84] The claimant need not, however, establish a failure of due diligence on the part of the carrier. Once the claimant has established that the ship was unseaworthy at the relevant time and that this was at least *a* cause of the loss, then the carrier will be liable, unless it can establish due diligence and so bring itself within the defence contained in Art IV(1). Subject to these points, the common law cases on what constitutes unseaworthiness will still be relevant in determining this issue as it arises under Art III(1). Indeed, subheadings (a), (b) and (c) merely confirmed the existing position under English law as to when a vessel would be unseaworthy.

In *The Hellenic Dolphin*,[85] cargo was damaged by an ingress of seawater through an indent in the vessel's plating. Had the indent been present before completion of loading, the vessel would have been unseaworthy. However, the evidence was such that the court was unable to decide whether the indent had been caused before or after loading. Therefore, cargo owners had failed to show a breach of Art III(1) and the shipowners were able to rely on two defences listed in Art IV(2).[86] The following passage from the judgment of Lloyd J[87] provides a succinct practical summary of the incidence of the burden of proof in cargo claims subject to the Hague or Hague-Visby Rules:

> The cargo owner can raise a prima facie case against the shipowner by showing that cargo which had been shipped in good order and condition was damaged on arrival. The shipowner

---

82   Compliance with Art III(1) is also a precondition for proceeding against a shipper for an indemnity against loading dangerous cargo under Art IV(6). See *The Fiona* [1994] 2 Lloyd's Rep 506, CA.
83   [1959] AC 589.
84   Op cit Tetley fn 31, pp 375–6, disputes this. However, the proposition was accepted by the Court of Appeal in *The Apostolis* [1997] 2 Lloyd's Rep 241.
85   [1978] 2 Lloyd's Rep 336.
86   On the facts, Lloyd J held that, even if he were wrong about the burden of proof in establishing unseaworthiness, the shipowners had established that they had taken due diligence and so would not have been liable in any event.
87   [1978] 2 Lloyd's Rep 336, 339.

can meet that prima facie case by relying on an exception [under Art IV(2)], for example, perils of the sea . . . The cargo owner can then seek to displace that exception by proving that the vessel was unseaworthy at commencement of the voyage and that the unseaworthiness was the cause of the loss. The burden in relation to seaworthiness does not shift. Naturally the court can draw inferences . . . [88] But if at the end of the day, having heard all the evidence and drawn all the proper inferences, the court is left on the razor's edge, the cargo owner fails on unseaworthiness and the shipowners are left with their defence of perils of the sea. If, on the other hand, the court comes down in favour of the cargo owners on unseaworthiness, the shipowners can still escape by proving that the relevant unseaworthiness was not due to any want of diligence on their part or on the part of their servants or agents.

Due diligence

The wording of Art III(1) does not impose an absolute obligation on the carrier to make the vessel seaworthy, as is the case at common law, but only an obligation to exercise due diligence to achieve this end. This is confirmed by Art IV(1), which also provides that the burden of proving due diligence rests on the carrier. This can be a formidable burden to discharge, as can be seen in *The Muncaster Castle*,[89] where the cargo was damaged by an ingress of seawater. Immediately prior to her outward voyage to the load port at Sydney, the ship had passed through her No 2 special survey and annual load line survey. The marine superintendent employed a reputable firm of ship repairers to open up all storm valves and inspection covers. After inspection, the repairers' fitter shut and secured each cover. Due to a fitter's negligence in not securing the nuts sufficiently, they were loosened by the working of the ship in rough weather and seawater got in. The owners had still failed to exercise due diligence. If the servant of the independent contractor was negligent, then the owners were still in breach of their duty. The duty was 'non-delegable', so, contrary to the general position in tort, it would not be satisfied merely by appointing a reasonably competent contractor.[90] However, this principle does not extend to the situation in which the ship is rendered unseaworthy by the fact that the shipper has caused dangerous cargo to be loaded.[91] Neither does the shipowner's duty under Art III(1) start until the vessel comes into its 'orbit', which term is coextensive with ownership, service or control. In *The Happy Ranger*,[92] the shipowner was not liable for the negligence of the shipbuilder prior to that date that had resulted in defects to the vessel's cranes. However, the shipowner had failed to exercise due diligence in relation to the period after the vessel came into its orbit by failing to proof test the hooks before loading began, having been aware that no such testing had been done by the shipbuilder.

However, the carrier need not take every conceivable precaution; it need only take such precautions as would be taken by a reasonable carrier. In *The Amstelslot*,[93] the vessel broke down due to a fatigue crack of an unknown cause. A careful inspection before the voyage had failed to reveal the defect, but the cargo owners argued that, had extra tests been carried out, it would have been revealed. The shipowners were held not to have breached their duty to exercise due diligence because the inspectors' failure to conduct these additional tests did not amount to negligence.

A similar conclusion was reached in *The Hellenic Dolphin*,[94] where Lloyd J was of the view that the shipowners had established due diligence by the following three factors. First, the vessel, at all

---

88 As in *The Theodegmon* [1990] 1 Lloyd's Rep 52, where the failure of the vessel's steering gear shortly after leaving the port of loading led to the inference that the vessel was unseaworthy on sailing.

89 [1961] AC 807, HL.

90 Reliance on the judgments of Classification Society surveyors will also be insufficient to discharge the burden of proving due diligence. See *The Toledo* [1995] 1 Lloyd's Rep 40.

91 *The Kapitan Sakharov* [2000] 2 Lloyd's Rep 255, CA.

92 [2006] EWHC 122 (Comm); [2006] 1 Lloyd's Rep 649.

93 *The Amstelslot* [1963] 2 Lloyd's Rep 223, HL.

94 [1978] 2 Lloyd's Rep 336.

material times, was fully classed and had undergone her annual dry-docking some nine months before the emergence of the indent to the shell plating. Secondly, there had been an intermediate examination of the vessel by a superintending engineer in Piraeus before she set out on the round voyage from Europe to Africa on which the cargo damage occurred. Thirdly, the master and chief officer had carried out routine inspections of the vessel during the course of the round voyage. The cargo owner's expert was of the view that there should have been a further examination by a superintending engineer at the turnaround point of the round voyage. Lloyd J was of the view that this was a counsel of perfection and not a course of action that would be obvious to a reasonable shipowner.

The effect of these decisions is that the carrier is unlikely to discharge the burden of proving that it took due diligence unless the unseaworthiness was caused by a latent defect not discoverable by a careful surveyor. However, a shipowner who fails to establish that it took due diligence to make the vessel seaworthy will still have a defence if it can prove that its failure to take due diligence did not cause the loss. In *The Yamatogowa*,[95] cargo owners tried to recover their salvage and general average contributions following the breakdown of the vessel due to failure of its reduction gears. Because of the way in which the gears were encased, they were very hard to examine. The previous year, the shipowners had inspected the gears, but had given them only a superficial scrutiny. Undoubtedly, they had failed to exercise due diligence, but the shipowners still succeeded because of the finding that even a thorough check of the gear would not have revealed the deficiency.

The doctrine of stages

Under Art III(1), the due diligence obligation attaches 'before and at the beginning of the voyage'. This imposes a continuous duty from the start of loading up to sailing, in contrast to the discrete stages of loading and sailing at common law. In *Maxine Footwear Co Ltd v Canadian Govt Merchant Marine Ltd*,[96] the fire took place between loading and sailing, yet still constituted a breach of the obligation.[97]

The implications for the bunkering stage were considered in *The Makedonia*.[98] The vessel suffered a breakdown on the voyage and, as a result, the cargo owners had to pay a share of the salvage costs and faced claims in general average, which they sought to recover by suing the shipowners under the bill of lading. The obligation to exercise due diligence before and at the start of sailing from the load port meant two things in the bunkering context. First, the shipowners must have adequately bunkered the vessel for the first stage of her voyage. Secondly, they must also have arranged for adequate bunkers of a proper kind to be available at the first and other intermediate ports on the voyage so as to enable the contractual voyage to be performed. On the evidence in this case, the owners had performed these obligations satisfactorily. Applying the common law doctrine of stages would have imposed a further duty on the shipowners to take due diligence to ensure that the actual bunkering operation at the intermediate port was done properly.[99]

Article III(2)

Where the claimant's loss is not due to the unseaworthiness of the vessel, it will need to base its claim on Art III(2), which provides that:

---

95 [1990] 2 Lloyd's Rep 39.
96 [1959] AC 589.
97 Cf *McFadden v Blue Star Line* [1905] 1 KB 697.
98 [1962] P 190.
99 However, the owners were in breach of Art III(1) in that the inefficiency of the engineers, which was the proximate cause of the loss, meant that the vessel was unseaworthy at the start of the voyage by reason of being improperly manned and were precluded from relying on the exemptions in Art IV(2).

Subject to the provisions of Art IV, the carrier shall properly and carefully load, handle, stow, carry, keep, care for, and discharge the goods carried.

The obligation, which is non-delegable,[100] requires the carrier to act both 'carefully' and 'properly'. The word 'carefully' is self-explanatory and it might be thought that nothing is added to it by the additional term 'properly'. However, the word 'properly' was held by the House of Lords, in *Albacora SRL v Westcott & Laurance Line (The Maltasian)*,[101] to impose an additional duty to adopt a system 'which is sound in light of all the knowledge which the carrier has or ought to have about the nature of the goods'. However, the carrier is not under an absolute duty to deliver goods in the same condition as that in which they were loaded. The case involved damage to a cargo of fish. The evidence at trial showed that, unless the fish were carried below 5°C, bacteria present before loading would inevitably cause damage. It was therefore held that there had been no breach of this duty by the shipowners, as neither they nor the shippers had any reason to suppose the fish could only be carried safely below that temperature. They had been told only to keep the cargo away from the ship's boilers and had not been informed that the cargo required refrigeration. Furthermore, the shipowners had no reason to know the cargo needed refrigeration. Where, however, the shipowner complies with the shipper's carriage instructions, but should have known that these were inadequate to ensure safe carriage of the cargo, a breach of Art III(2) will be established.[102]

The burden of proof under this Article is somewhat oblique. Does the claimant have to prove negligence, or does the defendant have to disprove it? The position is best put by the following statement of Lord Pearson in *Albacora SRL v Westcott & Laurance Line*:[103]

The scheme is, therefore, that there is a prima facie obligation under Art III(2), which may be displaced or modified by some provision of Art IV. The convenient first step is to ascertain what is the prima facie obligation under Art III(2) . . . It is not an obligation to achieve the desired result, ie, the arrival of the goods in an undamaged condition at their destination. It is an obligation to carry out certain operations properly and carefully. The fact that goods, acknowledged in the bill of lading to have been received on board in apparent good order and condition, arrived at the destination in a damaged condition does not in itself constitute a breach of the obligation, though it may well be in many cases sufficient to raise an inference of a breach of the obligation. The cargo owner is not expected to know what happened on the voyage, and, if he shows that the goods arrived in a damaged condition and there is no evidence from the shipowner showing that the goods were duly cared for on the voyage, the court may well infer that the goods were not properly cared for on the voyage.

It is submitted that, in practice, once the cargo owner establishes transit loss or damage, the burden shifts to the shipowner to establish either that it complied with its duties under Art III(2) or that it is entitled to rely on one of the exceptions under Art IV(2) or that its breach did not cause the loss in question.[104] In most cases, as in *Albacora SRL v Westcott & Laurance Line* itself, successful reliance on an exception will also enable the shipowner to rebut an allegation of breach of its duties under Art III(2).

In effect, the liability regime under Art III(2) is very similar to that applied by the common law to bailments by reward. However, unlike the position with a bailment for reward, there are two situations in which the shipowner may escape liability even though the loss has been caused by the

---

100 *Hourani v T&J Harrison* (1927) 32 Com Cas 305, KB.
101 [1966] 2 Lloyd's Rep 53, HL (Sc).
102 *The Mahia* [1955] 1 Lloyd's Rep 264, Can Ct.
103 [1966] 2 Lloyd's Rep 53, HL (Sc).
104 As in *The Polar* [1993] 2 Lloyd's Rep 478, QB.

negligence of its servants or agents. These are the situations covered by the exceptions in Art IV(2) (a) and (b).[105] In these situations, cargo interests will want to press home a claim for breach of Art III(1) so as to prevent the shipowner from relying on the exceptions. The influence of *The Glendarroch*[106] is still strong here in that, under English law, it is not for the carrier to prove compliance with Art III(1) before it can rely on the exceptions under Art IV(2). Instead, the carrier need only prove that the loss or damage falls within one of these exceptions. It is then for the claimant to prove not only that there was a breach of Art III(1), but also that it was at least a contributory cause of the loss or damage. Only if it successfully discharges this burden will the carrier lose the benefit of a defence that it has initially managed to establish under Art IV(2).

The carrier's defences under Art IV

Article IV(1) grants the carrier a 'due diligence' defence in respect of 'loss or damage' caused by unseaworthiness. Article IV(2) then goes on to grant the carrier immunity in respect of 'loss or damage' in respect of a list of causes, but these additional defences will be unavailable to a carrier where the loss or damage is caused by the carrier's failure to take due diligence to provide a seaworthy ship. On two occasions, the House of Lords has taken the view that 'loss or damage' extends beyond physical loss or damage to cargo: in *Renton (GH) & Co Ltd v Palmyra Trading Corp of Panama*,[107] in respect of trans-shipment costs; and in *Adamastos Shipping Co Ltd v Anglo-Saxon Petroleum Co Ltd*,[108] in respect of the economic loss consequent upon the reduction of the number of voyages that could be performed under a consecutive voyage charter.

The following are the defences available under Art IV(2). The first two listed allow the shipowner a defence in certain situations even where the loss has been caused by the negligence of its servants or agents. The remaining situations involve causes of loss that do not involve fault on the part of the carrier, its servants or agents. It has been suggested that to claim the benefit of exceptions (c)–(q) below, the carrier must not only prove that the loss falls within the exception, but it must also prove that the loss was not caused by its negligence. This additional requirement was doubted by Lords Pearce and Pearson in *Albacora SRL v Westcott & Laurance Line*.[109]

However, in practice, if a carrier can establish that it is entitled to the protection of any of the defences other than the first two listed, it will, in most cases, have also disproved negligence. In *Albacora SRL v Westcott & Laurance Line*, the same facts that enabled the carrier to rely on exception (m) below also enabled it to show that it had not been in breach of Art III(2).[110]

The burden of proof in relying on an exception falls on the carrier, who will be held liable for any loss or damage occurring within its period of responsibility that does not fall within an exception. This will require the carrier to establish the cause of the loss or damage. If the loss is caused partly by an excepted peril and partly by another cause which is not an excepted peril, the carrier must show how much of the loss has been caused by the excepted peril. If it is unable to discharge this burden, it will be liable in full for the loss.[111] If the loss is covered by an

---

105 Or conceivably (c), where the cargo owner lacks the requisite evidence to establish unseaworthiness, as in *The Hellenic Dolphin* [1978] 2 Lloyd's Rep 336.
106 [1894] P 226.
107 [1957] AC 149.
108 [1959] AC 133.
109 [1966] 2 Lloyd's Rep 53, HL (Sc).
110 A similar result was reached in *The Bunga Seroja* [1994] 1 Lloyd's Rep 455, Sup Ct (NSW), Admlty Div, where the defence in question was under heading (c), below.
111 *Gosse Millard Ltd v Canadian Government Merchant Marine Ltd (The Canadian Highlander)* [1929] AC 223; *Exportadora Valle de Colina SA (t/a Exportadora Santa Elena) v AP Moller-Maersk A/S (t/a Maersk Line)* [2010] EWHC 3224; *Milan Nigeria Ltd v Angeliki B Maritime Co* [2011] EWHC 892 (Comm).

exception, but has been aggravated by a breach by the carrier, the carrier will be liable to the extent of that aggravation.[112]

(a) Act, neglect, default of the master, mariner, pilot or the servants of the carrier in the navigation or in the management of the ship

This is the most controversial of the Hague Rules exceptions in that it allows the shipowner to escape liability in two situations, notwithstanding that there has been negligence on the part of its servants. The first is when the claim arises out of the ship's navigation. Navigation covers matters of seamanship, but the House of Lords held, in *The Hill Harmony*,[113] that it does not cover matters relating to the route the vessel is to take on the voyage. The master, however, retains overriding responsibility for the vessel's safety. His decisions as to how to sail on a particular route will therefore be navigational. So, too, will a decision on whether or not to set sail from a port in adverse weather conditions. In *The Tasman Pioneer*,[114] the Supreme Court of New Zealand held that the master's conduct in failing to take immediate remedial action after the vessel struck rocks on a voyage did not amount to barratry and that the carrier was protected by Art IV(2)(a) of the Hague-Visby Rules.[115] The second is when the claim arises out of the ship's management. In this connection, the neglect must relate to the ship, not to the cargo, as illustrated by *Gosse Millerd Ltd v Canadian Govt Merchant Marine Ltd*.[116] The ship sustained damage on her voyage. Repairs necessitated access to holds where tinplates were stowed. This meant that the hatches were left open and unprotected when rain fell. The shipowners could not rely on this exception, because what caused the damage was the misuse of tarpaulins, which were used solely to protect the cargo. There was no evidence that rain would have damaged an empty hold.

In contrast, in *International Packers London Ltd v Ocean Steam Ship Co Ltd*,[117] the carrier was able to rely on this defence when seawater entered a hold due to the failure of the crew to use the locking bars on the hatch covers when bad weather was encountered. The locking bars were regarded as for the protection of the ship due to the fact that the load line provisions applied to 'the whole of the appliances which go to make up a properly secured hatch in an exposed position . . .'. The fact that the crew's failure, in the circumstances of the case, did not, in fact, put at risk the safety of the vessel did not prevent the carrier from relying on the exception. What was critical was the fact that proper use of the locking bars was mandated by the Load Line Rules, which were directed at maintaining the safety of vessels at sea. In *The Iron Gippsland*,[118] however, management of an inert gas system on a tanker was held to be management of the cargo, as the system was needed to prevent the cargo from posing a danger to the safety of the ship.[119] However, failure to operate the vessel's refrigeration unit properly during the voyage will have no impact on the safety of the vessel and cannot therefore amount to 'management of the vessel'.[120]

Finally, it should be noted that the scope of this exception is likely to be substantially reduced in the future, as many instances of negligence in the navigation and management of the vessel may be attributable to a failure on the part of the shipowner to maintain adequate safety systems as required by the International Safety Management Code (the ISM Code). If cargo loss or damage can

---

112 In *Silver v Ocean SS Co* [1930] 1 KB 416, CA, at first instance, the carrier was able to rely on the defence of insufficient packaging contained in (n). However, it was held liable for 10 per cent of the loss because it had aggravated the damage by adopting an inappropriate method of discharging the packages.

113 [2001] 1 AC 638.

114 [2010] NZSC 37.

115 The test for establishing barratry as an implicit qualification to the exemption conferred by Art IV(a) was the same as under Art IV(5)(e) and Art IVbis(4), namely whether damage had resulted from an act or omission of the master or crew done with intent to cause damage, or recklessly and with knowledge that damage would probably result.

116 [1929] AC 223.

117 [1955] 2 Lloyd's Rep 218, QB.

118 [1994] 1 Lloyd's Rep 335, 358, Sup Ct (NSW).

119 In *The Eternity* [2008] EWHC 2480 (Comm); [2009] 1 Lloyd's Rep 107, Steel J held that the failure to close the isolation valves of the inert gas system or to maintain the valves in good condition did not constitute a failure in the management of the vessel, but rather in the management of the cargo.

120 *Foreman and Ellams Ltd v Federal SN Co* [1928] 2 KB 424.

be attributed to a breach of the shipowner's obligations under the ISM Code, which has led to negligence on the part of the crew, it is almost certain that the shipowner will be found to have been in breach of its obligations under Art III(1). In such a situation, it will be unable to rely on the exceptions contained in Art IV(2).

(b) Fire, unless caused by the actual fault or privity of the carrier

The exception will apply even if the fire is caused by the negligence of the carrier's servants or agents. However, it will be lost in two situations. The first is where the negligence is of a servant of such seniority as can be said to embody the 'carrier'. For example, in The Apostolis,[121] it was said, obiter, that the fault of the general manager of the shipowners constituted fault or privity of the carrier. Secondly, the carrier cannot rely on this exception if the fire renders the vessel unseaworthy and the shipowner cannot prove due diligence. This occurred in Maxine Footwear Co Ltd v Canadian Govt Merchant Marine Ltd,[122] where there was a fire in the cork lining of the ship's holds.

However, the mere fact that the cargo catches fire does not render the ship itself unseaworthy. In The Apostolis,[123] the Court of Appeal had to consider whether there had been a breach of Art III(1) when cargo was damaged by a fire that broke out during loading. The competing causes were a lighted cigarette having been thrown into the hold or sparks falling into the holds from welding work that was being carried out on deck. It was held that the first cause was the likeliest one and that was clearly not an instance of unseaworthiness. However, both Leggatt and Phillips LJJ went on to say that, even if the fire had been caused by ignition from a welding spark, that would not have been an instance of unseaworthiness as the vessel's holds were not intrinsically unsafe. This rather literal approach overlooks the possibility that the vessel was unseaworthy due to the system of operating the vessel by which the shipowner allowed welding work to take place on the vessel at a time when hatches containing cargo were left open.[124]

A British shipowner will, in addition, be able to rely on s 186 of the **Merchant Shipping Act 1995**,[125] where any property on board the ship is lost or damaged by fire. This defence will only be lost under Art 4 of the **1976 Limitation Convention** attached to the Act 'if it is proved that the loss resulted from his personal act or omission, committed with the intent to cause such loss, or recklessly and with knowledge that such loss would probably result'. It is probable that the carrier will be entitled to rely on this defence even if the fire is due to the unseaworthiness of the vessel.[126]

(c) Perils, dangers and accidents of the sea or other navigable waters

This reiterates the popular express exception discussed in the previous chapter. The exception was in common use well before the Hague Rules. The common law decisions as to its ambit, discussed previously at p 80, will, therefore, continue to be relevant to the scope of the exception as it appears in the Hague Rules. The English courts have, by and large, continued to apply the rule in The Glendarroch.[127] This means that the carrier will be entitled to rely on the defence if it can establish a sustainable case that the loss or damage constitutes a peril of the sea. The carrier will then escape liability unless the claimant can prove that the loss was caused by its negligence, the so-called 'exception upon the exception'.

---

121 [1996] 1 Lloyd's Rep 475, QB, overruled by the Court of Appeal [1997] 2 Lloyd's Rep 241, who overturned the finding that the fire had been caused by welding operations on the ship rather than by a cigarette.

122 [1959] AC 589.

123 [1997] 2 Lloyd's Rep 241.

124 Cf The Star Sea [1995] 1 Lloyd's Rep 651, QB.

125 Formerly s 18 of the Merchant Shipping Act 1979. The section also protects British shipowners in the event of the loss or damage of gold and valuables through theft, robbery or other dishonest conduct.

126 Louis Dreyfus & Co v Tempus Shipping Co [1931] AC 726, HL, which involved the interpretation of s 502 of the Merchant Shipping Act 1894, which was of similar effect to s 186 of the Merchant Shipping Act 1995.

127 [1894] P 226.

The rule has been criticised as placing an unduly onerous evidential burden upon cargo claimants in that, at least in theory, it allows for the possibility that the carrier can escape liability for unexplained losses that appear to fall within the exception. For example, the carrier could rely on the exception merely by proving that the cargo was damaged due to the ingress of seawater into the vessel during the voyage. It would then be for the claimant to prove that the carrier was negligent or that there had been a breach of Art III(1). This would require the claimant, first, to prove how the ingress had occurred. Given that evidence relating to the operation of the vessel is in the carrier's possession, it does not seem unreasonable that the burden of explaining exactly how the loss occurred should fall on the carrier. The position is compounded by the fact that, under English and Australian law, bad weather will fall within the exception notwithstanding that it was foreseeable that the vessel would encounter such weather on the voyage.[128] However, a different position has been taken by the courts of Canada,[129] the USA[130] and Israel.[131]

However, in many cases, the facts will be such that negligence, or lack of negligence, on the part of the carrier will be clearly established one way or another.[132] From a claimant's point of view, the harshness of the rule in *The Glendarroch* has been tempered somewhat by the willingness of the courts to infer unseaworthiness, as in *The Torenia*.[133] The fact that the vessel sank on the voyage led to an inference of unseaworthiness at the start of the voyage. The consequence was that the ingress of seawater, which damaged the cargo and which amounted to a 'peril of the sea', was only part of the cause of the loss. The excessive corrosion of the vessel's hull was a second, concurrent cause. The only exception in Art IV(2) that could cover it was subheading (p), but the shipowners were unable to establish that it was a 'latent defect not discoverable by due diligence'. Hobhouse J was prepared to accept that 'in all cases where a structural defect in the ship has contributed to the loss, the carrier has in effect to prove that he had exercised due diligence to make the ship seaworthy'.

This will not always be the case, however, as can be seen from the earlier decision of Lloyd J in *The Hellenic Dolphin*.[134] The ingress here came through a leaking seam due to the vessel's hull having received a severe blow at some point. No inference could be made that this blow occurred before the start of the voyage as it was equally likely that it could have occurred on the voyage itself. The shipowner was able to rely on the exception of 'peril of the sea'. Lloyd J also found that the shipowner had been able to establish that it took due diligence to make the vessel seaworthy before and at the beginning of the voyage. The judgment does not specify the significance of this finding to the shipowner's ability to rely on the exception of 'peril of the sea'. Suppose that the shipowner was unable to prove due diligence, but the claimant was still unable to prove a breach of Art III(1) because of the uncertainty as to when the vessel had sustained the blow to her hull. If the seawater ingress were regarded as the sole cause of the loss, then the shipowner would still have escaped liability. On the other hand, Hobhouse J's approach in *The Torenia* would entail viewing the loss as having been caused by two concurrent causes – the seawater ingress and the defective structure of the vessel. The fact that the defect might have occurred after the start of the voyage would not affect the shipowner's potential liability under Art III(2), which was what Hobhouse J was considering in *The Torenia*. There would now be two concurrent causes of loss and the shipowner would be able to escape liability only by proving that the second cause fell within the wording of exception (p). The result of these decisions is that the possibility of a carrier escaping liability under this exception

---

128 *The Bunga Seroja* [1999] 1 Lloyd's Rep 513. The view taken as to the ambit of this exception was, however, merely *obiter*, as positive findings were made that there had been no breach by the carrier of its obligations under either Art III(1) or (2).
129 *Good Fellow Lumber Sales Ltd v Verreault* [1971] 1 Lloyd's Rep 185.
130 *Thyssen Inc v SS Eurounity* [1994] AMC 1638 (2d Cir).
131 *Zim Israel Navigation v Israel Phoenix Ins*, noted (1999) LMCLQ 352.
132 As in *The Bunga Seroja* [1999] 1 Lloyd's Rep 513.
133 [1983] 2 Lloyd's Rep 210.
134 [1978] 2 Lloyd's Rep 336.

where there has been negligence on its part or that of its servants remains more theoretical than real.[135]

(d) Act of God

(e) Act of war

(f) Act of public enemies

(g) Arrest or restraint of princes, rulers or people, or seizure under legal process

(h) Quarantine restrictions

(i) Act or omission of the shipper or owner of the goods, his agent or representative

In *Ismail v Polish Ocean Lines*,[136] Lord Denning MR was of the view that this exception covered loss due to bad stowage, where the stowage had been performed under the directions of the charterer who was shipping the goods. However, the majority of the Court of Appeal based its decision on the grounds of estoppel. The distinction would be significant if the claimant in a similar situation was an indorsee of the bill of lading who had no knowledge of the shipper's officious intervention in the stowage of the cargo. In such a situation, no estoppel would affect the claimant. However, if Lord Denning's view is correct, the carrier would still have a defence under this exception.

(j) Strikes or lockouts or stoppage or restraint of labour from whatever cause, whether partial or general

(k) Riots and civil commotions

(l) Saving or attempting to save life or property at sea

This exception is a partial form of the much wider liberty to deviate that is granted by Art IV(4).

(m) Inherent defect, quality or vice of the goods

This defence covers loss that is due to the characteristics of the cargo rather than any defect in the mode of carriage. If the carrier properly follows the carriage instructions given by the shipper and the cargo cannot, in fact, safely be carried in accordance with them, the carrier will be able to rely on this defence. Thus, in *Albacora SRL v Westcott & Laurance Line (The Maltasian)*,[137] the shipowner, had it been in breach of Art III(2), would have been able to rely on this defence. The cargo in question could have been carried safely only if refrigerated. Not only did the shipper's carriage instruction not call for refrigeration, but the shipowner had no reason to suspect that the cargo required refrigeration.

The exception has recently been considered by the Supreme Court in *The Cendor MOPU*[138] in the context of an all risks marine insurance policy that excluded loss caused by inherent vice of the thing insured. The claim arose from the loss of an oil rig that was being carried on a barge from Texas to Malaysia. The rig, consisting of a platform and three legs, was carried with its legs in the air. During the voyage all of its legs broke off and fell into the sea. This was due to metal fatigue as a result of the motion of the waves, and the impact of a 'leg-breaking wave' which had caused the first leg to fail and which then caused greater stress to be placed on the remaining legs. The weather was within the range that could reasonably have been expected. The Supreme Court held that the

---

135 *The Stranna* [1938] P 69, CA, is just such a case, but was decided on common law principles. Had the Hague Rules applied, it is likely that the shipowner would have been held to have been in breach of Art III(1).
136 [1976] QB 893, CA.
137 [1966] 2 Lloyd's Rep 53, HL.
138 [2011] UKSC 5; [2011] 1 Lloyd's Rep 560.

loss did not fall within the exception of inherent vice. Under s 55(1) of the **Marine Insurance Act 1906**, whether a loss was covered by a marine insurance policy depended upon its proximate cause, which was not the cause that was closest in time to the loss, but that which was proximate in efficiency. Only where the fortuity operating on the goods came from the goods themselves could the proximate cause properly be said to be the inherent vice of the subject matter insured. Here the proximate cause was an external fortuitous accident or casualty of the seas, occurring under the influence of a leg-breaking wave of a direction and strength catching the first leg at just the right moment, leading to increased stress and collapse of the other two legs in turn. Where the only fortuity operating on the goods comes from the goods themselves, the proximate cause of the loss can properly be said to be the inherent vice or nature of the subject matter insured.

(n) Insufficiency of packing

The sufficiency of the packaging cannot be looked at in isolation, but has to be assessed in the light of the other cargo with which the package will be travelling. In *Silver v Ocean SS Co*,[139] packages of frozen eggs were held to be insufficient because their sharp edges would inevitably lead to them damaging each other during transit. The carrier's knowledge that the plaintiff's goods were insufficiently packed did not prevent it from relying on the exception. However, it was estopped from raising the defence because it had issued a clean bill of lading.

The position is less clear where the claimant's goods are damaged by insufficiently packed goods carried in the same vessel but which are not owned by the claimant. In *Goodwin, Ferreira & Co Ltd v Lamport & Holt*,[140] Roche J was of the view that the exception might extend to damage to the plaintiff's cargo when the damage was sustained by insufficiently packed goods carried in the same vessel, but not owned by the plaintiff. On the facts of the case, the carrier was able to rely on exception (q) below on proving that it had no reasonable means of discovering the defective condition of the adjacent package at the time of loading. However, if the carrier did have such knowledge, it is submitted that, *pace* Roche J, the exception in (n) should not apply.

(o) Insufficiency or inadequacy of marks

(p) Latent defects not discoverable by due diligence

This exception may appear to duplicate the 'due diligence' defence provided by Art IV(1). Nonetheless, Scrutton's view is that it covers defects that would not have been discoverable by due diligence, even if the shipowner could not show that he had, in fact, exercised due diligence.[141] However, this situation would probably not amount to a breach of Art III(1) in the light of the approach to the issue of causation adopted in *The Yamatogowa*.[142]

(q) Any other cause arising without the actual fault or privity of the carrier, or without the fault or neglect of the servants or agents of the carrier, but the burden of proof shall be on the person claiming the benefit of this exception to show that neither the actual fault or privity of the carrier nor the fault or neglect of the agents or servants of the carrier contributed to the loss or damage

This general exception is of limited use due to the proviso that the shipowner must establish that its fault or privity or by the fault or neglect of its servants or agents has not contributed to the loss.[143]

---

139 [1930] 1 KB 416, CA.
140 (1929) 34 Ll LR 192.
141 Scrutton, *Charterparties*, 20th edn, 1996, London: Sweet & Maxwell, p 450. Adopted by Branson J in *Corp Argentina de Productores de Carnes v Royal Mail Lines Ltd* (1939) 64 Ll L 188, 192, and quoted, without comment, by Staughton LJ in *The Antigoni* [1991] 1 Lloyd's Rep 209, CA.
142 [1990] 2 Lloyd's Rep 39, QB.
143 But it was successfully invoked in *Goodwin, Ferreira & Co Ltd v Lamport & Holt Ltd* (1929) 34 Ll L 192.

If the carrier's servants are even partially at fault, the carrier cannot rely on this exception. Although stevedores appointed to load or discharge the vessel are independent contractors, the men who they employ to discharge the cargo are regarded as servants of the shipowner for the purpose of subclause (q).[144]

However, in *Leesh River Tea Co Ltd v British India SN Co Ltd*,[145] damage was caused by the entry of water into a hold of tea due to the theft in the course of loading or discharging of one of the ship's storm valves by one or more of the stevedores. In these exceptional circumstances, the shipowners were able to rely on subclause (q); the stevedore, in committing the theft of part of the vessel, was not acting in the course of its employment by the shipowners and could not therefore be regarded as their servant or agent in respect of those acts. Had the theft been of cargo, the stevedore would have been acting within the course of its employment and the shipowner would have been unable to rely on the exception.[146]

If responsibility for loading or discharge is expressly allocated to the shipper or receiver by a 'free in' or 'free out' clause, stevedores will not be the servants of the shipowner, but of the shipper or receiver.[147] In this situation, cargo damage due to stevedore negligence will not be a breach by the shipowner of its obligations under Art III(2). It will therefore not need to rely on this exception, because it will not have been in breach of Art III(2) in the first place.

Deviation – Art IV (4)

An additional defence is given to the carrier, as follows: 'Any deviation in saving or attempting to save life or property at sea or any reasonable deviation shall not be deemed to be an infringement or breach of these Rules or of the contract of carriage, and the carrier shall not be liable for any loss or damage resulting therefrom'.[148] It is unclear whether a liberty clause will be rendered null and void by Art III(8) to the extent that it permits deviations other than those sanctioned by Art IV (4). The argument was raised in *Renton v Palmyra*[149] but in the House of Lords their Lordships expressed no view on it, holding that the clauses in issue were not provisions which permit deviations but which provide substituted ways of performing the contract in the event of strikes at the contractual loading or discharge ports.[150]

The one-year time limit – Art III(6) and (6)*bis*

This Article provides that:

> . . . the carrier and the ship shall in any event be discharged from all liability whatsoever in respect of the goods, unless suit is brought within one year of their delivery or of the date when they should have been delivered. This period may, however, be extended if the parties so agree after the cause of action has arisen.

---

144 RF Brown & Co Ltd v T & J Harrison (1927) 43 TLR 633.
145 [1967] 2 QB 250, CA.
146 As in Heyn v Ocean SS Co (1927) 137 LT 158.
147 The position pertaining in the absence of such a clause was set out by Erle CJ in Sack v Ford (1862) 13 CB (NS) 90, 100: 'Ordinarily speaking, the shipowner has by law cast upon him the risk of attending the loading, stowing and unloading of the cargo . . .'
148 See, also, the discussion of this provision in Chapter 4 at pp 89–92.
149 [1957] AC 149, HL.
150 In the Court of Appeal [1955] 2 Lloyd's Rep 744, Jenkins LJ, at 744, was of the view that the provision, by expressly permitting certain deviations, did not impliedly prohibit others. Hodson LJ, at 746, was of the view that the words 'properly and carefully' in Art III (2) '. . . relate to the manner and method of carriage and do not carry the implication that the discharge must take place at the port which is named in the bill of lading as the primary destination'. Another view, expressed by Wright J in Foreman and Ellams Ltd v Federal SN Co [1928] 2 KB 424, is that account would have to be taken of the terms of a liberty clause, subject to a reasonable interpretation, in determining whether or not there had been a reasonable deviation under Art IV(4).

The word 'whatsoever' does not appear in the Hague Rules and was added by the Hague-Visby Rules. Three other preliminary points should also be noted. First, time runs from 'delivery' and not from the completion of discharge. Where the cargo is delivered at a port other than the original port of discharge named in the bill of lading, 'delivery' will take place at the substituted port if it can still be said to have been made under the same transaction, albeit that the contract has been varied.[151] If this is not the case, time will run from the time at which delivery should have been made at the original port. Secondly, the time limit applies as regards claims against 'the carrier or the ship'. This wording, which also appears in Art III(8) and Art IV(3), was probably intended to do no more than cover claims that were made in *rem* against the ship rather than in *personam* against the carrier. Under English law, the time limit, and indeed the Rules in their entirety, can only be invoked by a carrier who has a contractual nexus with the claimant under a bill of lading.[152] Thirdly, under English law, the time bar applies equally to arbitration as to litigation.[153] The position is different under US law. However, if a contract subject to English law incorporates the provisions of the **US Carriage of Goods by Sea Act of 1936**, those provisions will be construed in the light of English law rather than of US law.[154]

Article III(6)*bis* of the Hague-Visby Rules, but not the Hague Rules, allows indemnity actions against third parties to be commenced outside the one-year period 'if brought within the time allowed by the law of the court seized of the case'. However, this time '*shall not be less than three months commencing from the day when the person bringing such action for indemnity has settled the claim or has been served with process in the action against himself*'. Although the contract under which the indemnity is sought must be subject to the Hague-Visby Rules, there is no requirement that the Rules must also govern the contract under which the claim was initially brought by the cargo owner. Thus, in *The Xingcheng and The Andros*,[155] a claim was made against the head carrier under a through bill, which was not subject to the Hague-Visby Rules. It then sought to claim an indemnity against the second carrier under the bill of lading that it had issued when the goods were trans-shipped. This bill was subject to the Hague-Visby Rules and therefore the first carrier was entitled to rely on Art III(6)*bis*.

The effect of the time bar is to extinguish the claimant's rights, not merely to bar its claim.[156] This was one of the reasons why the defendant in *The Aries*[157] was unable to set up by way of defence to a shipowner's claim for freight its cargo claim, which had become time-barred. The drastic consequences of becoming time-barred means that it is of the utmost importance that the claimant identify the correct defendant against which to issue its writ before the expiry of the one-year deadline. After the expiry of this period, it will not be possible to join the correct defendant, as was held in *The Jay Bola*.[158] The problem applies equally where proceedings are commenced by the wrong claimant. The correct claimant cannot be joined after the expiry of the time bar.[159]

Where the relevant contract provides for disputes to be resolved by arbitration, s 12 of the **Arbitration Act 1996**, which replaces s 27 of the **Arbitration Act 1950,** gives the court discretion to extend the time for commencing arbitration. This discretion is not exercisable when the time limit under Art III(6) applies by virtue of statute – for example, **COGSA 1971**[160] – because s 12 is

---

151 *The Sonia* [2003] EWCA Civ 664; [2003] 2 Lloyd's Rep 201, CA.
152 Or under a sea waybill where s 1(6)(b) of COGSA 1971 applies.
153 *The Merak* [1965] P 223, CA.
154 *The Stolt Sydness* [1997] 1 Lloyd's Rep 273, QB.
155 [1987] 1 WLR 1213, PC.
156 However, the one-year time bar does not operate to extinguish defences. Therefore, in *The Fiona* [1994] 2 Lloyd's Rep 506, CA, the shipper was successfully able to raise, as a defence to a claim against it by the shipowner under Art III(6) in respect of a shipment of dangerous goods, an allegation that the dominant cause of the damage had been the shipowner's breach of its obligations under Art III(1).
157 [1977] 1 WLR 185, HL.
158 [1992] 1 Lloyd's Rep 62, QB.
159 *The Leni* [1992] 2 Lloyd's Rep 62, QB.
160 As in *The Antares* [1987] 1 Lloyd's Rep 424, in which the Court of Appeal considered the equivalent provision, s 27, in the Arbitration Act 1950.

expressed to be without prejudice to any statutory provisions regarding the time for commencing arbitration proceedings. However, *dicta* of the Court of Appeal in *Nea Agrex SA v Baltic Shipping Co Ltd* (*The Agios Lazaros*)[161] relating to s 27 of the **Arbitration Act 1950** suggest that, where the Hague or Hague-Visby Rules apply purely by contractual incorporation, as with a clause paramount in a charterparty, the court will retain its discretion to extend time beyond the one-year limit contained in the Rules. This probably remains the position under s 12 of the **Arbitration Act 1996**.

Particular problems may arise in suing the correct defendant where the vessel is on demise charter, for what appears to be a shipowner's bill of lading will be a demise charterer's bill. In *The Stolt Loyalty*,[162] a claim under a 'shipowner's' bill of lading was directed to the demise charterers. Their solicitors gave the plaintiffs an extension of time on behalf of the 'owners' and this was held to refer not to the actual shipowner but to the 'owner' for the purpose of the bill of lading. Where a claim under a shipowner's bill is erroneously directed to the charterer, the charterer may be estopped from denying that it is a party to the bill if it continues to deal with the claim without alerting the claimant to its mistake.[163] However, there can be no estoppel where the defendant is unaware of the claimant's mistake.[164]

A less serious mistake is to plead the wrong cause of action against the correct defendant. In this situation, the cause of action pleaded may be amended after the expiry of the time bar. In *The Pionier*,[165] the plaintiff initially pleaded its claim under the bill of lading and then amended it to claim under the charterparty. It was allowed leave to re-amend after the expiry of the time bar to revert to its original claim under the bill of lading.[166]

If the correct defendant is sued in a competent jurisdiction within the time limit, the claimant may be able to take further proceedings in other jurisdictions outside the time limit. In *The Nordglimt*,[167] the plaintiff commenced proceedings in Belgium, where the cargo had been loaded, within the time limit. The Belgian court became a 'competent' court once the defendant submitted to its jurisdiction. The plaintiff was then able to arrest the defendant's vessel in England by serving a writ *in rem* after expiry of the time limit. Hobhouse J left open the question of whether the commencement of an action *in rem* within time would allow *in personam* proceedings to be commenced out of time. In *The Havhelt*,[168] Saville J held that an action brought in England in breach of a Norwegian jurisdiction clause was not a 'suit' for the purposes of Art III(6). Rix J reached a similar conclusion in *The Finnrose*[169] in respect of an action commenced in a competent jurisdiction but subsequently dismissed for want of prosecution.

The time bar applies to all liabilities whether derived from breaches of Art III(1) or (2). The Hague-Visby time bar, which applies to 'all liability whatsoever', has been held to cover a claim for quasi-deviation arising out of unauthorised deck stowage[170] and even a claim based on alleged theft of the cargo by the carrier, to which Art IV(2)(e)[171] would otherwise have applied.[172] However, the position is less clear where a misdelivery claim is involved. Article III(6), by its wording, is the only

161 [1976] QB 933, disapproving contrary *dicta* of Kerr J in *The Angeliki* [1973] 2 Lloyd's Rep 226.
162 [1993] 2 Lloyd's Rep 281, CA.
163 See *The Henrik Sif* [1982] 1 Lloyd's Rep 456, QB.
164 *The August Leonhardt* [1984] 1 Lloyd's Rep 322, where the shipowner's P&I Club gave a time extension conditional on charterers granting a similar extension and the plaintiff erroneously assumed that the Club would obtain this extension from the charterers that were also entered with it.
165 [1995] 1 Lloyd's Rep 223, QB.
166 See, also, *Anglo Irish Beef Processors International v Federated Stevedores Geelong* [1997] 1 Lloyd's Rep 207, Sup Ct of Victoria, CA (Aus), where an alternative claim in contract under the Hague Rules was allowed to be pleaded after the one-year limit, the initial tort claim having been commenced within that period.
167 [1987] 2 Lloyd's Rep 470, QB.
168 [1993] 1 Lloyd's Rep 523.
169 [1994] 1 Lloyd's Rep 559.
170 *The Antares* [1987] 1 Lloyd's Rep 424, CA.
171 The provision in the Hague-Visby Rules that removes the carrier's right to limit in the event of certain extremely serious breaches.
172 *The Captain Gregos* [1990] 1 Lloyd's Rep 310, CA. The carrier was able to rely on the Hague-Visby Rules by virtue of the doctrine of implied contract.

exception or limitation in the Rules that is capable of covering such a claim and it can plausibly be argued that the rewording of this provision in the Hague-Visby Rules was, by the addition of the word 'whatsoever', intended to cover just this sort of claim. The issue is whether the words 'all liability whatsoever in respect of the goods' refer to all liabilities under the bill of lading contract or merely to all liabilities imposed by the Hague-Visby Rules.[173] If the latter interpretation is correct, then this provision cannot cover misdelivery claims, as the shipowner's delivery obligations are not expressly mentioned in Art III(1), (2) and (3), which set out the carrier's obligations under the Rules. Such an interpretation, although probably correct linguistically, is liable to lead to the undesirable result that a suitably drafted express time-bar clause in a bill of lading that covers misdelivery claims would not be subject to Art III(8) in the event that it imposed a time limit of less than a year. On the other hand, the fact that the Article specifically applies the time limit from delivery as opposed to discharge could be taken as indicating that misdelivery claims do, in fact, fall within its ambit.[174] It is, however, arguable that misdelivery amounts to a breach of the carrier's duty properly and carefully to 'care for' the cargo under Art III(2), although, in many cases, there will be no breach because delivery will take place after discharge, outside the temporal ambit of the Rules.[175]

The one-year time limit may be extended by agreement between the claimant and defendant. On the other hand, if the bill of lading provides for a *shorter* time limit, the relevant clause is invalid, but only to the extent that it conflicts with the Rules. In *The Ion*,[176] a bill of lading incorporated a Centrocon charter with a three-month time limit in the arbitration clause. The clause was held to be void, but only to the extent that it conflicted with the Hague Rules. Therefore, the bill of lading was subject to arbitration, but with a one-year time limit under the Rules. However, a time limit of under one year will be valid to the extent that it regulates events arising outside the scope of the Rules, such as the carrier's liability for the cargo after its discharge.[177]

An additional time limit is provided by Art III(6), which provides that failure to give written notice to the carrier of the general nature of the loss or damage to the cargo within three days of delivery shall be prima facie evidence of the delivery by the carrier of the goods as described in the bill of lading. However, this provision is of little practical importance, as the cargo owner will almost certainly have some evidence as to the condition of the cargo on discharge that will displace the presumption. Indeed, without such evidence, the cargo claimant will be unable to prove receipt of damaged cargo and so be able to prove neither breach of the carriage contract nor any loss.

The package limitation

Hague Rules

Article IV(5) of the Hague Rules provides a limit on the amount recoverable from the carrier or ship of £100 sterling per package or unit. The limit is expressed to apply 'in any event'.[178] This limit may be avoided by the declaration, by the shipper, of the nature and value of the goods

---

173 Scrutton takes the view (op cit fn 141, p 435) that misdelivery claims probably fall outside the ambit of the Rules altogether.

174 See *Carver on Bills of Lading*, op cit fn 33, 9.162 and also *obiter dicta* of Kirby P in *The Zhi Jiang Kou* [1991] 1 Lloyd's Rep 493, Sup Ct (NSW), 516.

175 *The MSC Amsterdam* [2007] EWHC 944 (Comm); [2007] 2 All ER (Comm) 149, *per* Aikens J, *obiter*, at [106].

176 [1971] 1 Lloyd's Rep 541.

177 *The Zhi Jiang Kou* [1991] 1 Lloyd's Rep 493, Sup Ct (NSW).

178 In *The Happy Ranger* [2002] EWCA Civ 694; [2002] 2 Lloyd's Rep 357, the Court of Appeal held that these words have the effect that reliance on the package limitation is not dependent upon the fulfilment of any of the carrier's obligations under Art III. The Court of Appeal applied the same reasoning in *The Kapitan Petko Voivoda* [2003] EWCA Civ 451; [2003] 2 Lloyd's Rep 1, in holding that a carrier could still limit its liability even when the loss had been caused by unauthorised stowage of the cargo on deck.

on the face of the bill. This declaration is prima facie evidence, but is not binding or conclusive on the carrier.[179] Article IX provides that 'the monetary units mentioned in these Rules are taken to be gold value'. Uncertainty as to the effect of this provision on the £100 package limitation led to the adoption of the 'gold clause', which provided for an express limitation of £200 sterling per package.[180] The wisdom of adopting such a clause was confirmed in *The Rosa S*,[181] where the Hague Rules limit was held to refer to £100 gold value at current prices – namely, £6,630.50 at the date of the delivery of the cargo, 1 June 1984.

Article IV(5) concludes by providing that: 'Neither the carrier nor the ship shall be responsible in any event for loss or damage to or in connection with goods if the nature or value thereof has been knowingly misstated by the shipper in the bill of lading.' It might be thought that the effect of this provision is only to apply the limitation figure in circumstances when there has been a declaration of the nature and value of the goods with a view to avoiding the operation of the package limitation. In support of this construction is the fact that this provision appears in the Article dealing with limitation and refers to 'the nature and value' of the goods. These terms only appear in the Rules in the context of the declaration on the front of the bill, which will enable the claimant to avoid the effect of the package limitation. This was the view taken, *obiter*, in Australia in *Frank Hammond Pty Ltd v Huddart Parker Ltd and the Australian Shipping Board*.[182] However, the wording of this provision – in particular, the words 'in any event' – does clearly indicate that such a misstatement would give the carrier or ship a complete defence to an action, whether brought by the original shipper or by a third party, even though there was no causal nexus between the loss or damage and the misstatement. It would also appear that the defence would operate notwithstanding that the loss or damage had been caused by the breach by the carrier or ship of their own obligations under the Rules.

The Hague-Visby Rules

The Hague-Visby Rules also contain a package limitation, but it is subject to the following important differences.

Calculation of limitation

The package limit in the Hague Rules was fixed by reference to a fixed unit of currency. Over time, it was inevitable that the value of the package limit would be eroded by inflation. To solve this problem, the Hague-Visby Rules originally adopted a package limitation based on a fictitious currency, the Poincaré franc, the value of which was tied to that of a specific quantity of gold.[183] In December 1979, the Brussels Protocol replaced the Poincaré franc with the special drawing right (the SDR), which is currently based on a basket of four currencies: the pound, the dollar, the euro and the yen. The Protocol was implemented by the UK through s 2(4) of the **Merchant Shipping Act 1981**.[184] The limitation figure will be converted into the currency in which the loss was felt by the claimant.[185] The exchange rate will be that applicable at the date of the loss or damage. Article IV(5)(g) allows the parties to agree a different

---

179 Equivalent provisions exist in Art IV(5)(a) and (f) of the Hague-Visby Rules. The true value of the goods is rarely declared on the bill of lading, as to do so would attract a higher freight rate.
180 In *The Tasman Discoverer* [2004] UKPC 22; [2004] 2 Lloyd's Rep 647, PC (NZ), the incorporation of the Hague Rules was held not to bring in the provisions of Art IX when the bill of lading had an express clause dealing with limitation.
181 [1988] 2 Lloyd's Rep 574, QB.
182 [1956] VLR 496, Sup Ct (Vic).
183 The limitation figures were 10,000 Poincaré francs per package or 30 Poincaré francs per kilo.
184 It should be noted, however, that not all parties to the Hague-Visby Rules are party to the Brussels Protocol.
185 See *The Mosconici* [2001] 2 Lloyd's Rep 313, QB, where an Italian claimant was entitled to claim in US dollars on the grounds that it was a subsidiary company of a substantial US corporate group. This outweighed the fact that replacements for the lost cargo were made in Italy and paid for in lira.

limitation figure which results in a higher limit of liability than the amount provided for by the Hague-Visby Rules.[186]

Gross weight alternative

The Hague-Visby Rules provide an alternative limitation figure of two units of account per kilogram[187] of gross weight of the goods lost or damaged. This enables a defendant to limit its liability for damage to goods, such as bulk cargo, which are not carried in packages. Where goods are carried in packages, the claimant can rely on whichever limitation figure is the higher. In *The Limnos*,[188] Burton J held that the gross weight alternative must be calculated solely by reference to the weight of cargo that is physically lost or damaged and excludes the weight of cargo that has suffered a purely economic loss, even though such a claim is subject to limitation. Therefore, only the package limitation would apply to a claim for delay where the cargo arrives late, but in sound condition. With bulk cargo, no limitation figure could be set for such a claim.

Containers

The Hague-Visby Rules contain specific provision to deal with containerised goods and this will be examined in the following section on the application of the Rules to containers.

Containers and the Rules

Article III(1)

This Article imposes obligations on the shipowner not only as regards the ship and its crew, but also obliges the carrier to exercise due diligence to 'make the holds, refrigerating and cool chamber and all other parts of the ship in which the goods are carried, fit and safe for their reception, carriage and preservation'.

A question arises as to whether this obligation extends to containers. Where they are supplied by the carrier, there is no logical reason not to include them within the scope of Art III(1) and this would reflect the approach taken by a US court in *The Red Jacket*.[189] There, a defective container was supplied to the shipper who packed it prior to its being loaded onto the vessel. During the voyage, it broke loose during heavy weather and, as a consequence, a total of 43 containers were swept overboard. The court held that the obligations of seaworthiness imposed by the **US Carriage of Goods by Sea Act of 1936** applied to all of the ship's equipment, including a container supplied by the carrier. The decision leaves open the question of whether the obligation of seaworthiness extends to containers that are supplied by the shipper. It is possible that the obligation might still apply in these circumstances, at least as regards a claim for damage sustained by other shippers as a result of the defective condition of the container.

In any event, the carrier might still be liable for breach of its obligations under Art III(2) if, for example, it accepts, without entering a reservation on the bill of lading, a shipper's container that is in a patently bad condition. However, in *Empire Distributors Inc v US Lines*,[190] a carrier was successfully able to defend an action brought against it by a shipper who had supplied a cheaper, unrefrigerated

---

186 Theoretically this could be achieved by incorporation of the Hague Rules bringing in the £100 package limitation which would be valid to the extent that it resulted in a higher limit of liability than the amount provided for by the Hague-Visby Rules. However, it was improbable that rational commercial people could have intended a single contract of carriage to be covered simultaneously by two differing limitation of liability regimes, with differing provisions and accordingly the Hague Rules limitation figure was not applied. *The Superior Pescadores* [2014] EWHC 971 (Comm).

187 That is, 2,000 SDRs per ton.

188 [2008] EWHC 1036 (Comm); [2008] 2 Lloyd's Rep 166, noted [2008] LMCLQ 439.

189 [1978] 1 Lloyd's Rep 300, US Ct.

190 [1987] AMC 455, SD Ga 1986, US Ct.

container for the supply of wine that had been damaged by exposure to hot weather while awaiting shipment at the container terminal.

It is unlikely that the obligation under Art III(1) can apply to damage caused by a defective container prior to loading.[191] This could become an issue if the relevant contract extended the carrier's period of responsibility to the period during which the containers were being stored in a container depot prior to loading. The Hague-Visby Rules could have no relevance to any claim for damage caused during this period due to the defective condition of the container because of the provisions of Art I(b). The carrier's responsibility during the period of its contract that relates to storing the goods prior to their carriage by sea will be determined according to its status as a bailee, subject to any limitations contained in its contract with the shipper. The only statutory limitations placed on this contract as it relates to the pre-loading stage will be those imposed by the **Unfair Contracts Act 1977** – in particular, ss 2(2) and 3.

Article III(2)

Where the goods are damaged due to poor stowage within the container by the shipper, it is unlikely that the carrier will be found to be in breach of Art III(2). Furthermore, it should also be able to rely on the defences contained in Art IV(2)(i)(n) and (q). In the USA, it has been held[192] that the carrier is under no duty to open and inspect a shipper-supplied container and it is likely that an English court would come to the same conclusion.

Package limitation

Where goods are packed in containers, the bill of lading will usually note the shipment of the container 'said to contain' the relevant number of packages. What is the relevant package for the purpose of applying the limitation figure: the container or the packages said to be contained within it?

The Hague Rules

Until recently, there was no English authority on what constitutes a 'package' for the purposes of the Hague Rules. In *The Aegis Spirit*,[193] the US court held that goods in cartons stowed in the carrier's containers constituted the 'package' for the purpose of the US $500 package limitation, and not the container itself. The reason of the decision is given in the following extract of the judgment of Beeks DJ:

> I would liken these containers to detachable stowage compartments of the ship. They simply serve to divide the ship's overall cargo space into smaller, more serviceable *loci*. Shipper's packages are quite literally 'stowed' in the containers utilising stevedoring practices and materials analogous to those employed in traditional on board stowage. The logic of this view is made plainer yet upon noting . . . that Tokai's bill of lading covers every piece of cargo packaged by Matshushita/Japan but in no way affects title to the containers which remains in Tokai [the time charterer who issued the 'charterer's bills']. This fact underscores the fundamental distinction between shipper-packaged goods and the carrier-owned containers.

Applying this reasoning, it is possible that the container might be regarded as the package if it were owned by the shipper rather than the carrier.[194]

---

191 Although it would be extremely difficult to prove exactly when the damage occurred, if the container were sealed on stuffing and a bill of lading, claused 'said to contain', were issued.

192 *Reechel v Italia di Navigazione SpA* [1988] AMC 2748, 690 F Supp, D Md 1988, US Ct.

193 [1977] 1 Lloyd's Rep 93.

194 An interesting secondary issue in the case was whether the shipowner could rely on the same package limitation (incorporated into the charter by a clause paramount) by way of defence to a claim brought against it by the charterer Tokai in respect of damage to Tokai's container. The court held that it could not.

The Court of Appeal considered the issue in *The River Gurara*.[195] The bill of lading listed a number of containers 'said to contain' a specified number of separately packed items. The relevant 'package' under the Hague Rules was held to be not the container, but the separate packages within it. Initially, Colman J decided that the wording used on the bill of lading, notwithstanding the use of 'said to contain', indicated that the parties' intention was that the packages themselves, not the container, should constitute the 'package' for limitation purposes.[196] A clause in the bill of lading that stated that the container was to be regarded as the 'package' if the goods were stuffed by the shipper was held to be rendered void by Art III(8).[197] The Court of Appeal upheld the decision, but the majority did so on another ground. Phillips LJ held that if the consignee could objectively prove the number of containers loaded, then limitation should be based on that number, irrespective of the wording of the bill of lading.[198] These divergent approaches made no difference to the outcome of the case. The approaches would, however, lead to a different result when the bill of lading contains no enumeration as to the packages inside the container. Colman J's approach would lead to the container being treated as the package, which would equate with the position under Art IV(5)(c) of the Hague-Visby Rules, discussed below. In contrast, that of the Court of Appeal would entail that a separate package limit would still apply to each package that the claimant could prove to have been inside the container at the time of shipment. The Court of Appeal's approach also makes it less easy to decide on what constitutes the package when packages are packed within packages. Colman J's approach would simply require an examination of the wording of the bill. Thus, with one bill that recorded the loading of one container 'stc 8 pallets stc 1855 bundles . . . veneer', Colman J held that each bundle constituted a package because of the manner in which it had been described on the bill. The Court of Appeal's approach would require an assessment of whether a bundle could objectively be said to constitute a package.[199]

The Hague Rules package limitation will still be relevant if the claimant's claim is subject to the terms of the Hague Rules rather than the Hague-Visby Rules. This will be the case, for example, where cargo is discharged in the UK and loaded in a state that is a signatory to the Hague Rules but not to the Hague-Visby Rules.

The Hague-Visby Rules

The Hague-Visby Rules contain a new provision, Art IV(5)(c), dealing specifically with containers, in the following terms:

> Where a container, pallet or similar article of transport is used to consolidate goods, the number of packages or units enumerated in the bill of lading as packed in such article of transport shall be deemed the number of packages or units for the purpose of this paragraph as far as these packages or units are concerned. Except as aforesaid such article of transport shall be considered the package or unit.

Only where the number of goods packed within the container are not enumerated[200] would the container be capable of constituting the 'package'. It is likely that the goods are still 'enumerated', even if the statement in the bill of lading as to their number is qualified by wording such as 'said to contain'.[201] Any attempt to avoid this provision by including a clause in the bill of lading defining

---

195 [1997] 4 All ER 498.
196 [1996] 2 Lloyd's Rep 53.
197 See, also, *The Mormaclynx* [1971] 2 Lloyd's Rep 476, US Ct.
198 That part of Colman J's decision relating to Art III(8) was not challenged before the Court of Appeal.
199 Phillips LJ was of the view that, under this bill, each bundle would constitute a separate package.
200 Presumably, this 'enumeration' would cover enumeration under a 'said to contain' clause on the front of the bill of lading.
201 Op cit Scrutton fn 141, p 451; *Carver on Bills of Lading*, op cit fn 33, at 9.237. However, Carver, *Carriage of Goods by Sea*, op cit fn 33, Vol 1, p 557, took a contrary view.

the 'package' as the container, such as that used in *The River Gurara*, would be ineffective by virtue of Art III(8). In *The El Greco*,[202] it was held that 'said to contain' wording constituted the necessary 'enumeration' for determining what constituted a package. However, there had been no enumeration of the number of packages or units 'as packed'. These words meant that there had to be words in the bill of lading which made clear the number of packages or units separately packed for transportation. The bill of lading here stated that the container was said to contain '200,945 pieces, posters and prints' but gave no indication as to how these items were packed. Accordingly there had been no enumeration and the applicable limitation figure was either one package, the container, or the weight alternative for the damaged goods, which came to AUS\$38,250, whichever was the higher.

Loss of the right to limit

Under both sets of Rules, the package limitation is equally applicable to claims for breach of Art III(1) as to those for breach of Art III(2). As regards Art III(1), this has been confirmed by the decision of the Court of Appeal in *The Happy Ranger*.[203] The Court of Appeal has also held, in *The Kapitan Petko Voivoda*,[204] that the right to limit still applies notwithstanding that the cargo has been damaged by reason of its unauthorised carriage on deck, a 'quasi-deviation'. In both cases, the decision of the Court of Appeal was reinforced by reference to the wording of Art IV(5) that 'Neither the carrier nor the ship shall *in any event* be or become liable for any loss or damage to or in connection with the goods in an amount exceeding 100 pounds sterling per package or unit' (emphasis added). A potential drawback of the latter decision is that, under the Hague Rules, a carrier will still be entitled to limit in circumstances in which, under the Hague-Visby Rules, it would have lost the right to limit by virtue of Art IV(5)(e), discussed below.

The Hague-Visby Rules have introduced a new provision, Art IV(5)(e), which provides for the loss of the right to limit in the following circumstances:

> Neither the carrier nor the ship shall be entitled to the benefit of the limitation of liability provided for in this paragraph if it is proved that the damage resulted from an act or omission of the carrier done with intent to cause damage, or recklessly and with knowledge that damage would probably result.

It should first be noted that the provision demands an enquiry into the state of the mind of the carrier and not that of its servants. The requisite culpability must be shown in an individual of sufficient seniority in the carrier's management as to embody the carrier. The reference to 'the carrier' was held in *The European Enterprise*[205] not to encompass acts or omissions of the master. A contrary view was expressed by a New Zealand court in *The Pembroke*,[206] but this was not followed in *The Tasman Pioneer*,[207] where the issue was whether the carrier had lost its right to limit on the basis of tonnage limitation.

As regards the mental state that needs to be established, in the absence of authority on this provision, regard must be had to similar provisions in the international conventions that govern other modes of carriage. In *Goldman v Thai Airways*,[208] the Court of Appeal considered the equivalent section in the **Warsaw Convention**, which governs claims against air carriers. It stressed that the

---

202 [2004] 2 Lloyd's Rep. 537, Fed Ct (Aus).
203 [2002] EWCA Civ 694; [2002] 2 Lloyd's Rep 357.
204 [2003] EWCA Civ 451; [2003] 2 Lloyd's Rep 1, overruling the decision of Hirst J in *The Chanda* [1989] 2 Lloyd's Rep 494.
205 [1989] 2 Lloyd's Rep 185.
206 [1995] 2 Lloyd's Rep 290.
207 [2003] 2 Lloyd's Rep 713, NZ Ct.
208 [1983] 1 WLR 1186.

wording required not only that the act or omission be done 'recklessly', but also that it be done 'with knowledge that damage would probably result'. On the facts, the right to limit was not lost. Although the pilot was reckless, his state of mind was not such as to satisfy the second requirement. Accordingly, it will be very difficult to establish that a carrier should lose its right to limit under this provision.

Shipper's liability under the Rules

At common law, the shipper owes an absolute duty to notify the shipowner of any dangerous characteristics in the cargo to be shipped. The reason for imposing liability is that risks inherent in the cargo should be borne by the shipper, who is better able to ascertain them than the carrier. The shipper's lack of knowledge of the dangerous characteristics of the cargo will not amount to a defence.[209] However, it will have a defence if those characteristics were known, or ought to have been known, by the shipowner. Thus, in *The Athanasia Comninos*,[210] a time charterer was not liable to a shipowner in respect of an explosion that occurred in a cargo of coal due to emissions of methane. This was a risk inherent in the carriage of coal of which the shipowner ought to have been aware. Therefore, by consenting to carry coal, it assumed the risks attendant in carrying such a cargo. The shipowners had argued that this particular type of coal had a higher rate of methane emission than ordinary coal. Mustill J rejected this and held that this did not mean that the risk in carriage was different in kind from that associated with the carriage of ordinary coal; there was merely a difference in the degree of risk. Where, however, the cargo is due to some defect in its condition, of which the shipowner cannot be expected to be aware, rather than due to the risks inherent in the carriage of the cargo in its usual condition, the shipper will be liable.[211] A cargo can be inherently dangerous, or dangerous because it has not been appropriately treated. In *The Amphion*,[212] a shipper was liable under its charterparty for damage to the vessel caused by a cargo of bagged fishmeal that ignited during unloading. The shipper had failed to apply antioxidant treatment, which substantially reduces the risk of ignition, to the cargo. A cargo can also be physically safe, but still regarded as dangerous due to non-physical hazards associated with it. In *Mitchell, Cotts & Co v Steel Bros & Co Ltd*,[213] the shipper was liable for delays in the unloading of a cargo of rice at Piraeus during the First World War, due to its inability to obtain the necessary permission from the British government under wartime regulations.[214] It is likely that a cargo will be legally dangerous only when it is subject to a prohibition by the public authorities at the port of discharge. A cargo is not dangerous merely because its condition is such as to result in delays in the process of discharge.[215] In *Bunge SA v ADM do Brasil Ltda*,[216] Tomlinson J held that there was no general principle that cargo was to be regarded as dangerous if it was liable to cause delay to the vessel and/or to the carriage of other cargo, in the absence of some local legal obstacle to its carriage or discharge. A cargo of soyabean meal pellets that had been loaded along with rats did not constitute a dangerous cargo merely because it had caused delay to the carrier. The cargo plainly posed no threat of damage to the ship itself and did not pose a physical danger to another maize cargo on board; nor was the imposition of quarantine or dumping of the entire cargo to be expected.

---

209 *Brass v Maitland* (1856) 26 LJ QB 49, QB, Crompton J dissenting.
210 [1990] 1 Lloyd's Rep 277, QB.
211 As in *The Fiona* [1993] 1 Lloyd's Rep 257, QB; [1994] 2 Lloyd's Rep 506, CA.
212 [1991] 2 Lloyd's Rep 101, QB.
213 [1916] 2 KB 611.
214 See, further, on the definition of dangerous cargo, Rose, F, 'Cargo risks "dangerous goods"' (1996) 55 CLJ 601 and Girvin, S, 'Shipper's liability for the carriage of dangerous cargoes by sea' (1996) LMCLQ 487.
215 *Transoceanica Societa Italiana di Navigazione v H S Shipton & Sons* [1923] 1 KB 31.
216 [2009] EWHC 845 (Comm); [2009] 2 Lloyd's Rep 175.

Both the Hague and Hague-Visby Rules contain identical provisions on dangerous cargo in Art IV(6), which provides:

Goods of an inflammable, explosive or dangerous nature to the shipment whereof the carrier, master or agent of the carrier has not consented with knowledge of their nature and character, may at any time before discharge be landed at any place, or destroyed or rendered innocuous by the carrier without compensation and *the shipper of such goods shall be liable for all damages and expenses directly or indirectly arising out of or resulting from such shipment.* If any such goods shipped with such knowledge and consent shall become a danger to the ship or cargo, they may in like manner be landed at any place, or destroyed or rendered innocuous by the carrier without liability on the part of the carrier except to general average, if any. [emphasis added]

The emphasis indicates that the Rules essentially replicate the existing common law liability, as well as protecting the carrier if it has to land, destroy or render innocuous the dangerous cargo.

In *The Giannis NK*,[217] the House of Lords confirmed that liability under Art IV(6) was strict and, furthermore, could be imposed even when the cargo posed no direct physical risk to other cargo or to the ship. The shipper, therefore, was held liable for loading a cargo of groundnuts that, unknown to it, had been infected by khapra beetle, as a consequence of which the authorities, at the port of discharge, condemned the cargo, so requiring the shipowner to dump it at sea. However, it is perhaps unfortunate that their Lordships did not take the opportunity simply to equate liability under Art IV(6) with that pertaining at common law. Lord Lloyd declined to comment on whether Art IV(6) would apply when the cargo was physically safe but delay was caused by the operation of a local regulation relating to a characteristic of the cargo.[218]

The Rules appear to give the shipper, but probably not a third-party holder of the bill of lading,[219] a wide-ranging defence by virtue of Art IV(3), which provides:

The shipper shall not be responsible for loss or damage sustained by the carrier or the ship or resulting from any cause without the act, fault or neglect of the shipper, his agents or his servants.

However, in *The Giannis NK*, the House of Lords held that this provision did not qualify the shipper's obligations under Art IV(6). Article IV(3) will, therefore, be of limited use to a shipper.

The shipper can escape liability if it can show that the loss or damage was at least partly caused by the negligence of the carrier. In *The Fiona*,[220] the Court of Appeal exonerated the shipper on this basis when the shipowner's breach was the dominant cause of the loss. It also held that the one-year time limit under Art III(6) did not operate so as to preclude the shipper from invoking the carrier's breach of Art III(1) by way of defence to the carrier's claim under Art IV(6). In *The Kapitan Sakharov*,[221] the Court of Appeal confirmed that, for such a defence to operate, the shipper need not prove that the carrier's negligence was the dominant cause; it is enough if it can show that it is an effective cause, as would be the case where a claim is made against the carrier for breach of its duty under Art III(1). In the case, undisclosed dangerous goods were shipped in a container and ignited during the voyage.[222] The resultant fire spread to an inflammable cargo that had been wrongfully stowed under deck, in breach of Art III(1). The shipper was held liable for that part of the damage caused solely by the initial fire,

---

217 [1998] AC 605, noted (1998) LMCLQ 480.
218 Such pure economic loss is, however, recoverable at common law. See *Chandris v Isbrandtsen-Moller Co Inc* [1951] 1 KB 240.
219 *The Aegean Sea* [1998] 2 Lloyd's Rep 39, QB.
220 [1994] 2 Lloyd's Rep 506.
221 [2000] 2 Lloyd's Rep 255.
222 This rendered the vessel unseaworthy, but not so as to amount to a breach of Art III(1) by the shipowner.

but not for the consequent damage that resulted once the fire spread to the inflammable cargo stowed below deck. If a concurrent cause is the carrier's breach of its duty under Art III(2), the carrier will still be entitled to an indemnity if the breach falls within the exceptions in Art IV(2).[223]

Finally, one needs to address the question of whether this liability may be transferred to third parties.[224] At common law, it appears that this is indeed the case, provided that the third party triggers the provisions of s 3 of **COGSA 1992**, even though the third party will generally have no means of knowing about the dangerous characteristics of the cargo prior to taking delivery.[225] However, the reference in Art IV(6) to 'the shipper' makes it arguable that liability under the Rules is not transferable to subsequent holders of the bill of lading.[226] This analysis is borne out by the decisions of the Court of Appeal in *The Filikos*,[227] considering the term in Art IV(2)(i), and of Thomas J in *The Aegean Sea*,[228] considering the term in Art IV(3). However, both Lords Lloyd of Berwick and Steyn in *The Giannis NK* assumed that all of the shipper's original liabilities were transferred under the **Bills of Lading Act 1855**. Such transfer was by way of addition to the liability of the original shipper, rather than by way of substitution. The continuing liability of the shipper is now made explicit by the wording of s 3(3) of **COGSA 1992**.

---

223 *The Aconcagua*, per *obiter dicta* of Christopher Clarke J, [2009] EWHC 1880 (Comm); [2010] 1 Lloyd's Rep 1, aff'd [2010] EWCA Civ 1403; [2011] 1 Lloyd's Rep 683. On the facts the carrier's breach in stowing the dangerous cargo next to a fuel tank, which was heated during the voyage, was not causative of the explosion of the cargo.
224 See, further, Baughen, S and Campbell, N, 'Apportionment of risk and the carriage of dangerous cargo' [2001] 1 IML 3.
225 *The Berge Sisar* [1998] 2 Lloyd's Rep 475, CA.
226 On this basis, under a contract subject to the Hague or Hague-Visby Rules, a third party would be liable only in respect of a common law claim for pure economic loss of the sort made in *Chandris v Isbrandtsen-Moller Co Inc* [1951] 1 KB 240.
227 [1983] 1 Lloyd's Rep 9.
228 [1998] 2 Lloyd's Rep 39, 69.

Chapter 6

The Future? The Hamburg Rules and the Rotterdam Rules

Chapter Contents

The Hague and Hague-Visby Rules embody a compromise between the interests of shipowners and those of cargo owners. By and large, this compromise has succeeded in imposing a clear and uniform regime for dealing with cargo claims arising out of sea carriage. However, changing transport patterns have meant that the Rules are now starting to show their age. For example, the emergence of the sea waybill after the 1968 Visby amendments to the Hague Rules means that this document falls outside both the Hague and Hague-Visby Rules, which are focused exclusively on the bill of lading. Neither version of the Rules can deal with multimodal carriage. Indeed, the 'tackle to tackle' focus of the Rules means that they do not cover the whole of the sea carrier's period of responsibility under 'port to port' carriage. Furthermore, cargo interests have, for a long time, felt that the balance achieved in the Rules unduly favours sea carriers. In particular, they have criticised the burden of proof adopted by the Rules, as well as the fact that a carrier can escape liability under Art IV(2)(a) and (b) in circumstances in which cargo has been lost or damaged due to the negligence of its servants or agents. In this chapter, we shall examine two alternative regimes that have been, or are in the process of being, drafted to meet these criticisms. The first is the Hamburg Rules. The second is the Rotterdam Rules, an UNCITRAL convention that has been open for signing since September 2009.

The Hamburg Rules

The Hamburg Rules are an updated and more 'cargo-friendly' version of the Hague and Hague-Visby Rules. They came into force on 1 November 1992. However, they have not been adopted by any of the major trading nations, including the UK. Nevertheless, it is quite feasible that disputes involving the Hamburg Rules will come before English courts or arbitrators. This may be because the cargo claim arises out of a voyage where the state of loading is a Contracting Party to the Hamburg Rules.

Alternatively, the parties may voluntarily adopt the Hamburg Rules by a 'clause paramount'. As the Hamburg Rules are, in most respects, more onerous on carriers than the Hague-Visby Rules, such a voluntary incorporation would be effective even where the bill of lading was subject to the mandatory effect of the Hague-Visby Rules, by virtue of Art V of those Rules.[1]

A brief outline will now be given of the Hamburg Rules, pointing out the salient differences between their provisions and the equivalent provisions in the Hague-Visby Rules.

Ambit of operation

The Hague-Visby Rules attach to contracts covered by bills of lading; the Hamburg Rules attach to all 'contracts of carriage by sea' except charterparties.[2] Therefore, waybills will fall within the ambit of the Hamburg Rules, whereas they would generally fall outside the scope of the Hague-Visby Rules.

Under Art 2(1) of the Hamburg Rules, all contracts of carriage by sea between different states will be subject to their provisions if:

- the port of loading is in a Contracting State; or
- the port of discharge, including an optional port of discharge that becomes an actual port of discharge, is in a Contracting State; or

---

1 Even where the contract is subject to English law, the court may, pursuant to the provisions of Art 10(2) of the 1990 Rome Convention, take account of law in force in the country in which the contractual obligation will be performed, so far as it relates to the mode of performance. Thus, in *East West Corp v DKBS 1912* [2002] 2 Lloyd's Rep 535, QB, Thomas J considered the effect of Art 4(1)(3) of the Hamburg Rules in relation to a misdelivery claim that arose in Chile, which applies the Hamburg Rules.
2 Article 2(3).

- the bill of lading, or other document evidencing the contract of carriage, is issued in a Contracting State; or
- the bill of lading or other document evidencing the contract of carriage by sea incorporates the Hamburg Rules or the legislation of any State giving effect to them.

The major changes from the Hague-Visby regime are that the port of discharge is now significant and not only the port of loading, and contractual documents other than bills of lading are brought within the ambit of the Rules.

Who is liable?

Contractual claims

The Hague-Visby regime focuses on the liability of the 'carrier', which may be either a shipowner or a charterer, but not both simultaneously.[3] Under the Hamburg Rules, the position is changed, for Art 10 subjects both the 'contractual carrier' and the 'actual carrier' to the Rules. Under Art 10(1), the contractual carrier remains responsible for the part of the contract performed by another carrier ('the actual carrier'). Article 11(1) permits the contractual carrier to exclude its liability for loss or damage to the goods while in the custody of the 'actual carrier', provided that:

> the actual carrier is named in the contract of carriage
>
> AND details are given in the contract of carriage of that part of the contract of carriage to be performed by the named actual carrier
>
> AND judicial proceedings can be instituted against the actual carrier in a court competent under para 1 or 2 of Art 21.

The 'actual carrier' will be liable only for the part of the contract of carriage that it personally performs. This would cover other shipowners where the contracting carrier exercises a contractual liberty to trans-ship. It would also cover a shipowner where a time charterer's bill of lading is issued.[4] Article 10(2) extends 'all the provisions of this Convention governing the responsibility of the carrier' to the actual carrier.[5] This is emphasised by Art 11(2), which provides:

> The actual carrier is responsible in accordance with the provisions of para 2 of Art 10 for loss, damage or delay in delivery caused by an occurrence which takes place while the goods are in his charge.

Non-contractual claims

Article 7 contains similar provisions to those contained in Art IVbis of the Hague-Visby Rules. Article 7(2) purports to extend the protection of the Hamburg Rules to servants or agents of the carrier but does not refer to independent contractors.

Even without the specific exclusion of 'independent contractors' contained in Art IVbis(2) of the Hague-Visby Rules, this provision does not cover such third parties, for, under English law, an

---

3   The shipper's liability in respect of dangerous cargo is covered by Art 13, which is of similar effect to Art IV(6) of the Hague and Hague-Visby Rules.

4   It is doubtful whether the shipowner would be an 'actual carrier' where the vessel is on demise charter, as such a shipowner cannot realistically be said to 'perform' any part of the contract made by the charterer. See Luddecke and Johnson, *The Hamburg Rules*, 2nd edn, 1995, London: LLP, p 24.

5   Article 10(2)(d), by implication, must also extend to the actual carrier the benefit of any protective provisions of the Conventions, such as those contained in Arts 5 and 6.

independent contractor is neither a servant nor an agent. Article 7(2) does, however, have one advantage over the equivalent provision in the Hague-Visby Rules, in that 'servants or agents' will be protected in respect of a wider period of responsibility under the Hamburg Rules, by virtue of Art 4, than is the case under the Hague-Visby Rules.

Period of responsibility

The Hague-Visby Rules apply only to contracts of carriage *by sea*. Their ambit is limited to the period starting with the commencement of loading and terminating with the completion of discharge. In contrast, Art 4(1) of the Hamburg Rules provides that:

> The responsibility of the carrier for the goods ... covers the period during which the carrier is in charge of the goods at the port of loading, during the carriage and at the port of discharge.

Therefore, the Hamburg Rules will extend to any period of storage at the port of loading in the carrier's custody prior to actual loading and any equivalent period at the port of discharge prior to taking of delivery.

It is arguable that the Rules might apply when the carrier obtains custody at an inland point. Article 4(2) provides that:

> For the purposes of paragraph 1 of this article, the carrier is deemed to be in charge of the goods—
>
> (a)   from the time he has taken over the goods from:
>   (i)   the shipper, or a person acting on his behalf.

However, Art 4(2) has to be read in conjunction with Art 4(1), which makes specific reference to the carrier being in charge of the goods *at the port of loading*, and therefore it is probable that the words in Art 4(2)(a)(i) will not be extended to a taking over of the goods from the shipper at an earlier stage. Further support for this construction can be derived from the definition of 'contract of carriage by sea' in Art 1(6) as:

> ... any contract whereby the carrier undertakes against payment of freight to carry goods by sea *from one port to another*.

Basis of liability

The Hamburg Rules dispense with the two-pronged liability scheme of the Hague-Visby Rules in favour of a unitary system. Under Art 5, once the claimant can prove that the loss or damage took place while the goods were in the charge of the carrier, as defined by Art 4, the carrier will be presumed to be liable for the loss or damage. Delay is treated as a separate head of liability under Art 5(1) and has its own special limitation figure in Art 6. The presumption of liability under Art 5 can be rebutted only if the carrier proves that 'he, his servants or agents took all measures that could reasonably be required to avoid the occurrence and its consequences'. The exceptions provided by Art IV(2) of the Hague-Visby Rules have no equivalent in the Hamburg Rules. Consequently, a negligent carrier who could have relied on Art IV(2)(a) of the Hague and Hague-Visby Rules would no longer be able to escape liability under the Hamburg Rules. However, the wording of Art 5 leaves some residual uncertainty as to whether the carrier remains liable for the defaults of its independent contractors. The imposition of liability in such circumstances would depend on whether the courts were prepared to analyse the carrier's duties under the Hamburg Rules as being 'non-delegable' in the same way that they have been analysed in the context of the carrier's duty of due diligence under Art III(1) of the Hague and Hague-Visby Rules.

There is no specific provision relating to deviation. Article 5(6) exempts the carrier from liability 'where loss, damage or delay in delivery resulted from measures to save life or from reasonable measures to save property at sea'. This provision is narrower in ambit than the liberty given by the Hague-Visby Rules to make a 'reasonable deviation'. However, if a deviation were 'reasonable' under the Hague-Visby Rules, it is likely that the same facts would enable the carrier to prove what is required under the Hamburg Rules to displace the presumption of liability under Art 5(1). The Rules are silent as to the effects of deviation under a Hamburg Rules contract. If the UK were ever to become a Contracting State, the matter would be governed by the common law principles set out in Chapter 4.

The Hamburg Rules provide only two exceptions to the carrier who is unable to rebut the presumption of fault.

Fire

Where goods are lost or damaged by fire, Art 5(4) provides that the carrier will be liable only if the claimant can prove that the fire arose from the 'fault or neglect on the part of the carrier, its servants or agents'.

In some respects, the Hamburg Rules worsen the position of a claimant whose goods have been lost or damaged due to fire, for the burden of proof is placed on its shoulders and not those of the carrier, as is the case with the fire exception in the Hague-Visby Rules. However, the Hague-Visby exception can be lost only if the claimant can prove that the fire took place due to the fault or privity of the carrier. Under the Hamburg Rules, the claimant will succeed if it manages to prove fault or neglect on the part of the carrier's servants or agents. It must also be remembered that, under the Hague-Visby Rules, the claimant could prevent reliance on the fire exception if it could establish that the fire was due to the unseaworthiness of the vessel. In practice, the position of a claimant whose goods have been lost or damaged due to fire will be much the same under the Hamburg Rules as under the Hague-Visby Rules.

Live animals

With carriage of live animals, the carrier is not liable under Art 5(5) for loss, damage or delay arising out of 'any special risk inherent in that kind of carriage'. If the carrier can prove that the damage was caused by such a risk and that it complied with any special instructions given by the shipper, the burden of proof will shift to the claimant to prove negligence on the part of the carrier. If it fails to discharge this burden, the carrier will escape liability.

Deck cargo

Unlike the position with the Hague and Hague-Visby Rules, deck cargo under the Hamburg Rules is treated in exactly the same way as any other cargo in that its carriage cannot be taken outside the ambit of the Hamburg Rules. Article 9(1) provides that cargo may be carried on deck either in accordance with agreement with the shipper or the usage of a particular trade, or if required by statutory rules or regulations.

If loss occurs due to unauthorised carriage of cargo on deck, Art 9(3) provides that the carrier will be strictly liable for losses resulting solely from the carriage on deck. The carrier will not be able to rely on the defence under Art 5(1) that 'he, his servants or agents took all measures that could reasonably be required to avoid the occurrence and its consequences'. However, Art 9(4) provides that 'carriage of goods on deck contrary to express agreement for carriage under deck is deemed to be an act or omission of the carrier within the meaning of Art 8'. This will entail the carrier losing its right to rely on the limitation provisions in Art 6, although it will still be able to rely on the time bar in Art 20.

Package limitation

Article 6(1)(a) provides a package[6] limitation of 835 'units of account' (defined in Art 26 as the Special Drawing Right (SDR)) with an alternative of 2.5 units of account per kilogram of the gross weight of the goods. The claimant may choose whichever basis yields the higher figure. The Hamburg Rules limit amounts to a 25 per cent uplift of the equivalent Hague-Visby figures. Article 6(1)(b) provides for a separate limitation figure to cover the carrier's liability for delay of an amount equal to two-and-a-half times the freight payable for the goods delayed but not exceeding the total freight payable under the contract of carriage. Article 6(1)(c) provides that the total liability of the carrier under all heads cannot exceed the maximum limit on a total loss of the goods as calculated under Art 6(1)(a). The carrier's right to limit under international conventions such as the **1957** and **1976 Limitation Conventions** is preserved by Art 25(1).

As with the Hague-Visby Rules, the right to limit can be lost, by virtue of Art 8(1), if the carrier intentionally or recklessly causes the loss. This provision applies, *mutatis mutandis*, to the right to limit of any servant or agent of the carrier who relies on the Rules by reason of Art 7(2).

Time bar

Article 20(1) provides a two-year limitation period for any action 'relating to carriage of goods under this Convention',[7] extendable at any time within the period by a declaration in writing to the claimant by the defendant. The period commences on the date of delivery or, in the case of non-delivery, on the last day on which the goods should have been delivered.

Article 19 provides for the notice of the following claims to be given with a specified time:

(a)   claims by consignee for loss or damage – 15 consecutive working days after delivery;
(b)   claims by consignee for delay – 60 consecutive days after delivery;
(c)   claims by carrier/actual carrier against shipper for loss or damage – 90 consecutive days of either the occurrence or the delivery of the goods.

Failure to give the appropriate notice amounts to prima facie evidence of, respectively, delivery in good condition, delivery on time, absence of loss or damage to the carrier.

Bar on contracting out

Article 23(1) makes 'null and void' any:

> . . . stipulation in a contract of carriage by sea, in a bill of lading, or in any other document evidencing the contract of carriage by sea . . . to the extent that it derogates, directly or indirectly, from the provisions of this Convention.

The wording is wider than the equivalent provision, Art III(8), contained in the Hague and Hague-Visby Rules. It strikes down clauses that derogate *indirectly* from the Hamburg Rules. Moreover, it strikes down 'stipulations' and not just clauses '*relieving the carrier or ship from liability for loss or damage* . . .'.

---

6   'Package' is defined in similar fashion to the Hague-Visby definition in Art IV(5).
7   This wording makes it unclear whether Art 20 will cover claims for misdelivery.

The classification of a clause as an 'obligation' clause, as in *Renton (GH) & Co Ltd v Palmyra Trading Corp of Panama*,[8] would not suffice to remove it from consideration under Art 23(1). Such a clause might therefore be held void if it were to derogate directly or indirectly from the Hamburg Rules.

Jurisdiction

The Hague-Visby Rules contain no provisions dealing with jurisdiction, although provisions in the bill of lading referring disputes to a non-Hague-Visby jurisdiction have been held invalid by reason of Art III(8).[9] Article 21 of the Hamburg Rules expressly deals with jurisdiction and gives the claimant the option of suing the defendant in one of the following places:[10]

(a)   the principal place of business, or, in the absence thereof, the habitual residence of the defendant; or
(b)   the place where the contract was made, provided that the defendant has there a place of business, branch or agency through which the contract was made; or
(c)   the port of loading or the port of discharge; or
(d)   any additional place designated for that purpose in the contract of carriage by sea.

The Convention only gives the claimant the *option* of suing at one of these venues.[11] It does not itself confer jurisdiction on any of the venues. That issue still has to be established in accordance with the national law of the state concerned. An additional seat of jurisdiction is provided by Art 21(2), the courts of any port or place in a Contracting State at which the carrying vessel, or a sister ship, may have been arrested in accordance with the applicable rules of the law of that state and of international law. In this eventuality, the defendant may insist on the removal of the suit to one of the five venues specified in Art 21(1). However, the defendant must provide adequate security for the claim before the suit is removed from the place of arrest. The claimant's ability to choose from the venues specified in Art 21 may be curtailed by the effect of other international conventions such as the 1968 Brussels Convention, now EC Regulation 44/2001 on jurisdiction and recognition and enforcement of judgments in civil and commercial matters (the 'Judgments Regulation').

The wide range of possible seats of jurisdiction specified by the Hamburg Rules leaves open the possibility of a jurisdictional conflict when goods are carried between a Hague-Visby State and a Hamburg State. The courts of the state of loading would regard the contract as being mandatorily subject to the Hague-Visby Rules. However, the courts in the state of discharge would regard the contract as being mandatorily subject to the Hamburg Rules. Accordingly, a real risk exists of conflicting judgments coming into existence in relation to the same cargo claim. The claimant would proceed in the courts of the state of discharge, whereas the defendant would want to seek a declaration as to its liability in the courts of the port of loading. The Hamburg Rules lack any provision by which this potential impasse could be resolved. Much would depend on the domestic rules applied to questions of *lis alibi pendens* by each of the competing courts.[12]

Evidential status of shipping documents

Article 14 imposes an obligation on the carrier to issue a bill of lading to the shipper 'when the carrier or actual carrier takes the goods into his charge'. Article 15 goes on to specify the statements

---

8   [1957] AC 149, HL.
9   *The Hollandia* (sub nom *The Morviken*) [1983] 1 AC 565, HL.
10   Article 22 contains similar provisions relating to arbitration.
11   The permissible venues for arbitration proceedings are specified in Art 22(3).
12   If both courts were in States Parties to the Judgments Regulation, the *impasse* would be resolved in favour of the court 'first seised' in accordance with the provisions of Arts 27 and 28.

that must be contained in the bill of lading and is considerably wider in its ambit than the equivalent provision in Art III(3) of the Hague-Visby Rules.[13]

Article 16 deals with reservations in the bill of lading and the evidential effect of statements in the bill of lading. Article 16(1) requires the carrier or other person issuing the bill of lading to insert in the bill of lading a reservation specifying any inaccuracies, grounds of suspicion or the absence of reasonable means of checking particulars concerning the general nature, leading marks, number of packages or pieces, weight or quantity of the goods. Article 16(2) then goes on to provide that a bill of lading that fails to record the apparent order and condition of the goods is deemed to have recorded their shipment in 'apparent good order and condition'. Article 16(3) deals with the evidential effect of such statements in broadly similar terms to those adopted by Art III(4) of the Hague-Visby Rules, except for particulars in respect of which and to the extent to which a reservation permitted under Art 16(1) has been entered. Art 16(4) provides that bills of lading that do not expressly indicate that freight is payable by the consignee or do not set forth demurrage payable by the consignee at the port of loading are prima facie evidence that no such freight or demurrage is payable by the consignee. In the hands of a third party in good faith relying on absence of such statements in the bill of lading, proof to the contrary is not admissible by the carrier. This provision clarifies the existing law under which a 'lawful holder' of a bill of lading might be subject to a common law liability to freight if the bill of lading neither incorporates the terms of a charterparty nor is claused 'freight prepaid'.

Article 17(1) repeats the shipper's guarantee as to the accuracy of particulars relating to the general nature of the goods, their marks, number, weight and quantity as furnished by him for insertion in the bill of lading, and provides for an indemnity to the carrier in respect of loss resulting from inaccuracies in such particulars. The shipper's liability is to continue after it has transferred the bill of lading and the carrier's right to an indemnity does not affect its liability to parties other than the shipper. Article 17(2) deals with the effect of any indemnity or guarantee issued by the shipper to the carrier in relation to losses arising from issuing a bill of lading without entering a reservation relating to particulars furnished by the shipper for insertion in the bill of lading, or to the apparent condition of the goods. As regards third parties, including consignees, such an indemnity or guarantee is void and of no effect. However, under Art 17(3) the indemnity or guarantee is enforceable against the shipper, unless the failure to include a reservation in the bill of lading was done with the intention to defraud a third party acting in reliance on the bill of lading. If that is in respect of particulars furnished by the shipper the carrier has no indemnity under Art 17(1). Under Art 17(4) intentional fraud in failing to include a reservation in the bill of lading will have the additional consequence of removing the carrier's right to limit when sued by third parties, including the consignee, for the loss sustained in reliance on the description of the goods in the bill of lading.

Article 18 provides that statements in documents, other than bills of lading, have only prima facie evidential effect. Article 1(7) defines 'bill of lading' as 'a document . . . by which the carrier undertakes to deliver the goods against surrender of the documents', which, under English law, would cover a straight bill of lading, but not a sea waybill.

The Rotterdam Rules

The Hamburg Rules made several significant improvements to the scheme adopted by the Hague and Hague-Visby Rules. First, they covered the full period of the carrier's responsibility under 'port

---

13 For example, the name of the shipper and the name and principal place of business of the carrier must be included, as well as the number of original bills issued and the freight, if any, to be paid by the consignee.

to port' carriage, rather than being limited to the 'tackle to tackle' period. Secondly, they applied to all contracts of carriage by sea except charterparties, rather than being confined to 'bills of lading or other similar documents of title'. Thirdly, the imposition of liability on both the 'contracting carrier' and the 'actual carrier' reduced most of the problems associated with the identification of the single carrier under the Hague Rules. In addition, deck cargo was brought within the ambit of the Hamburg Rules. Fourthly, the Hamburg Rules applied mandatorily to carriage to a Contracting State and not just to carriage from a Contracting State. Fifthly, the Hamburg Rules contained specific provisions to deal with jurisdiction and arbitration, as well as the relationship of the Hamburg Rules to other international conventions. Sixthly, a unified system of liability was adopted, based on presumed fault as opposed to the two-tier system of the Hague Rules, with all its complications as to the allocation of the burden of proof. It is, perhaps, this final feature that has led to the fact that the Hamburg Rules can now be regarded as 'dead in the water' due to the fact that, to date, they have failed to be adopted by any major maritime nation.

Apart from the problems associated with such a major shift in favour of cargo interest, there is also the fact that the Hamburg Rules did not go far enough to address the realities of modern shipping practice. Three particular issues were either not addressed at all or addressed only sparingly. First, the wording of Art 7 extends the protection of the Hamburg Rules to the 'servants or agents' of the contracting carrier and the actual carrier, but makes no mention of the independent contractors engaged by these parties. Secondly, the Hamburg Rules are limited to 'port to port' carriage at a time when a significant amount of sea carriage forms part of 'door to door' carriage. Thirdly, the issue of electronic documentation is dealt with in only a limited fashion through Art 14(3), which recognises the validity of an electronic signature on the bill of lading.

In 1999, following three years of consultations among the international shipping community, the Comité Maritime International (CMI) started work on drafting a new convention on sea carriage. The CMI's draft outline instrument was completed in early 2001 and remitted to a working group of the UN Commission on International Trade Law (UNCITRAL) for further development. Work on the new convention was finalised in January 2008. On 3 July 2008, UNCITRAL approved the draft Convention on Contracts for the International Carriage of Goods Wholly or Partly by Sea, which was adopted by the Legal Committee of the General Assembly on 14 November 2008.[14] The signing ceremony for the Rotterdam Rules was held in Rotterdam from 20 to 23 September 2009. Since then, 24 countries have signed the Convention: Armenia, Cameroon, Congo, Democratic Republic of Congo, Denmark, France, Gabon, Ghana, Greece, Guinea, Luxembourg, Madagascar, Mali, the Netherlands, Niger, Nigeria, Norway, Poland, Senegal, Spain, Sweden, Switzerland, Togo and the United States of America. The Convention will come into force one year after ratification by the twentieth UN Member State. The Rotterdam Rules have so far been ratified by three states: Spain, Togo and Congo. Whether the new convention avoids the fate of the Hamburg Rules remains to be seen. The project is ambitious in that it is not confined to the familiar territory of the sea carrier's liability for cargo. It also tackles important associated issues that have, hitherto, been left exclusively to national law, such as: the cargo owner's title to sue and its liability under negotiable transport documents, as bills of lading are referred to in the Convention; the obligations of the consignee in respect of delivery of the cargo; and the cargo owner's right of control over the cargo during the voyage – particularly its right to vary the discharge port. The Convention has been drafted so as to allow electronic documentation to be covered in the same way as conventional paper documentation. It also covers multimodal carriage involving sea carriage, which raises difficult issues of how the new Convention will interact with existing carriage conventions such as CMR (UN Convention

---

14 http://www.un.org/News/Press/docs/2008/gal3359.doc.htm (accessed 10 December 2008). The English text of the Convention is to be found on the UNCITRAL website: http://www.uncitral.org/pdf/english/texts/transport/rotterdam_rules/09-85608_Ebook.pdf (accessed 29 April 2014).

Relative au Contrat de Transport International de Marchandises par Route). The Convention also contains optional chapters on jurisdiction and arbitration.

Chapter One – general provisions

Article 1 contains the salient definitions of the Convention in paras (1) to (30). 'Contract of carriage' in para (1) is defined as a contract whereby the carrier undertakes 'to carry goods from one place to another' against payment of freight. The reference to payment of freight causes a problem with a 'freight prepaid' bill under which the original bill of lading shipper has not undertaken to pay freight. Such a bill of lading will not constitute a 'contract of carriage' under the definition set out in para (1) and will therefore fall outside the Convention. Article 42 deals with 'Freight prepaid' statements, but treats them solely as creating an estoppel. It does not deal with the other function of such clausing, as seen in the Court of Appeal's decision in *Cho Yang Shipping Co Ltd v Coral (UK) Ltd*, that it amounts to evidence as to whether the original bill of lading holder ever undertook to pay freight.[15] Article 1(1) goes on to state that 'The contract shall provide for carriage by sea and may provide for carriage by other modes of transport in addition to the sea carriage'.[16] This definition means that there may be contracts of carriage that fall under the Convention as well as under another carriage convention, such as CMR. Articles 26 and 82 attempt, not entirely successfully, to deal with this issue. The overlap will only apply as regards the carrier under the contract of carriage. Sub-carriers that are not 'maritime performing parties' will incur no liability under the Convention.

'Carrier' is defined in para (5) as 'a person that enters into a contract of carriage with a shipper'. In para (6) a novel concept is introduced into the Convention – that is, the 'performing party', defined as:[17]

> . . . a person other than the carrier that performs or undertakes to perform any of the carrier's obligations under a contract of carriage with respect to the receipt, loading, handling, stowage, carriage, keeping, care, unloading or delivery of the goods, to the extent that such person acts, either directly or indirectly, at the carrier's request or under the carrier's supervision or control.

The term 'performing party' does not include any person who is retained by a shipper or consignee, or is an employee, agent, contractor, or subcontractor of a person (other than the carrier) who is retained by a shipper, documentary shipper, controlling party, or consignee. The definition brings within its scope *any* independent contractor engaged by the carrier to perform any of the carrier's responsibilities under its contract of carriage, to the extent that such a party actually performs such services. The carrier is responsible for the acts of performing parties, but the performing party itself will only fall under the Convention if it is a 'maritime performing party'. The term is defined in para (7) 'as a performing party to the extent that it performs or undertakes to perform any of the carrier's obligations during the period between the arrival of the goods at the port of loading of a ship and their departure from the port of discharge of a ship. An inland carrier is a maritime performing party only if it performs or undertakes to perform its services exclusively within a port area'. The application of the Convention to maritime performing parties entails a major expansion in its scope over that of the Hague Rules, which deal only with the 'carrier', and over that of the Hamburg Rules, which deal with the 'contracting carrier' and the 'actual carrier'.

15 [1997] 2 Lloyd's Rep 641.
16 The wording 'shall provide for carriage by sea' may lead to different interpretations by national courts, as has been the case with Art 1 of CMR. For example, if the contract of carriage does not specify the transport modes, but does in fact involve an element of sea carriage, will this fall within the scope of the Convention under Art 5?
17 The word 'keeping' was added to this paragraph in an amendment on 25 January 2013 (Depositary Notification C.N.105.2013. TREATIES-XI.D.8, Depositary Notification C.N.563.2012.TREATIES-XI.D.8).

On the cargo-owning side of the contract of carriage, the 'shipper' is defined in para (8) as 'a person that enters into a contract of carriage with a carrier'. The Convention also refers to the 'documentary shipper', who is defined in para (9) as 'a person, other than the shipper, that accepts to be named as the shipper in the transport document or electronic transport record'. This would cover a consignor who has no express contractual relations with the carrier, as is the case with a seller under a fob contract. Under English law, such a party is regarded as having a contract with the carrier under the terms of the bill of lading and would therefore fall within the Convention's definition of a 'shipper' in para (8) as 'a person that enters a contract of carriage with a carrier.' The position may be different in other jurisdictions, as can be seen by the Canadian decision in *The Roseline*.[18] The Convention's reference to the 'documentary shipper' will ensure that such a party will be subject to the obligations imposed by Chapter Seven. The 'holder' is defined in para (10) to cover persons in possession of a negotiable transport document. With an order document, the holder person must be identified in it as the shipper or the consignee, or the holder must be the indorsee. With a blank indorsed order document or bearer document, the holder is the bearer of the document.[19] The 'consignee' is defined in para (11) as 'a person entitled to take delivery of the goods under a contract of carriage or a transport document or electronic record'.

Article 1 then goes on to define the documentation covered by the Convention. 'Transport document' is widely defined in para (14) as: 'a document issued pursuant to a contract of carriage by the carrier or a performing party that (i) evidences the carrier's or a performing party's receipt of goods under a contract of carriage, or (ii) evidences or contains a contract of carriage'. The Convention distinguishes between negotiable and non-negotiable transport documents. The former are defined in para (15) as:

> ... a transport document that indicates, by wording such as 'to order' or 'negotiable' or other appropriate wording recognised as having the same effect by the law governing the document, that the goods have been consigned to the order of the shipper, to the order of the consignee, or to bearer, and is not explicitly stated as being 'non-negotiable' or 'not negotiable'.

The latter are defined in para (16) as being transport documents that are not negotiable transport documents.

The definition of a 'negotiable transport document', therefore, covers a traditional bill of lading but not a straight bill of lading. Similar definitions are used to cover negotiable and non-negotiable electronic records in paras (19) and (20), respectively. A negotiable electronic record must be subject to rules of procedure, 'which include adequate provisions relating to the transfer of that record to a further holder and the manner in which the holder of that record is able to demonstrate that it is such holder'.

Article 2 provides for regard to be had to the Convention's international character and the need to provide uniformity in its application and the observance of good faith in international trade. Article 3 provides for the various formalities required by the Convention, such as notices, agreements, and declarations, to be in writing. However, electronic communication may be used instead, 'provided the use of such means is with the consent of the person by which it is communicated and of the person to which it is communicated'.

---

18 [1987] 1 Lloyd's Rep 18.
19 Subparagraph (b) describes the holder of a negotiable electronic transport record as 'the person to which a negotiable electronic transport record has been issued or transferred in accordance with the procedures referred to in article 9, paragraph 1'.

Article 4 deals with non-contractual actions as against the carrier. Paragraph (1) provides:

> Any provision of this Convention that may provide a defence for, or limit the liability of, the carrier applies in any judicial or arbitral proceeding, whether founded in contract, in tort, or otherwise, that is instituted in respect of loss of, damage to, or delay in delivery of goods covered by a contract of carriage or for the breach of any other obligation under this Convention against:
>
> (a) The carrier or a maritime performing party;
> (b) The master, crew or any other person that performs services on board the ship; or
> (c) Employees of the carrier or a maritime performing party.

Paragraph (2) deals with non-contractual suits against the shipper, as follows:

> Any provision of this Convention that may provide a defence for the shipper or the documentary shipper applies in any judicial or arbitral proceeding, whether founded in contract, in tort, or otherwise, that is instituted against the shipper, the documentary shipper, or their subcontractors, agents or employees.

These provisions are wider than Art IVbis of the Hague-Visby Rules in that they extend the coverage of the Convention to non-contractual suits against the shipper and documentary shipper as well as to their subcontractors, agents and employees. They also extend the coverage of the Convention to non-contractual suits against maritime performing parties, so rendering redundant, as regards such parties, the esoteric jurisprudence that has built up around 'Himalaya' clauses and actions in bailment.

Chapter Two – scope of application

Article 5 of the Convention provides that it will cover:

> . . . contracts of carriage in which the place of receipt and the place of delivery are in different States, and the port of loading of a sea carriage and the port of discharge of the same sea carriage are in different States, if, according to the contract of carriage, any one of the following places is located in a Contracting State:
>
> (a) The place of receipt;
> (b) The port of loading;
> (c) The place of delivery; or
> (d) The port of discharge.

The additional requirement that the port of loading of a sea carriage and the port of discharge of the same sea carriage must be in different states means there must actually be sea carriage for the Convention to apply. It will not apply to a contract of carriage that gives an option to carry by sea, which is not, in fact, taken up, nor will it apply to a contract where there is sea carriage between ports in the same state (e.g. from Avonmouth to Southampton). Article 5 does not contain a provision equivalent to Art X(c) of the Hague-Visby Rules whereby the Rules apply when their provisions, or those of legislation giving effect to them, are incorporated into a bill of lading. Article 5 needs to be read in conjunction with the definition of 'contract of carriage' in Art 1.1.

Article 6 then takes out various contracts of carriage from this definition, most notably charterparties. Paragraph (1) deals with liner transportation[20] and excludes '(a) Charterparties; and

---

20 Article 1(3) defines liner transportation as 'a transportation service that is offered to the public through publication or similar means and includes transportation by ships operating on a regular schedule between specified ports in accordance with publicly available timetables of sailing dates'. Article 1(4) provides that non-liner transportation means any transportation that is not liner transportation.

(b) Contracts for the use of a ship or of any space thereon, whether or not they are charterparties.' Paragraph (2) provides that the Convention does not cover contracts of carriage in non-liner transportation except when:

(a) there is no charterparty or contract for the use of a ship or of any space thereon between the parties, whether such contract is a charterparty or not; and

(b) The evidence of the contract of carriage is a transport document or an electronic transport record that also evidences the carrier's or a performing party's receipt of the goods.

Thus, non-liner bills in the hands of third parties fall within the Convention, as do bills of lading in the hands of an original shipper that has not concluded an express contract of carriage with the carrier. It seems, however, that para (2)(a) excludes an express non-liner contract for the use of space on a ship that is evidenced by a transport document, such as a bill of lading. As regards the original contracting parties, such a contract would fall outside the Convention, although as regards these parties, such a contract of carriage would fall within the ambit of the Hague and Hague-Visby Rules.[21] Article 7 then goes on to exclude the exclusions in Art 6 as regards third parties and provides:

> Notwithstanding article 6, this Convention applies as between the carrier and the consignee, controlling party or holder that is not an original party to the charterparty or other contract of carriage excluded from the application of this Convention. However, this Convention does not apply as between the original parties to a contract of carriage excluded pursuant to article 6.

The effect of Arts 6 and 7 is that the Convention will cover traditional bills of lading, straight bills of lading and waybills, but not charterparties. However, in the non-liner trade, express contracts for the use of space on a ship that are evidenced by a non-transport document will fall outside the Convention as regards the original contracting parties. The Convention also contains a partial derogation from its provisions as regards volume contracts, in Art 80.

Chapter Three – electronic communication

Article 8 provides for the functional equivalence of transport documents recorded by using electronic communication 'provided the issuance and subsequent use of an electronic record is with the express or implied consent of the carrier and the shipper'. Article 9 requires the contract particulars to contain the agreed rules of procedure as to the transfer of the electronic record to a further holder, the manner in which the holder can demonstrate that it is a holder, and the way in which confirmation is given that delivery has been made to the consignee or that the electronic record has ceased to have effect, having been replaced by a paper document. Article 10 deals with a subsequent agreement between the carrier and the holder to switch from a negotiable transport document to its electronic equivalent, and vice versa. All originals of a negotiable transport document must be surrendered to the carrier when the switch is made to a negotiable electronic transport record. When the switch is made the other way, the negotiable transport document must contain a statement that it replaces the negotiable electronic transport record.

---

21 Anthony Diamond QC, 'The next sea carriage convention?' [2008] LMCLQ 135, 146, observes that the wording of Art 6(2):
  '. . . was intended to bring within the Convention so-called "on-demand" carriage in the bulk trades but it will give rise
  to some artificial considerations, such as whether the evidence of the contract of carriage is in the same document as,
  or a different document from, the carrier's receipt for the goods. Quite what the provision will achieve in practice is difficult to
  predict.'

Chapter Four – obligations of the carrier

Article 11 provides: 'The carrier shall, subject to this Convention and in accordance with the terms of the contract of carriage, carry the goods to the place of destination and deliver them to the consignee.' Delivery is specifically mentioned as an obligation of the carrier, unlike the position under the Hague-Visby Rules in which delivery is mentioned only in Art III(6). Article 12 provides for the carrier's period of responsibility to run from the receipt of the goods by the carrier or a performing party to the time of their delivery; an expansion from the 'tackle to tackle' rule that governs the ambit of the Hague and Hague-Visby Rules. The parties may agree as to the time and location of receipt and delivery of the goods, but such a provision will be void to the extent that it provides for receipt to be subsequent to the initial loading of the goods, and for delivery to be prior to their final unloading. The parties, therefore, are free to agree to contract on a 'tackle to tackle' basis where the contract involves sea carriage only.

The Convention has not adopted the simple 'presumed fault' model of the Hamburg Rules, but has based the obligations of the carrier on a modified version of the Hague Rules. Article 13 is an equivalent provision to Art III(2), but includes a reference to delivery. Paragraph 2 provides for the validity of 'fiost' (free in, out, stowed and trimmed) clauses whereby some of these functions may be performed 'by or on behalf of the shipper, the documentary shipper or the ·consignee', provided that this agreement is referred to in the contract provisions. Article 14 is an equivalent provision to Art III(1), but the carrier's due diligence obligation of seaworthiness now continues throughout the voyage. The obligation of seaworthiness is also expressly extended to containers that are supplied by the carrier.[22]

There then follow two provisions dealing with the carrier's right to decline to load cargo or to dispose of cargo already loaded. Article 15, in wording similar to that to be found in Art IV(6) of the Hague and Hague-Visby Rules, entitles the carrier or a performing party to decline to receive or to load, and to 'take such other measures as are reasonable, including unloading, destroying, or rendering goods harmless if the goods are, or appear likely to become during the carrier's period of responsibility an actual danger to persons, to property or to the environment'. Article 16 permits these parties, notwithstanding Arts 11, 13 and 14, to sacrifice goods at sea 'when the sacrifice is reasonably made for the common safety or for the purpose of preserving from peril human life or other property involved in the common adventure'.

Chapter Five – liability of the carrier for loss, damage, or delay

(i) Liability of the carrier

The carrier's liability is addressed in Art 17, para (1) of which states that the carrier shall be liable for loss of or damage to the goods, as well as for delay in delivery, if the claimant proves that the event or circumstance that caused or contributed to the loss took place during the carrier's period of responsibility. This restates the existing law about what the claimant must prove when making a cargo claim. However, the Article then goes on to contain a complex scheme for determining when the carrier may escape liability, involving a shifting burden of proof. Article 17 provides two ways for the carrier to escape liability. Paragraph (2) relieves the carrier of liability 'if it proves that the cause or one of the causes of the loss, damage, or delay is not attributable to its fault or to the fault of any person referred to in article 18'. This would cover misdelivery claims and would allow the

---

22 Article 1(26) defines a 'container' as 'any type of container, transportable tank or flat, swapbody, or any similar unit load used to consolidate goods, and any equipment ancillary to such unit load'. However, Glass, D, 'A sea regime fit for the 21st century?' (2008) 7(2) Shipping and Transport International 8, 12, observes: 'A problem remains, however, in respect of damage caused by a defective container where this occurs outside the period of the carrier's responsibility. This could arise where the carrier supplies the container but the shipper independently arranges for carriage to the terminal.'

carrier to avoid liability in situations such as arose in the *Motis* case, in which delivery was made against a convincing forgery of the bill of lading.[23]

Alternatively, the carrier may be relieved of liability under para (3) if it proves that the following circumstances caused or contributed to the loss, damage, or delay. There then follow a variety of exceptions in headings (a)–(o), along the lines of Art IV(2) of the Hague Rules. A notable omission from the list is the exception of neglect or default in the navigation or management of the vessel, which is to be found in Art IV(2)(a) of the Hague Rules. The 'catch-all' defence in Art IV(2)(q) has also been removed. New defences are provided under headings (i), (n) and (o).

(a) Act of God
(b) Perils, dangers, and accidents of the sea or other navigable waters
(c) War, hostilities, armed conflict, piracy, terrorism, riots and civil commotions[24]
(d) Quarantine restrictions; interference by or impediments created by governments, public authorities, rulers, or people including detention, arrest, or seizure not attributable to the carrier or any person referred to in Article 18[25]
(e) Strikes, lockouts, stoppages, or restraints of labour
(f) Fire on the ship[26]
(g) Latent defects not discoverable by due diligence
(h) Act or omission of the shipper, the documentary shipper, the controlling party, or any other person for whose acts the shipper or the documentary shipper is liable pursuant to Art. 33 or 34[27]
(i) Loading, handling, stowing, or unloading of the goods performed pursuant to an agreement in accordance with Art 13, para (2), unless the carrier or a performing party performs such activity on behalf of the shipper, the documentary shipper or the consignee
(j) Wastage in bulk or weight or any other loss or damage arising from inherent defect, quality, or vice of the goods
(k) Insufficiency or defective condition of packing or marking not performed by or on behalf of the carrier[28]
(l) Saving or attempting to save life at sea
(m) Reasonable measures to save or attempt to save property at sea
(n) Reasonable measures to avoid or attempt to avoid damage to the environment
(o) Acts of the carrier in pursuance of the powers conferred by Arts 15 and 16

If the carrier brings itself within para (3), it may still incur liability. The burden of proof now shifts to the claimant. Paragraph (4) provides that the carrier is liable for all or part of the loss, damage or delay, if the claimant can prove one of two things. The first is 'that the fault of the carrier or of a person referred to in Art 18 caused or contributed to the event or circumstance on which the carrier relies'. The second is 'that an event or circumstance not listed in paragraph 3 of this article contributed to the loss, damage, or delay, and the carrier cannot prove that this event or circumstance is not attributable to its fault or to the fault of any person referred to in article 18.4'. Paragraph (5) then provides that the carrier will still be liable if:

(a) The claimant proves that the loss, damage, or delay was or was probably caused by or contributed to by (i) the unseaworthiness of the ship; (ii) the improper crewing, equipping,

---

23 *Motis Exports Ltd v Dampskibsselskabet AF 1912 A/S (No 1)* [1999] 1 Lloyd's Rep 837, QB; [2000] 1 Lloyd's Rep 211, CA.
24 This consolidates exceptions in Art IV(2)(e), (f) and (k), and adds in piracy and terrorism.
25 This is a consolidation of Art IV(2)(g) 'Arrest or restraint or princes, rulers or people, or seizure under legal process' and (h) 'Quarantine restrictions'.
26 Cf Art IV(2)(b) of the Hague Rules, 'fire, unless caused by the actual fault or privity of the carrier'.
27 Cf Art IV(2)(1) 'Act or omission of the shipper of the goods, his agent or representatives'.
28 This is an expanded version of 'Inefficiency of packing' under Art IV(2)(n) of the Hague Rules.

and supplying of the ship; or (iii) the fact that the holds or other parts of the ship in which the goods are carried, or any containers supplied by the carrier in or upon which the goods are carried, were not fit and safe for reception, carriage, and preservation of the goods, and

(b) The carrier is unable to prove either that: (i) none of the events or circumstances referred to in subparagraph 5 (a) of this article caused the loss, damage, or delay; or (ii) that it complied with its obligation to exercise due diligence pursuant to article 14.

Paragraph (6) then provides that 'When the carrier is relieved of part of its liability pursuant to this article, the carrier is liable only for that part of the loss, damage or delay that is attributable to the event or circumstance for which it is liable pursuant to this article.' This leaves open the possibility that loss could be apportioned between the carrier and the cargo claimant, contrary to the position under English law in which the carrier is either liable in full or not liable at all, save where the carrier can establish that it is covered by an exception in the Rules as regards a specific part of the cargo that is lost or damaged.

Article 18 defines the parties for whom the carrier is responsible. These include not only any performing party, the master or crew of the ship, the employees of the carrier or a performing party, but also 'any other person, including a performing party's subcontractors and agents, who performs or undertakes to perform any of the carrier's responsibilities under the contract of carriage, to the extent that the person acts, either directly or indirectly, at the carrier's request or under the carrier's supervision or control'. However, although the carrier is responsible for the defaults of performing parties, not all performing parties fall under the Convention. Only maritime performing parties may incur liabilities under the Convention and may rely on the rights and immunities granted to the carrier by the Convention.

(ii) Liability of maritime performing parties

Article 19 provides for maritime performing parties to be subject to the same responsibilities and liabilities as those imposed on the carrier under the instrument for the period in which they have custody of the goods or at any other time to the extent that they are participating in the performance of any of the activities contemplated by the contract of carriage. They are also entitled to the carrier's rights and immunities during the same period. Under Art 19(1)(b) they will be liable if:[29]

> The occurrence that caused the loss, damage or delay took place: (i) during the period between the arrival of the goods at the port of loading of the ship and their departure from the port of discharge from the ship; and either (ii) while it had custody of the goods; or (iii) at any other time to the extent that it was participating in the performance of any of the activities contemplated by the contract of carriage.

A maritime performing party's responsibility will not be increased by the carrier accepting greater contractual responsibilities than those imposed by the Convention, unless the maritime performing party itself has also agreed to that increase.

Article 20 provides that the liability of the carrier and one or more maritime performing parties is joint and several, but only up to the limits provided in the Convention. Furthermore, their aggregate liability shall not exceed the overall limits of liability under the Convention. This is, however, without prejudice to the provisions of Art 61, which stipulate when a party will lose the right to limit its liability under the Convention.

---

29 The words 'and either' prior to heading (ii) were added by amendment on 25 January 2013 (Depositary Notification C.N.105.2013.TREATIES-XI.D.8, Depositary Notification C.N.563.2012.TREATIES-XI.D.8).

(iii) Calculation of loss and notice of loss

Article 21 deals with the carrier's liability for delay. 'Delay' is defined as occurring when 'the goods are not delivered at the place of destination provided for in the contract of carriage within the time agreed upon'. The 'time agreed upon' is not limited by reference to an express agreement, as was the case in the penultimate draft of the Convention, and therefore may cover a breach of the implied obligation to proceed on the voyage with reasonable dispatch. The Convention is pointedly silent about the shipper's liability for delay.

Article 22 provides that compensation for loss or damage to the goods is to be calculated by reference to the value of those goods at the place and time of delivery, which is fixed according to the commodity exchange price 'or, if there is no such price, according to their market price or, if there is no commodity exchange price or market price, by reference to the normal value of the goods of the same kind and quality at the place of delivery'. Article 59 provides that this measure of calculation also applies to claims for loss of or damage to the goods arising out of delay.

Article 23 establishes a presumption of delivery of the goods by the carrier in accordance with their description in the contract particulars,[30] 'unless notice of loss of or damage to the goods, indicating the general nature of such loss or damage, was given to the carrier or the performing party that delivered the goods before or at the time of the delivery'; alternatively, 'if the loss or damage is not apparent, within seven working days at the place of delivery after the delivery of the goods'. Such a notice is not required where the loss or damage has been established by a joint inspection of the goods. There is no compensation for delay unless 'notice of loss due to delay was given to the carrier within 21 consecutive days following delivery of the goods'. Notices given to the performing party that delivered the goods have the same effect as if they had been given to the carrier, and notices to the carrier have the same effect as if they had been given to a maritime performing party. Paragraph (2) provides that a failure to give the notices referred to in Art 21 shall not affect the right to claim compensation for loss of or damage to the goods under the Convention, nor will it affect the allocation of the burden of proof under Art 17. However, no reference is made here to claims for delay and claimants will need to take particular care to give the appropriate notice of such claims.

Chapter Six – additional provisions relating to particular stages of carriage

Article 24 provides that if a deviation constitutes a breach of the carrier's obligations, under applicable law, that will not prevent the carrier or a maritime performing party from relying on Convention defences or limitations, except as provided in Art 61, which specifies when the right to limit is lost. This alters the common law position whereby a deviation will deprive a carrier of its contractual rights and immunities and reduce it to the status of a common carrier from the moment of the deviation onwards, even if the deviation is not causative of the loss or damage claimed.

Article 25(1) permits carriage of deck cargo in three situations only: (a) such carriage is required by law; (b) the goods are carried in or on containers on decks that are specially fitted to carry such containers; (c) the carriage on deck is in accordance with the contract of carriage, or the customs, usages, and practices of the trade in question.[31] The carrier may not rely on this third heading as against good-faith third-party holders of a negotiable transport document, or electronic equivalent, unless the deck carriage is stated in the contract particulars. The Convention's provisions as to the carrier's liability apply to loss of, damage to or delay in the delivery of goods carried on

---

30 The presumption is subject to proof to the contrary.
31 In contrast, Art 1(c) of the Hague-Visby Rules merely excludes 'cargo which by the contract of carriage is stated as being carried on deck and is so carried' from its definition of 'goods' and is silent as to when it is permissible to carry cargo on deck.

deck as permitted by Art 25(1). However, in the first and third of the situations in which deck carriage is permitted, the carrier is not liable where the loss, damage or delay is caused by the special risks involved in the deck carriage. Where the deck carriage is not permitted under Art 25(1), the carrier is liable for loss, damage or delay that is exclusively caused by the carriage of the goods on deck, and may not rely on the defences in Art 17. Presumably, the burden of proving this will fall on the claimant. Where the cargo is carried on deck and the carrier has expressly agreed with the shipper to carry it under deck, para (5) prevents the carrier from limiting its liability 'to the extent that such loss, damage, or delay' resulted from the carriage of the goods on deck.

Article 26 deals with the situation in which the loss, damage, or the event causing delay, occurs during the carrier's period of responsibility, but solely before their loading onto the ship or solely after their discharge from the ship. In this event, the provisions of this Convention do not prevail over those provisions of another international instrument that, at the time of such loss, damage or event or circumstance causing delay:

(a)   pursuant to the provisions of such international instrument would have applied to all or any of the carrier's activities if the shipper had made a separate and direct contract with the carrier in respect of the particular stage of carriage where the loss of, or damage to goods, or an event or circumstance causing delay in their delivery occurred;

(b)   specifically provide for the carrier's liability, limitation of liability, or time for suit; and

(c)   cannot be departed from by contract either at all or to the detriment of the shipper under that instrument.

This attempts to provide a network solution to the problems of competing conventions that occur with multimodal carriage. Provisions of another international 'instrument' will prevail over the Convention, but only to the extent that they relate to the carrier's liability, limitation of liability and time for suit, cannot be departed from to the shipper's detriment under the terms of the other 'instrument' and would have applied to a hypothetical contract between the shipper and the carrier for the particular stage of carriage where the loss, damage, or event causing delay occurred.[32] Thus, provisions of the Convention relating to the right of control will still prevail over those in the other 'instrument' and will also prevail where the claimant is unable to prove where during the carriage the loss occurred. There is a more fundamental problem with the CMR in that a hypothetical road contract for, say, the pre-maritime leg of the carriage would, in many cases, fall outside the ambit of that Convention. For example, if goods were damaged on the UK road leg of a contract for road carriage from the UK to France involving roll-on, roll-off (ro-ro) carriage by sea, the hypothetical contract would be for domestic UK road carriage. This would not be 'international road carriage' as required by Art 1 of the CMR. However, it is possible to read Art 26 so that one looks at the hypothetical contract in its entirety for 'the particular stage of carriage where the loss of, or damage to goods . . . occurred'. The hypothetical contract would be the same as the actual contract of carriage, but a contract subject to the CMR. On this reading, the CMR would prevail as regards issues of liability, limitation and time for suit. However, conflicts would still arise as regards other issues, such as the right of control or jurisdiction. An example would be where there is a carriage by road and by sea between states that are parties to both the CMR and the Convention, but where only the state of delivery has opted into the jurisdiction regime contained in Chapter Fourteen of the Convention. The CMR, but not the Convention, permits suit to be commenced in the place where the branch or agency through which the contract was made is

32   The reference here is to 'instrument' rather than 'convention', which would cover, for example, a EU Regulation covering the carrier's activities.

located. The CMR and the Convention also contain rather different provision as regards arbitration and choice of law agreements.

Chapter Seven – obligations of the shipper

Article 27 sets out the shipper's obligations as regards the condition of the goods on delivery. They must be 'ready for carriage and in such condition that they will withstand the intended carriage, including their loading, handling, stowage, lashing and securing and discharge, and that they will not cause injury or damage'. This would probably cover a situation such as arose in *Transoceanica Societa Italiana di Navigazione v H S Shipton & Sons*,[33] where the goods are loaded in such a condition as to cause delay in the discharging process. A similar obligation is imposed by paragraph (3) in relation to goods that are delivered in or on a container or trailer packed by the shipper. Paragraph (2) provides that the obligations of the shipper and documentary shipper under 'fiost' contracts are to be performed properly and carefully. This provision may well give rise to a claim for detention against these parties, similar to that which arises under *Fowler v Knoop*,[34] although it is uncertain whether a carrier can claim against a shipper under the Convention in respect of economic loss resulting from delay. Article 28 requires the carrier and shipper to respond to requests from each other for information and instructions required for the proper handling and carriage of the goods. Article 29 requires the shipper to provide, in a timely manner, information, instructions and documents that are reasonably necessary for the handling and carriage of the cargo, compliance with rules and regulations relating to the intended carriage, and the compilation of the contract particulars and the issuance of the transport documents or electronic records. Unlike the information and instructions required under Art 28, this information must be provided by the shipper whether or not it is requested by the carrier.

Article 31 deals with the information that the shipper must supply for inclusion in the contract particulars and the transport document or electronic transport records. These include:

(a) the particulars referred to in Art 36(1);[35]
(b) the name of the party to be identified as the shipper in the contract particulars;
(c) the name of the consignee, if any; and
(d) the name of the person to whose order the transport document or electronic transport record is to be issued, if any.

The information must be provided in a timely manner and its accuracy at the time of its receipt by the carrier is guaranteed by the shipper, who is required to indemnify the carrier against loss or damage resulting from the inaccuracy of such information.[36] This is a provision that will become increasingly important in the light of the sanctions imposed for misdescription of containerised cargoes under customs measures such as the US 24 Hours Advanced Manifest Rule, which came into effect on 2 February 2003 in respect of all containerised cargo for discharge at US ports.

Article 32 is the counterpart to the first sentence of Art IV(6) of the Hague and Hague-Visby Rules, which refers to 'goods of an inflammable, explosive or dangerous nature'. However,

---

33 [1923] 1 KB 31. It is, however, uncertain whether economic loss due to delay can be recovered from the shipper under Art 30.
34 (1878) 4 QBD 299.
35 The contract particulars in the transport document or electronic transport record referred to in Art 35 shall include the following information, as furnished by the shipper:

    (a) a description of the goods as appropriate for the transport;
    (b) the leading marks necessary for identification of the goods;
    (c) the number of packages or pieces, or the quantity of goods; and
    (d) the weight of the goods, if furnished by the shipper.

36 The provision is an expanded version of Art III(5) of the Hague and Hague-Visby Rules. However, the shipper must not only guarantee the accuracy of the information, it must also provide it 'in a timely manner'.

Art 32 refers only to 'danger' and also introduces a reference to danger to the environment. This will bring in cargo that is legally dangerous by reason of any public law liability that the carrier may incur in carrying it due to the threat it poses to the environment. The power to dispose of dangerous goods, which is to be found in the second sentence of Art IV(6), is now to be found in Art 15. Subparagraph (b) makes it clear that the regime for dangerous cargo extends to compliance with legal requirements as to marking and labelling of the goods. These legal requirements are laws, regulations or other requirements and apply at any stage of the intended carriage, not just at the port of discharge. However, the provision does not cover legal requirements that prevent the cargo being unloaded at the port of discharge, of the sort encountered in *Mitchell Cotts & Co v Steel Bros Ltd*.[37] This type of 'legally dangerous' cargo would fall under Art 29 instead, and would be subject to a fault-based liability, rather than strict liability.

Article 30 imposes on the shipper and documentary shipper a fault-based liability regime for breaches of obligations under Chapter Seven. However, strict liability is imposed for breaches of the shipper's obligations under Arts 31 and 32. Liability is incurred only as regards 'the carrier' and not any other party, such as performing parties or owners of other cargo that sustain loss or damage as a result of the breach. Article 30 refers to the shipper's liability for 'loss or damage' sustained by the carrier, but there is no reference to economic loss sustained as a result of delay. Is delay covered by the words 'loss or damage'? It is likely that it is not. The Convention pointedly does refer to liability for delay, but only in respect of the liability of the carrier and of maritime performing parties.[38] An examination of the reports of Working Group III show that the issue of the shipper's liability for delay was subject to much discussion and it was proposed that references to such liability should be retained subject to the adoption of an appropriate limitation figure. This was not possible and the shipper is not able to limit its liability under the Convention. In these circumstances, the omission of any reference to the shipper's liability for delay must represent a clear intention by the drafters of the Convention that the shipper and the documentary shipper incur no such liability for breach of their obligations under Chapter Seven. The Working Group, at para 237, in recommending deletion of references to delay in this provision, suggested the possible inclusion of text clarifying that the applicable law relating to shipper's delay was not intended to be affected. However, no such clarifying text appears in the final draft of the Convention. The reports of the Working Group on this issue, as the *travaux préparatoires*, do not seem to provide the necessary 'bull's eye'[39] on this issue, which will have to be determined *de novo* by national courts.

Chapter Eight – transport documents and electronic transport records

Article 35 specifies the type of documents that the shipper and the documentary shipper are entitled to receive, and is the equivalent provision to Art VI of the Hague and Hague-Visby Rules. The shipper is entitled to obtain from the carrier, at the shipper's option, an appropriate negotiable or non-negotiable transport document or a negotiable or non-negotiable electronic transport record.[40] If the shipper consents, the documentary shipper is similarly entitled. This is subject to contrary agreement by the shipper and carrier, or to contrary customs, usages or practices in the trade.

---

37 [1916] 2 KB 610. The restrictions could be imposed by the authorities at the port of discharge or, as in *Mitchell Cotts*, by the authorities of the flag state.
38 Specific references to delay, in addition to 'loss' or 'damage', are to be found in Arts 17(1), 20 ('joint and several liability') and 23 ('notice in case of loss, damage or delay'). In contrast, Art 22 ('calculation of compensation') refers only to loss or damage. However, Art 60 provides that its provisions shall apply to compensation for loss or damage due to delay, whereas liability for economic loss due to delay is subject to its own limitation figure of two-and-a-half times freight.
39 These were the words used by Lord Steyn in *The Giannis NK* [1998] AC 605, 623F, to describe when the English courts would resolve an issue of interpretation in an international convention by reference to its *travaux préparatoires*.
40 The latter option is subject to the provisions of Art 8(a).

Article 36(1) specifies that there must be included in the transport document or electronic transport record the following contract particulars, furnished by the shipper. A far wider range of information must be included in the transport document than is the case under Art III(3) of the Hague and Hague-Visby Rules. There must be included:

(a)   A description of the goods;
(b)   The leading marks necessary for identification of the goods;
(c)   The number of packages or pieces, or the quantity of goods; and
(d)   The weight of the goods, if furnished by the shipper.

Paragraph (2) then requires the inclusion of the following additional particulars:

(a)   A statement of the apparent order and condition of the goods at the time the carrier or a performing party receives them for carriage;
(b)   The name and address of a person identified as the carrier;
(c)   The date on which the carrier or a performing party received the goods, or on which the goods were loaded on board the ship, or on which the transport document or electronic transport record was issued; and
(d)   If the transport document is negotiable, the number of originals of the negotiable transport document, when more than one original is issued.[41]

Paragraph (3) then refers to the inclusion of the name and address of the consignee, the name of the ship, and the place of receipt and, if known, of delivery.

Paragraph (4) defines 'apparent order and condition of the goods' as:

the order and condition of the goods based on:

(a)   A reasonable external inspection of the goods as packaged at the time the shipper delivers them to the carrier or a performing party; and
(b)   Any additional inspection that the carrier or a performing party actually performs before issuing the transport document or the electronic transport record.

Article 37 deals with the identity of the carrier. Paragraph (1) provides for the conclusive effect of any identification of the carrier by name in the contract particulars, notwithstanding 'any other information in the transport document or electronic transport record relating to the identity of the carrier . . .'. Paragraph (2) deals with the situation in which there is no such identification but the contract particulars state that the goods have been loaded onto a named ship, by creating a presumption that the carrier is the registered owner of the ship. The presumption is rebutted by the registered owner if 'it proves that the ship was under a bareboat charter at the time of the carriage and it identifies this bareboat charterer and indicates its address, in which case this bareboat charterer is presumed to be the carrier. Alternatively, the registered owner may rebut the presumption of being the carrier by identifying the carrier and indicating its address. The bareboat charterer may defeat any presumption of being the carrier in the same manner.' These provisions do not prevent the claimant from proving that any person other than the registered owner is the carrier.

Article 38 requires transport documents to be signed by the carrier or a person acting on its behalf and that electronic transport records are to include the electronic signature of the carrier or a person acting on its behalf.[42] Article 39 provides that the legal character or validity of the transport

---

41   Paragraph (2).
42   'Such electronic signature shall identify the signatory in relation to the electronic transport record and indicate the carrier's authorization of the electronic transport record.'

document or electronic transport record is not affected by the absence or inaccuracy of any of the contract particulars referred to in Art 36(1), (2) and (3). Paragraph (2) deals with the situation in which the contract particulars include the date, but fail to indicate its significance. The date is deemed to be:

(a) The date on which all of the goods indicated in the transport document or electronic transport record were loaded on board the ship, if the contract particulars indicate that the goods have been loaded on board a ship; or

(b) The date on which the carrier or a performing party received the goods, if the contract particulars do not indicate that the goods have been loaded on board a ship.

Paragraph (3) provides that if the contract particulars fail to state the apparent order and condition of the goods at the time that the carrier or a performing party receives them from the consignor, 'the contract particulars are deemed to have stated that the goods were in apparent good order and condition at the time the carrier or a performing party received them'.

Article 40(1) obliges the carrier to qualify the information required in Art 36(1) to indicate that the carrier does not assume responsibility for the accuracy of the information furnished by the shipper. The carrier must do this if:

(a) The carrier has actual knowledge that any material statement in the transport document or electronic transport record is materially false or misleading; or

(b) The carrier reasonably believes that a material statement in the transport document or electronic transport record is false or misleading.

Without prejudice to this provision, the carrier may qualify the information referred to in Art 36(1) to indicate that it does not accept responsibility for the accuracy of the information provided by the shipper in two situations.

First, paragraph (3) entitles this to be done where the goods are not delivered for carriage to the carrier or a performing party in a closed container (as will be the case where bulk cargo is loaded) or where they actually inspect goods that are received in a closed container, in one of two situations. The first is where the carrier had no physically practicable or commercially reasonable means of checking the information provided by the shipper. In this case, it must indicate which information it was unable to check. This will raise an issue with 'said to weigh' clausing in relation to bulk cargo as to whether the carrier had 'physically practicable or commercially reasonable means' of checking the weight provided by the shipper. The second is where the carrier 'has reasonable grounds to believe the information furnished to be inaccurate'. In this case, it may include a clause providing what it reasonably considers 'accurate information'.

Secondly, paragraph (4) permits qualification of the information required in Art 36(1)(a), (b) or (c), where the goods are delivered for carriage to the carrier or performing party in a closed container, subject to the following conditions:

. . . neither the carrier nor a performing party have actually inspected the goods inside the container; neither party otherwise has actual knowledge of the contents of the container before issuing the transport document or the electronic transport record.

The weight particulars referred to in Art 36(1)(d) may be qualified if:

• neither carrier nor a performing party have weighed the container or vehicle; and
• there was no physically practicable or commercially reasonable means of checking the weight of the container or vehicle.

The right to qualify the weight of a container does not apply where the shipper and the carrier have agreed prior to the shipment that the container or vehicle would be weighed and that the weight would be included in the contract particulars. The Convention does not define 'qualification', but it is likely that more is required than a printed 'said to weigh' or 'said to contain' statement in the transport document.

Subject to their qualification as set out in Art 40, the contract particulars are, by Art 41, stated as constituting prima facie evidence of the carrier's receipt of the goods, as stated in the contract particulars in the transport document or electronic transport record.[43] The contract particulars will have conclusive effect when included in:

(i)   a negotiable transport document or a negotiable electronic transport record that is transferred to a third party acting in good faith; or

(ii)   a non-negotiable transport document or a non-negotiable electronic transport record that indicates that it must be surrendered in order to obtain delivery of the goods and is transferred to the consignee acting in good faith.

Paragraph (c) then provides that certain particulars shall have conclusive effect when a consignee in good faith, under a non-negotiable transport document (such as a sea waybill) or electronic transport record, has acted in reliance on any of them. The particulars in question are: those referred to in Art 36(1) when furnished by the carrier; the number, type and identifying numbers of the containers, but not the identifying numbers of the container seals; and those referred to in Art 36(2).

This chapter concludes with Art 42, which deals with effect of 'freight prepaid' clausing, and is all that remains of a separate chapter, Chapter Nine, which dealt with freight under a previous draft of the Convention. It provides:

> If the contract particulars contain the statement 'freight prepaid' or a statement of a similar nature, the carrier cannot assert against the holder or the consignee the fact that the freight has not been paid. This article does not apply if the holder or the consignee is also the shipper.

This provision operates in favour of the holder or the consignee, but not in favour of the shipper. This would appear to restate existing law on the operation of such wording by way of estoppel. However, two points need to be made. First, under existing law, there may be situations in which a bill of lading holder that is not the original shipper may be unable to rely on such wording. Suppose that the bill of lading incorporates the terms of a subcharter and is then indorsed to the sub-charterer. The subcharterer would be unable to rely on the estoppel created by the wording because it would know for itself whether or not freight had been paid under the subcharter. In contrast, under Art 42, such a holder would be able to rely on the 'freight prepaid' wording. Secondly, the provision is directed at 'freight prepaid' wording in its estoppel role with its reference to 'the fact that the freight has not been paid'. It says nothing, however, about the impact of such clausing in determining whether the original shipper has undertaken any liability to pay freight in the first place. In Cho Yang Shipping Co Ltd v Coral (UK) Ltd,[44] such clausing was held to be an important part of the factual matrix, which rebutted the presumption that the bill of lading shipper had undertaken

---

43 Qualifications other than those permitted or required under Art 40 will therefore be ineffective. This deals with the problem that arose in *The Mata K* [1998] 2 Lloyd's Rep 614, regarding qualifications as to the weight of the cargo loaded, which were alleged not to comply with the proviso to Art III(3) of the Hague-Visby Rules. Anthony Diamond QC, op cit fn 21, p 169, raises a number of queries about the application of these provisions, in particular, as to who bears the burden of proof when a claimant challenges a qualification by the carrier, and as to how the provisions will work with carriage of bulk cargoes. As regards the latter, he writes: 'At the time of shipment the Convention will not apply if, as is usual, the bills of lading are issued in non-liner transportation. But the bills may subsequently be indorsed to one or more third parties, so that the Convention then applies. Will a clause that is valid on shipment subsequently be invalidated? I suspect that these and other questions will be answered differently in the courts of different countries.'

44 [1997] 2 Lloyd's Rep 641.

to pay freight. This issue will remain to be dealt with according to national laws, as the Convention does not deal with the shipper's liability for freight.

Chapter Nine – delivery of the goods

Chapter Nine deals with delivery of the goods and largely codifies the existing English law on this topic. Article 43 requires the consignee that demands delivery under the contract of carriage to accept delivery of the goods on arrival at their destination. It does not specify what remedy is available to the carrier in the event that such consignee fails to accept delivery of the goods. Article 44 requires the consignee to acknowledge receipt from the carrier or the performing party in the manner that is customary at the place of delivery, on the request of either of these parties. The carrier may refuse delivery if the consignee refuses to acknowledge such receipt.

There then follow a series of Articles that deal with delivery under three classes of transport documents: non-negotiable transport records/electronic transport records; non-negotiable transport documents under which surrender of the document is required to obtain delivery; and negotiable transport documents/electronic records. These provisions also deal with the carrier's rights and duties when the goods cannot be delivered as specified by the Convention, as when the party entitled to take delivery does not come forward to do so. The first of these three categories is covered by Art 45, which provides that the carrier shall deliver the goods to the consignee at the time and location referred to in Art 43, and may refuse delivery if the person claiming to be the consignee does not properly identify itself as the consignee on the request of the carrier. If the contract particulars do not specify the consignee's name and address, the controlling party must advise the carrier of these details before or upon the arrival of the goods. If the carrier does not know the consignee's name and address or if the consignee, having received notice of arrival, does not claim delivery of the goods from the carrier after their arrival, the carrier must so advise the controlling party. If, after reasonable effort, it is unable to locate the controlling party, it must notify the shipper.[45] These parties must then give the carrier delivery instructions. Delivery pursuant to the instructions of these parties then discharges the carrier from its obligations to deliver the goods under the contract of carriage.

The second category, non-negotiable transport documents and electronic transport records that require surrender, falls under Art 46, which provides that the consignee must not only produce proper identification at the carrier's request, but must also surrender the document. If more than one original has been issued, the surrender of only one original will suffice and the other originals will then cease to have any effect. If the consignee cannot be located, the carrier may deliver to the shipper, or documentary shipper if the shipper, too, cannot be located. Such delivery may be made without production of an original document. Delivery pursuant to the instructions of these parties then discharges the carrier from its obligations to deliver the goods under the contract of carriage. This is a significant change in the law relating to delivery under straight bills of lading.

The third category, negotiable transport documents and electronic transport records, falls under Art 47. The holder of such document or record is entitled to claim delivery of the goods from the carrier after they have arrived at the place of destination. In this event, the carrier shall deliver the goods at the time and location referred to in Art 43, to the holder, as appropriate. This shall be done upon surrender of the negotiable transport document and, additionally, if the holder is one of the persons referred to in Art 1(10)(a)(i),[46] upon proper identification. Surrender of one original of multiple original documents will suffice.[47] The others will then cease to have effect or validity.

---

45 If neither party can be located by the carrier, after reasonable effort, the documentary shipper is deemed to be the shipper.
46 The shipper, consignee or indorsee, where the document is an order document.
47 The existing common law position is somewhat different in that delivery against one original bill of lading will only provide the carrier with a defence to an action in conversion if it had no actual or constructive knowledge that another party had the immediate right to possession in the goods.

The holder of a negotiable electronic transport record must demonstrate, in accordance with the procedures referred to in Art 9(1), that it is the holder of that record. The electronic transport record will then cease to have any effect or validity upon delivery to the holder in accordance with the procedures required by Art 9(1). The carrier shall refuse delivery if these conditions are not met.

Paragraph (2) provides rules for delivery under negotiable transport documents/electronic records that expressly state that the goods may be delivered without the surrender of the transport document or electronic transport record. These rules are without prejudice to the rules regarding undelivered goods that are contained in Art 48. The rules under paragraph 2 contemplate the goods not being deliverable due to a failure of the holder to claim delivery at the place of destination after receiving a notice of arrival; or a failure of the holder properly to identify itself as one of the persons referred to in Art 1(10)(a)(i); or the inability of the carrier, after reasonable effort, to locate the holder in order to request delivery instructions. In these circumstances, the carrier may advise the shipper and request delivery instructions from it instead. If, after reasonable effort, the shipper cannot be located, the carrier may obtain instructions from the documentary shipper. Subparagraph (b) provides that delivery on the instructions of these parties in these circumstances will discharge the carrier from its contractual obligation to deliver to the holder, even if there has been no surrender of the negotiable transport document or compliance with the procedures set out in Art 9(1) regarding delivery to the holder of a negotiable electronic transport record. Subparagraph (c) entitles the carrier to an indemnity, against loss arising from liability from the holder under subparagraph (e), from the shipper/documentary shipper that gives delivery instructions in such circumstances. The carrier is entitled to refuse to follow the instructions of the shipper/documentary shipper if they fail to provide adequate security as the carrier may reasonably request.

Subparagraph (d) deals with the problem of 'spent' negotiable transport documents or negotiable electronic records. A person who becomes a holder of either of these after delivery pursuant to paragraph (b), but pursuant to contractual or other arrangements made before such delivery, acquires rights against the carrier under the contract of carriage, other than the right to claim delivery of the goods.[48] Subparagraph (e) then provides that, notwithstanding subparagraphs (b) and (d), the holder will acquire the rights incorporated in the negotiable transport document or negotiable electronic transport record provided that it did not have, or could not reasonably have had, knowledge of such delivery at the time that it became a holder. This will be presumed 'when the contract particulars state the expected time of arrival of the goods or indicate how to obtain information as to whether the goods have been delivered'.

Article 48 deals with the situation in which goods remain undelivered. Paragraph (1) provides that the goods shall be deemed to have remained undelivered at the place of destination only if:

(a) the consignee does not accept delivery of the goods pursuant to this chapter at the time and location referred to in Art 43;
(b) the controlling party or the shipper cannot be found or does not give the carrier adequate instructions pursuant to Arts 45, 46 and 47;
(c) the carrier is entitled or required to refuse delivery pursuant to Arts 44, 45, 46 and 47;
(d) the carrier is not allowed to deliver the goods to the consignee pursuant to the law or regulations of the place at which delivery is requested;
(e) the goods are otherwise undeliverable by the carrier.

---

48 The rule is in terms similar to those used with regard to 'spent' bills of lading in s 2(2)(a) of COGSA 1992. The rule, however, applies only to negotiable transport documents that expressly provide for delivery of the goods without surrender of the document.

Paragraph (2) then entitles the carrier,[49] at the risk and expense of the person entitled to the goods, to take such action in respect of the goods as circumstances may reasonably require. This includes: storing the goods at any suitable place; unpacking the goods if they are packed in containers, or to act otherwise in respect of the goods, including by moving the goods or causing them to be destroyed; and causing the goods to be sold in accordance with the practices, or pursuant to the law or regulations of the place where the goods are located at the time. Paragraph (3) states that these rights are subject to giving 'reasonable advance notice of arrival of the goods at the place of destination to the person stated in the contract particulars as the person, if any, to be notified of the arrival of the goods at the place of destination, and to one of the following persons in the order indicated, if known to the carrier: the consignee, the controlling party or the shipper'. Paragraph (4) requires the carrier to hold the proceeds of the sale 'for the benefit of the person entitled to the goods, subject to the deduction of any costs incurred by the carrier and any other amounts that are due to the carrier in connection with the carriage of those goods'. Paragraph (5) provides that the carrier shall not be liable for loss or damage to the goods occurring during the time that they are undelivered. However, the claimant may claim if it can prove that the loss or damage was the result of the carrier's failure to take reasonable steps to preserve the goods, and that the carrier knew or ought to have known that loss or damage would result from its failure to take such steps. Article 49 preserves any lien that may enure to the carrier or performing party under the contract of carriage or the applicable law.

Chapter Ten – rights of the controlling party

Chapter Ten sets out the rights of the controlling party. At common law, the consignor has the right to change the identity of the consignee up to the point at which the cargo is delivered. Where a negotiable document has been issued, that right will terminate upon transfer of that document. Under the Convention, the right of control exists during the entire period of responsibility of the carrier, as provided in Art 12. Article 50 provides that it may be exercised only by the controlling party and is limited to three rights: to give or modify instructions in respect of the goods that do not constitute a variation of the contract of carriage; to obtain delivery of the goods at a scheduled port of call or, in respect of inland carriage, any place en route; and to replace the consignee by any other person including the controlling party. The second of these rights does not currently exist under English law.

Article 51 then identifies the controlling party. Paragraph (1) sets out the basic rule whereby the shipper is the controlling party 'unless the shipper, when the contract of carriage is concluded, designates the consignee, the documentary shipper or another person as the controlling party'. The controlling party may transfer the right of control to another person and the transfer will bind the carrier upon its notification of the transfer by the transferor. The transferee then becomes the controlling party. The controlling party must produce proper identification when it exercises the right of control. This provision would appear to permit the consignee designating another party as a controlling party, so transforming a waybill, or its electronic equivalent, into a quasi-negotiable transport document.

There then follow three specific rules to deal with: non-negotiable transport documents that require surrender (straight bills of lading); negotiable transport documents (bills of lading); and negotiable electronic transport records. Paragraph (2) deals with the situation in which a non-negotiable transport document or a non-negotiable electronic transport record has been issued, requiring its surrender in order to obtain delivery of the goods. The shipper is the controlling party

---

49 'Unless otherwise agreed and without prejudice to any other rights that the carrier may have against the shipper, controlling party or consignee . . .'.

and may transfer the right of control to the consignee named in the transport document or the electronic transport record by transferring the document to this person without indorsement, or by transferring the electronic transport record to it in accordance with the procedures referred to in Art 9.[50] To exercise its right of control, the controlling party must produce all originals of the document, as well as proper identification.[51]

Paragraph (3) deals with the situation in which a negotiable transport document is issued. The controlling party is the holder of all of the original negotiable transport documents. The holder may transfer the right of control by transferring all of the original negotiable transport documents to another person in accordance with Art 57. To exercise the right of control, the holder must produce all of the negotiable transport documents to the carrier. If the holder of an order document is one of the persons referred to in Art 1(10h)(a)(i), they must also produce proper identification.

Paragraph (4) deals with the situation in which a negotiable electronic transport record is issued. The holder is the controlling party and may transfer the right of control to another person by transferring the negotiable electronic transport record in accordance with the procedures referred to in Art 9. To exercise the right of control, the holder must demonstrate that it is the holder, in accordance with the procedures referred to in Art 9.

Article 52 requires the carrier to execute the instructions referred in Art 50 subject to three conditions. First, the person giving such instructions is entitled to exercise the right of control. Secondly, 'the instructions can reasonably be executed according to their terms at the moment that they reach the carrier'. Thirdly, 'the instructions will not interfere with the normal operations of the carrier, including its delivery practices'. The carrier is entitled to be reimbursed by the controlling party for any expense that it may incur as a result of executing its instructions. It is also entitled to an indemnity 'against any loss or damage that the carrier may suffer as a result of executing any instruction pursuant to this article, including compensation that the carrier may become liable to pay for loss of or damage to other goods being carried'. The carrier may also obtain security from the controlling party 'for the amount of additional expense, loss or damage that the carrier reasonably expects will arise in connection with the execution of an instruction pursuant to this article'. If no such security is provided, the carrier is entitled to refuse to carry out the instructions. If the carrier fails to comply with the controlling party's instructions, as required by Art 52(1), its liability for resulting loss of or damage to the goods or for delay in delivery is subject to Arts 17–23. The amount of compensation payable is subject to Arts 59–61. Article 53 provides that goods delivered pursuant to such an instruction are deemed to be delivered at the place of destination, and the provisions of Chapter Nine relating to such delivery apply to such goods.

Article 54 deals with variations to the contract of carriage. Only the controlling party may agree with the carrier to variations to the contract of carriage other than those referred to in Art 50(1)(b) and (c). All contractual variations 'shall be stated in a negotiable transport document or incorporated in a negotiable electronic transport record, or, at the option of the controlling party, shall be stated in a non-negotiable transport document or incorporated in a non-negotiable electronic transport record'.[52] Such variations do not affect the rights and obligations of the parties prior to the date on which they are signed in accordance with Art 38. Article 56 also entitles the parties to the contract of carriage to vary the effect of Arts 50(1)(b) and (c), (2), and 52, and also to restrict or exclude the transferability of the right of control referred to in Art 51(1)(b).

---

50 If more than one original of the document was issued, all originals shall be transferred in order to effect a transfer of the right of control.

51 In the case of an electronic transport record, the holder shall demonstrate in accordance with the procedures referred to in Art 9 that it has exclusive control of the electronic transport record.

52 This preserves the existing law, under *Leduc v Ward* (1888) 20 QBD 475, whereby the terms of the contract between third-party holders of a bill of lading and the carrier are exclusively those contained in the bill of lading, and do not include any variations that may have been agreed between the original contracting parties.

Chapter Eleven – transfer of rights

Article 57 provides that the holder of a negotiable transport document may transfer the rights incorporated in the document as follows. Where the document is an order document, the transfer is through an indorsement to another person, or in blank. Transfer by indorsement is not required where the document is a bearer document or a blank indorsed document, or the document is made out to the order of a named person and the transfer is between the first holder and the named person. When a negotiable electronic transport record is issued, paragraph (2) provides that its holder may 'transfer the rights incorporated in it, whether it be made out to order or to the order of a named person, by transferring the electronic transport record in accordance with the procedures referred to in article 9, paragraph 1'. There is no provision defining the point at which a transfer of a negotiable transport document will cease to transfer the rights incorporated in that document. Presumably, the document would continue to be transferable at least until delivery of the goods and transfers of contractual rights would therefore continue to be possible during the final land carriage leg of a multimodal contract of carriage.[53] The Convention contains no provision divesting parties of rights of suit of the sort seen in s 2(5) of the **Carriage of Goods by Sea Act (COGSA) 1992**. The transfer of rights and liabilities under non-negotiable documents, such as straight bills and waybills, will continue to be dealt with under national laws.

Liability of third parties under negotiable transport documents or their electronic equivalents is dealt with under Art 58. The transfer of rights and liabilities under non-negotiable transport documents, or their electronic equivalents, or under delivery orders, falls outside the Convention and is left to be dealt with under national laws. Paragraph (2) sets out, as follows, the circumstances in which a third-party holder of such a document will become subject to liabilities under the contract of carriage:

> A holder that is not the shipper and that exercises any right under the contract of carriage assumes any liabilities imposed on it under the contract of carriage to the extent that such liabilities are incorporated in or ascertainable from the negotiable transport document or the negotiable electronic transport record.

Paragraph (1) provides that a holder that is not the shipper will not be liable if it does not exercise any right under the contract of carriage 'solely by reason of being a holder'. Paragraph (3) then provides two instances in which the holder that is not the shipper will not be taken to have exercised any right under the contract of carriage. The first is where 'It agrees with the carrier, pursuant to article 10, to replace a negotiable transport document by a negotiable electronic transport record or to replace a negotiable electronic transport record by a negotiable transport document.' The second is where it transfers its rights pursuant to Art 57.

These provisions will operate rather differently as regards third parties than is the case under existing law. Under s 3(1) of **COGSA 1992**, the lawful holder who satisfies one of the three triggers for liability becomes 'subject to the same liabilities under that contract as if he had been a party to that contract'. In contrast, Art 58 operates so that the holder 'assumes any liabilities imposed on it under the contract of carriage to the extent that such liabilities are incorporated in or ascertainable from the negotiable transport document or the negotiable electronic transport record'.[54] This would include any express liability for freight imposed by the terms of the bill of lading itself or through the incorporation of charterparty terms. It would not, however, subject the holder to any implied

---

53 The position regarding spent bills is dealt with under Art 47(2)(b) in terms similar to those to be found in s 2(2)(a) of COGSA 1992. This provision, however, applies only where the transport document expressly provides for delivery of cargo without surrender of the document.

54 Where the holder is also the charterer, as was the case in *The Dunelmia* [1970] 1 QB 289, it will fall outside the provisions of the Convention by virtue of Art 6.

obligation to pay freight that may have been imposed on the original shipper. Article 58 contains no provisions relating to the continuing liability of the original shipper, as is provided for in s 3(3) of **COGSA 1992**, and none relating to the divestment of liability from subsequent parties when they cease to be the holder of a negotiable transport document or negotiable electronic record.

One area of uncertainty that remains is what degree of incorporation or ascertainability is required in the wording of the negotiable transport document, to impose charterparty liabilities for freight and demurrage on the holder of the negotiable transport document. For example, will an express reference be needed to the relevant freight and demurrage provisions? Will it be necessary to go further and specify the amount of freight unpaid at the date on which the negotiable transport document is signed?

Chapter Twelve – limits of liability

Article 59 sets the limits of liability for the carrier's breaches of its obligations under the Convention at 875 SDRs per package or other shipping unit, or 3 SDRs per kilogram of the gross weight of the goods that are the subject of the claim or dispute, whichever amount is the higher.[55] The wording of the gross weight alternative differs from that used in the Hague-Visby Rules and should avoid the result in *The Limnos*,[56] where the gross weight was held to be limited to that of the cargo that was physically lost or damaged, notwithstanding that other cargo, although physically sound, had been economically damaged. Paragraph (2) adopts the Hague-Visby provision relating to the identification of the package of shipping unit when goods are carried in a container. Article 60 provides a separate limit of liability for economic loss due to delay. This is fixed at an amount equivalent to two-and-a-half times the freight payable on the goods delayed. Article 60 also provides that loss of or damage to the goods due to delay is calculated in accordance with Art 22. The total amount payable under Arts 59 and 60 must not exceed the limit that would apply under Art 59(1) in respect of a total loss of the goods concerned. Article 61 removes the right to limit from the carrier, or any of the parties listed in Art 18, if the claimant proves that 'the loss resulting from the breach of the carrier's obligation under this Convention was attributable to a personal act or omission of the person claiming a right to limit done with the intent to cause such loss or recklessly and with knowledge that such loss would probably result'. Article 61(2) contains a similar provision as regards the benefit of the limitation of liability for delay contained in Art 60. There are no limitation provisions in respect of the liabilities incurred under Chapter Seven by the shipper and the documentary shipper.

Chapter Thirteen – time for suit

Article 62(1) provides that 'No judicial or arbitral proceedings in respect of claims or disputes arising from a breach of an obligation under this Convention may be instituted after the expiration of a period of two years'.[57] Accordingly, the time bar may be relied on by the shipper and documentary shipper, and not just by the carrier and any maritime performing party. Article 62(3) provides that, notwithstanding the expiration of the two-year time bar under the Convention, 'one party may rely on its claim as a defence or for the purpose of set-off against a claim asserted by the other party'. Contrary to the position under *The Aries*,[58] it is likely that a cargo claim that had become

---

55 'Except when the value of the goods has been declared by the shipper and included in the contract particulars, or when a higher amount than the amount of limitation of liability set out in this article has been agreed upon between the carrier and the shipper.'

56 [2008] EWHC 1036 (Comm); [2008] 2 Lloyd's Rep 166.

57 The time bar operates procedurally rather than substantially, as under Art III(6) of the Hague Rules, which refers to the carrier and the ship being discharged from all liability.

58 [1977] 1 WLR 185.

time-barred could now be set off as against the carrier's claim for freight. The provision refers to 'a claim asserted by the other party' and does not limit such a claim to one that arises under the Convention. The time bar may be relied on not only by the carrier and a maritime performing party, but also by a shipper or documentary shipper that incurs a liability to the carrier under Chapter Seven. Article 63 provides for the possibility of extensions being granted by a declaration to the claimant. Article 64 deals with the time limits for indemnity actions. These may be instituted after the expiry of the time limit in Art 62 either within the time allowed by the applicable law of the jurisdiction in which proceedings are instituted, or within 90 days of the claim being settled by the person instituting indemnity proceedings or of that person being served with process in an action against itself. Article 65 contains similar provisions relating to actions against the bareboat charterer or the person identified as the carrier under Art 37(2). The 90 days run from the identification of the carrier or from when the presumption under Art 37(2) is rebutted.

Chapter Fourteen – jurisdiction

This chapter applies only if a Contracting State has opted into it under Art 91. Article 66(a) provides for actions against the carrier to be brought in the following places:

> In a competent court within the jurisdiction of which is situated one of the following places:
>
> (i)   The domicile of the carrier;
> (ii) The place of receipt agreed in the contract of carriage;
> (iii) The place of delivery agreed in the contract of carriage; or
> (iv) The port where the goods are initially loaded on a ship or the port where the goods are finally discharged from a ship.

Alternatively, subparagraph (b) permits proceedings to be brought in a court designated by an agreement between the shipper and the carrier. Article 67 provides that such a court will be exclusive only if the parties so agree and if their agreement:

> (a) Is contained in a volume contract that clearly states the names and addresses of the parties and either (i) is individually negotiated or (ii) contains a prominent statement that there is an exclusive choice of court agreement and specifies the sections of the volume contract containing that agreement; and
> (b) Clearly designates the courts of one Contracting State or one or more specific courts of one Contracting State.

Third parties to the volume contract are only bound by such an exclusive choice of court agreement if:

(a)   the court is in one of the places designated in Art 66, para (a);
(b)   that agreement is contained in the transport document or electronic transport record;
(c)   that person is given timely and adequate notice of the court in which the action shall be brought and that the jurisdiction of that court is exclusive; and
(d)   the law of the court seized recognises that that person may be bound by the exclusive choice of court agreement.

Article 68 gives the plaintiff the right to sue the maritime performing party under the Convention in a competent court situated in the domicile of the maritime performing party or 'the port where the goods are received by the maritime performing party, the port where the goods are delivered by the maritime performing party or the port in which the maritime performing party performs its activities with respect to the goods'. Under Art 72, after a dispute has arisen, the parties may agree to resolve it in any competent court. If the defendant appears before a competent court without contesting jurisdiction, that court has jurisdiction. Article 69 provides that there are no other bases of jurisdiction for proceedings under the Convention against either a carrier or a maritime performing party. Article 70 provides that the Convention does not affect jurisdiction with regard to provisional or protective measures, including arrest. However, the court in which such proceedings are taken has no jurisdiction to hear the case on the merits unless it falls with the requirements of Chapter Fifteen or is given such jurisdiction by an international convention that applies in that state.

Article 71 deals with consolidation and removal of actions where a single action is brought against the carrier and the maritime performing party arising out of a single occurrence. The consolidated action must be brought in a court that has jurisdiction under both Arts 66 and 68, and if there is none, then proceedings may be brought in a court falling under Art 68(b). This is subject to an exception where there is an exclusive choice of court agreement that is binding under Arts 67 or 72. Carriers or maritime performing parties that commence proceedings for a declaration of non-liability in a court authorised under this chapter must withdraw the action once the defendant has chosen their court, as permitted under Arts 66 or 68. Article 73 deals with enforcement and recognition of judgments given in Contracting States by other Contracting States, where both states have opted into the provisions of this chapter.

Chapter Fifteen – arbitration

This chapter applies only if a Contracting State has opted into it under Art 91. Article 75 permits the parties to refer disputes relating to the carriage of goods under the Convention to arbitration. Paragraph (2) provides that the proceedings shall take place, at the option of the person claiming against the carrier at:

(a) Any place designated for that purpose in the arbitration agreement; or
(b) Any other place situated in a State where any of the following places is located:
   (i) The domicile of the carrier;
   (ii) The place of receipt agreed in the contract of carriage;
   (iii) The place of delivery agreed in the contract of carriage; or
   (iv) The port where the goods are initially loaded on a ship or the port where the goods are finally discharged from a ship.

The agreed arbitration venue binds the parties to the agreement if it is contained in a volume contract that clearly states the names and addresses of the parties and is either individually negotiated or contains a prominent statement that there is an arbitration agreement and specifies the sections of the volume contract containing the arbitration agreement. Third parties are bound by the designation of the place of arbitration only if: the agreed place is situated in one of the places referred to in Art 75(2)(b); the agreement is contained in the transport document or electronic transport record; the person to be bound is given timely and adequate notice of the place of arbitration; and applicable law permits that person to be bound by the arbitration agreement. Any term of the arbitration agreement is void to the extent of any inconsistency with the provisions of Art 75.

Article 76 deals with arbitration agreements in non-liner transportation. The Convention does not affect the enforceability of such agreements where the Convention applies by reason of Art 7 or the parties' voluntary incorporation of the Convention into a contract of carriage that would otherwise fall outside the Convention. However, Art 76 provides that, where the Convention applies by reason of Art 7, the transport document or electronic record must identify the parties to, and the date of, the charterparty or other contract excluded from the application of this Convention by reason of the application of Art 6. The contract must also incorporate by specific reference the clause in the charterparty or other contract that contains the terms of the arbitration agreement.

Article 77 provides that, 'Notwithstanding the provisions of this chapter and chapter 14, after a dispute has arisen the parties to the dispute may agree to resolve it by arbitration in any place'.

Chapter Sixteen – validity of contractual terms

The Convention contains a provision similar to Art III(8) of the Hague and Hague-Visby Rules in Art 79(1), but also applies these principles against the cargo owner in Art 79(2), which provides:

> 2. Unless otherwise provided in this Convention, any term in a contract of carriage is void to the extent that it:
>
> (a) Directly or indirectly excludes, limits, or increases the obligations under this Convention of the shipper, consignee, controlling party, holder, or documentary shipper; or
> (b) Directly or indirectly excludes, limits, or increases the liability of the shipper, consignee, controlling party, holder, or documentary shipper for breach of any of its obligations under this Convention.

This provision would operate so as to prevent the obligations of the shipper and documentary shipper, which are imposed under Chapter Seven, from being extended to third-party holders of the transport document by reason of an express stipulation to that effect. It would also prevent an express contractual term from relieving the shipper or documentary shipper of their liability under Chapter Seven of the Convention.[59]

Article 80 allows for a limited exemption from the Convention as regards volume contracts. These are defined in Art 1(2) as 'a contract of carriage that provides for the carriage of a specified quantity of goods in a series of shipments during an agreed period of time. The specification of the quantity may include a minimum, a maximum or a certain range'.[60] As between the carrier and the shipper, a volume contract to which this Convention applies may provide for greater or lesser rights, obligations and liabilities than those imposed by this Convention. However, paragraph (2) sets out the following conditions for a derogation to be binding: the volume contract must contain a prominent statement that it derogates from this Convention; it must be individually negotiated or must prominently specify the sections of the volume contract containing the derogations; and the shipper must be given an opportunity and notice of the opportunity to conclude a contract of carriage on Convention terms without derogation. The derogation must not be incorporated by reference from another document, nor must it be included in a contract of adhesion that is not subject to negotiation. The obligations in Arts 14(a) and (b), 29 and 32 are not susceptible to derogation, and neither is any liability arising from an act or omission referred to in Art 61. Paragraph (5) then sets out the circumstances in which a volume contract that derogates from the Convention applies as between the carrier and a party other than the shipper. The third party must have received information that prominently states that the volume contract derogates from this Convention and have given its express consent to be bound by such derogations. Such consent must not be 'solely set forth in a carrier's public schedule of prices and services, transport document or electronic transport record'. The burden of proof that the conditions for derogation have been fulfilled falls on the party claiming the benefit of the derogation.

---

59 The penultimate draft of the Convention contained a specific provision directed at such cesser clauses, but this was deleted.
60 Article 80(3) provides that: 'A carrier's public schedule of prices and services, transport document, electronic transport record or similar document is not a volume contract pursuant to para 1 of this article, but a volume contract may incorporate such documents by reference as terms of the contract.'

Article 81 allows the carrier and the performing party to exclude their liability in two situations: first, where the goods are live animals, although liability will still be imposed where it is proved that the loss, damage or delay arose in circumstances that would lead to the loss of the right to limit; secondly, 'if the character or condition of the goods or the circumstances and terms and conditions under which the carriage is to be performed are such as reasonably to justify a special agreement'. This is subject to the provisos that 'ordinary commercial shipments made in the ordinary course of trade are not concerned and no negotiable transport document or negotiable electronic record is or is to be issued for the carriage of the goods'.

Chapter Seventeen – matters not covered by this convention

Article 82 attempts to deal with the problems of overlap between the Convention and existing unimodal conventions by providing that 'Nothing in this Convention affects the application of any of the following international conventions in force at the time this Convention enters into force that regulate the liability of the carrier for loss of or damage to the goods'. Subparagraph (a) refers to any convention dealing with the carriage of goods by air 'to the extent that such convention according to its provisions applies to any part of the contract of carriage'.

Subparagraph (b) deals with road carriage and its wording is rather different. Instead, it refers to 'any convention governing the carriage of goods by road to the extent that such convention according to its provisions applies to the carriage of goods that remain loaded on a vehicle carried on board a ship'. The CMR 'regulates the carrier's liability', so its application is unaffected by anything in the Draft Convention 'to the extent that such convention according to its provisions applies to the carriage of goods that remain loaded on a vehicle carried on board a ship'. If goods remain loaded on the ship, then Art 2 applies the CMR to the entire international contract of carriage by road (it is still such a contract even though another mode of transport is involved), subject to the proviso about maritime-specific loss. It would, therefore, seem as if only such maritime-specific loss will fall within the Convention. This leaves no role for Art 26 as regards multimodal carriage involving road and sea legs. However, Anthony Diamond QC interprets this provision as saying that the CMR will only apply to the extent that its provisions cover loss or damage occurring while the goods remain loaded on the ship – that is, to road-specific loss that happens to occur during the sea transit.[61] That would then give a possible role to Art 26 in relation to what happened before and after the sea leg. This seems to be supported by the *travaux préparatoires* of the Convention, which state that this provision was intended 'to eliminate only a very narrow and unavoidable conflict of convention between the relevant unimodal transport conventions and the convention'.[62]

Subparagraph (c) refers to any convention governing carriage of goods by rail 'to the extent that such convention according to its provisions applies to carriage of goods by sea as a supplement to the carriage by rail'. Similar wording is used in subparagraph (d) as regards conventions governing the carriage of goods by inland waterways.

Article 83 provides that the Convention shall not affect the application of any international convention on global limitation, while Art 84 provides that the Convention shall not affect 'the application of terms in the contract of carriage or provisions of national law regarding the adjustment of general average'. Article 85 excludes the operation of the Convention as regards contracts of carriage for passengers and their luggage, while Art 86 prevents liability arising under the Convention for damage due to a nuclear incident if the operator of the nuclear installation is liable under the specified international conventions or under national law applicable to such damage.

---

61 Diamond op cit fn 21, p 143.
62 A/CN.9/642, para 233.

Chapter Eighteen – final clauses

This chapter provides the procedure for the signature, ratification, acceptance or approval of the Convention. Article 94 provides for the Convention to come into effect one year after the deposit of the twentieth instrument of ratification, acceptance, approval or accession. Article 89 requires states that accept, approve or accede to the Convention to denounce existing maritime conventions to which they are a party – namely, the Hague Rules, the Visby Protocol and its 1979 amending Protocol, and the Hamburg Rules.

Chapter 7

Combined Transport

Chapter Contents

In this chapter, we will examine bills of lading other than the traditional ocean bill of lading involving a single ocean voyage. First, 'received for shipment' bills, where the sea carrier receives goods into its custody prior to their being loaded onto the vessel. Secondly, 'through bills', which involve two sea legs when the cargo is trans-shipped. Thirdly, 'combined transport' or 'multimodal' bills of lading, which involves a sea leg and at least one other mode of transport, such as road carriage.

Unimodal sea carriage

'Received for shipment' bills of lading

Where the sea carrier receives goods into its custody prior to shipment – for example, by reception of the goods into its warehouse at the port of loading – it will issue a 'received for shipment' bill of lading. This can be turned into a 'shipped' bill of lading by annotating it with the date of shipment. There is no clear authority as to whether such a bill of lading can constitute a document of title. Lloyd J, in The Lycaon,[1] assumed that it could be such a document, relying on the decision of the Privy Council in The Marlborough Hill.[2] However, the point in issue in that case was the definition of 'bill of lading' for the purposes of a statute conferring jurisdiction on the Admiralty Court. Diamond Alkali Export Corp v Fl Bourgeois[3] is claimed to be authority for the contrary proposition that such bills can be documents of title. Again, the issue never directly arose in the case, which merely decided that these documents did not amount to good tender under a cif sale, as they would not evidence the condition of the goods on shipment when risk passed.

The issue, therefore, remains in doubt, although such documents are expressly brought within the scope of the **Carriage of Goods by Sea Act (COGSA) 1992**. It is, in any event, almost indisputable that a 'received for shipment' bill that is turned into a 'shipped' bill by annotation of the date of shipment constitutes a document of title, as it then becomes indistinguishable from a 'shipped' bill of lading. At the other end of the spectrum is a 'received for shipment' bill of lading that is issued by someone other than the actual sea carrier, such as a freight forwarder. In The Maheno,[4] such a document was assumed not to be a document of title, although the actual decision proceeded on the basis that the forwarder had not contracted as carrier.

If a 'received for shipment' bill is a document of title, then annotation is the safest course for the sea carrier who wishes to turn it into a 'shipped' bill. A sea carrier who issues a separate set of 'shipped' bills runs the risk of being faced with competing claims for delivery under those bills and under the earlier 'received for shipment' bills. This was the problem that arose in The Lycaon, where the sea carrier decided not to deliver at all, and to carry the goods back to Germany and warehouse them there. It attempted to recover these costs by interpleading under Ord 17. However, it was denied recovery because the problem had only arisen due to the fault of its agent in issuing 'shipped' bills of lading without obtaining an adequate assurance that the 'received for shipment' bills had not been put into circulation. In fact, these bills had been passed on to the shipper in breach of a clear undertaking given by the freight forwarder to whom the agents had initially issued the bills.

Trans-shipment – 'through' bills of lading

When it is commercially inconvenient for the sea carrier to perform the entire sea voyage itself, it will arrange for the goods to be trans-shipped at an intermediate port (assuming that the contract

---

1 [1983] 2 Lloyd's Rep 548.
2 [1921] AC 444.
3 [1921] 3 KB 443.
4 [1977] 1 Lloyd's Rep 81, NZ Ct. A similar assumption was made in Carrington Slipways Pty Ltd v Patrick Operations Pty Ltd (The Cape Cormorin) (1991) 24 NSWLR 745, Sup Ct (NSW).

of carriage contains a liberty to trans-ship). The contract of carriage, although unimodal, now involves two separate sea voyages, as well as warehousing at the intermediate port. The contract of carriage can provide for trans-shipment in one of three main ways, two of which will involve the issue of two different original sets of bills of lading.

First, the carrier can undertake contractual responsibility for the entire voyage. The bill of lading that it issues on loading will be referred to as a 'pure' through bill.[5] Secondly, the carrier can undertake responsibility only for that part of the voyage which it personally performs, thereafter owing only the duty of a freight forwarder to exercise reasonable care in selecting a competent on-carrier. The bill of lading issued on loading will be referred to as a 'false' through bill. Thirdly, the carrier can act both as principal in respect of its own carrying voyage and also as agent for the second sea carrier. A single 'collective' through bill will be issued on loading. This will usually incorporate by reference the standard terms of each successive carrier in relation to that part of the contract that it personally performs.

In the first two examples, bills of lading will need to be issued once on loading, to the consignor, and again on trans-shipment, to the first carrier. The second set of bills of lading will generally evidence a contract of carriage solely between the first and second carriers. Cargo claimants wishing to sue the second carrier will have to do so in tort or bailment, as in *The Pioneer Container*.[6] Those entitled to delivery of the cargo will obtain delivery at the port of discharge by presenting the through bill to the second carrier. Even though the second carrier has not issued this document, the bill of lading that it *did* issue to the first carrier will usually contain a clause making delivery dependent on production of the through bill of lading. Without such a clause, problems on discharge should be avoided by making out the second bill of lading to the order of the first carrier. To avoid the risk of this negotiable document falling into the hands of someone not entitled to delivery under the through bill, the safest solution is for the second carrier to issue a waybill naming the first carrier as consignee.

If the first carrier contracts with the second carrier *as agent* for the shipper, as may exceptionally be the case with a 'false' bill of lading,[7] it will be obliged to surrender the second bill of lading on presentation of the through bill. The cargo claimant will have contractual claims against both carriers under each bill of lading in respect of that part of the contract that they have personally performed. The risks inherent in the creation of two different sets of bills of lading to cover the same shipment are a problem only for the first two types of through bills of lading. However, common to all three types of through bills are the following problems.

First, to what extent are the bills of lading issued by the initial sea carrier documents of title? 'Collective' and 'pure' bills of lading probably do constitute negotiable documents, although some doubts still attach to the status of a 'pure' bill. This is because, although it gives continuous contractual cover, its possessory function as the 'key to the warehouse' is dependent on the contractual arrangements made between the first and second carriers, and the cargo claimant's position is, therefore, less secure than if the entire carriage had been personally performed by the first carrier. The 'false' bill of lading is probably only a document of title as regards the initial sea leg because, in addition to the problems of constructive possession inherent in a 'pure' through bill, such a document confers contractual rights only as regards the first sea leg of the voyage. All three through bills, if issued by a shipowner or charterer, fall within the provisions of **COGSA 1992**.

Secondly, there is the problem that different liability regimes may govern the different sea legs. Under a 'false' through bill, the initial bill of lading may be issued in a Hague-Visby State, and the

---

5 Adopting the terminology used in De Wit, *Multimodal Transport*, 1995, London: LLP, Ch 6.
6 [1994] 2 AC 324, PC.
7 See *The Cape Cormorin* (1991) 24 NSWLR 745, where the first bill was issued by a freight forwarder.

second bill, issued to the first carrier as agent for the original shipper, may be issued in a state applying the Hague Rules or the Hamburg Rules or no international convention (such as the USA). With all three types of through bill, there will be a 'convention gap' in the period of storage at the port of trans-shipment, unless the provisions of the mandatory convention applicable to the first bill of lading can be extended to cover this period, as in *Mayhew Foods Ltd v Overseas Containers Ltd*.[8]

Thirdly, the issuer of a 'pure' bill of lading will wish to extend the protection of that contract to the subcontractors it engages. To achieve this result, it will need to include in the bill of lading either a 'Himalaya' clause or a 'circular indemnity' clause, both of which are discussed in Chapter 2, pp 52–7.

'Combined' or 'multimodal' transport

Most containerised shipments are now carried under 'door to door' contracts of carriage and will involve more than one mode of transport. The contractual carrier may well be a non-vehicle owning carrier ('NVOC') who undertakes the entirety of the carriage making use of subcontractors to perform the actual carriage. The contractual carrier will then take separate bills of lading, waybills, or other transport documents, naming it as the shipper, from the separate actual carriers it will engage to perform the carriage for each leg of the carriage. The cargo owner will have a contractual right of redress against the carrier under the combined transport bill of lading and the carrier will have a right of recourse against the actual carriers under the contracts it makes with them. These actual carriers will in turn use their own subcontractors to perform parts of their own carriage obligations to the combined transport carrier, for example, the use of stevedores to load and discharge the vessel on the sea leg.

The problems associated with 'received for shipment' bills of lading and with 'through' bills of lading occur with even greater severity when the carriage involves 'combined' transport, in that its performance will involve at least two different modes of carriage. This discussion will assume that one of those modes involves a sea leg. It will also assume that the carrier has undertaken responsibility for the entire carriage, as with a 'pure' through bill.

Combined transport bills are acceptable documents for the purposes of Art 19 of UCP 600 provided that they regulate all stages of the carriage, and the same applies as regards through transit bills of lading for the purposes of Art 20 of UCP 600.

Document of title?

A combined transport bill of lading will generally be a 'received for shipment' bill of lading. There is no clear authority as to whether such a bill of lading can constitute a document of title – a document whereby property[9] and possession[10] in the goods represented by the bill can pass during the sea voyage by negotiation without any attornment from the carrier.[11]

A received for shipment bill can be turned into a 'shipped' bill of lading by annotating it with the date of shipment. It will then be a shipped bill and will constitute a document of title. The fact that the bill of lading provides for delivery at an inland location will not prevent it being a

---

8 [1984] 1 Lloyd's Rep 317.
9 Established by *Lickbarrow v Mason* (1794) 5 TR 683.
10 Established by *Barber v Meyerstein* (1871) LR 4 HL 317.
11 See *The Marlborough Hill* [1921] AC 444, and *The Lycaon* [1983] 2 Lloyd's Rep 548, in favour of such a document being a document of title, and *Diamond Alkali Export Corp v Fl Bourgeois* [1921] 3 KB 443, for the contrary proposition.

document of title for the duration of the sea transit,[12] although it may not continue to be a document of title for the final land transit.[13]

A further possible objection to a combined transport bill of lading amounting to a document of title is that it may well be issued by someone other than the actual sea carrier, such as a freight forwarder.[14] It has been doubted whether such a document can confer constructive possession in the goods to which it refers when the contractual carrier has never taken them into its physical possession. However, this objection applies equally to a time charterer's bill of lading which is clearly accepted as a document of title and also to through bills of lading as regards the second sea leg. It is submitted that what matters is not the physical reception of the goods by the carrier, but its contractual capacity to control delivery by the performing carriers. This is borne out by the finding in *Spectra International plc v Hayesoak Ltd* that a party could become a bailee of goods, even without taking physical possession of them, by obtaining a right to give directions to the warehouseman as to their delivery.[15] Commercially, the contractual carrier does not actually need to be able to hand over the 'key to the warehouse'; it should be enough that he can direct the party who does have the key as to when it should be turned.

Combined transport documents and COGSA 1992

A related question is whether a combined transport bill of lading constitutes a bill of lading under **COGSA 1992**, so enabling consignees, indorsees and transferees of such a document to obtain rights to sue under it as lawful holders under s 2(1). **COGSA 1992** provides no definition of a 'bill of lading', although s 1(2)(b) provides that the Act applies to received for shipment bills. However, it is likely that this requires at least an indication of the designation of the carrying ship and of receipt by the sea carrier. Carver also argues that at common law a bill of lading refers only to a document containing or evidencing a contract for the carriage of goods by sea, a fact bolstered by the title of the Act itself, the **Carriage of Goods by Sea Act 1992**.[16] As against that, the definition of 'contract of carriage' in s 5(1) refers to the 'contract of carriage contained in or evidenced by the bill of lading' and makes no reference to that contract being by sea. It is possible that the Act might be construed so as to operate as regards transfers of the contract of carriage that take place between shipment and completion of the sea voyage, during which period the document will be a document of title, providing there is a notation as to shipment. The whole of the contract of carriage would be transferred, so allowing the lawful holder to sue in relation to loss or damage that occurred outside the period of sea carriage.

If the combined transport bill of lading is not a bill of lading, it may still fall within the provisions of **COGSA 1992** relating to waybills. However, there is a risk that such a document may fall outside a literal interpretation of the definition of sea waybill by s 1(3)(b) as a document that 'identifies the person to whom delivery of the goods is to be made by the carrier in accordance with that contract'. With a combined transport bill of lading, delivery is made against production of such a document, not on production of proof that one is the named consignee. The document

---

12 *Carver on Bills of Lading*, 3rd edn, 2011, London: Sweet & Maxwell, at 8-087, citing *Sutro & Co v Heilbut Symons & Co* [1917] 2 KB 348, *Johnson v Taylor* [1920] AC 144, although the point was not specifically addressed in either case.

13 The merchant jury in *Lickbarrow v Mason* found that there was a custom of merchants as to the negotiability of bills of lading so as to transfer property by way of indorsement and delivery or transmission by bills of lading: '. . . at any time *after such goods have been shipped, and before the voyage performed* . . .' [emphasis added].

14 *The Maheno* [1977] 1 Lloyd's Rep 81, NZ Ct.

15 [1997] 1 Lloyd's Rep 153. The point was raised before the Privy Council in *The Pioneer Container* in relation to the Scandutch claimants who had been issued with a bill of lading by a party who had never taken possession of the cargo. Their Lordships did not think it right to allow the point to be raised for the first time before them but Lord Goff of Chieveley observed: '. . . it is difficult to see why the shipowners should not, when they received the goods of the Scandutch plaintiffs into their possession, have become responsible as bailees to the owners of the goods even if the goods were never in the possession of Scandutch . . . and, if so, it is not easy to see why they should not be able to invoke against the owners any terms upon which the intermediary (Scandutch), with the owners' consent, entrusted the goods to them'.

16 *Carver on Bills of Lading*, 3rd edn, 2011, London: Sweet & Maxwell, at 8-080.

itself does not, strictly, identify the person to whom delivery of the goods is to be made, as a named consignee will be unable to claim delivery merely by being named as such in the bill. Furthermore, a 'sea waybill' is defined in s 1(3)(a) as 'such a receipt for goods as contains or evidences a contract for the carriage of goods by sea' (emphasis added), which would exclude combined transport waybills from the scope of the Act.[17]

The **Contracts (Rights of Third Parties) Act 1999** might prove useful in overcoming these residual uncertainties as to title to sue under such documents. Section 1(1) allows a person who is not a party to a contract to enforce the contract in its own right if: '(a) the contract contains an express term to that effect; or (b) . . . the contract purports to confer a benefit on the third party'. Under s 1(3), the third party has to be expressly identified in the contract either 'by name, as a member of a class or as answering a particular description', although it need not be in existence when the contract is entered into. In the light of these provisions, it should be a relatively straight-forward matter to draft a clause that allows a third-party holder of a combined transport bill of lading to claim the benefit of that contract.[18] However, standard form bills of lading, or waybills, for multimodal carriage do not include any clause conferring on third parties the right to sue under the contract.[19]

The Act will not apply to a 'a contract for the carriage of goods by rail or road, or for the carriage of cargo by air, which is subject to the rules of the appropriate international transport convention . . .' (s 6(5)). The combined transport bill of lading may well be a contract for the carriage of goods by one of these modes of transport and be subject to the applicable mandatory convention. Where the contract involves international road carriage within Europe, the applicable mandatory regime would be the CMR, which is considered in detail in Chapter 8. Where the sea carriage element is 'roll-on, roll-off', with the goods remaining on the lorry, the CMR will apply to the entire contract.[20] Where the goods are off-loaded from the lorry before the sea carriage, CMR will not apply to the sea leg but will apply to any international road carriage element in the contract. For example, with a contract of carriage from the UK to Germany with sea carriage to Holland, CMR would cover the international road carriage from Holland to Germany.[21]

Another solution is for the shipper to assign its rights under the combined transport bill of lading to the consignee, indorsee or transferee.[22]

Competing conventions

This problem may arise with pure sea carriage, as seen in the discussion of 'through' bills. With 'combined transport' bills of lading, the problem is more acute, as the differences between the applicable unimodal conventions are much wider than those between the competing versions of the sea conventions. Under UK law, the provisions of the applicable unimodal convention will apply to that part of the combined transport contract of carriage that falls within the ambit of that convention. The Hague-Visby Rules have been held to apply to the sea legs and to a period of storage at a port pending trans-shipment in a contract of combined transport carriage involving an initial road leg to the UK port of shipment.[23]

---

17 But see *Quantum v Plane Trucking* [2002] EWCA Civ 350; [2002] 2 Lloyd's Rep 24, where the road legs of a multimodal contract of carriage involving air carriage were subject to CMR as involving 'carriage by road'. On this basis, the sea leg covered by a combined transport waybill could be regarded as constituting a contract for the carriage of goods by sea.

18 These provisions will not, however, enable contractual liabilities to be transferred to the third party.

19 In contrast to the right to rely on the carrier's exceptions and limitations which is invariably provided for by a 'Himalaya' clause.

20 Subject to Art 2.

21 The exception in s 6(5) would take effect as regards the CMR part of the carriage contract. However, Art 13 of the CMR would give the consignee the right to sue the carrier in respect of loss or damage.

22 As in *The Kelo* [1985] 1 Lloyd's Rep 557, (QB).

23 *Mayhew v OCL* [1984] 1 Lloyd's Rep 317, 320. In *Bhatia Shipping and Agencies Pvt v Alcobex Metals* [2004] EWHC 2323 (Comm); [2005] 2 Lloyd's Rep 336, there is a brief dictum of Flaux J to the effect that they would not apply at all in such transport but this must be wrong.

The CMR has been held to apply to the international road legs of a combined transport contract of carriage where the first leg was carriage by air.[24] Moreover, there are an increasing number of stages covered by no convention, as can be seen in the following example:

(a)   Storage of goods following reception by the combined transport carrier in Birmingham.
(b)   Road carriage to the seaport, Felixstowe.
(c)   Storage of goods following reception by the sea carrier.
(d)   Sea carriage to Hook of Holland.
(e)   Storage of goods pending collection by road carrier.
(f)   Road carriage from Hook of Holland to customer's premises in Basel.

Mandatory conventions will apply only to stages (d) (the Hague-Visby Rules, if a bill of lading is issued) and (f) (the CMR). Most of the stages will be outside any mandatory convention and will be subject to the provisions of national law, such as **The Unfair Contracts Terms Act 1977** in the UK. The compensation payable to the cargo claimant will depend on where exactly the loss or damage occurred. Where the goods are containerised, this will often prove impossible to ascertain. Furthermore, if the shipper contracts with a freight forwarder who does not act as principal, the problem of localisation will also have a substantial impact on the question of which carrier is liable to the cargo claimant for the loss.

'Network' and 'uniform' solutions

There is no mandatory convention for combined transport currently in force, although some of the unimodal conventions have provisions dealing with combined transport.[25] In some respects, the CMR represents a multimodal convention in that, pursuant to Art 2, it continues to cover contracts for international road carriage where another mode of transport is used and where the goods are not unloaded from the road vehicle for that leg.[26] In 1980, the UN drew up the **Geneva Convention on International Multimodal Transport of Goods**. This applied a uniform system of liability based on the presumed fault regime of the Hamburg Rules, with a network system of limitation, with two regimes for unlocalised loss, depending on whether the contract involved carriage by sea or by inland waterways, and one regime for localised loss. However, the 1980 Convention has not come into force and is not likely to do so.[27] It is up to the parties to a 'combined transport' contract to come up with their own solutions to the problem.

A 'network' solution applies the mandatory regimes when applicable and freedom of contract in the 'convention gaps'. With containerisation, a pure 'network' solution is impossible to work and may be modified in cases of unlocalised loss by allowing the cargo claimant to claim on the basis of the convention that is most favourable to it. A 'uniform' solution applies one regime, irrespective of localisation of loss. To avoid conflicts with the mandatory conventions, the contractual regime must be at least as favourable to the cargo claimant as the most favourable of the mandatory conventions. This system has the benefit of predictability, but exposes the carrier to the risk of incurring a

---

24 *Quantum v Plane Trucking* [2002] EWCA Civ 350; [2002] 2 Lloyd's Rep 24.
25 For air transport, Art 31 of the Warsaw Convention and Art 38 of the Montreal Convention. For rail transport, Art 38 of COTIF-CIM 1999.
26 However, where loss is sustained during and by that other mode of transport, Art 2 provides that the road carrier's liability shall not be determined by CMR, but '. . . in the manner in which the liability of the carrier by the other means of transport would have been determined if a contract for the carriage of the goods alone had been made by the sender with the carrier by the other means of transport in accordance with the conditions prescribed by law for the carriage of goods by that means of transport'.
27 In 1991, the UN also drew up The Vienna Convention on the Liability of Transport Terminals in International Trade. This, too, has not come into force, nor is it likely to do so.

greater liability than it can recover from its sub-carriers under the mandatory conventions governing their mode of performance.

The **UNCTAD/ICC Rules for Multimodal Transport Documents 1992** came into effect on 1 January 1992 and provide a set of rules that parties may voluntarily incorporate into their transport documents. The Rules provide that when they are so incorporated, the Rules shall supersede any additional terms of the multimodal transport contract which are in conflict with these Rules, except insofar as they increase the responsibility or obligations of the multimodal transport operator. The Rules are based on the scheme of the 1980 Convention of a uniform system of liability coupled with a network system of limitation. They differ in that where the carriage involves carriage by sea or by inland waterways, the limitation figures in the Hague-Visby Rules or **US COGSA 1936** apply for unlocalised damage.

The ICC Rules provide that the multimodal transport operator ('MTO') undertakes to perform or to procure the performance of all acts necessary to ensure delivery of the goods. If the multimodal transport document is issued in negotiable form, delivery is to be against surrender of one original of the document by the holder, if a bearer document, or by the consignee or indorsee, if an order document. If the document is issued in non-negotiable form, delivery is to the person named as consignee in the document upon proof of his identity. The MTO is responsible for the goods from the time he has taken them into his charge to the time of their delivery and the MTO is liable for loss, damage and for delay in delivery.[28] The only defence is if the MTO can prove that no fault or neglect of his own, his servants or agents or any other person he uses to perform the contract caused or contributed to the loss, damage or delay in delivery. However, where loss, damage or delay in delivery arises during carriage by sea or by inland waterways, two additional defences are available to the MTO: (i) the nautical fault exception under IV.2 (a) of the Hague Rules, (ii) the fire exception under IV.2 (b) of the Hague Rules. Where loss or damage has resulted from unseaworthiness of the ship, reliance on these defences is subject to the MTO being able to prove that due diligence was exercised to make the vessel seaworthy at the commencement of the voyage.

The ICC Rules apply the Hague-Visby limitation figure of 666.67 SDRs per package or unit or 2 SDRs per kilogram of gross weight of the goods lost or damaged, whichever is the greater and adopt the Hague-Visby provision relating to goods carried in containers whereby the packages enumerated in the bill are deemed packages or shipping units. If there is no carriage by sea or inland waterways, the CMR package limit of 8.33 SDRs per kilogram of gross weight of the goods lost or damaged is applied. Where loss or damage is localised, the applicable limitation figure will be that contained in any international convention or mandatory law that would have applied had a separate contract been made for that stage. Loss due to delay or consequential loss other than loss or damage to the goods is limited to an amount not exceeding the freight. The right to limit will be lost in the same way as is the case under the Hague-Visby Rules. A nine-month time limit applies. The Rules apply whenever claims relating to the performance of the multimodal transport contract are made against any servant, agent or other person whose services the MTO has used in order to perform the multimodal transport contract, whether such claims are founded in contract or in tort. The final rule, Art 13 provides: 'These Rules shall only take effect to the extent that they are not contrary to the mandatory provisions of international conventions or national law applicable to the multimodal transport contract.' The nine-month time limit would therefore not apply if the Hague-Visby Rules or the CMR applied to the contract.

The Baltic and International Maritime Council (BIMCO) has produced two standard forms for multimodal transport documents. The first is Multidoc 1995, which is stated to be subject to the

---

28 Delay in delivery occurs when the goods have not been delivered within the time expressly agreed upon or, in the absence of such agreement, within the time which it would be reasonable to require of a diligent MTO, having regard to the circumstances of the case.

ICC Rules, but with three modifications. First, where loss, damage or delay in delivery arises during carriage by sea or by inland waterways, all the Hague Rule exceptions in Art IV(2) apply, except that in heading (q). Second, if **US COGSA 1936** applies, the package limit is US$500 per package or customary freight unit. Third, the MTO is not liable for delay unless the consignor has made a written declaration of interest in timely delivery which the MTO has accepted in writing.

The second form, Combiconbill, applies a modified network system to both liability and limitation. Clause 9 provides that the carrier is liable for loss of or damage to the goods occurring between the time when he receives the goods into his charge and the time of delivery, and is responsible for the acts and omissions of any person of whose services he makes use for the performance of the contract of carriage evidenced by the bill of lading, subject to eight specified defences.[29] Clause 10(3) stipulates a weight-based limitation figure of 2 SDRs per kilogram, but not a package limitation. Clause 12 provides that if the carrier is held liable for delay or consequential loss (which are not specifically referred to in the Hague-Visby Rules), the carrier shall also have a right to limit such liability limited to an amount not exceeding the freight or the value of the goods, whichever is the lesser. If **US COGSA 1936** applies, the package limit is US$500 per package or customary freight unit.

When it can be proved where the loss or damage occurred, these provisions give way to clause 11. The merchant is entitled to require that liability be determined under the provisions of any applicable mandatory unimodal convention or national law that would have applied had the merchant made a separate contract for that stage and received any document necessary for that convention or national law to have applied.[30]

Both forms contain 'Himalaya' and 'circular indemnity' clauses to protect the carrier's subcontractors. Both forms apply a nine-month time limit but this will be subject to the application of any mandatory unimodal convention.[31] Thus, if there is localised loss or damage during a sea leg to which the Hague-Visby Rules apply, or in the case of Combiconbill during any sea leg, the one-year time limit will apply.

---

29 (a) The wrongful act or neglect of the Merchant; (b) Compliance with the Instructions of the person entitled to give them; (c) The lack of, or defective conditions of packing in the case of goods which, by their nature, are liable to wastage or to be damaged when not packed or when not properly packed; (d) Handling, loading, stowage or unloading of the goods by or on behalf of the Merchant; (e) Inherent vice of the goods; (f) Insufficiency or inadequacy of marks or numbers on the goods, covering, or unit loads; (g) Strikes or lock-outs or stoppages or restraints of labour from whatever cause whether partial or general; (h) Any cause or event which the Carrier could not avoid and the consequence whereof he could not prevent by the exercise of reasonable diligence.

30 If there is no mandatory law applying to sea carriage in force, the Hague-Visby Rules are to apply and will apply to all goods, whether carried on deck or not, and also to carriage of goods by inland waterways as if such carriage were carriage by sea.

31 The nine-month limit will also be subject to national laws on contract terms, which in the case of the UK will be the Unfair Contract Terms Act 1977. In *Granville Oil & Chemicals Ltd v Davies Turner & Co Ltd* [2003] EWCA Civ 570; [2003] 1 All ER (Comm) 819 and *Rohlig (UK) Ltd v Rock Unique Ltd* [2011] EWCA Civ 18; [2011] 2 All ER (Comm) 1161, a nine-month time bar in the terms of the British International Freight Association (BIFA) has been held to satisfy the test of reasonableness under s 11.

Chapter 8

Carriage by Road – the CMR

Chapter Contents

International contracts for the carriage of goods by road have their equivalent of the Hague and Hague-Visby Rules in the CMR,[1] enacted by the **Carriage of Goods by Road Act 1965**. The main commercial differences between the two modes of carriage are that road carriage will frequently involve the use of sub-carriers, but will rarely involve sale of the goods in transit. With sea carriage, the position is generally reversed. These critical differences in the two modes of transport are reflected in the different structures of their respective mandatory codes.

Mandatory application of the CMR

The CMR governs contracts of carriage of goods by road, for reward, where the carriage is between two sovereign states, at least one of which must be a signatory to the CMR.[2] The CMR focuses on the terminus points of the contract rather than the nationality or domicile of the parties to the contract. The contract will still possess the international character necessary to attract the mandatory operation of the CMR, even if it is terminated before the goods leave the country of loading. In *Buchanan & Co v Badco Forwarding and Shipping (UK)*,[3] the contract was for the carriage of whisky from London to Paris. The whisky was stolen from the docks at Dover, but the contract was still treated as falling within the CMR, notwithstanding that no international carriage actually took place. Where the carrier is instructed to deliver to a different destination, the CMR may also continue to apply to that additional part of the carriage that is purely domestic. Thus, in *Moto-Vespa v MAT*,[4] goods destined for Barcelona were redirected to Madrid before arrival at their original destination. The CMR continued to govern the performance of the contract during the road journey from Barcelona to Madrid.

If part of the contract is carried out by sea carriage, as will generally be the case with carriage from the UK, Art 2 will apply. This provides that the CMR will continue to cover the whole carriage if the goods are not unloaded from their trailer for the sea leg. However, Art 2 then goes on to disapply the CMR:

> ... to the extent that it is proved that any loss, damage or delay in delivery of the goods which occurs during the other means of transport was not caused by an act or omission of the carrier by road, but by some event which could only have occurred in the course of and by reason of the carriage by that other means of transport.

In these circumstances, liability will be determined in the way in which it would have been assessed:

> ... if a contract for the carriage of the goods alone had been made by the sender with the carrier by the other means of transport in accordance with the conditions prescribed by law for the carriage of goods by that means of transport.

In the absence of such provisions, the loss will continue to be subject to the CMR.

Where the goods are unloaded from the road vehicle for carriage by another mode of transport, the CMR will not apply during that other mode of transport. However, it will still cover the international road legs of the carriage that come before and after the other mode of transport.

---

1 These initials are taken from the French title of the relevant international convention, *Convention Relative au Contrat de Transport International de Marchandises par Route*.
2 However, a voluntary incorporation of the CMR into a contract will take effect even though there is no international carriage by road as required by the CMR. See *Princes Buitoni Ltd v Hapag-Lloyd* [1991] 2 Lloyd's Rep 383.
3 [1978] AC 141.
4 [1979] 1 Lloyd's Rep 175.

In *Quantum Corp v Plane Trucking*,[5] the Court of Appeal rejected the notion that a carriage involving different modes of transport could only fall within the CMR if the carriage by road was the pre-dominant mode. A cargo of hard disk drives was to be carried from Singapore to Dublin. The air carrier flew them to Paris on two airline pallets. From Paris, the pallets were to be carried by road to Dublin, on a roll-on, roll-off basis. The goods were stolen during a staged hijack while being carried by road in England. The question was whether the road carrier was subject to the CMR or whether it could, instead, rely on the terms of a 'Himalaya' clause contained in the air waybill. The Court of Appeal held that, provided that carriage by road was permissible under the contract of carriage, the CMR was capable of applying to the international road leg of a larger contract of carriage. In such circumstances, the places of taking over and delivery to which Art 1(1) referred had to be construed so as to refer to the start and end of the road leg. The CMR therefore governed that part of the contract which was to be performed by road, the journey from Paris to Dublin.[6] A contrary view has been taken by courts in Germany and the Netherlands, to the effect that the CMR does not cover the international road stages that form part of a larger multimodal transport contract.[7]

The proviso to Art 2 was considered by Neill J in *Thermo Engineers Ltd v Ferrymasters Ltd*,[8] when a steam heat exchanger on a trailer hit the deckhead of the vessel while the trailer was being loaded onto the vessel. The damage took place once the trailer had passed the outboard ramp and crossed the line of the stern, and was held to have occurred during 'the other means of transport'. Even though loading had not been completed, the damage had occurred after the carriage by sea had begun with the loading of the trailer onto the vessel. The damage was not due to the fault of the road carrier[9] and was caused by an event that could only have occurred in sea carriage.

It was, however, not automatic that the carrier's liability would be on the terms of the Hague-Visby Rules, given that the Rules allowed the parties to reduce the shipowner's defences and increase its obligations. Another possibility, which was not considered by Neill J, was that the ocean carrier concerned may only have been prepared to contract on the basis that a waybill was issued. As the Hague-Visby Rules do not mandatorily apply to waybills, liability would, in the absence of 'such prescribed conditions', continue to be governed by the CMR.

Where the goods *are* unloaded from the trailer, Art 2 will not apply. Glass and Cashmore suggest that, in these circumstances, the contract would only become subject to the CMR, as an international contract of carriage by road within Art 1, after the conclusion of the sea leg.[10] Therefore, any road transport within the UK to the port of loading would fall outside the Convention. However, this will not be the case if a consignment note, which states that the contract is subject to the CMR is, in fact, issued at the start of the road carriage within the UK. Such a statement will incorporate the CMR contractually and such a purely contractual incorporation will have the effect of applying the CMR to purely domestic road carriage.[11]

---

5 [2002] EWCA Civ 350; [2002] 2 Lloyd's Rep 24.
6 Had the goods been unloaded from the trailer for the sea leg, it is difficult to see how there could be any international element in the road carriage, in which case CMR would not apply. The Court of Appeal refrained from commenting on this hypothesis.
7 [BGH] [Federal Court of Justice] Jul. 17, 2008 (I ZR 181/05), (2009) Eur Transp L 196 (Ger), Hoge Raad der Nederlanden [HR] [Supreme Court of the Netherlands] 1 juni 2012, NJ 2012, 516 mmt KFH (*Godafoss*) (Neth).
8 [1981] 1 WLR 1470.
9 For the purposes of Art 2, Neill J interpreted Art 3, which imposes liability on the carrier for the defaults of sub-carriers, so as not to cover the defaults of the ocean sub-carrier.
10 Glass and Cashmore, *Introduction to the Law of Carriage of Goods*, 1989, London: Sweet & Maxwell, at 3.14. See *Datec Electronic Holdings Ltd v United Parcels Service Ltd* [2007] UKHL 23; [2007] 2 Lloyd's Rep 114, where goods were carried from Luton to Amsterdam, by road to Luton airport then by plane to Cologne and then by road from Cologne to Amsterdam. The final road leg, involving international carriage, was subject to CMR.
11 *Princes Buitoni Ltd v Hapag-Lloyd* [1991] 2 Lloyd's Rep 383.

The identity of the contracting parties

The initial contract will be made between the 'sender' and the 'carrier'. Subsequently, the 'consignee' may obtain contractual rights against the carrier as well.

These parties are identified by applying the general law of contract and agency.

The sender

The sender is the party who makes the initial contract of carriage, the equivalent of the 'shipper' under a contract of ocean carriage evidenced by a bill of lading or by a sea waybill. However, this party may also contract as agent for the consignee, as in *Moto-Vespa v MAT*,[12] thus enabling the consignee to sue in contract, as an undisclosed principal. This agency will be presumed when title to the goods has already passed to the consignee at the time that the carriage contract is concluded.[13]

The consignee

This is the party named on the consignment note, the CMR equivalent of a sea waybill, as the party to whom delivery is to be made. Article 13 provides that if the goods are lost or delayed, the consignee can sue on the contract of carriage made by the sender. Title to sue in claims for *damage* will depend on a finding of agency, outlined in the paragraph above.

The carrier

The CMR, unlike the **Carriage of Goods by Sea Act (COGSA) 1992**, envisages the transfer of the 'burden' of the contract of road carriage down the chain of successive sub-carriers. These carriers may subcontract the whole of the journey or a particular geographical section of it. Irrespective of any subcontracting, the initial carrier will remain liable for the performance of the entire contract. This is because Art 3 makes the initial carrier liable for the acts of its agents and servants, including sub-carriers. The initial carrier is identified in accordance with the general principles of contract law.[14] The question at issue is whether the person dealing with the sender in connection with the carriage has undertaken to carry the goods or merely to arrange carriage.[15]

On the facts, it is quite possible for a party to contract to carry the goods as principal, even though it subcontracts the entirety of the performance of the contract. This occurred in *Ulster-Swift Ltd v Taunton Meat Haulage Ltd*,[16] where Taunton made the contract and subcontracted to Fransen, to which the consignment note was made out when it came to collect the goods. Taunton was sued for damage and claimed a CMR indemnity against Fransen. Fransen argued that Taunton made the contract as agent for Fransen, and Fransen was the first carrier; therefore Taunton had no rights against it under the CMR as a 'successive carrier'. Taunton was held to have been the first carrier, even though it never took possession of the goods.

A similar decision was reached in *Aqualon (UK) Ltd v Vallana Shipping Corp*.[17] The defendant was a freight forwarder, but was held not to have contracted in that capacity, but rather as a carrier.

---

12 [1979] 1 Lloyd's Rep 175.
13 *Texas Instruments v Nason (Europe) Ltd* [1991] 1 Lloyd's Rep 146.
14 Once the goods are accepted for carriage, there will be a contract subject to CMR, even though the value of the goods is such as would have entitled the carrier to refuse them under its standard terms and conditions. See *Datec Electronic Holdings Ltd v United Parcels Service Ltd* [2007] UKHL 23; [2007] 2 Lloyd's Rep 114.
15 A freight forwarder will be precluded from arguing that it is a carrier under CMR if it has argued before the courts of another country that it was a freight forwarder. See *Royal & Sun Alliance Insurance Plc v MK Digital FZE (Cyprus) Ltd* [2006] EWCA Civ 629; [2006] 2 Lloyd's Rep 110.
16 [1975] 2 Lloyd's Rep 502, QB; [1977] 1 WLR 625, CA.
17 [1994] 1 Lloyd's Rep 669.

Although it had deleted the reference to itself as carrier in the consignment note, the plaintiff was not aware of this practice. The fact that it made an all-in charge for the carriage pointed to its acting as principal, notwithstanding the reference in its invoices to the Netherlands Association for Forwarding and Logistics (FENEX) conditions, which covered freight forwarders.[18]

Successive carriers

Article 36 of the CMR allows the sender to sue either the first carrier, the last carrier or the carrier in whose custody the damage actually occurred. Under Art 34, each successive carrier becomes a party to the contract by accepting the consignment note,[19] while the first carrier, the original contracting party, remains liable by virtue of Art 3. If the consignment note is not passed on to a successive carrier, then CMR will not apply to that sub-carrier. However, it may indirectly apply through the doctrine of sub-bailment on terms, if that sub-carrier has contracted on CMR terms, in which case all the terms of CMR will govern the claim in bailment against that sub-carrier.[20]

If no consignment note is issued, or if one is not passed on to the successive carriers, the claimant will obtain no rights under the CMR against the sub-carriers. It will either have to proceed against them in tort or against the first carrier in contract. This contractual action will continue to be subject to the CMR despite the absence of any consignment note.

When a successive carrier becomes liable under the above provisions, Art 37 provides it with a right of indemnity against the carrier responsible for the loss.[21] Where the loss has been caused by two or more carriers, each is to bear an amount proportionate to its share of liability.[22] If it is impossible to say which carrier caused the loss, then the loss is apportioned amongst all of the carriers in proportion to the share of the payment for the carriage that is due to them.[23] Article 38 also applies this solution to the share of compensation due from a carrier who is insolvent. Article 39(2) provides that a carrier may bring an indemnity claim 'before the competent court or tribunal of the country in which one of the carriers concerned is ordinarily resident, or has his principal place of business or the branch or agency through which the contract of carriage was made. All the carriers concerned may be made defendants in the same action.' The claim made by the carrier seeking recourse cannot be disputed 'if the amount of the compensation was determined by judicial authority after the first mentioned carrier had been given due notice of the proceedings and afforded an opportunity of entering an appearance'.[24]

Where an extra-contractual claim is made against the carrier, Art 28 allows either the carrier or one of the sub-carriers[25] to rely on 'the provisions of this Convention which exclude his liability or which fix the compensation due'. In theory, a sub-carrier by sea could rely on this provision, although the application of CMR defences in the context of sea carriage might prove problematic.

---

18 A similar conclusion was reached in *Tetroc Ltd v Cross-Con (International) Ltd* [1981] 1 Lloyd's Rep 192.
19 Art 35 requires a successive carrier to give the previous carrier a signed and dated receipt and to enter his name and address on the second copy of the consignment note. However, where the successive carrier accepts the consignment note but does not comply with Art 35, he will still become a party to the contract under Art 34. *SGS-Ates Componenti Elettronici SpA v Grappo Ltd* [1978] 1 Lloyd's Rep 281 (QB).
20 *Sandeman Coprimar SA v Transitos y Transportes Integrales SL* [2003] EWCA Civ 113; [2003] QB 1270.
21 The indemnity under Art 37 does not operate where the sub-carrier is contractually obliged to make indemnity for loss of the goods while in the custody of the actual carrier. This indemnity would not be 'in compliance with provisions of the Convention', as the sub-carrier would have incurred no liability under CMR to either the sender or the first carrier. See *Rosewood Trucking Ltd v Balaam* [2005] EWCA Civ 1461; [2006] 1 Lloyd's Rep 429.
22 Article 37(b).
23 Article 37(b) and (c).
24 Article 39(1).
25 Under Art 28(2).

The contract documents

A consignment note in triplicate must be issued: one copy for the sender; one for the carrier; and one to accompany the goods and be handed over to each successive carrier, ending up in the hands of the consignee after delivery.[26] The consignment note resembles a sea waybill rather than a bill of lading. It is not a document of title, nor is delivery to be made against production of documents.

Information to be included in the consignment note

The CMR deals with the evidential status of the consignment note in Arts 6–9. Article 6 provides for the information to be contained in the consignment note, including:

(a)   the names and addresses of the sender, carrier and consignee;[27]
(b)   the date of the consignment note and the place at which it is made out;[28]
(c)   the place and the date of the taking over of the goods and the place designated for their delivery;[29]
(d)   a description of the goods and their packaging;
(e)   the number of packages and their special marks and numbers;[30]
(f)   the gross weight of the goods or their quantity otherwise expressed;[31]
(g)   the carrying charges.[32]

Article 7(1) makes the sender responsible 'for all expenses, loss and damage sustained by the carrier by reason of the inaccuracy or inadequacy . . .' of any of the above statements, save those as to the carrying charge and the name and address of the carrier. However, the carrier will be unable to rely on this provision where it has failed to check on certain particulars, as required by Art 8, below.

Carrier's duty to check particulars in consignment note

The consignment note must also contain a statement that it is subject to the CMR,[33] to protect the sender or the consignee in the event that they need to bring proceedings in a state that is not a party to the CMR. If this statement is omitted, Art 7(3) makes the carrier liable for 'all expenses, loss and damage sustained through such omission by the person entitled to dispose of the goods'.[34]

Article 8(1) obliges the carrier, on taking over the goods, to check:

(a)   the accuracy of the statements in the consignment note as to the number of packages and their marks and numbers; and
(b)   the apparent condition of the goods and their packaging.

Article 8(2) allows the carrier to enter reservations regarding the statements listed in (a) above where it has no reasonable means of checking their accuracy. The carrier is also entitled to make reservations regarding the statements in (b) above. However, the carrier must also enter the ground for any reservation that it makes. Article 8(3) gives the sender the right to require the carrier to

---

26 Article 5.
27 Article 6(b), (c) and (e), respectively.
28 Article 6(a).
29 Article 6(d).
30 Article 6(f).
31 Article 6(g).
32 Article 6(i).
33 Article 6(k).
34 Defined in Art 12.

check the gross weight of their goods, or their quantity or the contents of packages, but the carrier is entitled to claim the costs of such checking.

Contractual status of consignment note

Article 9 defines the contractual and evidential status of the consignment note.[35] Article 9(1) provides that the note is prima facie evidence of 'the making of the contract of carriage, the conditions of the contract and the receipt of the goods by the carrier'. Article 9(2) contains a presumption, unless the contrary is proved, as to the accuracy of statements in the note as to the number of packages, their marks and numbers, and their apparent order and condition, provided that no reservation has been entered in respect of any of these statements. The presumption is, however, rebuttable, in contrast to the conclusive evidence provisions of the Hague-Visby Rules and **COGSA 1992**, which enure to the benefit of third parties.

Non-compliance with Arts 6–9

If the note fails to comply with CMR formalities, as long as it is transmitted to successive carriers, those carriers will be within the CMR and its indemnity provisions. Thus, in *SGS-Ates Componenti Eletronici Spa v Grappo*,[36] the failure of a successive carrier to comply with the formalities of Art 35[37] on taking over the consignment note did not prevent it being treated as a successive carrier. On the other hand, if no note is issued, or it is not transmitted to successive carriers, the provisions of the CMR will not affect the successive carriers. However, there will still remain a CMR contract between sender and carrier, who will be liable for the defaults of sub-carriers under Art 3.

Terms of the contract

Contracting out

As with the Hague and Hague-Visby Rules, once it is established that the CMR regime applies, certain contractual terms are imported into the contract despite the actual agreement between the parties. Article 41 provides that, subject to the provisions of Art 40 described below:

> . . . any stipulation which would directly or indirectly derogate from the provisions of this Convention shall be null and void. The nullity of such a stipulation shall not involve the nullity of the other provisions of the contract . . .

This wording gives room for some doubt as to whether the parties may agree to increase the obligations of the carrier, or to reduce its defences, as is the case with the Hague-Visby Rules.

Article 40 preserves freedom of contract *between the carriers*, subject to their not being able to contract out of Arts 37 and 38 – that is, the indemnity provisions.

---

35 The additional Protocol to the Convention on the Contract for the International Carriage of Goods by Road (CMR) concerning the Electronic Consignment Note, Geneva, 20 February 2008, entered into force on 5 June 2011. The Protocol allows transport operators to use electronic consignment notes in the nine states that have currently ratified or acceded to it: Bulgaria, Czech Republic, Denmark, Latvia, Lithuania, Netherlands, Slovakia, Spain, Switzerland.
36 [1978] 1 Lloyd's Rep 281.
37 Article 35(1): 'A carrier accepting the goods from a previous carrier shall give the latter a dated and signed receipt. He shall enter his name and address on the second copy of the consignment note . . .'.

The parties' position during performance of the contract

Article 12 deals with the 'right of disposal' – that is, the right to alter the delivery instructions, regarding destination or consignees, while the goods are still in transit. Article 12(1) gives this right to the sender, provided that a consignment note has been issued. Article 12(5) sets out various preconditions before this right can be exercised, including an obligation to indemnify the carrier in respect of any expenses, loss or damage involved in carrying out the new instructions.

The right of disposal can be transferred to the consignee, either under Art 12(3), by stating this in the consignment note and sending the first copy to the consignee, or under Art 12(2), when the consignee receives the second copy of the consignment note along with the goods. Where the right of disposal enures to the consignee, it can name one new consignee, but, after that, Art 12(4) prevents that new consignee, in its turn, naming any further new consignee.

On delivery of the goods to the consignee, Art 13 gives it a right to demand the second copy of the consignment note. If it exercises this right, the consignee becomes liable to pay the carrier any outstanding freight due, irrespective of the terms of its agreement with the sender. As with sea carriage, cross-claims may not be set off against freight. However, under Art 13(2), the carrier can only obtain a lien on the goods by filling in the charges box on the consignment note. If this is not done, Art 41 prevents the carrier from relying on a lien expressly provided for in the contract of carriage.[38]

Where circumstances change in the course of performance of the contract of carriage, Arts 14–16 come into play. If it becomes impossible to carry out the contract in accordance with the terms laid out in the consignment note, Art 14(1) obliges the carrier to seek instructions from the person with the right of disposal. In the absence of such instructions, provided that the contract may still be performed under different conditions, Art 14(2) obliges the carrier to act in the best interests of such person. Article 15 applies a similar regime to circumstances preventing the delivery of the goods, for example, where the consignee refuses to take delivery.

Article 16 entitles the carrier in circumstances covered by Arts 14(1) or 15 to terminate the contract by unloading the vehicle and holding the goods on behalf of the person with a right of disposal. The carrier obtains a right to sell the goods under Art 16(3) where the goods are perishable or their nature warrants such a course, or where a reasonable time has elapsed and the carrier has received no instructions that it might reasonably be expected to carry out from the person with the right of disposal. Under Art 16(4), the carrier is entitled to deduct its charges from the proceeds of sale, the balance being held for the person with the right of disposal.

The carrier's liability for loss, damage or delay

Article 17(1) makes the carrier liable 'for the total or partial loss of the goods and for damage thereto occurring between the time when he takes over the goods and the time of delivery as well as for any delay in delivery'. The types of damage set out therein are not, however, exhaustive. In *Shell Chemicals UK Ltd v P & O Roadtanks Ltd*,[39] the driver collected the wrong tank of chemicals for carriage. This was pumped into the plaintiff's refinery, with consequential loss from the resultant damage to the refinery. This was held to be a breach of Art 17, notwithstanding that Art 17 refers only to loss or damage *to* the goods carried, and makes no specific mention of damage caused *by* the goods being carried.

The carrier's defences

If the claimant discharges the burden of proving that the loss occurred within the period set out in Art 17(1), the carrier will be liable unless it can rely on one or other of two sets of defences set out in Art 17. The primary defences are set out in Art 17(2) and the secondary ones in Art 17(4).

---

38 *T Comedy (UK) Ltd v Easy Managed Transport Ltd* [2007] EWHC 611 (Comm); [2007] 2 Lloyd's Rep 397.
39 [1993] 1 Lloyd's Rep 114, QB; aff'd on other grounds [1995] 1 Lloyd's Rep 297, CA.

The burden of proof required of the carrier if it is to rely on a defence is less onerous in respect to the secondary defences than it is in respect to the primary defences. This is because Art 18(2) gives rise to a presumption that the secondary defences apply:

> ... where the carrier establishes that in the circumstances of the case, the loss or damage *could* be attributed to one or more of the special risks referred to in Art 17, para 4 ...

The word 'could' imports a standard of proof that is lower than the balance of probabilities that is imposed on a carrier seeking to rely on one or more of the primary defences. The presumption is, however, rebuttable and the last sentence of the Article provides: 'The claimant shall however be entitled to prove that the loss or damage was not, in fact, attributable either wholly or partly to one of these risks.'

Delay is dealt with as a special head of loss under Art 19. Delay occurs when the goods are delivered outside an agreed time limit or, in the absence of an agreed limit, 'when ... the actual duration of the carriage ... exceeds the time it would be reasonable to allow a diligent carrier'. When loss is caused by delay, the carrier may rely only on the primary defences in Art 17(2). Article 20 contains provisions for when lengthy delays may be treated as amounting to a total loss of the goods.[40]

The primary defences

These are contained in Art 17(2) and are as follows:

(a) '... the wrongful act or neglect of the claimant' or '... the instructions of the claimant given otherwise than as the result of a wrongful act or neglect on the part of the carrier'. This exception probably continues to apply when the wrongful act is committed by the sender and the consignee is the party claiming against the carrier.

(b) '... inherent vice of the goods'. Most of the situations covered by this exception will overlap with the secondary defences in Art 17(4).

(c) '... circumstances which the carrier could not avoid and the consequences of which he was unable to prevent'.

The burden of proof in relying on this last exception is particularly onerous on the carrier. Proof that it took reasonable care of the goods will not entitle it to rely on this exception. It is required to do more than that, although it is not required to take every conceivable precaution. In *Silber Trading v Islander Trucking*,[41] goods were stolen from a lorry parked at a toll gate while the driver was resting in the cab. Mustill J held that the carrier could not rely on the defence. Although the driver had not been negligent, the carrier could still have done more to avoid the loss. Had a second driver been employed, the lorry could have been driven to a guarded lorry park without breaching EEC Regulations on drivers' hours. However, once the carrier establishes that the defence appears to cover the loss, Mustill J suggested that the onus falls on the plaintiff to suggest what further steps the carrier should have taken to avoid the loss.

Marr-Johnson J applied this test in *Cicatiello v Anglo-European Shipping Services Ltd*[42] and held that the carrier was not liable for the theft of a trailer stolen from an Italian service station by armed robbers.

---

40 The claimant will have this option either when the goods have not been delivered within 30 days of an agreed time limit or within 60 days from the carrier taking the goods over.
41 [1985] 2 Lloyd's Rep 243, QB.
42 [1994] 1 Lloyd's Rep 678.

The plaintiff suggested various additional anti-theft precautions that could have been taken, but the carrier still managed to establish that it had taken the utmost care. Furthermore, the precautions suggested by the plaintiff would still not have been sufficient to prevent the theft.[43]

The secondary defences

The presumption contained in Art 18(2) makes it easier for the carrier to rely on these defences than is the case with the primary defences. However, in certain situations, specified below, the carrier may lose the benefit of this presumption.

(a) Use of open, unsheeted vehicles, when their use has been expressly agreed and specified in the consignment note. By Art 18(3), this presumption ceases to apply in cases of abnormal shortage or loss of any package. In any event, the use of such vehicles must be expressly agreed and specified in the consignment note.

(b) The lack of, or defective condition of packing in the case of goods, which, by their nature, are liable to wastage or to be damaged when not packed or when not properly packed. The standard of packing required of the sender is not so high as to require it to anticipate negligence by the driver or abnormal delays. The carrier may lose the right to the defence if it fails to check the goods on taking them over, as required by Art 8, and make the appropriate reservation about their packaging.

(c) Handling, loading, stowage or unloading of the goods by the sender, the consignee or person acting on behalf of the consignee. To rely on this exception, the carrier will need to show who was responsible for these operations under the contract of carriage. If it was the sender/consignee, it is unclear whether the carrier need only prove that the other party, in fact, carried out the operations or whether it needs to go further and prove that the operations were carried out defectively. It is also unclear whether or not the carrier needs to inspect the operations performed by the other party.

(d) The nature of certain kinds of goods that particularly exposes them to total or partial loss or to damage, especially through breakage, rust, decay, desiccation, leakage, normal wastage, or the act of moth or vermin. Article 18(4) provides that 'If the carriage is performed in vehicles specially equipped to protect the goods from the effects of heat, cold, variations in temperature or the humidity of the air', the carrier loses the right to rely on this exception, 'unless he proves that all steps incumbent on him in the circumstances with respect to the choice, maintenance and use of such equipment were taken and that he complied with any special instruction issued to him'. The effect of this proviso is to impose a very hard burden on the carrier, as is illustrated by the *Ulster-Swift* case.[44] Pork was carried in a refrigerated trailer from Northern Ireland to Switzerland, where it arrived in a damaged condition. The Court of Appeal held that the onus fell on the carrier to show that the refrigeration machinery had been working properly. It would be unable to discharge this onus unless it could prove the exact cause of loss, which it could not do. Therefore it was not entitled to rely on this exception, even though it could show that it had taken proper care of the equipment.

(e) Insufficiency or inadequacy of marks or numbers on the packages. The carrier's right to rely on this exception may be lost if it fails to comply with the duty imposed on it

---

43 See, also, *Netstal-Maschinen AG and Securitas Bremer Allgemeine Versicherung AG v Dons Transporte AG, Stewart Height and David O'Neill*, 26 May 2004, English Mercantile Court, Central London, Hallgarten J. The carrier was able to rely on this defence when an accident occurred due to the driver swerving to avoid a wild boar on the road, which he thought to be a human being, and then having to swerve to avoid the car that had been disabled by impact with the wild boar. The driver was travelling at 55 mph on a Belgian dual carriageway at the time and would have to have been travelling at a speed grossly below 45 mph to take effective avoiding action.
44 [1975] 2 Lloyd's Rep 502, QB; [1977] 1 WLR 625, CA.

by Art 8 of checking the accuracy of the statements in the consignment note as to the above particulars.

(f)   The carriage of livestock. Article 18(5) allows the carrier to rely on this exception only if 'he proves that all steps normally incumbent on him in the circumstances were taken and that he complied with any special instructions issued to him'.

Apportionment of liability

Where loss is caused by competing factors, Art 17(5) provides that the carrier 'shall only be liable to the extent that those factors for which he is liable under this article have contributed to the loss, damage or delay'. The basis of such apportionment may either be related to the contribution of each cause to the loss, or be based on the degree of fault of each party.

Absolute liability for defects in the vehicle

The equivalent of Art III(1) of the Hague-Visby Rules is Art 17(3), which provides:

> The carrier shall not be relieved of liability by reason of the defective condition of the vehicle used by him in order to perform the carriage, or by reason of the wrongful act or neglect of the person from whom he may have hired the vehicle or of the agents or servants of the latter.

If the carrier would otherwise be able to rely on a primary or secondary defence, the claimant will still be able to make a recovery if it can prove that the loss or damage was caused by the facts set out in the Article. It may be quite difficult to predict whether a defect in the vehicle's special protective equipment falls under this Article or under Art 17(4). In the *Ulster-Swift* case,[45] Donaldson J disregarded Art 17(3) in the context of the vehicle's refrigeration unit. However, in *Walek & Co v Chapman and Ball*,[46] a defective canvas covering of a trailer was held to be 'equipment' within this Article.

Wilful misconduct

The defences[47] and limitations available to carriers and sub-carriers under the CMR, in both contractual and extra-contractual proceedings, will be lost under Art 29 if 'the damage was caused by his wilful misconduct or by such default on his part as, in accordance with the law of the court of tribunal seised of the case, is considered as equivalent to misconduct'. In *Lacey's Footwear (Wholesale) Ltd v Bowler International Freight Ltd*,[48] the majority of the Court of Appeal held that 'wilful misconduct' could be inferred from the surrounding circumstances, even though there was no direct evidence that the lorry driver knew that what he was doing was wrong when he was deceived by two criminals into delivering the consignment to another address. It is worth noting that Art 29 refers only to 'wilful misconduct' and does not contain the additional proviso, contained in Art IV(5)(e) of the Hague-Visby Rules, that it must be proved that 'the damage resulted from an act or omission of the carrier done with intent to cause damage, or *recklessly and with knowledge that damage would probably result*' (emphasis added). Theft by employees of the carrier will constitute wilful misconduct. In *Datec Electronic Holdings Ltd v United Parcels Service Ltd*,[49] the claimant was able to break limitation on this basis by proving, on the balance of probabilities, that the goods had been stolen by the carrier's employees, even though the employees in question could not be identified. Wilful misconduct is not established by the fact that the goods are damaged following an accident due to the driver falling asleep at the wheel. However, the position would have been different if there had been proof

---

45   Ibid.
46   [1980] 2 Lloyd's Rep 279, QB.
47   Including those provisions, such as Art 18(2), which shift the burden of proof.
48   [1997] 2 Lloyd's Rep 369.
49   [2007] UKHL 23; [2007] 2 Lloyd's Rep 114, noted [2008] JBL 184.

that the driver had exceeded his driving time limits or had received some prior warning of sleepiness, for example hitting the side of the road.[50]

Measure of damages

Article 23(1) provides that, in cases of total or partial loss of the goods, damages are to be calculated 'by reference to the value of the goods at the place and time at which they were accepted for carriage'.[51] This method of calculation, being based on the value of the goods at the start of the journey, excludes carrying charges. However, these are specifically recoverable under Art 23(4). The valuation of the goods is, by Art 23(2), to be fixed according to the commodity exchange price, or, if none, the current market price 'by reference to the normal value of goods of the same kind and quality'.

Where goods are damaged, Art 25(1) fixes the carrier's liability in accordance with the principles applied by Art 23 to claims for total or partial loss. Article 23(2) limits the compensation for damage to the whole or part of the consignment to the amount payable in respect of a total or partial loss, respectively.

Recovery of loss due to delay is limited by Art 23(5) to the carriage charges.

Package limitation

Article 23(3) applies a package limitation to claims for loss and damage of 8.33 SDRs per kilogram of gross weight short. Article 24 gives the sender the option to avoid the package limitation by declaring the value of the goods in the consignment note, 'against payment of a surcharge to be agreed upon . . .'. Similar provisions are contained in Art 26 concerning the fixing of a special interest in delivery.

The package limitation does not cover claims under Art 23(4) for 'carriage charges, customs duties and other charges incurred in respect of the carriage'. These are to be refunded in full in cases of total loss and in proportion to the loss sustained in cases of partial loss, 'but no further damages shall be payable'.[52] 'Other charges' was narrowly interpreted in *Tatton & Co Ltd v Ferrymasters Ltd*,[53] where the words were held not to cover the cost of returning goods to the UK, warehousing and inspection after damage to a trailer en route. However, the words received a wider interpretation in *Buchanan & Co v Badco Forwarding & Shipping (UK)*,[54] where they were held to cover the excise duty paid on the stolen whisky.

Jurisdiction and time limits

Article 31 contains provisions concerning the place in which a claimant may bring an action, resolution of the issue of *lis alibi pendens* where proceedings are commenced between the same parties on the same grounds in different jurisdictions, and enforcement of judgments. These provisions will displace the provisions of the Regulation (EU) No 1215/2012 on jurisdiction and recognition

---

50 *TNT Global SpA v Denfleet International Ltd* [2007] EWCA Civ 405; [2007] 2 Lloyd's Rep 504.
51 This method of valuation continues to apply even when there has been 'wilful misconduct'. See *Lacey's Footwear (Wholesale) Ltd v Bowler International Freight Ltd* [1997] 2 Lloyd's Rep 369, CA. However, the plaintiff there was able to make a recovery in excess of that due under the CMR because the carrier had also breached an undertaking to insure the goods for 110 per cent of their actual value.
52 These words do not apply when there has been 'wilful misconduct'. See *Lacey's Footwear (Wholesale) Ltd v Bowler International Freight Ltd* [1997] 2 Lloyd's Rep 369.
53 [1974] 1 Lloyd's Rep 203, QB.
54 [1978] AC 141.

and enforcement of judgments in civil and commercial matters (recast) ('**the Judgments Regulation**'), Art 71 of which provides that 'This Regulation shall not affect any conventions to which the Member States are parties and which in relation to particular matters, govern jurisdiction or the recognition or enforcement of judgments'.[55]

Under Art 31(1), the claimant may bring an action in any court or tribunal of a contracting country designated by the parties. In addition, it may proceed in the courts or tribunals of:

(a)   a country in which the defendant is ordinarily resident or has its principal place of business; or
(b)   the country in which the goods were taken over by the carrier; or
(c)   the country in which the place designated for delivery is situated.

The sender may proceed in no other courts or tribunals. Where jurisdiction is established over the first carrier, proceedings against successive carriers may be brought in that forum.[56] Article 31(1) applies not only to claims for enforceable relief but also to claims by a carrier for declaration that it is not liable.[57]

Article 31(2) provides: 'Where . . . an action is pending before a court or tribunal competent under [Art 31(1)] . . . no new action shall be started between the same parties on the same grounds unless the judgment of the court or tribunal before which the first action was brought is not enforceable in the country in which the fresh proceedings are brought.' This provision covers the same ground as Art 29 of the Judgments Regulation and will prevail over it in accordance with Art 71 of the Judgments Regulation. There are, however, no provisions of the CMR dealing with 'related actions' and these will fall under Art 28 of the Judgments Regulation.[58]

Article 31(3) provides: 'When a judgement entered by a court or tribunal of a contracting country in any such action as is referred to in paragraph 1 of this article has become enforceable in that country, it shall also become enforceable in each of the other contracting States, as soon as the formalities required in the country concerned have been complied with. These formalities shall not permit the merits of the case to be re-opened.'

The relationship between the CMR and the Judgments Regulation was considered by the Grand Chamber in *TNT Express Nederland BV v Axa Versicherung*.[59] Following non-delivery of cargo carried by road, the carrier sued the insurer of the goods in Rotterdam for a declaration that it was not liable over and above the limit set by the CMR. The insurer then sued the carrier in Munich for loss of the goods. The Munich court rejected a plea of *lis pendens* and gave judgment in respect of which the insurer obtained an enforcement decision in the Netherlands. The carrier appealed that decision on the basis that the CMR took precedence over the Regulation. The Dutch court referred this question to the European Court of Justice, which held that Art 71 of the Regulation must be interpreted as meaning that, in a case such as the main proceedings, the rules governing jurisdiction, recognition and enforcement that are laid down by a specialised convention, such as the *lis pendens* rule set out in Art 31(2) of the CMR and the rule relating to enforceability set out in Art 31(3) of that convention, apply provided that they are highly predictable, facilitate the sound administration of justice and enable the risk of concurrent proceedings to be minimised and that they ensure, under

---

55   Article 71 will have this effect even where the defendant enters no plea on the merits. *Nürnberger Allgemeine Versicherungs AG v Portbridge Transport International BV* Case C-148/03 [2005] 1 Lloyd's Rep 592, ECJ.
56   *British American Tobacco Switzerland SA and Others v Exel Europe Ltd* [2013] EWCA Civ 1319; [2014] 1 Lloyd's Rep 503. The cargo owner entered into a CMR contract of carriage with a carrier, based in England, and agreed exclusive English jurisdiction for disputes arising out of the contract of carriage. It was entitled to bring proceedings in England not only against the first carrier but also against successive carriers.
57   *Frans Maas Logistics (UK) Ltd v CDR Trucking* [1999] 2 Lloyd's Rep 179, QB.
58   *Sony Computer Entertainment Ltd v RH Freight Services Ltd and Ors* [2007] EWHC 302 (Comm); [2007] 2 Lloyd's Rep 463.
59   Case C-533/08, European Court of Justice, Opinion of Advocate General Kokott, 28 January 2010. Judgment of the Court (Grand Chamber) 4 May 2010.

conditions at least as favourable as those provided for by the Regulation, the free movement of judgments in civil and commercial matters and mutual trust in the administration of justice in the European Union (*favor executionis*). However, the Court did not have jurisdiction to interpret Art 31 of the CMR.

Subsequently, the CJEU has pronounced on the interpretation of Art 31(2) in the light of Art 71 of the Judgments Regulation. The case was *Nipponkoa Insurance Co. (Europe) Ltd v Inter-Zuid Transport BV*[60] and involved two sets of proceedings in respect of loss of goods carried under a contract for carriage by road subject to CMR. Proceedings were brought against the first carrier in Germany and subsequently the second carrier brought proceedings against the first carrier in the Netherlands and in 2009 it obtained a judgment declaring that it was responsible only up to the CMR limit in Art 23. In 2010, the German action settled for almost ten times that amount on the basis that the German court would find that the right to limit had been lost under Art 29. The first carrier's insurers then brought an indemnity action in the German court against the second carrier for the amount they had paid out under the settlement. The Third Chamber of the CJEU held that Art 71 of the Judgments Regulation must be interpreted as meaning that it precludes an interpretation of Art 31(2) of the CMR according to which an action for a negative declaration or a negative declaratory judgment in one Member State does not have the same cause of action as an action for indemnity between the same parties in another Member State. In effect, although, as in TNT *Express*, the Court acknowledged it had no power to interpret provisions of CMR, its interpretation of Art 71 of the Judgments Regulation means that effectively Art 31(2) of CMR is to be construed so that the action for indemnity and the negative declaratory judgment constitute the same cause of action.[61]

The time limits are set out in Art 32. The basic limit is one year, with three years where there has been 'wilful default'. A written claim will interrupt time until it is rejected. Article 39(4) applies these limits to indemnity claims as between carriers.[62] However, the time limits do not cover other, non-CMR claims, as between carriers, such as a claim for carriage charges as in *Muller Batavier v Laurent Transport Co.*[63]

A further limit is provided by Art 30, which deals with the failure of the consignee to send reservations to the carrier giving a general indication of loss, either at the time of delivery with apparent loss, or within seven days thereafter with non-apparent loss. Such failure shall amount to prima facie evidence that the consignee received the goods as described in the consignment note. This provision, like its equivalent in the Hague-Visby Rules, is of little practical value. Even without Art 30, the burden of proving that loss or damage took place within the carrier's period of responsibility falls on the claimant.

---

60 Case C-452/12.
61 This is contrary to the previous decision of the High Court in *Frans Maas Logistics (UK) Ltd v CDR Trucking* [1999] 2 Lloyd's Rep 179, QB.
62 Time starts to run '. . . either on the date of the final judicial decision fixing the amount of compensation payable under the provisions of this Convention, or, if there is no such judicial decision, from the actual date of payment'.
63 [1977] 1 Lloyd's Rep 411.

Chapter 9

Charterparties

Chapter Contents

Introduction

In this chapter, we shall consider the general nature of charterparties and matters common to all types of charterparty, on both the time and voyage formats.

Charterparties differ from bill of lading contracts in two important respects. First, they are not subject to the mandatory application of the Hague and Hague-Visby Rules. Secondly, they are not subject to the statutory assignment contained in the **Carriage of Goods by Sea Act (COGSA) 1992**. Theoretically, they are classified as a contract for the use of the vessel, as opposed to the bill of lading, which is classified as a contract for the carriage of goods.

There are various forms of charterparty. For example, there is the demise – or 'bareboat' – charter, under which the charterer not only has the use of the vessel, but also engages its own crew. However, more usual are those charterparties under which the crew are employed directly by the shipowner. There are two basic types of such charter: the voyage charter and the time charter. Charterparties are generally made by using a standard form applicable to the particular trade, and then amending its provisions and including typewritten addenda to reflect the particular agreement made between the parties. The most common standard forms are the 'Gencon' form for voyage charters and the New York Produce Exchange (NYPE) and Baltime forms for time charters. Where the carriage of oil is involved, it is likely that a specialised form will be used, such as Exxonvoy or Beepeevoy for voyage charters, and Shelltime for time charters.

The types of charter

Voyage charters

Under a voyage charter, the vessel is let out to the charterer for a specific voyage. The shipowner will be paid 'freight', which will cover its costs, including fuel and crew, as well as its profit. Legally, freight is a special type of payment, as the usual rules of set-off will not apply to it.[1] A set time, 'laytime', will also be provided for the loading and discharging operations. If these operations exceed the permitted laytime, the shipowner will be compensated by 'demurrage' at the rate set down in the charter. For its part, the shipowner owes the charterer the duty of proceeding with reasonable dispatch on the charterparty voyage, or voyages, in the case of a consecutive voyage charter.

Voyage charters frequently seek to extend the charterer's contractual obligations to the bill of lading holder as well. This will be done by virtue of a clause providing for the issue of bills of lading incorporating the terms of the charter. Such bills, provided that **COGSA 1992** effects the necessary statutory assignment, will link the shipowner contractually with the bill of lading holder on the terms of the charterparty, which is incorporated into the bill of lading. The charter will sometimes contain a further provision, a 'cesser' clause, by which the charterer is relieved from any obligations after the cargo has been loaded.

Voyage charters will usually contain two special remedies for the shipowner in the event of non-payment of freight or demurrage. These are the lien on cargo, a right to detain the cargo pending payment, and the lien on subfreights, a right to intercept subfreights due to the charterer from its subcharterer.

---

1   *Aries Tanker Corp v Total Transport Ltd (The Aries)* [1977] 1 WLR 185, HL.

Time charters

In contrast to a voyage charter, a time charter is defined not by a geographical voyage, but by a period of time, for example, six months. Payment is by means of 'hire', calculated daily, but usually payable in advance.[2] Hire, unlike freight, is subject to the usual rules of common law and equitable set-off.

Hire will start to run when the vessel is 'delivered' and will cease when she is 'redelivered', the charter specifying where and when these operations are to take place. Fuel consumed during the charter period will be paid for separately by the charterers in the following way. The charterers will take over and pay for the vessel's bunkers on delivery and the shipowners will do likewise on redelivery. The charterers will be paying for bunkers between delivery and redelivery and there may be problems if bunkers are supplied under a contract with a retention of title clause. If the unpaid bunker supplier still owns the bunkers at the time the vessel is redelivered, the shipowner is exposed to a potential liability in conversion. However, in *Angara Maritime Ltd v OceanConnect UK Ltd*,[3] his Honour Judge Mackie QC held that s 25(1) of the **Sale of Goods Act 1979** protected shipowners from what would otherwise be a claim for conversion, because they had purchased the bunkers from charterers upon delivery in good faith and without notice of any adverse right.

Delay is also treated differently under a time charter. There is no direct equivalent to laytime and demurrage. Instead, hire will run from the commencement of the charter, 'delivery', to its termination, 'redelivery'. However, its running may be interrupted by the operation of an 'off-hire' clause, which provides for the temporary cessation of hire brought about by the operation of any one of a number of specified causes.

Unlike the position under a voyage charter, the charterer will be more directly affected by any slow steaming on the voyages performed under the time charter in that this will restrict the total number of voyages that it will be able to perform within the charter period. To deal with this problem, most time charters contain an express clause, such as that contained in cl 8 of the NYPE form, which obliges the shipowner to prosecute voyages with the utmost dispatch. In addition, the charterparty will generally contain a warranty as to the speed at which the vessel will be able to proceed.[4] In the light of such express clauses, there will generally be no need for a charterer to argue in favour of an implied term that voyages be prosecuted with reasonable dispatch. There is no good reason why such a term should not be implied, although there is no authority directly on the point.[5]

Time charters do not usually envisage any contractual transfer of liability such as that which voyage charters achieve with 'charterparty bills of lading' and 'cesser' clauses. The norm is for bills of lading to be issued that do not contain any such words of incorporation. Such bills are frequently marked 'freight prepaid'. This wording will prevent the shipowner from being able to exercise a lien on cargo. The cargo will not usually be owned by the time charterers and the bills of lading will contain no reference back to the terms of the time charter. The lien on subfreights is likely to be of more use. Time charters usually provide for a further remedy, which is not to be found with voyage charters – that is, the right of 'withdrawal'. This amounts to an option to terminate the charter if hire is not paid punctually in full.

Finally, different rules on frustration apply depending on whether the contract is a voyage or a time charter. The **Law Reform (Frustrated Contracts) Act 1943** does not apply to voyage charters, but does apply to time charters.

---

2 The Baltime form specifies a period of 30 days, whereas the NYPE 93 form specifies a period of 15 days.
3 [2010] EWHC 619 (QB); [2011] 1 Lloyd's Rep 61.
4 Most time charters will also contain a warranty by the shipowner as to the fuel consumption of the vessel.
5 See *The Democritos* [1976] 2 Lloyd's Rep 149, where the Court of Appeal held that the shipowner owed a duty to proceed with due diligence to meet the cancellation date specified in the time charter.

Hybrids – the 'trip charter'

A charter may be concluded for a specific voyage, which uses the form of a time charter. Hire, not freight, will be paid and the charter will usually provide a minimum and maximum period for the voyage. There will be no laytime, and demurrage provisions and delay will be dealt with by means of off-hire. Such charters have been classified as time charters.[6] This is of significance in the context of the operation of the **Law Reform (Frustrated Contracts) Act 1943**, which does not apply to voyage charters.

Conversely, what is, in effect, a time charter may be concluded on voyage charter forms, as with the consecutive voyage charters in *Suisse Atlantique Société d'Armement Maritime SA v NV Rotterdamsche Kolen Centrale*.[7]

The interest conferred by a charterparty

A charterer obtains no proprietary interest in the chartered vessel, although a charterer by demise will obtain a possessory interest in the vessel. Therefore, when a vessel is sold in mid-charter, the new owner will be bound by its terms only if a demise charter is involved.

However, in some situations, the non-demise charterer can still obtain an injunction to prevent the new owner dealing with the vessel inconsistently with the charter.[8] In *Swiss Bank Corp v Lloyds Bank Ltd*,[9] Browne-Wilkinson J was of the view that this remedy can be founded on two grounds. The first is the tort of inducing a breach of contract, which requires the purchaser to have actual knowledge of the charter. The second is a constructive trust, which would be imposed when a vessel is sold expressly 'subject to' the existing charter.

Matters common to both types of charter

This chapter will now consider those matters that are common to both types of charter.[10] Such matters fall under two broad headings. First, there is the issue of what orders the charterer may give the shipowner and what happens if the shipowner suffers loss in consequence of obedience of those orders. Secondly, there is the issue of the shipowner's duties in relation to the commencement of the charter. When must the vessel be put at the disposal of the charterers and what will happen if the shipowner is late in doing so?

Charterers' orders

The terms of the charterparty will determine how the charterer can use the vessel during the currency of the charter. Generally, a charterer will have substantially greater freedom as to the use of the vessel under a time charter than under a voyage charter, in which the voyage and the cargo to be carried will be set out by the contract itself. If a voyage charter does give the charterer the right to nominate ports and cargoes, that right is likely to be very limited in extent. Those orders that fall within the scope of the charterparty are 'legitimate' orders. The most important types of order are those relating to the type of bills of lading to be issued, the type of cargo to be loaded and the ports between which the vessel should trade. Failure to comply with a 'legitimate' order may

---

6 *The Eugenia* [1964] 2 QB 226.
7 [1967] 1 AC 361.
8 *Lord Strathcona SS Co v Dominion Coal Co* [1926] AC 108, PC; doubted by Devlin J in *Port Line Ltd v Ben Line Steamers Ltd* [1958] 2 QB 146.
9 [1979] Ch 548.
10 The implied obligations in relation to seaworthiness, etc., are matters common to both bill of lading contracts and charterparties. These have already been discussed in Chapter 4, pp 81–92.

amount to an anticipatory breach of charter by the shipowner, which will justify the charterer in terminating the charter, depending on the seriousness of the consequences of the breach to the charterer. Thus, in The Nanfri,[11] the shipowner refused to comply with the charterer's order to issue 'freight prepaid' bills of lading and the consequences of this breach were sufficiently serious to entitle the charterers to terminate the charter.

Orders that fall outside the scope of the charterparty are 'illegitimate' and amount to a breach of charter by the charterer. This is so, notwithstanding the 'employment' clause that is found in most time charters. An example of such a clause is to be found in cl 8 of the NYPE form and reads: 'The Captain (although appointed by the owners) shall be under the orders and directions of the charterers as regards employment and agency.' This type of clause, and the similar clause to be found in cl 9 of the Baltime form, does not oblige the captain to follow orders that the charterers are not entitled to give under the terms of the charter;[12] nor does it mean that the captain ceases to be regarded as the shipowner's servant for the purpose of determining the liability of the shipowner for the captain's negligence.[13] The shipowner is entitled to disregard an illegitimate order and call on the charterer to replace the order with a legitimate one. Failure to do this will amount to an anticipatory breach, entitling the shipowner to treat the charter as at an end.[14] On the other hand, the shipowner may comply with the illegitimate order and seek to recover any consequent losses from the charterer for its breach of contract. This is the most prudent course if there is any doubt as to the legitimacy of the order, for, if the order is later judged to have been legitimate, the shipowner's refusal will amount to a breach of charter.

The above analysis of charterers' orders is framed in terms of breach of contract. There is, however, an alternative way in which a shipowner may claim against the charterer for losses it suffers as a result of obeying the charterer's orders – namely, by way of an indemnity against the consequences of obeying the charterer's orders as to the employment of the vessel. The indemnity may be express, as in the Baltime charter, or may be implied in a time charter, such as the NYPE form, where there is no express provision for an indemnity. The Court of Appeal in The Island Archon[15] confirmed that an indemnity would be implied in such circumstances, because one was justified under a time charter as a quid pro quo for the charterer's extensive contractual rights to dictate the employment of the vessel. For this reason, express indemnities are rarely found in voyage charterparties and it would be unusual for an indemnity to be implied into such a contract.[16] However, Evans LJ stressed that a rigid distinction could not be drawn between time and voyage charters. For example, an indemnity might not be implied into a 'trip' charter that gave the charterers very little control over the employment of the vessel, whereas it might be implied into a voyage charter that gave the charterers a wide range of options as to the vessel's use.

The indemnity will operate even if the charterer has not been in breach of charter, provided that the shipowner can show that its losses are consequent upon the shipowner's acting on the charterer's legitimate orders.[17] However, such an indemnity is limited by the following factors.

Employment, as opposed to navigational, matters

The indemnity covers orders as to employment, but not as to navigational, matters. For example, the charterers may order the shipowners to proceed to a particular port, but the indemnity will

11 [1979] AC 757.
12 The Sussex Oak (1950) 83 Ll L Rep 297, 307, per Devlin J.
13 The Aquacharm [1980] 2 Lloyd's Rep 237, 241, per Lloyd J.
14 The Gregos [1994] 1 WLR 1465, HL, noted (1995) LMCLQ 318.
15 [1994] 2 Lloyd's Rep 287, noted (1996) LMCLQ 15, approving dicta of Mustill J in The Athanasia Comminos [1990] 1 Lloyd's Rep 277.
16 See The C Joyce [1986] 2 Lloyd's Rep 285, where Bingham J refused to imply an indemnity into a Gencon form voyage charter.
17 Express indemnities in charters for the benefit of charterers will be construed so as to be coextensive with any liability of the shipowner for breach of contract. See The Eurus [1996] 2 Lloyd's Rep 408, QB, noted (1996) LMCLQ 438.

not extend to how the master executes that order. In *Larrinaga SS Co Ltd v R*,[18] a vessel requisitioned to the government under time charter in the Second World War was ordered to proceed from Newport to St Nazaire and thence to Cardiff for her pre-delivery survey. The Sea Transport Officer ordered her to proceed to Quiberon Bay to join a convoy to Cardiff, despite bad weather. The vessel set out and grounded. The indemnity did not apply as the damage was not due to compliance with charterer's orders, but due to compliance with the Sea Transport Officer's orders as to how and when the vessel should navigate to Cardiff and so execute those orders. The distinction is sometimes difficult to draw in practice. This can be illustrated by *The Hill Harmony*,[19] where the charterer ordered the vessel to proceed to a port by the quicker of two usual routes. The master had experienced navigational problems on this route on a previous voyage and, before setting out on the voyage, decided to disregard the charterer's orders and take the alternative route. The majority of the arbitrators found as a matter of fact that the master had acted unreasonably in doing so. The charterers sued the shipowner for damages consequent upon the master's failure to obey a legitimate order. Clarke J and the Court of Appeal both held that the shipowner was not liable to the charterer, as the master's decision as to which route to take was to be regarded as a navigational matter, not an employment one, provided that the decision was made bona fide on the grounds of the vessel's safety. The fact that the master had made this decision before setting out on the voyage did not alter the position. However, the House of Lords has now allowed the appeal, categorising the decision as to which route to follow as an employment, rather than a navigational, matter, while stressing that the master would still be entitled to refuse to obey orders that endangered the safety of the crew and the vessel. The decision is to be welcomed in that it prevents time charterers from having to bear the financial risks, in terms of loss of time, of a bona fide but unreasonable decision of a master to decline to follow the route that they have specified.

Causation

Charterer's orders must be the proximate cause of the loss. Intervening negligence on the part of the shipowner is a classic example of something that will break the chain of causation. In *The Aquacharm*,[20] the vessel took on too much cargo, due to the fault of the master, and had to trans-ship some of it before being allowed to transit the Panama Canal. It was held that the shipowners were not entitled to an indemnity, because these trans-shipment costs were not incurred as a direct consequence of obeying charterer's orders to proceed through the Panama Canal; rather, the true cause of the loss was the master's negligence in overloading the vessel.

In contrast, in *The Island Archon*,[21] the necessary causal link was made out where the shipowners incurred losses due to abnormal cargo claims arising out of trading to Iraq. The claims arose due to the peculiar legal system then in operation in Iraqi ports, whereby the port authority routinely issued short landing certificates even where the cargo had been discharged in full.

Relationship with other charter provisions

The indemnity may be excluded or limited by contrary provisions in the charter. In *The Berge Sund*,[22] delay occurred due to the need to clean the vessel's holds following contamination that was the fault of neither party. The indemnity was held not to operate where the charterer was not at fault in

---

18 [1945] AC 246.
19 (1999) LMCLQ 461; [1999] QB 72; [2000] QB 241, CA; [2000] 3 WLR 1954, HL, noted (1998) LMCLQ 502.
20 [1982] 1 Lloyd's Rep 7, CA. See, also, *The White Rose* [1969] 2 Lloyd's Rep 52, QB.
21 [1994] 2 Lloyd's Rep 287.
22 [1993] 2 Lloyd's Rep 453, CA.

giving orders partly because the off-hire clause was phrased so as not to operate if the off-hire events were due to the fault of the charterer.

The indemnity will also be excluded in respect of risks that the shipowner has voluntarily assumed. This element was stressed in *The Island Archon*.[23] However, on the facts, the shipowner had not voluntarily assumed the risk of the Iraqi system of manufacturing cargo claims. This had only come into existence some time after the signing of the charter and was not reasonably foreseeable at that date. So, too, in *The Athanasia Comminos*,[24] the shipowner was unable to recover by way of indemnity in respect of losses caused by an explosion on board the vessel caused by emissions of methane from a cargo of coal. The risk of explosion was known to be attendant on the carriage of coal and, therefore, by agreeing to carry such a cargo, the shipowner had assumed these risks. In *The Kitsa*,[25] Aikens J held that there could be no recovery under an implied indemnity in respect of losses that were the foreseeable consequence of complying with a legitimate order. Time was lost as a result of bottom fouling due to the vessel being inactive for 22 days at a warm water port to which she had been ordered to load. This was a risk that the shipowners had undertaken.

We shall now consider three specific types of charterer's order relating to: the bill of lading; the cargo to be loaded; and the ports between which the vessel is traded.

The bill of lading

Dealings with the bill of lading

The terms of the charter will regulate what bills of lading the charterer may order the shipowner to issue. If, for example, the charterparty provides for the issue of 'charterparty bills', the shipowner would be entitled to refuse to issue a bill that did not incorporate the terms of the charter.[26]

With time charters, it is more common to provide that the master should sign bills of lading 'as presented', in which case, the form of the bill of lading is entirely a matter for the charterer. Usually, a time charterer will require 'freight prepaid' bills of lading, but if any freight is due on delivery under its own contract with the shipper, it will require the bills of lading to incorporate the terms of its subcharter.[27]

Any attempt to strip charterers of their authority to issue their chosen form of bill will amount to a breach of charter, entitling the charterer to terminate the charter.[28] A charter provision that bills are to be issued 'without prejudice' to the charter does not qualify the charterer's freedom as to the form of bill to be issued. What it does is to provide the shipowner with an indemnity if the form of bill exposes it to any greater liability than it would be subject to under the terms of the charter. So, for example, where the charterparty provides that deck cargo is to be at 'shipper's risk' and the charterer fails to ensure that this notation appears on the bill of lading, it is liable to indemnify the shipowner in respect of liabilities created under the bill of lading, which would have been validly excluded had the bill been properly claused.[29] In *The Caroline P*,[30] the primary basis of such a claim was held to be on the basis of an indemnity. However, the court did not rule out a secondary basis of breach of charter. This analysis must be suspect, as it would entitle the shipowner to refuse to issue any bill that imposed greater liabilities on it than were imposed by the charter. When it comes

23 [1994] 2 Lloyd's Rep 287.
24 [1990] 1 Lloyd's Rep 277, QB.
25 [2005] EWHC 177 (Comm); [2005] 1 Lloyd's Rep 432, noted [2006] LMCLQ 129.
26 However, the shipowner may not go on to insist that such bills should be further claused with details of a subsisting claim against the charterer. See *The Anwar el Sabah* [1982] 2 Lloyd's Rep 261, CA.
27 The shipowner will be in breach if the master inserts the date of the wrong charterparty, as in *The Mathew* [1990] 2 Lloyd's Rep 323, QB.
28 *The Nanfri* [1979] AC 757.
29 *The Imvros* [1999] 1 Lloyd's Rep 849, QB, noted (2000) LMCLQ 295.
30 [1984] 2 Lloyd's Rep 466.

to the contents of the bill, as opposed to the form, the position changes somewhat. The shipowner is entitled to insist on a bill of lading that accurately reflects the quantity and condition of the cargo loaded. In *The Boukadoura*,[31] the shipowners were held to be entitled to insist on the right figures for quantity of cargo loaded being entered on the bill of lading; time lost by their insistence was held to be for the account of the charterers.

If a clean bill of lading is issued as a result of the master signing clean mate's receipts for damaged cargo, the master's negligence will preclude any claim against the charterers on an indemnity basis. In *The Nogar Marin*,[32] a clean bill of lading was issued after the master signed a clean mate's receipt in respect of rusty coils. The master's negligence barred the shipowners from claiming an indemnity from the time charterers in respect of the resulting cargo claim. But the master's failure will give the charterers no right of recourse against the shipowner. In *The Arctic Trader*,[33] the Court of Appeal held that time charterers had no recourse against the shipowners when they suffered loss as a consequence of a clean bill of lading being issued as a result of the master failing to clause the mate's receipts. No term could be implied to the effect that the shipowners had to inform the charterers of the condition of the goods on loading. The charterers would have this knowledge in any event, through the knowledge of the shippers, who would be treated as their agents.

However, where the charterparty requires bills of lading to be in conformity with the mate's receipts, as is the case under cl 8 of the NYPE form, and it is the charterer who signs a shipowner's bill of lading, then if that bill of lading is not in conformity with the mate's receipt, the charterer will become liable to the shipowner in respect of any cargo claims that result from this non-conformity.[34] It is likely that a term to this effect would be implied even without the express reference to the mate's receipts in such a clause.

The shipowner is also entitled to refuse orders relating to the bill, after its issue, which may expose it to liability to the bill of lading holder. In *The Sagona*,[35] it was held that the shipowners were entitled to insist on delivery against the bill of lading because of this need to protect themselves against possible claims for misdelivery (for which there would be no P&I cover). Although the usual practice is to discharge against a suitable indemnity,[36] in *The Houda*,[37] the Court of Appeal held that the shipowner is not obliged to do so, even if a suitable indemnity is offered. It also held that the shipowner was entitled to a reasonable time in which to verify the legitimacy of the orders being given by the charterers. The shipowners were held not to have been in breach by delaying in obeying orders given by Kuwaiti charterers after the invasion of Kuwait by Iraq in 1990, when time was needed to check the new source of the orders. A related problem arose in *The Wiloni Tanana*,[38] where the shipowners were allowed to correct the dates on incorrectly dated bills of lading in their possession, although new bills could be issued only with the consent of the charterers. Claims arising out of the inaccurate dating of the bills of lading would also have been outside the shipowner's P&I cover.

The standard form of indemnity will require the party requesting delivery to provide an indemnity against claims arising out of the delivery of the cargo and also will require them to provide security in the event that the vessel is arrested or detained in respect of such claims. The letter of indemnity will require delivery to a specified party and delivery to that party is a

31 [1989] 1 Lloyd's Rep 393, QB.
32 [1988] 1 Lloyd's Rep 412, CA. But charterers may still be liable under Art III(5) of the Hague Rules, or equivalent, if there is a 'clause paramount'. See *The Paros* [1987] 1 Lloyd's Rep 269, QB.
33 [1996] 2 Lloyd's Rep 449. See, also, *The Almak* [1985] 1 Lloyd's Rep 557, where no term was implied into a charterparty that the shipowner take reasonable care in presenting correctly dated bills of lading to the master for signature.
34 *The Hawk* [1999] 1 Lloyd's Rep 176, QB.
35 [1984] 1 Lloyd's Rep 194, QB.
36 As is also the case where the charterer orders the shipowner to discharge at a port other than the one named on the bill of lading.
37 [1994] 2 Lloyd's Rep 541.
38 [1993] 1 Lloyd's Rep 41.

precondition of a claim being made under the indemnity.[39] Delivery will be effected by the ship-owner under a bill of lading and does not require physical delivery to the party designated in the indemnity. Owners must effectively divest themselves of the power to compel any dealing in or with the cargo which could prevent the designated party from obtaining possession.[40] Where the vessel is arrested in connection with the delivery of the cargo, the court may make an order for specific performance in respect of the obligation of the provider of the indemnity to put up security to secure the release of the vessel from arrest.[41] The obligation to put up security is not discharged by the owners putting up security and obtaining release of the vessel. In these circumstances, an order for specific performance can be obtained requiring the party providing the indemnity to provide bail or other security in place of that provided by the shipowner.[42] Where the indemnity is provided to the owners by the charterers, and the charterers in their turn take an indemnity from the receivers, the owners may be able to rely on the receivers' indemnity pursuant to s 1(1)(b) of the **Contracts (Rights of Third Parties) Act 1999**, as the indemnity given to the charterers purports to confer a benefit on the owners who act as the charterer's agents in performing the delivery of the cargo requested under the letter of indemnity and who are the party that will be sued in the event of a misdelivery. In *The Laemthong Glory (No 2)*,[43] the receivers' indemnity was addressed to the charterers, providing that in consideration of their request for delivery they would indemnify 'you, your servants and agents'. The owners were also able to rely on the clause requiring the receivers to put up security in the event of the vessel's arrest or detention in connection with delivery of the cargo, which made no reference to the charterer's agents.[44]

Apportionment of resulting cargo claims

A claim under a shipowner's bill of lading will generally be directed at the shipowner. After settling the claim, the shipowner will seek to recover from the charterer under the terms of the charter. When will the shipowner (or charterer if it settles a claim under a 'charterer's bill') be able to make such a recovery?

Specific provisions relating to cargo claims

The 'clause paramount'

The first step is to see if the charter contains any specific clauses dealing with apportionment of cargo claims. The most common is the 'clause paramount', some form of which is found in the majority of voyage and time charters. The clause effects a voluntary incorporation into the charter of the Hague or Hague-Visby Rules or the legislation of a particular state giving effect to them.[45] The effect of such a clause is to equate the charterer's position with that of a cargo claimant under a bill of lading subject to the Rules.[46]

Where the charter contains a printed clause paramount, such as the NYPE form time charter, which incorporates the provisions of the **US Carriage of Goods by Sea Act of 1936**, its provisions will supplement those contained in the other printed terms and will prevail in the case of conflict

---

39 *The Bremen Max* [2008] EWHC 2755 (Comm); [2009] 1 Lloyd's Rep 81.
40 *The Jag Ravi* [2012] EWCA Civ 180; [2012] 1 Lloyd's Rep 637, where delivery occurred when the owners discharged the cargo into the custody of the port authority, instructing it to deliver the cargo to the designated party without production of the bills of lading.
41 *The Laemthong Glory (No 2)* [2005] EWCA Civ 519; [2005] 1 Lloyd's Rep 688.
42 *The Bremen Max* [2008] EWHC 2755 (Comm); [2009] 1 Lloyd's Rep 81.
43 [2005] EWCA Civ 519; [2005] 1 Lloyd's Rep 688.
44 A similar finding was made in *The Jag Ravi* [2012] EWCA Civ 180; [2012] 1 Lloyd's Rep 637, where the receivers gave an indemnity to the charterers addressed to 'The Owners/Disponent Owners/Charterers'. The offer was directed to all three parties specified and constituted a contract with the charterers when delivery was made to the specified party by the shipowners, as their agents.
45 Such as the US Carriage of Goods by Sea Act of 1936 in the case of the NYPE form charter.
46 Where the paramount clause does not specify either the Hague or the Hague-Visby Rules or any equivalent national legislation. See *The Bukhta Russkaya* [1997] 2 Lloyd's Rep 744, QB.

between them.[47] However, in the event of a conflict between a printed clause paramount and typed clauses, the latter will prevail. Thus, in *The Satya Kailash*,[48] the typed clauses imposed an absolute warranty of seaworthiness, which took priority over the due diligence obligation that would otherwise have applied by virtue of the clause paramount.[49]

Incorporation of the Rules, or of the relevant statute bringing them into effect, causes linguistic problems in that the language of the Rules is framed in the context of bill of lading contracts. The courts have been prepared to manipulate the language of the Rules so that they can make sense in a charterparty context. Otherwise, an over-literal reading of the wording of the Rules would deprive the 'clause paramount' of any effect.

In *Adamastos Shipping Co Ltd v Anglo-Saxon Petroleum Co Ltd*,[50] the House of Lords considered the effect of a 'clause paramount' added to a charterparty by a typed slip in the following wording: 'This bill of lading shall have effect subject to the provisions of the United States Carriage of Goods by Sea Act 1936.' The Act applied a similar regime to the Hague Rules to bills of lading contracts in respect of voyages into and out of the USA. The charterers had lost potential voyages under their time charter due to delay caused by the alleged unseaworthiness of the vessel on a ballast voyage. The shipowners wanted to rely on the 'due diligence' defence in the Act, as well as the equivalent defences to those found in Art IV of the Hague Rules. The charterers' argument was based on the following propositions:

(a) The 'clause paramount' referred to 'this bill of lading' and therefore could have no application to claims under the time charter.

(b) Even if it did apply the Act to the charterparty, the language of the Act did not apply in a charterparty context. In particular, s 5 stated that the Act should not apply to charterparties.

(c) Even if the Act's language could be extended to charterparties, its provisions could only apply to voyages under the charter into or out of the USA, to match the provisions of the Act regarding bills of lading.

(d) Even if the Act extended to all voyages under the charter, the exceptions in s 4 in respect of 'loss or damage' were limited to claims for loss or damage in respect of cargo and did not cover economic loss caused by events on a non-cargo-carrying voyage.

The House of Lords unanimously rejected the charterers' arguments on the first two points, and, by a 3:2 majority, rejected their arguments on the last two points as well. The majority were clearly determined to give effect to the clear commercial intentions of the parties, and to manipulate the language of the statute in whatever way necessary to achieve that end. An important consequence of the decision is that shipowners may rely on the defences in Art IV(2), or its equivalent, even when the charterer's claim is not related to loss of or damage to cargo.[51]

Linguistic problems have also arisen when applying the one-year time limit under Art III(6) in the context of a charterparty that contains a clause paramount. A claim for consequential losses due to delays in loading by reason of the vessel presenting for loading with tanks requiring cleaning has been held to be subject to the time bar,[52] but not one for delay in the issue of bills of lading.[53] The issue was most recently reviewed in *The Marinor*,[54] where it was held that the time bar was not

47 *Nea Agrex SA v Baltic Shipping Co Ltd (The Agios Lazaros)* [1976] 2 Lloyd's Rep 47, CA, 59, *per* Shaw LJ.
48 [1984] 1 Lloyd's Rep 588, CA.
49 See, also, *Metalfer Corp v Pan Ocean Shipping Co Ltd* [1998] 2 Lloyd's Rep 632, QB, where a 30-day time limit in an arbitration clause prevailed over the one-year time limit in the Hague Rules, which were incorporated by a printed 'clause paramount'.
50 [1959] AC 133.
51 See *The Satya Kailash* [1984] 1 Lloyd's Rep 588, CA.
52 *The Ot Sonja* [1993] 2 Lloyd's Rep 435, CA.
53 *The Standard Ardour* [1988] 2 Lloyd's Rep 159, QB.
54 [1996] 1 Lloyd's Rep 301, QB, noted (1996) LMCLQ 173.

limited to claims of a nature that could have been made against the shipowners by a bill of lading holder. However, the claims did have to be 'in respect of goods' and therefore had to relate to physical or economic loss suffered by a particular cargo, which the charterers had ordered the shipowners to load. The facts of the case clearly illustrate this distinction. Problems had arisen with contaminated outturns of sulphuric acid cargoes under the charter. The charterers decided to charter in other vessels for future consignments and to order the chartered vessel to make a test voyage to Tampa, where the cargo could be disposed of as fertiliser, even if contaminated (the cargo was, in fact, discharged contaminated). The claims arising out of the chartering in of substitute vessels were outside the time bar, but those arising out of the test voyage were within it.[55] A further problem is the extent to which the presence of a 'clause paramount' in a time charterparty alters the common law position that the warranty of seaworthiness attaches only on delivery of the vessel. Under Art III(1), the obligation to take due diligence attaches 'before and at the beginning of the voyage'. Does this mean that if there is a 'clause paramount', the obligation attaches at the start of each voyage performed under a time charter? There is no direct authority on the point. The House of Lords did, however, hold, in *Adamastos Shipping Co Ltd v Anglo-Saxon Petroleum Co Ltd*,[56] that the **US Carriage of Goods by Sea Act of 1936**, which was the subject of the 'clause paramount' in question, applied to each voyage under a charter for consecutive voyages.

The 'Inter-Club Agreement'

Another very common clause in time charters is the 'Inter-Club Agreement' (ICA). The agreement began as an agreement between the P&I Clubs as to how they would recommend settlement of cargo claims as between shipowners and charterers where the NYPE form time charter is used. It is now common for the agreement to be specifically incorporated into the time charter. Indeed, the NYPE 1993 form contains a printed cl 27 to this effect.

The 1984 ICA adopts the following system of apportionment of claims, which are initially pursued under a bill of lading that is subject to the Hague or Hague-Visby Rules. Damage due to unseaworthiness is apportioned 100 per cent to shipowners. 'Unseaworthiness' bears the same meaning as it does in the Hague-Visby Rules. It is not limited to the inability of the ship to withstand the hazards of navigation, but extends to uncargoworthiness. Whether or not a cargo claim is due to unseaworthiness depends on an objective ascertainment of the facts and not on the way in which the claim is presented by the third-party claimant.[57] Unseaworthiness has to be a cause of the loss; it does not have to be the effective cause. In *The Kamilla*,[58] seawater ingress through the hatch covers damaged 1 per cent of the cargo. The Algerian authorities, however, condemned the entire cargo. The arbitrators found that the action of the authorities was 'by no means unprecedented in our experience', and was therefore not too remote. The charterers were entitled to recover the entire loss from the shipowners under the Inter-Club Agreement. Damage due to bad stowage and bad handling are apportioned 100 per cent to charterers unless cl 8 of the NYPE form is amended with the addition of the words 'and responsibility', in which case the loss is shared equally between the parties. Claims arising out of short delivery are also apportioned on a 50/50 basis, irrespective of any amendment to cl 8. The ICA will continue to apply notwithstanding the fact that antedated bills of lading have been issued.[59] Where trans-shipment bills are issued, the ICA will only apply if

55 See, also, *The Casco* [2005] EWHC 273 (Comm); [2005] 1 Lloyd's Rep 565. The charter provided that any claim arising out of 'any loss of or damage to or in connection with cargo' would be subject to the provisions of the Hague Rules. This covered only claims of the sort that were normally brought by bill of lading holders claiming loss or damage arising in relation to the cargo and measured by reference to the cargo. It did not cover charterers' claims for loss of freight and wasted bunkers resulting from cancellation of the sub-charter.

56 [1959] AC 133.

57 *The Benlawers* [1989] 2 Lloyd's Rep 51, QB.

58 [2006] EWHC 509; [2006] 2 Lloyd's Rep 238.

59 *The Elpa* [2001] 2 Lloyd's Rep 596, QB.

the charterers can prove that the shortages occurred during the sea transit on the shipowner's vessel.[60] The provisions of the ICA will prevail over those of a clause paramount where the two coexist in the same charter.[61]

The 1996 ICA makes certain amendments to the 1984 version. It now covers cargo claims pursued under any authorised contract of carriage, including waybills and voyage charters, provided that their terms are no less favourable than those contained in the Hague or Hague-Visby Rules, or the Hamburg Rules, where compulsorily applicable. The ICA is extended to claims for delay and claims arising out of negligent navigation or management, and covers a residual category of 'all other cargo claims whatsoever'. For the first time, customs dues and fines, and costs reasonably incurred in defending or settling cargo claims, come within the ambit of the ICA. The 1996 amendment also makes it clear that, for the ICA to apply, cargo claims must be paid and not merely be pending, and that cargo claims that are mandatorily subject to the Hamburg Rules are covered.

The 1996 ICA has now been amended and will be referred to as the 'Inter-Club New York Produce Exchange Agreement 1996 (as amended September 2011)' (the '2011 Agreement'), and applies to charterparties entered into on or after 1 September 2011, where the charterparty refers to either 'the ICA 1996 (as amended September 2011)' or 'the ICA 1996 or any amendments thereto', or wording to that effect. The 2011 Agreement contains a new provision, cl 9, which grants a party which has given security to a cargo claimant the right to claim security from the other party to the charterparty, regardless of whether a right to apportionment has arisen. The party demanding security must give the other party to the charterparty written notification of the cargo claim within the relevant period specified in cl 6,[62] and must reciprocate by providing acceptable security for an equivalent amount to the other party in respect of the cargo claim if requested to do so.

No special clauses relating to cargo claims

In the absence of any special clauses, one needs to read the charter to see who has responsibility for what activities, and link up the cause of the damage with a breach of one of those activities. At common law, the shipowner is obliged to load, stow, trim and discharge the cargo.[63] These obligations are frequently modified by express provisions of the charter. The terms of a time charter as to fitness to carry a cargo or as to seaworthiness are capable of embracing legal fitness to carry the cargo. In *The Elli and the Frixos*,[64] the shipowners were held to be in breach of charter after the coming into force of new regulations for double-hulled vessels, with which their vessels did not comply, under the **Convention for the Prevention of Pollution from Ships 1973 (MARPOL)**. Clause 1(g) of Shelltime 4 required the vessels to have on board the documents required 'from time to time' by any applicable law to enable her to perform the charter service, even though cl 1 began as follows: 'At the date of delivery of the vessel under this charter . . .'. However, this is not the case regarding 'Rightship' approval, which is a private vetting system set up by three major companies in the coal and iron markets. In *The Silver Constellation*,[65] such approval was held not to be required under cl 1 of the NYPE form, nor under cl 31, which required the vessel to have the necessary certificates to be 'eligible' for trading to permitted ports. However, the charterers were entitled to require the shipowners to have a Rightship inspection, as this would be an order as regards

---

60 *The Holstencruiser* [1992] 2 Lloyd's Rep 378, QB. The decision also contains *dicta* that 'legal costs' referred to in the ICA cover the costs of the bill of lading claimants, but not the charterers, and that it does not cover customs fines.
61 *The Strathnewton* [1983] 1 Lloyd's Rep 219, CA, where the one-year Hague Rules time limit was held to have no application to a claim by charterers under the ICA.
62 24 months from the date of delivery of the cargo or the date the cargo should have been delivered, 36 months when the cargo claim is subject to the mandatory application of the Hamburg Rules.
63 *The Filikos* [1983] 1 Lloyd's Rep 9, CA.
64 [2008] EWCA Civ 584; [2008] 2 Lloyd's Rep 119.
65 [2008] EWHC 1904 (Comm); [2008] 2 Lloyd's Rep 440.

employment under cl 8. The charter may also provide that the charterer is responsible for stowage. In these circumstances, if the shipowner has to settle a cargo claim under the bill of lading that results out of bad stowage, it will be able to recover the costs of the settlement from the charterer by way of damages.

Liability for stowage is not always clearly allocated by the express terms of the charter. Particular problems arise under the NYPE form charter, cl 8 of which provides that the charterers are to 'load, stow, trim and discharge the cargo under the supervision of the master'.[66] At common law, the first three of these operations fall on the shipowners.[67] In *Court Line Ltd v Canadian Transport Co Ltd*,[68] the House of Lords held that cl 8 shifted liability for them onto the charterer. The reference to the 'supervision' of the master allowed for a shift back to the shipowners if the loss was caused by a want of care in matters within the master's province, such as the stability of the vessel, or the master actually supervised the stowage and the loss was caused by that supervision. If the defective stowage renders the vessel uncargoworthy, but does not imperil the safety of the vessel or the crew, the charterer will remain liable.[69] Sometimes, the loss or damage will be caused partly by a breach of the charterer's obligation to stow and partly by a breach of the shipowner's warranty of seaworthiness, which affects the safety of the vessel or the crew. In such a case, it is likely that the shipowner will be solely liable, provided that its breach is an effective cause of the loss or damage, even if it is not necessarily the dominant cause.[70] However, in *Compania Sud American Vapores v MS ER Hamburg Schiffahrtsgesellschaft mbH & Co KG*,[71] Morison J held that the charterer remained fully responsible under unamended cl 8 of the NYPE form, where they had stowed the vessel in such a way as to render it unseaworthy.

Clause 8 is frequently amended by the insertion of the words 'and responsibility' after the word 'supervision'. The effect of this amendment was held, in *The Argonaut*,[72] to throw liability for bad stowage back onto the shipowners if damage is caused by bad stowage by the charterer's servants, the stevedores, as opposed to any officious intervention by the charterers themselves. The time charterer will owe a duty to employ a reasonably competent firm of stevedores, but will not be obliged to ensure that they carry out their work competently.[73] Whichever version of cl 8 is used, the charterers will remain responsible for the costs of loading and discharge, but not for the costs of reloading and trans-shipment.[74]

Exceptions clauses

The charter's provisions as to who does what are not exhaustive of the question of how cargo claims are to be apportioned. The charter may contain a wide exceptions clause, such as cll 9[75] and 13 of the Baltime charter. A similarly worded provision appears in cl 2 of the Gencon charter. As with the Baltime form, a wide exceptions clause is necessary in the absence of a clause paramount in the printed form. In contrast, where the printed form contains a clause paramount, the printed exceptions clause is likely to be very restricted in its ambit, as is the case with cl 16 of the NYPE form, which provides: 'The act of God, enemies, fire, restraint of Princes, Rulers and People, and all

---

66 These problems led to the drafting of the ICA.
67 Although the charterers may be estopped from making a claim based on bad stowage if the stowage was done in accordance with instructions given by their representative. See *The Santamana* (1923) 14 Ll L Rep 159 and *Ismail v Polish Ocean Lines* [1976] 1 Lloyd's Rep 489, CA.
68 [1940] AC 934.
69 *The Imvros* [1999] 1 Lloyd's Rep 849, QB.
70 See *The Kapitan Sakharov* [2000] 2 Lloyd's Rep 255, CA, in the context of loss caused by a combination of the shipowner's breach of Art III(1) and the shipper's breach of Art IV(6) of the Hague Rules.
71 [2006] EWHC 483 (Comm); [2006] 2 Lloyd's Rep 66, noted [2007] LMCLQ 1.
72 [1985] 2 Lloyd's Rep 216, QB.
73 *The Clipper San Luis* [2000] 1 Lloyd's Rep 645, QB.
74 *The Aquacharm* [1982] 1 WLR 119, CA.
75 'The Owners not to be responsible for shortage, mixture, marks, nor for number of pieces or packages, nor for damage to or claims on cargo caused by bad stowage or otherwise . . .'.

dangers and accidents of the Seas, Rivers, Machinery, Boilers and Steam Navigation, and errors of Navigation throughout this Charter Party, always mutually excepted.'

Clause 13 of the Baltime charter provides that:

> . . . the owners only to be responsible for delay in the delivery of the Vessel or for delay during the currency of the Charter and for loss or damage to goods onboard, if such delay or loss has been caused by want of due diligence on the part of the Owners or their Manager in making the vessel seaworthy and fitted for the voyage or any other personal act or omission or default of the Owners or their Manager. The Owners not to be responsible in any other case nor for damage or delay, whatsoever and howsoever caused even if caused by the neglect or default of their servants . . .

In *The Brabant*,[76] it was held that the clause limits the liability of the shipowner to *personal* want of due diligence, so avoiding the effect of *The Muncaster Castle*,[77] in which the shipowner was held liable for unseaworthiness caused by the default of an independent contractor.

However, such clauses need to be read with care, as the courts may construe the exception more narrowly than might at first be apparent to the party seeking to rely on it. In *The TFL Prosperity*,[78] the House of Lords held that the second sentence of cl 13 of the Baltime form, quoted above, referred back to the matters contained in the first sentence. These were limited to physical loss or damage to goods and, therefore, cl 13 did not afford the shipowners a defence to the charterer's claim for financial losses suffered pursuant to a misdescription in the charter of the height of the main deck. Where the charterparty does not contain a printed clause paramount, as is the case with the Baltime form, the presence of a typed clause paramount will entail its taking precedence over the printed exceptions clause in the charter.[79]

Deck cargo

Carriage of cargo on deck involves hazards over and above those encountered in the carriage of cargo below deck. For this reason, it is common to find specific provisions in charterparties that transfer the risk of damage to deck cargo back to the charterer. The most common clause is one that provides that deck cargo is to be carried at 'charterer's risk'. In *The Fantasy*,[80] the Court of Appeal upheld the decision of Evans J that this wording could exclude the shipowner's liability in respect of loss or damage caused by the negligence of its servants. A similar result follows where the clause is strengthened by specific wording that the shipowner is not to be responsible for loss or damage to deck cargo 'however caused'.[81] Furthermore, in *The Imvros*,[82] Langley J held that these words also protected the shipowner where the negligence of the crew in lashing the deck cargo had been such as to make the vessel unseaworthy in the sense of being uncargoworthy. The principles of construction adopted in these decisions are markedly more liberal than those that are applied in general contract law.[83] These principles were applied by the Canadian Court of Appeal in *Belships v Canadian Forest Products Ltd*,[84] when it held that a general exclusion of liability for deck cargo does not cover negligence, as the clause could also cover the strict liability imposed on carriers independently of negligence.

---

76 [1967] 1 QB 588, QB.
77 [1961] AC 807, HL.
78 [1984] 1 Lloyd's Rep 123.
79 *Adamastos Shipping Co Ltd v Anglo-Saxon Petroleum Co Ltd* [1958] 1 Lloyd's Rep 73.
80 [1991] 2 Lloyd's Rep 391, QB; [1992] 1 Lloyd's Rep 235, CA.
81 *The Danah* [1993] 1 Lloyd's Rep 351, QB.
82 [1999] 1 Lloyd's Rep 849, QB, noted (2000) LMCLQ 295.
83 See pp 81–3.
84 (1999) 45 Lloyd's Alert Service.

The effect of a clause paramount incorporating the Hague Rules was considered in *The Socol 3*.[85] Hamblen J held that although it is generally necessary to read the phrases 'bill of lading' or 'contract of carriage' in the Hague Rules as referring to the governing charterparty, there was no principle or rule that this must always be so. The construction of the phrase 'contract of carriage' in the Rules depends on the context in which it is being used, and in the context of Art I(c) 'contract of carriage' could only sensibly apply to the bill of lading since it is only the bill of lading which is ever likely to contain an on-deck statement. As the bill of lading had stated the quantity of cargo carried on deck, the deck cargo was not covered by the Hague Rules. Its loss fell to be determined under the other provisions of the charter, which was on the NYPE form, with cl 8 unamended. There were three causes of the loss of the deck cargo: an inadequate method of stowage of the deck cargo; unsatisfactory lashing equipment and inadequate care of the lashings during the voyage; and the instability of the vessel. Although the master's right to supervise under cl 8 did not involve a duty to intervene, the case fell under the exception to that rule where the loss or damage was attributable to want of care in matters (such as the stability characteristics of the ship) of which the master was aware but the charterers were not. The shipowners were unable to claim an indemnity from the charterers under cl 13(b) of NYPE form 1993 'for any loss and/or damage and/or liability of whatsoever nature caused to the Vessel as a result of the carriage of deck cargo and which would not have arisen had deck cargo not been loaded'. The risks inherent in the carriage of deck cargo gave the clause a realistic content regardless of negligence or breach of the seaworthiness obligation.

Deck cargo clauses may be modified so as to throw some of the risks of the carriage of deck cargo back onto the shipowner. In *The Fantasy*, the clause provided that the crew were to check and protect the deck cargo during the voyage, and in *The Visurgis*[86] the crew were required to perform the lashing of the cargo. In such situations, the clause would cease to protect the shipowner where the charterer established that the loss or damage to the deck cargo had occurred due to negligence of the crew in performing these services, unless, as in *The Imvros*, the clause further provided that the crew in performing these services were to be regarded as servants of the charterer.

Such clauses not only protect the shipowner in respect of cargo claims arising out of loss or damage to deck cargo, but also entitle it to recover the costs of re-stowing deck cargo, which it might not otherwise be entitled to under the basic provisions of the cargo relating to loading, stowing and discharging. This was the case in *The Darya Tara*,[87] where the costs of re-stowing deck cargo would otherwise have fallen on the shipowner, the vessel being chartered on the NYPE form with cl 8 amended to include the words 'and responsibility'. However, the shipowners in that case also advanced a claim for hire lost and bunkers consumed during a deviation to a port of refuge for the purpose of re-stowing deck cargo. These claims were held not to fall within the deck cargo claim and were not recoverable, because the amendment to cl 8 had made it impossible for the shipowners to attribute these losses to any breach of charter by the charterers. The shipowners' claim to recover these items by way of indemnity also failed due to the fact that they had voluntarily undertaken the risks inherent in the carriage of deck cargo.

Finally, it should be noted that a shipowner obtains less protection under a clause that merely states that cargo is loaded 'at shipper's risk' than under one that refers to 'charterer's risk'. Such a clause was considered in *The Danah*[88] and was held not to provide the shipowners with a blanket defence to a claim against them by the charterers for an indemnity in respect of a cargo claim. It would only provide a defence if the claim could have been avoided by putting such a clause into the bill of lading. It therefore provided no defence to the charterers' claim in respect of salvage

---

85 [2010] EWHC 777; [2010] 2 Lloyd's Rep 221.
86 [1999] 1 Lloyd's Rep 219, QB.
87 [1997] 1 Lloyd's Rep 42, QB.
88 [1993] 1 Lloyd's Rep 351, QB.

claims that had been made against them by the Dutch authorities resulting from containers stowed on deck being washed overboard.

Indemnity actions

Exceptions clauses create defences. It does not necessarily follow that they also create positive rights of indemnity. In *The C Joyce*,[89] the shipowners attempted to reclaim from charterers by way of an indemnity the costs that they had incurred in settling cargo claims. They based their argument on the fact that cl 2 of the Gencon charter gave them a defence to any cargo claims brought against them by charterers, other than those arising from unseaworthiness. Bingham J rejected the argument and held that cl 2 gave the shipowners no rights of indemnity against the charterer.

However, where a time charter is involved, it is likely that the courts will imply a right of indemnity in favour of the shipowner. In the limited situations already discussed in this chapter, this will enable the shipowners to make a recovery from charterers in respect of cargo claims where there has been no breach of charter by the charterer, as in *The Island Archon*.[90]

Type of cargo to be loaded

This issue has already been examined in detail in Chapter 5. However, to recapitulate, the charterer must not order the shipowner to load cargo outside the permitted range of cargoes specified in the charter. If the charterer orders the shipowner to load a permitted cargo, it must inform the shipowner of any special risks attaching to the cargo of which the shipowner has no actual or constructive knowledge. Although the charterer will not incur liability if the shipowner suffers loss due to the inherent dangers of a cargo that it has consented to carry,[91] it will be liable in such circumstances if the cargo in question is one the carriage of which is not authorised by the terms of the charterparty.[92] The charterer's duty extends to notifying the shipowner of any purely financial risks that it may incur by loading the cargo. Thus, in *Mitchell Cotts & Co v Steel Bros & Co Ltd*,[93] shippers of a cargo of rice chartered for voyage to Piraeus knew that the rice could not be discharged there without permission of the British government (it being wartime), although they thought that they might obtain it. They were unable to get it and this caused delay, for which the shipper was held liable.[94]

Permitted ports

Charterer's right to nominate ports

A voyage charter may simply specify a loading and a discharging port. If that is the case, then the charterer cannot order the shipowner to proceed to any port other than that named in the charterparty. If the shipowner does agree to obey such an illegitimate order, it will be able to recover additional freight on a *quantum meruit* basis.[95]

With time charters, and, to a lesser extent, with some voyage charters, the charter will not specify particular ports, but will give the charterer the right to nominate loading and discharging

---

89 [1986] 2 Lloyd's Rep 285.
90 [1994] 2 Lloyd's Rep 287. But note that an indemnity is unlikely to be implied into a voyage or trip charter.
91 *The Athanasia Comninos* [1990] 1 Lloyd's Rep 277, QB.
92 *Chandris v Isbrandtsen-Moller* [1951] 1 KB 240.
93 [1916] 2 KB 610.
94 See, also, *The Greek Fighter* [2006] EWHC 1729 (Comm); [2006] 2 CLC 497. The charterers were in breach of a lawful merchandise warranty under a charter when the vessel was detained and sold by the UAE authorities for having on board some oil of Iraqi origin in contravention of UN sanctions then applicable to Iraq.
95 *The Batis* [1990] 1 Lloyd's Rep 345, QB.

ports from within a given geographical range of ports.[96] Nomination of a port outside the range will be an illegitimate order.[97]

The express warranty of safety

The charterer's right to nominate ports is usually coupled with an express warranty as to the safety of the nominated port. The courts will give effect to an express safe port warranty, even when the port is specified in the charter and is not nominated by the charterer.[98] By implication, this warranty will probably also extend to the berths within the port. The standard of safety for a berth will be the same as that for a port. The express warranty of safety may be excluded, by virtue of other clauses in the charter. In *The Evia (No 2)*,[99] this was held to be the effect of the war risks clause in the Baltime charter, which was intended to provide an exhaustive set of provisions to regulate the parties in the event of a nominated port becoming unsafe. In contrast, the war risks clause in the Shelltime 3 form used in *The Chemical Venture*[100] was held not to constitute a complete code and therefore did not exclude the safe port warranty. In *The Ocean Victory*,[101] a provision in a demise charter that the demise charterer take out marine, war and P&I insurance in the joint names of itself and the owners did not constitute a complete code and exclude the safe port warranty. Clear words are necessary before the court will hold that a contract has taken away rights or remedies that one of the parties would otherwise have had, either at common law or under other parts of the contract.

The implied warranty of safety

In the absence of an express warranty, the courts may be prepared to imply one, but they will not do so where the port is specified in the charter and there is no right to nominate; nor will they do so where the charter gives the charterers a right to trade the vessel in a known war zone. In *The APJ Priti*,[102] the charter allowed the charterer to nominate one of three ports in the Persian Gulf at the time of the war between Iran and Iraq. It contained an express warranty as to the safety of the berth nominated, but none as to the nominated port. The vessel was hit by a missile on her approach voyage to the nominated port. It was held that there was no implied warranty as to the safety of nominated ports on these facts. Of particular significance was the fact that all of the ports from which the charterer could make its nomination were situated in an area that was already subject to hostilities at the time that the charter was concluded.

The circumstances in which a safe berth warranty will be implied were considered in *The Reborn*.[103] The vessel was chartered on a Gencon form for a voyage from Chekka in Lebanon to Algiers. In cl 1 of Gencon the word 'safely' had been struck through in relation to the load port. At Chekka the vessel's hull was damaged by an underwater projection at the loading berth nominated by the charterers. It was held that there was no implied term that the berth nominated by the charterers would be safe. There was a contrast with safe port charterparties where the port must be prospectively safe for the vessel to use, which included a safe loading berth, so that a safe berth was implicit in the express warranty of safety of the port. In the present case where there was no safe port warranty, it did not follow from the mere fact that charterers were under a duty to nominate

---

96 In *The Aegean Sea* [1998] 1 Lloyd's Rep 39, Thomas J held that the right of nomination, and any consequent liability if the nominated port proves to be unsafe, adheres to the charterer and not the bill of lading holder.

97 With time charters, an order to proceed to a port within the geographical range will also be illegitimate if compliance with the order means that the vessel will be redelivered outside the charter period.

98 *The Livanita* [2007] EWHC 1317 (Comm); [2008] 1 Lloyd's Rep 86; *The Archimidis* [2008] EWCA Civ 175; [2008] 1 Lloyd's Rep 597, noted [2008] JIML 78.

99 *The Evia (No 2)* [1983] 1 AC 736, HL.

100 [1993] 1 Lloyd's Rep 508, QB.

101 [2013] EWHC 2199 (Comm); [2014] 1 Lloyd's Rep 59.

102 [1987] 2 Lloyd's Rep 37, CA. The circumstances prevailing at the time of the charter will also be relevant for assessing danger in the context of any express warranty of safety as in *The Product Star* [1993] 1 Lloyd's Rep 397.

103 *Mediterranean Salvage & Towage Ltd v Seamar Trading & Commerce Inc* [2008] EWHC 1875 (Comm); aff'd [2009] EWCA Civ 531; [2009] 2 Lloyd's Rep 639.

a berth that they also warranted that the berth was safe. A significant factor in this finding was cl 20 of the charterparty, whereby owners guaranteed that the vessel would be compliant with the port's specifications and restrictions including draft, and agreed to investigate the named port, or take the risk of any damage in getting into and out of it or in using it. The clause was inconsistent with the implication of a safe berth warranty. Furthermore, charterers' options for nomination had been circumscribed with the stipulation that the berth nominated must comply with the saltwater draft of 27 feet.

What constitutes 'unsafety'?

The classical definition of a safe port was given by Sellars LJ in *The Eastern City*, where he stated that a port would be safe if:[104]

> . . . in the relevant period of time . . . the particular ship (can) reach it, use it, [and] return from it without, in the absence of some abnormal occurrence, being exposed to danger which cannot be avoided by good navigation or seamanship.

'Danger' can encompass both physical and political unsafety. Ports have been found to be physically unsafe where they are liable to the sudden onset of high winds that could not be predicted and that might cause the anchor to drag,[105] or where the vessel is liable to be damaged by inadequate fendering to protect her from the pier at which she is moored.[106] In *The Marinicki*,[107] a port was held to be unsafe due to an underwater obstruction in the dredged channel constituting the designated route into the port, notwithstanding that the shipowner could not prove that it had been in existence at the time that the orders were given. The port's unsafety was due to the fact that there was no proper system in place at the port for investigating and removing obstacles, and to give proper warnings as to obstacles. In *The Ocean Victory*[108] the port of Kashima was held to be prospectively unsafe for a Capesize vessel because of the risk that such a vessel might have to leave the port on account of long waves or bad weather at a time when the wind and sea conditions in the channel were such that the vessel might not be able to leave the port safely, together with an absence of any system to ensure that the vessel could safely leave the port when weather conditions required it do so. The warranty was one of safety, and not 'reasonable safety'. An abnormal occurrence was one that was unrelated to the characteristics of the port and the causes. Although the concurrence of long waves and gale force winds from the north was a rare event, it flowed from the characteristics of the port. Ports have also been found to be politically unsafe where vessels have been detained there following the outbreak of war.

The risk of unsafety must be more than negligible, otherwise the risk becomes an 'abnormal occurrence' within the definition of Sellars LJ, and the charterers will not be liable. This factual issue may pose difficulties when it is alleged that a port is prospectively unsafe due to political reasons, as this will inevitably involve a more subjective judgment than is the case with physical characteristics of the port. These difficulties are well illustrated by comparing the approach of the first-instance judge in *The Saga Cob*[109] with that adopted by the Court of Appeal.[110] The vessel was ordered to proceed to the Ethiopian port of Massawa on 26 August 1988 and suffered a seaborne attack by Eritrean guerillas, the EPLF, on 7 September 1988, while anchored

---

104 [1958] 2 Lloyd's Rep 127, 131.
105 *The Eastern City* [1958] 2 Lloyd's Rep 127.
106 *Reardon-Smith Line v Australian Wheat Board (The Houston City)* [1956] AC 266, HL.
107 [2003] EWHC 1894 (Admlty); [2003] 2 Lloyd's Rep 655, QB.
108 [2013] EWHC 2199 (Comm); [2014] 1 Lloyd's Rep 59.
109 [1992] 2 Lloyd's Rep 398.
110 [1992] 2 Lloyd's Rep 545.

off the port. Diamond J found the port to be prospectively unsafe, because, at the date of the charterer's nomination:

> . . . it was a characteristic of the port of Massawa that vessels proceeding to or from the port or lying at anchor outside the port could be subject to seaborne attack by the EPLF. This characteristic may not have involved a high degree of risk but equally the risk cannot properly be regarded as negligible.

In coming to this conclusion, Diamond J had been chiefly influenced by the fact that another vessel, *The Omo Wonz*, had been subject to a seaborne attack by guerillas on 31 May 1988.

The Court of Appeal overruled his decision. In doing so, it discounted the relevance of the earlier attack because it did not show that the precautions adopted by the Ethiopian authorities were inadequate. *The Omo Wonz* was attacked because the security system was not properly carried out and the vessel had got too far away from her escort frigate. The Court of Appeal supported its conclusion by reference to the fact that there was no subsequent attack of any kind on shipping off the coast of Ethiopia until early 1990. In assessing the degree of risk required before a port became unsafe, Parker LJ stated that the 'political' risk must be sufficient for a reasonable shipowner or master to decline to send or sail its vessel there.

In *The Chemical Venture*,[111] Gatehouse J expressed reservations about this formulation on the ground that it added another element to the definition of Sellars LJ. It is submitted that these reservations are unfounded and that the statements of Parker LJ should be read as clarifying, rather than adding to, the definition propounded by Sellars LJ. Gatehouse J was also unhappy with the willingness of the Court of Appeal to consider events after the incident.[112] There is much to be said for his view from the point of strict logic. If the issue is the prospective safety of the port at the date of nomination, a charterer can only base its judgment on an assessment of events up to the date of nomination.

The assessment of danger is further complicated when the permitted trading area is already hazardous at the time that the charter is signed. The Court of Appeal in *The Product Star*[113] held that the 'danger' of proceeding to a nominated port in the Persian Gulf in 1987 during the Iran/Iraq war had to be assessed by comparing the danger of the port as at the date of the charter with the danger as at the date of the order. The port would be dangerous only if conditions had worsened in this period. Furthermore, a discretion given by the charter to the shipowners to refuse to proceed to dangerous ports was also held to be valid only if (a) the port was prospectively more dangerous than was the case at the time of the signing of the charter, and (b) the shipowners' discretion had not been exercised capriciously. The shipowners' refusal failed on both counts, their decision not being actuated by any true concern about the safety of the ship, but being prompted by a dispute with the charterers regarding over-age insurance.

The nature of the warranty

The warranty of safety is not, as was held in *The Mary Lou*,[114] a continuing warranty. In *The Evia* (No 2),[115] the House of Lords held that the warranty crystallises at the time that the nomination is made. At this time, the port must be prospectively safe for the anticipated time of the vessel's stay there. If circumstances subsequently change, the charterers must renominate an alternative safe

---

111 [1993] 1 Lloyd's Rep 508.
112 Nonetheless, his own finding that Mina Al Ahmadi was prospectively unsafe at the time of nomination on 22 May 1984 was based not only on the fact that three Saudi or Kuwait flagged vessels had been attacked by Iranian aircraft shortly prior to that date, but also that a further 11 were attacked in the five months after the attack on *The Chemical Venture*.
113 [1993] 1 Lloyd's Rep 397.
114 [1981] 2 Lloyd's Rep 272, QB.
115 [1983] 1 AC 736, HL.

port. If they are unable to do so, as in the present case in which the vessel was already in Basra when the Iran/Iraq war broke out, the charterers will not be in breach. Their Lordships expressed no firm view as to whether this secondary duty would arise in a voyage charter where the charterer, generally, has no right to alter a nomination, once made. Cooke describes the unappealing consequences of this conclusion as follows: '. . . the vessel must encounter the new danger or wait until that danger is passed or wait until an unreasonable period or frustrating period has elapsed or will inevitably elapse.'[116] However, a duty to renominate on grounds of unsafety is quite a different matter from a right to renominate on grounds of commercial convenience.[117] It is submitted that the secondary duty to renominate should be imposed wherever the primary warranty exists. If the charter contains a 'near' clause, the position may be altered somewhat. Should the shipowner exercise the liberty, it is likely that it will be taken to have warranted the safety of the alternative port. Should it fail to do so, it may be regarded as having debarred itself from pleading the frustration, as any frustration will be self-induced. Alternatively, it may be unable to claim demurrage incurred in waiting outside the original port on the ground that it has failed to mitigate its losses.

Changed circumstances that amount merely to a worsening of a pre-existing incident of unsafety will not prevent the port being regarded as having been unsafe at the time of its nomination. In *The Lucille*,[118] the charterers ordered the vessel into Basra on 20 September 1980. At that date, the port was prospectively unsafe due to the outbreak of the Iran/Iraq war. On 22 September, the Shatt al Arab waterway was closed, which led to the subsequent trapping of the vessel in Basra once she had completed her loading on 23 October. The closure of the Shatt al Arab was not to be regarded as a separate abnormal event for which the charterers were not responsible. It was intrinsically linked to the state of affairs prevailing on 20 September when the charterers ordered the vessel to proceed into Basra to load.

In some charters, the charterer is obliged only to take due diligence to nominate a safe port. In *The Saga Cob*,[119] Parker LJ was of the view, *obiter*, that such a clause might exonerate the charterer, even when the port was prospectively unsafe. He gave as an example the situation in which a charterer who was unsure of the position inquired of a number of owners who used the port and was advised by all of them that the risk was so small that they would discount it. In *The Chemical Venture*,[120] Gatehouse J was of the view that, in the above example, it is unlikely that the port would have been prospectively unsafe anyway. He interpreted the views of Parker LJ as requiring the charterer to come up with some evidence to justify its order, which, on the facts before him, it had failed to provide.

Where the charterer's duty is limited to one of 'due diligence', that duty will be regarded as non-delegable. Thus, in *Dow-Europe v Novoklav Inc*,[121] the time charterer was held liable for the negligence of the port authority to which it had delegated its duty of nominating a safe berth.

The consequences of breach of the warranty

Breach of the warranty will expose charterers to a liability to pay damages to the shipowners in respect of losses sustained by reason of entering the unsafe port. The charterers will be liable in respect of any physical damage suffered by the vessel in consequence of entering the unsafe port. They will also be liable in respect of the economic consequences.[122] Thus, if the vessel is trapped in

---

116 Cooke, Young, Taylor, Kimball, Martowski and Lambert, *Voyage Charters*, 2nd edn, 2001, London: LLP, at 5.56. It is possible that losses incurred by the shipowner in such a situation might be recovered from the charterer by way of an implied indemnity, given that the losses flow directly from a choice made by the charterer.

117 As in *The Jasmine B* [1992] 1 Lloyd's Rep 39, QB.

118 [1984] 1 Lloyd's Rep 387, CA.

119 [1992] 2 Lloyd's Rep 398.

120 [1993] 1 Lloyd's Rep 508.

121 [1998] 1 Lloyd's Rep 306, QB.

122 In *The Vine* [2010] EWHC 1411 (Comm); [2011] 1 Lloyd's Rep 301, the charterers were liable for time lost in waiting to berth, even though laytime did not run though the period of delay due to the operation of a laytime exception.

a port in a war zone, then the charterers will be unable to rely on the doctrine of frustration. The charter will continue and, instead, they will be liable to pay the shipowners hire or demurrage, as the case may be, up to the end of the charter, and damages for detention for any subsequent period during which the vessel remains trapped.

At the time that the charterer nominates a prospectively unsafe port, the shipowner is entitled to refuse the nomination and call for a new one. But the risks at the time may be difficult to assess, particularly where 'political' risks are involved. The shipowner may decide to accept the nomination and claim damages for breach of the warranty if things subsequently turn out badly. It does not necessarily lose its right to claim damages by complying with such an order. The effect of compliance with an illegitimate order was considered by the House of Lords in *The Kanchenjunga*.[123] Once the shipowner has agreed to act on such an illegitimate order, it cannot subsequently change its mind and call for a fresh nomination, but it will still be able to recover damages unless its conduct is such as to allow the charterer to rely on waiver or promissory estoppel as a defence. The charterer was able to do this in *The Chemical Venture*[124] by reference to the shipowners' conduct, in negotiating with them for the provision of war bonuses to encourage the crew to sail into an area in which they would be at risk of air attack.

However, although the shipowner may not have waived its right to claim damages, it may lose its entitlement to damages if its compliance with the orders is so unreasonable as to amount to a break in the chain of causation. This proposition, which was accepted by Lord Goff in *The Kanchenjunga*, stems from dicta of Morris LJ in *The Stork*, where he stated:[125]

> The owners must not throw their ship away. If, having the opportunity to refrain from obeying the order, and having the knowledge that the ship had been wrongly directed to run into danger, those responsible for the ship allowed her to be damaged, when they could have saved her, it would be contrary to reason if damages could be recovered . . . they would not be the result of the breach of contract, but of the deliberate and unnecessary act of those in control of the ship. Further, there is a duty to behave with ordinary reasonable prudence so as to minimise damages, and the readily attainable minimum may in some cases be nil . . .

In practice, it will be very difficult to establish that the compliance with the order was so unreasonable as to have this effect. In *The Stork* itself, the master sought and obtained reassurances from the pilot sent by the charterers to meet the vessel and the chain of causation was not broken.[126] Morris LJ stressed that the shipowner did not need to verify every order given by the charterers by seeking information beyond that ordinarily available to a reasonable and prudent shipowner.

Finally, it must be noted that even if the charterer is not in breach of its duty to nominate a safe port, the shipowner may still be able to recover by way of an indemnity. In *The Evaggelos Theta*,[127] Donaldson J held that the warranty, which there related to the purely marine characteristics of the berth, had not been broken, but remitted the case to the arbitrators to consider this issue. The decision was premised on the assumption that the charterer would be in breach only if it nominated a prospectively unsafe port. In the light of *The Evia (No 2)*,[128] it is clear that a time charterer, at least, also owes a secondary duty to renominate if circumstances change. It might be thought that this duty would leave little room for a claim based on an indemnity in unsafe port cases. Nonetheless, a claim by way of indemnity was held to be possible in the case of damage due to physical unsafety

123 [1990] 1 Lloyd's Rep 391, noted Reynolds, F (1990) LMCLQ 453.
124 [1993] 1 Lloyd's Rep 508.
125 [1955] 2 QB 68, 104.
126 Notwithstanding the fact that, though paid for by the charterers, a pilot is usually regarded as the shipowner's servant.
127 [1971] 2 Lloyd's Rep 200.
128 [1983] 1 AC 736, HL.

in Port Harcourt, Nigeria, in *The Erechthion*[129] (decided after *The Evia (No 2)*). After *The Island Archon*,[130] it must be borne in mind that the issue in an indemnity claim is no longer solely one of causation, but will also involve consideration of the risks voluntarily assumed by the shipowner at the time that the charter was signed. This will further complicate the relationship between an indemnity claim and liability for breach of the duty to renominate.

Shipowners' obligations in getting to the load port

Reasonable dispatch

It is a term implied into every voyage charterparty that the shipowner must proceed with reasonable dispatch not only on the contract voyage itself, but also on the approach voyage.[131] Such a term is also implied into the time charter as regards the approach voyage to the place of delivery.[132] The approach voyage is the voyage from the place at which the vessel is situated when the charter is signed to the loading port/place of delivery specified in the charter. This term is an innominate term. Breach will only justify the charterer in terminating the contract if the consequences thereof are sufficiently serious to 'frustrate the commercial purposes of the contract'.[133]

Statements as to vessel's position and expected readiness

The implied obligation to proceed with reasonable dispatch will frequently be fleshed out with statements in the charter designed to give the charterer a more concrete idea as to when performance of the charter is likely to commence. Examples of such statements are:

(a)   'vessel now in the port of Amsterdam';[134]
(b)   'vessel now sailed or about to sail from a pitch pine port to UK';[135]
(c)   'vessel expected ready to load 1 July'.[136]

Such statements amount to conditions, any breach of which will entitle the charterer to terminate the contract as well as to damages. The shipowner will be in breach if the statement is untrue or, in the case of statement (c), if it had no reasonable grounds to believe the statement at the date of the charter.[137] If the charterer knows that the statement is untrue and proceeds with the charter, it will be taken to have waived its right to repudiate, but not its right to damages.[138]

When combined with the obligation to proceed with reasonable dispatch, the effect of such a condition is to oblige the shipowner to start from 'wherever she may happen to be, at a date when, by proceeding with reasonable dispatch, she will arrive at the port of loading by the expected date'.[139] The obligation will generally be subject to exceptions clauses in the charter as regards delays that happen after, but not before, the commencement of the approach voyage.[140] Therefore,

---

129 [1987] 2 Lloyd's Rep 180, QB.
130 [1994] 2 Lloyd's Rep 227, CA.
131 *Freeman v Taylor* [1831] 8 Bing 124; *MacAndrew v Chapple* (1866) LR 1 CP 643.
132 *The Democritos* [1976] 2 Lloyd's Rep 149, CA.
133 Per Devlin J in *Universal Cargo Carriers Corp v Citati* [1957] 2 QB 401.
134 *Behn v Burness* [1863] 3 B & S 751.
135 *Bentsen v Taylor* [1893] 2 QB 274.
136 *The Mihalis Angelos* [1971] 1 QB 164, CA.
137 A warranty as to the duration of a trip charter that was made 'without guarantee' was held to have the same effect in *The Lendoudis Evangelos II* [1997] 1 Lloyd's Rep 404, QB.
138 *Bentsen v Taylor* [1893] 2 QB 274.
139 Per Devlin J in *Evera SA Commercial v North Shipping Co Ltd* [1956] 2 Lloyd's Rep 367, QB.
140 *Monroe Bros Ltd v Ryan* [1935] 2 KB 28, CA.

if, at the date of the new charter, the vessel is performing a previous charter, any delays under the previous charter will be outside the protection of exceptions clauses in the new charter.[141]

Although the charterparty exceptions cover the approach voyage, the obligation itself attaches from the signing of the charter and not from the time at which the vessel leaves the discharging port under the previous charter. In *The Baleares*,[142] the subcharter contained an estimated time of arrival (ETA) of 31 January 1987. The vessel was unable to make that date and the subcharterers exercised their right to cancel. They claimed damages on the basis of the increase in the price of propane from their suppliers, which took place between 20 January and the beginning of February, and which affected the profitability of their contracts with their own sub-purchasers. At the date of the charter, 12 January 1987, the vessel was already employed on a voyage from the Gulf to Tarragona, in Spain, where the vessel arrived on 4 February, completing discharge on 7 February. It would then take 22 hours to sail from Tarragona to the Algerian load port under the new charter. The shipowners argued that those 22 hours had to be subtracted from midnight on 31 January to ascertain the time at which they breached their duty to proceed with reasonable dispatch – namely, 0200 on 31 January 1987.

The shipowners put their case in this way so as to identify the time of their breach as occurring at the latest possible point. This was because most of the increase in the price of propane from the Algerian suppliers had taken place before 31 January 1987. Initially, Webster J found for the shipowners. The Court of Appeal, however, rejected their argument and held that the shipowners had been in breach of their obligation at least from 20 January, which is when the charterers started to incur losses. The combination of the ETA date with the obligation to proceed with reasonable dispatch produced an obligation to 'start in time' to reach the load port by 31 January. By 20 January, it was clear that the shipowners would be unable to start in time from Tarragona so as to reach the load port before midnight on 31 January.

The Court of Appeal left open the issue of whether there had also been a distinct breach of the ETA provision. On the facts, it is quite likely that there would have been such a breach, which would have been committed at the date that the charter was signed. The vessel lost 24 hours due to an engine breakdown, but the arbitrators' award makes no mention of any other factors that would explain why the vessel was unable to proceed from Tarragona until 7 February.

The cancellation clause

Most charters commonly contain a cancellation clause. This gives the charterer the option to cancel if the vessel has not arrived, ready to load, at the load port by a certain date. The charterer will need this facility to enable it to recharter if delays under the original charter are likely to put it in breach of its obligations under its contract of sale as to the time within which the cargo is to be loaded.

The exercise of the option to cancel depends on the terms of the option, not on whether the shipowner has been in breach. Cancellation will discharge the contract for both parties, but will not necessarily mean that the charterer can also sue the shipowner for breach of contract. In *The Democritos*,[143] the Court of Appeal held that the shipowner would be liable in damages only if its failure to meet the cancelling date was due to a failure to proceed with reasonable dispatch on the approach voyage. The charterer's right to cancel is not conditional on its having nominated a delivery port.[144]

---

141 *Louis Dreyfus & Co v Lauro* (1938) 60 Ll L Rep 94. The same principle applies even if the previous charter is specifically mentioned in the new charter. See *Evera SA Commercial v North Shipping Co Ltd* [1956] 2 Lloyd's Rep 367, QB.
142 [1993] 1 Lloyd's Rep 215, CA.
143 [1976] 2 Lloyd's Rep 149.
144 *The Ailsa Craig* [2009] EWCA Civ 425; [2009] 2 Lloyd's Rep 371. At the time the charterer cancelled, the vessel was still at Piraeus undergoing modification works and the charterer had not nominated a delivery port in the Ghana/Nigeria range. In any event, the obligation would not arise until the vessel had reached its 'deviation point' on the approach voyage from Piraeus at Las Palmas off Liberia. The time for the charterer to make its nomination had, therefore, never arrived.

Until the option is exercised, the contract remains alive. The shipowner must continue to proceed to the load port with reasonable dispatch, even if it knows that it will miss the cancellation date. The charterer must exercise its option within a reasonable time of its arising, but need not declare its intentions before, or even after, the due date.[145] It must not exercise its right before the due date, even if it is certain that the shipowner will not make the cancelling date. Premature cancellations are not only ineffective;[146] they also amount to a repudiatory breach by the charterer, although damages may well be nominal.[147] If the shipowner waives the repudiation, the House of Lords held in *The Simona*[148] that the charter, including the cancellation clause, survives. The charterer may therefore have a second bite at the cherry and validly cancel when the right to do so arises.

The right to cancel is not qualified by charter exceptions clauses.[149] It subsists even if the charterers themselves are not ready to load at the cancelling date,[150] unless the lack of 'readiness' is in some way the fault of the charterer. In *Armement Adolf Deppe v John Robinson & Co Ltd*,[151] the vessel, which was under a port charter, moored at the buoys. The charterer wanted delivery at berth, not buoys, and argued that the vessel was not 'ready', due to the fact that her gear was not rigged. The only reason that the shipowners had not taken on board a stevedore gang to do this was that the receivers were not willing to discharge at the buoys. There was nothing to prevent her being made ready at once, if desired, and, therefore, she was 'ready' for the purposes of starting laytime.

Although the vessel must be 'ready' to load, 'readiness' needs to be distinguished from 'fitness' to load. In *Vaughan v Campbell, Heatley & Co*,[152] the charter allowed for various cargoes to be loaded. The charterer elected to load a wheat cargo, which required the holds to have protective lining. The absence of the lining meant that the vessel was not 'fit' to load the wheat, but the vessel was still 'ready' and therefore the cancellation clause did not apply. Many of the permitted cargoes would not have required lining and the charter contained no provisions regarding lining. Had wheat been the sole permitted cargo, the vessel would not have been 'ready' to load and the charterer could have cancelled. Similarly, in *Noemijulia SS Co v Minister of Food*,[153] the Court of Appeal distinguished between readiness of the cargo spaces and readiness of the ship's equipment. For the purpose of the cancellation clause, the ship would be 'ready' if its gear could be made ready by the time at which the charterers would need to use it.

The presence of a cancellation clause does not necessarily exclude the operation of the doctrine of frustration. In *Bank Line v Capel (Arthur) & Co*,[154] the charter was frustrated when the vessel was requisitioned by the British government in the First World War for an indefinite period. Although the charter contained a clause giving an option to cancel in the event of requisition, this was held not to exclude the doctrine of frustration, as neither party had contemplated when they signed the charter that the vessel might be requisitioned for an indefinite period. Nor is a cancellation clause a factor to consider when assessing damages suffered as a result of the shipowner's failure to prosecute the carrying voyage with reasonable dispatch. In *The Heron II*,[155] the shipowner argued that the cargo owner had suffered no loss. This was because, had the vessel arrived just before the cancelling date, she would not have arrived at the discharge port before the fall in the market for the cargo of sugar, even if the shipowner had proceeded with reasonable dispatch. This argument was rejected.

---

145 *Moel Tryvan Ship Co v Andrew Weir & Co* [1910] 2 KB 844.
146 *The Madeleine* [1967] 2 Lloyd's Rep 224, QB.
147 *The Mihalis Angelos* [1971] 1 QB 164, CA. However, there, the premature cancellation was retrospectively justified as termination for breach of the 'expected readiness to load' provision.
148 *The Simona* [1989] AC 788, HL.
149 *Smith v Dart* (1884) 14 QBD 105.
150 *The Tres Flores* [1974] 1 QB 264, CA, especially Roskill LJ.
151 [1917] 2 KB 204.
152 (1885) 2 TLR 33, CA.
153 [1951] 2 KB 223.
154 [1919] AC 435, HL.
155 *The Heron II* [1969] 1 AC 350 at 426.

Chapter 10

Voyage Charterparties – Payment of Freight

Chapter Contents

What is freight?

The primary payment obligation under a voyage charter is freight. Freight is a fixed price for a particular voyage carrying a particular cargo or cargoes. It includes the shipowner's operating costs, such as crew wages, the fuel consumed on the voyage and the shipowner's profit margin.

It can be calculated either on a lump-sum basis, for example, £200,000, or by reference to the quantity loaded or discharged, for example, £20 per ton. The latter mode of calculation will usually be accompanied by a clause specifying the minimum and maximum cargo to be loaded, or one requiring the charterer to load 'a full and complete cargo'. If less than the minimum is loaded, the shipowner can claim freight on the shortfall, subject to de minimis.[1] This is known as *deadfreight*. In *The Archimidis*,[2] a tender of the full amount of cargo by the charterers was held not to prevent their incurring a liability for deadfreight as it was, in fact, not possible to load that quantity of cargo given draft restrictions at the port of loading. The charterers could have loaded the full quantity by taking up an option of loading by ship-to-ship transfer at anchorage, but they chose not to do so. Deadfreight will not accrue under a charter where lump-sum freight is payable, as the charterer will be under no obligation to load any particular quantity of cargo. Additional freight on a *quantum meruit* basis will be payable if the shipowner agrees to load a non-charter cargo[3] or proceed to a non-charter port.[4]

The freight provisions in a charter will frequently be accompanied by warranties by the shipowner as to the vessel's cargo-carrying capacity, its 'deadweight'. The warranty does not relieve the charterer of its obligation to load a 'full and complete cargo' where the charterer can, in fact, load in excess of the stated deadweight.[5] However, if the charterer is unable to load up to the deadweight figure, it will be entitled to claim a rebate on lump-sum freight provided that the wording of the deadweight warranty relates to the particular cargo to be carried on the voyage.[6] Even if the wording does relate to the particular cargo, the charterer's claim will fail if it tenders a cargo that is not of the proper description, even though such a tender may not amount to a breach of charter.[7]

Set-off

Charterers must pay freight in full and are not entitled to deduct counterclaims from it by relying on the usual rules of common law and equitable set-off. The House of Lords, in *The Aries*,[8] confirmed that freight is a special obligation that is not subject to either of these rules.[9] Any cross-claims made by charterers must be made by counterclaim or by separate action. This ruling was fatal to the charterers' claim because they had allowed their cargo claims against the shipowners to become time-barred under the Hague Rules before the shipowners commenced their action for freight. Attempts

---

1 This principle did not apply in *Margaronis Navigation Agency Ltd v Henry W Peabody & Co of London Ltd* [1965] 2 QB 430, CA. The vessel was capable of loading 12,600 tons of maize and the charterers were liable for deadfreight when they loaded only 12,588 tons, a 12-ton shortfall.
2 [2008] EWCA Civ 175; [2008] 1 Lloyd's Rep 597.
3 *Stevens v Bromley* [1919] 2 KB 722.
4 *The Batis* [1990] 1 Lloyd's Rep 345, QB.
5 *Hunter v Fry* (1819) 2 B & Ald 421.
6 *W Millar & Co Ltd v Owners of SS Freden* [1918] 1 KB 611, CA.
7 *Robert Mackill v Wright Brothers & Co* (1884) 14 App Cas 106, HL.
8 *The Aries* [1977] 1 WLR 185.
9 Affirming the previous strand of authority relating to common law set-off as evidenced in *Dakin v Oxley* [1864] 15 CB (NS) 646, where the charterers abandoned the damaged cargo on the vessel, but were still liable for freight, and also *The Brede* [1973] 2 Lloyd's Rep 333, CA.

to set off claims for short delivery of cargo,[10] and for damages consequent upon a repudiatory breach by the shipowner,[11] have also failed.

However, freight will not be payable if the damage is so severe as to transform the goods into a different type of goods altogether.[12] In this situation, the shipowner will have failed to deliver the contract goods. It will therefore have failed to satisfy the condition precedent to its entitlement to freight due on 'right and true delivery'. Whether or not the goods are merely damaged or have changed their intrinsic character involves a very difficult assessment of the facts. In *The Caspian Sea*,[13] the question arose as to whether freight was payable on delivery of a cargo of Bachaquero Crude, which the charterers alleged was contaminated with the residues of a previous cargo. Donaldson J set out the appropriate factual inquiry as follows:

> The arbitrators will have to consider what is meant by the description 'Bachaquero Crude'. Does it mean a paraffin free crude? If it does, 'Bachaquero Crude contaminated by paraffin' is a contradiction in terms and the owners will not be entitled to freight. Or does it mean a 'crude from the Bachaquero region' which in its natural state contains no paraffin? If so, there is no necessary contradiction in 'Bachaquero Crude contaminated by paraffin'. In that event, the fact of contamination will not of itself deprive the owners of their right to freight. However, the arbitrators would have to consider the degree of contamination. They would have to ask themselves the question: 'Is the oil so contaminated that it has ceased to be even contaminated Bachaquero Crude?' If so, the right to freight has gone. No doubt a relevant factor will be the cost and practicability of extracting the paraffin, but there may well be other criteria.

When and where is it payable?

Freight was traditionally paid at the end of the voyage on 'right and true delivery' of the cargo. Now, the usual practice is for most of the freight to be paid soon after the cargo is loaded (*advance freight*), with a small balance being paid on delivery. Splits ranging between 80 per cent/20 per cent and 95 per cent/5 per cent are quite common. Once advance freight is due, it cannot be recovered should the shipowner subsequently fail to make 'right and true delivery'.[14] The charterer's remedy will be to sue the shipowner for breach of contract, reclaiming by way of damages any freight that it has paid in respect of cargo that is not delivered.

Freight that is payable on 'right and true delivery' will not become due if delivery is made instead at an intermediate port. Although the shipowner may have committed no breach of contract, it will not be entitled to freight even on a pro rata basis.[15] However, freight will become payable on this basis when the charterer agrees to discharge at another port, although this will not be the case if the agreement is made 'without prejudice' to the provisions of the charter.[16] Where the charterer refuses to take delivery of the cargo at the discharge port, the shipowner will not only be entitled to full freight, but will also be able to claim back freight to cover the cost of returning the cargo to

---

10 *The Tarva* [1973] 2 Lloyd's Rep 385, Singapore Ct. The problem can be avoided by a clause making freight payable on outturned quantities. Freight paid on non-delivered cargo can be recovered by way of damages in the separate action brought by the charterer in respect of the non-delivery of the cargo.

11 *The Dominique* [1989] 1 Lloyd's Rep 431, HL, where the vessel sailed from the loading port and was arrested by her creditors at an intermediate bunkering port. The charterers elected to terminate but, by then, 95 per cent of the freight had already become due.

12 *Asfar & Co v Blundell* [1896] 1 QB 123.

13 [1980] 1 Lloyd's Rep 91.

14 See, on this point, *Allison v Bristol Marine Insurance Co* (1876) 1 App Cas 209, especially 223 and 226.

15 *Hopper v Burness* [1876] 1 CPD 137. No freight was due on goods sold by the master at an intermediate port under the justifiable exercise of his agency of necessity.

16 *The Lefthero* [1991] 2 Lloyd's Rep 599.

the port of loading.[17] Full freight is also payable where the action of the charterer prevents the completion of the voyage.[18]

With a 'lump-sum' freight, the full amount of freight will be due even if only part of the cargo is delivered at the discharge port. In *Thomas v Harrowing SS Co*,[19] the vessel was wrecked outside the discharge port. However, two-thirds of the cargo was washed ashore and this was held to constitute the 'right and true delivery' necessary to entitle the shipowner to claim the full amount of the lump-sum freight. If insufficient cargo is delivered to amount to a 'right and true delivery', freight will be paid on the quantity actually delivered on either a *quantum meruit* basis or as a proportion of the contractual lump sum.

Non-lump-sum freight is traditionally based on the quantity actually delivered. Therefore, freight would not be payable in respect of any cargo not delivered.[20] However, any provision for advance freight must be based on intaken quantity and many charters now provide for the entire freight to be calculated on such a basis. In *The Metula*,[21] the effect of such provision was held to be that the shipowners were entitled to the full freight based on the intaken quantity, even though less than that quantity was actually delivered.

Special clauses

The principles stated above as to when freight becomes due will be modified if any of the following special clauses appear in the charter.

The 'deemed earned' clause

This clause provides that freight shall be deemed to have been earned on loading, although the time for payment may not arise until some time afterwards. Some versions of the clause go on to state 'vessel and/or cargo lost or not lost'. The need for the clause was shown by *The Lorna 1*.[22] A vessel sank shortly before payment of advance freight became due. The charter was frustrated and therefore the loss lay where it fell. The shipowner was unable to recover any freight at all, as the obligation to pay freight had not accrued by the time that the vessel sank and the charter became frustrated. Being a voyage charter, it was outside the provisions of the **Law Reform (Frustrated Contracts) Act 1943**.

The clause operates by separating out the time when freight is deemed to be 'earned' from the time when it becomes 'payable'. Full freight will be deemed earned on loading, even though the advance freight may not be payable until a few days have elapsed and the balance of freight will not be payable until 'right and true delivery' has been accomplished. In *The Karin Vatis*,[23] the clause was construed so as to entitle the shipowner to the balance due on delivery when the vessel sank before reaching her discharge port. The contractual timetable for payment of such balance was replaced by an obligation on the charterer to make the payment within a reasonable time. The shipowner in *The Lefthero*[24] was also able to

---

17 *Cargo ex Argos* (1873) LR 5 PC 134.
18 *Cargo ex Galam* (1863) 33 LJ Ad 97 at 100.
19 [1915] AC 58, HL. An unusual feature of the decision is the stress placed on the fact that the inability of the ship to come into port to discharge was covered by an exceptions clause. Even if the shipowner had been in breach of charter, that should be irrelevant to the question of entitlement to freight in the light of the reasoning in *The Aries* [1977] 1 WLR 185.
20 However, it must be noted that the charterer would not be entitled to set off the value of the short-delivered cargo from the freight due. See *The Tarva* [1973] 2 Lloyd's Rep 385, Singapore Ct.
21 [1978] 2 Lloyd's Rep 5, CA.
22 [1983] 1 Lloyd's Rep 373, CA.
23 [1988] 2 Lloyd's Rep 330, CA.
24 [1991] 2 Lloyd's Rep 599, QB; rev'd on other grounds [1992] 2 Lloyd's Rep 109, CA.

rely on the clause where it had discharged at an alternative port under a 'without prejudice' agreement with the charterer.[25]

In neither of these cases was the shipowner's inability to reach the contractual discharge port a breach of contract. But what if the shipowner fails to reach the nominated discharge port due to a breach of charter on its part? In the light of the decision of the House of Lords in The Aries,[26] the answer should be that the shipowner is entitled to rely on the clause to claim its freight and that the charterers have a counterclaim for damages. This conclusion is supported by the shipowner's successful reliance on the clause in The Dominique[27] to recover 95 per cent advance freight that had become payable after the charterers had elected to terminate the charter by reason of the shipowner's breach of contract. However, the shipowners advanced no claim in respect of the 5 per cent balance that would have become payable on delivery of the cargo.

The 'near' clause

This clause qualifies the discharge port nominated in the charter with the following words: '. . . or so near thereto as she may safely get and lie always afloat'. In certain circumstances, the clause will entitle the shipowner to discharge at a nearby alternative port if the charter port is unusable and thereby claim the freight due on 'right and true delivery' of the cargo. It will also entitle it to claim demurrage if loading or discharge at the alternative port exceeds the permitted laytime.

To rely on the clause, the alternative port must be within the 'ambit' of the named port. The meaning of this term was considered in The Athamas.[28] The vessel was chartered for a voyage from India to two named ports in South East Asia – Saigon and Phnom Penh. After discharging about two-thirds of her cargo in Saigon in March 1959, the local pilotage authority unexpectedly refused to take the vessel up the Mekong River to Phnom Penh during the low-water season, which lasted until August. The reason was that the pilotage authority required the vessel to maintain a minimum speed of 10 knots, which was beyond her capacity. The shipowners accordingly discharged the balance of the cargo in Saigon. The Court of Appeal held that they were entitled to rely on the near clause because Saigon, although 250 sailing miles distant from Phnom Penh, was the nearest safe port that was a viable alternative discharge port for this particular cargo off this particular vessel. It also held that where the charter provides for discharge at two named ports, discharge at the first named port can entitle the shipowner to claim freight under the clause if discharge at the second named port is prevented.

In contrast, in Metcalfe v Britannia Ironworks,[29] the shipowner was not entitled to rely on the clause when faced with a similar period of delay in getting to the charter discharge port of Taganrog. This was located in the Sea of Azov, which had frozen up and would remain so for three months. This eventuality was foreseeable by both parties, unlike the requirement by the port authorities in The Athamas that the vessel maintain a minimum speed of 10 knots when navigating the vessel in the low-water season. Moreover, the parties had addressed this eventuality by inserting ice clauses into the charter.[30]

Even if the clause appears to cover the facts of the case, there is still a further hurdle that the shipowners must surmount if they are to be able to rely on it to claim their freight. The shipowners

---

25 That is, the parties agreed that, notwithstanding discharge at the alternative port, their position on the issue of what constituted the correct port of discharge should still be determined under the provisions of the charterparty.
26 [1977] 1 WLR 185.
27 [1989] 1 Lloyd's Rep 431, HL.
28 [1963] 1 Lloyd's Rep 287.
29 (1877) 2 QBD 423, CA.
30 In Dahl v Nelson (1881) 6 App Cas 38, 44–5, Lord Blackburn appears to suggest that the clause might avail a shipowner, even where the obstruction was foreseeable. However, this must be read in the light of Lord Watson's view of the situation, expressed at 63, that although some delay was foreseeable, the extent of the delay was not.

must establish that the time they would have to wait before they could enter the contractual port would amount to an 'unreasonable' period of delay. In deciding this, the court must balance out the costs to the shipowners in lost time if they have to wait for the obstacle to clear, against the trans-shipment costs to charterers in allowing discharge to take place at a non-contractual port or berth. In both *Dahl v Nelson*[31] and *The Athamas*,[32] the scales tipped in favour of the shipowners.

However, there may well be cases in which the scales tip in favour of the charterers. In such cases, the shipowners will be unable to rely on the clause.

By whom is it payable?

Most voyage charters impose joint liability for freight on the voyage charterer and the bill of lading holder. They achieve this by providing for the issue of bills of lading, which incorporate the terms of the charter. Provided that the wording of the charter freight clause does not impose a liability on the charterer alone, the holder of a bill of lading that incorporates the terms of the head charter will thereby become jointly liable with the charterer for freight due under the head charter. Payment by the bill of lading holder to the charterer will not discharge this liability, for the charterer will receive the freight as principal rather than as agent for the shipowner.[33]

The position is different where a shipowner's bill of lading incorporates the terms of the subcharter. This will generally happen where a time charterer wishes to secure payment of freight due it under a subcharter.[34] However, contractually, the freight due under such a bill of lading becomes due to the shipowner, not the charterer. The shipowner is entitled to claim the outstanding freight under the bill of lading and may claim the full amount that is due, even though a lesser sum is due to it under the head charterparty.[35] This remains the case even if the freight clause in the subcharter provides for payment to a third party. The shipowner may make its demand for freight against the bill of lading holder at any time before the subcharterer has paid the charterer. However, the shipowner must account to the charterer for any surplus between the amount due under the head charter and the freight received under the bill of lading incorporating the subcharter.[36] Payment to the charterer before the owner makes a demand for freight will discharge the apparent liability of the bill of lading holder to the shipowner, for the charterer is regarded as the shipowner's agent when it receives the payment.[37] Where the terms of a subcharter are incorporated into the bill of lading, the shipowner is bound by the terms of any variation agreed between the parties to the subcharter. Thus, when the shipowner claimed freight under the bill of lading in *The Spiros C*,[38] it was unable to object either to the fact that the freight had been paid to the time charterer before the time specified in the subcharter or that the payment was subject to agreed deductions other than those permitted by the terms of the subcharter.

In the absence of such words of incorporation, the bill of lading holder may still be liable for freight on a *quantum meruit* basis. This reflects the position when a shipper deals directly with a

---

31 Ibid.
32 [1963] 1 Lloyd's Rep 287.
33 *The Constanza M* [1980] 1 Lloyd's Rep 505, QB.
34 Time charterers will have no right to compel the shipowner to sue for the freight due under the bill of lading or to exercise a lien for it. *The Mathew* [1990] 2 Lloyd's Rep 323 (QB).
35 *The Bulk Chile* [2013] EWCA Civ 184; [2013] 1 WLR 3440, applying *dicta* of Rix LJ in *The Spiros C* [2000] 2 Lloyd's Rep 319. It is possible that the shipowner could intervene and claim the bill of lading freight even when there is no default under the head charter. However, Tomlinson LJ at [28] regarded it as arguable that a time charterer could restrain the shipowner from claiming freight in these circumstances 'on the simple ground that until such time as the charterer is in default the shipowner has, by reason of clause 8 of the NYPE Form, or a similar employment clause, agreed to delegate collection of freight to the charterer'.
36 *Wehner v Dene* [1905] 2 KB 92 at 99.
37 *Wehner v Dene SS Co* [1905] 2 KB 92.
38 [2000] 2 Lloyd's Rep 550, CA.

shipowner and no freight is expressly agreed.[39] There is no direct authority covering the situation in which freight is due under a charter and the shipowner wishes to recover from a third party who holds the bill of lading. However, there does seem to be a tacit assumption that such a right does, in fact, exist.[40] To avoid this result, bills of lading that do not incorporate the terms of the charter[41] will usually be claused 'freight prepaid'.[42] Such bills are most likely to be issued when the vessel is on time charter.

'Freight prepaid' clausing generally operates by way of estoppel, so that it has no effect on a pre-existing liability for freight that the holder of the bill of lading owes to the shipowner. Thus, in *The Indian Reliance*,[43] the bill of lading holder, who was a subcharterer, could not rely on the clausing to defeat a claim by the shipowner for outstanding freight under a bill of lading that incorporated that subcharter, as it knew the clausing was inaccurate and could not therefore have relied on it to its detriment. However, the clausing does not always derive its effect from estoppel. In *Cho Yang Shipping Co Ltd v Coral UK Ltd*,[44] a shipowner claimed freight against the consignor named in the bill of lading, which did not incorporate the terms of any charterparty, pursuant to a default by an inter-mediate party standing between the shipowner and the consignor. The Court of Appeal held that the issue was whether the consignor had undertaken any liability for freight and held that the 'freight prepaid' clausing was an important part of the factual matrix that showed that the consignor had never undertaken any liability to pay freight to the shipowner. There had been a chain of carriage contracts with each party contracting as principal, and not as agent, whereby the charterer paid freight to the shipowner and the shipper paid freight to the charterer. The analysis adopted in the case would be inapplicable where the bill of lading incorporated the terms of a charterparty. Such incorporation, in itself, would make clear the parties had intended that the bill of lading holder should be subject to the freight obligations set out in the charterparty.[45]

Some voyage charters go further and attempt to achieve a complete transition of charter obligations from the charterer to the bill of lading holder once the cargo has been loaded. This may be particularly useful to a fob seller who has chartered the vessel and wants its buyer to take over responsibility for some or all of the charterer's obligations under the charters.

Two steps are required to achieve this result. First, a mechanism is needed whereby the receiver can be made liable on the terms of the charterparty to the shipowner. This is achieved by incorporation of charterparty terms into bills of lading. Subject to s 3 of the **Carriage of Goods by Sea Act (COGSA) 1992**, the bill of lading holder will become liable to the shipowner on the terms of the bill of lading. As this will incorporate the terms of the charter, the holder of the bill of lading will indirectly have been made subject to the terms of a contract, the charter, to which it was not directly party. Secondly, the charter itself must provide for the premature termination of the charterer's obligations under the charter. This is achieved by the 'cesser' clause, which provides for the charterer's liability to cease at some point during the charter, usually on completion of loading.

A cesser clause will only relieve a charterer of its obligations under the charter to the extent that the shipowner acquires, in exchange for the rights that it is surrendering, an effective lien against the bill of lading holder in respect of those obligations. The effectiveness of the lien will depend on the following factors.

---

39 As in *Dommett v Beckford* (1833) 5 B & Ad 521.
40 See *The Jalamohan* [1988] 1 Lloyd's Rep 443, where the shipowner's allegation, that *quantum meruit* freight could be recovered from the shipper if the bill of lading turned out to be a time charterer's bill, went unchallenged.
41 As will be the case with bills of lading issued under most time charters.
42 This wording will also exclude the shipowner's common law right to lien the cargo for freight due on delivery of the cargo.
43 [1997] 1 Lloyd's Rep 52, QB.
44 [1997] 2 Lloyd's Rep 641, CA.
45 See Baughen, S, 'Does a freight prepaid bill of lading mean what it says?' [1999] Shipping and Transport Lawyer 12.

(a) The shipowner must have a contract with the bill of lading holder. The cesser clause will not operate if **COGSA 1992** fails to transfer a bill of lading contract to the bill of lading holder. In *The Silva Plana*,[46] a subcharterer was, therefore, unable to rely on a cesser clause, as against the head charterer, when a shipowner's bill of lading was issued. Such a bill of lading constituted a contract between its holder and the shipowner, but effected no contract between the holder and the head charterer.

(b) The bill of lading must properly incorporate the lien provisions of the charterparty. The charterparty must provide for the issue of bills of lading incorporating its terms.[47] If it does so, general words of incorporation will bring its lien clause into the bill of lading.[48] The lien will still be effective, even if the charter's language is such that no personal liability is imposed on the bill of lading holder in respect of obligations arising under the charter.[49]

(c) The shipowner's rights under the bill of lading contract must be as effective as those it has given up *vis-à-vis* the charterer. For example, the lien given by the charterparty must work as effectively against the bill of lading holder under the bill of lading contract as it would against the charterer under the charterparty. If the bill of lading allows a lien for a lesser amount of freight than that due under the charterparty, in that respect, the bill of lading will be less effective as a contract than the charter. The cesser clause will not apply to the extent of that ineffectiveness;[50] so, too, if the lien is ineffective at the discharge port due to local law and practice.[51] The bill of lading may also be less effective as a contract if the courts at the country of discharge ignore the provisions of the incorporated charter when dealing with cargo claims arising under the bill of lading. In such a situation, the cesser clause will not apply.[52]

Remedies for non-payment

The usual remedies for non-payment of freight are to proceed for summary judgment under CPR Pt 24 or, where the charter contains a reference to arbitration, to apply to the arbitrators for an interim final award.[53] Wherever possible, these actions should be backed up by obtaining a freezing order over the charterer's assets. However, such remedies take time, and the shipowner may be better served by relying on two 'self-help' remedies, which are commonly to be found in both voyage and time charters. These are the remedies of lien.

The nature of a lien

There are two types of lien: a lien on cargo and a lien on subfreights. Both legally and practically, they operate in quite different ways.

The lien on *cargo* is possessory – that is, a right to detain the cargo until freight is paid. At *common law*, there is an implied right to lien for freight and general average. It is doubtful whether this

---

46 [1989] 2 Lloyd's Rep 371, QB.
47 This was not the case in *Jenneson v Sec of State for India* [1916] 2 KB 702, and, accordingly, the cesser clause did not operate.
48 If the shipowners fail to incorporate the terms of the charter in such circumstances, the cesser clause will still be effective. See *Fidelitas v V/O Exportchleb* [1963] 2 Lloyd's Rep 113, 124, *per* Pearson LJ. Pearson LJ also considered that charterers would be liable to the owners in damages if they were responsible for issuing the bills of lading, and failed to incorporate the terms of the charter into them, as required by the charter.
49 See *The Miramar* [1983] 2 Lloyd's Rep 319, 324.
50 *Hansen v Harrold Bros* [1894] 1 QB 612.
51 *The Sinoe* [1972] 1 Lloyd's Rep 201, CA.
52 *The Aegis Brittanic* [1987] 1 Lloyd's Rep 119, QB. The cesser clause in question preserved the charterer's liability for freight, deadfreight and demurrage incurred at both loading and discharge ports. The dispute was as to whether the shipowners could proceed against the charterers in respect of cargo claims which arose at the port of discharge.
53 Under the Arbitration Act 1996, it is no longer possible to proceed against the charterer under CPR Pt 24 in respect of a claim for unpaid freight to which the charterer has no good arguable defence. *The Halki* [1998] 1 Lloyd's Rep 49, QB.

includes advance freight.[54] *Contractually*, the parties can provide for a right to lien for other charges, for example, advance freight, deadfreight or demurrage. The common law lien binds third parties;[55] the contractual one does not.

Therefore, if a contractual lien in a charter is to bind a bill of lading holder, the bill must incorporate the terms of the charter and the language of the charter lien clause must be apt to cover a lien against both charterer and bill of lading holder. However, the lien will still be effective against the bill of lading holder even if it incurs no personal liability in respect of the charterparty claims in respect of which the lien may be exercised.[56] If the bill of lading incorporates the terms of a subcharter, the shipowner may lien the cargo for sums due to the head charterer under its subcharter, but is not obliged to do so.[57] Where the bill of lading is a charterer's bill, it is difficult to see how the shipowner can exercise either a common law or a contractual lien on the cargo at the request of charterers.[58]

Even a common law lien will be excluded, by the doctrine of estoppel, if the bill is claused 'freight prepaid', as is the case with most bills issued when the vessel is on time charter. However, such clausing will not affect the shipowner's rights as against a contracting shipper who has not, in fact, paid the freight.[59]

The lien on *subfreights* is a right of the shipowner to require payment to him by the subcharterer of subfreights up to the amount due under the head charter, before payment is made to the head charterer. The lien may also be expressed to apply to sub-hires but there is a divergence of first-instance authority as to whether a lien on subfreights extends to sub-hires.[60] The right may be exercised in respect of freight, or hire, due from a sub-sub-charterer if the subcharter contains a lien on subfreights or sub-hire.[61] Judicial opinion is divided as to how the lien on sub-freights operates.[62] In *The Western Moscow*,[63] Christopher Clark J held that it operates by way of equitable assignment, noting: 'Further, if the right is only some form of sui generis contractual right it is one of restricted use. It would give the owners no direct claim against the sub-charterer; but only a right to have the charterers restrained from receiving the sub-charter hire or ordered to direct its payment to the owners or to a blocked account.'

Exercising a lien

The lien on cargo

The usual mode of exercise is to discharge into bonded warehouses. If local conditions make this impossible in practice, the lien can be exercised by waiting outside the discharge port.[64] Such conduct will constitute a breach of the bill of lading contract if the lien is not validly incorporated

---

54 *Kirchner v Venus* (1859) 12 Moo PC 361.
55 *The Exeter Carrier Case* (1702) 2 Ld Raym 867.
56 *The Miramar* [1983] 2 Lloyd's Rep 319, 324.
57 *The Mathew* [1990] 2 Lloyd's Rep 323, QB.
58 Channell J adverted to these difficulties in *Wehner v Dene SS Co* [1905] 2 KB 92.
59 Per Hobhouse LJ in *Cho Yang Shipping Co Ltd v Coral (UK) Ltd* [1997] 2 Lloyd's Rep 641, 643.
60 In *The Cebu* [1983] 1 Lloyd's Rep 302, it was held that sub-hires were subject to the lien, but in *The Cebu (No 2)* [1990] 2 Lloyd's Rep 316, it was held that they were not. Many charters will now provide for the lien to lie against all subfreights and sub-hires, as is the case with line 260 of NYPE 1993.
61 *The Cebu* [1983] 1 Lloyd's Rep 302, QB; *The Western Moscow* [2012] EWHC 1224 (Comm); [2012] 2 Lloyd's Rep 163 [61], Christopher Clarke J holding that this is the effect of the charter clause giving a lien on 'all subhires'.
62 This view derives from *dicta* of Lord Russell in *The Nanfri* [1979] 1 Lloyd's Rep 201 at 210, and has been applied at first instance in *The Ugland Trailer* [1986] Ch 471, *The Annangel Glory* [1988] 1 Lloyd's Rep 45; [1988] 1 Lloyd's Rep 439, and *The Cebu (No 2)* [1990] 2 Lloyd's Rep 316. A contrary argument was propounded by Dr Fidelis Oditah in his article 'The juridical nature of a lien on sub-freights' [1989] LMCLQ 191 to the effect that the lien on subfreights is a personal contractual right of interception analogous to an unpaid seller's right of stoppage in transit, and not a charge or proprietary right at all. This view has been endorsed by Lord Millett, in *Agnew v Commissioners of Inland Revenue* [2001] 2 AC 710 (PC), at paras 38–41.
63 [2012] EWHC 1224 (Comm); [2012] 2 Lloyd's Rep. 163.
64 *The Chrysovolandou Dyo* [1981] 1 Lloyd's Rep 159, QB.

into the bill of lading. It will also constitute a deviation that will vitiate P&I cover. What is less certain is whether it will also constitute a breach of the charter itself. There are conflicting first-instance *dicta* on this point.[65] Where a shipowner's bill of lading incorporates a subcharter under which freight is due to the charterer, there is no implied obligation on the shipowner to exercise its lien on the charterer's behalf.[66]

Usually the lien only gives a right to detain the cargo. The cargo may subsequently be sold in accordance with the provisions of the local law in force at the port of lien.[67] However, at common law, the cargo may be sold if continued detention will result in its deteriorating in quality and the master cannot communicate with the cargo owner and receive its instructions.[68]

It used to be thought that the costs of exercising a lien – for example, warehousing charges – could not be recovered by the party exercising the lien, unless there was a specific contractual provision authorising such recovery. The authority for this proposition was *Somes v British Empire Shipping Co*,[69] a case involving an artificer's lien. However, the charterer might become liable in demurrage or in damages for detention in respect of time spent in the reasonable exercise of the lien.[70] Warehousing costs might also be recovered if it could be shown that the shipowner had acted reasonably by warehousing the cargo in reducing the costs that would otherwise have accrued, by way of demurrage, had the cargo remained on the vessel.[71] The Court of Appeal in *The Lehmann Timber* has now held that *Somes* has no application to the exercise of a lien in a shipping context.[72] In *Somes* there was only a failure to pay, and the customer was not in breach of contract in failing to take back his property. With contracts of carriage the failure to pay will lead to the shipowner retaining possession of the goods at the port of discharge in exercise of the lien and this will lead to the cargo owner being in breach of its obligation to discharge its cargo, which constitutes the basis for the recovery of the expenses of exercising the lien.[73] The case involved costs involved in the exercise of a lien to obtain a general average bond, but the reasoning of the Court of Appeal would apply equally to liens on cargo under charterparties. Provided the costs of exercising the lien are reasonable, they will now be recoverable by the shipowner.

The lien on subfreights

The right is exercised by giving notice to the subcharterer, or to other charterers further down the chain. The shipowner can only use the lien to claim amounts due under the head charter at the date on which the notice is given. The notice will be effective only if the subcharterer has not paid the

---

65 In *The Aegnoussiotis* [1977] 1 Lloyd's Rep 268, Donaldson J held that the exercise of a lien in such circumstances was valid against the charterer. Mocatta J found to the contrary in *The Agios Georgios* [1976] 2 Lloyd's Rep 192.

66 *The Mathew* [1990] 2 Lloyd's Rep 323, QB.

67 Where that port is a UK port, the position used to be covered by ss 492–501 of the Merchant Shipping Act 1894, but these provisions were repealed by the Statute Law (Repeals) Act 1993 and have not been replaced.

68 Boyd, Burrows, and Foxton, *Scrutton on Charterparties*, 20th edn, 1996, London: Sweet & Maxwell. The duty to sell will arise only where the master is unable to obtain the instructions of the cargo owner. See *The Olib* [1991] 2 Lloyd's Rep 108, QB. On the facts, however, there was no evidence that the condition of the cargo was in any danger.

69 (1858) El, Bl & El 353.

70 *Lyle Shipping v Cardiff Corp* (1899) 5 Com Cas 87; *The Boral Gas* [1988] 1 Lloyd's Rep 442.

71 Per Bailhache J *Anglo-Polish Lines v Vickers* (1924) 19 Lloyd's Rep 121, 125. 'As I understand it, if the goods were held in a place for the hire of which under the contract between the parties payment would have to be made, as for instance in a ship or warehouse, then the person who is exercising the lien is entitled to claim payment for the detention of his ship it he holds the goods in the ship or, if less expensive, he clears them out of the ship and puts them into a warehouse and in my opinion the expenses of keeping them in the warehouse.'

72 [2013] EWCA Civ 650; [2013] 2 Lloyd's Rep 541. Rix LJ stated: 'In my judgment, the *Somes* principle is a narrow one, applicable to an artificer's lien but of doubtful status outside that context. It appears to be founded in the technical doctrine that a right of lien does not carry with it any cause of action to recover an indemnity for the expenses of exercising it in the absence of some other basis for recovery, such as in contract or bailment or tort', at [122].

73 Rix LJ also noted that if the contract had come to an end, as in *The Kos* [2012] UKSC 17; [2012] 2 Lloyd's Rep 292, the ship would in any event be entitled to claim the cost of taking care of cargo and to continue to enforce any lien it has. The arbitrators' award had not made clear whether the contract had come to an end at the time the cargo was discharged into warehouses ashore, in which case the claim would have been in bailment.

freight as at the date of the notice. There is no right to trace the payment of freight into the hands of the charterer or its agent.[74] It remains an open question whether this is also the case where the freight is paid to a third party.[75] The lien will still be effective when a 'freight prepaid' bill of lading is issued, provided that the freight has not, in fact, been paid at the date of the notice. This is because the claim operates by way of an equitable assignment of the charterer's rights under the subcharter and not through the bill of lading. The lien on subfreights, therefore, unlike a direct claim under the bill of lading, does not depend for its validity upon the operation of s 3(1) of **COGSA 1992**. In many respects, however, the lien on subfreights operates in a similar fashion to the shipowner's right to claim freight under a bill of lading that incorporates the terms of a subcharter. In both instances, the shipowner must make its demand before the freight due has been paid by the subcharterer to the charterer.[76] However, the lien on sub-freights can only be exercised in respect of sums that are due under the head charter, whereas the shipowner has a contractual right to claim the full amount of freight due under a shipowner's bill of lading which incorporates a subcharter.[77]

If the subcharterer, having received notice, then pays the charterer, it is at risk of having to make a double payment to the shipowner if the shipowner later substantiates its claim against the head charterer. In such an event, the subcharterer can protect its position by paying the money into court pursuant to the interpleader provisions of Ord 17. In the event of competing claims to the subfreights – for example, by a prior assignee – the claim of the first assignee to give notice will prevail, even if its assignment was not the first in time.[78]

Where the charterer is an English registered company, the lien, as an equitable assignment, must be registered in accordance with the relevant provisions of the **Companies Act 1985**.[79] These provisions will eventually be repealed when s 93 of the **Companies Act 1989**, adding s 396(2)(g) to the **Companies Act 1985** to deal with liens on freight, is brought into force. In Cosco Bulk Carrier Co Ltd v Armada Shipping SA,[80] Briggs J held that it was appropriate for a dispute over entitlement to sub-hire to be arbitrated in London notwithstanding the recognition in the UK jurisdiction of the Swiss bankruptcy of the charterer. All the underlying issues were issues of English shipping law and the true analysis of the claim was that there were two competing proprietary or contractual claims in relation to a single asset, namely a party's obligations to make payments under the subcharter.

---

74 *Tagart Beaton & Co v James Fisher & Sons* [1903] 1 KB 391, CA.
75 *Samsun Logix Corporation v Oceantrade Corporation* [2007] EWHC 2372 (Comm); [2008] 1 Lloyd's Rep 450. This point, however, did not need to be decided, once it was found that payment to the charterer's solicitor, pursuant to a variation of a freezing order, constituted a payment to the charterer's agent.
76 A payment to the head charterer will be regarded as having been made to the shipowner's agent for the receipt of bill of lading freights and will discharge the bill of lading holder of its liability for such freight. *The Indian Reliance* [1997] 1 Lloyd's Rep 52, QB; *The Spiros C* [2000] 2 Lloyd's Rep 319, CA.
77 If the shipowner recovers more by way of freight than is due to it under the head charter it must account for the balance to the charterer. *Wehner v Dene SS Co* [1905] 2 KB 92.
78 *The Attika Hope* [1988] 1 Lloyd's Rep 439, QB.
79 Sections 395(1) and 396(1)(f); *The Annangel Glory* [1988] 1 Lloyd's Rep 45, QB.
80 [2011] EWHC 216 (Ch); [2011] 2 All ER (Comm) 481.

Chapter 11

Voyage Charters – Laytime and Demurrage

The secondary payment obligation of the voyage charter arises out of the loading and discharging operations. This is best understood by dividing the performance of the voyage charter into four distinct parts, two of which are to be performed by the shipowner and two by the charterer. The duties of the shipowner are: first, to proceed with reasonable dispatch on the 'approach voyage' to the loading point designated by the charter (which may be either a port or a berth within a port); and secondly, to proceed with reasonable dispatch on the 'carrying voyage' to the discharge point designated by the charter. The duties of the charterer are: first, to nominate within a reasonable time a port or berth, where appropriate, for loading or discharge; and secondly, to load and discharge the cargo at that berth or port within a reasonable time, on completion of the approach or the carrying voyage.[1] If the charterer fails to perform either obligation, it will be liable to the shipowner in damages for detention at the market rate.[2]

The second of the duties owed by the charterer is usually more precisely delineated in the charter. A 'reasonable time' is replaced by a set period of 'laytime'. The charter will usually contain an exceptions clause, which provides for the suspension of laytime on the occurrence of various events interfering with loading or discharging, for example bad weather.

If loading or discharge takes longer than the permitted laytime, the charterer will generally be made liable for 'demurrage'. This is a pre-agreed daily rate of liquidated damages, which replaces the common law liability for detention, assessed at the market rate. The laytime and demurrage calculations will cease with the completion of loading or discharge as the case may be. To encourage charterers to complete loading and discharge as soon as possible, many charters contain a 'dispatch' clause under which charterers become entitled to payment by the shipowner in the event that they finish these operations before the expiry of their allotted laytime. Payment is usually at half the daily rate of demurrage.

The laytime provisions of the charter will identify the point at which the approach and carrying voyages end. This may be when the vessel reaches the port, in which case the charter will be a port charter. Alternatively, it may be when the vessel reaches a berth within the port, in which case it will be a berth charter. Charterers will generally pay for the cost of the loading and discharging operations. The issue under consideration in this chapter is identifying the party who is to pay for the time used in these operations. In answering this question, the following enquiries need to be made:

(a)   How much laytime is available?
(b)   When does laytime commence?
(c)   When will laytime be interrupted?
(d)   What are the shipowner's remedies when laytime is exceeded?

Calculating the available laytime

There are various ways of calculating the length of laytime. One is to make the calculation by reference to a fixed number of days. The presumption is that 'days' means 'calendar' days and that where only part of a day is worked, that counts as a whole day's laytime. However, the presumption is easily rebutted[3] and the 'calendar' day gives way to the more normal 'conventional' day. This is a day of 24 hours, running from the start of laytime. If time starts at 0600 on a Monday and loading

---

1   At common law, the cost of and responsibility for these operations is apportioned between the parties in accordance with the principles set out in Chapter 4, pp 88–9. The shipper may also be under an implied obligation to load the vessel within a reasonable time, and the receiver under a similar obligation in respect of discharge. See *The Spiros C* [2000] 2 Lloyd's Rep 550, CA. The obligation will only arise if the shipper or receiver has undertaken to load or discharge the vessel, as the case may be.
2   The difficulties of establishing such a claim are well illustrated by *Hulthen v Stewart* [1903] AC 389.
3   For example, in *Leonis SS Co Ltd v Rank (Joseph) Ltd (No 2)* [1908] 1 KB 499, by a provision that time should start 12 hours after giving of a notice of readiness to load (NOR).

completes at 1200 on a Thursday, under a 'calendar' day, four laydays would be used. Under a 'conventional' day, only three-and-a-quarter laydays would be used.

Alternatively, laytime may be calculated by reference to a daily rate of loading/discharge, for example, 300 tons per day. Sometimes the rate will be expressed as one being 'per working/available hatch', as in *The Sandgate*.[4] A working hatch means an upper deck hatch under which there is cargo for loading or discharging, as the case may be. The hatch will not be workable if the person responsible for loading or discharging is disabled from working. In making the calculation, the court will disregard any unevenness in loading or discharge that arises because of the order in which the shipper wants to load the hatches.[5] In most cases, the hatch that is to take the largest quantity of cargo will be the 'critical' hatch and the laydays will be the result of dividing the cargo for that hatch by the average rate specified by the charter. Therefore, if the average rate is 500 tons per day and the charterer loads 1,000 tons into hatch one, 800 into hatch two and 200 into hatch three, the charterer will have available a total of two laydays, calculated by dividing cargo loaded into hatch one by the daily rate. In *The General Capinpin*,[6] the House of Lords held that a variant of the clause that read 'at the average rate of 1,000 metric tons basis five or more available workable hatches pro rata, if less number of hatches' fixed an overall discharge rate of 1,000 tons per day.

Separate laytime calculations have to be drawn up for loading and discharge. A saving of time on one operation cannot be used to offset demurrage incurred on the other, unless there is an express clause to this effect in the charter. This might be done by allowing the laytime to be averaged, in which case two separate statements are drawn up, but time saved on one operation can be credited against the other. Alternatively, laytime may be 'reversible', in which case the charterer is given the option to compile an aggregate laytime statement for both loading and discharge ports and to apply as the laydays the total of those allowed for loading and discharge. These provisions will be more beneficial to charterers than 'dispatch' provisions, as these usually allow charterers a credit at only half the demurrage rate in the event that loading or discharge is completed before the expiry of the laydays.

A charterer will usually wish to complete loading before expiry of laytime so as to avoid liability for demurrage. But completion of loading before expiry of the laydays may sometimes cause problems to the charterer if it means that bills of lading are dated earlier than the date specified in their sale contract. What the charterer cannot do is to delay the presentation of the bills for signature. Bills of lading must be presented within a reasonable time of completion of loading. Any delay caused by a charterer's failure to comply with this obligation will be compensated by damages for detention, and not at the demurrage rate.[7] However, it is quite legitimate to spin out the loading operation so that the bills of lading eventually issued bear the date that is in accordance with the charterer's sale contract. In *Margaronis Navigation Agency Ltd v Henry W Peabody & Co of London Ltd (The Vrontados)*,[8] the charterer delayed the loading of the final 1 per cent of the cargo so that a January bill of lading could be issued in respect of the whole cargo. It was held that the charterer was entitled to have the fixed time to load and was under no duty to accelerate the rate of loading to shorten the time to which it was otherwise entitled. More controversially, in *The Eurus*,[9] Rix J accepted the findings of the arbitrators that charterers can legitimately order the shipowner to delay the start of loading or discharge.[10]

---

4 [1930] P 30.
5 *The Aegis Progress* [1983] 2 Lloyd's Rep 570.
6 [1991] 1 Lloyd's Rep 1.
7 *Nolisement (Owners) v Bunge y Born* [1917] 1 KB 160. A vessel loaded 19 days prior to the expiry of laydays. Bills of lading were not presented until three days after completion of loading, whereas, on the facts, a reasonable time for presenting bills of lading for signature would have been no more than one day.
8 [1965] 1 QB 300, especially 322–6. See, also, *The Ulyanovsk* [1990] 1 Lloyd's Rep 425.
9 [1996] 2 Lloyd's Rep 408.
10 Criticised by McCarter, P (1997) LMCLQ 483.

It must be stressed that the charterer's duty is to load within the laytime allowed. The charterer owes no further duty to load or discharge with 'reasonable dispatch'. This is illustrated by *Hudson v Ede*,[11] where, in the middle of the laydays, the river, down which the charter cargo was to be brought, froze up. A laytime exception of 'detention by ice' operated even though the charterer, by exercising greater diligence, might have loaded before the freeze-up.

When is charterer's duty to load or discharge triggered?

The vessel must first complete its approach or carrying voyage – that is, have arrived at the port or the berth – depending on the provisions of the charter. The vessel must also be 'ready' to load the cargo, which will involve similar considerations to those relevant to the operation of cancellation clauses.[12] At the load port, the shipowner is, by custom, obliged to give a 'notice of readiness' (NOR) to the charterer to commence the running of laytime. There is no customary obligation to submit NOR on discharge,[13] although the charterparty may expressly oblige the shipowner to do so.

Giving notice of readiness

Unless stated to the contrary in the charterparty, NOR need not be in any specific form. There must merely be an accurate statement that a vessel is ready to load or discharge as the case may be.[14] The notice must be a notice of actual, not anticipated, readiness. The facts entitling NOR to be given must exist when it is given and not just at the expiry of the notice.[15] NOR will be effective only if the vessel is, in fact, 'ready' to load and discharge at the time it is given. Thus, in *The Tres Flores*,[16] the Court of Appeal held that where the holds required fumigation after the notice was given, such a NOR is invalid, even though the work necessary to make the vessel ready takes only a short time and is completed before a loading berth becomes available.[17] The Court of Appeal did recognise, however, that a valid NOR could be given, even though some preliminary routine matters, such as removal of hatch covers, still needed to be attended to, provided that they were unlikely to cause any delay. A similar distinction appears in cases involving readiness in the context of cancellation clauses. In *Noemijulia SS Co v Minister of Food*,[18] the Court of Appeal distinguished between readiness of the cargo spaces and readiness of the ship's equipment. As regards disabled ship's gear, the decision would appear to be inconsistent with *The Tres Flores* unless the following distinction is made. Preparation of the ship's gear will not entail the vessel being unready in either a cancelling or a laytime context, providing the gear itself is in working order. On the other hand, where the gear is not in working order but can be repaired without loss of time to the charterer, it seems that the vessel may be ready as regards the cancellation clause but not for the purpose of giving a valid NOR.

A more lenient approach has been adopted where the notice itself is accurate and the only defect is that it has been tendered to the charterer's agents outside the time specified in the charter.

---

11 (1868) LR 2 QB 566, aff'd (1868) LR 3 QB 412, CA.
12 'Readiness' relates to the readiness of the vessel and not the cargo. Therefore, the vessel will be 'ready' for the purpose of starting laytime, even if discharge is delayed due to the need to fumigate the cargo. See *The Epaphus* [1987] 2 Lloyd's Rep 215, CA.
13 *Houlder v General SN Co* (1862) 3 F & F 170. But NOR must be given where a party is specified in the bill of lading as 'notify party' (*Clemens Horst v Norfolk and NW American SN Co* (1906) 11 Com Cas 141), or when the shipowner intends to rely on a 'near' clause (*The Varing* [1931] P 79, 87, per Scrutton LJ).
14 A requirement that NOR be in writing is satisfied by giving NOR by email. *The Eagle Valencia* [2010] EWCA Civ 713; [2010] 2 Lloyd's Rep 257.
15 *Christensen v Hindustan Steel* [1971] 1 Lloyd's Rep 395.
16 [1974] QB 264.
17 However, the charterer's lack of cargo may be relevant after laytime starts in that it will preclude the charterer from relying on a laytime exception if it is in fact the true cause of the delay. See *The Nikmary* [2003] EWHC 46 (Comm); [2003] 1 Lloyd's Rep 151, QB.
18 [1951] 2 KB 223.

In *The Petr Schmidt*,[19] the charter provided that the notice had to be tendered within the charterer's office hours. The master sent the notice, which was, in all other respects, in complete conformity with the terms of the charter, outside these hours. The notice was held to become valid when the charterer's agents received it the following day within the hours specified in the charter. However, where the notice itself is defective, there is no question of its being cured by a subsequent change in circumstances. Thus, in *The Agamemnon*,[20] the notice was given at a place other than that stipulated in the charter. It did not subsequently become valid once the vessel had moved to the designated place. The issue of waiver may also arise where the vessel arrives early at the load port and the charterer consents to loading commencing before the time specified in the charter. The Court of Appeal considered this issue in *The Front Commander*.[21] Rix LJ was of the view that, ordinarily, the charterer cannot require a vessel to load early if it arrives early. If, however, the charter requires the master to give NOR on arrival, as is the case with cl 6 of the Asbatankvoy form, the master must do so even if the vessel arrives early.[22] The notice period in the NOR will then start to run whether the charterer orders the vessel to load early or not. The charterer is entitled, but not obliged, to start loading before the earliest layday. If the charterer does so, the laytime provisions will start to run against the charterer.[23]

Most charters require the shipowner to obtain *free pratique* before giving the NOR. Free pratique is a health clearance of the ship and the crew conducted by the port authority's medical officer. Provided that the master believes that it will be a mere formality to obtain this clearance, he may give NOR before free pratique has actually been obtained.[24] The common law position may be modified by specific terms in the charterparty, such as cl 22 of the Shellvoy 5 form which provides that the notice of readiness is not valid if owners fail to obtain free pratique within six hours of giving NOR. In such a situation, the owners should give a fresh NOR when free pratique is obtained.[25]

An invalid NOR may be treated as valid if the charterer's agents accept it without protest. In *The Shackleford*,[26] the charterparty required the vessel to have obtained customs clearance before giving NOR. The master gave NOR before this was obtained and the charterers were held to be estopped from challenging the validity of the NOR. This was because their agents had accepted the premature NOR and the shipowners had suffered a consequent detriment by not attempting to procure customs clearance as soon as they would otherwise have done. Another instance of waiver is provided by *The Helle Skou*.[27] There the charter provided that the vessel's holds must be clean and free from smell before NOR could be tendered. Charterers were held to have accepted the premature NOR once they started loading the vessel. They were not entitled to retract it once they became aware of the smell some time after the loading had commenced. However, in *The Mexico 1*,[28] the Court of Appeal held that waiver would not be established simply because the charterer's agents had accepted the invalid notice without protest. For there to have been a waiver, the agents must have known of the facts rendering the notice invalid. This was not the case here, as the agents were unaware that at the time NOR was given the cargo was inaccessible, being overstowed by a cargo carried under another contract. In contrast, in *The Northgate*, the charter provided that NOR could be

---

19 [1997] 1 Lloyd's Rep 284, QB; [1998] 2 Lloyd's Rep 1, CA.
20 [1998] 2 Lloyd's Rep 675, QB.
21 [2006] EWCA Civ 944; [2006] 2 Lloyd's Rep 251.
22 In contrast, in *The Eurus* [1996] 2 Lloyd's Rep 408, the charterers were held to be entitled to order the master to delay presenting NOR, so as to delay berthing.
23 This was the position under cll 5 and 6 of the Asbatankvoy form and was not altered by additional specific cll 31 and 33 in the charter.
24 *The Delian Spirit* [1971] 1 Lloyd's Rep 506, CA.
25 *The Eagle Valencia* [2010] EWCA Civ 713; [2010] 2 Lloyd's Rep 257.
26 [1978] 2 Lloyd's Rep 154, CA.
27 [1976] 2 Lloyd's Rep 205.
28 [1990] 1 Lloyd's Rep 507, noted (1990) LMCLQ 383.

given to the terminal at the load port that had the implied authority of the charterers to waive a defect in it.[29] Waiver occurred through the terminal accepting the NOR with knowledge of the facts that rendered it defective. There was no additional requirement that the terminal should also have been aware of the terms of the charter regarding the giving of NOR. The consequences of a failure to give a valid NOR were considered by the Court of Appeal in *The Happy Day*.[30] NOR was given while the vessel was waiting at anchorage to discharge at Cochin. The vessel berthed a day later and began discharge. The NOR was held to be invalid as the charter was a berth charter with a 'wibon' clause and there had been no congestion at the time that the notice was given. Accordingly, Langley J held that laytime never began and not only were the shipowners not entitled to demurrage for any part of the three months it took the charterers to discharge the vessel, but the charterers were also entitled to claim dispatch. Langley J rejected the idea that the notice became valid once discharge commenced, as the concept of 'inchoate' notice had been rejected by the Court of Appeal in *The Mexico 1*.[31] He also rejected the argument that there was no need to serve a second NOR at the start of discharge, as such a notice would be futile: it would be informing the charterers of a fact of which they were already aware. Although the receivers had signed a statement of facts on completion of discharge that noted that the NOR had been 'accepted', this was insufficient material from which to spell out a variation of the charter.

The Court of Appeal upheld the decision on these points. However, it managed to find that laytime commenced, in accordance with the charter provisions, once discharge began.[32] The receivers, whom the charter authorised to accept NOR on behalf of the charterers, had waived the charterers' right to require service of a fresh NOR by allowing discharge to begin without reserving the charterers' position in this regard. Had such a reservation been made, the shipowners would then have been alerted to the need to serve a second NOR. The failure to object, in conjunction with knowledge that discharge had started, were the two elements that constituted the waiver. Some charters expressly provide for the cessation of laytime in the event that, on berthing, the vessel proves not to be ready after all. The effect of such a provision is to validate the NOR provided that, at the time that it was given, the master bona fide believed the vessel to be ready to load.[33]

The termination point of the approach and carrying voyages

In any voyage charter, it is of the utmost importance to ascertain what the charter provides for the termination of the approach and carrying voyages. Until these voyages are concluded, NOR cannot be given and laytime cannot start to run. The two most usual possibilities are that the voyage will end either when the vessel reaches the port of loading or discharge – a 'port' charter – or when she reaches the actual berth at which she will load or discharge – a 'berth' charter. The charter will need careful reading to decide what sort of charter it is. What seems to be a 'port' charter may, in fact, turn out to be a 'berth' charter, as in *Stag Line Ltd v Board of Trade*.[34] The charter there provided for loading at 'one or two safe ports E[ast] Canada/Newfoundland, place or places as ordered by charterer'. The charterer nominated Miramichi. The vessel arrived and gave NOR. The charterer's agents then told her to load at Millbank, one of the four loading places in the port. No berth was available

29 [2007] EWHC 2796 (Comm); [2008] 1 Lloyd's Rep 511, noted [2008] JIML 383.
30 [2002] EWCA Civ 1068; [2002] 2 Lloyd's Rep 487.
31 [1990] 1 Lloyd's Rep 507, CA.
32 Laytime would be calculated on the assumption that a second NOR had been given when discharge started. Laytime would then commence after the expiry of the time referred to in the NOR clause. Earlier authorities such as *Pteroti Cia Nav SA v National Coal Board* [1958] 1 QB 469, QB, and *The Mass Glory* [2002] EWHC 72 (Comm); [2002] 2 Lloyd's Rep 244, in which it was held that the commencement of loading or discharge did not amount to a waiver, must now be regarded as wrongly decided.
33 *The Linardos* [1994] 1 Lloyd's Rep 28, CA; *The Jay Ganesh* [1994] 2 Lloyd's Rep 358, QB.
34 [1950] 2 KB 194, CA.

for six days. As the charterer had the express right, on the vessel reaching the port, to load at a particular place within the port, the vessel was held not to have 'arrived' until she berthed.[35] The classification of a charterparty as a port or berth charter was recently considered in *The Merida*.[36] Clause 1 defined the contractual destinations in a manner which, if it stood alone, must mean that it was a berth charterparty in that the opening term was in a form which identified the destination as the berth and which provided expressly for charterers to nominate the berth. Clause 2, however, referred to both safe ports and berths but did not qualify cl 1. There was no apparent reason why the charterparty would have started out in cl 1 as a berth charterparty and then undergone a fundamental alteration in cl 2 to become a port charterparty. If instead cl 2 were to be viewed as introducing a safe port warranty and reiterating the safe berth warranty, then there would be no inconsistency between the two clauses.

Charterer's duty to provide a cargo does not generally arise until laytime begins. However, in exceptional circumstances, this duty can arise at an earlier stage, if the non-availability of the cargo prevents the vessel reaching the relevant geographical point at which laytime would begin. In *The Aello*,[37] a ship awaiting a cargo of maize was compelled to wait in Buenos Aires roads and excluded from the dock area unless the cargo was immediately available. The roads were not the place where ships waiting delivery of grain usually lay. The vessel was unable to reach that place and become 'arrived' unless cargo was immediately available (this part of the decision was subsequently overruled by the House of Lords in *The Johanna Oldendorff* [38]). However, where the provision of cargo was necessary to enable a ship to become 'arrived', the charterer owed an absolute obligation to provide a cargo or a reasonable part of it in time to enable the ship to perform its obligation under the contract. It was not enough to show that it had taken all reasonable steps to provide a cargo. The shipowners were therefore able to recover the lost time as damages for breach of this implied term.

A term will also be implied obliging the charterers to take all reasonable steps to allow the vessel either to become 'arrived' or to leave the port on the completion of loading or discharge. In *The Atlantic Sunbeam*,[39] the issue was whether the charterers or the consignee had delayed taking the necessary steps to obtain the 'jetty challan' without which the vessel would not be allowed to enter the port. The onus of proof lay on the shipowner to show unreasonable delay by the charterer,[40] although inferences could be drawn from unexplained periods of delay or inactivity. If the shipowner could discharge this burden, damages for detention would be awarded in respect of any delay in entering the port over and above that which was reasonably to be expected.

Port charters

Under a port charter, the approach and carrying voyages will terminate when the vessel reaches the port. If the vessel can proceed directly to berth, NOR cannot be given until reaching the berth.[41] If the vessel cannot proceed to her berth on reaching the port, NOR may now be given and the vessel will become an 'arrived' vessel. All of the time that is subsequently lost in waiting to berth, including 'shifting' time spent sailing from any waiting place to berth, will count as laytime. However, it has not always been clear what geographical location the vessel must reach before it can be regarded as 'arrived'. In *Leonis SS Co Ltd v Rank (Joseph) Ltd (No 2)*,[42] laydays under a 'port' charter were held to start

---

35 The shipowner may also have the right to discharge at an alternative port or berth if the charter contains a 'near' clause, as discussed in Chapter 10, pp 215–16.
36 [2009] EWHC 3046 (Comm); [2010] 1 Lloyd's Rep 274.
37 [1961] AC 135.
38 [1974] AC 479, HL.
39 [1973] 1 Lloyd's Rep 482, QB.
40 The charterer would not, however, be in breach to the extent that any delay was attributable to the port authority.
41 *The Johanna Oldendorff* [1974] AC 479 at 557.
42 [1908] 1 KB 499.

as soon as the shipowner put the vessel at the disposal of the charterer in the port as a ship ready, as far as she is concerned, to discharge. The vessel will still be at the disposal of the charterer, even though congestion prevents it from naming the berth at which loading or discharging is to take place. In *The Aello*, the House of Lords adopted a more restricted definition in holding that a vessel did not become 'arrived' until she reached that part of port where a ship could be loaded when a berth was available.

Their Lordships overruled this part of the decision in *The Johanna Oldendorff*.[43] The vessel had anchored at the Mersey Bar, which was the usual waiting place for ships discharging at Liverpool. This place was within the legal and commercial limits of the port, but 17 miles off the docks. It was held that the vessel must reach the place where she is at the immediate and effective disposition of the charterer. If she is at a place where waiting ships usually lay, she would be in such a position unless extraordinary circumstances were to prevail, in which case the burden of proof would be on the charterer. It makes no difference if the waiting area is, or is not, inside that part of a port where a ship can be loaded. From a practical and commercial standpoint, there is no longer anything to choose between these locations, given the instantaneous nature of modern ship-to-shore communications and the greater speeds and manoeuvrability of modern ships.

The practical reasons behind the decision might suggest that a vessel should become 'arrived' even if the usual waiting place was outside the port limits. However, the House of Lords rejected this suggestion in *The Maratha Envoy*.[44] Under a 'wibon'[45] port charter, the vessel proceeded to the Weser estuary. Brake was the nominated port, some miles from its mouth. The only waiting area for large vessels was the Weser lightship, 25 miles seaward of the mouth of the river, and outside the legal and commercial limits of the port of Brake. All berths were full. Although the vessel made two voyages up river to qualify as an 'arrived' vessel, then returning to the lightship, the House of Lords held that a vessel cannot be considered to be 'arrived' when she reaches a waiting place short of the named port. In a port charter, the 'wibon' clause is, therefore, superfluous. A solution to this problem may be found by using 'wipon' (whether in port or not) clauses or 'time lost' clauses (time lost in waiting for berth to count as laytime), although the latter, and probably the former too, will only serve to throw the risk of delay due to congestion onto the charterer.[46]

'Berth' charters and special modifying clauses

Under a berth charter, laytime cannot commence until the vessel has actually berthed at her loading or discharging berth. Any delay in getting into berth, together with shifting time, will be for the shipowner's account. To avoid this result, special clauses have evolved at the instigation of shipowners in an attempt to throw some of the risks inherent in a berth charter back onto the charterer. The two most common clauses are the 'wibon' clause, which provides that laytime is to count 'whether in berth or not', and the 'time lost' clause, whereby 'time lost in waiting for berth [is] to count as laytime'.

'Wibon' and 'time lost' clauses

These clauses do not simply turn a berth charter into a port charter. The courts have drawn an important distinction between delay due to congestion and delay due to bad weather. In *The Kyzikos*,[47] there was a Gencon charter to load steel in Italy to discharge in the US Gulf, '1/2 always afloat,

43 [1974] AC 479, especially Lord Reid at 531 and Lord Diplock at 556–60.
44 *The Maratha Envoy* [1978] AC 1.
45 A 'wibon', 'whether in berth or not', clause effects a limited transformation of a 'berth' charter into a 'port' charter.
46 See *The Kyzikos* [1989] 1 Lloyd's Rep 1, HL.
47 [1989] 1 Lloyd's Rep 1, HL.

always accessible berth(s) ... each port, wipon, wibon, wifpon and wccon' (whether in port or not, whether in berth or not, whether in free pratique or not, whether customs cleared or not). Clause 6 provided: 'Time lost in waiting for berth to count as discharging time.' A berth was always available, but was not reachable due to fog and the consequent closure of the pilot station. The House of Lords held that the shipowner's claim for demurrage must fail as the effect of the 'time lost' clause was not to turn a berth charter into a port one, but to shift liability for delay due to congestion alone onto the charterers. Where a berth is unavailable and bad weather would also have prevented the vessel from proceeding to berth, time will run under a 'wibon' clause.[48]

With a port charter, the 'time lost' clause is superfluous once the vessel becomes an arrived ship, but will start laytime running if there is congestion at the port and the vessel is waiting to berth at a waiting place which is outside the port limits. In this case, the 'time lost' clause will ensure that laytime runs subject to the laytime definitions and exceptions.[49] In contrast, a 'wibon' clause only takes effect once the vessel is within port limits, and is completely superfluous in a port charter.[50] Another difference between the two clauses is that, although NOR must be given to start laytime under a 'wibon' clause, this is not the case with a 'time lost' clause. This gives rise to the question of whether such a clause can operate when the vessel is physically unready. There are two conflicting first-instance decisions on this point, both of which arose in the context of charterer's cargo being overstowed by a fill-up cargo. In *The Massalia* (No 2),[51] Diplock J held that the clause could operate in such circumstances. However, Donaldson J took a different view in *The Agios Stylianos*:[52] until the other cargo was discharged, no time was lost waiting for a berth to discharge the charterer's cargo. Although both cargoes were discharged at the same berth, the charterers could have used another berth and would not have been obliged to nominate a berth until their cargo had become accessible.

When the clause operates, the charterer will still be able to rely on the laytime exceptions.[53] A 'wibon' clause merely starts the laytime clock running. It does not affect the ability of the charterer to rely on a laytime exception. In *Carboex SA v Louis Dreyfus Commodities Suisse SA*,[54] Field J held that a wibon clause did not have the effect of throwing the risk of all delays, other than those caused by congestion, onto the charterer. The charterer was, accordingly, entitled to rely on a laytime exception which provided that time should not run for the purposes of demurrage where delay in discharge had been caused by congestion after a strike.

The position is somewhat different if the clause provides that the time lost is to count as 'used laytime'. In *The Stainless Emperor*,[55] this wording prevented the charterer from excluding Fridays and holidays from laytime where the relevant exception excluded such days 'unless used'. As the clause referred to 'used laytime', these periods were treated as used, even if that was not, in fact, the case.

Reachable on arrival

Clause 9 of the Asbatankvoy charter form obliges the charterer to nominate a berth 'reachable on the vessel's arrival'[56] at the loading or discharging port. It works by expanding the charterer's duty to nominate a berth. While the clause operates, the shipowner is entitled to demurrage and the

---

48 *Suek AG v Glencore International AG* [2011] EWHC 1361 (Comm); [2011] 2 Lloyd's Rep 278, a case involving liability for laytime under a cif sale.
49 *The Darrah* [1977] AC 157.
50 *The Maratha Envoy* [1978] AC 1.
51 [1960] 2 Lloyd's Rep 352.
52 [1975] 1 Lloyd's Rep 426.
53 *The Darrah* [1977] AC 157, HL.
54 [2011] EWHC 1165 (Comm); [2011] 2 Lloyd's Rep 177.
55 [1994] 1 Lloyd's Rep 298, QB.
56 'Arrival' does not have its technical meaning of reaching the commercial and legal limit of the port. See *The President Brand* [1967] 2 Lloyd's Rep 338. Cf the 'time lost' clause.

charterer is not entitled to the benefit of any laytime exceptions.[57] In interpreting the clause, the courts, in sharp contrast to their approach to 'time lost' and 'wibon' clauses, have not distinguished between congestion and bad weather. In *The Fjordaas*,[58] berthing was delayed due first to a port prohibition on night navigation, then to bad weather and then to a strike by tug officers. The ship-owner's claim for demurrage succeeded. The 'reachable' clause had to be given its ordinary meaning and not reworded as 'reachable on arrival without delay due to physical causes'.

Although, technically, a 'reachable on arrival' clause is distinct from the laytime and demurrage provisions, the relationship between the two obligations is less straightforward than might at first appear to be the case. For a start, although breach of the clause will render the charterers liable in damages for detention at the market rate, this sum may, in fact, be assessed by reference to the demurrage rate. There is also the question of whether charterers may use their laytime allowance to reduce their liability for breach of the 'reachable' clause. The answer to this question depends on whether the period of delay is experienced before the vessel can reach the end of the carrying voyage, either by becoming an 'arrived' ship under a port charter or by reaching the berth under a berth charter.

In *The President Brand*,[59] the clause operated so as to make the charterers liable for detention, without the benefit of any laytime exceptions, from arrival at the waiting place outside the port limits until the time at which the vessel had shifted to a waiting place within the port limits and given NOR so as to become an arrived ship. Thereafter, delay was dealt with by the laytime provisions and the charterer was entitled to rely on any laytime exceptions. The decision was followed by the Court of Appeal in *The Delian Spirit*,[60] where it held that the clause had no application in a port charter when the vessel was delayed at a waiting place within the port limits, so enabling her to become an 'arrived' ship. Delay in this situation was governed exclusively by the laytime provisions and the charterer was entitled to the full benefit of the laytime provisions.

Once the laytime regime takes over, the charterer's breach of the 'reachable' obligation may still have consequences as to its ability to rely on a laytime exception, as was the case in *The Laura Prima*.[61] The vessel was chartered on an Exxonvoy form charter, cl 6 of which provided for NOR to be given on arrival at load port, 'berth or no berth', but with time not to count in the event of delay due to circumstances beyond the charterers' control. Clause 9 contained a 'reachable' provision. The vessel was delayed in berthing at the loading port due to congestion and was, in fact, an arrived ship for the period of such delay. The House of Lords upheld the decision of Mocatta J that the general laytime exception in cl 6 had to be read in the light of the 'reachable' provisions in cl 9 and that compliance with the latter was a precondition to reliance on the former. The charterer would be protected only in the event that the berth was 'reachable' at the time that it had procured it and had subsequently become 'unreachable' by virtue of an intervening event within the wording of cl 6. Thus, in *The Afrapearl*,[62] cl 6 did not operate when the vessel shifted to anchorage to allow for repairs to a leak in the pipeline through which the vessel was discharging, as the leak had existed before the vessel's arrival at the discharge port.

The decision in *The Laura Prima*, however, leaves it unclear as to which other laytime exceptions may be qualified in similar fashion by the existence of a 'reachable' clause. It is likely that the decision is confined to the specific exception in cl 6, whereby 'berth' in the earlier part of the clause is qualified by the 'reachable' provision in cl 9, and that, once laytime starts to run, the charterer will still be able to rely on laytime exceptions, such as 'weather working day' provisions, notwithstanding the breach of the obligation contained in the 'reachable' clause. This conclusion is

---

57 *The President Brand* [1967] 2 Lloyd's Rep 338, QB.
58 [1988] 1 Lloyd's Rep 336. See, also, *The Sea Queen* [1988] 1 Lloyd's Rep 500, QB, but cf *The Kyzikos* [1987] 2 Lloyd's Rep 122, QB.
59 [1967] 2 Lloyd's Rep 338, QB.
60 [1971] 1 Lloyd's Rep 506, CA.
61 [1982] 1 Lloyd's Rep 1, HL.
62 [2003] EWHC 1904 (Comm); [2003] 2 Lloyd's Rep 671, QB.

supported by the fact that, in *The Delian Spirit*, the charterers were held to be entitled to the full benefit of the laytime provisions in a clause that not only set out the total amount of laytime, but also provided, 'Sundays and holidays excepted, weather permitting'.[63]

Suspending laytime

Once laytime begins, it will run continuously against the charterer unless: (a) there is an express provision in the charter to interrupt the running of laytime; or (b) delay is caused by the fault of the shipowner; or (c) the shipowners remove the ship for their own purposes. The charter will usually contain a provision defining the days that are to count for laytime, such as a provision that the charterers are to be allowed a set number of 'weather working days' to load or discharge.

The charter will also contain specific laytime exceptions that will list certain eventualities that will interrupt the running of laytime, such as 'unavoidable hindrances delaying the discharge of the cargo', or 'Strikes, frost . . . or any other unavoidable accidents preventing the loading.' Where the provision is an exception to laytime, the burden is on the charterer to establish that loading or discharging of the vessel in question has been affected by the excepted peril. There is no principle of construction that the eventualities listed in the clause must have been outside the control of the charterer.[64] Nor is there a principle of construction that laytime exceptions have effect only once the vessel is in berth.[65] General charterparty exceptions clauses will not usually suspend the running of laytime.[66]

If laytime begins while a vessel is waiting for a berth, it will run in the same way as if the vessel were at the berth. In *The Darrah*,[67] the vessel arrived at Tripoli roads and gave NOR. The charter provided 'Time lost in waiting for berth to count as laytime' and provided for discharge 'at the rate of 625 metric tons per weather working day of 24 consecutive hours, Fridays and holidays excepted'. The charterers said that while the vessel was waiting to berth time should count in accordance with the laytime definitions. The shipowners relied on *The Radnor*[68] and argued that the 'time lost' clause constituted an independent code for the counting of time which was not subject to the laytime definitions. The House of Lords held that the charterers were right and overruled *The Radnor*. Lord Diplock stated that under a 'time lost' clause '. . . there are to be excluded all periods which would have been left out in the computation of permitted laytime used up if the vessel had actually been in berth', as was the case when the vessel was an arrived ship under a port charter. The same applies as regards the application of laytime exceptions.[69]

Laytime definitions and exceptions

Weather working day

This is the most common laytime definition in voyage charters and involves a consideration of two issues. The first involves defining a 'working day'. In *Reardon-Smith Line Ltd v Ministry of Agriculture,*

---

63 For further discussion of this issue, see Schofield, *Laytime and Demurrage*, 6th edn, 2011, London: Informa Law, pp 4.453–81 and Baughen, *Summerskill on Laytime*, 5th edn, 2013, London: Sweet & Maxwell, pp 6–43.

64 *The Vine* [2010] EWHC 1411 (Comm), 16 June 2010.

65 *Carboex SA v Louis Dreyfus Commodities Suisse SA* [2012] EWCA Civ 838; [2013] QB 789. A laytime exception in respect of strikes in the AmWelsh charter was held to apply to a vessel that was unable to berth, provided the strike was the effective cause of the delay.

66 *The Johs Stove* [1984] 1 Lloyd's Rep 38. See, also, *The Lefthero* [1992] 2 Lloyd's Rep 109, CA, and *The Solon* [2000] 1 Lloyd's Rep 293, QB. The principle applies equally to delays that start during laytime and continue once the vessel goes on demurrage as to delays that arise only once the vessel is already on demurrage.

67 [1977] AC 157.

68 [1955] 2 Lloyd's Rep 668, CA.

69 *The Radauti* [1988] 2 Lloyd's Rep 416.

Fisheries and Food,[70] the question arose as to how a Saturday at Vancouver should be classified. The House of Lords held that it would either be a 'working' day or a 'non-working' day. On the basis of a 'conventional' day,[71] once Saturday was classified as a working day, time ran for the full 24 hours of the day, irrespective of the normal hours of work for that day.

The second involves the effect of bad weather on a working day. This element was addressed by Pearson J in *Compania Naviera Azuero SA v British Oil and Cake Mills Ltd,*[72] in which he defined a weather working day as '. . . a day on which the weather permits the relevant work to be done, whether or not any person avails himself of that permission; in other words, so far as the weather is concerned, it is a working day'. In *Reardon-Smith Line Ltd v Ministry of Agriculture, Fisheries and Food,* their Lordships were of the view that if a 'conventional' day is being used, time lost due to bad weather needs to be assessed by reference to the impact of the weather on the normal working hours for the port. Therefore, if two hours are lost due to rain, laytime is not suspended for two hours out of 24; rather, a fraction must be obtained by comparing the time lost with the normal working hours for that day and then applying the fraction to the 24 hours of the calendar day. If the normal working hours are eight, then laytime will be suspended for one-quarter of the 24-hour 'conventional' day. This process must be applied, even if no work is actually taking place on a working day, for example when there is a strike.[73] No deduction is made in respect of bad weather occurring outside the normal working hours. In a port which works a 24-hour day, laytime will be suspended for the actual time by which work is interrupted due to bad weather. If laytime starts under a port charter while the vessel is waiting for a berth, the laytime definitions will operate in the same way as if the vessel were at the berth. Therefore, if bad weather prevents loading or discharge at the berth, laytime will have to be reduced, even though the vessel is not directly affected as it is waiting to berth.

Weather permitting

Another common laytime description is 'weather permitting'. In *The Vorras,*[74] the Court of Appeal held that weather which prohibited any vessel of this general type from loading would interrupt laytime, even though the relevant vessel was not directly affected by the weather in that it was waiting for a berth during the period of the bad weather. Under this clause the actual amount of bad weather that prohibits loading or discharge is excluded from laytime, unlike the apportionment required with a 'weather working day' definition.

Laytime exceptions

There are a variety of specific laytime exceptions. The Gencon charter contains a detailed regime for dealing with the effect of strikes at the loading and discharge ports. Many charters also contain some form of *force majeure* clause under which laytime will not run when time is lost due to circumstances beyond the charterer's control. Where the charter contains a 'reachable on arrival' clause, the charterers will be unable to rely on such an exception if they have failed to nominate a berth reachable on the vessel's arrival.[75]

Strikes, frost . . . or any other unavoidable accidents preventing the loading

'Loading' will be construed narrowly, as can be seen in *Grant v Coverdale.*[76] The vessel arrived and loaded part of her cargo, when a frost rendered a canal communicating with the dock impassable.

---

70 [1963] AC 691, HL.
71 The charter provided for laytime to start 24 hours after the giving of NOR.
72 [1957] 2 QB 293, 303.
73 Where the clause refers to a weather working day of 24 consecutive hours, the ratio method is not used. Instead, a deduction is made of the actual amount of time that has been lost, or, in the case of a vessel waiting to berth, would have been lost.
74 [1983] 1 Lloyd's Rep 579, CA.
75 *The Laura Prima* [1982] 1 Lloyd's Rep 1, HL.
76 (1884) 9 App Cas 470.

The rest of the cargo was ready at a wharf on the canal and could not, for several days, be brought in lighters to the dock; it could be brought into the dock by carting or otherwise, but only at an unreasonable expense. The dock was not frozen and had the cargo been there, loading might have proceeded. The delay was held to be outside the exceptions clause. Lord Bramwell stated that frost did not prevent 'loading'; it merely prevented the particular cargo that charterers had provided from being brought to the place where the loading would not have been prevented.

'Loading' would, however, have been prevented had the canal been the only way in which cargo could have been brought to the port, as was the case in *Hudson v Ede*,[77] where there was an exception in respect of 'detention by ice'. The vessel arrived at Sulina to load grain. There were no storehouses there, as grain was stored higher up the Danube, from where it could only be brought down by lighters, there being no connecting railway or other practicable means of land transport. NOR was given and after six days, when no cargo had been supplied, the river froze up for two months. This exception was held to cover the detention by ice of the lighters coming downriver to load the ship, irrespective of the ignorance of the shipowner as to the circumstances of the port.

If the charterparty calls for the loading of more than one cargo, an exception that covers one cargo will not protect the charterer from failing to load an alternative cargo specified in the charter, which is not covered by the exception. However, in *Brightman & Co v Bunge y Born Limitada Socieda*,[78] the charterers were allowed a 'reasonable time' to make arrangements for loading of the alternative cargo, during which laytime was suspended. The position is different if the charterparty provides for one basic cargo and gives the charterers an option to load alternatives. In *Reardon-Smith Line Ltd v Ministry of Agriculture, Fisheries and Food*,[79] the duty to load 'a full and complete cargo . . . of wheat in bulk . . . and/or barley in bulk and/or flour in sacks' was qualified by a subsequent clause giving the charterers the option to load up to one-third of the cargo with barley and one-third with flour on paying an increased rate of freight. The basic contractual cargo was wheat and, as loading of that cargo was prevented by a laytime exceptions clause, the charterers were not obliged to load barley or flour.[80] The essential distinction between this case and the previous one lies in the fact that the charter provided for a different freight rate for the alternative cargoes and also specified a limit to the quantity that could be loaded from them.

Unavoidable hindrances delaying the discharge of the cargo
This exception has been held to cover foreseeable hindrances. In *The Radauti*,[81] a berth charter provided 'Time lost in waiting for berth to count as laytime', and also contained a *force majeure* clause. Discharge was delayed as the vessel could not get to berth due to congestion. The phrase 'hindrances . . . delaying the discharge of the cargo' in the *force majeure* clause was given its normal meaning, which included congestion, even if foreseeable.

Fault of the shipowner

If the loading or discharge is interrupted without the fault of the charterer, laytime will still run unless the charterer can either bring itself within a laytime exceptions clause or can show that the interruption was caused by the fault of the shipowner.[82] An example of the latter is provided by the

---

77 (1868) LR 2 QB 566; aff'd (1868) LR 3 QB 412.
78 [1924] 2 KB 619, CA.
79 [1963] AC 691.
80 Even if they had exercised their option, they would only have been able to load two-thirds of the vessel's capacity.
81 [1988] 2 Lloyd's Rep 416, CA.
82 It is possible that laytime may be suspended even if the shipowner's fault is non-actionable in the sense that the shipowner is protected by an exceptions clause in the charter. The reasoning of Parker J in *The Union Amsterdam* [1982] 2 Lloyd's Rep 432, which concerned the suspension of demurrage due to the fault of the shipowner, would suggest that this is indeed the case.

conduct of the shipowner in *The Fontevivo*.[83] The vessel was part of the way through discharging her cargo at Lattakia in Syria when she sailed away, due to her crew becoming nervous about war risks. Three days later, she sailed back to Lattakia. The charterer established a prima facie case of the shipowner's fault by reference to the vessel's leaving Lattakia for three days. The shipowners had failed to rebut that case and laytime was accordingly suspended for those three days. However, in *The Sinoe*,[84] discharge was delayed due to the incompetence of the stevedores. The charterparty provided that stevedores were to be appointed by the charterers but 'considered as owner's servants'. This wording was held to be insufficient to make the shipowners responsible for the defaults of the stevedores and laytime was not thereby suspended.

Where loading is interrupted due to the fault of neither the shipowner nor the charterer, it follows that laytime will not be suspended. In *William Alexander & Sons v Aktieselskabet Dampskibet Hansa*,[85] discharge, which was to be a joint operation by shipowners and charterers, using the same stevedores, was delayed, due to a labour shortage at the port. As the delay could not be attributed to the fault of the shipowner, laytime was not suspended.

Nor will the shipowner be at fault if loading is delayed because the charterer's cargo is stowed below that of another charterer. In *Porteus v Watney*,[86] bills of lading, incorporating the terms of the voyage charter, were issued to several shippers. It was held that delays in discharge due to the negligence of other consignees whose cargo was stowed above that of the defendants could not be attributed to the fault of the shipowners. The laydays were not to be apportioned between all of the bill of lading consignees, nor was the demurrage rate to be apportioned between them. However, subsequent decisions have modified the hardship caused by the case. In *The Massalia (No 2)*,[87] Devlin J construed the NOR provisions relating to 'cargo' as relating only to the understowed cargo, although the shipowners were still able to claim demurrage in full by relying on a 'time lost' clause. This part of the decision was distinguished in *The Agios Stylianos*,[88] where Donaldson J held that a 'time lost' clause in a charter for the carriage of cement on a vessel that was also carrying vehicles under another charter, meant 'time lost in waiting for a cement berth'.[89]

Removal of vessel for shipowner's purposes

Laytime and demurrage will not run in respect of time during which the vessel is not at the disposition of the charterers. In *Stolt Tankers v Landmark*,[90] the vessel tendered a NOR off Bombay anchorage under a port charter. The master was advised that the intended berth would not be available for 15 days. Accordingly, the vessel left her anchorage to discharge other cargo being carried under concurrent charters. She then returned to the waiting anchorage only to leave again to load cargo under another charter. Andrew Smith J held that the charterers could not be liable for demurrage in respect of these two periods during which the shipowners had used the vessel for their own purposes, notwithstanding that demurrage would have accrued had they simply waited idly at the anchorage. Similarly, demurrage will be interrupted if the vessel shifts to take on bunkers, even though no cargo is available for loading during that time.[91] However, an interruption that is necessary for the safe discharge of the cargo will not interrupt demurrage.[92]

83 [1975] 1 Lloyd's Rep 399.
84 [1971] 1 Lloyd's Rep 514; aff'd [1972] 1 Lloyd's Rep 201, CA.
85 [1920] AC 88, HL.
86 (1878) 3 QBD 534, CA.
87 [1962] 2 QB 416.
88 [1975] 1 Lloyd's Rep 426.
89 See, also, *The Sea Pioneer* [1982] 1 Lloyd's Rep 13, CA and *The Oriental Envoy* [1982] 2 Lloyd's Rep 266.
90 [2002] 1 Lloyd's Rep 786, QB.
91 *Re Ropner Shipping Co Ltd & Cleeves Western Valleys Anthracite Collieries Ltd* [1927] 1 KB 879.
92 *Houlder v Weir* [1905] 2 QB 267, where demurrage was held to run continuously while ballast was being put into a ship to enable her to discharge in safety.

The shipowner's remedies for delays in loading and discharge – demurrage

Once the laydays expire, the vessel will go on demurrage until the completion of loading or discharge, as the case may be.[93] Demurrage is primarily due from the charterer, but recovery may also be made from a bill of lading holder, provided that the bill of lading incorporates the terms of the charter and the demurrage clause is worded so as to encompass the liability of a bill of lading holder. The shipowner's remedy against either the charterer or the bill of lading holder is limited to a claim for demurrage, even if the delay is so serious as to entitle it to repudiate the charter.[94] If the shipowner elects to keep the contract alive, then it is bound by all of the terms of the contract, including the demurrage clause. The position is the same, even if the breach is wilful and deliberate.[95] Where the charterers delay for an unreasonable period in giving orders as to the discharge port, the shipowner must accept the repudiation by the charterer. It must then mitigate its losses by discharging at the port that, in the master's opinion, would be the one most likely to have been selected by the charterers.[96]

The charterer's obligations regarding loading and discharge are innominate terms. Therefore, the shipowner will not generally be entitled to terminate the charter and sail off at the expiry of laytime.[97] The right to terminate will arise only when the period of delay after the expiry of laytime may either be expressed as a period of 'unreasonable delay'[98] or of delay such as to 'frustrate the commercial purposes of the contract'.[99]

Under the doctrine of anticipatory breach,[100] the right to terminate will arise once it becomes inevitable that the vessel will not be loaded before the expiry of an 'unreasonable' or 'frustrating' period of delay, and the shipowner need not wait until the end of the period of delay. In some circumstances, the shipowner may therefore terminate the charter before the expiry of laytime. In *Universal Cargo Carriers Corp v Citati*,[101] the shipowners terminated on 18 July, shortly before the expiry of laytime. There had been no renunciation by the charterers but the owners could justify their conduct provided that they could show that, on that date, the charterer had wholly and finally disabled itself from finding a cargo before a period of time that would be so long as to frustrate the commercial purpose of the contract. The determination of whether this had happened was to be made in the light of all events occurring before and after the critical date of 18 July.

Irrespective of the charterer's breach, the shipowner who is unreasonably delayed from entering the port or berth nominated for discharge may have a further remedy if the charter includes a 'near' clause. Subject to the principles set out in Chapter 10, this clause will entitle it to discharge at an alternative port. Discharge at an alternative port or berth in reliance on the clause will be subject to the same laytime and demurrage provisions as would have governed discharge at the contracted port or berth.

---

93 If the charter gives the shipowner an option to trans-ship, and this is exercised, the charterer will remain liable for any demurrage incurred in discharge by the second vessel, even if that vessel is not in the same ownership as the original vessel. See *The Christos* [1995] 1 Lloyd's Rep 106, QB.
94 *Ethel Radcliffe SS Co v Barnet* (1926) 24 Ll L Rep 277, 279.
95 *Suisse Atlantique Société d'Armement Maritime v NV Rotterdamsche Kolen Centrale* [1967] 1 AC 361, HL.
96 Per Bankes LJ in *Ethel Radcliffe SS Co v Barnet* (1926) 24 Ll L Rep 277, 279.
97 *Wilson & Coventry Ltd v Otto Thoresen Linie* [1910] 2 KB 405.
98 *Inverkip SS Co v Bunge* [1917] 2 KB 193, CA.
99 *Universal Cargo Carriers Corp v Citati* [1957] 2 QB 401.
100 To rely on an anticipatory breach of the charterparty, the owners must show that there had been a renunciation by the charterer of his liabilities, whereby by his conduct he has shown an intention not to go on with the charterparty or impossibility of performance created by his own act.
101 [1957] 2 QB 401. The arbitrators had found that the charterer was willing to perform and Devlin J remitted the issue of impossibility to the arbitrators. However, the Court of Appeal held [1958] 2 Lloyd's Rep 17, that there was sufficient material before the judge for him to infer that performance by the charterers was impossible at the date of termination by the owners.

Two further issues relating to demurrage will now be considered: whether demurrage may be suspended by laytime exceptions; and whether demurrage covers all losses suffered by the shipowner by reason of delays in the loading and discharge processes.

Laytime provisions and demurrage

Laytime definitions and exceptions are presumed not to apply to demurrage, hence the adage 'once on demurrage, always on demurrage'. This was applied in *The Dias*,[102] where a vessel was waiting in the roads. After expiry of laytime, the cargo was required to be fumigated. Under cl 15, the charterers had the option to fumigate at the discharge port, 'time so used not to count', but this provision was held to apply only while laytime was still running. The charterer could no longer rely on it once the vessel had gone on demurrage.

Laytime exceptions will cover demurrage only if they are expressly worded to have that effect. General charter exceptions will not cover demurrage unless they would be meaningless if demurrage were not covered. This was not the case in *The Kalliopi A*,[103] where a berth charter, with a wibon clause, had no laytime exceptions clause. The general exceptions clause mutually excluded liability due to 'unavoidable hindrances', but was held not to exclude liability for demurrage caused by non-availability of a berth causing the vessel to wait within the port at the pilot station. To cover demurrage, such a consequence must clearly follow from the language used in the clause.[104] This was not the case here and the clause could take effect quite apart from dealing with liability for demurrage.[105]

There is, however, one situation in which the charterer will be able to avoid its liability for demurrage – that is, where the delay in the loading or discharging operations is due to the fault of the shipowner. This will be the case even if the shipowner's fault is rendered non-actionable by an exceptions clause. Accordingly, in *The Union Amsterdam*,[106] demurrage was interrupted during a period of delay caused by the negligent grounding of the vessel, even though such negligence was protected by the incorporation of the **US Carriage of Goods by Sea Act of 1936** with its exemption in respect of negligence in the navigation and management of the vessel. However, while the decision may be correct on the grounds that the wording of the particular clause paramount did not cover claims by the shipowner for demurrage, the wider proposition deduced by Parker J that non-actionable fault will interrupt demurrage is inconsistent with the approach to non-actionable fault in general average cases applied in *Louis Dreyfus & Co v Tempus Shipping Co*.[107]

The time credited against demurrage as a result of time lost due to breach by the shipowner will be limited by the general contractual principles governing remoteness of damage, which are discussed in Chapter 13. Although each case will turn on its own facts, the facts of two arbitration awards give a useful indication of how the principles may be applied in practice.[108]

In *London Arbitration 29/84*,[109] laytime ran from 29 December to 31 December. The vessel was then on demurrage until 5 January, during which period there fell a weekend and the New Year holiday. It later transpired that the shipowners, in breach of contract, had delayed sailing from the load port due to a temporary absence by the chief engineer on personal grounds. Had the vessel

---

102 [1978] 1 WLR 261.
103 [1988] 2 Lloyd's Rep 101.
104 It is likely that this is also the case where a claim for detention is made on the grounds that such a claim is in essence the same as one for demurrage, save that damages in the latter case are liquidated. See *Moor Line Ltd v Distillers Co Ltd* (1912) SC 514.
105 Such as the clause in *Moor Line Ltd v Distillers Co Ltd* (1912) SC 514, which was worded as follows: '. . . in case of any delay by reason of a strike . . . no *claim for damages* to be made' (emphasis added).
106 [1982] 2 Lloyd's Rep 432.
107 [1931] AC 726. See Schofield, op cit fn 63, pp 4.85–93. However, the Court of Appeal in *The Lefthero* [1992] 2 Lloyd's Rep 109 assumed the correctness of the wider proposition.
108 See Schofield, op cit fn 63, pp 4.33–5, 4.38.
109 LMLN 20 December 1984.

sailed at once, she would have arrived on 23 December and completed discharge by 30 December. On this calculation, both the weekend and the holidays would fall within the laydays. However, the arbitrators were not prepared to allow a deduction from demurrage, for the following reason:

> There is a possibility that a weekend will fall within laytime rather than within a demurrage period, but since the ship will be carrying only a small quantity of cargo which will not take more than about 36 hours to discharge, and only 48 hours' laytime is being allowed, it is not likely that such a happening will occur.

In *The Forum Craftsman*,[110] a vessel on demurrage was removed from berth due to seawater damage to the cargo to be discharged. It took another 79 days before she reberthed and most of this time was lost due to bureaucratic delays. The arbitrators allowed only seven days against demurrage.[111]

Demurrage and other breaches of charter

Other breaches of charter may cause delays in the loading or discharging of the vessel. Such breaches are not automatically within the demurrage provisions. For example, delay may also be caused by the charterer's failure to nominate a berth or a port within a reasonable time. This is the duty onto which the 'reachable on arrival' clause fastens. Once a nomination has been made, the charterer has no right to alter it in the absence of any express provision in the charter.[112] The right to renominate must be expressly provided for in the charter and is not to be implied from a clause requiring the charterer to pay extra expenses incurred pursuant to a change in the loading or discharge port.[113]

Damages in respect of this breach will be at large and will not be governed by the demurrage clause.[114] In *The Timna*,[115] the charterers failed to nominate the port of discharge. The master went to one port and gave NOR, but the charterers eventually ordered the vessel to another port. It was held that no demurrage was earned at the port where the master gave NOR as there was no implied term that the master could nominate a discharge port if the charterers failed to do so. However, the ship-owner could claim damages for detention as the charterer had been in breach of its duty to give orders for the first discharge port. It was liable for the time that elapsed from when the orders should have been given to when they were given. The shipowners were under no duty to prove that, had the charterer ordered the vessel to a port, they could have got close enough in to be 'arrived'. If the charterers were to show that the shipowners had suffered no loss, it was incumbent upon them to prove that there was no charter port at all at which the vessel could have become an 'arrived' ship.[116] Damages were also awarded at the demurrage rate in *The Vine*,[117] where the delay was the result of the charterer's breach of the safe berth warranty. The substantial delay in berthing

---

110 LMLN 273 2 June 1990.

111 See, also, *The Eurus* [1996] 2 Lloyd's Rep 408, where the arbitrators' finding that loss due to the operation of the 'eight-hour' rule in Nigerian ports was too remote, even though it had been in operation there for some 18 years. The rule provided that where loading was completed before 0800, the bill of lading should bear the date of the preceding day.

112 As in *The Jasmine B* [1992] 1 Lloyd's Rep 39, QB. Once a port has been nominated, the position is as if it had been written into the charter *ab initio*. However, although the option given could be exercised after giving of NOR at the original port, it could not be used to send the vessel to a port 'for orders'.

113 *The Antiparos* [2008] EWHC 1139 (Comm); [2008] 2 Lloyd's Rep 237, which involved cl 4(c) of the Asbatankvoy form.

114 But note that the demurrage clause may specifically apply to these types of delay, as in *Ethel Radcliffe SS Co v Barnet* (1926) 24 Ll L Rep 277. In most instances, there will be very little difference between the market rate and the demurrage rate. See *The Boral Gas* [1988] 1 Lloyd's Rep 342, 346, per Evans J.

115 [1971] 2 Lloyd's Rep 91, CA.

116 See, also, *The Mass Glory* [2002] EWHC 72 (Comm); [2002] 2 Lloyd's Rep 244, where the vessel was delayed in proceeding to berth due to charterers' inability to ensure that the cargo documentation was in order. Moore-Bick J held that the shipowners could claim damages for detention for this period of delay. However, once the vessel berthed, any subsequent delay fell under the laytime provisions.

117 [2010] EWHC 1411 (Comm); [2011] 1 Lloyd's Rep 301.

was due to the fact that out of three berthing dolphins, the middle and forward ones had been damaged in two separate incidents, and required repairs before the vessel could berth. Teare J held that the charterers had nominated an unsafe berth, requiring more than ordinary navigation and seamanship to avoid the dangers inherent in the defective dolphins. Although there had been no breach of the obligation to load within the laydays, due to the operation of a laytime exception, this did not disable the shipowners from claiming the agreed rate of damages for delay caused by breach of another obligation.

Even delays in loading or discharge may give rise to losses that fall outside the demurrage provisions. For example, the delay may cause less cargo to be loaded than required by the charter. This will give rise to a claim for deadfreight. Although the delayed loading caused the under-loading, the shipowner's damages will not be confined to demurrage for exceeding the laydays. In *Akt Reidar v Arcos*,[118] due to delay in the loading of the vessel, only five-eighths of the cargo could be loaded, as she would be unable to reach the discharging port by the end of October and could not carry more than the cargo loaded without infringing s 10 of the **Merchant Shipping Act 1906**. If the vessel had carried a larger deck cargo than the cargo loaded and arrived after 31 October, she would have been fined, but had the charterer loaded a full cargo without delay, she could have been discharged before 31 October and so avoided a fine. It was held that the demurrage clause did not affect the shipowner's rights to deadfreight as the claim was distinct from one for detention.

If, however, the loss manifests itself as a loss of time in the loading or discharge, damages will be assessed in relation to the demurrage clause. In *Chandris v Isbrandtsen-Moller*,[119] the cargo was to consist of lawful general merchandise excluding 'other dangerous cargo'. In breach of charter, turpentine was loaded, but with the knowledge of the master. Because of the dangerous nature of the cargo, the vessel had to unload it in the river into barges. This was held to be a breach of charter. The fact that the master consented to load the cargo did not amount to a waiver of the shipowner's right to claim damages. However, these were governed by the demurrage clause. Loss of time due to detention in an unsafe port is also compensated in accordance with the demurrage clause and not by way of damages for detention.[120]

Where non-charter cargo is loaded, an additional rate of freight may become due from the charterer. In *Stevens v Bromley*,[121] a vessel was chartered to load steel billets at a set rate. The cargo actually loaded consisted in part of general cargo, the current rate for which exceeded the charter rate. Although the demurrage clause covered any delay in loading, the shipowner was not prevented from making a further claim for additional freight by reason of agreeing to load a non-charter cargo. The demurrage provisions do not cover every loss resulting from breach of the charter provisions as to loading and discharge, but only such losses that are felt as a loss of time in such operations.

Demurrage time bars

Many charterparties require demurrage claims to be submitted within a specified period of time. For example, cl 15(3) of Part II of Shellvoy 5 provides that, if owners fail to submit any demurrage claim 'fully and correctly' documented within 90 days, charterers' liability for any such claim 'shall be extinguished'. In *The Eagle Valencia*,[122] the shipowners submitted their demurrage claim within 30 days and after 90 days the charterers rejected it on the grounds that the NOR was invalid under cl 22 because free pratique had not been granted until more than six hours after NOR

---

118 [1927] 1 KB 352.
119 [1951] 1 KB 240.
120 *The Hermine* [1979] 1 Lloyd's Rep 212, CA.
121 [1919] 2 KB 722.
122 [2010] EWCA Civ 713; [2010] 2 Lloyd's Rep 257.

was given. The charterers contended that time did not start to run until the vessel berthed. The shipowners submitted an alternative claim based on a second NOR given after the vessel obtained free pratique, while still waiting to berth, but the Court of Appeal held that this claim was time barred by cl 15(3). The shipowners' initial demurrage claim had not been 'fully and correctly' documented in that the shipowners had attached a copy of the initial, invalid NOR, and had not included a copy of the second, valid, NOR.

Where there is a failure to submit documentation relating to part of the demurrage claim within the time limit, there are conflicting first instance decisions as to whether the entire demurrage claim is barred or only that part to which the missing documentation relates. For example, pumping logs are required under BPVoy4 cl 19 in respect of any discharge which had taken place at a terminal. Failure to provide pumping logs signed by the terminal representative led to the barring of the entire composite demurrage claim in The Sabrewing[123] but the decision was not followed in The Eternity.[124]

123 [2007] EWHC 2482 (Comm); [2008] 1 Lloyd's Rep 286.
124 [2008] EWHC 2480 (Comm); [2009] 1 Lloyd's Rep 107.

Chapter 12

Time Charters

The principal differences between time and voyage charters have already been discussed in Chapter 9. In this chapter, we shall consider two of those differences in more detail. First, we shall consider the remedy of withdrawal, which is available to the shipowner in the event of non-payment of hire under a time charter. Secondly, we shall consider the different contractual mechanisms adopted for allocating the risk of loss of time during the currency of the charter.

The shipowner's right of withdrawal

If the charterer fails to pay the hire on time or in full, this will amount to a breach of charter. Only in exceptional circumstances will it amount to such a serious breach as to justify the shipowner terminating the charter.[1] For this reason, most time charters contain a clause that gives the shipowner the option of withdrawing the vessel from the service of the time charterer if hire is not paid in full on the due date.

A shipowner that wishes to exercise its option to terminate the charter must give the charterer notice that it is withdrawing the vessel from its service. The notice becomes irrevocable once it is given and cannot be withdrawn without the consent of the time charterer. Unless expressly stated, a withdrawal clause cannot be used to effect a *temporary* withdrawal of the vessel from the charter.[2]

Until the notice is given, the charter will remain in force. In *The Mihalios Xilas*,[3] the charterers made an underpayment on an instalment of hire payable in advance. The shipowners accepted it and then took four days to make their decision to withdraw the vessel. They were required to return the charterers' tendered payment, which covered a period after the withdrawal of the vessel, after which the charter and the obligation to pay hire ceased.[4] They were, however, allowed to retain a sum covering the four days during which they were making their mind up on whether or not they should exercise their option to withdraw. For this period, the charter remained in force, as did the obligation to pay hire.

It therefore follows that legitimate orders given by the charterer prior to the withdrawal remain valid and must be obeyed. The risk for the shipowner is that if it withdraws the vessel, it will still have to perform bill of lading commitments made prior to the withdrawal.[5] Furthermore, it will be unable to claim freight from either the charterer[6] or the bill of lading holder, if, as is likely, a 'freight prepaid' bill has been issued. Sometimes, the shipowner faced with this dilemma will seek to persuade the bill of lading holders to contribute towards the costs of the voyage. Such a course of action runs the risk that the agreement will be rendered unenforceable by reason of duress, as was the case in *The Alev*.[7] The courts will certainly find duress if there is any suggestion that the agreement was procured by reason of threats by the shipowner not to continue the voyage unless such payments were made.

A withdrawal will terminate the charterparty and the shipowner will be entitled to claim unpaid hire up to the date of withdrawal with interest. However, it may incur additional expenses

---

1 In *The Afovos* [1983] 1 WLR 195, Lord Diplock was of the view that the doctrine of anticipatory breach by conduct which disables a party to a contract from performing one of his primary obligations under the contract had no application to a breach of a clause as to the punctual payment of hire. The threatened non-performance in a failure to pay a single instalment of hire on time would not have the effect of depriving the shipowner of substantially the whole benefit of the contract then remaining unperformed.

2 *International Bulk Carriers v Evlogia Shipping (The Mihalios Xilas)* [1978] 2 Lloyd's Rep 186, QB. The 1993 NYPE form gives the shipowner a right of temporary withdrawal once it has given notice to withdraw under the 'anti-technicality' clause.

3 [1979] 1 WLR 1018, HL.

4 However, where hire is assigned to a third party, the charterer cannot recover from the assignee any overpaid hire. *The Trident Beauty* [1994] 1 Lloyd's Rep 365, HL.

5 This will certainly be the case if shipowner's bills are issued, and may also be the position where charterer's bills are issued, as held by the Admiralty Court of New South Wales in *The AES Express* [1990] 20 NSWLR 57.

6 *The Tropwind (No 2)* [1982] 1 Lloyd's Rep 232, *per dicta* of Lord Denning MR.

7 [1989] 1 Lloyd's Rep 138.

following the withdrawal, such as the costs of performing existing contracts of carriage under bills of lading issued pursuant to charterer's orders before the withdrawal. The relationship between shipowners and charterers where the vessel is withdrawn with cargo on board has recently received consideration in the Supreme Court. In *The Kos*,[8] the shipowners withdrew at a time when the ship had just loaded a cargo. The charterers threatened to arrest the vessel for wrongful withdrawal and the shipowners provided a guarantee for $18 million. The shipowners claimed compensation for the use or detention of the ship between notice of withdrawal and discharge of the cargo, for fuel consumed during that time and used to unload the cargo, and for the costs of providing and maintaining the guarantee. The Supreme Court (Lord Mance dissenting) held that these items could be claimed from the charterers under the indemnity clause in the charter as these expenses were the direct result of the master's compliance with the charterer's order to load the cargo.[9] The reasoning of the Supreme Court would apply equally to costs incurred in fulfilling voyages under freight prepaid bills of lading issued on charterers' orders prior to withdrawal, contrary to what has hitherto been assumed to be the law.[10] The Supreme Court unanimously held that the costs were also recoverable in bailment. Where the property was originally bailed under a contract of carriage and the carrier had no choice but to remain in possession after the contract had ended, the existence of a continuing duty to care for the cargo was a sufficient basis for imposing on its owner an obligation to pay. This had also been the view of the House of Lords in *The Winson*,[11] where a claim in bailment for expenses incurred by salvors was upheld because: (i) the cargo was originally bailed to the owners under a contract which came to an end while the cargo was still in their possession; (ii) as a matter of law their obligation to look after the cargo continued notwithstanding the termination of the charterparty; (iii) that the only reasonable or practical option open to them once the charterparty had come to an end was to retain the cargo until it could be discharged at the port where the vessel was then located. These factors were all present in *The Kos*, and justified a claim for remuneration in bailment. Under the **Senior Courts Act 1981** the shipowners were also entitled to recover the costs of providing the guarantee they had provided to the charterers, as costs of the action.

There are conflicting first instance decisions as to whether shipowners may claim damages from the time charterer for loss of bargain or for loss of earnings over the unperformed balance of the charterparty following a withdrawal. In *The Brimnes*,[12] the shipowners' claim for damages failed. The charterer's failure to make punctual payments of hire was held not to amount to a repudiation of the charter. However, in *The Astra*, shipowners were able to recover damages on two grounds.[13] First, there had been a repudiatory breach of the charter by the charterer who had made repeated requests for reduction of the hire rate, made late payments, and repeatedly advised owners that unless the rate of hire was reduced, it would be forced to declare immediate bankruptcy. Secondly, the obligation to make punctual payment of hire was a condition of the charter. *The Brimnes* was distinguished on the grounds that the present charter contained an anti-technicality clause.[14]

---

8 [2009] EWHC 1843 (Comm); [2010] EWCA 772 (Comm); [2010] WLR (D) 173.
9 Lord Mance dissented on the ground that the loss was not effectively caused by the failure to pay hire because the shipowner's decision to withdraw the ship had broken the chain of causation.
10 Lord Denning MR addressed this point briefly in *dicta* in *The Tropwave*: 'If there is cargo on board at the time of the notice of withdrawal – and the shipowner carries it to its destination – he does so by way of fulfilling the original charter or bill of lading – and not by way of any new request by the charterer. So he cannot recover the market rate either on a *quantum meruit* or otherwise.' [1982] 1 Lloyd's Rep 232, 237.
11 [1982] AC 939.
12 [1973] 1 WLR 386; aff'd [1975] QB 929, CA.
13 [2013] EWHC 865 (Comm); [2013] 2 Lloyd's Rep. 69.
14 Flaux J also stated that there did not seem to be anything in the judgments in the Court of Appeal in *The Brimnes* on the question of whether cl 5 of the NYPE form was a condition.

Following a withdrawal, the shipowners may also claim *quantum meruit* remuneration from subcharterers who request that the cargo be carried to its destination, notwithstanding that this is a service that the shipowners were obliged to perform under the bill of lading.[15]

The withdrawal clause will now be examined in more detail as it relates to late payments and to underpayments.

Late payment

Withdrawal clauses are construed strictly and are not subject to equitable relief against forfeiture.[16] In *The Laconia*,[17] the hire was due on a Sunday and was paid on the Monday. The shipowners were entitled to withdraw, notwithstanding that there was no practical way in which the charterers could have effected payment on the due date. A further issue arose out of the fact that the late payment was initially accepted by the shipowners' agents. The charterers argued that this amounted to a waiver of the shipowners' right to withdraw in respect of this particular late payment. The argument was rejected, as the agents had no authority to accept the late payment, and the shipowners instructed them to return the payment as soon as they became aware of what had happened. However, if a shipowner makes a practice of accepting hire late, such conduct may waive its right to withdraw on account of a future late payment, unless notice is given to charterers that, in future, the shipowner will insist on timely payment.[18]

The 'anti-technicality' clause

To counteract the harsh effects of the decision in *The Laconia*, most time charters now contain an 'anti-technicality' clause, which obliges the shipowner to give the charterer notice of its intention to withdraw if the breach is not remedied within 48 hours. Such provisions are as strictly construed as the withdrawal provisions themselves. The notice must be in the correct form[19] and given at the correct time. In *The Afovos*,[20] the charter contained such an 'anti-technicality' clause. If hire were not paid, then the shipowners were to give the charterers 48 hours' notice to rectify the default. The notice was given at 1640 on the date on which hire fell. The notice was given after working hours, so there was no longer any practical possibility of the charterer making payment on the due date. However, technically, the notice was given too early, as the charterers had, in theory, until midnight to pay. As the shipowners had not strictly complied with the terms of the withdrawal clause, their withdrawal was ineffective and therefore a repudiatory breach of charter.

One common form of anti-technicality clause provides that notice must be given where there is 'any failure to make punctual and regular payment due to errors or omission of Charterers' employees, bankers or agents or otherwise for any reason where there is absence of intention to fail to make payment'. In *Owneast Shipping Limited v Qatar Navigation QSC*,[21] Christopher Clarke J held that 'intention' did not include recklessness. The charterers had intended to make a payment that

---

15 *The Bulk Chile* [2013] EWCA Civ 184; [2013] 1 WLR 3440. In Australia in *The Lakatoi Express* (1990) 19 NSWLR 285, Carruthers J held that the subcharterers were obliged to pay the shipowner a reasonable remuneration for the use of the vessel after the repudiation, and had a claim for damages against the time charterer. However, the shipowners had no right of lien in respect of this right to *quantum meruit* remuneration over the freight payable under the time charterer's bill of lading.

16 *The Scaptrade* [1983] 2 AC 694, HL, following *dicta* in *The Laconia* [1977] AC 850, HL. Relief against forfeiture may, however, be given where the vessel is on demise charter. See *The Jotunheim* [2004] EWHC 671. However, due to the unmeritorious conduct of the charterers, relief was not given.

17 [1977] AC 850, HL.

18 *The Brimnes* [1975] QB 929, CA.

19 In *The Li Hai* [2005] EWHC 735 (Comm); [2005] 2 Lloyd's Rep 389, the notice was ineffective as it failed to state that to avoid withdrawal the charterers would have to pay the hire in full within the period specified by the 'anti-technicality' clause. It was also unclear from previous correspondence with the charterers as to what the owners were demanding as the price of avoiding withdrawal.

20 [1983] 1 WLR 195.

21 [2010] EWHC 1663 (Comm); [2011] 1 Lloyd's Rep 350.

involved a calculation of a deduction made in bad faith, but then failed to make that underpayment due to their incompetence. However, the shipowners were not required to give notice under the clause because of the charterers' intention to make a payment that involved a calculation of a deduction that was made in bad faith. For the purposes of assessing the validity of a notice to withdraw, it was held in *The Pamela*[22] that the relevant time is not the time at which the notice was sent but the time at which it was likely to be received by the charterers. Accordingly, a notice by telex sent at 2341 on the Friday on which hire became due was not invalid, because the charterers would not read it until the start of business on the Monday.[23] The decision is distinguishable on its facts from *The Afovos*, where the premature notice was actually received by the charterers before midnight on the day of payment. However, it is inconsistent with the reasoning of the House of Lords in that case to the effect that a valid notice could not be *given* before midnight on the day of payment.[24]

Some charters will allow withdrawal for breaches of charter other than those connected with payment of hire, but the withdrawal provisions may not operate as harshly as in the hire cases. In *The Tropwind* (No 1),[25] the owners withdrew for late payment of an additional insurance premium required to maintain the vessel's war risks cover. The charter allowed withdrawal 'for any other breach of charter', but this was held not to cover delayed payments and to apply only to an unjustified *refusal* to pay. However, this decision was not followed in *The Athos*,[26] where the right to withdraw for 'any breach' was held to crystallise at the moment of breach.

Underpayment – charterers' rights to make an 'equitable' set-off

Hire must not only be paid punctually, it must also be paid in full. *The Chikuma*[27] throws light on what is meant by 'payment in full'. The charterers paid on the due date by an irrevocable transfer to an Italian bank. However, had the owners wanted to get their hands on the money on that date, they would have had to pay up to US$100 bank charges. Therefore, the payment did not amount to a payment in full. The irrevocable transfer was equivalent to an overdraft, not cash.

However, there will be some situations in which the charterer will be justified in making less than a full payment. In contrast with the position relating to freight, charterers may deduct certain counterclaims from hire payments. In *The Nanfri*,[28] the Court of Appeal held that they could invoke the doctrine of equitable set-off to deduct from hire their valid cross-claims, quantified by a reasonable assessment made in good faith, without the necessity of first obtaining the owners' consent.

Not every cross-claim may be deducted from hire. The doctrine of set-off requires a close connection between the primary claim and the cross-claim. Accordingly, the time charterer's claims must arise out of the owner's wrongful deprivation of the charterer's use of the vessel, as this is what hire is paid for. This definition includes claims such as those for speed and consumption.[29] It does not include cargo claims or claims for consequential loss following loss of use of the vessel.[30]

---

22 [1995] 2 Lloyd's Rep 249, QB.
23 The notice was, however, invalid in that it failed to require the charterer to remedy the breach within 48 hours, as required by the 'anti-technicality' clause.
24 This reasoning was applied by the arbitrators in *The Western Triumph* [2002] EWCA Civ 405; [2002] 1 WLR 2397, where the notice of withdrawal had been sent by email before hire became due but, due to some fault in the system, had not entered the charterer's mailbox until after the hire became due.
25 [1977] 1 Lloyd's Rep 397, QB.
26 [1983] 1 Lloyd's Rep 127, CA.
27 [1981] 1 WLR 314, HL.
28 [1978] QB 927.
29 *The Chrysovolandou Dyo* [1981] 1 Lloyd's Rep 159, QB.
30 *The Aditya Vaibhav* [1991] 1 Lloyd's Rep 573, QB. In *The Li Hai* [2005] EWHC 735 (Comm); [2005] 2 Lloyd's Rep 389, charterers were held not to be entitled to set off a claim to be reimbursed for a bunker cancellation fee as this claim did not affect their use of the vessel.

Furthermore, charterers cannot deduct for claims relating to wrongful deprivation of the vessel, which will arise after the hire date.[31]

If the charterers tender a lesser amount of hire on the due date, the shipowners are faced with a dilemma. It may subsequently transpire that the charterers were justified in making their set-offs, in which case any 'withdrawal' by the shipowners will be unjustified and will amount to a repudiation by them of the charter. On the other hand, if they accept the tendered payment, will they be taken to have 'waived' their rights to withdraw?

Some answers are given in *The Mihalios Xilas*,[32] where the charterers' final hire statement showed a lower balance due than the shipowners expected. The charterers had not itemised their deductions. The charterers transferred the amount due under their statement to the shipowners' agents one day before the deadline. The next day, the shipowners received details of the deductions and requested further details within four days, failing which the vessel would be withdrawn. The details were not provided and the vessel was duly withdrawn. Retention of hire was held not to be a waiver, as the shipowners were entitled to a reasonable time before deciding whether or not to withdraw. The charterers' deduction was not made reasonably, and was therefore not justified under the principles of equitable set-off set out in *The Nanfri*.[33] It was not enough that it was made bona fide.

It is quite possible that a charterer will make several deductions from hire, only some of which amount to valid set-offs. This happened in *The Chrysovolandou Dyo*.[34] The charterers validly deducted sums from the final hire statement, which were made up of reasonable estimates of the bunkers likely to be left on redelivery and of their speed claim against the shipowners. However, despite giving an estimated redelivery date of 13 September, their last hire payment on 1 September only covered the period up to 10 September. This underpayment was not a valid set-off, even though the charter allowed the charterers to pay an 'approximate' amount of hire on the last payment. Accordingly, the shipowner was entitled to withdraw on account of the underpayment.

Loss of time under a time charter – 'off-hire'

Delay under a time charter is primarily dealt with by an 'off-hire' clause. Such a clause suspends the running of hire if time is lost in consequence of certain causes set out in the clause. However, the cost of bunkers consumed during an off-hire period will be deductible only if the clause specifically permits the deduction. A charterer, to place the vessel off-hire, must establish three things. First, it must show that the shipowner has been unable to perform the services required of it by the charterer. Secondly, it must show that the inefficiency complained of was caused by an event listed in the off-hire clause. Thirdly, it must then show how much time was lost in consequence of the inefficiency. Whether or not a vessel goes off-hire depends entirely upon the construction of the off-hire clause in question and is not dependent on time being lost due to a breach of charter by the shipowner. It follows that no account is to be taken of exceptions clauses in the shipowner's favour when construing the off-hire clause.[35]

---

31 *The Lutetian* [1982] 2 Lloyd's Rep 140, QB. Bingham J also held that where the vessel is off-hire when an instalment of hire falls due, the charterer's obligation to pay hire is suspended until the vessel goes back on hire. The uncertainty that such a rule is likely to engender means that this part of the decision should be regarded with circumspection. In *The Li Hai* [2005] EWHC 735 (Comm); [2005] 2 Lloyd's Rep 389, charterers were held not to be entitled to make a set-off against hire a period of off-hire for drydocking that was certain to occur after the hire became due.

32 [1979] 1 WLR 1018, HL.

33 [1978] QB 927.

34 [1981] 1 Lloyd's Rep 159, QB.

35 Per Staughton J in *The Ioanna* [1985] 2 Lloyd's Rep 164, 167. See, also, the US decision in *Clyde Commercial SS Co v West India SS Co* 169 F 275 278 (2d Cir 1909), cert denied 214 US 253.

Inefficiency of the vessel

The charterer must first show that it has actually lost time, in that the ship has been prevented from performing a service that is one of the usual incidents of a time charter. This is the effect of words such as 'preventing the full working of the vessel', which appear in cl 15 of the NYPE form, or the reference to 'the service immediately required', in cl 11 of the Baltime form.

In order to assess whether charterers have, in fact, lost time, the court must first decide what constitutes 'full working of the vessel' or a 'service immediately required'. Cleaning of the vessel's holds is one such service, and the charterer cannot put the vessel off-hire by arguing that the holds should not have needed cleaning and that therefore the ship is not able to comply with the charterer's order to load. The Court of Appeal rejected this argument in The Berge Sund[36] and refused to differentiate between ordinary and extraordinary cleaning.[37] A similar result was reached in The Aquacharm.[38] The master had negligently disobeyed the charterer's orders and taken on too much cargo, with the consequence that the vessel had to discharge some cargo into lighters before her draught was at a level to allow her to transit the Panama Canal. Nonetheless, lightening of cargo was a usual incident of a time charter and the charterer was unable to place the vessel off-hire for the period of the lightening. In contrast, in The TS Singapore,[39] the vessel was held not to be performing the service required by the charterers, and remained off-hire, when proceeding to a repair port, even though for part of that voyage the vessel was on the same route as she would have been had she been carrying out the charterers' orders. The vessel left Yokahama on 6 September 2007, under orders to discharge at Shanghai. However, she sustained damage soon after leaving Yokohama and was obliged to remain there until 22 September. The classification society then required her to proceed direct to Hong Kong to discharge the entire cargo, and then to sail to Guangzhou for repairs. On 28 September, charterers cancelled the charterparty pursuant to a clause giving them the right to cancel should the vessel be off-hire for 20 consecutive days. The owners argued that the vessel had not been off-hire 20 consecutive days on 28 September because for one and a half days after leaving Yokohama the vessel was on the common route to Shanghai and Hong Kong and had come back on hire. However, Burton J rejected this argument. The important question to ask was under what instructions the vessel was operating at the relevant time. Even while she was on the common route for Hong Kong and Shanghai, the vessel was not following charterers' instructions to proceed to the discharge port, Shanghai, but, rather, was following the instructions of the classification society.

There has been some divergence in judicial approach as to whether a vessel needs to be *physically* inefficient before the charterer can place it off-hire. A vessel may be physically efficient, yet still incapable of performing the task required by the charterers due to a *legal* prohibition imposed by the local port authorities.

A wide approach was adopted by Lloyd J in The Mastro Georgis,[40] so as to cover delay due to arrest by the receivers of damaged cargo. In contrast, a more restricted approach was adopted by Webster J in The Roachbank,[41] where the delay was due to the vessel being kept outside port, having taken on Vietnamese refugees. This type of delay was held to fall outside the clause, as it was the result of extraneous circumstances. The vessel herself was perfectly capable of performing the services ordered by the charterers, if only the port authorities had been prepared to admit her to port. An example of circumstances that were not extraneous to the vessel is provided by The Apollo,[42] where

---

36 [1993] 2 Lloyd's Rep 453, CA.
37 Any time lost in cleaning the holds could be recovered only if the necessity for hold cleaning could be traced to a breach of charter by the shipowner, which, on the facts, it could not.
38 [1982] 1 WLR 119, CA.
39 [2009] EWHC 933 (Comm); [2009] 2 Lloyd's Rep 54.
40 [1983] 2 Lloyd's Rep 66, QB.
41 [1987] 2 Lloyd's Rep 498.
42 [1978] 1 Lloyd's Rep 200, QB.

the clause was held to cover a period of delay due to fumigation, which was caused by suspected typhus on the vessel.[43] To date, all authority is at first-instance level. In *The Roachbank*,[44] the Court of Appeal declined to endorse either view, merely observing, when upholding the decision of Webster J, that the same decision would have been reached even if the wider approach of Lloyd J had been adopted. Rix J, *obiter*, in *The Laconian Confidence*,[45] has forcefully put the view that the NYPE off-hire clause should not be limited to physical inefficiency, provided that the off-hire event is covered by one of the causes listed in the clause.[46]

Off-hire events

Once the charterer has established that the 'full working of the vessel' has been prevented,[47] it then needs to prove that the delay is due to one of the specific causes listed in the off-hire clause. The burden of proving that a cause listed in the clause has supervened is on the charterer.[48] The cause must be fortuitous and not merely a natural consequence of the charterer's use of the ship. In *The Rijn*,[49] time lost due to an accretion of marine growth during a protracted period of waiting to load a cargo was held not to amount to off-hire. In construing an off-hire clause, the courts will take account of the division of responsibility between owner's matters, relating to the ship, and charterer's matters, relating to their orders as to the vessel's employment. In *The Doric Pride*,[50] the clause provided for hire to be suspended if the vessel was detained by any authority or legal process during the currency of the charter, unless this was caused 'by reason of cargo carried or calling port of trading under this charter'. The vessel was on trip charter from the US Gulf, and the charterers nominated New Orleans. The vessel, as a first-time caller to the USA, was required to be inspected under US anti-terrorist measures. The scheduled inspection was delayed due to a collision between two other vessels in the south-west pass into New Orleans. The time lost was held to fall within the off-hire clause. The reason for detention was a matter for which the ship was responsible – that is, the fact that the vessel was a first caller to a US port. The vessel would have been subject to inspection at whichever US Gulf port the charterer had nominated, so the inspection was not due to the vessel's port of trading.

The NYPE off-hire clause lists the following events:

> ... deficiency of men or stores, fire, breakdown or damages to hull, machinery or equipment, grounding, detention by average accidents to ship or cargo, drydocking for the purpose of examination or painting bottom, or by any other cause preventing the full working of the vessel ...

We shall now consider some of these events in more detail.

---

43 So, too, in *The Bridgestone Maru (No 3)* [1985] 2 Lloyd's Rep 62, QB, where a vessel went off-hire when detained by port authorities acting reasonably and properly pursuant to their suspicions as to the vessel's physical inefficiency.

44 [1988] 2 Lloyd's Rep 337.

45 [1997] 1 Lloyd's Rep 139.

46 See, also, Davies, M, 'The off-hire clause in the New York Produce Exchange time charterparty' (1990) LMCLQ 107, where the author argues that the problem with the NYPE clause is not so much the specific off-hire events that it contains, but rather the phrase 'preventing the full working of the vessel'.

47 There will be no element of prevention of the charterer from making use of the vessel against its will when the charterer agrees to the vessel being taken temporarily out of service for use by the shipowner, as was the case in *The Fu Ning Hai* [2006] EWHC 3250 (Comm); [2007] 2 Lloyd's Rep 223. Accordingly, the charterer could not cancel pursuant to a clause giving it an option to cancel if the vessel had been off-hire for a period of more than 30 days.

48 *Royal Greek Government v Minister of Transport* (1948) 82 Ll L Rep 196 at 199 per Bucknill LJ, and from *The Doric Pride* [2006] EWCA Civ 599; [2007] 2 CLC 1042 at 1050 per Rix LJ.

49 [1981] 2 Lloyd's Rep 267, QB.

50 [2006] EWCA Civ 599; [2006] 2 Lloyd's Rep 175.

Detention by average accidents to ship or cargo

This cause focuses on the vessel's ability to work. In *The Mareva AS*,[51] there was a 15-day delay in discharge, due to wet damage to cargo during the voyage. This cause was not within the clause as the *vessel* could still perform every service required of her. In *The Saldanha*,[52] Gross J held that time lost due to the detention of the vessel by Somali pirates was not 'detention by average accidents to ship or cargo', as detention by pirates could not naturally be described as an 'accident'. It was not 'default and/or deficiency of men', as 'default of men' did not include a failure to take recognised anti-piracy precautions and did not extend to the negligent or inadvertent failure to perform the duties of the master and crew. Rather, there would have to be a refusal by the master and crew to perform their duties. Nor did it fall under 'any other cause', as piracy was not *ejusdem generis*.

Any other cause preventing the full working of the vessel

In *The Laconian Confidence*,[53] these words were held to be subject to the *ejusdem generis* principle of construction. The vessel had been detained for 18 days by the port authorities in Chittagong because of the presence remaining on board of residue sweepings. However, this delay could not be related back to 'detention or average accidents to ship or cargo' and the vessel did not go off-hire. The rule will be excluded by the addition of the word 'whatsoever', in which case the vessel will go off-hire for any period during which her full working is prevented.[54] In most charters, the inclusion of this word will be essential if the charterer is to have any prospect of success in placing the vessel off-hire for non-physical inefficiency. This is because the events listed in most off-hire clauses are all examples of *physical* inefficiency of the vessel.

Time deductible following an off-hire event

The time deductible in consequence of an off-hire event will depend on the wording of the off-hire clause. There are two principal types of clause: the 'period' and the 'net' clause.

'Period' clauses

These start the interruption of hire with a specific event and end it with another. In *Hogarth v Alexander Miller Bros & Co*,[55] the vessel went off-hire due to an engine breakdown, which required the vessel to be towed into the discharge port. Once there, she was once again 'in an efficient state to resume her service' and hire restarted. The engine breakdown had no effect on the vessel's ability to discharge once she had got to the discharge port.

'Net' clauses

An example of such a clause is to be found in the NYPE form, the off-hire clause of which reads 'payment of hire shall cease for the time *thereby lost*', and the Baltime form, which has '*any time lost thereby*'. The clause will operate quite differently when time is lost due to partial inefficiency of the vessel. A 'period' clause gives partial inefficiency the effect of total inefficiency, whereas under a 'net' clause the vessel is only off-hire to the extent time is actually lost by partial inefficiency. Thus, in *Hogarth v Alexander Miller Bros & Co*,[56] no allowance was made for the assistance given to the tow by the vessel's own low-pressure engine and the whole period during which the vessel was under tow counted as off-hire.

---

51 [1977] 1 Lloyd's Rep 368, QB.
52 [2010] EWHC 1340; [2011] 1 Lloyd's Rep 187.
53 [1997] 1 Lloyd's Rep 139.
54 *The Apollo* [1978] 1 Lloyd's Rep 200, QB; *The Mastro Georgis* [1983] 2 Lloyd's Rep 66, QB.
55 [1891] AC 48, HL.
56 Ibid.

The different effect of the two clauses is well illustrated by *The HR Macmillan*.[57] Time was lost due to crane breakdowns in three of the Munck gantry cranes on the vessel. The charter contained five separate off-hire clauses. The relevant ones were cl 15, the standard NYPE off-hire clause, and cl 38, which applied to periods of 'inefficiency' due to 'breakdowns' of the cranes. Cranes 2 and 3 were deliberately taken out of commission for examination. This did not count as a 'breakdown' and was therefore governed by cl 15. The relevant test for this clause was to ask how much earlier the vessel would have finished loading or discharging had these cranes been available throughout these operations. In practice, it may be quite difficult to compute this period.

In contrast, crane 1 did suffer a 'breakdown', and time lost was governed by cl 38, operating a 'period' clause. To find the appropriate period of off-hire, one simply adds up the number of days for which the crane was out of action and divides by a third. Off-hire was not suspended during periods when the vessel should have been loading or discharging but would not have been able to do so due to rain or strikes.[58] However, the vessel would not be off-hire when engaged on a service, such as shifting between berths, in which the use of cranes was not required. In such a situation, the vessel would be performing a service that was a usual incident of a time charter and would not, therefore, be 'inefficient'.

However, under both a 'net' and a 'period' clause, once the vessel is again fully efficient, hire resumes. The 'but for' calculation required under a 'net' clause ceases with the resumption of the physical efficiency of the vessel. Consequential loss of time will not be covered by the clause. Thus, in *The Marika M*,[59] the vessel was due to berth on 18 July. She grounded on 17 July and refloated on 27 July, but was not able to proceed to berth until 6 August. The delay between 27 July and 6 August was held to fall outside the 'net' off-hire clause.[60] In calculating how much time has been lost as a result of the vessel's inability to perform the service required by the charterer, account is not to be taken of events after the end of the off-hire event. In *The Athena*,[61] the Court of Appeal held that the enquiry into what time has been lost pursuant to the NYPE off-hire clause relates to the service immediately required of the vessel and it is not relevant that time would have been lost for other reasons at another stage in the charterparty. The vessel was ordered to discharge in Libya and to proceed to the roads off Benghazi. However, the owners instructed the master to wait in international waters outside Libya where the vessel drifted for 10.9 days until proceeding to Benghazi. The arbitrators held that had the vessel proceeded directly to Benghazi it would not have berthed any earlier than it did but found that the vessel was off-hire for the 10.9 days. This finding was overruled at first instance but the arbitrator's finding was reinstated by the Court of Appeal. The net off-hire clause in cl 15 of NYPE was concerned with the service immediately required of the vessel, and not with the chartered service as a whole or the entire maritime adventure. The Court of Appeal rejected the approach adoped by Tuckey J in *The Ira*,[62] in which he had taken account of events occurring after the end of the off-hire event in determining whether any time had been lost.[63] It must be possible at the conclusion of the off-hire event to determine what net time has been lost in consequence of the event and therefore regard should not be had to events occurring after the end of the off-hire event.

---

57 [1974] 1 Lloyd's Rep 311, CA.
58 These periods would have to be taken into account for the purpose of making a calculation of 'time lost thereby' under a 'net' clause.
59 [1981] 2 Lloyd's Rep 622, QB.
60 Excluding time lost due to extraneous factors is consistent with the constructional approach adopted in *The Roachbank* [1988] 2 Lloyd's Rep 337, CA, to the issue of non-physical inefficiency.
61 [2013] EWCA Civ 1723.
62 [1995] 1 Lloyd's Rep 103, QB.
63 After discharging in Ravenna, the vessel had been ordered to drydock in Piraeus, pursuant to cl. 21 of the charterparty, and on conclusion of the drydocking, the vessel was ordered to load at a port in the Black Sea. Tuckey J had held that the time spent proceeding from Ravenna to Piraeus was not 'lost' so as to put the vessel off-hire under cl 15 of the NYPE charter because Piraeus was only slightly off the direct route from Ravenna to the Black Sea loading port. However, the decision was correct because the vessel had not been performing the service required by the charterers when proceeding from Ravenna to Piraeus for drydocking.

Other remedies for delay

An off-hire clause does not exclude the operation of a charterer's ordinary rights to sue a ship-owner for damages due to breach of contract. Therefore, delay outside the clause may still be recoverable if it is not too remote a consequence of a breach by the shipowner.[64] However, the breach may often be covered by an exception clause, as in *The Aquacharm*[65] and *The Marika M*.[66] In particular, where there is a clause paramount, many instances in which delay occurs due to deficiencies in the ship or its equipment will fall within Art IV(2)(a) or its equivalent, unless the charterer can prove that the deficiency constituted a breach of Art III(1). Article IV(2)(a) will also protect the ship-owner where time is lost due to the master's negligence in carrying out the charterer's orders as to the vessel's employment.[67] However, it will not cover a situation in which the master simply refuses to follow such orders, unless the master's conduct can be objectively justified by reference to the safety of the vessel and the crew.[68]

Conversely, if the vessel goes off-hire as a result of a breach by the charterer, the shipowner will either be able to recover the lost hire by way of damages or to argue that hire was never suspended in the first place.[69] If hire is lost as a result of the need to re-stow deck cargo, the shipowner will need to prove a breach of some charter provision if hire is to be recovered from the charterer by way of damages. The mere existence of a clause that deck cargo is to be carried at charterer's or shipper's risk will not give rise to such a right, nor will the shipowner be able to recover the lost hire by way of indemnity.[70]

Redelivery

A time charter starts with the delivery of the vessel to the charterer and ends with its redelivery to the shipowner after the expiry of the period of time specified by the charter. What happens if the vessel is redelivered after this time? One suggestion is that charter hire ceases to be payable during the period of overshoot and is replaced by an obligation to pay hire on the basis of the current market rate.[71] This will suit the shipowner if the current market rate exceeds the charter rate, but will disadvantage it if the market rate has fallen below the charter rate.

For this reason, the suggestion was rejected by the House of Lords in *The London Explorer*.[72] Hire continued to be payable at the charter rate until the actual time of redelivery. However, if the current market rate exceeds the charter rate, the shipowner may be able to claim the difference between the two rates for the overshoot period as damages for the late redelivery of the vessel. The view of the majority was that this liability occurred simply by reason of the late redelivery of the vessel. Lords Reid and Cross, however, were of the view that the charterer would be liable only if, at the time that the charterer had given its order for the final voyage under the charter, there had been no reasonable prospect of its being completed before the redelivery deadline set in the charter.

---

64 In this connection, see the discussion in Chapter 11, pp 237–8, concerning interruption of demurrage due to delay caused by breach of the shipowner, and the general discussion of remoteness in Chapter 13.
65 [1982] 1 WLR 119, CA.
66 [1981] 2 Lloyd's Rep 622, QB.
67 *The Aquacharm* [1982] 1 WLR 119, CA.
68 *The Hill Harmony* [2000] 3 WLR 1954, HL.
69 *Lensen Shipping Ltd v Anglo-Soviet Co* (1935) 52 Ll L Rep 141, CA.
70 *The Darya Tara* [1997] 1 Lloyd's Rep 42, QB.
71 The shipowner may also seek to recover any damages it has to pay out to a new charterer by reason of late delivery consequent upon late redelivery under the old charter. However, such an action might fail on the grounds that the liability incurred to the new charterer is too remote.
72 [1972] AC 1.

For many years, it was widely thought, following the minority in *The London Explorer*, that the charterer's only obligation was to give orders for a 'legitimate' last voyage. The Court of Appeal decisively rejected this approach in *The Peonia*.[73] The issue arose in the context of the construction of an exceptions clause. The charterers argued that the clause could only have any meaning if it covered late redelivery pursuant to an 'illegitimate' last order. This was because, on the view of the minority in *The London Explorer*, they were already protected by any late redelivery due to unexpected circumstances following the giving of orders for a 'legitimate' last voyage. However, the Court of Appeal followed the majority view in *The London Explorer* and rejected this argument. Once it was accepted that there were two redelivery obligations on the charterers, the clause was needed to protect them in the event of late redelivery on a 'legitimate' last voyage. These were a duty to give 'legitimate' last orders and a duty not to redeliver late.[74]

Consequently, a charterer may be in breach of the second duty, even if it is not in breach of the first, if, for example, the last voyage is delayed due to unforeseen circumstances. In *The Paragon*,[75] the charterers gave illegitimate orders for the last voyage which the shipowners had executed. The shipowners argued that the giving of the illegitimate orders had constituted a repudiatory breach that brought the charter to an end and that, therefore, they should be compensated on a *quantum meruit* basis for the performance of the illegitimate final voyage. The Court of Appeal held that the obligation to give legitimate orders for the last voyage was not a condition and if illegitimate orders were given the shipowners would be entitled to decline to perform them. If the shipowners agreed to perform the voyage, the charterparty remained in force and their remedy would lie in damages on the usual basis for the period of the overshoot.

If circumstances do change between the giving of the orders and their coming to be acted upon, the charterers must give fresh orders. Failure to do so was held by the House of Lords in *The Gregos*[76] to amount to an anticipatory breach, giving the shipowner the option to terminate the charter. If the shipowner opts to continue the charter and to obey the order, it will not be taken to have waived its right to damages for late redelivery.

A shipowner claiming damages for late redelivery will always need to identify the precise charter deadline. The charter may have an express margin, for example, 'redelivery 1 January plus or minus 15 days at charterer's option'. In the absence of an express margin, a 'reasonable margin' will be implied, unless the charter is worded so as to exclude any implied margin. If the charter does contain an express margin, no further margin will be implied.[77] Some charters may give the charterer the option, in effect, to order the vessel to perform an 'illegitimate' last voyage. This was the effect of the clause in *The World Symphony and The World Renown*,[78] where particular significance was attached to the description in the clause of the period of overrun as 'extended time'. In contrast, in *The Black Falcon*,[79] the words 'charterers having option to complete last round voyage under performance prior to delivery . . .' were held to protect the charterers only in the event of delays on a legitimate last voyage.

The measure of damages to be awarded in respect of a late redelivery was considered by the House of Lords in *The Achilleas*.[80] The shipowner suffered an unusual loss in that market rates had risen substantially by the time that the vessel should have been redelivered, but had then fallen back

73 [1991] 1 Lloyd's Rep 100, CA, noted (1991) LMCLQ 173.
74 Where the minimum and maximum periods specified in a 'trip' charter are expressed to be 'without guarantee', the charterer will not be liable simply because it redelivers outside those parameters. For it to be liable, the shipowner must also prove that, at the time that the charter was signed, the charterer had no reasonable expectation of being able to deliver within those parameters. *The Lendoudis Evangelos II* [1997] 1 Lloyd's Rep 404.
75 [2009] EWCA Civ 855; [2009] 2 Lloyd's Rep 688.
76 [1994] 1 WLR 1465.
77 *The Dione* [1975] 1 Lloyd's Rep 115, CA.
78 [1992] 2 Lloyd's Rep 115, CA.
79 [1991] 1 Lloyd's Rep 77, QB.
80 [2006] EWHC 3030 (Comm); [2007] 1 Lloyd's Rep 19; [2007] EWCA Civ 901; [2007] 2 Lloyd's Rep 555.

somewhat by the time that the vessel was actually redelivered. The shipowner had to renegotiate the follow-on charter at a lower hire rate to avoid cancellation. At first instance, and before the Court of Appeal, damages were awarded on the basis of the difference between the agreed rate and the lower rate for the whole period of the charter, and not just the difference between the market rate and the hire rate under the old charter for the period of the overshoot. The type of loss was within the contemplation of the parties and was recoverable in full, notwithstanding that the quantum of the loss was not such that could have been expected at the time of the contract. The decision, however, was reversed by the House of Lords.[81] The decision was unanimous, but their Lordships adopted a variety of approaches to reach this conclusion. As a result, it is now clear that damages for late redelivery will be assessed at the market rate for the period of overrun. Any clause in the charterparty that provides for compensation at a higher rate will be regarded as a penalty and have no effect.[82]

The charterer will also be liable in damages if it redelivers prematurely,[83] or if it fails to redeliver the vessel in the same good order and condition as on redelivery.[84] It will also be liable in damages if it redelivers the vessel outside the geographical range specified for redelivery. Damages will be based on the hire that the vessel would have earned had redelivery been made within the permitted geographical range. In making this calculation, the court will assume a notional voyage in ballast from the place of actual redelivery to the nearest safe port at which redelivery could legitimately have taken place.[85] Any profit actually earned by the shipowner during the period of this notional voyage must be deducted from the additional hire payable by the charterer.

---

81 [2008] UKHL 48; [2008] 2 Lloyd's Rep 275. See Foxton, D, 'Damages for late or early redelivery under time charterparties' [2008] LMCLQ 461.
82 *The Paragon* [2009] EWCA Civ 855; [2009] 2 Lloyd's Rep 688.
83 Premature redelivery by the charterer will constitute a repudiatory breach and the shipowner may elect to keep the charter alive and claim hire until the end of the charter, provided it has a legitimate interest in doing so. *The Alaskan Trader* (No 2) [1983] 2 Lloyd's Rep 645, QB.
84 *The Puerto Buitrago* [1976] 1 Lloyd's Rep 250, CA. The Court of Appeal held that the shipowners were not entitled to refuse to accept the redelivery, keeping the vessel on hire, until the charterers had effected the repairs.
85 *The Rijn* [1981] 2 Lloyd's Rep 267, QB.

Chapter 13

Damages and Frustration

Chapter Contents

Damages

Once the claimant has established that its loss resulted from a breach of contract by the defendant, the amount of damages that will be recoverable will be assessed by reference to the general principles of causation and remoteness applicable to claims in tort and contract. The same principles will apply, irrespective of whether the claim is made under a charterparty or a bill of lading, although the factual contexts may differ.

Tort and contract compared

Losses suffered by the claimant will be recoverable only if they satisfy the relevant tests of causation and remoteness. These differ, depending on whether the action is brought in contract or in tort.

If the action is brought in tort, the relevant question of causation is: 'What would have happened if there had been no breach of duty?' The relevant question of remoteness is: 'Which of those consequences were reasonably foreseeable *at the time of breach?*'

If the action is brought in contract, the two questions are posed in significantly different ways. The causation question now becomes, 'What would be the position if this contract had been performed?' and the remoteness question, 'Which of those consequences would have seemed *not unlikely* to a reasonable man with the knowledge of the contract breaker *at the date of the contract?*'

Therefore, different limits govern the direct consequences of the breach that may be recoverable in damages, depending on whether the action is brought in tort or in contract. The reason for the different tests of remoteness was said, in *The Heron II*,[1] to be that with contracts, but not torts, the parties have the opportunity to anticipate certain breaches and can estimate in advance the damage that they will cause. This enables the parties to negotiate contractual terms to cover such situations. This advance planning is not possible with torts such as negligence, hence the need for a wider range of direct consequences to be recoverable by way of damages.

Another important difference between contract and tort is that the **Law Reform (Contributory Negligence) Act 1945** only applies to tort, unless the breach of contract would give rise to a duty of care in tort, independent of the existence of the contract.[2] Therefore, if loss under a contract is caused by a combination of breaches by both parties, there is no possibility of apportioning the loss. The court will have to decide which of the two breaches was the proximate cause of the loss and then attach the totality of that loss to that breach.[3] There is also the possibility that the chain of causation leading from a breach may be broken by the subsequent act of the party not in breach, even if that act is not itself a breach.[4] In particular, if an innocent party fails to mitigate its loss, some or all of its loss may be attributed not to the breach, but to its unreasonable reaction to it.

When the same act gives rise both to a breach of duty in tort and a breach of contract, the contractual remedy prevails and the recovery in tort will be limited with reference to exclusion and limitation clauses in the contract.[5] However, an action in tort will be governed by tortious principles as to the recovery of damage.

The parties may include a clause that defines the amount payable in the event of a breach of charter. Such a clause will be valid if it is a genuine pre-estimate of the likely amount of damages,

---

1 [1969] 1 AC 350, HL.
2 *Forsikringsaktieselskapet Vesta v Butcher* [1989] AC 852, HL. However, where pure economic loss is being claimed, there will usually be no duty of care in negligence independent of that owed under the contract.
3 Where the shipowner's breach is a breach of its warranty of seaworthiness, it is likely that the loss will be attributed to the shipowner provided its breach is an effective cause of the loss, even though it may not be the dominant cause. See *The Kapitan Sakharov* [2000] 2 Lloyd's Rep 255, CA.
4 See the discussion of *novus actus interveniens* in *The Eastern City* [1958] 2 Lloyd's Rep 127, CA, in the context of claims for breach of the safe port warranty.
5 *Pyrene Co Ltd v Scindia Navigation Co Ltd* [1954] 2 QB 402; *Tai Hing Cotton Mill Ltd v Liu Chong Hing Bank* [1986] AC 80, PC.

as is the case with demurrage clauses. However, if this is not the case, the clause will be invalid as a penalty clause. In *The Paragon*,[6] the Court of Appeal held that a clause providing that the hire rate would be the market rate for the last 30 days of charter until redelivery if the charterers redelivered later than the final terminal date was a penalty and unenforceable. The legal measure of damages must apply, which for an illegitimate last voyage was the charter rate until the final terminal date and thereafter the market rate, as per *The Achilleas*.

Contractual measure of damages

The rule for remoteness of damages in contract was set out in *Hadley v Baxendale*.[7] Recovery is possible in respect of two sets of direct consequences of the breach of contract. First, there are those consequences of which a 'reasonable man' would have had knowledge at the time the contract was made. Secondly, there are those consequences of which the defaulting party had actual knowledge at the time that the contract was made. After *Victoria Laundry (Windsor) Ltd v Newman Industries Ltd*,[8] these may be better looked at as two aspects of the same test.

Regarding the first set of consequences, the House of Lords in *The Heron II*[9] disliked the use of 'reasonably foreseeable' in *Victoria Laundry* in that it failed to differentiate the rules of remoteness in contract from those of tort. Various alternative formulations were proposed, perhaps the most helpful being 'not unlikely', put forward by Lord Reid. Accordingly, recovery will be possible in tort, but not in contract, in respect of consequences that are foreseeable, but that occur only in a small number of cases.

Applying the contractual rules on remoteness to cargo claims

Cargo claims arising from breach of contracts of carriage may arise from non-delivery, damaged delivery, late delivery, or a combination of any of these factors. How the loss is felt will depend on how the claimant intends to use the goods. The claimant will either want to resell them or to use them for its own purposes. We shall now consider how the rules on remoteness of damage apply to these two different situations.

Claimant resells the goods

There are two usual ways of assessing a cargo claim: one is by reference to the invoice value of the goods; the other is by reference to their sound arrived value at the date on which they should have been delivered at the discharge port.[10] The latter will usually be the correct measure, although each case depends on its particular facts. In *The Heron II*,[11] the cargo owner succeeded in its claim for damages resulting from the fall in the market value of sugar between the time at which the cargo should have been delivered at Basra and the time of its actual (late) delivery. On the facts, it was 'not unlikely' that it would sell the sugar at Basra where there was a market in sugar. In most cases, the claimant will be able to satisfy this burden. However, it will be relieved of the burden altogether where the claim is subject to the Hague-Visby Rules, as Art IV(5)(b) expressly provides for damages to be assessed by reference to the sound arrived value of the goods at the port of discharge.

---

6 [2009] EWCA Civ 855; [2009] 2 Lloyd's Rep 688.
7 (1854) 9 Ex D 341.
8 [1949] 2 KB 528, CA, especially 536–7.
9 [1969] 1 AC 350, HL.
10 Whichever basis is used, the salvage value of the cargo must always be deducted in quantifying a claim for damage to cargo.
11 [1969] 1 AC 350, HL; not following, on this point, *The Parana* (1877) 2 PD 118, CA.

Damages will not usually be assessed by reference to any sub-sales that the claimant may have made, unless the defendant has actual knowledge of these at the time that the contract is concluded. Sub-sales may become relevant as evidence of market value where there is no market for the goods in question at the discharge port. However, a sub-sale will not constitute such evidence if it is concluded substantially before the time at which the goods were or ought to have been delivered.[12]

Claimant uses the goods itself

The courts have generally been more willing to impute knowledge of the intended use of the goods by the claimant to sellers than to carriers. In *Hadley v Baxendale*,[13] the land carrier had no imputed knowledge as to the critical nature of the mill shaft to the defendant's factory. In contrast, the seller in *Victoria Laundry (Windsor) Ltd v Newman Industries Ltd*[14] was taken to know that the buyer would use the boilers in their laundry business and was liable for loss of usual profits on its regular contracts, although not for the loss of particularly lucrative ones.

If the carrier has no imputed knowledge of the intended use by the cargo owner of the goods, then damages for delay will be limited to interest on the value of the goods. In *British Columbia Saw-Mill Co Ltd v Nettleship*,[15] a box of a cargo of machinery for a new mill was lost and the acquisition of replacement parts caused a lengthy delay. Damages were calculated on the basis of interest for the period of delay calculated on the cost to the shipper of the replacements for the missing parts.

In calculating damages on a replacement cost basis, regard must be had to the way in which the claimant actually intends to use the goods. In *The Alecos M*,[16] a second-hand vessel was sold without a spare propeller. At first instance, damages were assessed on the basis of replacement value, even though the plaintiff never intended to acquire a replacement. The Court of Appeal overruled this assessment and held that the appropriate measure was the scrap value of the undelivered propeller.[17]

Following *The Heron II*, the distinction between sale and carriage contracts is less significant as regards recovery for loss of profit than used to be the case. Such damages are no longer inherently too remote to be recovered in actions arising out of delay in the performance of carriage contracts. In *The Pegase*,[18] due to a delay in the delivery of raw materials, a processing plant lost profits on sales, lost goodwill and incurred expenses in buying in substitute material.[19] The particular circumstances of the plaintiff were such that it had very low stocks of the raw material, so had to buy in replacements at an earlier stage than would usually be expected. The replacement goods had to be purchased from competitors at a high price. All of these items of loss were peculiar to the special circumstances surrounding the plaintiff's business. As the carrier had no actual knowledge of these circumstances, these consequential losses were irrecoverable. However, Goff J went on to express the view that 'no doubt the [carriers] could, on their knowledge at the time of making the contract, reasonably have contemplated as not unlikely that . . . the receivers, would, after a delay so great . . . lose some resale profits'.[20]

One must also distinguish between the kind of damage and its quantum. The latter does not have to have been in the guilty party's contemplation at the time of the contract. *Wroth v Tyler*[21] involved loss to a house purchaser due to the vendor's refusal to complete. Damages due to a rising

---

12 *The Arpad* [1934] P 189.
13 (1854) 9 Ex D 341.
14 [1949] 2 KB 528.
15 (1868) LR 3 CP 499.
16 [1990] 1 Lloyd's Rep 82, QB; rev'd [1991] 1 Lloyd's Rep 120, CA.
17 The House of Lords in *Ruxley Electronics v Forsyth* [1995] 3 WLR 118, noted McMeel, G (1995) LMCLQ 456, adopted the same approach to damages based on 'cost of cure'.
18 [1981] 1 Lloyd's Rep 175.
19 The defendant conceded that it would be liable on the basis of interest on the invoice value of the goods.
20 [1981] 1 Lloyd's Rep 175, 186.
21 [1974] Ch 30.

property market were the kind of damages within the purchaser's contemplation when contracts were exchanged. However, the *extent* of the market rise could not have been contemplated. Nonetheless, the defaulting vendor was liable for the purchaser's loss in full. In cases like *Victoria Laundry* and *The Pegase*, the actual losses suffered, and not recovered, must be regarded not as part of the quantum of one kind of loss – namely, profits – but as a separate kind of loss, namely, *exceptional* profits, or losses, as in *The Pegase*.

These principles now need to be reviewed in the light of the decision of the House of Lords in *The Achilleas*.[22] Their Lordships unanimously held that a shipowner whose time-chartered vessel had been redelivered late could not claim the losses that they had suffered on the follow-on fixture, but were limited to damages based on the difference between the market rate at the time of redelivery and the hire rate, for the period by which the charterers overshot the contractual date of redelivery. Their Lordships adopted a variety of approaches to reach this result. Lords Hoffmann and Hope based their decision on the ground that *Hadley v Baxendale* required account to be taken of the type of liability that the parties could be said to have undertaken. Here, it was commonly assumed in the shipping industry that late redelivery would sound only in damages for the difference between hire and the market rate for the period of overshoot. Lord Hoffmann made the analogy with the assumption of risk in tort cases such as *Banque Bruxelles Lambert SA v Eagle Star Insurance Co Ltd (sub nom South Australia Asset Management Corpn v York Montague Ltd)*.[23] Lord Hope stressed the need for the parties to have information about potential liabilities before them so as to enable them to provide for that in the contract. The loss here was due to how the shipowner had dealt with the follow-on charterer and this was completely unpredictable and went beyond mere market fluctuations. This approach adds a completely new element into the process of calculating what damages may be awarded for breach of contract – that is, the type of liability that the parties could be taken to have undertaken under their contract.

Lord Rodger of Earlsferry based his decision on the more orthodox ground that this type of loss was not within the contemplation of the parties. The parties would contemplate that although the shipowners might lose a fixture due to late redelivery, market availability of substitute fixtures would protect them. There might, however, be some scope for awarding a general sum for loss of business where the late redelivery of a particular vessel in a particular area at a particular time might mean that there was a poor market for its services. However, even this approach is at odds with the existing law in that the *type* of loss in issue, loss of a follow-on fixture, clearly was within the contemplation of the parties. What was not within their contemplation was the extent of such loss, due to unforeseeable market fluctuations at the end of the charter. However, previous authority is clearly to the effect that a loss that is within the parties' contemplation is recoverable in full, notwithstanding that the *extent* of the loss is unusually large.[24]

Lord Walker held that the charterer had not contracted on the basis that they would be liable for any loss, however large, caused by late redelivery where the charterer had no knowledge or control over the shipowner's forward fixture. Baroness Hale, along with Lord Hope, had initially been inclined to uphold the judgment of the lower courts. She preferred Lord Rodger's solution. The parties had not contemplated this particular type of loss. The loss was caused by extreme market volatility. This type of loss could not be said to be 'not unlikely', in contrast to that caused by missing a fixture. She did not take the approach adopted by Lords Hoffmann and Lord Hope of determining whether the contemplation of the parties had encompassed the particular type of liability for which the claim was being made. This would introduce a new element into the *Hadley v Baxendale* analysis, by importing into contract law the principles seen in tort law in the context of liability for professional negligence. Baroness Hale's views mean that the majority *ratio* of the

---

22 [2008] UKHL 48; [2008] 2 Lloyd's Rep 275, noted [2008] JIML 295.
23 [1997] AC 191.
24 *Christopher Hill Ltd v Ashington Piggeries Ltd* [1969] 2 Lloyd's Rep 425; *Brown v KMR Services* [1995] 2 Lloyd's Rep 513.

decision is that the loss was not recoverable because it was not of the type that was within the contemplation of the parties at the date of the conclusion of the contract.

Their Lordships' decision has since been considered in two decisions. In *The Amer Energy*,[25] arbitrators awarded charterers over US$750,000 damages for the shipowner's breach of charter in arriving at the load port after the expiry of the laycan dates.[26] The shipowners appealed on the grounds that the tribunal had failed to consider the opinions in *The Achilleas* which had been delivered after the hearing but before the award was issued. The shipowners' application was rejected. Flaux J held that the House of Lords had not intended to lay down some completely new test as to recoverability of damages in contract and remoteness different from the existing rule and the tribunal had correctly applied the law as to remoteness of damage. A similar approach was manifested in *The Sylvia*,[27] where the charterers were able to claim damages for loss of a fixture caused by the shipowners' failure to exercise due diligence in repairing holds as ordered by the port state. The loss was foreseeable and fell under the first limb of *Hadley v Baxendale*. Hamblen J held that the decision in *The Achilleas* had not provided a new generally applicable legal test of remoteness in damages. The test in *The Achilleas* should be applied only in exceptional circumstances, and in most cases it would not be necessary specifically to address the issue of assumption of responsibility which was the broader approach adopted in *The Achilleas* to the issue of remoteness of damage. However, in unusual cases, such as *The Achilleas* itself, the context, surrounding circumstances or general understanding in the relevant market might make it necessary specifically to consider whether there had been an assumption of responsibility. That would be most likely to be where the application of the general test in *Hadley v Baxendale* might lead to an unquantifiable, unpredictable, uncontrollable or disproportionate liability or where there was clear evidence that such a liability would be contrary to market understanding and expectations.

The Hague and Hague-Visby Rules

The Hague Rules contained no provision on valuation, but Art IV(5)(b) of the Hague-Visby Rules provides:

> The total amount recoverable shall be calculated by reference to the value of the said goods at the place and time at which the goods are discharged from the ship in accordance with the contract or should have been so discharged. The value of the goods shall be fixed according to the commodity exchange price, or, if there be no such price, according to the current market price, or if there be no commodity exchange price or current market price, by reference to the normal value of goods of the same kind and quality.

This provision could be interpreted as covering all claims for breach of the Hague-Visby obligations, in which case it would exclude recovery of claims for consequential loss. However, in *The Subro Valour*,[28] damages were awarded in respect of such losses incurred under a bill of lading that was subject to the Hague-Visby Rules, although no point was taken on the application of this Article. The loss in question was loss due to fluctuation in EC subsidies on the cargo during the period of delay and this was held to be within the imputed knowledge of the carrier. A similar result occurred in *The Ardennes*,[29] which was, of course, not a Hague-Visby case, where a claim was successfully made in respect of additional import duty that had become payable on the goods during the period of delay.

---

25 [2009] 1 Lloyd's Rep 293.
26 A laycan clause in a voyage charter specifies the time at which laytime can start and the date at which the charterer can cancel the charter if the vessel is not ready.
27 [2010] EWHC 542 (Comm); [2010] 2 Lloyd's Rep 81.
28 [1995] 1 Lloyd's Rep 509, QB.
29 [1951] 1 KB 55, KB.

Charterparty claims and damages

Similar principles govern the recovery of damages for breach of charter. They will be particularly relevant in deciding which consequences of delay by a shipowner can be attributed to its breach of contract. For example, in *Monarch SS Co Ltd v A/B Karlshamns Oljefabriker*,[30] in the summer of 1939, the voyage was delayed by unseaworthiness. As a consequence of this delay, the shipowner was unable to deliver at the contractual port. By then, the Second World War had broken out and the British government ordered the vessel to discharge at a British port. This was held to be a consequence of the shipowner's breach of its warranty of seaworthiness and therefore precluded it from arguing that the contract had been frustrated. The relevant factor was that, at the time that the contract was made, the outbreak of world war was something that the shipowner could reasonably have anticipated.[31]

The manner in which claims for repudiation of a voyage charter are calculated is illustrated by *The Concordia C*.[32] The claim will generally be based on the difference between the anticipated profit under the repudiated charter and the actual profit under the replacement charter for the prospective duration of the old charter.[33] Where a time charter is repudiated, damages are based on the difference between the charter rate and the market rate for the unexpired residue of the repudiated charter. If a market rate cannot be ascertained, then account will be taken of actual earnings made during this period. No account will be taken of the market rate if a market subsequently re-emerges in the period of the unexpired residue of the time charter.[34]

In some circumstances, account must be taken of events occurring after the notional termination date of the old charter. In *The Noel Bay*,[35] Staughton LJ noted:

> But one problem that almost invariably arises, and does in this case, is that the substitute voyage lasts for longer than the voyage under the original charter-party. The solution commonly adopted is to take a proportion of the profits on the substitute voyage to set off against the profits lost on the original voyage; otherwise one would be involved in calculations to the end of the ship's working life. Another problem is that the vessel may have been better – or worse – placed for future employment at the end of one voyage than at the end of the other.

In *The Elbrus*,[36] the charterers wrongfully terminated a time charterparty, and but for the repudiation, the vessel would have been redelivered at Houston 39 days later on 13 May. As there was no available market for the vessel at the place of repudiation, off the coast of West Africa, the owners decided to sail her to Portugal in order to prepare her for the next fixture and the vessel commenced employment under the subsequent charter on 6 May, earning a higher rate of hire than under the charter at issue. In calculating what the owners had lost as a result of the repudiation, it was legitimate to take into account benefits they had received as a result of the repudiation, and account could be taken of benefits arising after the notional date of redelivery, such as earning a higher rate of hire earlier than would otherwise have been the case. In doing so, the arbitrators had compared what the owners would have earned had the vessel not been repudiated and what they actually

30 [1949] AC 196, HL.
31 See, also, the discussion of this issue at pp 234–5, in the context of interruptions to demurrage due to delays caused by breach of contract by the shipowner.
32 [1985] 2 Lloyd's Rep 55.
33 But not where the state of the freight market, combined with the unseaworthiness of the vessel on redelivery, make it reasonable for the shipowner not to seek an alternative fixture, but to lay the vessel up instead and attempt to sell her. See *The Griparion* (No 2) [1994] 1 Lloyd's Rep 533, QB.
34 *Glory Wealth Shipping Pte Ltd v Korean Line Corporation* [2011] EWHC 1819 (Comm).
35 [1989] 1 Lloyd's Rep 361, 363.
36 [2009] EWHC 3394; [2010] 1 CLC 1.

earned on the substitute fixture up to 10 July, the date the vessel would have been delivered had she been redelivered at Houston on 13 May under the original fixture.

Where one party repudiates the contract, the other party is entitled to reject the repudiation and keep the contract alive, subject to two conditions: it must be able to perform its obligations under the contract without the cooperation of the repudiating party; it must have a legitimate interest in performing the contract.[37] Otherwise, the innocent party must accept the repudiation or other breach, such as redelivery of a vessel in a damaged state,[38] and claim damages. Where a time charterer repudiates the contract, the first condition is satisfied[39] and the second condition requires the contract breaker to show that damages would be an adequate remedy and that the innocent party's wish to maintain the contract was 'wholly unreasonable'. In *The Aquafaith*,[40] the owners were held to have a legitimate interest in keeping a five-year time charter alive when the charterers repudiated 94 days before the end. The repudiation came in a difficult market where a substitute time charter was impossible, and trading on the spot market very difficult.[41] In contrast in *The Alaskan Trader (No 2)*,[42] the charterers redelivered eight months early and instead of rechartering, the shipowners kept the vessel idle for that period, with full crew, and claimed hire. Lloyd J declined to interfere with the arbitrator's conclusion that such conduct was a commercial absurdity and held that the owners were not entitled to keep the charter alive.[43] This is an application of the 'duty to mitigate', a phrase that is something of a misnomer, as the innocent party who fails to mitigate has committed no breach of contract. Mitigation is more a matter of causation. If an innocent party reacts unreasonably to a breach of contract, then consequences that flow from its unreasonable conduct cannot be said to have any causative link with the breach of contract itself.

Mitigation principles also govern the ability of a shipowner to claim damages on the basis of 'cost of cure', rather than on the diminution of the market value of its ship. In *The Rozel*,[44] the vessel was redelivered with a repair to the entablature of the generator leaving her with a mention in the Class memoranda, although the Classification Society had not actually required any action to be taken. The shipowners were not entitled to recover the notional cost of repairs, but were limited to damages based on any diminution in the vessel's value due to the mention in the memoranda. In *Omak Maritime v Mamola Challenger*,[45] the shipowners claimed costs incurred in preparing the vessel for the charterparty even though, following the charterers' repudiation, they were able to let the vessel out at a better rate than they would have earned from the charterers. The shipowners claimed the costs as wasted expenses on a reliance rather than an expectancy basis. The court, however, held that this was a case where there would be a breach of the compensatory principle if the owners were to recover as they had not suffered any overall loss.

If the innocent party, by mitigating its loss, actually improves its position over and above that which would have pertained in the absence of a breach, it will be unable to claim damages. However, purely fortuitous consequences of the breach will be disregarded in assessing damages. In *The Fanis*,[46] following a repudiation by the shipowners, the charterers refixed and redelivered to the second shipowner with a surplus of bunkers. The resulting profit was held to be unrelated to the repudiation of the charter and was not, therefore, to be credited against the damages

---

37 *White and Carter (Councils) Ltd v McGregor* [1962] AC 413.
38 *The Puerto Buitrago* [1976] 1 Lloyd's Rep 250, CA.
39 This is not the case with a demise charter – see obiter dictum of Orr LJ in *The Puerto Buitrago* [1976] 1 Lloyd's Rep 250, 256, CA.
40 [2012] EWHC 1077 (Comm); [2012] 2 Lloyd's Rep 61.
41 The contract is not affirmed merely because the innocent party requests the guilty party to reconsider its repudiation. See *Yukong Line v Rendsberg Investments* [1996] 2 Lloyd's Rep 604, QB.
42 [1983] 2 Lloyd's Rep 645, QB.
43 In *The Puerto Buitrago* [1976] 1 Lloyd's Rep 250, CA, the charterers redelivered with the vessel needing repairs and it was held that the shipowners were not entitled to refuse to accept the redelivery, keeping the vessel on hire, until the charterers had effected the repairs.
44 [1994] 2 Lloyd's Rep 161, QB.
45 [2010] EWHC 2026 (Comm); [2011] 1 Lloyd's Rep 47.
46 [1994] 1 Lloyd's Rep 633, QB.

recoverable by the charterer in respect of that breach.[47] Similarly, in *The North Prince*,[48] there was a chain of charterparties under which the subcharterers redelivered 173 days early. The head charterer redelivered the vessel to the shipowners 22 days before the earliest redelivery date under the subcharterparty. The head charterer was entitled to claim damages for the 22 days because the early redelivery by them was an independent speculation and not caused by the subcharterers' breach. In *The New Flamenco*,[49] the charter was repudiated in 2007 following which the owners sold the vessel for nearly $24 million. Had the charter not been repudiated, the vessel would have been redelivered in 2009 at which time its value would have been $7 million due to the intervening collapse of the freight market. In assessing owners' damages no account was to be taken in the benefit to owners of being able to sell the vessel in 2007, as this was not a benefit legally caused by charterer's breach. The change in capital value had nothing to do with the income rights that the owners had lost as a result of charterer's breach.[50]

Although the date of the breach is critical for fixing the amount of compensation, the duration of the unexpired residue of the time charter may be reduced by reason of events that have occurred between the date of the breach and the date of trial. Subsequent events may give the repudiating party a legitimate reason to terminate the contract, which it did not have at the time of repudiation. The effect that this will have on assessing damages for repudiation of a charter can be seen in *The Golden Victory*.[51] A vessel was time-chartered for seven years in 1998. Clause 33 of the charterparty provided that if war should break out between certain named countries, both parties would be entitled to cancel the charter. However, the charterers repudiated the charter in December 2001 by redelivering the vessel to the shipowners, who accepted the repudiation. Damages for breach came to be considered by an arbitrator, by which time the second Gulf War had broken out. That event would have entitled the charterer to cancel the charter had it still been current. The arbitrator determined that the outbreak of war in March 2003 placed a temporal limit on the damages, none being recoverable after 21 March 2003. The arbitrators' findings were upheld by the House of Lords. Four of their Lordships found for the charterer, recognising that considerations of certainty and finality would have to yield to the greater importance of achieving an accurate assessment of the damages based on the loss actually incurred. Lord Carswell stated that:[52]

> If the second Gulf War had not broken out by the time the arbitration was held, the arbitrator would have had to estimate the prospect that it might do so and factor into his calculation of the appellants' loss the chance that the charter would be cancelled at some future date under cl 33. The loss, which would have been sustained over the full period of the charter, would then have been discounted to an extent that would have reflected the chance, estimated at the time of the assessment, that it would be so terminated. As events happened, however, the arbitrator did not come to assess damages until after the outbreak of war, when, as he found, the respondents would have cancelled the charter. The outbreak of the second Gulf War was then an accomplished fact, which was highly relevant to the amount of damages, and in my opinion the arbitrator was correct to take it into account in assessing the appellants' loss.

However, Lord Bingham, dissenting, stressed the importance of certainty and predictability in commercial transactions. In his view, the owners were entitled to compensation for the value of

---

47 See, also, *Aitken v Ernsthausen* [1894] 1 QB 773.
48 *Glory Wealth v North China Shipping* [2010] EWHC 1692 (Comm); [2011] 1 All ER (Comm) 641.
49 [2014] EWHC 1547 (Comm).
50 Popplewell J observed that the relevant benefit flowing from the lost contractual rights, in terms of the vessel's capital value, would be the difference in value between a sale of the vessel in 2007 for immediate delivery, and a sale at that date for delivery at the expiry of the charter in 2009.
51 [2007] UKHL 12; [2007] 2 Lloyd's Rep 164.
52 *Ibid* [66].

what they had lost on the date that it was lost and pointed out that, had the charterers promptly honoured their obligation to pay damages, the matter would have been settled before the Second Gulf War became a reality. In *The Glory Wealth*,[53] the compensatory principle referred to in *The Golden Victory* was applied in a case of an accepted repudiation which did not involve a right of cancellation that would have been exercised had the contract not been repudiated. It was held that the disponent owners were only entitled to substantial damages if they could prove that they would have been able to perform the contract, assuming that the party in breach had performed its obligations.[54]

Frustration

What amounts to frustration?

A change of circumstances occurring after the conclusion of the contract[55] may be sufficient to discharge the parties from further performance of their contract. The change of circumstance must be so fundamental as to alter the whole commercial basis of the contract, not merely such as to involve one or other of the parties in increased expenditure in performing its obligations.[56] The test involves a similar assessment of the *factual consequences* of the supervening event to that used for deciding whether an innocent party may terminate the contract when the other has broken an innominate term.[57] However, in the latter instance, the innocent party will also be able to claim damages from the guilty party for losses that it has sustained due to the premature termination of the contract. If the contract is frustrated, neither party can claim damages from the other in respect of the termination of the contract.

The decisions relevant to carriage contracts mainly arise out of government requisition of vessels in the First World War, the blocking of the Suez Canal in 1956 and 1967, pursuant to the wars between Israel and Egypt, and the trapping of vessels in Basra following the 1980 war between Iran and Iraq.

In assessing whether a charterparty has been frustrated, the courts have taken into account the following factors: whether there is a clause in the contract that makes full provision for the effect of the supervening event – if it does there will be no frustration;[58] whether the charter is impossible of fulfilment, which will be the case if the vessel sinks;[59] whether the charter specifies a particular route for the voyage, and that route is now unusable;[60] and whether the new situation poses a peril

---

53 [2013] EWHC 3153 (Comm); [2014] 2 WLR 1405.

54 The disponent owners and the charterers had entered into a contract of affreightment for the carriage of cargoes over three years. The charterers failed to declare laycans in two of the three years, which amounted to a repudiatory breach of the contract. The charterers argued that, as a result of the collapse in the freight market, the disponent owners' financial position had deteriorated to such an extent that, had the laycans been declared, the disponent owners would have been incapable of providing the required vessels. The arbitrators found as a fact that that the disponent owners would have been able to perform.

55 Changed circumstances in existence at the date of the contract are dealt with by the law relating to common mistake.

56 *Davis Contractors Ltd v Fareham UDC* [1956] AC 696, HL, especially Lord Radcliffe at 728–9.

57 See *Hong Kong Fir Shipping Co Ltd v Kawasaki Kisen Kaisha Ltd* [1962] 2 QB 26, CA.

58 *Bank Line v Capel (Arthur) & Co* [1919] AC 435, HL: a clause allowing the charter to cancel in the event of the vessel's requisition did not have this effect when the government requisition was indefinite in its prospective duration. See, also, *The Florida* [2006] EWHC 1137 (Comm); [2007] 1 Lloyd's Rep 1, where a liberty clause did not make full provision for the effect on a voyage charter for the carriage of vegetable oil of a supervening import ban by the Nigerian authorities on such a cargo. An example of where a contractual clause has allocated the risk of a supervening event to one of the contractual parties is *The Kyla* [2012] EWHC 3522 (Comm); [2012] 2 CLC 998, where a clause in a time charter requiring charterers to maintain full hull and machinery cover created an assumption of risk and responsibility on the part of the owners to repair the hull damage up to the insured figure of US$16 million. Accordingly, the contract was not frustrated when the vessel was damaged without owner's fault and the cost of repair exceeded the vessel's sound market value.

59 *The Lorna 1* [1983] 1 Lloyd's Rep 373, CA.

60 See *The Massalia* [1961] 2 QB 278, where this rather spurious interpretation of the charter provisions enabled the facts to be distinguished from those in *The Eugenia* [1964] 2 QB 226.

to ship, crew or cargo.[61] This last factor is more likely to be relevant to voyage charters than to time charters. If the time-chartered vessel cannot perform a particular voyage, the charterer can always charter in a substitute vessel.

One of the most important factors is the length of any delay in performance caused by the new circumstances when set against the anticipated time for performance of the contract. Delay will be particularly significant to the assessment of whether a time charter has been frustrated. Such an assessment involves a comparison of the period of delay with the duration of the charter. With a voyage charter, one needs to ask how long the voyage, as a whole, will take after the change in circumstances and compare it with the time that it would have taken, as a whole, had there been no change in circumstances.

In *The Eugenia*,[62] a voyage charter was held not to have been frustrated by the closure of the Suez Canal in 1956. The charter was concluded on 9 September 1956, by which time Nasser had nationalised the Suez Canal and there was a risk that the Canal might become closed during the voyage. However, no express clause was drafted to cover this eventuality, the parties deciding to 'leave it to the lawyers to sort out'. The vessel was delivered at Genoa on 20 September 1956 and proceeded to load at Odessa, whence she sailed on 25 October 1956. The part of the voyage from Odessa to India would have taken 26 days via the Canal and 56 via the Cape. The total voyage from Genoa to India would have taken 108 days via the Suez Canal, and 138 days via the Cape. The whole voyage was taken for the purposes of this comparison and not just the portion remaining at the time that the Canal became unusable.

However, delay will not always be determinative of whether a charter has been frustrated. In *The Sea Angel*,[63] a maritime pollution incident occurred off Karachi, following which salvors were engaged on LOF 2000, containing the SCOPIC clause. The salvors concluded a 20-day trip charter for a vessel to assist in the trans-shipment of oil from the stricken vessel. Three days before the end of the charter, after conclusion of these services, the vessel was detained by the refusal of the port authority to issue a certificate confirming that no port dues were outstanding. This was a cover for the general strategy of the port authority to detain any vessels connected with the casualty to obtain security for the pollution and clean-up expenses. Three months later, after litigation in the local courts, the vessel was eventually able to leave and to be redelivered under the time charter. The shipowners argued that the charter had been frustrated because the probable length of the delay had greatly exceeded the unexpired portion of the charter. This argument was rejected. The Court of Appeal held that a multifactored analysis had to be brought to bear on the issue of frustration. A comparison of the likely delay with the unexpired portion of the charter was only one of the factors to be considered. It was outweighed by the following factors. First, the supervening event had occurred at the very end of a charter, with redelivery as essentially the only remaining obligation. Secondly, the risk of detention by the Pakistani authorities arising out of a salvage situation in which there was a concern about pollution was, in general terms, foreseeable, even if the particular way in which that risk manifested itself was not foreseeable. This type of risk was within the scope of cl 9(iii) of the SCOPIC clause, which formed part of the salvage contract. The vessel chartered in by the salvors had been specifically contracted for salvage services at a price that was intended to reflect their risks.

The assessment of whether the supervening event amounts to frustration should be made by reference to the facts available to the parties at the time of the event. This was the approach adopted

---

61 *Tsakiroglou & Co v Noblee Thorl GmbH* [1962] AC 93, HL, a cif contract in which frustration was unsuccessfully argued on the ground that the closure of the Suez Canal and the subsequent need for rerouting round the Cape had gone to the root of the contract.

62 [1964] 2 QB 226. This decision was reluctantly followed in a similar case of delay due to closure of the Suez Canal, this time in the 1967 Arab/Israeli war, in *The Captain George K* [1970] 2 Lloyd's Rep 21, QB.

63 *Edwinton Commercial Corporation, Global Tradeways Limited v Tsavliris Russ (Worldwide Salvage & Towage) Ltd* [2006] EWHC 1713 (Comm); [2007] EWCA Civ 547; [2007] 2 Lloyd's Rep 517, noted (2007) S & TI, 6(4), 24.

in *Bank Line v Capel (Arthur) & Co*,[64] where the fact that a government requisition, when made, was likely to be of indefinite duration was decisive in finding that the contract was frustrated, even though the actual period of requisition was only four months out of a one-year charter. However, in *The Evia (No 2)*,[65] no criticism was made of the approach of the arbitrator in judging this issue with the benefit of hindsight.

The effect of breach

If the change of circumstances is caused by the breach of contract of one of the parties, the defaulting party may not argue that those changed circumstances amount to frustration; hence the question of whether there had been a breach of the safe port warranty was critical to the issue of frustration in *The Evia (No 2)*.[66] If the charterers had been found to have broken their secondary duty of renomination, the trapping of the vessel in Basra would have been a consequence of that breach of duty, rather than the extraneous event of the outbreak of the Iran/Iraq war. The charterers, but not the shipowners, would therefore have been precluded from relying on the doctrine of frustration. In *DGM Commodities Corp v Sea Metropolitan SA*,[67] voyage charterers were unable to argue that the contract was frustrated due to a six-month delay at the discharge port due to receivers refusing to discharge cargo in a particular hold which included contaminated cargo. The charterers were under a non-delegable duty to discharge the cargo, and remained liable for its breach even if that duty had been delegated to the receivers.[68]

If the change of circumstances is caused by the action of one of the parties, even if there is no breach of contract, then that party is also precluded from arguing frustration. In *The Super Servant Two*,[69] the shipowner was given the option to nominate one of two tugs to perform the contract. The nominated tug sank, the sinking being covered by an exceptions clause, and the shipowner was unable to perform the contract, the other tug being committed at the time to another contract. The shipowner was unable to rely on the doctrine of frustration, as the problem could be traced to its action in the exercise of its option to nominate *The Super Servant Two* rather than *The Super Servant One*.

The consequences of frustration

Frustration stops the contractual clock from running. Both parties are discharged from obligations arising after the contract is frustrated, but remain liable for obligations accruing before that date. Therefore, in *The Lorna 1*,[70] the shipowners were unable to recover any freight, because at the date of the frustrating event, the sinking of the vessel, the obligation to pay freight had not accrued. If the contract is held to have been frustrated, and the parties still perform it, the post-frustration performance is paid for on a *quantum meruit* basis, as in *The Massalia*.[71]

At common law, advance payments in general lie where they fall and are only recoverable if there is a total failure of consideration.[72] This will not be the case in most voyage charters where at least some services, such as loading the cargo, will have been performed before the right to advance

---

64 [1919] AC 435, HL. The case is also of interest in that the doctrine of frustration was not excluded by reason of an option to cancel in the event of frustration which the charter gave to the charterers.
65 [1983] 1 AC 736, HL.
66 Ibid. Cf the question in *Monarch SS Co Ltd v A/B Karlshamns Oljefabriker* [1949] AC 196, HL, as to whether the delay could be attributable to the breach of the warranty of seaworthiness.
67 [2012] EWHC 1984 (Comm); [2012] 2 Lloyd's Rep. 587.
68 A similar period of delay in *The Adelfa* [1988] 2 Lloyd's Rep 466, QB amounted to frustration. There the vessel was detained by an arrest by the receivers and there was no undertaking in the charterparty, express or implied, that cargo receivers would not arrest the vessel or seek to do so.
69 [1990] 1 Lloyd's Rep 1, CA. See, also, *Maritime National Fish Ltd v Ocean Trawlers Ltd* [1938] AC 524, PC.
70 [1983] 1 Lloyd's Rep 373, CA.
71 [1961] 2 QB 278.
72 As in *Fibrosa Spolka Akcyjna v Fairbairn Lawson Combe Barbour Ltd* [1943] AC 32.

freight arises. Such a situation would amount only to a partial failure of consideration. Under a time charter, hire paid in advance before the frustrating event would not be recoverable by the charterer. Conversely, services performed before the accrual of a right to payment, which falls after the frustrating event, would attract no right to compensation, as in *The Lorna 1*.[73]

The **Law Reform (Frustrated Contracts) Act 1943** amends these rules, save as regards voyage charters and any contracts for the carriage of goods by sea other than a charterparty. Trip charters are regarded as time charters, and so fall within the operation of the statute.[74] Section 1(2) provides for the return of payments made before the frustration of the contract subject to a discretion in the court to allow such payments to be retained in whole or in part to cover expenses incurred by the payee in performance of the contract. Section 1(3) gives the court the power to order a suitable payment to be made when one party has conferred a 'valuable benefit' on the other, due to its performance of the contract prior to the date of its frustration. Such performance will only constitute a 'valuable benefit' in the light of the other party's position *after* the frustrating event.[75] An award under s 1(3) will be for such sum 'as the court considers just, having regard to all the circumstances of the case', but such sum will be capped by the amount of 'valuable benefit' obtained by a party as a result of the other's pre-frustration performance.

The combination of these provisions will enable the court to achieve a just apportionment of loss in respect of an advance payment of hire that covers the period during which the contract was frustrated. The court may exercise its discretion under s 1(2) to order the return of less than the full amount of advance payments if the facts are such that no payment can be made to the payee under s 1(3) because its contractual performance prior to frustration was not such as to confer a 'valuable benefit' on the other party.[76]

Furthermore, s 2(4) gives the court power to sever part of a frustrated contract from the rest of the contract and treat that part as not having been frustrated. Thus, if a twelve-month charter is frustrated in month six, the court would be likely to use this proviso to sever the first five months and apply the provisions of s 1(2) and (3) only to the hire instalment in the sixth month, during which the frustrating event occurred.

---

73 [1983] 1 Lloyd's Rep 373, CA.
74 *The Eugenia* [1964] 2 QB 226.
75 *BP Exploration Co (Libya) v Hunt* [1979] 1 WLR 783; aff'd [1983] 2 AC 352.
76 *Gamerco SA v ICM/Fair Warning (Agency) Ltd* [1995] 1 WLR 1226.

Part **2**

Wet Shipping

Chapter 14

Collisions

Chapter Contents

Collisions at sea are a staple of 'wet' Admiralty work. Such actions are subject to two procedural peculiarities that distinguish them from ordinary shipping actions proceeding in the Commercial Court or the Admiralty Court. The first is the collision statement of case, formerly known as the 'preliminary act'. This is a document containing various questions relating to the collision, for example: the ships involved; the weather; the course steered; and the angle of contact.[1] Under CPR Pt 61.4(5), every party must file a completed statement of case in form Adm 3 within two months of the defendant filing an acknowledgment of service.[2] The answers contained in the statement of case will constitute admissions of fact for the purpose of the litigation. The second is the role of the assessors, who are usually chosen from the 'elder brethren' of Trinity House. They sit with the judge to advise on nautical matters. They cannot be cross-examined and their role substantially restricts the right of the parties to call their own expert nautical evidence.

As a matter of substantive law, collisions at sea involve the application of the law of negligence in just the same way as collisions on the road. Collisions are the car crashes of the sea. The existence of a duty of care is rarely a problem and can easily be established under the general 'neighbour' principles set out in *Donoghue v Stevenson*.[3] The difficult issues of law arise in the context of establishing: whether that duty has been breached; how liability is to be apportioned when both vessels are, to some extent, at fault; and what losses may be recovered by way of damages. However, the starting point of any inquiry is to establish which human agencies were responsible for the collision and whether their faults can be attributed to the defendant shipowner. This will involve the application of the principles of vicarious liability.

Vicarious liability

In most instances, collisions result from the negligence of the crew. The shipowner will be vicariously liable for such negligence, as the crew are its employees. The shipowner will remain responsible for the crew's defaults unless they can be said to constitute a 'frolic of their own', so taking their conduct outside the remit of their employment. This is extremely difficult to prove, but was established in *The Druid*,[4] when the master, believing himself to be owed money for towing the SS *Sophie* into dock, ambushed her on her way out and dragged her up and down the river.

The crew will also be personally liable. In *Adler v Dickson*,[5] a passenger on a cruise ship was injured while disembarking and successfully sued the master of the ship whose fault had contributed to the accident. Although the master was not vicariously liable for the faults of the crew involved in berthing the ship, he was personally liable in failing to supervise the berthing.

Where the negligence is that of someone other than a member of the crew, it becomes critical to establish whether the wrongdoer was acting as a servant or agent of the shipowner, or as an independent contractor. If the latter is proved to be the case, the shipowner will be liable only if it is proved to have not taken reasonable care in choosing the contractor. The relevant test to be applied was set out in *Mersey Docks and Harbour Board Ltd v Coggins & Griffiths (Liverpool) Ltd and MacFarlane*.[6] The appellant owned and managed various cranes, which it hired out to stevedoring companies at the docks. It appointed and paid for the drivers, which it hired out with the cranes.

---

1   The questions to be answered are set out in form Adm 3 contained in the Practice Direction to CPR Pt 61.
2   Where the defendant disputes the jurisdiction of the court under CPR Pt 11, the time runs from when the defendant files the further acknowledgment of service referred to therein.
3   [1932] AC 562.
4   (1842) 1 W Rob 391.
5   [1955] 1 QB 158.
6   [1946] 2 All ER 345.

It was held vicariously liable when a crane driver negligently injured some other workers on the dock. The fact that the appellant had the right to control the driver's operation of the cranes, although it did not exercise that right in practice, was critical to the finding that the crane driver had been acting as its servant.

Applying these principles, one finds crew members, who are clearly servants of the shipowner, at one end of the spectrum and salvors, who are clearly independent contractors, at the other. However, it is less easy to draw the line with intermediate categories. Particular problems arise with collisions involving vessels under tow.

Tugs and tows

The maxim 'tug is servant of the tow' suggests that the ship under tow will always be vicariously liable for the defaults of the tug. It was applied in The Niobe,[7] even when the tow itself was not directly involved in the collision between the tug and the other ship. This maxim, however, is a rule-of-thumb guideline rather than a hard-and-fast rule. The true test is the extent to which the tow controls the actions of the tug and the resulting liability is best seen as a primary liability rather than a vicarious one.[8] Thus, in The Devonshire,[9] a dumb barge was sunk following a collision between its tug and The Devonshire. Although the tug was partly to blame for the collision, the tow was wholly innocent. The tug had sole control and management of the navigation. The owners of the dumb barge were therefore able to recover in full from the owners of The Devonshire and their recovery was unaffected by the fault of the tug.

Circumstances may arise where the tow is only partly responsible for a collision between a tug and another vessel. In The Panther and The Ericbank,[10] The Panther was towing The Ericbank when it collided with The Trishna, which was then holed by contact with The Panther's revolving propeller. The causes of the damage to The Trishna were threefold. First, The Trishna had been attempting to pass The Ericbank on a bend in the Manchester Ship Canal in breach of the canal bylaws. Secondly, the owners of The Ericbank had failed to respond to The Trishna's whistle by warning The Panther of her approach. Thirdly, The Panther had been at fault through the failure of its crew to stop its engines as soon as it made contact with The Trishna. The owners of The Ericbank, the tow, were held liable in respect of the second cause but not the third. The manoeuvre involved was within the province of the tugmaster and outside the general navigational control of those on the tow's bridge. The absence of navigational control meant that there could be no liability on the part of The Ericbank for The Panther's manoeuvre. The owners of The Trishna, as third parties, were unaffected by any terms in the towing contract providing for the tow to indemnify the tug.

Pilots

Another problematic area is the extent to which shipowners are liable for the negligence of pilots. The professional independence of pilots means that, in most situations, they will be regarded as independent contractors. However, s 16 of the **Pilotage Act 1987**, replacing s 15(1) of the **Pilotage Act 1913**, renders the shipowner vicariously liable for the default of compulsory pilots. Under s 15(1) of the **Pilotage Act 1913**, the shipowner was held to be 'answerable' for the negligence of a compulsory pilot. In Workington Harbour and Dock Board v Towerfield (Owners),[11] this wording was held to

---

7 (1888) 13 PD 55.
8 In The Niobe, the tow's liability was based on its failure to keep a proper lookout and warn the tug.
9 [1912] AC 634.
10 [1957] P 143.
11 [1951] AC 112.

have the additional effect of precluding any claim by the shipowners against the pilot in respect of damage to their vessel. The word 'answerable' is omitted from s 16 of the **Pilotage Act 1987**, so that a shipowner may now be able to claim against a negligent compulsory pilot. However, such a course of action is unlikely to be fruitful, given the very low limits of liability that pilots can invoke.

Standard of care

The conduct of those navigating a ship involved in a collision will be judged by the standards of prudent seamanship. This is a question of fact, and the findings of the first-instance judge will only exceptionally be challenged, such as where various reasons are given as to why a vessel is to blame and the appellate court finds some of them not to be valid, or where the judge misapprehends a vital fact bearing on the matter.[12]

An important factor in assessing compliance with those standards will be the extent to which the Collision Regulations have been followed. In 1840, Trinity House published a set of advisory regulations to provide clear 'rules of the road' to help to avoid collisions. These were given statutory effect by the **Steam Navigation Act 1846**. Collision Regulations are now produced and revised internationally by the International Maritime Organisation (IMO). The Collision Regulations include 38 rules divided into five sections: Part A – General; Part B – Steering and Sailing; Part C – Lights and Shapes; Part D – Sound and Light Signals; and Part E – Exemptions. There are also four Annexes containing technical requirements concerning lights and shapes and their positioning, sound signalling appliances, additional signals for fishing vessels when operating in close proximity, and international distress signals. The 1972 Regulations[13] are given effect in English law by the Merchant Shipping (Distress Signals and Prevention of Collisions) Regulations 1996[14] and apply to UK registered ships in any waters whatsoever and to all other ships when they are within the UK or its territorial waters. The 1972 Regulations also include traffic separation schemes adopted by the IMO. Compliance with such schemes is required by the principles of good seamanship, even if, as with foreign ships outside UK waters, compliance is not compulsory.[15]

Where a collision occurs in international waters, the English courts will apply English law. However, where it occurs in the territorial waters of a foreign state, the English courts will apply the law of that state. Both the Collision Regulations and the unwritten rules of good seamanship will apply only to the extent provided for by the law of the state in question. Thus, in *The Esso Brussels*,[16] it was held that a ship that was in Belgian waters at the time of the collision was not at fault for failing to use sound attention signals. Although these were required by the Collision Regulations, their use was positively prohibited in the particular circumstances of the case by the local port regulations.

A detailed treatment of the Regulations is outside the scope of this book, being a navigational, rather than a legal, matter. However, the following general outline will be given. The Regulations contain rules relating to: the use of lookouts; safe speeds; the use of lights; shapes; and the giving of signals by light and sound. They contain special provisions to deal with navigation in restricted visibility, or along the course of narrow channels. They impose a duty to use all means, including radar, if fitted, to determine whether or not there is a risk of collision and, if there is such a risk,

---

12 *The Macgregor* [1943] AC 197.
13 These came into effect on 15 July 1977 and have since been amended, as follows. In 1981, r 10 was amended. The 1987 amendments dealt with crossing traffic lanes, the 1989 amendments with unnecessary use of the inshore traffic zone, and the 1993 amendments with positioning of lights. In 2001 they were amended in respect of WIG (wing-in ground) craft. In 2007 Annex IV regarding distress signals was amended.
14 SI 1996/75.
15 *The Genimar* [1977] 2 Lloyd's Rep 17.
16 [1973] 2 Lloyd's Rep 73, CA.

impose a further duty to take positive action to avoid collisions in accordance with the principles of good seamanship. Rule 2 provides that nothing in the Regulations is to exonerate the ship from the consequences of neglecting to take any precaution required by the ordinary practice of seamen or by special circumstances.[17]

The Regulations also deal with overtaking and head-on situations. When ships are in sight of one another, the overtaking ship must keep out of the way of the ship being overtaken. A ship is deemed to be overtaking when it is coming up with another ship from a direction more than 22.5 degrees abaft her beam. Where power-driven ships are approaching each other in a head-on situation, each must alter course to starboard to pass on the port side of the other. Where power-driven ships are crossing one another, if there is a risk of collision or a close proximity between ships in an overtaking situation,[18] the ship that has the other on her own starboard side must keep out of the way. This ship is known as the 'give way' ship and must take early and substantial action to keep well clear of the other ship.[19] That ship is known as the 'stand on' ship and her duty is to keep her speed and course.[20] Rule 17(a)(ii) authorises the 'stand on' vessel to 'take action to avoid collision by her manoeuvre alone, as soon as it becomes apparent to her that the vessel required to keep out of the way is not taking appropriate action in compliance with these Rules'. Rule 17(b) then provides: 'When, from any cause, the vessel required to keep her course and speed finds herself so close that collision cannot be avoided by the action of the give-way vessel alone, she shall take such action as will best aid to avoid collision.' Accordingly, some fault may be attributed to a 'stand on' vessel that fails to take appropriate action once it becomes clear that the 'give way' vessel is not going to alter course.[21]

The early statutes in the nineteenth century treated breach of the Collision Regulations as creating a presumption of fault. This presumption was abolished by s 4(1) of the **Maritime Conventions Act 1911**, which brought into effect the provisions of the **1910 Brussels Collision Convention**. A shadow of the presumption of fault continued in English law with the decision in *The Aeneas*[22] that once a breach is shown to have been committed by those navigating a ship, her owners must then show that the breach did not contribute to the collision. The decision was overruled in *The Heranger*.[23] *The Heranger* and *The Diamond* collided. *The Diamond* was in breach of r 33 of the Port of London river bylaws. Once the owners of *The Diamond* had proved some fault on the part of *The Heranger*, and vice versa, the court was free to come to a conclusion as to causation and the division of loss. The owners of *The Diamond* were not saddled with the additional burden of showing that her breach of r 33 had not contributed to the collision.

Both colliding shipowners will have to prove that the other was in breach of its duty of care. However, in *The Merchant Prince*,[24] the Court of Appeal held that the mere fact of a collision will be sufficient to attract the operation of the doctrine of *res ipsa loquitur*, so creating a rebuttable presumption of negligence. There, the ship had collided with the plaintiff's vessel at anchor in the Mersey. The cause of the collision was the failure of the mechanical steering gear on the defendant's ship. Part of the gear had recently been renewed and was liable to stretch, although it had been in a satisfactory condition when tested prior to leaving anchorage. The defendant, however, was unable to rebut the presumption of negligence. The stretching of the gear was foreseeable. The defendant, therefore, should have had on board manual steering gear, ready to use at a moment's notice. The presumption will be rebutted where the cause of the collision can be shown to be due to the fault

---

17 As in *The Vysotsk* [1981] 1 Lloyd's Rep 439.
18 *The Nowy Sacz* [1977] 2 Lloyd's Rep 91.
19 Rule 16.
20 Rule 17.
21 This situation arose in *The Mineral Dampier and The Hanjin Madras* [2001] 2 Lloyd's Rep 419, CA, where the 'stand on' vessel was held 20 per cent to blame for the resulting collision.
22 [1935] P 128.
23 [1939] AC 94.
24 [1892] P 179.

of a third party for whom the defendant is not responsible. This was the case in *The Virginian Dollar*,[25] where the cause of the collision was the snapping of a steel bollard at Genoa to which the colliding ship had been properly moored.

The doctrine of *res ipsa loquitur* can be invoked only in relation to the case actually pleaded by the claimant. In *Esso Petroleum Co Ltd v Southport Corp*,[26] a ship grounded in a river estuary, following an unexplained defect in the steering gear. The master decided to refloat her by jettisoning some of the cargo of oil, which then contaminated the foreshore. The action was pleaded solely on the basis of the fault of the master, for which the shipowner would be vicariously liable, in discharging the oil. *Res ipsa loquitur* could not be invoked as regards the grounding, as that would involve a claim against the shipowner itself, which had not been pleaded.

A shipowner whose crew have failed to meet the standards of prudent seamanship will be able to exonerate itself if the failure can be shown to have arisen in 'the agony of the moment'. In *The Bywell Castle*,[27] the pleasure steamer *The Princess Alice* very suddenly, and without warning, turned sharp to port under the bows of *The Bywell Castle* as that vessel was about to pass her. The master of *The Bywell Castle*, instead of turning away from *The Princess Alice*, turned into her, and she sank with great loss of life. The owners of *The Bywell Castle* were held to be not liable for the collision. The reason for this was given by Brett LJ, who said:

> . . . when one ship, by her wrongful act, suddenly puts another ship into a position of difficulty of this kind, we cannot expect the same amount of skill as we should under other circumstances.

The principle was subsequently applied in *The Highland Loch*.[28] The defendants' ship was due to be launched in the Mersey, which had been cleared of craft. The plaintiff's ketch fouled her mooring chains there and refused to drop anchor unless the defendants made themselves answerable for it, which they refused to do. The defendants then went ahead with the launch, deeming it dangerous to life and property to postpone it and judging the risk of colliding with the ketch to be slight. Unfortunately, as their ship turned down river, it struck the ketch. The defendants were held not to be liable, because they had been put in an impossible situation by the unreasonable demands of the plaintiff. The defendants had not been unreasonable in taking the risk that they had taken. The principle cannot, however, be relied on by a shipowner when the fault of its crew has actually contributed to the situation causing the 'agony of the moment'.[29]

Causation

Even if the claimant establishes breach by the defendant, it must still prove that its loss was actually caused by that breach, in that the loss would not have occurred but for the breach. If the claimant succeeds in doing so, the defendant may then attempt to show that the chain of causation was broken by some intervening event, a *novus actus interveniens*. However, this will be difficult to establish where the intervening event is factually bound up with the breach itself. For example, in *The Oropesa*,[30] a collision occurred due to the fault of both vessels. The master of one of them took out a boat to discuss salvage with the other master. The boat overturned and lives were lost. The master's action in taking out the boat was reasonable and did not constitute a *novus actus*

---

25 (1926) 25 Ll L Rep 227.
26 [1956] AC 218.
27 (1879) 4 PD 219.
28 [1912] AC 312.
29 *The Winona* (1944) 77 Ll L Rep 156.
30 [1943] P 32.

interveniens. The chain of causation between the collision and the subsequent loss of life was, therefore, unbroken.

Similarly, in *The Zaglebie Dabrowskie* (No 2),[31] the chain of causation was unbroken when, following a collision in fog, one of the vessels sank three hours later. Her master had abandoned her 20 minutes after the collision, and it was argued that he might have saved her had he beached her on the nearby Fairy Bank. It was held that where a vessel was badly holed due to a collision and sank due to water ingress, a prima facie case has been made out that the collision was the cause of the loss. The owners of the other vessel had failed to rebut this by proving intervening negligence on the part of those on board the vessel that sank. The chain of causation may even survive the subsequent negligence of the defendant. In *The Calliope*,[32] two ships collided in the Seine. One of them grounded and refloated. The following day, while under a salvage tug, she re-grounded due to the negligence of her crew. The effect of the initial negligence of the colliding ship was held to be still continuing at the time of the second grounding, because it had put the defendant in a situation in which its ship would have to attempt a difficult manoeuvre it would not otherwise have attempted.

These principles of causation have found expression in the so-called 'last opportunity' rule. The rule proposes that the ship that had the last opportunity to avoid the collision shall be regarded as the sole cause of the collision. In practice, most acts of negligence on the part of colliding ships are so intertwined as to make the rule unworkable. In *The Volute*,[33] the collision was due to the failure of *The Volute* to give the appropriate whistle signal when she ported and the fact that *The Radstock*, in the resulting position of danger, had then gone full ahead. The two acts of negligence were so mixed up with each other that the rule could not be applied. Viscount Birkenhead posited a spectrum between two situations. The first is where the second act of negligence is severable, in which case the ship initially negligent recovers in full. The second is where the second act of negligence is covered by the rule in *The Bywell Castle*,[34] in which case the ship initially negligent will be liable in full. Nearly all collisions at sea will fall in between these points and the rule of 'last opportunity' will have no application.[35]

The rule is more likely to apply to collisions between a moving ship and a stationary one. In *The Kate*,[36] a ship collided with one of a flotilla of barges that were moored outside the entrance to the Surrey Docks. The ship was held wholly to blame for the collision, as it should have been aware of the obstruction and taken avoiding action. Even if the barge had been negligently moored, which was not the case, such negligence would have had no causal impact on the collision. However, even where a ship collides with another ship at anchor, the rule is not invariable. In *The Eurymedon*,[37] a ship was anchored in the Thames so as to obstruct the fairway. Another ship saw her lights, but did not identify them as anchor lights due to that vessel's unexpected position and the presence of shore lights behind her. Both ships were to blame, as the negligence of the stationary ship had assisted the colliding ship in being negligent. So, too, in *The Margaret*,[38] where cargo on board the moving ship was damaged following a collision with a moored barge. Both ships were held to blame as the colliding ship had been holed by the barge's anchor, which was left swinging from its hawse with its stock not awash, contrary to local bylaws.

---

31 [1978] 1 Lloyd's Rep 573.
32 [1970] 1 All ER 624.
33 [1922] 1 AC 129.
34 (1879) 4 PD 219.
35 See, also, *The Boy Andrew (Owners) v The St Rognvald (Owners)* [1948] AC 140, where the rule was not applied when the accident was caused by the synchronous faulty navigation of both vessels.
36 (1936) 54 Ll L Rep 120.
37 [1938] P 41.
38 (1881) 6 PD 76.

Apportionment of liability

The majority of collisions will involve some degree of fault on the part of all of the colliding ships. When this happens, s 187 of the **Merchant Shipping Act 1995** – formerly, in part, s 1 of the **Maritime Conventions Act 1911** – gives the court the power to apportion liability between the ships, applying similar principles to those now applied in general tort law by virtue of the **Law Reform (Contributory Negligence) Act 1945**. Under s 187, liability is to be 'in proportion to the degree in which each ship was in fault'. If the relative degrees of fault cannot be ascertained, the court is directed to apportion fault equally. Apportionment of 'loss' under the Act covers not only physical damage, but also liability to third parties.[39]

In multiple collisions, each ship's contribution must be assessed separately. The faults of one or more ships must not be amalgamated to form a single 'unit' for the purpose of applying the Act in relation to a third ship. In *The Miraflores v The George Livanos (Owners) and Ors*,[40] *The Miraflores* and *The Abadesa* collided in the Scheldt. A third ship, *The George Livanos*, went aground in trying to avoid the colliding vessels. All three ships were at fault. In assessing the share of blame attributable to *The George Livanos*, the first-instance judge treated the initial collision as a single causal unit, which was 50 per cent to blame for the grounding of *The George Livanos*. *The George Livanos* was therefore 50 per cent to blame for the grounding. The other 50 per cent attributable to the colliding vessels was split one-third as to *The Miraflores* and two-thirds to *The Abadesa*. The House of Lords held that this was the wrong approach, because it failed to take into account the degree of blame attributable to *each* ship, and its causal link with the grounding. Their Lordships reapportioned fault 40 per cent to *The Abadesa*, 20 per cent to *The Miraflores* and 40 per cent to *The George Livanos*.

Where initial negligence results in separate incidents of damage, and there has been no *novus actus interveniens*, two apportionments may need to be made in respect of each separate head of damage. Thus, in *The Calliope*,[41] fault for the initial grounding damage that followed the collision was split 45 per cent and 55 per cent as between *The Carlsholm* and *The Calliope*. The initial collision was also held partly responsible for the re-grounding damage suffered the following day during salvage operations. No accurate apportionment was possible, so equal division was applied. Therefore, *The Carlsholm* was responsible for 22.5 per cent of the re-grounding damage, being half of the initial 45 per cent apportionment.

Apportionment under s 187 is only possible where there have been faults connected with the navigation of ships, although the ship at fault need not actually have been one of the colliding vessels.[42] The Act can be used to apportion as between a tug and tow, as in *The Panther and the Ericbank*,[43] provided that the tug and tow were not jointly participating in the negligent operation.[44]

Where the fault of a party such as a harbour authority, which is not involved with the navigation of a vessel, is involved, apportionment in respect of its share of blame will be effected under the **Law Reform (Contributory Negligence) Act 1945**. The principle is illustrated by *The Sobieski*,[45] which involved a collision occurring before the enactment of the 1945 Act. The collision occurred in fog between *The Sobieski* and *The Esperance*, two ships forming part of a wartime convoy. The senior escort officer was on board *The Loch Alvie* and failed to warn *The Sobieski* of the presence nearby of *The Esperance*, which he had picked up by radar. The senior escort officer could not rely on s 1, as his fault could not be attributable to that of a ship. Although he was on board *The Loch Alvie* at the time of his negligence, he took no part in her management or navigation.

---

39 *The Cairnbahn* [1914] P 25.
40 [1967] 1 AC 86.
41 [1970] 1 All ER 624.
42 *The Cairnbahn* [1914] P 25, where it was held that the old common law rule that there could be no contribution between joint tortfeasors was to be disregarded when affecting an apportionment under s 1 of the Maritime Conventions Act 1911.
43 [1957] P 143.
44 As in *The Socrates and the Champion* [1923] P 76.
45 [1949] P 313.

Where a wholly innocent ship is involved in a collision, the Act will not apply, as s 187 requires 'two or more ships' to be at fault. This proviso would not be satisfied even in a three-ship collision where two of the ships are at fault, as *all* of the ships must be at fault for the Act to apply. In such a situation, the innocent ship could make full recovery from either of the guilty ships as joint tortfeasors. Apportionment of the resulting award of damages as between the guilty ships will be effected under the **Civil Liability (Contribution) Act 1978**.

Where all of the ships involved are to blame to some extent, the question arises as to the extent to which innocent parties connected with either of the guilty ships will be identified with the fault of that ship. This is certainly the case with claims by cargo owners. Their claim in tort against the colliding ship will be reduced in accordance with the degree of blame attributed to the carrying ship. Thus, in *The Drumlanrig*,[46] *The Tongariro* and *The Drumlanrig* collided and were equally at fault. Cargo on *The Drumlanrig* was damaged and its owners sued the owners of *The Tongariro*, but were unable to recover more than half their loss. In theory, the balance is recoverable under the contract of carriage with the carrying ship. In practice, this right will be frustrated by the defence provided by Art IV(2)(a) of the Hague and Hague-Visby Rules in respect of loss due to the 'act, neglect or default of the master, mariner, pilot or the servant of the carrier in the navigation and management of the ship'.

However, this principle was not applied in *The Devonshire*,[47] where a wholly innocent tow, which was sunk in a collision caused partly by the fault of its tug, was able to recover in full from the colliding ship. The tow's damages were not reduced by identifying it with the fault of the tug. Personal injury and death claimants are also unaffected by the principle.[48] By s 188 of the **Merchant Shipping Act 1995** – formerly, in part, s 2 of the **Maritime Conventions Act 1911** – they may sue either of the guilty ships for their full claim. If recovery is made in full against one of the guilty ships, it may, by virtue of s 189 – formerly, in part, s 3 of the 1911 Act – recover a contribution from the other guilty ship, according to that vessel's share of blame.

Damages

Recovery of loss is governed by the usual principles of negligence law. Not only must the losses be directly caused by the negligent act, but they must also not be too remote – that is, they must have been foreseeable by a reasonable person at the time of the negligence. An illustration of losses that were held to be too remote is provided in the *The Liesbosch Dredger v SS Edison (Owners)*.[49] A dredger was engaged on constructional work in Patras harbour and was rendered a total loss following a collision. The owners of *The Liesbosch* lacked the funds to acquire a replacement dredger and instead, after some delay, hired in a dredger at an exorbitant rate. Their recovery was limited to the cost of replacing the dredger. The actual losses suffered were not truly caused by the collision, but by the plaintiff's lack of funds, and were therefore not recoverable.

Furthermore, recovery is possible only in respect of physical damage and financial loss consequent thereon.[50] There is no recovery in respect of pure economic loss. Thus, a time charterer of a vessel involved in a collision can make no recovery in tort against the colliding vessel.[51] This is because it lacks either a proprietary or a possessory interest in the vessel that it has chartered. The principle even extends to shipowners whose claim is in a capacity other than that as owners. In *The Mineral Transporter*,[52] the shipowner, Mitsui, demise chartered its vessel to Matsuoka. They, in turn,

---

46 [1911] AC 16.
47 [1912] AC 634.
48 *The Bernina* (1886) 12 PD 36.
49 [1933] AC 449.
50 Loss of personal use of a vessel following a collision will generally not give rise to a separate head of damages, but is, instead, subsumed in the award of interest. See *The Baltic Surveyor* [2002] EWCA Civ 89; [2002] 2 Lloyd's Rep 623, CA.
51 Confirmed in *TheWorld Harmony* [1967] P 341.
52 [1985] 2 All ER 935.

time chartered the vessel back to the shipowner. Mitsui were unable to recover in respect of their loss of profits during the period in which the vessel was having collision damage repaired. Their losses as shipowners were off-hire under the demise charter. However, this was compensated by the off-hire provisions of the time charter back to themselves. The loss of profits was incurred purely in Mitsui's capacity as time charterer and was therefore irrecoverable, as being pure economic loss. On the other hand, claimants have recovered when they have shown the necessary proprietary or possessory interest. Examples include claims by demise charterers, by salvors in possession of a wreck[53] and by cargo interests claiming in respect of their liability for general average.[54]

The assessment of damages for physical and consequential loss will differ, depending on whether or not the collision has rendered the claimant's ship a total loss. If it has, then damages will be awarded on the basis of the ship's value at the date of the collision, rather than at the end of her planned voyage.[55] On the other hand, if the vessel can be repaired, the costs of repair will form the principal head of damages. Damages will not be reduced by reason of any fortuitous benefit that enures to the claimant by reason of the need to repair its ship. In The Bernina,[56] the full cost of repairing the collision damage was allowed, even though some of the repairs would shortly have become necessary in any event to enable the ship to pass her Classification Society survey.[57] The application of similar principles has also denied defendants any credit for the fact that repairs may increase the ship's value by the building into her of new materials.[58]

Irrespective of whether the ship is rendered a total loss, an additional sum will be awarded to compensate the claimant for loss of freight or profits at the end of the voyages fixed by the ship's existing charters, subject to deductions for contingencies and wear and tear. The aim of damages is to effect restitutio in integrum. The usual method of doing this is the 'ballast/laden' method adopted in The Argentino.[59] The lost charter would have involved a ballast voyage to the new load port and a laden voyage under the fixture. A time charter equivalent rate is calculated for this period and then a similar calculation is made for the substitute fixture for the period in which it coincides with what would have been the period of the cancelled fixture. Damages are awarded on the difference between the two rates for the duration of the ballast and laden voyages on the cancelled fixture. However, this method is not invariably used. In The Vicky 1, the Court of Appeal held that the Registrar had correctly adopted an alternative method based on 'time equalisation'.[60] This involved a calculation of the earnings that the vessel would have made between the time at which the lost fixture would have ended and the time at which the longer substitute fixture actually ended. This method was more suitable for vessels that had one major loading area, the Arabian Gulf, which meant that it was commercially important to discharge cargo as close as possible to that area. The method was also able to take account of the difference in voyage lengths between the cancelled and the substitute fixtures.

Where the claimant is not trading its vessel, it will still be awarded some compensation for its loss of use. Thus, in The SS Mediana v Lightship Comet,[61] the plaintiff's lightship was damaged in a collision. While it was being repaired, the plaintiffs used a substitute lightship that they had on hand. They were awarded substantial damages for loss of the services of the original lightship. Lord Shand took the view that part of the expense to the plaintiffs of maintaining a lightship in reserve should be reflected in the damages, while Lord Brampton considered that damages should reflect the value

---

53 *The Zelo* [1922] P 9.
54 *Morrison SS Co v Greystoke Castle (Cargo Owners) (The Greystoke Castle)* (1947) 80 Ll L Rep 55.
55 *The Philadelphia* [1917] P 101.
56 (1886) 12 PD 36.
57 See, also, *The Acanthus* [1902] P 17, where no credit was given to the defendant for the fact that the plaintiff took advantage of the drydocking required for repairing the collision damages to fix new bilge keels to the ship.
58 *The Gazelle* (1844) 2 W Rob 279.
59 (1889) 14 App Cas 519.
60 [2008] EWCA Civ 101; [2008] 2 Lloyd's Rep 45.
61 [1900] AC 113.

of the services provided by the substitute lightship.[62] In addition, there is a convention in the Admiralty Court that a shipowner can claim 1 per cent on its claim in a collision action to cover interruption to its business, without the necessity of proving the same. This convention is not available to cargo claimants in a collision action.[63]

Statutory liability

Apart from the common law liability for negligence set out above, shipowners[64] will also be subject to statutory liability under s 74 of the **Harbour Docks and Piers Clauses Act 1847** in respect of damage caused by their ships to harbours, docks and piers owned by public authorities. Liability is strict, even if the harbour authority has contributed to the accident,[65] and extends to 'works connected therewith', which has been held to include electric cables located at the bottom of a channel connecting two docks.[66] Damages cover the costs of reinstatement and repair, but not consequential loss, which is recoverable only in negligence.[67] The only defence permissible is where no human agency is involved in the incident, as was the case in *River Wear Commissioners v Adamson*,[68] where a ship drifted against a pier after it had been abandoned by the crew in a storm.

Time bar

A two-year time bar is imposed on collision actions by s 190 of the **Merchant Shipping Act 1995** – formerly, s 8 of the **Maritime Conventions Act 1911** – in respect of:

. . . any proceedings to enforce any claim or lien against a ship or her owners:

(a) in respect of damage or loss caused by the fault of that ship to another ship, its cargo or freight or any property on board it; or

(b) for damages for loss of life or personal injury caused by the fault of that ship to any person on board another ship.[69]

Fault is immaterial to the operation of the time bar. A counterclaim is subject to the two-year limitation period in the **Merchant Shipping Act 1995** s 190(3),[70] as is a claim against a sister-ship.[71] Under s 190(5), 'Any court having jurisdiction in such proceedings may, in accordance with rules of court, extend the period allowed for bringing proceedings to such extent and on such conditions as it thinks fit.' There is a mandatory provision for extending time in in rem proceedings, but not in in personam proceedings,[72] under s 190(6), which provides:

---

62 See, also, *The Astrakhan* [1910] P 172, where damages were awarded to compensate for the loss of use of a Danish warship during the 22 days that it took to repair the collision damage. The plaintiff was held to be under no obligation to prove that it would have used the warship during those 22 days.

63 *The Kumanova (Owners) v Owners of The Massira* [1998] 2 Lloyd's Rep 301, QB.

64 'Owner' under s 74 means the registered owner and does not cover charterers or bareboat charterers. See *The Chevron North America* [2002] 2 Lloyd's Rep 77, HL.

65 *Workington Harbour and Dock Board v Towerfield (Owners)* [1951] AC 112.

66 *Great Western Railway Co v Owners of SS Mostyn* [1928] AC 57.

67 *Workington Harbour and Dock Board v Towerfield (Owners)* [1951] AC 112.

68 (1877) 2 App Cas 743.

69 Where loss of life or suffering did not occur at the same time as the causative maritime incident, time for suit does not begin to run until the date when the injury was suffered. *Sweet v RNLI* [2002] EWHC 117 (Admlty); (2002) 99(10) LSG 32.

70 *The Jebel Ali* [2009] EWHC 1365 (Admlty); [2010] 2 All ER (Comm) 64.

71 *The Preveze* [1973] 1 Lloyd's Rep 202 (QB).

72 *The Stolt Kestrel* [2014] EWHC 1731 (Admlty).

Any such court, if satisfied that there has not been during any period allowed for bringing proceedings any reasonable opportunity of arresting the defendant ship within –

(a) the jurisdiction of the court, or
(b) the territorial sea of the country to which the plaintiff's ship belongs or in which the plaintiff resides or has his principal place of business,

shall extend the period allowed for bringing proceedings to an extent sufficient to give a reasonable opportunity of so arresting the ship.

The mandatory provision in s 190(6) also applies to claims against sister-ships.[73] It is open to the parties to a collision action to agree to extend the two-year time limit. In *The Theresa Libra*,[74] a settlement provided that a shipowner 'shall pay' the agreed percentage of the other's claim and this precluded each party from relying on the two-year time bar. The demise charterers were also a party to the agreement and were precluded from asserting that the application to add them as a party to the claim form had been made 'after the end of a period of limitation'.

Jurisdiction

Collision actions can be heard only in the Admiralty Court.[75] Jurisdiction is governed by the **1952 Collision and Civil Jurisdiction Convention**, Art 1 of which provides that:[76]

An action for collision occurring between seagoing vessels, or between seagoing vessels and inland navigation craft, can only be introduced:

(a) either before the court where the defendant has his habitual residence or a place of business;
(b) or before the court of the place where arrest has been effected of the defendant ship or of any other ship belonging to the defendant which can be lawfully arrested, or where arrest could have been effected and bail or other security has been furnished;
(c) or before the court of the place of collision when the collision has occurred within the limits of a port or inland waters.

Category (b) allows the Admiralty Court to assume jurisdiction over collisions that have no connection with England, provided that the ship in question is, or could have been, arrested in England or Wales. The allocation of jurisdiction does not prevent the defendant from subsequently applying to stay the substantive proceedings on the grounds of *forum non conveniens*.

Actions *in personam* are restricted by s 22(1) of the **Supreme Court Act 1981** to situations covered by (a) and (c) of Art 1 of the 1952 Convention. An action *in personam* may also be brought where 'an action arising out of the same incident or series of incidents is proceeding in the court or has been heard and determined in the court'. Similar provisions relating to the granting of leave to serve such a claim form out of the jurisdiction are to be found in CPR Pt 61.4(7).[77]

---

73 Ibid.
74 [2013] EWHC 2792 (Admlty); [2013] 2 Lloyd's Rep 597.
75 CPR Pt 61.2(b).
76 Article 1(2) allows the claimant to choose in which of the above courts it is to commence proceedings. Once proceedings are begun, Art 1(3) bars the claimant from bringing another action against the defendant on the same facts in another jurisdiction, unless it discontinues the first action.
77 The order also permits service of a defendant where it has submitted or agreed to submit to the jurisdiction of the High Court.

Chapter 15

Salvage

Chapter Contents

Salvage is a concept unique to maritime law. If a person voluntarily saves the property of another on land, English law entitles them to no reward for their efforts. However, if the same service is performed at sea, the person saving the property, 'the salvor', will be entitled to a reward, not exceeding the value of the property saved. The public policy reason behind this difference between salvage services on land and at sea lies in the need to provide financial encouragement to vessels to assist other vessels in distress.

The sources of salvage law

The framework of the current law of salvage was first established by the decisions of the Admiralty Court in the eighteenth and nineteenth centuries. In general, a salvage reward would become payable whenever maritime property was saved from danger by a 'volunteer', a person who was not debarred from claiming salvage by virtue of some pre-existing relationship with the property in question. The reward could never exceed the salved value of the property, for otherwise its owner would derive no benefit from the exertions of the salvor. At the time that these decisions were made, salvage was still largely a matter of purely voluntary services, often non-contractual, rendered by ordinary ships that happened to be passing the distressed ship. The end of the nineteenth century saw the emergence of a professional salvage industry and, today, nearly all salvage work is performed by professional salvors. The heyday of such salvors was in the 1970s. Since then, improvements in the safety of vessels have led to a declining demand for their services, and this has provided the background to some of the current controversies in the law that we shall be reviewing.

A particular form of contract – Lloyd's Open Form (LOF) – developed, and proved popular with professional salvors. The contract has been judicially categorised as one for work and labour that is only subject to the principles of salvage law in so far as these have been expressly or impliedly incorporated into it.[1] Nonetheless, the contract does incorporate many of the salient features of the general law of salvage – in particular, the principle of 'no cure, no pay' – although there are important differences that will be examined later in this chapter. One important feature of the contract is that the quantum of any award is left 'open' to be determined subsequently in London before Lloyd's arbitrators, applying English law. Another crucial feature is that, under LOF, salvage is admitted, thereby obviating the need for the salvor to show that the vessel was in danger at the time that the agreement was made. The contract has frequently been updated, most recently in 2000 (LOF 2000). This version has been shortened so that it contains only the provisions directly relevant to the salvage services. These are now in lettered, not numbered, form. The new form incorporates by reference Lloyd's Standard Salvage and Arbitration clauses (LSSA clauses), which contain provisions of an administrative or procedural nature.

LOF 1980 contained important provisions recognising the environmental risks that often attend modern salvage, especially where oil tankers are in distress. For the first time, a salvor became entitled to some payment, even if no property was salved, provided that its services had minimised oil pollution from the casualty. Moreover, if property was salved, the salvor's efforts in minimising oil pollution became a factor enhancing the amount of the eventual salvage award.

The changes introduced by LOF 1980 were to exert a powerful influence on the form of the **1989 Salvage Convention** drawn up by the Comité Maritime International (CMI) to replace its previous convention, the **1910 Brussels Salvage Convention**. In reply, LOF 1990 incorporated the principal Articles of the new Convention.[2] The **1910 Brussels Salvage Convention** received a large number of ratifications and accessions. However, it was never incorporated into English law,

---

1 *The Unique Mariner (No 2)* [1979] 1 Lloyd's Rep 37, QB.
2 Articles 1, 8, 13 and 14.

as its 11 Articles were regarded as being essentially declaratory of existing English law. In contrast, the **1989 Salvage Convention** became part of English law as of 1 January 1995.[3] By s 224 of the **Merchant Shipping Act 1995**, the Convention is to have 'the force of law'. Unlike other mandatory codes, such as the Hague-Visby Rules, the Convention itself, in Art 6(1), allows for parties to a salvage contract to contract out of most of its provisions.[4] To take account of these changes, LOF 1995 simply incorporates the 1989 Convention in its entirety. Internationally, the 1989 Convention came into force on 14 July 1996, although its application may differ from state to state, due to the power given to the Contracting States to make reservations in respect of specific Convention provisions.

This chapter will analyse the law of salvage by considering the following questions in turn:

(a)   What property can be subject to salvage?
(b)   What are the geographical limits of salvage?
(c)   Who can claim as a salvor?
(d)   What services lead to entitlement to a salvage award?
(e)   What principles govern the relationship between salvor and salvee?
(f)   How is any salvage award to be calculated?
(g)   What remedies are available to salvors?
(h)   How do the salvage principles apply to wreck?

Each step of the inquiry will consider, first, the pre-1995 law of salvage, and then, the extent to which it has been modified either by contractual provisions of LOF or by the **1989 Salvage Convention**.

It must be noted that some services that formerly qualified as salvage services, such as those rendered under the doctrine of 'engaged services', have no equivalent in the Convention. It is likely, therefore, that they can no longer be regarded as salvage, although remuneration may still be possible under the doctrine of implied contract. An important consequence of the demotion in status of such claims is that they would no longer create maritime liens. However, they would still be subject to the in rem jurisdiction of the Admiralty Court by virtue of the amended s 20(2)(j) of the **Supreme Court Act 1981**, which gives the Admiralty Court jurisdiction over claims:

(a)   under the 1989 Convention; and
(b)   under a contact for or in relation to salvage services; and
(c)   in the nature of salvage not falling within (a) and (b) above.

This final heading should cover 'demoted' salvage claims.

What property can be salved?

Maritime property

Ship, cargo and freight – the traditional categories

Only 'maritime property' can be salved. According to Lord Esher MR in *The Gas Float Whitton* (*No 2*), such property is limited to the 'ship, her apparel and cargo ... and the wreck of

---

3   By virtue of the Merchant Shipping (Salvage and Pollution) Act 1994, now consolidated in s 224, Sched II to the Merchant Shipping Act 1995.
4   The exceptions are the power of the court under Art 7 to modify and annul salvage contracts, and the environmental obligations imposed on the parties by Art 8.

these and freight'.[5] The case involved a salvage claim in respect of an unmanned lightship moored in tidal waters to give light to vessels, after it had gone adrift in a storm. Both the Court of Appeal and the House of Lords were of the view that the lightship was not a proper subject of salvage. It was certainly not cargo, nor was it a ship. Under s 742 of the **Merchant Shipping Act 1894**,[6] 'vessel' was defined as including 'any ship or boat, or any other description of vessel used in navigation' and 'ship' as including 'every description of vessel used in navigation not propelled by oars'.[7] Neither definition covered the lightship, which was not intended or fitted for navigation, although it was shaped like a boat. Lord Macnaghten asked himself whether there was a navigational interest to preserve these beacons from destruction and concluded:[8]

> But these beacons are for the most part, if not always, left unguarded – they are easily set adrift. And the hope of earning reward by the restoration of lost property is not perhaps the best preservative against loss. Then, too, one must bear in mind the inconveniences which might arise from the legal right of salvors in regard to detention of property when that property is the subject of salvage.

Their Lordships' definition of 'ship' makes it difficult to assess whether new types of oil exploration and exploitation structures that have emerged since 1897 can be the subject of salvage. Mobile structures, particularly if manned, probably do fall within the definition. Fixed structures, such as oil rigs, almost certainly fall outside it. Article 1 of the 1989 Convention defines 'vessel' as 'any ship or craft or any structure capable of navigation'. It has been suggested that the CMI report that led to the drafting of the Convention intended the phrase 'structure capable of navigation' to include mobile offshore structures, such as LANBYs (large automatic navigation buoys), the modern unmanned equivalents of lightships.[9] Article 3 expressly excludes fixed or floating platforms or mobile offshore drilling units when 'on location and engaged in exploration, exploitation or production of sea bed mineral resources'.

The other main category of maritime property is cargo carried on board the vessel. Cargo is a subject of salvage, irrespective of whether it is owned by the shipowner or by a third party, or whether or not it is carried under a bill of lading. *Dicta* of Lord Herschell in *The Gas Float Whitton* (No 2) suggest that 'cargo' might extend to goods in tow. Freight, although mentioned by Lord Esher in his definition, will rarely be a separate subject of salvage. It will usually be at the risk either of the shipowner, if payable at destination, or of cargo, if prepaid. In both cases, it will come into account in valuing the property salved at the place of safety. However, freight may be payable to charterers, in which case, in principle, a salvage claim in respect of it should be possible against them.[10] Both freight and cargo are included in the following definition of property adopted by Art 1(c) of the **1989 Salvage Convention**: 'Property means any property not permanently and intentionally attached to the shoreline and includes freight at risk.'

Where the property salved belongs to the Crown, s 230 of the **Merchant Shipping Act 1995** allows the salvor to claim a salvage reward in the same way as is permissible against a private person. However, s 29 of the **Crown Proceedings Act 1947** prohibits in rem proceedings from being brought against the Crown.

---

5 [1897] AC 337, HL.
6 Now, in part, s 313 of the Merchant Shipping Act 1995. The new Act attempts to assimilate the two terms and only defines 'ship'. However, this term 'includes every description of vessel used in navigation'.
7 A vessel's bunkers are covered within the term 'ship'. See The Silia [1981] 2 Lloyd's Rep 534.
8 [1897] AC 337, 349.
9 Shaw, R, 'The 1989 Salvage Convention and English law' (1996) LMCLQ 202, 208.
10 See The Pantanassa [1970] P 187.

Non-traditional categories – aircraft, lives

Aircraft do not constitute 'maritime property', but may form the subject of salvage by virtue of s 87(1) of the **Civil Aviation Act 1982**. A salvage award was made in respect of a Harrier jump jet that landed on the Spanish vessel *Alraigo* in June 1983 when it ran out of fuel.

The saving of human lives, 'life salvage', will not, by itself, justify a claim for salvage if it is not connected with the salvage of some 'maritime property'. The reason for this was given by Brett MR in *The Renpor*, as follows:[11]

> . . . there is one element invariably required by Admiralty law in order to found an action for salvage, there must be something saved more than life, *which will form a fund from which salvage may be paid* . . . [emphasis added]

In the past, where 'maritime property' was saved, the saving of lives was a factor taken into account by the court in increasing the amount of the salvage award, although a pure life salvor who had saved no property obtained no independent right to claim salvage. Such a right was given by s 544(1) of the **Merchant Shipping Act 1894**[12] in respect of salvage of any vessels within British waters and of British vessels outside British waters. In *Cargo ex Schiller*,[13] it was held that this right also applied where property was saved but not salved, as where the cargo owners subsequently raised their own property from the ocean bed.[14] Furthermore, s 544(2) gave life salvors priority over all other salvors.

These provisions have now been repealed. The entitlement of life salvors is now governed by Art 16 of the **1989 Salvage Convention**. This allows life salvors to share in the eventual award given to the property salvors 'for salving the vessel or other property or preventing or minimising damage to the environment'. However, it gives them no independent right of action against the owners of the salved property, or any priority over the property salvors. Such a parasitic right may pose problems for life salvors in the event either of the insolvency of the property salvor or of the possible reduction of their award due to misconduct. Property salvors, too, may be inconvenienced by the risk that any award obtained before the expiry of the two-year time limit for instituting proceedings may need to be shared with life salvors, without the initial award having been enhanced by reason of the life salvage.

Where insufficient property is salved to give an adequate reward to life salvors, the Department of Transport may use its discretion to make payments out of the Mercantile Marine Fund.[15] The discretion exists only in relation to salvage services in British waters. For salvage services outside such waters, the discretion is exercisable only in relation to salvage services rendered to British vessels.

Contractual salvage of non-maritime property

The definition of 'maritime property' is significant only in that it limits the types of property that can be salved by a pure 'volunteer' salvor. It is always open to parties to contract expressly that property other than 'maritime property' be the subject of salvage. This happened with the recovery by Wijsmuller, pursuant to a contract on an LOF form, of the oil rig *Orion*, which ran aground on rocks in the Channel Islands in January 1978. However, this type of self-styled salvage is purely contractual and will not amount to salvage for the purposes of creating a maritime lien. Claims arising out of such a contract would not easily fit within the list of permitted claims in *rem*, although a reference to English law would potentially render the claim subject to the *in personam* jurisdiction of the High Court.

---

11 (1883) 8 PD 115, 117.
12 Replacing s 458 of the Merchant Shipping Act 1854.
13 (1877) 2 PD 145.
14 The general rule is that one cannot salve one's own property.
15 Schedule II, Pt II, para 4 of the Merchant Shipping Act 1995, formerly s 544(3) of the Merchant Shipping Act 1894.

The requirement of danger

'Maritime property' must also satisfy one further condition before it can be the subject of salvage. It must be in danger when the services are rendered. Exposure to danger is critical, because the preservation of property from danger is the underlying policy reason justifying the rewards given to maritime salvors. If some property is exposed to danger, but other property is not, the latter will not be liable in respect of salvage. Thus, in *The Geertje K*,[16] cargo was not exposed to danger and its owners were not liable in respect of the salvage reward.

In assessing danger to maritime property, the salvor must prove that a reasonably prudent and skilful person in charge of the venture would not have refused the salvor's help. However, where LOF has been signed, the shipowner will be estopped from disputing the existence of danger.[17] 'Danger' usually entails physical danger to the maritime property. Non-physical danger, such as the possibility of that property incurring liability to third parties, is probably insufficient on its own to constitute danger, but, when combined with physical danger, will be a factor tending to enhance a salvage award.[18]

The danger need not be a present one. A reasonable apprehension of future danger will also suffice. This is illustrated by *The Aldora*,[19] where a vessel ran aground outside a dredged channel leading into Blyth harbour. At that point, the vessel was held to be in a position of danger because it was unlikely that she would have refloated without assistance. Even if she had been able to do so, it was unlikely that she would have been able to keep clear of the west bank of the dredged channel.

Once initial danger is proved, it becomes necessary to establish when the vessel has reached a place of safety, for, at that point, the salvage services will cease.[20] This was the issue in *The Troilus v The Glenogle*,[21] where a vessel lost the use of her propeller in the Indian Ocean. She was towed 1,050 miles to an anchorage at Aden. There were no facilities there to repair the vessel or to discharge or store the cargo on board. Accordingly, a second tow was arranged to her destination in the UK. Repairs in the Mediterranean would have involved difficulty. The initial tow was clearly a salvage service and the salvage services continued throughout the second tow. The services lasted as long as the master continued to act reasonably for the combined benefit of ship and cargo.

Lord Porter considered the following factors to be relevant to this issue, which are summarised by Kennedy:[22]

> ... the lesser ability of a disabled vessel to deal with emergencies such as fire or being set adrift; the danger of deterioration of ship and cargo (especially if perishable) if not removed; the facility for repairs at the place in question; the possibility of safely discharging and storing the cargo and sending it on to its destination; the possibility of expenses and the effect of delay upon both ship and cargo; and the possibility of repair at convenient ports and the time involved and safety of the operation to ship and cargo.

Their Lordships upheld the first-instance decision of Lord Merriman P that the second tow constituted a salvage service. However, they stressed that there was no general principle that an immobilised vessel remained in danger until it had regained its means of propulsion.

Clause A of LOF 2000 leaves open the question of whether the place agreed by the parties for redelivery of the salved property to its owners is, in fact, a place of safety.[23] Clause H, however,

---

16 [1971] 1 Lloyd's Rep 285.
17 *The Beaverford (Owners) v The Kafiristan (Owners)* [1938] AC 136.
18 *The Whippingham* (1934) 48 Ll L Rep 49.
19 [1975] QB 748.
20 Per Bucknill LJ in *The Troilus v The Glenogle* [1951] AC 820, HL, this burden falls on the owner of the property salved.
21 Ibid.
22 Kennedy, *Law of Salvage*, 15th edn, 1985, London: Stevens, para 339.
23 Unlike LOF 1990, which contained a provision deeming such a place to be a safe place.

provides that 'The Contractors' services shall be deemed to have been performed when the property is in a safe condition at the place of safety'. It goes on to provide that the property shall be regarded as being in a safe condition 'notwithstanding that the property (or part thereof) is damaged or in need of maintenance if (i) the Contractors are not obliged to remain in attendance to satisfy the requirements of any port or harbour authority, governmental agency or similar authority and (ii) the continuation of skilled salvage services from the Contractors or other salvors is no longer necessary to avoid the property becoming lost or significantly further damaged or delayed'.

Before leaving the issue of danger, consideration must be given to the question of whether property may be salved other than at the express request of its owners. The answer would seem to be a qualified 'yes', provided that the situation in which the ship finds herself is one in which a prudent person would accept the services on offer.[24] In such a situation, the salvor will still be entitled to its reward, even if it performs the services in the face of the objections of the owner of the property in question.[25]

Article 19 of the **1989 Salvage Convention** deals with the issue by giving the shipowner, but not the owners of cargo on board, the right to make an express and reasonable prohibition of salvage services. This right is also given to 'the owner of any other property in danger which is not and has not been on board the vessel'. This proviso is intended to cover property that is not intentionally and permanently attached to the shoreline, such as buoys or navigational aids.[26]

What are the geographical limits of salvage?

Prior to 1995, English law limited salvage to assistance rendered in tidal waters,[27] and this was confirmed when the House of Lords in The Goring[28] rejected a claim for salvage in respect of services rendered in the non-tidal reaches of the River Thames. The **1989 Salvage Convention**, however, defines salvage so as to include assistance 'in navigable waters or in any other waters whatsoever'. To preserve the effect of the pre-existing geographical limitation, the UK adopted the right of reservation contained in Art 30 of the Convention so as to exclude salvage claims in 'inland waters'. Part II, para 2(1) of Sched 11 to the **Merchant Shipping Act 1995** excludes the provisions of the Convention regarding both:

(a)   any 'salvage operation which takes place in inland waters[29] of the United Kingdom and in which all the vessels involved are of inland navigation'; and

(b)   any 'salvage operation which takes place in inland waters of the United Kingdom and in which no vessel is involved'.

Who can be a salvor?

A salvage claim may be made by the owners of the vessel rendering assistance. It may also be made by the crew of the salving vessel and by any other person who renders personal assistance or who allows their property to be used in rendering assistance. In appropriate circumstances, even the

---

24 The Annapolis (1861) Lush 295; The Vandyck (1882) 5 Asp MLC 17, CA.
25 The August Legembre [1902] P 123. See, also, The Jonge Bastian (1804) 5 C Rob 322, 323.
26 Shaw, op cit fn 9, p 226, suggests that to give the proviso this meaning, the words 'the vessel' need to be read as 'a vessel'.
27 That is, beyond the ebb and flow of the tide at ordinary spring tides.
28 [1988] 1 AC 831.
29 Paragraph 2(2) defines these so as to exclude any waters 'within the ebb and flow of the tide at ordinary spring tides or the waters of any dock which is directly or (by means of one or more other docks) indirectly, connected with such waters'.

owners of cargo carried on board the salved vessel may perform services entitling them to claim a salvage reward.[30] Where a vessel is salved by the exertions of more than one salvor, a single award will be made, which will be apportioned between them, with a further apportionment being made between the owners and crew of each vessel.

If the vessel is on demise charter, the demise charterer will claim in place of the shipowner. Where the vessel is chartered other than by demise, the charterer will have no entitlement to salvage, although the terms of the charter may provide for some apportionment of any award between itself and the shipowner. However, such an agreement will have no effect on third parties, such as the owners of the property salved.

The entitlement to salvage will be lost if the person rendering assistance cannot be shown to have acted as a 'volunteer' – that is, where the assistance was rendered pursuant to a prior duty owed towards the owners of the salved property arising before the onset of the danger. Thus, the performance of salvage services under a contract of salvage, such as LOF, will not deprive the salvor of its status as a 'volunteer'. At the time that such contract was concluded, the salvor would have owed no prior duty to assist the ship in distress.

Contractual duties

The prior duty may be contractual. The crew of the salved vessel may assist in its preservation, but will not thereby become entitled to salvage. Their efforts will be regarded as no more than the performance of their pre-existing duties under their contracts of employment. They will only become entitled when they perform services after the vessel has been abandoned by the master, thereby discharging these prior duties. There are four elements to a valid 'abandonment'. First, it must take place at sea, and not upon the coast. Secondly, it must be without hope of return or recovery. Thirdly, it must be bona fide and for the purpose of saving lives. Fourthly, it must be by order of the master in consequence of danger by reason of damage to the ship and the state of the elements.

An example of crew becoming entitled to salvage following an abandonment is given by *The San Demetrio*.[31] A ship in a wartime convoy was carrying a cargo of petrol and was set on fire. The master gave the order to abandon ship. Some of the crew later sighted the ship from their lifeboat and decided to reboard her. They then put out the fires, restarted her engines, and sailed the ship and her cargo 700 miles to the port of refuge.

Services performed under contracts of towage will also fail to qualify for salvage if they amount to no more than the performance of the service contracted for. However, if the services go beyond those called for by the particular contract of towage, salvage may become payable. This happened in *The Aldora*,[32] where tugs were engaged to tow a ship into harbour. The ship then went aground and the tugs rendered services to refloat her that went beyond the services contemplated by the prior contract of towage. Accordingly, salvage became due in respect of services rendered while the vessel was in danger, with the towage contract regulating the parties' relations once the vessel was out of danger. Contractual services were also turned into salvage in *The Star Maria*,[33] where a steering tug assisted a tug rendering salvage services under LOF. When the towage connection between this tug and the casualty broke, the steering tug assisted the casualty, which was in danger of grounding, by pulling her stern out of shallow waters and holding her in position. These services went beyond those contemplated in the contract and were not foreseeable at the time that the tug was engaged as a steering tug. Accordingly, the steering tug was entitled to salvage remuneration at common law,

---

30 *The Sava Star* [1995] 2 Lloyd's Rep 134.
31 (1941) 69 Ll L Rep 5.
32 [1975] QB 748.
33 [2002] EWHC 1423 (Admlty); [2003] 1 Lloyd's Rep 183.

in respect of services rendered to the casualty from the time at which she lost her connection with the salving tug until the time at which that connection was resumed.

In contrast, in *The Texaco Southampton*,[34] a contract was made specifically to tow a disabled vessel in danger. Salvage, therefore, could not be claimed by the head contractor as the services to be performed would not go beyond the ambit of those for which it had been engaged under its particular contract of towage. For the same reason, neither the subcontractor that actually towed the vessel, nor its crew, were entitled to claim salvage.[35]

Article 17 of the **1989 Salvage Convention** maintains the existing law by providing:

> No payment is due under the provisions of this Convention unless the services exceed what can be reasonably considered as due performance of a contract entered into before the danger arose.

Public duties

The prior duty may also be a public duty. In *The Bostonian and Patterson v The Gregerso (Owners)*,[36] a public authority was unable to claim salvage in respect of the use of one of its tugs to remove a vessel that had stranded in the fairway to Boston harbour. The harbour authority was under a public duty to use its statutory powers of wreck removal. Only if it had provided services beyond the ambit of its public duty would it have been able to claim a salvage reward. In contrast, in *The Mbashi*,[37] the emergency arose outside the harbour and therefore the assistance of the port authority vessel could not be attributed to performance of its pre-existing public duty of removing obstructions to the harbour.

However, salvage may still be claimed even though the salving vessel is performing a statutory duty to assist other vessels in distress. In *The Tower Bridge*,[38] the defendant's vessel was in danger in an ice field and sent out an SOS. The plaintiff's vessel proceeded towards her and got to within six miles of her. Her condition was now not so serious as first thought. The plaintiff refused the defendant's request to stand by and see her into the next port. However, it radioed advice as to the course that she should steer to get to clear water. The plaintiff's assistance earned it a salvage reward, even though it had, in one sense, merely been complying with the duty to answer a distress call imposed on it by s 26 of the **Merchant Shipping (Safety and Load Line Conventions) Act 1932**.[39]

In coming to this conclusion, the court was aided by the fact that s 22 expressly provided that it should not affect the provisions of s 6 of the **Maritime Conventions Act 1911**.[40] This imposes a general duty of assistance and specifically preserves the right to claim salvage. There is no equivalent saving provision in respect of the duty to stand by imposed on colliding vessels by s 422 of the **Merchant Shipping Act 1894**. Nonetheless, it has been held that the performance of this duty, in itself, does preclude entitlement to a salvage award.[41]

The **1989 Salvage Convention** deals with the performance of public duties in Art 5(3), which states:

> The extent to which a public authority under a duty to perform salvage operations may avail itself of the rights and remedies provided for in this Convention shall be determined by the law of the State where such authority is situated.

---

34 [1983] 1 Lloyd's Rep 94, CA (NSW).
35 See, also, *The Tramp* [2007] EWHC 31 (Admlty); [2007] 2 Lloyd's Rep 363. A tug may make a salvage claim where the vessel to be towed is impeded in manoeuvring and is effectively immobilised, so that a reasonable person would not refuse salvage assistance in such circumstances.
36 [1971] 1 Lloyd's Rep 220.
37 [2002] 2 Lloyd's Rep 502.
38 [1936] P 30.
39 Now s 93 of the Merchant Shipping Act 1995.
40 Now replaced by Art 10 of the 1989 Salvage Convention.
41 *The SS Melanie and The SS San Onofre* [1925] AC 246; *The Beaverford (Owners) v The Kafiristan (Owners)* [1938] AC 136.

Self-interest

Performance of salvage services out of pure self-interest may also have the effect of disentitling that person to the status of 'volunteer'. Passengers, therefore, will generally be unable to claim in respect of salvage, as will the owners of the salving vessel where they are also the owners of either the ship or the cargo that they salve. However, the prohibition does not extend to the crew of the salving vessel where they perform services beyond those required by their contracts of service. Neither does it debar the shipowner from claiming salvage from cargo interests on a sister ship to which it renders assistance.

Furthermore, self-interest is no bar to a claim to salvage where a person performs services over and above those to be expected from someone in their position. Thus, in The Lomonosoff,[42] British and Belgian soldiers, who had been assisting the 'White' Russians in the civil war, escaped from Murmansk, which was about to fall to the Bolsheviks, by boarding a steamship that they navigated to safety and handed over to its owners after their escape. The soldiers were entitled to a salvage award for saving the vessel, even though, in doing so, they had also saved their own lives. Hill J stated that 'where in a case like the present the salvor has two means of saving himself and elects one which also saves maritime property I have no doubt that qua that property he is a volunteer'. More recently, in The Sava Star, Clarke J allowed a claim for salvage by the owners of cargo on board the distressed ship.[43] He regarded the motives of the potential salvor as being irrelevant. Provided that the cargo owners did more than could be expected of someone in their position, such as merely relaying information to the shipowner regarding the cargo, there was nothing to debar them from claiming salvage.

The **1989 Salvage Convention** contains no prohibitions on claims for salvage in respect of one's own property and 'sister ship' salvage is specifically permitted under Art 12(3).[44] It is therefore likely that, in future, persons who render salvage services within the definition contained in Art 1(a) will be debarred from claiming a salvage reward under the Convention only if they fall within Art 5(3) in relation to the performance of public duties, or Art 17 in relation to contractual ones.

What services qualify for salvage?

The general rule of 'no cure, no pay'

The would-be salvor's services must, to some extent, be successful if they are to form the basis of a salvage award. If the assisted vessel is lost, there can be no claim for salvage. In The Renpor,[45] a vessel in distress asked another to stand by her. The two masters made an agreement for a fixed sum that the sound vessel would remain by the damaged vessel until she was in a safe position to get to port. When the distressed vessel was about to sink, her crew were taken onto the other vessel. However, no claim for life salvage was sustainable by this assistance. The vessel had sunk and therefore there was no fund out of which an award could be made.

Where the distressed vessel is saved, it is usually a requirement that the efforts of the assisting vessel actually contributed to her preservation. Such assistance may be purely passive, as in The Alraigo.[46] Entitlement to salvage will not be lost if the property is destroyed after it has been brought to a place of safety.[47] The general rule was put by Lord Phillimore as follows in The SS Melanie and The SS San Onofre:[48]

---

42 [1921] P 97.
43 [1995] 2 Lloyd's Rep 134.
44 Although such a claim would not give rise to a maritime lien, as a claimant in an Admiralty action is still unable to apply for the arrest of its own property.
45 (1883) 8 PD 115.
46 Noted (1984) LMCLQ 696.
47 The Bormarsund (1860) Lush 77, where the ship was subsequently damaged due to the negligence of the pilot.
48 [1925] AC 246.

Services which rescue a vessel from one danger but end by leaving her in a position of as great or nearly as great danger though of another kind, are held not to contribute to the ultimate success and do not entitle to salvage reward. In considering these questions whether the service has been meritorious, the court has leant towards supporting a claim for salvage.

Where doubt exists as to the value of the service, the court will resolve it in favour of the salvor.[49]

The rule can sometimes lead to injustice, as in The Benlarig.[50] The Vesta was to tow The Benlarig to Gibraltar. After 130 miles, The Benlarig's hawser broke and fouled The Vesta's anchor. The Vesta was now disabled, so her master disengaged from The Benlarig and proceeded to Gibraltar to give information as to the position and condition of The Benlarig. Another vessel set out and successfully salved The Benlarig. The Vesta was awarded nothing for her efforts, which had left The Benlarig temporarily in greater danger than when the tow commenced. No credit was given for the information given to the eventual salvor, nor to the fact that The Vesta's efforts had left The Benlarig considerably nearer her destination.[51] However, if the vessel is left at a place of greater comparative safety, the first salvor may be entitled to salvage remuneration if she is eventually salved.[52]

An exception to the rule occurs when the distressed vessel requests services that are then provided, even though the services do not contribute to the saving of the distressed vessel. In The Undaunted,[53] a ship parted from both anchors and engaged a steamer to go onshore and bring back an anchor and chain. The steamer placed the anchor and chain on board two luggers and, for three days, they all looked for the distressed ship. When the steamer fell in with her, she was no longer in a condition of imminent distress. The steamer towed her to port. The luggers only arrived with the anchor and chain after the steamer had arrived in port. The master of the distressed vessel was no longer interested in taking the anchor and chain. Nonetheless, both the steamer and the luggers were entitled to remuneration for the whole of their efforts. Dr Lushington gave the reason for this decision as follows:[54]

> Salvors who volunteer, go out at their own risk for the chance of earning reward, and if they labour unsuccessfully, they are entitled to nothing: the effectual performance of salvage service is that which gives them a title to salvage remuneration. But if men are engaged by a ship in distress, whether generally or particularly, they are to be paid according to their efforts made, even though the labour and service may not prove beneficial to the vessel . . . The engagement to render assistance to a vessel in distress, and the performance of that agreement so far as necessary or so far as possible, establish a title to salvage reward.

The exception will apply only if the distressed property is, in fact, salved. In The Tarbert,[55] a tug was engaged to tow in-shore a damaged vessel that struck a bank before completion of the towage. Although £17,000 worth of cargo was recovered from the vessel as she lay on the bank, it was proved that, had the vessel been allowed to sink in deep water, an equivalent value of cargo could have been salved. The tug was therefore not entitled to salvage, nor to her contractual remuneration, as she had failed to complete her indivisible obligation of towing the vessel to safety. In contrast, in The Westbourne,[56] a tug was engaged to tow a disabled vessel to Gibraltar. Following a hurricane on the journey, which left the tug short of ropes, it was decided to tow only to Cartagena. The contractual

---

49 The EU (1853) 1 Ecc & Ad 63.
50 (1888) 14 PD 3.
51 The tug was, however, awarded a quantum meruit sum for the services performed in towing the distressed ship.
52 The Camellia (1883) 9 PD 27.
53 (1860) Lush 90.
54 Ibid, 92.
55 [1921] P 372.
56 (1889) 14 PD 132.

service had not been completed and so nothing was due under the contract. However, the tug received salvage in excess of its contractual remuneration for its extra-contractual services that led to the successful preservation of the tow during and after the hurricane.

Under the **1989 Salvage Convention**, it is doubtful whether the exception survives, at least as a claim to salvage. Article 12(1) provides that 'Salvage operations which have had a useful result give right to a reward', and Art 12(2) goes on to state that 'Except as otherwise provided, no payment is due under this Convention if the salvage operations have had no useful result'. Where the performance of the engaged services does not contribute at all to the eventual salvage, as was the case on the facts of The Undaunted, they will have had no 'useful result' and cannot therefore give rise to a payment under the Convention. It is likely that a court would reward such services by awarding a quantum meruit payment under an implied contract. However, the rights created thereby would be contractual, and not in the nature of salvage. They could not, therefore, give rise to a maritime lien.[57]

It should be noted that it is always possible to contract on the basis that remuneration will be paid on an alternative basis in the event of unsuccessful salvage. Such a provision was found in a towage contract considered by the House of Lords in Admiralty Commissioners v m/v Valverda. Their Lordships held that the agreement was nonetheless a salvage agreement. Lord Roche said:[58]

> It is true enough that 'no cure, no pay' is the essence of salvage. Unless the res is saved and a claimant to salvage brings about or contributes to its safety he is not ordinarily entitled to claim salvage remuneration in the proper sense; but there is no reason in principle or upon any authority why a person should not alternatively be a salvor entitled to salvage remuneration or a labourer worthy of some hire. That alternative position may arise by reason of any agreement antecedent to any salvage services, as in the familiar case of a towage agreement . . . In such a case salvage remuneration may be earned if the circumstances warrant it, but if it is not, the towage money will be payable . . .

If payment becomes due on a non-salvage basis, then that claim will not constitute a maritime lien.

Environmental salvage

An exception to the principle of 'no cure, no pay' has developed since 1980 with regard to the efforts of salvors to prevent oil pollution from the vessels they attempt to salve. Salvors of oil tankers face particular problems. Oil may escape during the salvage operations and they may be held liable for the resultant pollution. They may lose any entitlement to salvage if the operations are unsuccessful; for example, if a neighbouring government orders the destruction of the vessel. Even if they are successful, the salved value of the tanker may not be sufficiently high to encourage salvors to run these risks.

For these reasons, LOF 1980 introduced the twin concepts of the 'enhanced award' and the 'safety net'. Both concepts apply only to the salvage, or attempted salvage, of oil tankers, laden wholly or in part with a cargo of oil. Clause 1(a) imposed a duty on the salvor to use its best endeavours to prevent the escape of oil from the vessel while performing the services of salving. The prevention of oil pollution during the salvage services was singled out as a factor that would 'enhance' any ultimate award. When the operations were not successful, and the salvor therefore lost its entitlement to a traditional salvage award, LOF 1980 provided a 'safety net' whereby the salvor should be awarded its reasonably incurred expenses, together with a profit element of up to 15 per cent thereof. These 'safety net' expenses were to be payable only by the shipowner, and not

57 In this respect, see Gaskell, Current Law Statutes 1995, 1995, London: Sweet & Maxwell, Vol 2, at pp 398–9.
58 [1938] AC 173, 202.

by cargo interests. The provisions would not apply when the lack of success was attributable to the negligence of the salvor.

Modified versions of the 'enhanced award' and the 'safety net' appear in Arts 13 and 14 of the **1989 Salvage Convention**, which were specifically incorporated into LOF 1990.[59] Unlike their LOF 1980 precursors, these provisions are not limited to laden tankers. Article 13(1)(b) lists 'the skill and efforts of the salvors in preventing or minimising damage to the environment' as one of the factors to be considered in assessing any salvage award, although it does not specifically state that any priority be given to it over the other listed factors.[60] However, the provision is worded to reward success. Therefore, the skill and efforts of salvors in attempting to minimise damage to the environment will fall outside the provision if those efforts turn out to be of no avail.

'Damage to the environment' is defined in Art 1(d) as 'substantial physical damage to human health or to marine life or resources in coastal or inland waters or areas adjacent thereto', which falls within one of the following listed headings: 'Pollution, contamination, fire, explosion or similar major incidents.' It should be noted that this definition is limited to 'substantial' damage, which must be 'physical'. Furthermore, unlike the 'safety net' provisions in LOF 1980, the Convention's environmental provisions are geographically limited to damage in coastal waters.[61]

Article 14(1) and (2) provide the Convention's 'safety net' equivalents. Article 14(1) gives a salvor 'special compensation', based on the salvor's expenses as defined in Art 14(3), if it has failed to earn an award under Art 13 at least equivalent to such 'special compensation'. This shortfall between any award and the expenses-based 'special compensation' is to fall entirely on shipowners. Their liability insurers, the P&I Clubs, are thereby made directly concerned with any salvage award involving environmental considerations.

'Special compensation' is available 'if the salvor has carried out salvage operations[62] in respect of a vessel which by itself or its cargo threatened damage to the environment . . .'.[63] Article 14(1) will entitle the salvor to 'special compensation', even if the salvage operation fails to prevent or minimise damage to the environment, but this will be limited to its expenses as defined in Art 14(3).[64] If, however, the salvor does manage to prevent or minimise damage to the environment, Art 14(2) gives the tribunal power to increase the 'special compensation' payable by up to a maximum of 30 per cent of the salvor's expenses. However, if the tribunal considers it fair and just to do so, it may make a further increase up to a total increase of 100 per cent of the salvor's expenses.

Article 14(3) defines the salvor's expenses for the purposes of Art 14(1) and (2) as:[65]

> . . . out of pocket expenses reasonably incurred by the salvor in the salvage operation and a fair rate for equipment and personnel actually and reasonably used in the salvage operation taking into consideration the criteria listed in Art 13(h), (i) and (j).

These provisions were considered by the House of Lords in *The Nagasaki Spirit*.[66] Services were rendered under LOF 1990, which incorporated Arts 13 and 14, to a tanker on fire after a collision in the Malacca Strait. The main question at issue was how a 'fair rate' for tugs used should be calculated. Their Lordships endorsed the judgment of the Court of Appeal that the assessment should

---

59 LOF 1995 incorporates the Convention in its entirety.
60 Tribunals are not obliged to specify what proportion of their award is made up of this 'enhanced' element.
61 Where there is the threat of oil pollution outside coastal areas from a laden tanker in distress, salvors may be better advised to contract on LOF 1980, which would be permissible under Art 6(1).
62 As defined in Art 1(a).
63 Pure cargo recovery operations, therefore, fall outside the scope of Art 14.
64 Cf the requirement of success in Art 13(1)(b). Gaskell (op cit fn 57, p 408) argues that the salvor may become entitled under Art 14(1) in respect of expenses incurred in relation to a reasonably perceived environmental threat, even though it subsequently transpires that there was in fact no such threat.
65 Namely, the promptness, availability, and readiness and efficiency of the salvor's equipment.
66 [1997] 1 Lloyd's Rep 323, noted (1997) LMCLQ 321.

cover the overhead costs of the salvors in maintaining salvage craft in readiness. However, it should not include any profit element, as the tribunal has an opportunity to award this under the 'mark-up' provisions of Art 14(2) if the operations successfully prevent or minimise damage to the environment. Their Lordships also held that Art 14 expenses are not limited to those incurred in attempts to minimise pollution, but cover all of the expenses incurred in the salvage operation. The decision has been bitterly criticised by the salvage industry as providing an inadequate recompense for the costs of maintaining salvage tugs in readiness during a period of general decline in demand for their services.

Article 14(4) provides that special compensation under Art 14 shall be paid 'only if and to the extent that such compensation is greater than any reward recoverable by the salvor under Art 13'. Accordingly, the tribunal must first fix both a salvage award under Art 13 and the amount of special compensation under Art 14. The latter amount starts with an assessment of the amount of the salvor's expenses under Art 14(3), to which a mark-up is applied under Art 14(2) if the salvor has successfully minimised or prevented damage to the environment.

Strictly speaking, the award under Art 13 must be assessed separately from the amount of any special compensation payable under Art 14. However, some cross-checking is permissible, and indeed inevitable, given that the assessment of Art 14 compensation will involve the consideration of factors that are also relevant to the assessment of the award under Art 13.[67] The tribunal, in making this initial dual assessment, is also to be guided by the Common Understanding to the **1989 Salvage Convention**. This appears in para 4 of Pt II of Sched 11 to the 1995 Act and provides that:

> . . . in fixing a reward under Art 13 and assessing special compensation under Art 14 . . . [the tribunal] is under no duty to fix a reward under Art 13 up to the maximum salved value of the vessel and other property before assessing the special compensation to be paid under Art 14.

Its purpose is as a reminder of the need for tribunals to hold a fair balance between salving and salved interests.

Having separately assessed the sums due under Arts 13 and 14, the tribunal must then check whether the sum awarded under Art 13 exceeds that under Art 14. If so, the Art 14 sums are disregarded. Thus:

Salvage award under Art 13	US$800,000
Salvor's expenses under Art 14(3)	US$700,000

Only the salvage award is payable.

If, however, the Art 14 sums exceed those awarded under Art 13, the difference between them becomes payable solely by the shipowner under Art 14(4).[68] The award under Art 13 will be apportioned pro rata between ship, cargo and freight in the usual way.

Salvage award under Art 13	US$800,000
Salvor's expenses under Art 14(3)	US$700,000
30% mark-up under Art 14(2)	US$210,000
Total payable under Art 14	US$910,000
Balance payable by shipowner	US$110,000

---

67 Per Clarke J in the first-instance decision in *The Nagasaki Spirit* [1995] 2 Lloyd's Rep 44. This part of his decision was not subject to the subsequent appeals to the Court of Appeal and the House of Lords, which were purely concerned with the correct assessment of a 'fair rate' under Art 14.

68 However, Art 14(6) preserves the shipowner's right of recourse against third parties, such as the other vessel involved in a collision, in respect of its liability for Art 14 special compensation. By virtue of Sched VII, Pt II, para 4 of the Merchant Shipping Act 1995, the other vessel may not limit in respect of such a claim.

The SCOPIC clause

As a result of discontent by salvors at the calculation of Art 14 remuneration after *The Nagasaki Spirit*, in 1999, a new clause was drafted to give salvors an alternative basis of remuneration. The clause was the Special Compensation P&I Club clause (the SCOPIC clause) and, although its provisions only affect the relationship between the salvor and the shipowner, the International Group of P&I Clubs has agreed a code of conduct giving its backing to the clause whenever a ship entered with the International Group is salved by a member of the International Salvage Union (the ISU). The salient features of the clause, which received clarificatory amendment in 2000, are as follows:

- For the clause to operate, it needs to be specifically incorporated into an LOF contract, of whatever form. LOF 2000 contains a box to be ticked if the parties agree to the incorporation of the SCOPIC clause. If the clause is incorporated, it then needs to be invoked by the salvor.[69] This can be done even if there is no threat to the environment. Invoking the clause completely replaces the right of the salvor to claim under Art 14, even in respect of services performed before the invocation of the clause.[70] The provisions of Art 14(5) and (6), however, continue to remain effective. Within two days of the clause being invoked, cl 3 obliges the shipowner to put up security for the salvor's claim under the clause in the amount of US$3 million. If the shipowner fails to do so, cl 4 entitles the salvor to withdraw from the SCOPIC clause, provided that the security is still outstanding at the date of withdrawal.

- Clause 5 provides that SCOPIC remuneration is to be calculated by reference to an agreed tariff of rates that are profitable to salvors, calculated by reference to the horsepower of the salvage tug(s) employed.[71] It also covers the salvor's out-of-pocket expenses. An uplift of 25 per cent is applied to both these heads of claim. Clause 6 provides that SCOPIC remuneration is payable only in the event that it exceeds the amount of the award under Art 13. To deter salvors from invoking SCOPIC too readily, cl 7 provides that, in the event of SCOPIC remuneration falling below the amount of the Art 13 award, that award shall be discounted by 25 per cent of the difference between the award and the SCOPIC remuneration. Thus, where the Art 13 award is for US$1 million and the SCOPIC remuneration is only US$600,000, the Art 13 award will be reduced by US$100,000, being 25 per cent of the difference between the two sums, giving the salvor a net award of US$900,000. The SCOPIC clause now incorporates Art 18 of the **1989 Salvage Convention**.

- The SCOPIC clause also provides for the termination of both the SCOPIC provisions and the LOF in two situations. First, the salvor can terminate if the cost of its services less any SCOPIC remunerations exceeds the value of the salved property.[72] Secondly, the shipowner can terminate by giving five days' notice.[73] These termination provisions do not apply if the contractor is restrained from demobilising its equipment by a public body with jurisdiction over the area where the services are being performed.[74] Once the clause has been invoked, the shipowner is entitled to appoint a Special Casualty Representative (SCR) to monitor the salvage services.[75] The SCR does not impinge on the authority of the salvage master, but does have the right to be kept fully informed about the progress of the salvage operations. This provision improves the flow of information back to the P&I Club, the interests of which will ultimately be affected by the salvage services.

---

69 Clause 2.
70 Clause 4.
71 Appendix A contains the daily tariff rates for personnel, tugs and other craft, and portable salvage equipment, fixed by reference to US dollars. The tariffs have been regularly increased since the introduction of SCOPIC in 1999, most recently on 1 January 2011.
72 Clause 9(i).
73 Clause 9(ii).
74 Clause 9(iii).
75 Clause 11.

What principles govern the relationship between salvor and salvee?

The law of salvage emerged as a way of rewarding non-contractual services by which maritime property was rescued. Today, however, salvage operations are usually performed on a contractual basis, although non-contractual claims may still recur. The services remain salvage services despite their contractual underpinning. By far the commonest form of salvage contract is the LOF. The principal characteristics of the LOF are as follows. First, the parties agree to refer the amount of the award, and any disputes relating to the services performed under the agreement, to arbitration in London, subject to English law. The salvor's entitlement to a reward is dependent on the principle of 'no cure, no pay', as is the case at common law. Secondly, the parties accept that the services are salvage services, thereby preventing the owner of the salved property from arguing that its property was not in danger. Thirdly, the obligations of the salvor to the salvee are spelt out with more clarity than is the case at common law. In particular, the salvor undertakes to use its best endeavours to salve the vessel and/or her cargo, bunkers and stores and to take her either to a specified place or to a place of safety. There is no equivalent duty imposed on the salvor at common law. Fourthly, under cl 13 of the LSSA clauses, the salvor is granted an express right to subcontract, although it will remain liable for performance of the salvage contract.

The relationship between salvor and salvee gives rise to the following issues, which will be considered both from the standpoint of the LOF contract and from the non-contractual position at common law:

(a)   the parties bound by the signing of a salvage agreement;
(b)   the power of the Admiralty Court to set aside a salvage agreement, and the consequences of its exercising this power;
(c)   the effect of negligence both prior to and during the salvage operations;
(d)   the right of the salvee to terminate the salvage services;
(e)   the right of the salvor to remuneration for services performed after the termination of the salvage operations.

The parties bound by the signing of a salvage agreement

At common law, the master has ostensible authority to bind the owners of the salved vessel when signing a salvage agreement[76] and also the crew, as regards prospective, but not accrued, rights to salvage.[77] However, this authority does not extend to other interests concerned in the salvage operation, such as cargo. LOF 1980 attempted to address this problem by stating that the contract is made by the captain of the salved vessel for and on behalf of its owners and of cargo on board. At common law, the captain cannot constitute himself the agent of cargo merely on his own 'say so' and the signing of LOF 1980 cannot therefore bind cargo interests. This conclusion was confirmed by the Court of Appeal in *The Choko Star*,[78] where it held that the master had no implied or ostensible authority to bind cargo.[79] The master could bind cargo only if facts existed that would justify the finding of an agency of necessity and this issue was remitted to the Admiralty

---

76 *The Unique Mariner (No 1)* [1978] 1 Lloyd's Rep 438.
77 *The Inchmaree* [1899] P 111.
78 [1990] 1 Lloyd's Rep 516.
79 See, also, *Marine Blast Ltd v Targe Towing Ltd* [2004] EWCA Civ 346; [2004] 1 Lloyd's Rep 721. A towage contract made between the charterer and the tug owner was held not to be binding on the shipowner. The charterer had no implied authority to contract on the shipowner's behalf, even though there had been a sub-bailment, or a non-contractual bailment, of the tow to the tug.

judge.[80] In the absence of any agency of necessity, the salvors would have to claim against cargo in a separate action under the general common law principles of salvage. In such an action, they would not be able to rely on the arbitration and English law provisions of LOF, nor on its contractual assumption as to the existence of the state of danger necessary to justify an award of salvage.

The decision has now been reversed by Art 6(2) of the **1989 Salvage Convention**, which gives the master the authority to conclude salvage contracts not only on behalf of the owners of the ship, but also on behalf of owners of the cargo carried on board. In *The Altair*,[81] Gross J held that Art 6(2) was not limited to a salvage contract made by the master or shipowner personally, or by an employee of the shipowner. It also applied to a salvage contract made by other agents, such as an employee of the shipowner's managers, provided that they had the necessary authority from the shipowners. Accordingly, the salvors were able to enforce an arbitration award, as a judgment, against the Iranian cargo owners, who had not participated in the arbitration. It was irrelevant that Iran was not a party to the **1989 Salvage Convention**. What mattered was that the LOF provided for arbitration in London and the Convention had the force of law in the UK. However, salvors may still face problems in holding cargo to a salvage agreement when proceeding in a jurisdiction where the Convention has not been ratified. Furthermore, it may be possible for cargo interests to avoid the effects of Art 6 if they can establish the absence of danger at the time that the contract was made. Without danger, there can be no salvage as defined by Art 1 of the Convention and therefore Art 6(2), which applies to the master's authority to 'conclude contracts for salvage operations', ceases to apply as there have been no 'salvage operations'. Should such an argument succeed, the disappointed salvor would have an action against the shipowner for breach of warranty of authority where a contract, such as LOF, had been used, which stated that it was made on behalf of both ship and cargo.[82]

Setting aside a salvage agreement

The Admiralty Court possesses inherent jurisdiction to set aside salvage agreements on general grounds of unfairness, but imposes a high burden on the party seeking to do so. Butt LJ, in *The Rialto*,[83] set out two factors that had to be established to overcome the presumption that the agreement was valid: first, the parties must be on unequal footings; and secondly, the sum insisted on must be exorbitant. A fixed sum for salvage will not be regarded as exorbitant merely because it exceeds the salved value of the vessel.[84] If a contract is set aside, the salvor will still be able to claim in respect of salvage services on a non-contractual basis, but no costs will be awarded to it.[85] However, in the event of fraud, a party who has been directly privy to the fraud is likely to lose any entitlement to salvage. The inherent jurisdiction also extends to inequitable settlements made after the services have been rendered. These principles are reflected in Art 7 of the **1989 Salvage Convention**. It is unclear whether Art 7 applies to contracts made between suppliers of salvage vessels and salvors.[86]

---

80 See *The Pa Mar* [1999] 1 Lloyd's Rep 338, QB, for an example of where an agency of necessity has been found on the facts where the master has acted reasonably in signing LOF and has had no practical means of communication with the cargo interests. However, cargo interests were not bound by a subsequent variation of the LOF to specify the place of redelivery.
81 [2008] EWHC 612 (Comm); [2008] 2 Lloyd's Rep 90.
82 Gaskell, op cit fn 57, pp 384–6.
83 [1891] P 175.
84 *The Inna* [1938] P 148.
85 *The Generous* (1868) LR 2 A & E 57.
86 In *Svitzer Salvage BV v Z Energy Ltd* [2013] NZHC 2584; [2014] Lloyd's Rep Plus 19, the High Court of New Zealand held that the applicability of Art 6 of the Convention to a charterparty concluded between a specialist vessel and a salvor was not a suitable issue for summary judgment as there was insufficient authority as to whether an agreement between a third party and a salvor was capable of being regarded as relating to a 'salvage operation', and further, it did not appear to ever have been judicially considered whether Art 7 could apply to charterparties concluded for salvage operations.

An agreement may also be set aside on the general contractual principles governing mistake and misrepresentation. This, too, imposes a heavy burden on the party trying to get shot of the agreement, as can be seen in *The Unique Mariner (No 1)*.[87] A vessel stranded and her master was told by the shipowner's agents that a tug would be coming from Singapore. Another tug then offered to help, and the master accepted, under the mistaken impression that it was the tug referred to by the ship's agents. When the master found out his error, he dismissed the tug. Brandon J held that there had been no misrepresentation by the captain of the salvage tug, whose evidence on this point he preferred to that of the master of the distressed vessel; nor had there been any unilateral mistake, the tug master being unaware of the master's mistake.[88]

Salvage contracts are also subject to the provisions of s 2(1) of the **Unfair Contracts Terms Act 1977**, and are excluded from the effect of sections 2(2), 3, 4 and 7 except in favour of a person dealing as consumer.[89] They are also subject to Pt II of the **Supply of Goods and Services Act 1982**.

The effect of negligence

At common law, salvor and salvee owe a duty of care both to each other and to third parties. Negligence may occur in three instances during salvage operations.

The first is where the salvor suffers loss due to the negligence of the salvee. An example of this is provided by *The Valsesia*,[90] where two tugs contracted to beach a ship that had grounded on the rocks. During the operations, the distressed ship failed to slip its cable, with the consequence that it re-grounded. As the tugs were unable to complete their salvage services, they failed to become entitled to the lump sum due under their contract. However, they were able to recover an equivalent amount from the owners of the distressed ship by way of damages for negligence.[91]

The second is where the salvor itself negligently causes the danger that necessitates the salvage services. In *Cargo ex Capella*,[92] such negligence was held to deprive the salvor of any entitlement to a reward for its services. In *The Beaverford (Owners) v The Kafiristan (Owners)*,[93] however, the House of Lords held that the principle did not debar a claim for salvage by a vessel in the same ownership as the vessel that had collided with the salved vessel. Moreover, Lord Wright was of the view that even colliding vessels should be entitled to salvage remuneration for salvage services, subject to a cross-claim in damages by the salved vessel in respect of the negligence that necessitated those services in the first place.

The third is where the salvor negligently damages the salved property during the salvage operations. Where a non-contractual salvor is involved, the action will sound in tort.[94] Where a contractual salvor is involved, the action will sound in contract. What difference, if any, does the existence of a salvage contract make to the salvor's liability in negligence?

This question was to be answered by the House of Lords in *The Tojo Maru*.[95] A tanker that was being salved was badly damaged by an explosion caused by the negligence of the salvor's chief diver, who had fired a bolt gun into her shell plating. The salvors argued that because they had contracted on a 'no cure, no pay' basis, under LOF, the only consequence of their negligence should be to affect the amount of their salvage reward. Their Lordships rejected this argument, and held

---

87 [1978] 1 Lloyd's Rep 438.
88 [1927] P 115.
89 Schedule 1(2).
90 [1927] P 115.
91 Ibid, *per* Hill J, *obiter*, at 120, who thought that the negligence of the crew would not affect cargo interests.
92 (1867) LR 1 A & E 356.
93 [1938] AC 136.
94 *Anglo-Saxon Petroleum Co v The Admiralty and Damant (The Delphinula)* (1947) 82 Ll L Rep 459. Until the House of Lords' decision in *Mersey Docks and Harbour Board v Turner (The Zeta)* [1893] AC 468, the Admiralty Court had proceeded on the mistaken assumption that the only tort cases over which it had jurisdiction where those involving collisions, as in *The Thetis* (1869) LR 2 A & E 365.
95 [1972] AC 242.

that the owners of the salved vessel were entitled to bring a counterclaim for negligence in the salvage proceedings, even though it was likely to exceed the amount of any salvage award.

Lord Diplock analysed the contract as one for work and labour under which a duty of care would ordinarily be imposed on the contractor. The contract's special nature as one of salvage derived from the fact that it was on the basis of 'no cure, no pay', with remuneration fixed on a *quantum meruit* basis and capped by the salved values of the property salved. None of these factors was sufficient to displace the duty of care that arose under an ordinary contract for work and labour.

Not surprisingly, their Lordships held that professional salvors would have to meet a higher standard of care than non-professionals. Given the rescue nature of salvage, it will generally be very difficult to persuade a court that salvors were negligent. To avoid excessively penalising the salvors,[96] their Lordships held that the salvage award should be assessed on the hypothesis that there had been no negligence and then deducted from the damages. They rejected the views of the Court of Appeal that damages should only be awarded if the salvors had done 'more harm than good'.[97]

The principles set out in *The Tojo Maru* have been followed by Art 8 of the **1989 Salvage Convention**, which imposes duties on the salvor and salvee towards each other.[98] Although the Convention provides no express sanction for breach of these obligations, it cannot have been intended to impose duties without sanctions. The obvious sanction would be a claim in damages, although an issue might remain as to whether this should be assessed on a contractual or a tortious basis. Where the duty corresponds with an equivalent duty in a contract such as LOF, it is submitted that the contractual measure should be applied.

Article 8(1) imposes the following duties on the salvor:

(a)   to carry out the salvage operations with due care;[99]
(b)   in performing the duty specified in (a), to exercise due care to prevent or minimise damage to the environment;[100]
(c)   whenever circumstances reasonably require, to seek assistance from other salvors; and
(d)   to accept the intervention of other salvors when reasonably requested to do so by the owner or master of the vessel or other property in danger, provided that the amount of his reward shall not be prejudiced should it be found that such a request was unreasonable.

Article 8(2) imposes the following duties on the salvee:

(a)   to cooperate fully with the salvor in the course of the salvage operations;[101]
(b)   in so doing, to exercise due care to prevent or minimise damage to the environment; and
(c)   when the vessel or other property has been brought to a place of safety, to accept redelivery when reasonably requested by the salvor to do so.[102]

---

96 By reducing the amount of the award due to salvorial misconduct, and also by having lower salved values due to the lowered value of the vessel after the explosion.
97 Calculated as follows, where U = the unsalved value of the vessel before commencement of salvage services, A = the actual salved value of the vessel, USV = the undamaged salved value of the vessel: A minus U gives the measure of 'good'; USV minus A gives the measure of 'harm', damages being the amount by which the latter exceeds the former.
98 Their duties to third parties would continue to be governed by the general law of negligence.
99 This duty is of a lower order than the contractual duty imposed by LOF whereby the salvor undertakes to use its 'best endeavours' to salve the ship and cargo.
100 'Damage to the environment' is defined in Art 1(d).
101 Although no such duty is expressly imposed on the salvor by the Convention, one would almost certainly be implied to render the salvee's obligation workable. Clause 3 of LOF 1995 imposed a mutual duty of cooperation on the contracting parties. Clause F(ii) of LOF 2000 specifies that: 'The Contractors shall be entitled to all such information as they may reasonably require relating to the vessel or the remainder of the property provided such information is relevant to the performance of the services and is capable of being provided without undue difficulty or delay.'
102 'Redelivery' means the completion of the salvage services.

The **1989 Salvage Convention** also contains two provisions under which salvorial misconduct may have the effect of reducing or extinguishing any entitlement to a salvage award or to special compensation. Article 18 provides that:

> A salvor may be deprived of the whole or part of the payment due under this Convention to the extent that the salvage operations have become necessary or more difficult because of fault or neglect on his part or if the salvor has been guilty of fraud or other dishonest conduct.

Article 14(5) provides that:

> If the salvor has been negligent and has thereby failed to prevent or minimise damage to the environment, he may be deprived of the whole or part of any special compensation due under this article.

Although neither Article refers to the possibility that misconduct may expose the salvor to a liability in damages exceeding the amount of any salvage award, their language is not such as to exclude liability under Art 8(1) as an additional consequence of salvorial misconduct.

Termination of the salvage services

The position of a salvor dismissed before it can complete its services was extensively considered by Brandon J in *The Unique Mariner (No 2)*.[103] The master of the distressed ship had engaged the first set of salvors under the mistaken impression that they were the salvors being sent by the vessel's agents. When these salvors actually arrived, the master dismissed the first salvors, although they were willing and able to continue their services. Brandon J considered the rights of the dismissed salvors on the assumption, first, that the salvage had been non-contractual, and secondly, that it had been contractual.

With non-contractual salvage, the salvor and salvee owe only minimal duties towards one another. The salvor owes a duty of care in respect of any services that it actually performs, but it owes no duty to perform those services. It is free to cease work at any time it chooses. The corollary of this is that the salvee is free to dismiss the salvor at any time, for whatever reason, justified or not. However, the dismissed salvor will be able to participate in any eventual salvage award. Its share of the award will be calculated on the basis of its expenses up to the time of its dismissal. If the salvor was willing and able to continue with the services, it will also be entitled to 'some' compensation for the loss of the opportunity to earn a full salvage award by completing the salvage services. However, it will not be entitled to full compensation for loss of this opportunity. The policy reason behind this entitlement is to encourage non-contractual salvors to render salvage services, despite the risk of supersession.

The position is quite different with a contractual salvor, such as the salvor in the present case, where LOF had been signed. LOF imposes an additional duty on the salvor to use its best endeavours to salve the ship and its cargo. The salvor would, therefore, no longer have the freedom unilaterally to terminate the services before the ship had reached a place of safety. A term therefore needed to be implied into LOF that, so long as the salvor was both willing and able to continue with the services, the salvee should continue to engage it.[104] In the present case, this term had been broken and the owners of the distressed ship became liable to the first salvors in damages. Damages were to be assessed on the basis of the award that would have been made had the salvor been able

---

103 [1979] 1 Lloyd's Rep 37.
104 Clause 4 of LOF 1995 expressly gives the owner of the salved vessel the right to terminate the salvage services when there is no prospect of a useful result. Clause G of LOF 2000 extends this right of termination to salvors as well as to the shipowner.

to complete the services, subject to deductions for expenses not incurred and risks not run. The claim sounded in general contract rather than salvage, so that the availability of damages was not dependent on the eventual salving of the distressed ship. In *The Valsesia*,[105] similar principles were applied when the hoped-for salvage award was lost due to the negligence of the crew of the distressed ship in cooperating with the salvors in the salvage operations.

The decision in *The Unique Mariner* (No 2) may now need to be reconsidered in the light of the provisions of the **1989 Salvage Convention**. Article 19 provides that there shall be no payment under the Convention in respect of services rendered 'notwithstanding the express and reasonable prohibition of the owner or master of the vessel . . .' and Art 8(1)(d) obliges the salvor to accept the intervention of other salvors 'when reasonably requested to do so'.[106]

Where a contractual salvor is unreasonably dismissed, the effect of these provisions would probably be similar to the actual decision in *The Unique Mariner* (No 2). However, the right of a non-contractual salvor who is dismissed to share in the eventual salvage award must now be regarded with suspicion. Pre-termination services that contributed to the eventual salving of the property could still give rise to a share in the eventual award as constituting 'an act or activity undertaken to assist a vessel or any other property in danger' under Art 1(a), which gives a 'useful result' under Art 12(1).

However, compensation in respect of the future prospect of a salvage award would no longer fit in with the requirement of 'useful result'. Nor could there be compensation by way of damages, as there would be no breach of the salvee's obligations under Art 8(2). Article 8(1)(d) would not assist either, for although it provides that the amount of a salvor's reward shall not be prejudiced by an unreasonable request to accept the intervention of other salvors, Art 12 would have the effect that such reward could be assessed solely by relation to the pre-supersession services.[107]

Post-termination services

Salvage services end when the maritime property concerned has reached a place of safety. Services rendered after that time will be compensated under principles of bailment rather than salvage. The matter was considered by the House of Lords in *The Winson*.[108] A ship was stranded outside Manila harbour. Her master signed LOF as agent for ship and cargo interests. The salvor took the cargo off the vessel and sought instructions from cargo as to its disposal. When none were forthcoming, the salvor stored it at its own expense in Manila. Shortly afterwards, the shipowners notified the cargo interests that they were abandoning the voyage. A month later, the salvors abandoned their efforts to salve the ship. The cargo was eventually released to its owners on production of a guarantee.

Cargo interests denied liability for the storage charges on the grounds that these were shipowners' items. At the time that the cargo had been salved, by being brought safely into Manila harbour, the contract of carriage was still afoot. The cargo was, therefore, deliverable to the shipowners, who had the immediate right to its possession by virtue of their lien for freight under the charterparty. Their Lordships rejected this argument on the ground that the shipowners lost their possessory lien on parting with the cargo by allowing it to be unloaded onto the salvor's lightening vessels. A relationship of bailor and bailee then arose between cargo and salvors. While the salvage services were continuing, it was a bailment for reward pursuant to the salvage contract signed on cargo's behalf; thereafter, it became a gratuitous bailment. Where a gratuitous bailee owed the bailor a duty to take reasonable steps to preserve the cargo, it was, in return, entitled to be

105 [1927] P 115.
106 Gaskell, op cit fn 57, pp 391–3.
107 Ibid, pp 422–3.
108 [1982] AC 939.

reimbursed for the expenses that it had reasonably incurred in preserving the cargo. Their Lordships declined to consider whether the salvor could also base its claim as an agent of necessity.

Under the **1989 Salvage Convention**, cargo interests in such a situation would probably also be liable in damages for breach of their obligation under Art 8(2)(c) to accept redelivery 'when reasonably requested by the salvor to do so' when their property has been brought to a place of safety.

How is any salvage award calculated?

Salved values

Salvage is awarded because maritime property has been saved. The value of the property salved forms the fund out of which the salvage award becomes payable. It follows that the award can never exceed the value of the property salved. Accordingly, the first step in assessing any reward for salvage is to fix the value of the salved property at the time that it arrived at the place of safety following the successful conclusion of the salvage operations. Not only does this put a 'cap' on the overall amount of any award, but it also determines the respective contributions to any award of the different owners of the maritime property that has been salved. Each interest will contribute pro rata according to the salved value of its property.[109] No account will be taken of differences of degree of risk or difficulty regarding that property, unless they are such as to justify the making of a separate award in respect of each item salved. Liability will fall not only on the owners of the property in question, but also on those with a possessory interest in it.[110]

Thus, if the salved value of the ship is US$2 million and that of the cargo is US$4 million, the total award cannot exceed US$6 million. Ship and cargo will contribute one third and two thirds, respectively. If the ultimate award were to be US$300,000, the ship's contribution would be US$100,000 and the cargo's US$200,000. If the award is enhanced because of life salvage, the amount of such enhancement will be apportioned rateably between the owners of the maritime property salved. But if, say, cargo alone is salved, any enhancement due to the saving of life will be borne solely by cargo interests. It is important to note that each owner of maritime property is liable only for its share of a salvage award. If, say, cargo interests have not been made a party to the proceedings, the salvors will be unable to recover their share of the award from the shipowners.[111]

The salved property must be valued at the time and place at which the salvage services terminate, and the burden of proving its value lies on the salvors. If separate salvage services are rendered closely together in time, it will generally be appropriate to arrive at a single salved value at the time and place at which the maritime property reached a place of safety. In *The Ningpo*,[112] a vessel was stranded on a reef in the China Sea. Assistance was rendered to her by various salvors and she finally reached a place of safety when she was beached at Weihaiwei. She was then towed to Shanghai, where she was sold for £11,600. Her owners unsuccessfully argued that this figure should be taken to be her salved value, from which should be deducted, for each salvor's claim, the expenses incurred after its services had terminated. Hill J held that there had been a single salvage and therefore there could only be one salved value, to be fixed at Weihaiwei, where the ship had first come

---

109 This principle was most recently applied in *The M Vatan* [1990] 1 Lloyd's Rep 336, where no exception was admitted in circumstances when an LOF was signed that expressly recorded the fact that the master lacked authority to sign for cargo interests.

110 As in *The Five Steel Barges* (1890) 15 PD 142, as regards ship's share of the award, and in *Cargo ex Port Victor* [1901] P 243, where the time charterer was made liable for cargo's share, in its capacity as bailee.

111 *The Geestland* [1980] 1 Lloyd's Rep 628.

112 (1923) 16 Ll L Rep 392.

to a place of safety. However, where there is a distinct gap between the separate salvage services, separate salvage awards may be made, in which case the salved value of the property must be separately assessed at the termination of each service.

Events subsequent to termination that reduce the value of the property, such as changes in the market value of cargo,[113] will be disregarded. In *The Josefina Thorden*,[114] a Finnish tanker was salved in the Second World War. After security had been posted and while the vessel was under repair, Finland was declared to be enemy territory and the vessel seized as prize. This obviously diminished her value, but had no effect on the assessment of her salved value. Salved values may even be assessed on the basis of the value of the property *before* it arrives at a place of safety where the value is depressed by the misconduct of the salvee. In *The Germania*,[115] a trawler towed a disabled steamship off to Aberdeen and called for a pilot and tug to take her into harbour. The steamship improperly refused this assistance and drifted ashore. The resulting repairs and cost of refloating reduced her value to £1,750, yet the salvage award was based on a salved value for the steamship of £8,500. This represented the value that she would have had at Aberdeen, had she accepted the assistance offered to get her into harbour.

Ship's value

The ship will usually be valued at her value in sound condition less the costs of placing her in such a condition. Alternatively, the ship may be valued by reference to her scrap value if this produces a higher valuation.

Repair costs are easily proved, but the assessment of the vessel's sound value is more problematic. There is a divergence of authority as to how this should be assessed. One approach would be simply to assess the ship's value on the open market. In the absence of a sale of the salved vessel, this is proved by reference to evidence of sales of similar ships sold at about the time the salvage services came to an end.[116] Another approach requires the ship's existing charter commitments to be taken into account as well. The former approach was taken in *The San Onofre*,[117] where no allowance was made for the fact that the ship was on a long time charter at a low rate of hire. In contrast, in *The Castor*,[118] charterparty commitments that increased the value of the ship were taken into account in assessing her salved value. The reasoning in the two cases is contradictory, which rules out a simplistic resolution based on a rule that charter commitments will only be considered when they raise the value of the ship.

From the ship's value, the following items are deductible: survey costs; the cost of delivery to either the port of repair or to the scrapyard as the case may be; the costs of discharging cargo if this responsibility falls on the shipowners; the costs of repairing any damage to the ship whether or not it was caused during or prior to the casualty; port charges; pilotage; towage; additional insurance premiums; and running expenses incurred during any repair period.

Cargo's value

Cargo can be valued either by taking the value of sales of comparable goods at the port of destination or by reference to the price at the port of shipment. If the latter method is adopted, a sum for freight and insurance must be added to the fob price, and a profit margin, say 10 per cent, to the cif price. Freight is not to be deducted from the salved value of cargo.[119]

---

113 *The Gaupen* (1925) 22 Ll L Rep 371.
114 [1945] 1 All ER 344.
115 [1904] P 131.
116 This mode of assessment may need to be varied when government restrictions affect the use the shipowner can make of the proceeds of sale of the ship. See *The Eisenach* (1936) 54 Ll L Rep 354.
117 [1917] P 96.
118 [1932] P 142.
119 *The Charlotte Wylie* (1846) 2 W Rob 495, 497, and also *The Fleece* (1850) 3 W Rob 278, 282.

Where the cargo is brought to a port of refuge and carried on to the port of destination in another vessel, the cargo is valued as at the port of refuge. In *The George Dean*,[120] this valuation was reached by allowing some deduction from the sale price eventually realised at the destination, deducting freight and other charges for the on-carriage, but allowing a pro rata freight for the voyage up to the port of refuge.

Freight's value

Although freight is often referred to as a separate head of salvage, this is not really the case; rather, any freight that becomes payable by reason of the salvage operations will form part of the salved value of the ship. Freight that is due on delivery at the contractual destination will be preserved for the shipowner if the salvage services terminate at that place. The full amount of such outstanding freight will be added to the ship's salved value at that place. Where freight is pre-paid, it will be at the risk of cargo interests. This will not be considered in assessing the salved value of cargo, but will be reflected in the cif value of the cargo at the port of refuge.

Where the services terminate short of the contractual discharge port, the shipowners will be entitled to full freight if the cargo owner has prevented them from carrying the cargo on to its destination.[121] Alternatively, pro rata freight will become due if the cargo owner requests delivery at the intermediate port.[122] In both of these situations, freight will have become payable due to the exertions of the salvors and, accordingly, the freight saved will be added to the salved value of the ship. If the shipowner carries the salved cargo to its destination, it will become entitled on delivery to the full freight due at that point. Strictly speaking, none of this freight should affect the salved value of the vessel at the port of refuge, because, at that point, no freight would have been due to the shipowner. However, some part of the freight due at destination will still be allowed in calculating the salved value of the vessel at the port of refuge.[123] This will be on the basis of a pro rata apportionment, less deductions for the shipowner's expenses incurred in the further voyage from the port of refuge to the port of destination.

Those who benefit from the preservation of freight will be liable in respect of its salvage. The shipowner is, in the majority of cases, the obvious party to benefit from its preservation. Cargo, too, will be subject to arrest, as entitlement to freight is dependent upon its preservation. If cargo pays the share of salvage due on freight, it may either deduct that amount from freight when paying the shipowner, or, if it has already paid the shipowner in full for the freight due at destination, it may recover such amount from the shipowner. Whoever pays the salvor in respect of freight will discharge all other interested parties from any further liability to the salvor, thereby precluding any double recovery.[124]

Fixing the award

Once salved values have been ascertained to fix a cap on any award, the next step for the court or arbitrators is to assess the award to be made to the salvor. It is rare for an award to exceed 50 per cent of the total salved value, although an award may end up exceeding the sale value of the salved property in the event that its sale is delayed pending an arrest.[125] LOF 2000 provides that 'the currency of payment shall be in US dollars where no alternative currency has been agreed between the parties'.

---

120 (1857) Swa 290.
121 *Cargo ex Galam* (1863) 2 Moo PCC (NS) 216.
122 *Christy v Row* (1808) 1 Taunt 300.
123 *The Norma* (1859) Lush 124; *The James Armstrong* (1875) 3 Asp MLC 46. In *The Dorothy Foster* (1805) 6 C Rob 89, 91, Lord Stowell went further and allowed the full amount of such freight in the salved value of the ship.
124 Kennedy, op cit fn 22, paras 1179–80.
125 *The Lyrma (No 2)* [1978] 2 Lloyd's Rep 30.

The circumstances material to this exercise were classified as follows in *The Charlotte*.[126] As regards the salved property, the court should consider the degree of danger both to life and to property. In assessing the degree of danger, the court may make separate awards if the ship and cargo were exposed to different risks. In *The Velox*,[127] the ship ran out of coal and had to be towed to her destination. An award was made whereby cargo and freight contributed more than their salved values bore to the whole fund, because the cargo of herring would have become value-less had it remained at sea for 48 hours longer than, in fact, it did. Potential liabilities to third parties will also be taken into account, as well as physical danger to maritime property.[128] The value of the property salved is also relevant. High values will justify liberal awards, as in *The Queen Elizabeth*.[129] However, in *The Amerique* Sir James Colville stated that 'The rule seems to be that though the value of the property salved is to be considered in the estimate of the remuneration, it must not be allowed to raise the *quantum* to an amount altogether out of proportion to the services actually rendered'.[130] In *The Ocean Crown*,[131] this principle was held to apply equally to all cases and was not disapplied in complex and comprehensive cases. Therefore, the high value of the fund must not be allowed to raise the quantum of a salvage award to an amount altogether out of proportion to the services actually rendered.

As regards salvors, the following factors will be relevant: the degree of danger to life in the services; the classification, skill and conduct of the salvors; the degree of danger to the salvors' property; the time occupied and the work done in the service;[132] responsibilities incurred in the service;[133] and loss and expenses incurred in the service. Particular generosity will be shown to professional salvors. However, in *The Ocean Crown*,[134] Gross J held that future economic conditions are not to be taken into account in fixing the award. The date of termination of services is the relevant cut-off point.

Serious misconduct by salvors may result in a reduction, and, in extreme cases, a forfeiture of any award, even though the services may have been successful either wholly or in part.[135] To have this effect, the misconduct need not result in any actual damage being sustained by the maritime property.[136] However, the burden of proving misconduct lies on the owners of the maritime property in question and the standard of proof is such as leaves no reasonable doubt.[137]

The 'disparity principle' states that, in salvage cases where there is only immobilisation, and there exists no great urgency and only straightforward towage is required to effect a cure, it is important that the sum awarded should not be wholly out of line with commercial towage rates. The principle was regarded as fundamentally flawed by the arbitrator in *The Voutakos*. However, David Steel J held that commercial rates were admissible and relevant, but that their significance would depend on the facts of each case: 'In the simplest of towage cases they may be particularly influential and provide, subject to values, a floor to any award that could begin to be regarded as encouraging'.[138] The award was remitted to the appeal arbitrator for reconsideration.

---

126 (1848) 3 W Rob 68, 71.
127 [1906] P 263.
128 *The Whippingham* (1934) 48 Ll L Rep 49.
129 (1949) 82 Ll L Rep 803.
130 (1874) LR 6 PC 468, 475.
131 [2009] EWHC 3040 (Admlty); [2010] 1 Lloyd's Rep 468.
132 Services that occupy only a short time will not, for that reason alone, justify a small award. See *The General Palmer* (1846) 5 Notes of Cases 159.
133 For example, potential deviation liabilities incurred by reason of the salvage services. See *Scaramanga v Stamp* (1880) 5 CPD 295.
134 [2009] EWHC 3040 (Admlty); [2010] 1 Lloyd's Rep 468.
135 *The Magdalen* (1861) 31 LJ Adm 22; (1861) 5 LT 807.
136 *The Glory* (1850) 14 Jur 676.
137 *The Atlas* (1862) Lush 518, 529; *The Charles Adolphe* (1856) Swab 153, 156.
138 [2008] EWHC 1581 (Comm) 10, [45].

Similar principles are applied by Art 13 of the **1989 Salvage Convention**, which lists the following factors as being relevant to the assessment of any award:

(a)   the salved value of the vessel and other property;
(b)   the skill and efforts of the salvors in preventing or minimising damage to the environment;
(c)   the measure of success obtained by the salvor;
(d)   the nature and degree of the danger;
(e)   the skill and efforts of the salvors in salving the vessel, other property and life;
(f)   the time used and expenses and losses incurred by the salvors;
(g)   the risk of liability and other risks run by the salvors or their equipment;
(h)   the promptness of the services rendered;
(i)   the availability and use of vessels or other equipment intended for salvage operations;
(j)   the state of readiness and efficiency of the salvor's equipment and the value thereof.

In addition, Art 18 provides that misconduct may have the effect of reducing or extinguishing any award.

Salvage claims are claims for debt and are therefore subject to interest,[139] but the rate and period of interest remains discretionary.[140] The practice of Lloyd's arbitrators used to be to start awarding it from six months after the conclusion of the services at a rate of 1 per cent over base rate. Since 1990 Lloyd's Open Form has provided that interest is to start to run from the date on which the services terminate, and this principle has also been applied to salvage services that are not rendered on these forms.[141] Clause 8(2) of the LSSA clauses provides that compound interest may be awarded 'if the Contractors have been deprived of their salvage remuneration or special compensation for an excessive period as a result of the Owner's gross misconduct or in other exceptional circumstances'.

Apportioning the award between salvors

Where more than one salvor is involved in contemporaneous salvage services, their respective shares are determined by the same principles as apply to the assessment of the whole award.[142] Where the salvors have rendered separate services at different times, special favour is usually shown to the first salvors. However, second salvors will receive a larger share of the award if their efforts contributed more towards the eventual preservation of the ship or cargo.[143] If the second salvors dispossess the first salvors, who are willing to continue their services, then the second salvors will be entitled to a reward only if they can prove that there was no reasonable probability of the first salvors saving the vessel on their own.

Any award to the owners of a salving vessel will also be apportioned between the owners and the crew, with the crew usually receiving a quarter-share. Of that share, the master will normally receive one third and the remainder will be shared among the crew according to their rates of pay. Radio officers who are not paid by the ship will be ranked as second or third officers and entitled to a share accordingly.[144] Article 15(2) of the **1989 Salvage Convention** provides that such apportionment is to be determined by the law of the flag of the salving vessel.

---

139 *The Aldora* [1975] QB 748.
140 Article 24 of the 1989 Salvage Convention provides that the salvor's right to interest is to be determined by the law of the state in which 'the tribunal seized of the case is situated'.
141 *The Yolaine* [1995] 2 Lloyd's Rep 7.
142 Cf Art 15 of the 1989 Convention, which applies the criteria listed in Art 13(1) to this apportionment.
143 *The American Farmer* (1947) 80 Ll L Rep 672.
144 *The Albionic* [1942] P 81.

What remedies are available to salvors?

Security for the claim

Claims for salvage constitute maritime liens and can be pursued by arrest of the ship, cargo and freight[145] in respect of the share of the award due from each interest. Article 20(1) provides:

> Nothing in this Convention shall affect the salvor's maritime lien under any international Convention or national law.

Under LOF, the salvor can demand that security be provided to the Committee of Lloyd's,[146] and if this is done, it waives its right to arrest or detain the salved property.[147] A similar provision is to be found in Art 20(2) of the **1989 Salvage Convention**, which provides:

> The salvor may not enforce his maritime lien when satisfactory security for his claim, including interest and costs, has been duly tendered or provided.

However, a salvor must remember that the liability of the various interests salved is several and not joint. Therefore, the shipowner cannot be made to pay for or put up security for cargo's share of an award, and vice versa.[148] For this reason, LOF, and now Art 21(2) of the **1989 Salvage Convention**, imposes on the shipowner an obligation, before releasing the cargo, to use 'best endeavours' to ensure that its owners provide security to the salvors in respect of their share of the eventual award. In *The Tesaba*,[149] it was held that a breach by the shipowners of this obligation did not give rise to a claim 'in the nature of salvage' and so fell outside the jurisdiction of the Admiralty Court. The decision has been reversed by the amendment to the definition of salvage contained in s 20(2)(j) of the **Supreme Court Act 1981**.

Another provision adopted from LOF by the **1989 Salvage Convention** is Art 21(3), which provides:

> The salved vessel and other property shall not, without the consent of the salvor, be removed from the port or place at which they first arrive after the completion of the salvage operations until satisfactory security has been put up for the salvor's claim against the relevant vessel or property.

Time bar

The time limit for commencing claims in connection with salvage was fixed by s 8 of the **Maritime Conventions Act 1911** at two years.[150] The Act allowed for time to be extended when the plaintiff had not had a reasonable opportunity to arrest the salved vessel within the jurisdiction of the Admiralty Court or in the territorial waters of the state in which the plaintiff's ship belonged or in which the plaintiff resided or had its principal place of business.

---

145 Freight at shipowner's risk can be arrested by arresting the cargo. See *The Leo* (1862) Lush 444.
146 Under the LSSA clauses, Lloyd's must now enforce such security if payment of an award is not made within 56 days of its publication.
147 In doing so, the salvor must not demand an unreasonable amount of security. In *The Tribels* [1985] 1 Lloyd's Rep 128, an injunction was issued against the salvors whose demand was for three times the amount of any award that they might reasonably expect to receive on their best case.
148 However, if the shipowner chooses to pay the entirety of the award, it may proceed against cargo for its contribution. See *Briggs v Merchant Traders' Ship Loan and Insurance Association* (1849) LR 13 QB 167.
149 [1982] 1 Lloyd's Rep 37.
150 Now replaced by s 190 of the Merchant Shipping Act 1995.

Article 23 of the **1989 Salvage Convention** maintains the two-year time limit, but omits this proviso. Instead, it provides for time to be extended by a 'declaration' by the defendant. It is also worded to cover 'any action relating to payment under this Convention', which leaves it uncertain as to whether the time bar covers only claims under Arts 13 and 14 or also extends to other claims, such as those for breach of the obligations imposed by Art 8 or 21.

LOF 2011

On 9 May 2011 Lloyd's introduced LOF 2011, which sees the following changes in the accompanying LSSA clauses. Three provisions apply to salved cargo insofar as it consists of laden containers. Clause 13 provides for notification to the party that has provided salvage security to constitute notification to the owners of such property. Clause 14 provides that where 75 per cent, by value, of the salved fund reaches an amicable settlement with the salvors, subject to the arbitrator's consent these settlements can bind unrepresented interests. Clause 15 provides for the omission from the salved fund of low-value cargo and its excusing from salvage liability where 'the cost of including such cargo in the process is likely to be disproportionate to its liability for salvage'. This is subject to the express approval of the arbitrator. In addition, LSSA cl 6.6 gives arbitrators power to order the provision of security, for sum or sums determined by them, in respect of their reasonable fees and expenses, with cl 10.8 giving a similar power to the appeal arbitrator.

There are also two changes to the 'Important Notices' on the reverse of the form. Notice 3 now makes awards under LOF 2011 available on the Lloyd's website, with access being available through subscription. Notice 4, 'Notification to Lloyd's', provides:

> The Contractors shall within 14 days of their engagement to render services under this agreement notify the Council of Lloyd's of their engagement and forward the original agreement or a true copy thereof to the Council as soon as possible. The Council will not charge for such notification.

How do salvage principles apply to wreck?

Wreck may be salved, provided that it is in a position of danger.[151] This will not always be the case. In *Simon v Taylor*,[152] the Singapore High Court held that some three-and-a-half tons of mercury recovered by divers from a German U-boat, which had rested on the ocean bed since being torpedoed in 1944, was not in danger.

Where the wreck is classed as 'derelict', in that it has been abandoned at sea with no *animus revertendi* on the part of the master at the time of abandonment, the position of the salvors will change in two respects. First, they will obtain possessory rights over the wreck, which can be asserted against other salvors.[153] Secondly, they may, in some circumstances, even be able to claim a finder's title over the property salved. By s 236(1) of the **Merchant Shipping Act 1995**, 'wreck', which is defined by s 255(1) as including 'jetsam, flotsam, lagan and derelict found in or on the shores of the sea or any tidal water', must be surrendered to the Receiver of Wreck both when it is found within UK waters and when it is brought within UK waters, having been found outside those waters. Under s 241, wreck found within UK waters becomes the property of the Crown if it remains unclaimed by its owner within one year of delivery to the Receiver of Wreck.

---

151 Salvage in UK waters of historic wrecks or wrecks that constitute a danger to life or property may be prohibited by the Secretary of State under the Protection of Wrecks Act 1973.
152 [1975] 2 Lloyd's Rep 338.
153 *The Tubantia* [1924] P 78.

However, in *The Lusitania*[154] it was held that the Crown's rights do not extend to unclaimed wreck that is found outside UK waters. In such a case, the finder will acquire a possessory title to the wreck, good against all but its owner. In *Simon v Taylor*, the plaintiff, who had purchased the sunken U-boat from the West German government, conceded that its claim against the divers would fail if the U-boat were classed as derelict, which it was not.[155] This concession needs to be read in the light of the following statement of Lord Finlay in *Bradley v Newsum*[156] that the fact that the vessel is derelict:

> . . . does not involve necessarily the loss of the owner's property in it, but any salvors by whom such a vessel is picked up have the right to possession and control . . .

---

154 [1986] 1 Lloyd's Rep 132, QB.
155 The U-boat commander had no intention of abandoning the craft when it was torpedoed.
156 [1919] AC 16, 27.

Chapter 16

General Average

Chapter Contents

General average is a right of contribution as between the various interests in a sea voyage: the ship; the cargo owners; and the party entitled to freight. It is imposed throughout the world as part of the law of the sea. It is a form of mutual insurance that developed before the emergence of marine insurance. The right arises whenever extraordinary sacrifices have been made or extraordinary expenses incurred by one interest for the preservation of the other interests in the common adventure. The cost of such sacrifices or expenses must be borne proportionately among all of the interests in the voyage, including the interest that made the sacrifice or bore the expense. That interest will then have a direct action against the other interests in respect of their proportionate contributions.

Thus, if A's cargo has to be jettisoned to prevent the ship from sinking, with the loss of both the ship and the other cargo, the value of A's cargo will be apportioned among all of the other cargo owners and the ship in accordance with the value of their respective interests. The apportionment will include the value of A's cargo, so that A will not receive full reimbursement. This is only fair, as the aim of general average is to spread the cost of such sacrifices equitably among all of the interests in the voyage. The process of assessing the contributions of the interests is called an 'adjustment', as it is usually performed by professional average adjusters.

At common law, rights to general average are regulated by the law of the port of discharge at which the common adventure terminates. However, in most cases, general average is governed by express provisions in bills of lading or charterparties, which will usually incorporate the York Antwerp Rules. These are a set of rules establishing how general average is to be applied in particular situations. In some countries, they are enforced by law, but in others, such as the UK, they are enforced only by virtue of their express incorporation into the contract. They have been frequently updated and amended, most recently in 1974, 1994 and in 2004. The Rules consist of seven lettered rules, A to G, which establish general principles, and 22 numbered rules, I to XXII, which detail with particular instances of general average. A Rule of Interpretation provides:

> In the adjustment of general average the following lettered and numbered Rules shall apply to the exclusion of any Law and Practice inconsistent therewith.

> Except as provided by the numbered Rules, general average shall be adjusted according to the lettered Rules.

Thus, the numbered rules must override the lettered ones to the extent that there is any inconsistency between them.

We shall now examine the basic principles of general average with reference to common law and to the provisions of the York Antwerp Rules where they diverge from the common law. We shall start with the definition of general average given by s 66(2) of the **Marine Insurance Act 1906**:[1]

> There is a general average act where any extraordinary sacrifice or expenditure is voluntarily and reasonably made or incurred in the time of peril for the purpose of preserving the property imperilled in the common adventure.

We shall examine, in turn, each of the constituent elements of this definition:

---

1   Cf Rule A of the York Antwerp Rules: 'There is a General Average act when, and only when, any extraordinary sacrifice or expenditure is intentionally and reasonably made or incurred for the common safety or for the purpose of preserving from peril the property involved in a common maritime adventure.'

(a)   there must be an extraordinary sacrifice or expenditure;
(b)   it must have been voluntarily and reasonably made or incurred;
(c)   it must be made or incurred in a time of peril; and
(d)   it must be made or incurred for the specific purpose of preserving the property imperilled in the common adventure.

A loss that does not satisfy each of these conditions will amount to 'particular average' and the party sustaining it will have no right to contribution from the other interests. We shall conclude by considering the process of apportionment and the rights and liabilities *inter se* of the parties to a common maritime adventure in respect of a general average act.

Extraordinary sacrifices and expenses

A loss must be 'extraordinary' to be recoverable in general average. Losses sustained by reason of the ordinary incidents of the voyage cannot therefore amount to general average. The dividing line depends on the facts of each case and is not always easy to draw. In *Société Nouvelle d'Armement v Spillers & Baker Ltd*,[2] a tug was engaged to tow a French ship from Ireland to England during the First World War to minimise the risk of her being attacked by U-boats. The additional costs of this operation were not allowable in general average, as the risk of such attack was not extraordinary for a time of war. In contrast, in *Robinson v Price*,[3] a ship sprang a leak that required her to maintain constant pumping to stay afloat. Consequently, she used up all of her coal supplies earlier than would otherwise have been the case, and the ship's spars and the cargo had to be used as fuel. The cost of these items was allowed in general average, as these sacrifices were regarded as not forming part of the usual incidents of the voyage.

Sacrifices

Cargo

The most common instance of cargo being sacrificed for the common safety of the adventure is when it is jettisoned. However, jettison of deck cargo will give rise to a general average contribution only when carried in accordance with a recognised custom of the trade or with the agreement of all of the interests in the voyage.[4]

Other cargo losses that give rise to a claim in general average include the burning of cargo as fuel as in *Robinson v Price*, its loss or damage during operations necessary to extinguish a fire on board,[5] such as the dousing of the holds with water, or even the scuttling of the ship.[6] Cargo may also depreciate in value, even though it is physically undamaged. This too will amount to a sacrifice of cargo as in *Anglo-Argentine Live Stock Agency v Temperley SS Co*,[7] where a ship carrying a cargo of livestock bound for England was forced to call at a Brazilian port for repairs. Due to an Order in Council then in force, this call had the effect of making it impossible to land the livestock in England. Instead, they were discharged and sold at Antwerp, and realised a lower price than they would have done in England.

---

2   [1917] 1 KB 865.
3   (1877) 2 QBD 295.
4   As would be the case where all cargo was carried under bills of lading that gave the shipowner a liberty to carry on deck. See, also, Rule I of the York Antwerp Rules, which requires any jettisoned cargo to be carried in accordance with the recognised custom of the trade.
5   *Stewart v West India & Pacific SS Co* (1873) LR 8 QB 362; *Greenshields, Cowrie & Co v Stephens* [1908] AC 431, HL. See, also, Rule III of the York Antwerp Rules.
6   *Papayanni and Jeronica v Grampian SS Co Ltd* (1896) 1 Com Cas 448.
7   [1899] 2 QB 403.

Ship

The ship or part of her equipment may be sacrificed when intentionally used in an abnormal way. Thus, she may be scuttled to extinguish a fire,[8] her engines may be strained in an attempt to refloat after grounding,[9] or part of her equipment used as fuel to maintain the constant working of pumps following a leak.[10] Under Rule V of the York Antwerp Rules, an intentional stranding can also amount to general average.[11] The 1974 revision to the Rules made it clear that an intentional stranding will still amount to general average, notwithstanding that the ship might have stranded anyway due to the intervention of the weather. The position is probably similar at common law, although there is no direct authority on the point.[12]

A sacrifice may also arise where the shipowner incurs a liability to a third party in respect of a manoeuvre undertaken for the common safety of those interested in the voyage. In *Austin Friars SS Co v Spillers & Baker Ltd*,[13] a ship was drifting without motive power on a strong ebb tide and her pilot decided to try to get her in between two piers. In doing so, she struck the piers and the shipowners became strictly liable for the damage thereto. The amount of that liability was held to be recoverable in general average.[14] However, where the loss is caused by the ordinary use of the ship, there can be no claim in general average.[15]

Freight

Freight will be sacrificed when it is payable on delivery of cargo that is itself sacrificed or that sustains such damage that it cannot be carried to its destination. It will be a loss suffered by the party entitled to freight.

Expenses

Salvage

The shipowner will also be able to claim a contribution in general average in respect of extraordinary expenses that it incurs in the common interest. An example of such an expense would be a payment made to salvors engaged by the shipowner when the safety of the whole adventure is imperilled. At common law, a distinction is made between contractual and non-contractual salvage. General average is recoverable only in respect of the former, and then only to the extent that the contractual sum is reasonable.[16]

The York Antwerp Rules 1974 introduced a new Rule VI, allowing salvage expenditure as general average, whether incurred contractually or not, provided that 'the salvage operations were carried out for the purpose of preserving from peril the property involved in the common maritime adventure'. In 1990, this rule was amended to take account of the provisions of the **1989 Salvage Convention**. Enhancement of the award under Art 13(1)(b) is to be allowable as general average, but not 'special compensation' under Art 14.[17]

The relative contribution of ship and cargo to a salvage award will not always coincide with their contribution for general average. This is because, for salvage purposes, the interest will be

---

8 *Papayanni and Jeronica v Grampian SS Co Ltd* (1896) 1 Com Cas 448.
9 *The Bona* [1895] P 125. See, also, Rule VII of the York Antwerp Rules.
10 *Robinson v Price* (1877) 2 QBD 295. See, also, Rule X of the York Antwerp Rules.
11 'Stranding' requires the ship to touch bottom (*The Seapool* [1934] P 53), but the master need not have intended to beach the ship at a particular point, provided that he intended to beach her. See *Anglo-Grecian Steam Trading Co v T Beynon & Co* (1926) 24 Ll L Rep 122.
12 *Arnould's Law of Insurance and Average*, 16th edn, 1981, London: Stevens, Vol 2, at 15 para 943.
13 [1915] 3 KB 586.
14 A similar result was reached by the Court of Appeal in *Australian Coastal Shipping Commission v Green* [1971] 1 QB 456, in respect of liabilities incurred by the shipowner under a contract of towage.
15 *Wilson v Bank of Victoria* (1867) LR 2 QB 203, 212, per Blackburn J.
16 *Anderson, Tritton & Co v Ocean SS Co* (1884) 10 App Cas 107.
17 But note the changes introduced by the York Antwerp Rules 2004, which are discussed at the end of this chapter.

valued once they have reached a place of safety, whereas for general average purposes, valuation will take place at the termination of the voyage.

Port of refuge costs

Another common instance in which the shipowner may incur extraordinary expenditure is when it puts into a port of refuge to repair damage to the ship. The repairs themselves will not amount to general average, unless they are needed to make good a general average sacrifice of part of the ship. However, at common law, there has been uncertainty as to the extent to which associated costs can be allowed in general average. These consist mainly of the inward and outward port charges, and the costs of unloading and warehousing cargo. In *Atwood v Sellar*,[18] the Court of Appeal allowed all of these costs in general average when the ship was forced into a port of refuge in consequence of a general average incident. In contrast, in *Svendsen v Wallace*,[19] the ship was forced into the port of refuge in consequence of a particular average incident. The House of Lords allowed only the inward charges and the costs of discharging cargo as general average. They reasoned that, after this point, the cargo was safe, and further expenditure could not therefore be said to relate to the common safety of both ship and cargo. This reasoning would apply equally to the situation in *Atwood v Sellar*.

The conflict between these authorities has lost much of its importance, due to the widespread use of the York Antwerp Rules. Rule X allows as general average all of the costs associated with a port of refuge[20] and does not require a general average incident to have been the cause of the ship having to seek refuge.[21] The effect of the Rule of Interpretation is that these costs can amount to general average, even though they might not be covered by the definition of general average in Rule A.[22] Furthermore, Rule XI allows the shipowner the additional wage and fuel costs caused by the prolongation of the voyage, due to the stay at the port of refuge.[23] Recovery under Rule XI is not, however, possible in respect of costs incurred at the port of discharge. In *The Trade Green*,[24] no recovery was allowed under this rule in respect of tug costs incurred when a fire broke out on the vessel during discharge, which led to the port authority ordering tugs to remove her from the berth. The shipowners attempted to claim such costs as 'port charges' under Rule XI(b). However, their argument failed, as they first had to show that the vessel had been 'detained' in the port by reason of repairs necessary for 'the safe prosecution of the voyage', which they were unable to establish as the voyage had terminated at the time that the fire broke out. Consequently, their only prospect of recovering these costs in general average would have been under Rule A. For the purpose of this rule, the 'common maritime adventure' would still have been afoot at the time of the fire. However, recovery would still not have been possible as the tug assistance could not be described as having been for the common benefit of the ship and cargo, as the fire could more readily have been extinguished had the vessel stayed at berth.

If the ship is condemned or the voyage abandoned, no costs incurred after that date are allowable under either rule. Rule XII allows damage to cargo when damage results from operations at the port of refuge, where the cost of such operations is itself allowable as general average under Rules X or XI.

---

18 (1880) 5 QBD 286.

19 (1885) 10 App Cas 404.

20 Or a second port of refuge if repairs cannot be effected at the first place.

21 However, Rule X(b) excludes costs incurred solely for restowage due to shifting during the voyage, unless such restowage is necessary for the common safety.

22 In *Vlassopoulos v British and Foreign MI (The Makis)* [1929] 1 KB 187, decided prior to the adoption of the Rule of Interpretation, a claim under Rule X was disallowed for this very reason.

23 These are not allowable at all at common law. As regards crew wages, see *The Leitrim* [1902] P 256. But note the changes introduced by the York Antwerp Rules 2004, which are discussed at the end of this chapter.

24 [2000] 2 Lloyd's Rep 451, QB.

Environmental costs

The 1994 Rules introduced a new Rule X(d) to allow the costs of measures to prevent or minimise damage to the environment when incurred in any of the following four specific situations:

(i)   as part of an operation performed for the common safety that, if it had been undertaken by a party outside the common maritime adventure, would have entitled such party to a salvage reward;
(ii) as a condition of entry into or departure from any port or place in the circumstances prescribed in Rule X(a);
(iii) as a condition of remaining at any port or place in the circumstances as prescribed by Rule X(a), provided that when there is an actual escape or release of pollutant substances, the cost of any additional measures required on that account to prevent or minimise pollution or environmental damage shall not be allowed as general average;
(iv) necessarily in connection with the discharging, storing or reloading of cargo whenever the cost of those operations is admissible as general average.

Substituted expenses

Expenditure that does not strictly qualify for general average may nonetheless be allowable as such if it is incurred to prevent greater expenses being incurred that would amount to general average. Such expenses are known as 'substituted expenses' and are allowable to the extent that they represent a saving on expenses that would otherwise have been allowable in general average. However, the substituted expenditure will not be allowable if the shipowner was under a contractual duty to incur it. This causes problems at common law when the shipowner effects temporary repairs at the port of refuge, so saving the costs and time that would be wasted were it to effect permanent repairs. These expenses, which would, at first glance, appear to be allowable as 'substituted expenses', are, in fact, not so allowable, because, by effecting temporary repairs, the shipowner is regarded as doing no more than is necessary to fulfil its pre-existing contractual duty to prosecute the voyage.[25]

The position is different under the York Antwerp Rules. Rule F is the general provision on substituted expenses, and, in the 1994 Rules, reads as follows: 'Any additional expense incurred in place of another expense which would have been allowable as general average shall be deemed to be general average and so allowed without regard to the saving, if any, to other interests, but only up to the amount of the general average expense avoided.' Rule XIV goes on specifically to allow temporary repairs that have not themselves been necessitated by a general average incident, 'but only up to the saving in expense which would have been incurred and allowed in general average if such repairs had not been effected there'.[26]

The process of making such a hypothetical comparison can cause difficulties, as can be seen from the facts of The Bijela.[27] The ship was engaged on a voyage from Providence to Kandla and grounded shortly after sailing. She put into Jamestown, the nearest anchorage, and was faced with the choice of either effecting temporary repairs there, or discharging the cargo into barges while she proceeded to New York for permanent repairs, for which there were no suitable facilities at either Providence or Jamestown. The shipowners chose the former option, which cost US$282,000, whereas the latter option would have resulted in general average expenditure of US$535,000.

Cargo owners submitted that, in making the calculation required by Rule XIV, one was forced to the conclusion that there had been no saving in general average as a result of the temporary repairs. This is because, had permanent repairs been undertaken in New York, the associated costs

---

25 *Wilson v Bank of Victoria* (1867) LR 2 QB 203.
26 But note the changes introduced by the York Antwerp Rules 2004, which are discussed at the end of this chapter.
27 [1994] 1 WLR 615, HL.

would not have been allowable in general average under Rule X(b) as those repairs would not have been 'necessary for the safe prosecution of the voyage', which could have been achieved by temporary repairs in Jamestown.

This very literalist argument was accepted at first instance as well as by the Court of Appeal. However, the House of Lords adopted a more purposive approach and found for the shipowner. Lord Lloyd held that, for the purposes of the comparison required by Rule XIV, the only assumption that needed to be made in construing Rule X(b) was that temporary repairs were not, in fact, made. On that assumption, repairs at New York would have been necessary for the safe prosecution of the voyage and the port of refuge costs there would have been allowable in general average. As these exceeded the actual cost of the temporary repairs, it followed that the cost of the latter must be allowable under Rule XIV.

Similar problems arise with trans-shipment costs. If these are to be allowable as 'substituted expenses', they must produce a saving over the expenses otherwise allowable in general average. The problem is that the port of refuge expenditures, if not in themselves required for the common safety, are allowable under Rules X and XI, only if the repair of the ship is 'necessary for the safe prosecution of the voyage'.[28] This is no longer the case once a decision has been made to trans-ship the goods. To avoid this problem, a shipowner who wishes to trans-ship will try to persuade cargo interests to sign a 'non-separation' agreement. This is an agreement to allow, in general average, the port of refuge costs that would have been allowable had the cargo, in fact, been carried to its destination in the original ship.

The benefit to the shipowner is obvious, but such an agreement also benefits the cargo owner in that it allows it to have its cargo trans-shipped without delay rather than being required to wait for it to be carried in the original carrying vessel after completion of repairs. The agreement will provide for valuation of the ship at the port of refuge and of cargo on the basis of its value at delivery at the original port of destination unless sold or otherwise disposed of short of that destination. From the 1980s onward, it became common for such agreements to contain a 'Bigham' clause. This has the effect of capping cargo's contribution under the agreement to a figure not exceeding the costs of trans-shipment had the cargo owners taken delivery of the cargo at the port of refuge and arranged its trans-shipment themselves. The difference between cargo's proportion of general average and the amount of the cap will be regarded as part of the shipowner's proportion of general average and will accordingly be recoverable from its hull underwriters.[29] The new third paragraph of Rule G of the 1994 York Antwerp Rules has similar effect to a non-separation agreement, while the new fourth paragraph reproduces the effect of the 'Bigham' clause. Rule XVII of the 1994 York Antwerp Rules contains an additional paragraph to reflect the valuation provisions of a 'non-separation' agreement. However, an express non-separation agreement will still be required for any trans-shipment where the contracts of carriage incorporate one of the previous versions of the Rules.

Voluntariness

Extraordinary sacrifices and expenses will not constitute general average unless they are made intentionally. Losses due to the actions of the elements will amount only to particular average, no matter how abnormal their nature. The distinction is well illustrated in considering damage due to fire. The use of water to extinguish the fire is an intentional act. Water damage may, therefore, be allowable in general average, whereas damage due to the fire itself remains particular average,

---

28 And at common law are severely restricted by *Svendsen v Wallace* (1885) 10 App Cas 404.
29 *The Abt Rasha* [2000] 2 Lloyd's Rep 575, CA. The decision also confirms that, depending on the circumstances of each case, such an agreement is a reasonable one for cargo and ship to make, for the purpose of binding their respective underwriters.

having arisen by accident. Smoke damage is not allowable in general average as it is impossible to distinguish smoke damage due to the fire itself from that caused by the application of water.

The intentional act must either be that of the master or be one that he has sanctioned.[30] An action forced on the master is not voluntary and the losses resulting from it cannot therefore amount to general average. Thus, in *Athel Line v London & Liverpool WRA*,[31] delays consequent upon compliance with the order of a convoy commander in the Second World War could not amount to general average, as they were caused by the master's legal duty to obey such orders.

The master's intentional act must also be reasonable if the consequent losses are to amount to general average. The master's act will be reasonable if done in the interests of all concerned in the voyage, even if the act is inherently hazardous. In *The Seapool*,[32] a ship at anchor was caught up in a sudden gale and was at risk of losing her propellers and breaking her back. To avoid this, the master engaged in a risky manoeuvre designed to get her out to sea and, although he was successful, he caused damage to the ship and the pier in the process. These losses were held to amount to general average.

All direct losses that flow from the intentional act of the master are capable of amounting to general average.[33] There is no additional requirement that the particular losses that flow from the intentional act should also be intended by the master. In *McCall v Houlder Bros*,[34] the master needed to repair the ship at a port of refuge. The cargo was perishable and had to stay on board the ship. To facilitate the repairs, the master set the ship down by the head and this led to seawater running into the hold. The resultant damage to cargo was allowable in general average, although the master had not intended it as a consequence of his manoeuvre. In *Australian Coastal Shipping Commission v Green*, another case involving Rule C of the York Antwerp Rules, Lord Denning took the view that the chain of causation would not be broken when the subsequent accident would have been a 'distinct possibility' to the master at the time that he took his action, but might be broken when it would have been only a 'remote possibility'.[35]

Time of peril

The master's intentional act must be made at a time of actual peril. If the master is mistaken as to the existence of a peril, losses sustained in consequence of his actions cannot amount to general average. In *Watson (Joseph) & Sons Ltd v Fireman's Fund Insurance Co*,[36] the master mistook vapour from a fractured pipe for smoke and put steam into the holds, thereby damaging the cargo. It was held that there could be no general average as there had been no real danger. If the master acts unreasonably in the face of real danger, that will not necessarily preclude a claim in general average.[37] To deal with this problem, a 'Rule Paramount' was introduced into the York Antwerp Rules 1994 to the effect that 'in no case shall there be any allowance for sacrifice or expenditure unless reasonably made or incurred'.

Although the danger must be real, it need not be immediate. In *Vlassopoulos v British and Foreign MI Co*,[38] the ship put into a port of refuge to repair a fouled propeller. The resulting expenses were allowable in general average, for although the ship was not in actual danger at the time that she entered the port of refuge, the action was justified in avoiding potential danger later in the voyage.[39]

---

30 *Papayanni and Jeronica v Grampian SS Co Ltd* (1896) 1 Com Cas 448.
31 [1944] KB 87.
32 [1934] P 53.
33 See Rule C of the York Antwerp Rules.
34 (1897) 66 LJQB 408.
35 [1971] 1 QB 456, 482–3.
36 [1922] 2 KB 355.
37 *The Alpha* [1991] 2 Lloyd's Rep 515.
38 [1929] 1 KB 187.
39 See, also, *Daniolos v Bunge & Co* (1938) 62 Ll L Rep 65.

Common safety

To amount to general average, expenses and sacrifices must be made for the common safety of the adventure. Two consequences follow from this. First, expenses incurred after an interest has been brought to safety cannot be claimed in general average against that interest. In *Royal Mail Steam Packet v English Bank of Rio de Janeiro*,[40] a ship stranded and a valuable, but low-weight, cargo of specie was removed into lighters solely with a view to preserving the cargo. It was held that cargo was not obliged to contribute in general average towards the subsequent costs of refloating the ship. Secondly, general average depends on the ultimate success of the adventure. Thus if, as in *Chellew v Royal Commission for the Sugar Supply*,[41] a ship incurs port of refuge expenses, and ship and cargo are subsequently lost before reaching the discharge port, no claim in general average can be sustained in respect of those expenses.

Fault

If the loss is caused by the fault of an interest, that interest loses its rights to claim in general average. However, the loss does not lose its general average character and the other interests retain their rights of contribution against each other.[42] Under English law, the fault needs to be actionable.[43] Thus, in *The Carron Park*,[44] the shipowner retained a right to contribute because it was able to rely on an exception covering crew negligence. A similar result occurred when the shipowner was able to rely on the fire defence contained in s 502 of the **Merchant Shipping Act 1894**.[45]

The position is otherwise under US law and, accordingly, many contracts contain a *Jason* clause, which expressly restores the shipowner's rights to general average in the event of its non-actionable fault.

Valuing losses and assessing contributory values

At common law, the basic rule is that the relevant interests are valued at the termination of the adventure with discharge at the port of destination.[46] This is the case both for valuing sacrifices and for establishing each interest's share of general average. Where the voyage is abandoned at a port of refuge, either by agreement or because the underlying contracts of carriage have become frustrated, the relevant values are those pertaining at the time and place of abandonment.[47]

What is the position if the ship is carrying cargoes for different destinations? Cargo for an intermediate port and freight thereon will contribute only in respect of general average incurred prior to discharge and will contribute on the basis of values at that port. However, the ship and the remaining cargo will contribute on the basis of their values at the ultimate destination.[48]

---

40 (1887) 19 QBD 362.
41 [1922] 1 KB 12.
42 *Strang Steel and Co v Scott* (1889) 14 App Cas 601.
43 The common law position is maintained by Rule D of the York Antwerp Rules.
44 (1890) 15 PD 203.
45 *Louis Dreyfus & Co v Tempus Shipping Co* [1931] AC 726.
46 See Rule G of the York Antwerp Rules as regards loss and contribution, and Rule XVII as regards contributory values.
47 However, the voyage is not abandoned if the shipowner forwards the goods to their destination at its own expense. See *Shipton v Thornton* (1838) 9 Ad & E 314.
48 Per Roche J in *Green Star Shipping Co Ltd v The London Assurance* [1933] 1 KB 378, 385.

Sacrifices

Cargo

Where cargo is sacrificed, the loss is valued by reference to what would have been its net market value at the termination of the adventure. From this figure, there must be deducted the expenses incurred subsequent to the sacrifice that would have been needed to realise this price. Examples of such expenses would be freight due on delivery and landing expenses.

Where the York Antwerp Rules apply, Rule XVI values cargo sacrifices on the net value of the cargo at the port of discharge. This is to be:

> ... ascertained from the commercial invoice rendered to the receiver or if there is no such invoice from the shipped value. The value at the time of discharge shall include the cost of insurance and freight except insofar as such freight is at the risk of interests other than cargo.

The owner of jettisoned cargo will never receive reimbursement in full, as the aim of general average is to spread the loss equally among all interests. Thus, if the common adventure consists of ship, cargo A and cargo B, all worth US$300,000 at the port of discharge, and cargo B is jettisoned, equal contribution will mean that ship and cargo A each contribute US$100,000 to the loss. Cargo B will therefore receive US$200,000 and bear US$100,000 of the sacrifice itself.

In the above example, the contribution of cargo B will be further reduced if general average expenditure is incurred subsequent to its sacrifice. Thus, if cargo A and ship incur a salvage liability of US$90,000, that must be split equally between all three interests according to their contributory values at the port of discharge. It follows that cargo B will now receive only US$200,000 less US$30,000, its share of the salvage award.

Freight

Freight will be sacrificed when it is due on delivery from cargo that is itself jettisoned. Its gross value is taken less the expenses saved, such as the cost of discharge.[49] Freight that is prepaid, or payable on a lump-sum basis, will not be sacrificed following jettison of the cargo on which it was due. Only freight due under bills of lading will constitute a general average sacrifice, and not charter freight.

Ship

Sacrifices of part of the ship are assessed on the basis of reasonable repair costs less an allowance of 'new for old'. Where the York Antwerp Rules apply in their 1974 and 1994 versions, Rule XIII applies a one-third 'new for old' allowance in respect of repairs to ships over 15 years old, but none in relation to ships under that age.

Expenditure

General average expenses are based on their actual cost to the shipowner at the port of refuge, although no recovery will be possible if the common adventure is not, in fact, completed. This will be the case where ship and cargo subsequently sink between the port of refuge and the port of discharge.

---

49 See Rule XV of the York Antwerp Rules.

Contributory values

Cargo will be valued according to its market value at the port of discharge. If cargo is discharged damaged, its value in damaged condition will be the relevant value for assessing its share of general average. From this value, there must be deducted any expenses that would have been saved had the adventure been totally lost, such as freight payable on delivery, import duty or salvage charges.

Where the York Antwerp Rules apply, Rule XVII values cargo for contribution purposes in the same way as cargo sacrifices are valued under Rule XVI. The commercial invoice submitted to the receiver will fix the value of the cargo at the time of discharge.

Freight contributes only if it is at the risk of the carrier and is, in fact, earned. The relevant rate is that due from the cargo owners. Freight at the risk of a time charterer will contribute and will be apportioned between the time charterer and the shipowner in accordance with their respective interests therein.[50]

The ship is valued on the basis of its sound market value at the termination of the adventure, plus any sum made good in general average for ship sacrifices. From this figure there is then deducted the cost of any repairs already carried out subsequent to the general average act. Where the York Antwerp Rules apply, Rule XVII provides that the ship's value is to be assessed without reference to its charter commitments.[51] The 1994 version of this Rule provides that no deduction can be made from the ship's value in respect of its liability for payments under Art 14 of the **Salvage Convention 1989**. It further provides that, in the event of trans-shipment contemplated by the revised Rule G, 'the ship shall contribute upon its actual net value at the time of completion of discharge of the cargo'.

Rights and remedies of the interests *inter se*

All of the interests in the common adventure have rights of action against one another in respect of general average contributions. The shipowner's right lies against the owners of the cargo at the time that the sacrifice was made or the expenditure incurred.[52] Subsequent owners, however, can be made liable if there is a clause to that effect in the bill of lading.[53] Any contractual rights to general average will be lost if the ship deviates.[54] The shipowner may also claim against those taking delivery of the cargo by virtue of the separate contract that will come into existence when the master releases the lien on the cargo in return for the provision of a general average bond. The right to lien a cargo will be valid, notwithstanding a deviation on the voyage, provided that the owner of the cargo at the time of the deviation has waived its rights to terminate its contract of carriage.[55]

Subject to contractual provisions to the contrary, general average will be adjusted in accordance with the law prevailing at the place at which the common adventure terminated. This is usually the port of discharge, but, exceptionally, can be the port of refuge. This can be illustrated by *The Olympic Galaxy*.[56] Claims arose out of the grounding of a vessel under pilotage off Sri Lanka. The ship's ownership had changed three days before, so the cargo owners had no contractual claim under the bill of lading. A general average bond was issued and provided that it was to be prepared in accordance with the provisions of the contract of affreightment governing the carriage of the goods, or,

---

50 See Rule XVII of the York Antwerp Rules.
51 So avoiding the uncertainties in the common law position revealed by the conflicting authorities on the valuation of the ship for salvage purposes.
52 *Scaife v Tobin* (1832) 3 B & Ad 523.
53 This principle was applied in *Walford de Baedermaeker v Galindez* (1897) 2 Com Cas 137 to impose liability for cargo's share of general average on the shippers as opposed to the owners of the cargo at the time of the general average act.
54 *Hain SS Co v Tate & Lyle Ltd* (1936) 41 Com Cas 350, HL.
55 Ibid.
56 [2006] EWCA Civ 528; [2006] 2 All ER (Comm) 902; [2006] 2 Lloyd's Rep 27.

failing any such provision, in accordance with the law and practice of the place where the common maritime adventure ended. The Court of Appeal held that leave to serve out of the jurisdiction should not have been given to the shipowner. Even if the bond was itself governed by English law, there was a substantial argument that the rights and wrongs of the claims and cross-claims for general average contribution and indemnity for being exposed to general average or salvage claims would fall to be determined in accordance with the law of Sri Lanka as the place where the adventure ended.[57]

The shipowner has a possessory lien over the cargo in respect of general average contributions owed both to itself and by the cargo owners among themselves.[58] The lien is normally discharged by the provision of a general average bond backed up by a guarantee.[59] The shipowner is entitled to require both a general average bond and a guarantee.[60] The wording of the guarantee may oblige the guarantor undertaking to pay such an amount as might be ascertained to be due under the adjustment, rather than an undertaking to pay the sum which was properly and legally due from cargo interests.[61]

The shipowner's lien is not solely a means of enforcing his own claims to general average contribution. He also owes a duty to exercise it in favour of contributions owed to the owners of jettisoned cargo.[62] The reasonable costs of exercising the lien are recoverable from the owners of the liened cargo.[63]

Claims for general average contribution give rise to a statutory, but not a maritime, lien. The time limit is the contractual limit of six years. In *The Potoi Chau*, the Privy Council held that for causes for action for contributions in general average arising under a provision in the bill of lading that required general average to be adjusted according to York-Antwerp Rules, time ran from the time of the general average act and not from the time of the general average adjustment.[64] However, the general average bond will create separate contractual rights. The cargo owner's contractual obligation under the bond is to make payment of a liquidated sum at a future date which would not arrive until the general average statement had been completed by an average adjuster appointed by the shipowners. Accordingly, that was the earliest date at which the shipowner's cause of action against the cargo owner under the average bond for payment of general average contribution arose. Where cargo is carried under bills of lading subject to the Hague Rules, the one-year time bar under Art III(6) has been held not to apply to its claim against the ship in respect of general average contributions.[65]

---

57 Even if English law undoubtedly applied to the general average claims, it would not necessarily follow that the disputes should be determined in England. The Sri Lankan courts were well used to applying English law, and the English law factor was only one factor among many to be considered.

58 The lien is enforceable at the expense of the shipowner.

59 The discharge of the lien is good consideration for the average bond even when the shipowner has committed a deviation, provided that the predecessor in title to the bill of lading holder has waived the deviation. See *Hain v Tate & Lyle Ltd* (1936) 41 Com Cas 350, HL.

60 *The Lehmann Timber* [2013] EWCA Civ 650; [2013] 2 Lloyd's Rep 541. The lien was not discharged by the shipowner accepting the insurer's guarantee.

61 *St Maximus Shipping Co Ltd v AP Moller-Maersk A/S* [2014] EWHC 1643 (Comm), where the undertaking was 'to pay the proper proportion of any general average and/or special charges which may hereafter be ascertained to be due from the cargo, or the shippers or owners thereof under an adjustment'.

62 *Crooks v Allan* (1879) 5 QBD 38.

63 *The Lehmann Timber* [2013] EWCA Civ 650; [2013] 2 Lloyd's Rep 541. It had previously been assumed, following *Somes v British Empire Shipping Co* (1858) El, Bl & El 353, that such costs could not be recovered absent a specific provision in the bill of lading. The Court of Appeal held that *Somes* was a case involving an artificer's lien and was not of general application to liens that arose in a shipping context.

64 [1983] 2 Lloyd's Rep 376, PC.

65 *Goulandris Bros Ltd v B Goldman & Sons Ltd* [1958] 1 QB 74, QB. It follows that a clause in a bill of lading requiring claims for general average to be made within a period less than 12 months from discharge would not fall foul of Art III(8). The position would be likewise with the Hague-Visby Rules.

The York Antwerp Rules 2004

The latest version of the York Antwerp Rules, which was finalised in June 2004, has made various amendments, the most important of which are as follows:

(1)   Rule VI now excludes salvage from general average unless a party has paid a salvage award for all of the interests concerned.

(2)   Rule XI has been amended to exclude from general average the wages and maintenance of the master, officers and crew incurred while a vessel is detained in a port of refuge.

(3)   The second paragraph of Rule XIV now provides that 'for the purposes of this paragraph only, the cost of temporary repairs falling for consideration shall be limited to the extent that the cost of temporary repairs effected at the port of loading, call or refuge, together with either the cost of permanent repairs eventually effected or, if unrepaired at the time of the adjustment, the reasonable depreciation in the value of the vessel at the completion of the voyage, exceeds the cost of permanent repairs had they been effected at the port of loading, call or refuge'. This is aimed at preventing shipowners from benefiting unduly from a situation in which temporary repairs enable permanent repairs to be effected more cheaply elsewhere than would have been the case had they been effected at the port of refuge.

(4)   Rule XX is amended so as to remove the former allowance of a commission of 2 per cent on disbursements other than crew wages and maintenance and fuel and stores not replaced during the voyage.

(5)   Rule XXI allows interest at a rate of 7 per cent in general average on expenditure, sacrifices and allowances. The figure is subject to annual review by the CMI.

(6)   Rule XXIII provides for a one-year time limit in respect of claims for general average.

Chapter 17

Marine Pollution

Chapter Contents

At common law, the liability of shipowners for maritime pollution is dealt with by the torts of nuisance and negligence. However, in practice, negligence has proved an inadequate compensatory response to widespread pollution damage such as that which occurred in the aftermath of the *Torrey Canyon* disaster in 1967. Not only do persons who have suffered loss have to prove negligence on the part of the shipowner, they may also find that they receive inadequate compensation due to the shipowner's ability to limit its liability.[1] Furthermore, the existing law of negligence does not allow claims for pure economic loss in such circumstances, nor are claims for environmental damage easily assimilated into its structure. Trespass and nuisance have also proved of limited value.[2]

The response of the international community was twofold. First, there was the public law response under the **International Convention Relating to Intervention on the High Seas in Cases of Oil Pollution Casualties 1969**. This Convention enabled States to take both preventive and remedial actions in relation to actual or potential oil pollution on the high seas. These measures, which are outside the scope of this book, were enacted into English law by the **Prevention of Pollution Act 1971** and are now contained in ss 128–51 of the **Merchant Shipping Act 1995**.

Secondly, there was the private law response under the **International Convention on Civil Liability for Oil Pollution Damage 1969 (CLC)**. This set up a compensation regime that was far more generous than that allowed by the existing tort of negligence. The Convention was followed by the **International Convention on the Establishment of an International Fund for Compensation for Oil Pollution Damage 1971** (the 1971 Fund). This provided for a fund, financed by levies on the oil industry, to compensate victims of pollution damage who fell outside, or were inadequately compensated by, the new system of statutory liability imposed on shipowners in respect of oil pollution. The 1992 Protocols updated both the CLC regime and the Fund provisions and came into force on 30 May 1996. It is these private law responses that this chapter will now examine.

The CLC

The CLC was brought into English law by the **Merchant Shipping (Oil Pollution) Act 1971** (hereafter referred to as 'the 1971 Act'), subsequently ss 152–70 of Sched 4, Ch III to the **Merchant Shipping Act 1995**. Under English law, claims arising after 30 May 1996 are subject to the 1992 CLC and it is this regime that shall be examined in this chapter.[3] However, as many states still adhere to the 1969 CLC, the differences between the two regimes will be highlighted at the appropriate places in the following analysis of the 1992 CLC.

Strict liability

Under s 153(1), strict liability is imposed on all shipowners, irrespective of their nationality or flag, in respect of discharges or escapes of 'persistent oil' from laden bulk oil tankers. In such circumstances, the registered shipowner will be liable:

(a) for any damage caused outside the ship in the territory of the United Kingdom by contamination resulting from the discharge or escape; and

---

1   The damage caused by the *Torrey Canyon* oil spill came to about £6 million, whereas her limitation figure was only £1.25 million.
2   See *Esso Petroleum Co Ltd v Southport Corp* [1955] 2 Lloyd's Rep 655, HL. It is, however, possible that pure economic loss may be recoverable in an action for public nuisance. *Mitchell v Milford Haven Port Authority* [2003] EWHC 1246 (Admlty).
3   From that date until 15 May 1998, the two regimes coexisted, with claims being met initially under the 1969 CLC and then the 1971 Fund, with any balance being met under the 1992 CLC and the 1992 Fund.

(b)   for the cost of any measures reasonably taken after the discharge or escape for the purpose of preventing or minimising any damage so caused in the territory of the United Kingdom by contamination resulting from the discharge or escape; and

(c)   for any damage caused in the territory of the United Kingdom by any measures so taken.

Under s 153(4), liability is extended to escapes of oil from oil tankers on ballast voyages following the carriage of oil, 'unless it is proved that no residues from the carriage of any such oil remain in the ship'. Liability is also imposed in respect of escapes from combination bulk carriers, for example, oil, bulk, ore carriers (OBOs). Under s 170(1), 'damage' is defined so as to include loss. 'Oil' means persistent hydrocarbon mineral oil. 'Registered Owner' means the person or persons registered as the owner of the ship or, in the absence of registration, the person or persons owning the ship, except that, in relation to a ship owned by a state that is operated by a person registered as the ship's operator, it means the person registered as its operator.[4] 'Ship' means any seagoing vessel or seaborne craft of any type whatsoever.

A trio of cases have considered the meaning of the words 'damage caused . . . by contamination' contained in s 153(1)(a) and s 175 of Sched IV to the **Merchant Shipping Act 1995**, applying the provisions of the 1969 CLC and 1971 Fund. In *Landcatch Ltd v International Oil Pollution Compensation Fund*,[5] Lord Gill, in the Scottish Outer House, held that, although this statutory liability was capable of encompassing economic loss, it could do so only to the extent to which such loss was recoverable under the general law. Accordingly, the Fund had been entitled to reject the claims of a smolt supplier located 500 km from the oil spill in the Shetlands, which claimed that it had lost business from the Shetland salmon farms as a result of the oil spill from *The Braer*. As a claim arising out of mere contractual rights in the property damaged was not recoverable under the general law of Scotland and England, an *a fortiori* claim arising out of expectations of contractual rights must also be excluded. Nor was the position altered by the fact that previous decisions of the Fund had admitted claims for pure economic loss wider than those allowable under the general law. Applying these principles, the Scottish Outer House in *P & O Scottish Ferries Ltd v The Braer Corp Times*[6] also rejected claims of loss of business suffered by the sole ferry company serving the Shetland Islands at a time when the Islands were subject to bad publicity due to the oil spill from *The Braer*.

Similar issues came before the Court of Appeal in *The Sea Empress*.[7] A claim against the Fund was made by a whelk processor in Devon whose business was adversely affected as a result of an oil spill off the south coast of Wales in February 1996, which led to the Secretary of State prohibiting the removal of whelks from the affected area. The claimant had contracted with fishermen operating in this area for its supply of whelks and, accordingly, was unable to export whelks as a result of the prohibition. The claimant accepted the correctness of the principles set out in *Landcatch*, but sought to distinguish the case on two grounds. The first was that the pursuers in *Landcatch* had no concluded contracts with the affected salmon farms, whereas, here, the claimant did have existing contracts with whelk fishers. The second was that, in *Landcatch*, the smolt had never been contaminated and the prohibition was on their entering the fish farms in the affected area. The Court of Appeal held that neither distinction was material. It stressed that a strong causal link was needed as a screening mechanism to ensure that those claims that could be made against the Fund were likely to be met in full. Economic loss claims could be made in circumstances in which a claim at common law would fail, even if negligence were proved. However, the relevant causal link would be satisfied only when there was a very close relationship between the person claiming on the Fund and the waters

---

4   Section 153 originally referred to the 'owner' but was amended when the provisions of the 2001 Bunker Oil Pollution Convention were implemented. In Chapter III of the Merchant Shipping Act 1995, the term 'owner' is now used in relation to liabilities arising under that Convention.

5   [1998] 2 Lloyd's Rep 552, Sc Ct.

6   [1999] 2 Lloyd's Rep 535, Sc Ct.

7   [2003] EWCA Civ 65; [2003] 1 Lloyd's Rep 327.

affected by the contamination. This would be the case where the claim was made by fishermen who fished in those waters. However, the activities of the claimant in the present case, like those of the pursuer in *Landcatch*, lacked the necessary nexus with the contaminated waters.[8]

The 1992 CLC contains two new provisions on liability. The first relates to measures designed to deal with an imminent *threat* of an escape or discharge of oil. In the event of 'a grave and imminent threat of damage being caused outside a ship . . . by the contamination that might result if there were a discharge or escape of oil from the ship . . .', s 154(2) provides for the shipowner to be liable:

(a) for the cost of any measures reasonably taken for the purpose of preventing or minimising any such damage in the territory of the United Kingdom; and

(b) for any damage caused outside the ship in the territory of the United Kingdom by any measures so taken;

and in this Chapter any such threat is referred to as a relevant threat of contamination.

The second provision clarifies how pollution damage may be recovered following an oil spill. Section 156(3) provides that:

The liability of the owner of a ship under section 154 . . . for any impairment of the environment shall be taken to be a liability only in respect of—

(a) any resulting loss of profits, and

(b) the cost of any reasonable measures of reinstatement actually taken or to be taken.

Accordingly, if no reinstatement works are actually taken, no claim can be made. The section is also interesting in that the words 'other than loss of profit' impliedly recognise claims for pure economic loss. However, the word 'resulting' makes it likely that such claims are still subject to the causal link referred to in *Landcatch* in respect of the shipowner's liability under s 153.

Geographical ambit

Under the 1969 CLC, liability was geographically limited to 'any damage caused in the area of the United Kingdom by contamination resulting from the discharge or escape' and 'the cost of any measures reasonably taken after the discharge or escape for the purpose of preventing or reducing any such damage in the area of the United Kingdom'. It also covered damage caused in the area of the UK in consequence of such 'clean-up' measures. A shipowner who was liable under these provisions was, by s 153(2), also made liable for any equivalent damage or costs incurred in the area of any other Convention territory.

Under the 1992 CLC, references to the territory of any country are, by s 170(4), expressed to include its territorial sea and, in the case of the UK, 'any area specified by virtue of section 129(2) (b)', which refers to areas designated pursuant to s 1(7) of the **Continental Shelf Act 1964**. In the case of any other Liability Convention country, 'territory' also extends to 'the exclusive economic zone of that country established in accordance with international law'. In the absence of such a zone, the extension is to 'such area adjacent to the territorial sea of that country and extending 200 nautical miles from the baselines from which the breadth of that sea is measured as may have been determined by that State in question in accordance with international law'. It follows that shipowners can now be made liable in respect of oil spills much further out on the high seas than was hitherto the case.

---

8 The activities of the ferry company in *P & O Scottish Ferries Ltd v The Braer Corp* [1999] 2 Lloyd's Rep 535 would have a closer nexus with the contaminated waters, but would still be distinguishable from the activities of fishermen in that the ferry company was not actually prohibited from carrying out its activities.

Defences

Although liability is strict, s 155 allows the shipowner to escape liability if it can prove that the discharge or escape or the threat of contamination:

(a) resulted from an act of war, hostilities, civil war, insurrection or an exceptional, inevitable and irresistible natural phenomenon; or

(b) was due wholly to anything done or left undone by another person, not being a servant or agent of the owner, with intent to do damage; or

(c) was due wholly to the negligence or wrongful act of a government or other authority in exercising its function of maintaining lights or other navigational aids for the maintenance of which it was responsible.

In respect of s 155 (b) and (c), the word 'wholly' is particularly important. If the shipowner can only prove that the damage fell partly within the events listed, it will be unable to claim the exemption. Liability is also excluded under s 167(1) in respect of 'any warship or any ship for the time being used by the government of any State for other than commercial purposes'.

If the claimant itself had contributed to the loss or damage, the shipowner, if it were not at fault, is, by s 153(8), entitled to invoke the provisions of the **Law Reform (Contributory Negligence) Act 1945** as if it had been at fault. Where an oil spill occurs from two or more ships, with each ship being liable under s 153, and the resultant damage cannot be separately apportioned to each owner, s 153(5) imposes joint liability on each of the owners 'for the whole of the damage or cost for which the owners together would be liable under this section'.

'Channelling' of liability

Under s 156, where oil is discharged or escapes from a ship or there arises a relevant threat of contamination, the shipowner shall not be liable otherwise than under s 153, whether or not it actually incurs a liability under that section. Furthermore, under s 156(2), claims 'for any such damage or cost' may not be made against any of the following persons:

(a) any servant or agent of the owner of the ship;

(b) any person not falling within paragraph (a) above but employed or engaged in any capacity on board the ship or to perform any service for the ship;[9]

(c) any charterer of the ship (however described and including a bareboat charterer) and any manager or operator of the ship;

(d) any person performing salvage operations with the consent of the owner of the ship or on the instructions of a competent public authority;

(e) any person taking any such measures as are mentioned in subsection (1)(b) or (2)(a) of section 153 or 154;

(f) any servant or agent of a person falling within paragraph (c), (d) or (e) above.

Claims against such persons will, however, be possible in the circumstances in which limitation could be broken – that is, when the damage or cost has 'resulted from anything done or omitted to be done by [such person] either with intent to cause any such damage or cost or recklessly and in the knowledge that any such damage or cost would probably result'.[10] Recourse actions by the shipowner against third parties are expressly preserved by s 169. The party sued by the shipowner/

---

9 For example, independent contractors such as pilots, surveyors or service engineers.
10 The equivalent provision under the 1969 CLC was limited to claims against servants or agents of the shipowner.

insurer by way of a recourse action will be able to limit its liability in accordance with the provisions of the **1957** or **1976 Limitation Convention**.[11]

However, a public law liability may arise under EC legislation that exceeds the amount of compensation payable under the CLC and the Fund. In *Commune de Mesquer v Total France SA and Total International Ltd*,[12] the Grand Chamber of the European Court of Justice held that an oil spill was capable of involving the provisions of Directive 75/442 on waste. Heavy fuel oil was not waste while it was being carried, but was waste once it had been spilled. For the purposes of the Directive, the shipowner could be regarded as the 'holder' of the waste. A national court could also find that the seller of the fuel or the charterer of the ship were producers of the waste. If the costs of disposing of the waste exceeded what was recoverable under the CLC and from the Fund, the producer of the product could be held liable if their conduct contributed to the risk of pollution due to shipwreck.

Limitation of liability

The 1969 CLC established its own separate system of limitation with higher limits than those in force under the **1957 Limitation Convention**, which were expressly excluded from operating in respect of CLC claims. As was the case under the 1957 Convention, CLC limits could be broken if the discharge or escape occurred with the 'actual fault or privity' of the shipowner. The limits, initially expressed in gold francs, were 133 SDRs per ton, subject to a global maximum of 14 million SDRs.

Under the 1992 CLC, these were first raised, as follows: an initial flat rate of 3 million SDRs for vessels the gross tonnage of which did not exceed 5,000 tons; for vessels the gross tonnage of which exceeded 5,000 gross tons, but did not exceed 140,000 gross tons, the figure was 3 million SDRs plus 420 SDRs for each additional gross ton over 5,000 gross tons; for vessels the tonnage of which exceeded 140,000 gross tons, the figure was a flat rate of 59.7 million SDRs. A simplified, 'tacit acceptance', procedure has been adopted for increasing these figures. The 2000 Protocols were introduced under this procedure and came into force on 1 November 2003 and effect a 50 per cent rise in the 1992 limits. For the CLC, the new limits are:

- for vessels not exceeding 5,000 gross tons, a flat rate of 4.51 million SDRs;
- for vessels between 5,000 and 140,000 gross tons, 4.51 million SDRs plus an additional 631 SDRs for each additional gross ton above 5,000 gross tons;
- for vessels of 140,000 gross tons and above, the limit is 89.77 million SDRs.

Ships registered with a State that still applies the 1969 CLC will also be issued with certificates in respect of the 1992 CLC to enable them to continue trading to State Parties to the 1992 CLC, which require such certificates.

The procedure for establishing a limitation fund is dealt with under s 158, while s 159 provides for the release of vessels from arrest following the establishment of a limitation fund. Section 160 deals with the interaction of CLC limitation with ordinary tonnage limitation in respect of concurrent liabilities of a shipowner under s 153 and of another party, otherwise than under s 153. If the shipowner has shown he is entitled to limit under CLC and has paid the limitation amount into court and the other party is entitled to limit under 1976 LLMC, no proceedings shall be taken against the other person in respect of his liability, although the shipowner retains the right to proceed against that party by way of recourse.

---

11 In *The Aegean Sea* [1998] 2 Lloyd's Rep 39, QB, oil pollution claims brought by shipowners by way of recourse were held to fall within Art 2(1) of the 1976 Limitation Convention.
12 Case C-188/07 [2008] 3 CMLR 16.

Under s 157(3), the right to limit is now lost in the same way as is the case under the **1976 Convention on Limitation of Liability for Maritime Claims (LLMC)**. The old 'fault or privity' test has been replaced with a test by which the claimant needs to prove that the damage or cost 'resulted from anything done or omitted to be done by [such person] either with intent to cause any such damage or cost or recklessly and in the knowledge that any such damage or cost would probably result'. The wording of the 1992 Protocols refers to the 'personal' acts or omissions of the shipowner. This word is omitted from the Act, which adds 'any' to the words 'such damage', which appear in the Protocols. It is probable that these two linguistic differences between the Act and the Protocols will not prove significant.

Compulsory insurance

All ships carrying in bulk a cargo of more than 2,000 tons of persistent oil are, by s 163, required to supply a certificate confirming liability insurance covering their CLC liabilities. Without such a certificate, the ship will not be permitted to enter or leave any UK port or terminal in the territorial sea of the UK. Under s 165(1), third parties are given a direct right of action against liability insurers and, under s 165(5), are excluded from the effect of the **Third Parties (Rights against Insurers) Act 1930**. Under s 165(2), the insurer is given a defence if it can prove that the discharge or escape or threat of contamination was due to the wilful misconduct of the shipowner itself. Under s 165(3), the insurer is permitted to limit its liability in the same way as was available to the shipowner, although its right to limit will not be affected by the fact that the shipowner has lost the right to limit under s 157(3). Ships registered with a State that still applies the 1969 CLC or a State that applies no version of the CLC may apply to a 1992 CLC State for a certificate in respect of the 1992 CLC to enable them to continue trading to State Parties to the 1992 CLC.[13]

Time limits

Under s 162, claims must be made no later than three years from when the claim first arose and no later than six years 'after the occurrence or first of the occurrences resulting in the discharge or escape by reason of which the liability was incurred'. In *Gray v The Braer Corp*,[14] the Scottish Outer House confirmed that the three-year limit was applicable to all claims, with a long-stop provision that after the lapse of six years from the date of the relevant occurrence, no other action could be brought to enforce any claim whether for losses already suffered or for losses apprehended.

Jurisdiction

Section 166 assigns to the Admiralty Court jurisdiction over statutory oil pollution claims, provided that the loss or damage has not been wholly sustained in a Convention State other than the UK. This is the effect of s 166(2), which prevents any court in the UK from entertaining any action, to enforce a claim arising from 'any relevant damage or cost' where:

(a) any oil is discharged or escapes from a ship but does not result in any damage caused by contamination in the territory of the United Kingdom and no measures are reasonably taken to prevent or minimise such damage in that territory, or

13 Section 164(1).
14 [1999] 2 Lloyd's Rep 540, Sc Ct.

(b) any relevant threat of contamination arises but no measures are reasonably taken to prevent or minimise such damage in the territory of the United Kingdom.[15]

Under s 166(4), Pt I of the **Foreign Judgments (Reciprocal Enforcement) Act 1933** applies to any judgment given by a court in a Liability Convention country to enforce a claim in respect of a liability incurred under any provision corresponding to s 153.[16]

The Fund

The Fund Convention set up a fund to compensate victims of oil pollution who were unable to receive adequate recompense from the shipowner under the CLC regime. It was brought into English law by the **Merchant Shipping Act 1974** (the 1974 Act), the provisions of which subsequently became ss 172–81 of Sched 4, Chapter IV to the **Merchant Shipping Act 1995**. The UK is a party to the 1992 Protocols, which set up a new fund with higher limits and provided for the eventual winding up of the 1971 Fund. From 16 May 1998, members of the 1992 Fund had ceased to retain membership of the 1971 Fund. On 24 May 2002, the 1971 Fund ceased to be in force. Some states that still apply the 1969 CLC are parties to the 1992 Fund.

The Fund's liability

Section 175(1) provides that the Fund is liable for pollution damage in the territory of the UK where the claimant has been unable to obtain full compensation under s 153 for one of the following three reasons.

(1) The shipowner has escaped liability by reliance on one of the exceptions permitted under the CLC.

(2) The shipowner is financially incapable of meeting its CLC liabilities and has inadequate liability insurance.

(3) The damage exceeds the shipowner's liability under the CLC.

Under s 175(6), a claim might also be made on the Fund in respect of 'Expenses reasonably incurred, and sacrifices reasonably made, by the owner voluntarily to prevent or minimise pollution damage'. The Fund also has a right to intervene in proceedings against owners under the CLC.[17]

In two situations, set out in s 175(2), proceedings may be made against the Fund in respect of pollution damage that occurs in a Fund Convention country. The first is where the headquarters of the Fund are in the UK[18] and proceedings under the CLC have been brought in a country that is not a Fund Convention country.[19] The second is where the incident has caused pollution damage in the territory both of the UK and of another Fund Convention country and CLC proceedings have been brought in a country that is not a Fund Convention country or in the UK. The purpose of this provision is to plug the potential loophole that might exist when proceedings were commenced in a country that had only ratified the CLC.

---

15 'Relevant damage or cost' is defined in s 166(3) as covering damage caused in the territory of another Liability Convention country, preventive measures taken to reduce or minimise damage or the threat of damage in the territory of another Liability Convention country or any damage caused by any such measures.

16 In its application to such a judgment, that Part shall have effect with the omission of s 4(2) and (3) of that Act.

17 CPR 61 PD 11.3 giving effect to Art 7.4, 'Each Contracting State shall ensure that the Fund shall have the right to intervene as a party to any legal proceedings instituted in accordance with Article IX of the 1992 Liability Convention before a competent court of that State against the owner of a ship or his guarantor.'

18 As is currently the case.

19 In this situation, there is no requirement for any loss or damage to have occurred within the territory of the UK.

Defences available to the Fund

Under s 175(7), the Fund will not be liable in three situations:

(1)   where damage was suffered in a non-member state;
(2)   where the pollution damage resulted from an act of war or was caused by a spill from a warship;
(3)   where the claimant was unable to prove a causal link between its loss and a spill from one or more ships of the type that are potentially liable under the CLC.

Under s 175(8), the Fund is also entitled to reduce or extinguish its liability if it can prove that the pollution damage resulted wholly or partly '(a) from anything done or omitted to be done with intent to cause damage by the person who suffered the damage, or (b) from the negligence of that person'. The Fund is also entitled, under s 175(9), to rely on the provisions of the **Law Reform (Contributory Negligence) Act 1945** in the same way as is available to a shipowner under s 153(8). However, s 175(10) precludes reliance on the defences in s 175(8) and (9) 'where the pollution damage consists of the costs of preventive measures or any damage caused by such measures'. Salvage costs may qualify for compensation against the 1992 Fund as preventive measures if their primary purpose is to prevent pollution damage, but not if salvage operations have another purpose, such as saving the ship and/or the cargo. Where salvage operations are undertaken for the dual purposes of preventing pollution and saving the ship and/or the cargo, but their primary purpose cannot be established, the costs are apportioned between pollution prevention and salvage.[20]

Limitation

Under Pt 1, Sched 5 to the **Merchant Shipping Act 1995**, the overall Fund limit under the 1992 Protocols was initially fixed at 135 million SDRs, with a tacit acceptance procedure for raising the limits. In accordance with this procedure, on 1 November 2003, the 2000 Protocol came into force, raising the limit to 203 million SDRs. It also contains a provision that if three states contributing to the Fund receive more than 600 million tons of oil per annum, there should be a further increase to 300.704 million SDRs. An additional tier of compensation is provided by the 2003 Protocol, which came into force on 3 March 2005. This establishes a supplementary fund with an overall limit of 750 million SDRs for each incident for pollution damage in the territory of the State Parties to the Protocol.[21] It will only cover claims for incidents that occur after the Protocol has entered into force for the state concerned. The financing of this extra tier of compensation falls on the oil industry. To redress this imbalance, the International Group of P&I Clubs, the 13 members of which provide liability insurance to 98 per cent of the world's tanker fleets, introduced, on 20 February 2006, two voluntary agreements: the Small Tanker Oil Pollution Indemnification Agreement (STOPIA 2006); and the Tanker Oil Pollution Indemnification Agreement (TOPIA 2006). Oil spills covered by these agreements will still be dealt with by the 1992 Fund and the Supplementary Fund, but the Funds will then be indemnified by the shipowner under the agreements. STOPIA 2006 provides for a limitation figure of 20 million SDRs for tankers up to 29,548 gross tonnage for damage in 1992 Fund Member States. The owners of such tankers agree to indemnify the 1992 Fund in respect of the Fund's liability for the difference between the shipowner's limit of liability under CLC 92 and 20 million SDRs. Under TOPIA 2006, the Supplementary Fund is indemnified for half the amount it has paid in respect of incidents involving ships covered

---

20   IOPC 1992 Fund Claims Manual October 2013, 3.1.15.
21   There are currently 21 Contracting States.

by the agreement. Indemnification shall not be payable for: (1) the costs of any preventive measures to the extent that the participating owner is exonerated from liability under Art III, para 3 of the Liability Convention, and for which the Supplementary Fund is liable by virtue of the Protocol; (2) any other pollution damage to the extent that liability is incurred by the Supplementary Fund but not by the participating owner. TOPIA also excludes indemnification for payments in respect of pollution damage caused by any act of terrorism, save to the extent, if any, that such amounts are covered by any insurance or reinsurance in force at the time of the incident.

Time limits

Under s 178, the time limit for commencing an action[22] against the Fund in the UK is three years after the claim against the Fund arose and not later than six years after 'the occurrence, or first of the occurrences, resulting in the discharge or escape, or (as the case may be) in the relevant threat of contamination, by reason of which the claim against the Fund arose'.

Subrogation

Under s 179(1), the Fund obtains a right of subrogation in respect of 'any rights in respect of the damage which the recipient has, or but for the payment would have had, against any other person'. Unlike the position under the 1971 Fund, these rights of subrogation can come into existence before any judgment is given against the shipowner.[23]

Jurisdiction

Under s 177, Admiralty jurisdiction extends to claims for damage done by ships to claims against the Fund and provides for the finality of judgments against shipowners/insurers subject to their being notified to the Fund. It also extends the provisions of Pt I of the **Foreign Judgments (Reciprocal Enforcement) Act 1933** to render enforceable judgments against the Fund given in other Fund Convention countries.

Non-tanker oil spills

Persistent oil may also escape or be discharged from ships that are not bulk oil carriers. Such spills fall outside both the 1969 and the 1992 CLC regimes. However, s 154 of the **Merchant Shipping Act 1995**[24] imposes a statutory liability on the registered shipowner when any oil is discharged or escapes from a ship other than a ship to which section 153 applies.[25] The liability regime under s 154 is equivalent to that imposed by the 1992 CLC regime which is implemented through s 153. There are, however, the following important differences:

(1)   There is no requirement of compulsory liability insurance.[26] However, s 16 of the **Merchant Shipping and Maritime Security Act 1997** inserts a new s 192A into the **Merchant Shipping**

---

22 Alternatively, the claimant can give the Fund a third-party notice of an action to enforce a claim against the owner or its guarantor in respect of the same damage.
23 The Merchant Shipping Act 1995 also applied this amendment to the 1971 Fund regime.
24 Formerly s 6 of the Merchant Shipping (Salvage and Pollution) Act 1994.
25 Section 154 originally referred to the 'owner' but was amended when the provisions of the 2001 Bunker Oil Pollution Convention were implemented. In Chapter III of the Merchant Shipping Act 1995, the term 'owner' is now used in relation to liabilities arising under that Convention.
26 The absence of liability insurance can cause problems in recovering the costs of any clean-up operation, as with the spill following the grounding of the Russian fish factory *Pionersk* on 31 October 1994, reported in Lloyd's List on 11 November 1994.

Act 1995 empowering the Secretary of State to make regulations requiring ships in UK waters to have liability insurance.

(2) There is no liability where damage or the costs of preventive measures (and any resulting damage) are incurred outside the territory of the UK.

(3) Under s 168, limitation in respect of s 154 liability is under the property damage provisions of the **1976 Limitation Convention** rather than under those imposed under the CLC. Any liability incurred under s 154 is deemed to be a liability to damages in respect of such damage to property as is mentioned in Art 2(1)(a) of the 1976 Limitation Convention. This provision is necessary to remove any doubts as to whether the costs of preventive measures would fall under the 1976 Limitation Convention.

(4) Unlike s 153, this section covers non-seagoing vessels.

The 2001 Bunker Oil Pollution Convention

This Convention came into force on 21 November 2008 and in the UK was implemented by the **Merchant Shipping (Oil Pollution) (Bunkers Convention) Regulations 2006** (SI 2006/1244), which makes the necessary amendments and additions to Chapter III of the **Merchant Shipping Act 1995**. There are currently 25 Contracting States, including the UK. The Convention does not provide for ratification by the EU. Accordingly, ratification must be made by individual EU Member States, notwithstanding the fact that they have lost their national competence in this area by reason of the **Judgments Regulation**, EC Reg 44/2001. To meet this objection, on 19 September 2002, the Council authorised the Member States to sign or ratify the Convention.

The Convention covers bunker oil spills[27] outside the vessel,[28] wherever they occur, which cause damage in the territory of State Parties.[29] Under Art 2, 'territory' includes the territorial sea and exclusive economic zone of a State Party. As with the CLC, a strict liability regime applies to the ship-owner. In the UK this is implemented through s 153A of the **Merchant Shipping Act 1995**. The Convention, however, defines 'shipowner' in terms wider than those used by the CLC, as 'the owner, including the registered owner, bareboat charterer, manager and operator of the ship'. The new provisions of the **Merchant Shipping Act 1995** which implement the Convention refer to 'the owner of the ship', which s 153A(7) defines in accordance with the Convention. Sections 153 and 154 have been altered so as to refer to 'the registered owner'. As with the 1992 CLC, compensation for impairment of the environment other than loss of profit is limited to the costs of reasonable measures of reinstatement actually undertaken or to be undertaken. Apart from pollution damage, the shipowner will be liable for the costs of preventive measures and further loss or damage caused thereby. The Convention contains the familiar CLC exclusions and also excludes claims falling under the CLC. Unlike the CLC, the Convention contains no channelling provisions. However, in the UK these are included in s 156A (2)(A) and (B) of the **Merchant Shipping Act 1995**.

There is no separate provision for limitation of liability. Instead, claims under the Convention will fall to be limited under either the **1957** or **1976 Limitation Conventions**. Article 7 provides that for vessels over 1,000 gross tons, the registered owner, but not the other persons falling within the definition of 'owner', must maintain insurance equal to the amounts of liability under the

---

27 Bunker oil is defined as 'hydrocarbon mineral oil, including lubricating oil used for the operation or propulsion of the ship, and any residues of such oil'. In contrast, 'oil' in s 153 and s 154 of the Merchant Shipping Act 1995 is defined as 'persistent hydrocarbon mineral oil'. Spills of persistent hydrocarbon mineral oil used as bunkers on oil tankers will fall under the 1992 CLC and not under the 2001 Bunker Oil Pollution Convention. Spills of non-persistent hydrocarbon mineral oil from such tankers will fall within the 2001 Bunker Oil Pollution Convention.

28 Defined as 'any seagoing vessel and seaborne craft, of any type whatsoever'.

29 A bunker spill from an oil tanker will be subject to the CLC where the bunkers are persistent oil, but will fall under the 2001 Convention for spills of non-persistent bunker oil.

applicable national or international limitation regime applicable in the flag state, but not exceeding the limits in the 1976 Convention, as may be amended.[30] This assumes that claims under the Convention will, in fact, fall within the types of claim covered by the Limitation Conventions. This is a doubtful assumption in relation to claims that do not involve physical damage or an infringement of rights. In the UK s 168 of the **Merchant Shipping Act 1995** provides that any liability incurred under s 153A shall be deemed to be a liability to damages in respect of such damage to property as is mentioned in Art 2(1)(a) of the 1976 LLMC.

As with the CLC, Art 7 gives a direct right of action to the claimant against the insurer, with the insurer maintaining a right to limit even if this has been lost by the registered owner. The insurer may rely on any defences available to the shipowner and may avoid liability on proof that the damage resulted from the wilful misconduct of the shipowner. The IMO has also recommended that states legislate to exempt from liability persons taking reasonable measures to minimise or prevent the effects of oil pollution, save in situations in which the right to limit would be lost (personal act or omission with intent to cause loss or damage or recklessness).

The Convention adopts the CLC time limits. Claims may be pursued before the courts of the state where the pollution has occurred, or in the state where security has been posted. Alternatively, claims may be brought before the courts of the state where preventive/minimising measures have taken place. The Convention makes no provision for a Fund to cover claimants who have been unable to obtain adequate recompense for losses due to bunker oil pollution.

Hazardous and Noxious Substances (HNS) Pollution

In 1996, an international convention was drawn up to apply a regime, similar to that applicable to oil pollution, to non-oil pollution from hazardous and noxious substances. The **International Convention on Liability and Compensation for Damage in Connection with the Carriage of Hazardous and Noxious Substances by Sea 1996** will not come into force internationally until it has been ratified by at least twelve states, of which at least four must each have a fleet totalling more than 2 million gross tons.[31] In addition, the Secretary General of the Fund must be satisfied that potential Fund contributors have received in the preceding year not less than 40 million tons of contributing cargo.

Section 14 of the **Merchant Shipping and Maritime Security Act 1997** inserts a new s 182B into the **Merchant Shipping Act 1995**. This allows the government to give effect to the Convention by means of Order in Council on or after its ratification by the UK, even though the Convention may not yet have come into force internationally.[32] The UK has not yet ratified the Convention and is pressing for concerted ratification by the major European States. On 18 November 2002, Member States were authorised to ratify the HNS Convention, and have subsequently been required to do so by June 2006. However, this has yet to happen.

Liability

Strict liability is imposed on shipowners who carry HNS cargoes, defined in Art 1(5) by reference to lists of substances listed in various existing sources, such as the International Code for the Construction and Equipment of Ships Carrying Dangerous Chemicals in Bulk 1983. The Convention

---

30 The UK has implemented this provision through s 163A of the Merchant Shipping Act 1995.
31 Article 46.
32 This was the way in which the provisions of the 1989 Salvage Convention became part of domestic law before the Convention came into force internationally.

does not apply to damage caused by certain radioactive materials or to pollution damage, as defined in the 1969 CLC, as amended.[33]

'Damage' is defined by Art 1(6) as covering:

(a) loss of life or personal injury on board or outside the ship carrying the hazardous and noxious substances caused by those substances;

(b) loss of or damage to property outside the ship carrying the hazardous and noxious substances caused by those substances;

(c) loss or damage by contamination of the environment caused by the hazardous and noxious substances, provided that compensation for impairment of the environment other than loss of profit from such impairment shall be limited to costs of reasonable measures of reinstatement actually undertaken or to be undertaken; and

(d) the costs of preventive measures and further loss or damage caused by preventive measures.[34]

Article 5 gives State Parties the right to declare that the Convention does not apply to small ships not exceeding 200 gross tons, which carry HNS substances only in package form on domestic voyages. Neighbouring states may agree to extend this exception to voyages by small ships between ports in their territories.

Geographical ambit

By Art 3, the Convention applies exclusively to any damage caused in the territory, including the territorial sea, of a State Party and to environmental damage caused in the exclusive economic zone of such state. The Convention also covers damage, other than environmental contamination, which is caused outside the territory or territorial sea of a State Party where it is caused by an HNS substance carried on board a ship registered in a State Party.[35] The Convention applies to preventive measures wherever taken.

Shipowners' defences

Article 7 reiterates the familiar CLC defences and adds a new one where:

the failure of the shipper or any other person to furnish information concerning the hazardous and noxious nature of the substances shipped either

(i) has caused the damage, wholly or partly; or

(ii) has led the owner not to obtain insurance in accordance with article 12;

provided that neither the owner nor its servants or agents knew or ought reasonably to have known of the hazardous and noxious nature of the substances shipped.[36]

Article 7 also contains 'channelling' provisions similar to those in the CLC regime, which apply not only to claims against the shipowner, but also to claims against a similar list of associated persons as is provided in the CLC regime. Where an incident involves two or more ships carrying HNS, Art 8 makes each owner, unless exonerated under Art 7, jointly and severally liable for such damage as

---

33 Article 4(3).
34 'Preventive measures' is defined in Art 1(7) as 'any reasonable measures taken by any after an incident has occurred to prevent or minimise damage'.
35 Or, with unregistered ships, with ships entitled to fly the flag of a State Party.
36 Article 7(2)(d).

is not reasonably separable. The owners shall be entitled to the limits of liability applicable to each of them and their rights of recourse *inter se* are expressly preserved.

Limitation

Article 9 provides for limitation as follows: ships not exceeding 2,000 gross tons limit on a flat rate basis of 10 million SDRs; for ships over 2,000 gross tons, there is an additional rate of 1,500 SDRs per gross ton; for gross tonnage in excess of 50,000 gross tons, the additional rate comes down to 360 SDRs per gross ton. The maximum aggregate amount is 100 million SDRs. Following the 2010 Protocol, Art 9 provides for a 15 per cent increase in the limitation figures for incidents involving packaged HNS cargo as follows: ships not exceeding 2,000 gross tons limit on a flat rate basis of 11.5 million SDRs; for ships over 2,000 gross tons, there is an additional rate of 1,725 SDRs per gross ton; for gross tonnage in excess of 50,000 gross tons, the additional rate comes down to 414 SDRs per gross ton. The maximum aggregate amount is 115 million SDRs. Claims in respect of death and personal injury are to have priority over other claims for the first two-thirds of the limitation fund and thereafter are to share equally with other claims.[37]

The limitation fund can be established by provision of a bank guarantee in the courts of any State Parties under which the action is brought, or could be brought, under Art 38.[38] The fund can be established by the liability insurer on behalf of the shipowner.[39] Once a fund is established, the courts of the state where it is established shall obtain exclusive jurisdiction to determine all matters relating to its apportionment and distribution.[40]

Where the shipowner or the liability insurer pays a claimant prior to the distribution of the fund, they will be subrogated to the claimant's rights against the fund.[41] The right to limit will be lost in the same way as under the **1976 Limitation Convention**.[42]

Unlike CLC claims, HNS claims are not excluded from the **1976 Limitation Convention**. An HNS claim, therefore, will involve two parallel limitation regimes. However, the 1996 Protocols to the 1976 Limitation Convention will give a State Party the option to exclude HNS claims from the ambit of the 1996 Protocols. It is likely that any state adopting the HNS Convention will also adopt the 1996 Protocols to the 1976 Limitation Convention so as to take advantage of this option. It will need to do so if it is to avoid the conflict in treaty obligations that would otherwise occur where it sought to impose the higher HNS limits against vessels flying the flag of a state that adheres to the 1976 Limitation Convention, but which does not apply the 1996 HNS Convention.[43]

Compulsory liability insurance

Article 12(1) requires ships registered in a State Party to maintain insurance against HNS liabilities. Article 12(11) requires each State Party to ensure, under its national law, that insurance against HNS liabilities is in force in respect of any ship, wherever registered, entering or leaving a port in its territory, or arriving at or leaving an offshore facility in its territorial sea. Article 12(8) provides for direct actions against liability insurers. The insurers may rely on the limitation figure applicable to the ship, even though the shipowner may have lost the right to limit. The insurer:

---

37 Article 11.
38 Article 9(3).
39 Article 9(11).
40 Article 38(5).
41 Article 9(5).
42 Article 9(2).
43 See, further, Griggs, P, 'Extending the frontiers of liability: the proposed Hazardous Noxious Substances Convention and its effect on ship, cargo and insurance interests' (1996) LMCLQ 145.

. . . may further invoke the defences (other than the bankruptcy or winding up of the owner) that the owner would have been entitled to invoke. Furthermore, the defendant may invoke the defence that the damage resulted from the wilful misconduct of the owner, but the defendant shall not invoke any other defence which the defendant might have been entitled to invoke in proceedings brought by the owner against the defendant.

Jurisdiction

Article 38 requires HNS claims to be brought in the courts of the state or states in which the incident occurred. Where liability arises in respect of an incident causing damage exclusively outside the territory or territorial sea of any state, an action may be commenced in one of the three following places:

(1)   the State Party where the ship is registered or, if unregistered, the state the flag of which the ship would be entitled to fly; or

(2)   the State Party where the owner has habitual residence or where the principal place of business of the owner is established; or

(3)   the State Party where a fund has been constituted in accordance with Art 9(3).

Time bars

Article 37(1) extinguishes the right to HNS compensation 'unless an action is brought . . . within three years from the date when the person suffering the damage knew or ought reasonably to have known of the damage and of the identity of the owner'. An absolute maximum of ten years from the date of the incident that caused the damage is imposed by Art 37(3).

The HNS Fund

The Convention establishes a fund financed by contributions collected after the event. As with the oil pollution fund, its purpose is to cover losses that are not recoverable either because the shipowner has a defence or because it is 'financially incapable' of meeting its obligations. The overall fund limit is 250 million SDRs. Claims against the Fund must be notified within three years from the date on which the person suffering the damage 'knew or ought reasonably to have known of the damage'[44] and are subject to the same overall ten-year limit that governs HNS claims against shipowners.

The Protocol to the HNS Fund

The **1996 HNS Convention** has received only a few ratifications and a working group was set up in October 2007 to suggest amendments in three particularly problematic areas. The first is the definition of the receiver of general cargo. It has been proposed that general cargo should no longer be regarded as contributing cargo under the HNS Convention, although it would still be possible to receive compensation from the HNS Funds in incidents involving general cargo if the compensation amount were to exceed the shipowner's financial liability limit. It has been proposed to raise the shipowner's financial liability limit for damage to general cargo. Secondly, there is a problem of how to ensure payments for the Convention's LNG (Liquefied Natural Gas) accounts. The 1996 HNS Convention places contributing responsibility on the party that is the owner of the LNG

---

44 Article 37(2).

immediately before it is loaded, which causes problems when such owner is in a Member State that has not ratified the Convention. The current proposal is that the receiver of LNG should be the contributing party. Thirdly, a mechanism is needed to ensure compliance by Member States on their obligation to submit information as to the quantity of contributing cargo that they have received. It has been proposed that sanctions should be imposed on the Member States for failure to submit such information. Ratification of the Convention and entitlement of Member States to compensation will be conditional on compliance with this obligation.

The 2010 Protocol to the HNS Convention was adopted in April 2010 and was open for signature from 1 November 2010 until 31 October 2011. Thereafter, it will remain open for accession. As of 31 October 2011 Canada, Denmark, France, Germany, Norway and Turkey have signed subject to ratification and the Netherlands has signed subject to acceptance. It will enter into force eighteen months after the date on which the following conditions are fulfilled: (a) at least twelve States, including four States each with not less than two million units of gross tonnage, have expressed their consent to be bound by it; and (b) the Secretary-General has received information in accordance with Art 20, paras 4 and 6, that those persons in such States who would be liable to contribute pursuant to Art 18, paras 1(a) and (c), of the Convention, as amended by the Protocol, have received during the preceding calendar year a total quantity of at least 40 million tonnes of cargo contributing to the general account. Once the 2010 HNS Protocol enters into force, the 1996 Convention, as amended by the 2010 Protocol, will be called: 'the International Convention on Liability and Compensation for Damage in Connection with the Carriage of Hazardous and Noxious Substances by Sea, 2010'.

The three salient features of the Protocol are as follows. First, shipowner compensation limits, for packaged HNS only, have been increased by 15 per cent with a maximum aggregate limit of 115 million SDRs (around US$172.5 million). Secondly, no compensation shall be paid by the HNS Fund for damage in the territory of a state that has not fulfilled its obligations to report contributing cargo. Thirdly, the provisions relating to payment of contributions for LNG cargoes have been amended.

Pollution from oil rigs

The *Deepwater Horizon* incident in April 2010 provided a stark reminder that oil pollution is not only caused by ships. A fire and explosion occurred on the rig which was located 41 miles off the southeast coast of Louisiana. The well to which the rig was connected leaked oil into the sea for 87 days, causing substantial damage to the marine environment.[45] There are, however, no international agreements which regulate the liability of operators of oil rigs.

Rigs operating in UK waters are subject to a voluntary agreement between the major offshore operators, the Offshore Pollution Liability Agreement (OPOL), which came into force on 1 May 1975.[46] OPOL defines offshore facilities to include: oil and gas wells; pipelines connected to such wells; offshore rigs and drilling ships; and mobile installations used to treat, store or transport crude oil from the seabed. The operator is strictly liable up to a maximum of US$250 million, of which half is allocated to preventive measures and half to pollution damage. 'Pollution damage' is

---

45 A year before, in 2009, in the '*Montara*' incident, a blowout occurred on a rig 400 miles west of Darwin, Australia, leading to oil pollution of 70,000 square metres of the Pacific Ocean.

46 The agreement has been subsequently extended to cover offshore facilities in Denmark, Faroe Islands, France, Germany, Ireland, Isle of Man, Netherlands and Norway. OPOL was initially conceived as an interim measure until the coming into force of the 1977 Convention on Civil Liability for Oil Pollution Damage Resulting from Exploration and Exploitation of Seabed Mineral Resources. The Convention has, however, received no ratifications to date.

defined as 'direct loss or damage by contamination which results from a discharge of oil.' The wording would seem to exclude pure economic loss claims and pure ecological damage claims. 'Oil' covers only crude oil. In January 2014, Art IV was amended so that operators would be liable for the costs of reasonable remedial measures undertaken by them following a discharge of oil from an offshore facility operated by them. The costs of these measures will count towards the US$125m aggregate cap for remedial measures

OPOL is a voluntary agreement and there is nothing to prevent a claim being made in tort in the UK courts in the event of a UK 'Deepwater'.[47] This would raise the issue of whether the operator could limit his liability under the LLMC 1976. Article 15(5) excludes 'floating platforms constructed for the purpose of exploring or exploiting the natural resources of the seabed or subsoil thereof', but this provision does not appear in the **Merchant Shipping Act 1995**, which implements the 1976 Convention. Notwithstanding this omission, the operator of an oil rig would probably be unable to limit liability as an oil rig would not fall within the definition of a ship in para 12, Sched 7, Pt II of the **Merchant Shipping Act 1995**, which provides: 'References in this Convention and in the preceding provision of this Schedule to a ship include references to any structure (whether completed or in the course of completion) launched and intended for use in navigation as a ship or part of a ship.'

A related issue is whether oil pollution from an offshore rig would fall within the 1992 CLC. Article 1(1) states that the Convention applies to 'any seagoing vessel and any sea-borne craft of any type whatsoever constructed or adapted for the carriage of oil in bulk'. In October 1999, the Assembly of the 1992 IOPC Fund decided that offshore craft are to be regarded as a ship only when they carry oil as cargo on a voyage to or from a port or terminal outside the oil field in which they operate.[48]

The Environmental Liability Directive 2004/35/EC

The Environmental Liability Directive 2004/35 put in place an EU-wide framework for remediation of environmental damage, which was implemented in England by the **Environmental Damage (Prevention and Remediation) Regulations 2009** No 153. 'Environmental damage' under the Directive means damage to:

(a) protected species or natural habitats, or a site of special scientific interest,[49]

(b) surface water or groundwater,[50] or

(c) land.

The Directive sets out two complementary public law regimes to require remediation of environmental damage, or any imminent threat of such damage, by operators, neither of which has retroactive effect. The first is a strict liability regime which applies to operators who professionally conduct risky, or potentially risky, activities listed in Annex III. Those relevant to shipping are:

● Manufacture, use, storage, processing, filling, release into the environment and onsite transport of: (a) dangerous substances as defined in Art 2(2) of Council Directive 67/548/EEC, as last

---

47 The UK courts will have jurisdiction over claims involving oil rigs within the UK's exclusive economic zone under Art 5(3) of the Judgments Regulation (now Art 7(3)). *Conocophillips (UK) Ltd v Partnereederei Ms Jork* [2010] EWHC 1214 (Comm).

48 Record of Decisions of the Third Extraordinary Session of the 1992 Fund Assembly (92FUND/A/ES 3/21).

49 This refers to damage to protected species and habitats protected under the 1979 Birds Directive and the 1992 Habitats Directive. The ambit of this heading extends to the seabed of the continental shelf and anywhere other than the seabed in the continental shelf.

50 This refers to waters covered by the 2000 Water Framework Directive, which covers all water resources within the EU, including coastal waters and extends to all water up to one nautical mile seaward from the baseline.

amended by Directive 2008/98/EC, on the approximation of the laws, regulations and administrative provisions of the Member States relating to the classification, packaging and labelling of dangerous substances.

- Transport by road, rail, inland waterways, sea or air of dangerous goods or polluting goods as defined in: (c) Council Directive 93/75/EEC concerning minimum requirements for vessels bound for or leaving Community ports and carrying dangerous or polluting goods, as last amended by Directive 2002/84/EC.

The first category would cover oil rigs, while the second would cover carriage of hazardous substances. A second, fault-based regime covers damage to protected species or natural habitats or a site of special scientific interest caused by all professional activities, including those outside Annex III, where the operator is at fault or negligent. Therefore, the Directive does not cover damage to surface water or groundwater or to land by an activity outside Annex III. The Directive excludes an incident in respect of which liability or compensation falls within the scope of the 1992 CLC, or the 1992 Fund Convention, or the 2001 Bunker Oil Pollution Convention. The Directive also provides that it is without prejudice to the right of an operator to limit liability in accordance with the **Convention on Limitation of Liability for Maritime Claims 1976**. The Directive also excludes liability in relation to environmental damage caused by: (a) an act of terrorism; (b) an exceptional natural phenomenon, provided the operator of the activity concerned took all reasonable precautions to protect against damage being caused by such an event; (c) activities the sole purpose of which is to protect from natural disasters.

There is no upper limit of liability for an operator under either of these regimes, but operators are not required to obtain liability insurance. In the event that they cannot meet the costs of remediation, there is no obligation that the Member State in question must effect the remediation of such 'orphan damage' instead. The Directive's regimes are based on public law and require public authorities to identify liable polluters and to ensure that such operators undertake, or finance, the necessary preventive and remedial measures contemplated by the Directive. Civil claims fall outside the Directive and remain subject to national laws.

The effect of the Directive in the maritime sphere has so far been limited by the geographical ambit of damage to surface water. However, that will change with the implementation of Directive 2013/30 on safety of offshore oil and gas operations. Article 38 amends the Environmental Liability Directive so that the ambit of damage to surface water covers all EU waters including the exclusive economic zone (about 370 km from the coast) and the continental shelf where the coastal Member States exercise jurisdiction. Member States have until 19 July 2015 to implement this provision. The new Directive also requires Member States to ensure that the licensee is financially liable for the prevention and remediation of environmental damage caused by offshore oil and gas operations carried out by, or on behalf of, the licensee or the operator.[51]

Wreck removal

Statutory powers of wreck removal

Under s 252 of the **Merchant Shipping Act 1995**, harbour authorities are given the power to remove any vessel that is sunk, stranded or abandoned in, or near any approach to, any harbour or

---

51 Article 7.

tidal water under their control. If the vessel is likely to become an obstruction or danger to navigation or to lifeboats in that harbour or water or the approach thereto, the harbour authority may take possession of, raise, remove or destroy the wreck in whole or in part. In the interim, it may light or buoy the vessel.

It may then sell the vessel and reimburse itself for its expenses out of the proceeds of sale, with any balance going to its owner. Seven days' notice must be given of any sale, save where perishable property is involved, and, within this time, the owner is entitled to reclaim its vessel on payment of its fair market value.

The 2007 Nairobi International Convention on the removal of wrecks

This IMO Convention, which was adopted on 22 May 2007, aims to provide a set of uniform international rules to ensure the prompt and effective removal of wrecks located beyond the territorial sea but within the exclusive economic zone of a State Party, with State Parties being given the option of applying certain provisions to their territory, including their territorial sea.

The Convention contains provisions, *inter alia*, on:

- criteria for determining the hazard posed by wrecks, including environmental criteria (Art 6);
- reporting and locating ships and wrecks (Art 7);
- marking wrecks (Art 8);
- measures to facilitate the removal of wrecks, setting out when the shipowner is responsible for removing the wreck and when a state may intervene (Art 9);
- settlement of disputes between State Parties (Art 15).

Article 10(1) makes shipowners liable for the costs of locating, marking and removing the wreck under Arts 7, 8 and 9 respectively,[52] unless the registered owner 'proves that the maritime casualty that caused the wreck: (a) resulted from an act of war, hostilities, civil war, insurrection, or a natural phenomenon of an exceptional, inevitable and irresistible character; (b) was wholly caused by an act or omission done with intent to cause damage by a third party; or (c) was wholly caused by the negligence or other wrongful act of any Government or other authority responsible for the maintenance of lights or other navigational aids in the exercise of that function.' Article 10(2) allows shipowners to limit under the applicable limitation regime. Article 10(3) provides that 'No claim for the costs referred to in paragraph 1 may be made against the registered owner otherwise than in accordance with the provisions of this Convention.' Article 11(1) then provides that the registered owner will not be liable for such costs if, and to the extent that, such liability would conflict with one of the following conventions, provided that convention is applicable and in force:

(a)   the **International Convention on Civil Liability for Oil Pollution Damage 1969**, as amended;

(b)   the **International Convention on Liability and Compensation for Damage in Connection with the Carriage of Hazardous and Noxious Substances by Sea 1996**, as amended;

(c)   the **Convention on Third-Party Liability in the Field of Nuclear Energy 1960**, as amended, or the **Vienna Convention on Civil Liability for Nuclear Damage 1963**, as amended, or national law governing or prohibiting limitation of liability for nuclear damage; or

---

52 Under Art 2 such costs must be reasonable and proportionate to the hazard faced.

(d) the **International Convention on Civil Liability for Bunker Oil Pollution Damage, 2001**, as amended.[53]

Article 11(2) deals with salvage, as follows: 'To the extent that measures under this Convention are considered to be salvage under applicable national law or an international convention, such law or convention shall apply to questions of the remuneration or compensation payable to salvors to the exclusion of the rules of this Convention'.[54] Article 12 will require the owners of a ship of over 300 grt (gross register tonnage) which is registered in a signatory state to take out insurance or provide other financial security to cover the costs of wreck removal. Such ships must carry a certificate of insurance in approved form, failing which they will not be permitted to operate at any time. Article 13 provides a time limit for recovery of costs under the Convention of three years from the date of the hazard's determination in accordance with the Convention. In no case can an action be brought after six years from the maritime casualty that caused the wreck.

The Convention, opened for signature on 19 November 2007, entered into force on 14 April 2015, 12 months after it had been ratified by ten states: Bulgaria, Denmark, Germany, India, Iran, Malaysia, Morocco, Nigeria, Palau and the United Kingdom.[55]

---

53 In addition, Art 4 provides that the Convention will not apply to measures taken under the International Convention relating to Intervention on the High Seas in Cases of Oil Pollution Casualties 1969, as amended, or the Protocol relating to Intervention on the High Seas in Cases of Pollution by Substances other than Oil 1973, as amended; nor shall the Convention apply to 'any warship or other ship owned or operated by a State and used, for the time being, only on Government non-commercial service, unless that State decides otherwise'.
54 Article 12(10) will provide State Parties with a right of direct action against insurers of liabilities arising under the Convention.
55 The Wreck Removal Convention Act 2011 provides for the future incorporation of the Convention's provisions into UK law through insertion in a new Part 9A of the Merchant Shipping Act 1995 after s 255. The Act will come into force in accordance with provision made by the Secretary of State by order made by statutory instrument.

Part 3

Jurisdiction, Choice of Law, Security and Limitation

Chapter 18

Jurisdiction, Arbitration and Applicable Law

Chapter Contents

The ultimate success of any shipping claim is dependent not only on the merits of the claim itself, but also on the claimant's ability to obtain a judgment or arbitration award that can readily be enforced against the defendant's assets. To this end, a claimant will seek to invoke the jurisdiction of the English courts for two purposes. The first is to have the substantive dispute heard. The second is to obtain security for any eventual judgment or arbitration award, even though it may not be intended that the substantive claim itself be heard in the English courts.

This chapter will consider the jurisdiction of the English courts over the substantive dispute and the system of law that will be applied. It will start by examining the basis on which the English courts assume jurisdiction over matters and will outline the relevant procedure. It will then consider the grounds on which the English courts may decline to exercise a jurisdiction with which they are vested. It will conclude by examining the question of what law will be applied by the English courts in the event that they hear the substantive dispute between the parties.

Jurisdiction of the English High Court

Historically, the jurisdiction of the English courts has been based on the claimant's ability to serve proceedings on the defendant, if the action is brought in *personam*, or on its property within the jurisdiction, if the action is brought in *rem*.

Under the domestic rules governing jurisdiction, service of an in *personam* claim form (formerly, a 'writ') can be effected, without permission of the court, on any defendant who is physically present in England and Wales or who has agreed to accept service of High Court proceedings. In other cases that have a strong English connection, the claimant, with permission of the court, may also serve a defendant who is outside the jurisdiction. Service of an in *rem* claim form is effected by arresting the defendant's ship at any port in England and Wales. The claimant must also establish that its claim falls within the types of claim listed in ss 20–21 of the **Senior Courts Act 1981** (formerly the **Supreme Court Act 1981**), which provides the statutory definition of the in *rem* jurisdiction of the Admiralty Court.

Service of proceedings in accordance with the domestic rules will establish the jurisdiction of the English courts, although, in certain cases, the defendant can subsequently apply to stay the proceedings on the grounds of *forum non conveniens*. The jurisdiction of the English courts has also been affected by the accession of the UK to various international conventions that govern jurisdiction, such as the **1952 Arrest Convention**, the **1952 Collision Jurisdiction Convention**, the **1976 Limitation of Liability for Maritime Claims Convention** and the conventions governing shipowners' liability for oil pollution. Their provisions, for the most part, have been given effect by appropriate amendments to the domestic sources of law relating to jurisdiction.

However, the most important development relating to the jurisdiction of the English courts has been the implementation of the **1968 Brussels Convention** by the **Civil Jurisdiction and Judgments Act 1982**. This Convention dealt with the allocation of jurisdiction and the enforcement of judgments as between the states of the European Union. Its provisions had 'the force of law' and came into force on 1 January 1987. Its provisions were to be construed in the light of the principles of the **Treaty of Rome** and, under the **Luxembourg Convention 1971**, the European Court of Justice (now the Court of Justice of the European Union) was given jurisdiction to rule on the interpretation of the Convention.

A modified version of the Convention governed jurisdictional matters as between courts in different parts of the UK, such as England, Scotland and Northern Ireland. The 1988 **Lugano Convention** applied substantially the same provisions as the Brussels Convention and its signatories were the former EFTA states.[1] However, the European Court of Justice had no jurisdiction to rule on the interpretation either of the Lugano Convention or of the intra-UK modified Brussels Convention.

The Convention expanded the existing jurisdiction of the English courts. Where the Convention allocated jurisdiction to the English courts, in most cases, defendants who were not present within the jurisdiction might be served without permission of the court, in accordance with the former Rules of the Supreme Court (RSC) Ord 11(2). The Convention also restricted the pre-existing jurisdiction of the English courts. This could only be ascertained by reference to the Convention itself. Service might be effected in accordance with the domestic sources of law, but if the matter fell under the Convention and the Convention allocated jurisdiction to another Convention State, then the English courts would not have jurisdiction over the matter.

As of 1 March 2002, the Brussels Convention was replaced by **EC Regulation 44/2001** on jurisdiction and recognition and enforcement of judgments in civil and commercial matters ('the **EC Judgments Regulation**').[2] This applies an expanded and modified version of the Brussels Convention among the Member States. Although Denmark originally abstained from participating in the adoption of the Judgments Regulation, following an agreement with the European Community in June 2007, the provisions of the Regulation have now been extended to Denmark, thereby restoring the uniformity that existed before the Regulation came into force.[3] The Regulation has since been amended, with consequential renumbering of its articles, by **Regulation (EU) No 1215/2012** on jurisdiction and recognition and enforcement of judgments in civil and commercial matters (recast) ('the **Judgments Regulation**') which applies to legal proceedings instituted on or after 10 January 2015.

Accordingly, the question of jurisdiction must now be approached first by asking whether the matter falls within the provisions of the Judgments Regulation. If it does, jurisdiction is decided exclusively in accordance with those provisions. If the matter falls outside the Judgments Regulation, jurisdiction is still established by service of proceedings in accordance with the domestic rules. The issue is somewhat complicated by the fact that the Judgments Regulation itself provides that jurisdiction in some matters that fall within its scope is nonetheless to be decided on non-Regulation grounds – that is, by application of the 'domestic' rules governing jurisdiction. We shall now consider the bases by which the English courts may be assigned jurisdiction in matters subject to the Judgments Regulation and then go on to examine the domestic bases of jurisdiction in non-Regulation matters.

Jurisdiction under the Judgments Regulation (EU 1215/2012)

The Judgments Regulation, by virtue of Art 1(1), governs 'civil and commercial matters'. Matters that are not 'civil and commercial' do not therefore fall within the provisions of the Judgments Regulation. What amounts to 'civil and commercial matters' is to be determined autonomously,[4] and by referring to both the objectives of the Judgments Regulation and the general principles that stem from the corpora of the national legal systems.[5] In any case, actions based on the exercise of public as opposed to private powers will almost certainly fall outside of this definition,[6] such as claims for damages suffered as a result of the acts of a Member State's armed forces.[7] By Art 1(2)(d)

---

1 The Convention was implemented into UK law by The Civil Jurisdiction and Judgments Act 1991.
2 Implemented in the UK by the Civil Jurisdiction and Judgments Order 2001.
3 The Brussels Convention also applies to the territories of Member States that are within its territorial scope, but which are excluded from the Jurisdiction Regulation pursuant to Art 299 of the Treaty of Amsterdam.
4 Case 29/76 *LTU Lufttransportunternehmen GmbH & Co KG v Eurocontrol* [1976] ECR 1541, 1551, [3].
5 Case C-292/05 *Lechouritou v Germany* [2007] ILPr 14, [29].
6 Case 814/79 *Netherlands State v Rüffer* [1980] ECR 3807.
7 Case C-292/05, fn 5.

(formerly Art 1(4)), arbitration is also excluded from the provisions of the Judgments Regulation. The extent of this exclusion was considered by the European Court of Justice in *Marc Rich & Co AG v Societa Italiana Impianti (PA) (The Atlantic Empress)*.[8] It was held that: 'If, by virtue of its subject matter, such as the appointment of an arbitrator, a dispute falls outside the scope of the Convention, the existence of a preliminary issue which the court must resolve in order to determine the dispute cannot, whatever the issue may be, justify the application of the Convention.' On this footing, the European Court of Justice held that disputes concerning the existence and validity of agreements to arbitrate fall outside of the scope of the Brussels regime. Applying this test, applications for interim relief, such as freezing orders,[9] in support of arbitration proceedings, have been held to fall within the scope of the Judgments Regulation, on the basis that the subject matter of such applications is the preservation of a legal or factual state of affairs, rather than the arbitration of the primary dispute.[10]

The Judgments Regulation assigns jurisdiction to Member States in one of four ways. First, jurisdiction may be allocated on the basis of the defendant's domicile in a Member State. Secondly, the claimant may be given the option of suing the defendant in a jurisdiction other than that of the defendant's domicile. Thirdly, jurisdiction may be allocated, irrespective of the defendant's domicile. Fourthly, in some situations, the Judgments Regulation itself provides that jurisdiction is to be based on non-Regulation grounds – that is, by application of the 'domestic' rules governing jurisdiction.

Jurisdiction based on defendant's domicile

Article 4 – defendant domiciled in another Member State[11]

The underlying principle of the Judgments Regulation is that a defendant is, subject to the provisions of the Judgments Regulation, entitled to be sued in the place of its domicile where that is in a Member State. If jurisdiction is assigned to the state in which the defendant is domiciled, it follows that no other Member State can have jurisdiction over the matter.[12]

Where the defendant is a corporation, its domicile is defined in Art 63 (formerly Art 60) as the place where it has its '(a) statutory seat, or (b) central administration, or (c) principal place of business'. For the purposes of the UK and Ireland, 'statutory seat' means 'the registered office or, where there is no such office anywhere, the place of incorporation or, where there is no such place anywhere, the place under the law of which the formation took place'. The European Court of Justice in *Group Josi Reinsurance Co SA v Universal General Insurance Co*[13] has confirmed that the claimant is entitled to rely on this provision, even though it is not domiciled in a Convention State.

Two points need to be made about the references to 'the defendant' in Art 4. First, a potential defendant may sometimes be able to initiate litigation against a potential claimant. Thus, a shipowner anticipating that it will be sued by cargo claimants might initiate limitation proceedings before the cargo claimants bring their proceedings. Alternatively, it might bring a claim for a negative declaration – that is, a ruling by the court that it is not liable. Such an action can be brought before the English courts and those of many other Member States.[14] In both of these actions, the shipowner will reverse the parties to the expected action. The shipowner will now be the claimant[15]

---

8 [1992] 1 Lloyd's Rep 342, 351.
9 See, generally, Chapter 19.
10 Case C-391/95 *Van Uden Maritime BV v Kommanditgesellschaft in Firma Deco-Line* [1998] ECR I-7091.
11 Formerly Art 2.
12 Where the proceedings are undefended, Art 26(1) requires the court to dismiss them on its own motion where the courts of another Member State have jurisdiction under Art 4.
13 Case C-412/98 [2001] QB 68.
14 In *Messier-Dowty Ltd v Sabena SA* [2000] 1 WLR 2040, the Court of Appeal held that there was no jurisdictional ground for excluding claims for negative declarations from being brought before the English courts. The remedy, however, was an unusual one in that it reversed the usual position of the parties, and was subject to the exercise of the court's discretion.
15 The term 'plaintiff' was used in the Brussels Convention and in the 2001 Judgments Regulation. The 2012 Recast Regulation now uses the term 'claimant'.

and the cargo claimant the defendant. If the cargo claimant is domiciled in a Member State, the shipowner will be entitled to commence proceedings in the courts of that state under Art 4.

Secondly, it is not immediately obvious who constitutes 'the defendant' in an action in *rem*. The claim form will name a ship and, until the action is defended, when it will proceed as a parallel action in *personam* against the shipowner, it could be argued that the only defendant is that ship.[16] This fiction formed the basis of the judgment of Hobhouse J in *The Nordglimt*,[17] in the context of the application of Art 21 of the **Brussels Convention** (now Art 29 of the Judgments Regulation). However, the Court of Appeal was to take a radically different approach in *The Deichland*.[18] For the purposes of Art 4, it held that 'the defendant' in an in *rem* action, even at a stage when the action was proceeding solely in *rem*, was the person who would be interested in defending the action – that is, the person potentially liable in *personam*. On the facts, that person was the demise charterer of the vessel at the time that the cargo claim arose. As they were domiciled in Germany, they were entitled to be sued in Germany under Art 4 and the Admiralty Court had no jurisdiction over the claim against them.

Article 4 is followed by Art 5 (formerly Art 3), which provides: 'Persons domiciled in a Member State may be sued in the courts of another Member State only by virtue of the rules set out in Sections 2 to 7 of this Chapter'. Section 2 'Optional Allocation of Jurisdiction' covers Arts 7–9. Section 3 'Jurisdiction in Matters Relating to Insurance' covers Arts 10–16. Section 4 'Jurisdiction over Consumer Contracts' covers Arts 17–19. Section 5 'Jurisdiction over Individual Contracts of Employment' covers Arts 20–23. Section 6 'Exclusive Jurisdiction' covers Art 24. Section 7 'Prorogation Jurisdiction' covers Art 25–28. Articles 7, 8, 9, 24 and 25 are the provisions most likely to concern the shipping practitioner and these will now be discussed.

Article 7 – contract, tort and salvage claims against freight and cargo[19]

Under Art 7(1)(a), contract disputes may also be brought before the courts of the Member State where the obligation in question should have been performed.[20] The court whose jurisdiction is invoked must fix the place of performance of the obligation in question[21] by reference to its own choice of law rules,[22] even if the forum so designated turns out not to be the one with the closest connection with the dispute.[23] If the court has jurisdiction under Art 7, it has no power to stay its own proceedings and is required to hear the case.[24]

Where a contractual claim is made under a bill of lading in respect of a cargo claim, one cannot assume that the place of performance will always be at the place of discharge. In *The Sea Maas*,[25] the cargo claim was due to initial unseaworthiness, which meant that the place of performance was the place at which the cargo was loaded. Article 7(1)(b) provides that:

> . . . for the purpose of this provision and unless otherwise agreed, the place of performance of the obligation in question shall be:

---

16 The nature of in *rem* proceedings, and their relation to in *personam* proceedings, is discussed later in this chapter in the section dealing with domestic sources of jurisdiction, at pp 360–6.

17 [1988] 1 QB 183.

18 [1990] 1 QB 361.

19 Formerly Art 5.

20 This paragraph will not apply when the contract – in this case, a general average guarantee – gives a choice to pay one of two parties, one of whom is within the jurisdiction, the other outside the jurisdiction. See *Mora Shipping Inc v Axa Corporate Solutions Assurance SA* [2005] EWCA Civ 1069; [2005] 2 Lloyd's Rep 769.

21 Viz the contractual obligation forming the basis of the legal proceedings, see Case 14/76 *Ets A de Bloos SPRL v Société en commandite par actions Bouyer* [1976] ECR 1497.

22 Case 12/76 *Industrie Tessili Italiana Como v Dunlop AG* [1976] ECR 1473.

23 Case C-288/92 *Custom Made Commercial Ltd v Stawa Metallbau GmbH* [1994] ECR I-2913.

24 *Oceanfix International Ltd v AGIP Kazakhstan North Caspian Operating Co NV* [2009] ScotSC 9.

25 [1999] 2 Lloyd's Rep 281, QB.

- in the case of the sale of goods, the place in a Member State where, under the contract, the goods were delivered,
- in the case of the provision of services, the place in a Member State where, under the contract, the services were provided or should have been provided.[26]

In *Scottish & Newcastle International Ltd v Othon Ghalanos Ltd*, the House of Lords confirmed that the courts are to continue to rely on the law that is applicable to the contract in question in order to identify the place of delivery of goods or provision of services. If Art 7(1)(b) does not apply, then the basic rule set out in Art 7(1)(a) applies.[27]

Under Art 7(3), tort disputes may also be brought before the courts of the Member State where the harmful event occurred or may occur.[28] This provision was significantly extended by the European Court of Justice in *Handelskwekerij GJ Bier BV v Mines de Potasse d'Alsace SA* to include both the place where damage occurred and the place of the event(s) giving rise to that damage.[29]

Under Art 7(7), salvage actions against cargo and freight may be brought in the courts of the Member State in which the cargo or freight has been arrested or could have been arrested but for the provision of security. The provision shall apply only 'if it is claimed that the defendant has an interest in the cargo or freight or had such an interest at the time of salvage'. The provision is needed to maintain the existing admiralty jurisdiction over salvage claims against cargo and freight. The **1952 Arrest Convention** confers jurisdiction in relation to salvage claims, but only in relation to claims against ships.

Article 8 – co-defendants and third parties[30]

This Article allows a person domiciled in a Member State to be sued:

(a) where he is one of a number of defendants, in the courts for the place where any one of them is domiciled, provided that the claims are so closely connected that it is expedient to hear and determine them together to avoid the risk of irreconcilable judgments resulting from separate proceedings;

(b) as a third party in an action on a warranty or guarantee or in any other third-party proceedings, in the court seised of the original proceedings, unless these were instituted solely with the object of removing him from the jurisdiction of the court that would be competent in his case;

(c) on a counter-claim arising from the same contract or facts on which the original claim was based, in the court in which the original claim is pending;

(d) in matters relating to a contract, if the action may be combined with an action against the same defendants in matters relating to rights in rem in immovable property, in the court of the Member State in which the property is situated.

As regards Art 8(1), the European Court of Justice in *Kalfelis v Bankhaus Schroder, Munchmeyer, Hengst & Co*[31] has ruled that when the claimant sues different defendants, there must be a connection between the actions such that it is expedient to determine them together so as to avoid the risk of irreconcilable judgments.[32] The wording of para 50 of the judgment of the European Court of Justice in *Réunion*

---

26 Article 7(1)(c).
27 [2008] UKHL 11; [2008] 2 Lloyd's Rep 462, noted (2008) LMCLQ 358.
28 The words 'or may occur' did not appear in the equivalent provision in the Brussels Convention.
29 Case 21/76 [1976] ECR 1735].
30 Formerly Art 6.
31 Case C-189/87 [1988] ECR 5565.
32 This condition has now been reproduced in the wording of Art 6(1) of the Judgments Regulation.

Européenne SA v Spliethoff's Bevrachtingskantoor BV[33] led to uncertainty as to whether the requisite connection can ever exist when the claimant claims against one defendant in contract and against a co-defendant in tort. The Court of Appeal in *Watson v First Choice Holidays*[34] remitted this issue to the European Court of Justice, but the case was ultimately settled. The European Court of Justice has, however, clarified this area in *Freeport Plc v Arnoldsson*,[35] where it held that neither the text of Art 8(1) nor the contested passage in *Réunion Européenne* provided support for the assertion that the operation of this provision is limited to claims with the same legal base.

At least one of the defendants must be domiciled in the Member State in which proceedings have been commenced.[36] The issue of domicile is determined by reference to the time at which proceedings are issued, rather than when they are served,[37] and this is also the case in determining the domicile of a defendant who is subsequently added to the proceedings.[38] Article 8(1) will cease to apply once proceedings are discontinued against the co-defendant that is domiciled in the Member State of the court before which those proceedings have been brought.[39]

Article 9 – limitation actions[40]
Article 11 of the **1976 Limitation Convention** entitles the defendant to constitute a limitation fund 'in any State Party in which legal proceedings are instituted in respect of claims subject to limitation', but gives the shipowner no right to launch a 'pre-emptive' strike. However, it does not prevent the shipowner doing so, provided that it can establish jurisdiction in its chosen court under either domestic grounds or, where appropriate, on Judgment Regulation grounds.

Accordingly, a shipowner can rely on Art 4 to proceed against the cargo owner in the courts of a Member State in which it is domiciled.[41] However, such a shipowner would not be able to initiate limitation proceedings in the Member State in which it was itself domiciled. Article 9 allows it to do this. It provides that:

> Where by virtue of this Regulation a court of a Member State has jurisdiction in actions relating to liability arising from the use or operation of a ship, that court, or any other court substituted for this purpose by the internal law of that State, shall also have jurisdiction over claims for limitation of such liability.

Article 24[42]
Article 24 confers jurisdiction on courts in Member States, regardless of domicile, in respect of a list of proceedings, such as those that have as their object rights in rem in immovable property. The only proceedings that are likely to concern the shipping practitioner are those listed in Art 24(5): '. . . proceedings concerned with the enforcement of judgments' where jurisdiction is assigned to 'the courts of the Member State in which the judgment has been or is to be enforced'.

Article 25 – jurisdiction clauses[43]
Article 25 confers exclusive jurisdiction on any Member State that the parties have agreed should have jurisdiction 'to settle any disputes which have arisen or which may arise in connection with a

---

33 Case C-51/97 [1999] CLC 282.
34 [2001] 2 Lloyd's Rep 339, CA.
35 Case C-98/06 [2008] 2 WLR 853, noted (2008) LMCLQ 113.
36 Article 8(1) cannot therefore apply where none of the defendants are so domiciled. See Case C-51/97 *Réunion Européenne SA v Spliethoff's Bevrachtingskantoor BV* [1999] CLC 282.
37 *Canada Trust Co v Stolzenberg* (No 2) [1998] CLC 23, CA.
38 *Petrotrade Inc v Smith* [1998] CLC 298, QB.
39 *The Xing Su Hai* [1995] 2 Lloyd's Rep 15.
40 Formerly Art 7.
41 It can also rely on Arts 7 and 8.
42 Formerly Art 22.
43 Formerly Art 23.

particular legal relationship . . .'. This provision applies where one or more of the parties are domiciled in a Member State. The agreement must be either:

(a) in writing or evidenced by writing; or
(b) in a form according with practices that the parties have established between themselves; or
(c) in international trade or commerce, in a form that accords with a usage of which the parties are or ought to have been aware and which in such trade or commerce is widely known to, and regularly observed by, parties to contracts of the type involved in the particular trade or commerce concerned.

A jurisdiction clause in a charterparty will fall within subheading (a).[44] A jurisdiction clause in a bill of lading is more problematic, in that the initial contract of carriage may have been made orally prior to the issue of the bill of lading. In *The MS Tilly Russ*,[45] the European Court of Justice held that subheading (a) would cover the case if the parties' agreement to the bill of lading had been expressed in writing or there had been prior oral agreement to the jurisdiction clause. If this were not the case, the clause would fall under subheading (b) if the carrier and the shipper have a continuing business relationship that is regulated by the carrier's general conditions, which include the clause in question. The position of third-party holders of the bill is determined by the application of this provision to the relationship of the shipper and the carrier. A clause might also fall within subheading (c), as was the case in *Trasporti Castelletti v Hugo Trumpy*.[46] The European Court of Justice held that the requirements of the subheading would be satisfied if the usage were regularly followed in the particular branch of international trade in which the parties operated. A sub-bailment on terms has been held not to constitute an 'agreement' and so falls outside Art 25.[47]

Article 25(2) provides that 'any communication by electronic means which provides a durable record of the agreement shall be equivalent to writing'.

In order that Art 25 be relied upon, the court must be satisfied that there is a good arguable case that a contract containing the jurisdiction agreement came into existence between the parties.[48] In this regard, where the contract signed by both parties expressly refers to general conditions, one of which includes a clause conferring jurisdiction, the requirements of Art 25 will be satisfied. It is not necessary that the general conditions form part of the contractual document itself, nor that there be express reference to the jurisdiction clause in the principal document.[49] In *Deutsche Bank AG v Asia Pacific Broadband Wireless Communication Inc* Longmore J held that the doctrine of separability applies, whereby

> . . . disputes about the validity of the contract must, on the face of it, be resolved pursuant to the terms of the clause and, indeed, the last sentence of the clause expressly so provides. It is only if the jurisdiction clause is itself under some specific attack that a question can arise whether it is right to invoke the jurisdiction clause. Examples of this might be fraud or duress alleged in relation specifically to the jurisdiction clause.[50]

Where none of the parties are domiciled in a Member State, Art 25(3) provides that 'the courts of other Member States shall have no jurisdiction over their disputes'. A reference to a jurisdiction in a non-Member State falls outside Art 25. Where the jurisdiction clause is non-exclusive,

---

44 In *Polskie Ratownictwo Okretowe v Rallo Vito & C SNC* [2009] EWHC 2249 (Comm); [2010] 1 Lloyd's Rep 384, Hamblen J held that an oral agreement fell within the subheading when it was subsequently evidenced by a written recap.
45 Case 71/83 [1984] ECR 2417; [1985] 1 QB 931.
46 Case C-159/97 [1999] IL Pr 492.
47 *Dresser UK Ltd v Falcongate Freight Management Ltd, 'The Duke of Yare'* [1992] QB 502.
48 *Bols Distilleries BV v Superior Yacht Services Ltd* [2006] UKPC 45; [2007] 1 WLR 12, Privy Council.
49 *7E Communications Ltd v Vertex Antennentechnik GmbH* [2007] EWCA Civ 140; [2007] 1 WLR 2175, CA.
50 [2008] EWCA Civ 1091; [2008] 2 Lloyd's Rep 619, para 24.

such as a clause that lists more than one jurisdiction, the claimant may still rely on Art 25 and will not be compelled to sue the defendant in the courts of the Member State in which it is domiciled.[51]

Article 26 – submission to the jurisdiction[52]
This Article provides that:

> Apart from jurisdiction derived from other provisions of this Regulation, a court of a Member State before which a defendant enters an appearance shall have jurisdiction. This rule shall not apply where appearance was entered solely to contest the jurisdiction, or where another court has exclusive jurisdiction by virtue of Article 24.

The European Court of Justice has ruled that the defendant will not be taken to have submitted under this Article where it raises a defence on the merits at the same time as it disputes jurisdiction.[53] The provisions of Art 26 are very similar to the domestic rules on establishing jurisdiction by submission. There is uncertainty as to whether Art 26 requires one or both of the parties to be domiciled in a Member State. Although Art 26 appears in the same section of the Judgments Regulation as Art 25, which only requires one of the parties to be domiciled in a Member State, such a condition does not appear in the text of Art 26. With respect to English law, however, such a debate is academic, since even if a submission to proceedings is regarded as falling outside of the Judgments Regulation, it will be accepted under the common law rules.[54]

The internal hierarchy of competing grounds of jurisdiction under the Judgments Regulation
It is quite feasible for courts in different Member States to have jurisdiction over a particular matter based on different provisions in the Judgments Regulation. How is the court before which the case is proceeding to decide which competing ground of jurisdiction under the Judgments Regulation is to prevail, assuming proceedings have not already been brought in the courts of another Member State?[55] To start with, jurisdiction based on Art 4 is specifically expressed to be 'subject to the provisions of this Regulation'. This ground of jurisdiction will therefore yield to other jurisdiction grounds found elsewhere in the Regulation, including Art 7.[56] In particular, the superior nature of the jurisdiction bases in Arts 24 and 25 is confirmed by the references therein to 'exclusive jurisdiction'.[57]

In *Elefanten Schuh GmbH v Jacqmain*,[58] the European Court of Justice ruled that the provisions of Art 18 of the Brussels Convention (now Art 26 of the Judgments Regulation) should take priority over those of Art 17 (now Art 25 of the Judgments Regulation).

Jurisdiction to be decided on a non-Regulation basis
The Judgments Regulation provides for jurisdiction to be determined on a non-Regulation basis in two situations. The first is under Art 6, where the defendant is not domiciled in a Member State. The

---

51 *Kurz v Stella Musical Veranstaltungs GmbH* [1992] Ch 196.
52 Formerly Art 24.
53 Case 150/80 *Elefanten Schuh GmbH v Jacqmain* [1981] ECR 1671.
54 See p 357, 'Domestic sources of jurisdiction'.
55 In which case, the court will be subject to the *lis alibi pendens* provisions of the Judgments Regulation, contained in Arts 27–30, formerly Arts 21–3 of the Brussels Convention.
56 See *Hough v P & O Containers* [1998] 2 Lloyd's Rep 318, QB, where it was held that Art 6(2) overrides Art 2, and Art 17 (now Art 23) overrides both of them.
57 Article 24 begins with the words 'Apart from jurisdiction derived from other provisions of this Regulation . . .' so as to provide an alternative jurisdiction base to those contained elsewhere in the Regulation. Article 23 may be relied upon to endow the courts of a Member State with exclusive jurisdiction over a dispute even where the jurisdiction agreement is explicitly non-exclusive. See *Kurz v Stella Musical Veranstaltungs GmbH* [1992] Ch 196.
58 [1981] ECR 1671.

second is under Art 71 – formerly, Art 57 of the Brussels Convention – where the jurisdiction of a Member State can be based on the provisions of another Convention governing jurisdiction.

Article 6: defendant not domiciled in a Member State[59]
This Article provides:

> If the defendant is not domiciled in a Member State, the jurisdiction of the courts of each Member State shall, subject to Article 18(1), Article 21(2) and Articles 24 and 25, be determined by the law of that Member State.

In most cases, the effect of Art 6 is to take outside the Judgments Regulation actions against a defendant that is not domiciled in a Member State. Jurisdiction will be based on the principles of domestic law applied by the courts in which the claimant has commenced proceedings. However, it should be noted that this result follows from the provisions of the Judgments Regulation itself. Furthermore, Art 24 will still have mandatory effect, even where the defendant is domiciled in a non-Member State; so too will Art 25 where the claimant is domiciled in a Member State and the parties have agreed to submit to the exclusive jurisdiction of the courts of a Member State. It is possible that Art 26 may also apply when a defendant domiciled in a non-Member State submits to the jurisdiction of a Member State.[60]

Article 6 also provides that as against a defendant who is not domiciled in a Member State:

> . . . [a]ny person domiciled in a Member State may, whatever his nationality, avail himself in that Member State of the rules of jurisdiction there in force, and in particular those of which the Member States are to notify the Commission pursuant to point (a) of Article 76(1), in the same way as nationals of that Member State.

A claimant domiciled in a Contracting State may therefore take advantage of the UK rules allowing jurisdiction to be founded on the presence of the defendant within the jurisdiction or the seizure of its assets within the jurisdiction, provided that the defendant is not domiciled in a Member State. This provision does not, by implication, prevent a claimant who is not domiciled in a Member State from taking advantage of these rules.[61]

Article 71 and other conventions governing jurisdiction[62]
Article 71(1) of the Regulation preserves the effect of other conventions that govern jurisdiction, in the following terms:[63]

> This Regulation shall not affect any conventions to which the Member States are parties and which, in relation to particular matters, govern jurisdiction or the recognition or enforcement of judgments.

---

59 Formerly Art 4.
60 Article 26(1) provides: 'Apart from jurisdiction derived from other provisions of this Regulation, a court of a Member State before which a defendant enters an appearance shall have jurisdiction. This rule shall not apply where appearance was entered to contest the jurisdiction, or where another court has exclusive jurisdiction by virtue of Article 24.'
61 *The Po* [1991] 2 Lloyd's Rep 206.
62 Formerly Art 57 of the Brussels Convention.
63 The equivalent passage in Art 57(1) of the Brussels Convention contained the additional words 'or will be' before 'parties'. This made it clear that the rules contained in that convention did not preclude the application of different rules to which the Contracting States would agree in the future through the conclusion of specialised conventions. However, Art 71(1) of the Regulation, which omits these words, does not enable the Member States to introduce, by concluding new specialised conventions or amending conventions already in force, rules which would prevail over those of the Regulation.

Article 71(2)(a) then provides:

> . . . this Regulation shall not prevent a court of a Member State which is party to a convention on a particular matter from assuming jurisdiction in accordance with that convention, even where the defendant is domiciled in another Member State which is not party to that convention. The court hearing the action shall, in any event, apply Article 28 of this Regulation;

The interpretation of Art 71 of the Judgments Regulation, formerly Art 57 of the Brussels Convention, was, for a time, a matter of some uncertainty. One view was that its effect was to exclude the provisions of the Brussels Convention whenever jurisdiction was established by the provisions of a competing Convention. This interpretation was rejected by the European Court of Justice when the issue came before it in *The Tatry*.[64] The case involved a cargo claim in which proceedings for a negative declaration were commenced in the Dutch court by the shipowner, followed by an arrest of a 'sister ship' in England by the cargo owners. Looked at in isolation, the provisions of the **1952 Arrest Convention** would confer jurisdiction on the Admiralty Court. Did that, then, mean that the effect of Art 57 was to exclude the lis alibi pendens provisions of the Brussels Convention, Arts 21 and 22 (now Arts 29 and 30)? The European Court of Justice ruled that Art 57 did not have this effect. Instead, it should be interpreted so that the provisions of the Convention should govern any matters that were not covered by a specific provision in the competing convention. Effectively, the Convention fills in any gaps left in the other conventions. Therefore, it held that the specific provisions of the Convention relating to lis alibi pendens governed the case before it, as there were no equivalent provisions in the 1952 Arrest Convention.[65]

The relationship between the Convention and the **1952 Arrest Convention** and the **1952 Collision Jurisdiction Convention** has given rise to particular difficulties with actions in rem. Neither Convention has been directly enacted into English law, although many of their provisions are contained in the **Senior Courts Act 1981**, and were contained in its predecessor, the **Administration of Justice Act 1956**. Suppose that the English courts have jurisdiction under ss 20–21 of the **Senior Courts Act 1981**, but those of another Convention State have jurisdiction under the Convention: how then is this conflict to be resolved? To answer this question, one needs to distinguish between situations in which service of in rem proceedings have been effected by an arrest and those in which there has been no arrest.

Service by arrest
A claim in rem will be regarded as having been effectively served if a claim form in rem is served on any solicitor authorised to accept service,[66] or if the owner acknowledges service before service has actually been effected,[67] or in the event that a contractually agreed method of service has been complied with.[68] Such proceedings may also be correctly served by attaching the claim form to the outside of the res in a position that may reasonably be expected to be seen.[69] Where service of in rem proceedings accompanies an arrest, the provisions of the **1952 Arrest Convention** need to be considered. Article 2 of that Convention provides that '[a] ship flying the flag of one of the Contracting States may be arrested in the jurisdiction of any of the Contracting States in respect of

---

64 Case C-406/92 [1994] ECR I-5439; [1995] 1 Lloyd's Rep 302, noted (1995) LMCLQ 161.
65 Cf the position with the CMR, which contains such provisions in Art 31. The Grand Chamber has held in *TNT Express Nederland BV v Axa Versicherung AG*, Case C-533/08; [2011] RTR 11, that the rules governing jurisdiction, recognition and enforcement that are laid down by a specialised convention, such as the lis pendens rule set out in Article 31(2) of the CMR and the rule relating to enforceability set out in Article 31(3) of that convention, apply, rather than the provisions of the Regulation.
66 CPR PD 61 para 3.6(5).
67 CPR Pt 61.3(6).
68 CPR PD 61 para 3.6(6).
69 CPR PD 61 para 3.6(1)(a).

a *maritime claim* but in respect of no other claim' (emphasis added). Article 7 then goes on to give jurisdiction to the courts of the arresting country to determine the case on its merits if:

> ... [t]he domestic law ... gives jurisdiction to such courts or ... (a) if the claimant has his habitual residence or principle [sic] place of business in the country in which the arrest is made, or (b) if the claim arose in the country in which the arrest was made.

The Court of Appeal in *The Deichland*[70] held that Art 7 of the **1952 Arrest Convention** took effect only where an arrest had actually been effected.[71] In *The Anna H*,[72] the Court of Appeal was asked to consider the effect of an arrest that was made, not to obtain security, but purely to establish jurisdiction. The defendant shipowner and demise charterer were domiciled in Germany. They claimed that Art 2 of the Brussels Convention (now Art 4 of the Judgments Regulation) required that they be sued in Germany and that no alternative convention gave jurisdiction to the English courts so as to bring Art 57 (now Art 71) into operation. They argued that the provisions of Art 7 of the 1952 Arrest Convention were limited by the definition of 'Arrest' in Art 1(2) of that Convention as 'the detention of a ship by judicial process *to secure a maritime claim*' (emphasis added).

The Court of Appeal rejected this argument. In applying Art 57, one should read the provisions of the competing convention as if it had been incorporated into the Brussels Convention itself. On this basis, an interpretation of Art 7 of the 1952 Arrest Convention, which restricted its application to arrests used to obtain security, would be to conflict with Art 3 of the Convention.[73] This set out a general rule that the attachment of property as security is not a sufficient basis to establish jurisdiction under the Convention.[74] Glidewell LJ then went on to say that:[75]

> It is not therefore obtaining the security which makes the Admiralty jurisdiction exceptional. The identifying features are that the property attached is a ship and that the claim is a maritime claim.

The Court of Appeal also held that 'domestic law' in Art 7 of the 1952 Arrest Convention did not cover 'treaty law', even where a treaty had been given statutory force.

The effect of *The Anna H* is that, for most purposes, effecting an arrest will trigger the provisions of the 1952 Arrest Convention, irrespective of the motives behind the arrest. However, in accordance with the approach of the European Court of Justice in *The Tatry*,[76] the matter should still be governed by specific provisions of the Convention if there are no equivalent provisions in the 1952 Arrest Convention. This issue arose in *The Bergen*,[77] where the claim arose under a bill of lading that contained a clause referring all disputes to the jurisdiction of the courts of the country in which the carrier had its principal place of business. As this was in a Contracting State, Germany, the carrier argued that the Admiralty Court had no jurisdiction by virtue of Art 17 of the Brussels Convention (now Art 25 of the Judgments Regulation). However, Clarke J held that as the Admiralty Court would have jurisdiction under the 1952 Arrest Convention, Art 57 prevented the application

---

70 [1990] 1 QB 361.
71 In this respect, the 1952 Arrest Convention is narrower than the domestic grounds on which the *in rem* jurisdiction of the Admiralty Court can be established, as jurisdiction can be established by acknowledgment of service as well as by arrest.
72 [1995] 1 Lloyd's Rep 11.
73 Now Art 5(2) of the Recast Regulation which provides: 'In particular, the rules of national jurisdiction of which the Member States are to notify the Commission pursuant to point (a) of Article 76(1) shall not be applicable as against the persons referred to in paragraph 1.'
74 The rule in *The Dictator* [1892] P 304, 20, *per* Hobhouse LJ, whereby a shipowner who defends an action *in rem* thereby submits to the *in personam* jurisdiction of the Admiralty Court, conflicts directly with Art 3 of the Convention and has been implicitly qualified by the Civil Jurisdiction and Judgments Act 1982.
75 [1995] 1 Lloyd's Rep 11, 24.
76 [1995] 1 Lloyd's Rep 302.
77 [1997] 1 Lloyd's Rep 380.

of Art 17 and the matter was subject to the principles of *forum non conveniens*. It is submitted that this decision is inconsistent with *The Tatry* and should be regarded as wrongly decided.[78]

Service without arrest

Where service of *in rem* proceedings is effected without an arrest, the application of the Convention will depend on whether or not the cause of action arises out of a collision. Unlike the **1952 Arrest Convention**, Art 1(1)(b) of the **1952 Collision Jurisdiction Convention** also confers jurisdiction on the courts of the state in which an arrest *could* have been effected.[79] This difference was to prove significant in *The Po*,[80] where, following a collision, *in rem* proceedings were served on a shipowner domiciled in Italy. No arrest, however, was effected. The Court of Appeal held that the effect of Art 57 (now Art 71) was that Art 2 (now Art 4) of the Brussels Convention gave way to the specific provisions of Art 1(1)(b) of the 1952 Collision Jurisdiction Convention.[81] It rejected the argument that this Article should be disregarded as it had never been implemented into English law. What mattered, for the purposes of Art 57 of the Brussels Convention, was that the UK was a party to the 1952 Collision Jurisdiction Convention.

Domestic sources of jurisdiction

In personam proceedings in the Commercial Court without the permission of the court

Claimants wishing to bring proceedings in the English courts against defendants that are not domiciled in a Member State are, by virtue of Art 6 of the Judgments Regulation, required to satisfy the court that it has jurisdiction under the common law rules. The same is required of matters falling outside of the material scope of the Regulation.[82] Under the common law rules, the claimant may serve an *in personam* claim form on a defendant without the permission of the court: where the defendant is present within the jurisdiction;[83] where the defendant has agreed to submit to the jurisdiction of the court; and pursuant to CPR Pt 6.33, which specifies when the claim form may be served on a defendant out of the UK without the permission of the court.[84] First:

> ... where each claim made against the defendant to be served and included in the claim form is a claim which the court has power to determine under the Judgments Regulation and –
>
> (a) no proceedings between the parties concerning the same claim are pending in the courts of any other part of the United Kingdom or any other Member State; and
>
> (b) (i) the defendant is domiciled in the United Kingdom or in any Member State;
>
> (ii) the proceedings are within Art 22 [now Art 24] of the Judgments Regulation; or
>
> (iii) the defendant is a party to an agreement conferring jurisdiction, within Art 23 [now Art 25] of the Judgments Regulation.[85]

---

78 As argued by Siig (1997) LMCLQ 362.
79 Cf *The Deichland* [1990] 1 QB 361.
80 [1991] 2 Lloyd's Rep 206.
81 For the purposes of both the Convention and the 1952 Collision Jurisdiction Convention, it was irrelevant that the plaintiff was domiciled in the USA, which was a party to neither Convention.
82 See pp 347–8.
83 Even a temporary and fleeting presence will suffice. See *Maharanee of Baroda v Wildenstein* [1972] 2 QB 283.
84 Service on a defendant in Scotland or Northern Ireland is dealt with under CPR 6.32.
85 Para 2. A similar provision is to be found in para 1, in relation to proceedings falling under the Brussels Convention.

Secondly:

> ... where each claim made against the defendant to be served and included in the claim form is a claim which the court has power to determine other than under the 1982 Act or the Judgments Regulation, notwithstanding that –
>
> (a) the person against whom the claim is made is not within the jurisdiction; or
> (b) the facts giving rise to the claim did not occur within the jurisdiction.[86]

With permission of the court under CPR Pt 6.36

In all other cases, CPR Pt 6.36 provides that service on the defendant is possible only with the permission of the court. The situations in which permission may be given are set out in Practice Direction (PD) 6b 3.1.[87]

Procedure for applying for permission

The procedure for applying for permission is set out in CPR Pt 6.37.[88] Since there is no defendant on the record, an application to the court for permission to serve a claim form out of the jurisdiction should be made *ex parte* and without notice. Although permission should generally be sought before the claim is served, the court retains the discretion to grant retrospective permission in this regard.[89] The claimant will need to swear an affidavit showing how its claim satisfies the requirements first laid down by the House of Lords in *Seaconsar Far East Ltd v Bank Markazi Jomhouri Islami Iran*.[90] In this regard, the claimant must satisfy the court that there is a good arguable case that its application falls under one of the heads of PD 6b 3.1, and that there is a serious issue to be tried on the merits. In addition, CPR Pt 6.37 (3) provides that: 'The court will not give permission unless satisfied that England and Wales is the proper place in which to bring the claim.'

Similar principles apply as will govern an application by the defendant to stay a claim on the ground of *forum non conveniens*. These principles will be discussed below in connection with the defendant's right to apply for a stay under CPR Pt 11.[91] However, at this stage, the burden of proof is entirely on the claimant, whereas in applications for a stay of proceedings on the basis of *forum non conveniens*, the burden of proof is shared between the claimant and the defendant. The defendant is entitled to appeal against the grant of permission to serve out. In such a case, the burden of proof stays with the claimant.

General grounds

Of the general grounds on which applications for permission to serve out of the jurisdiction are based, two heads are of particular interest. First, under PD 6b 3.1(1), a claim form may be served out of the jurisdiction with permission of the court if it is made for a remedy against a person domiciled within the jurisdiction. This is the common law analogue to Art 4 of the Judgments Regulation, and will only be relied upon in circumstances falling outside of the Regulation's material scope. Secondly, under PD 6b 3.1(3), permission to serve out may be sought with respect to claims made against someone on whom the claim form has been or will be served, and:

(a) there is between the claimant and that person a real issue that it is reasonable for the court to try; and
(b) the claimant wishes to serve the claim form on another person who is a necessary or proper party to that claim.

---

86 Para 3.
87 Formerly RSC Ord 11(1)(1).
88 The grounds for service with permission of the court are to be found in PD 6b 3.1.
89 *Nesheim v Kosa* [2006] EWHC 2710 (Ch); [2006] LTL 4/10/06.
90 [1994] 1 AC 438.
91 Formerly RSC Ord 12(8).

PD 6b 3.1(3) operates in much the same manner as Art 8 of the Judgments Regulation with respect to claims involving more than one defendant. However, the former is evidently less stringent in its application, since it does not require at least one of the defendants to be domiciled in a Member State.[92]

Claims for interim remedies

PD 6b 3.1(5) allows permission to be sought to serve out of the jurisdiction claim forms for interim (formerly, 'interlocutory') remedies under s 25(1) of the **Civil Jurisdiction and Judgments Act 1982**. This provision is of particular importance for claimants seeking orders to freeze a defendant's assets pending the outcome of the parties' substantive dispute, which may not be taking place on English soil.[93]

Contractual claims

PD 6b 3.1(6)[94] applies to a contract that:

(a)   was made within the jurisdiction;[95] or
(b)   was made by or through an agent trading or residing within the jurisdiction; or
(c)   is governed by English law; or
(d)   contains a term to the effect that the court shall have jurisdiction to hear and determine any claim in respect of the contract.

Therefore, permission would probably be given to serve a foreign defendant in respect of a claim under a bill of lading where the underlying contract was made in England, such as when the voyage commences at an English port. Alternatively, permission would probably be given where the bill of lading had no connection with England but was either subject to English law or contained an English High Court jurisdiction clause.[96] However, if the bill of lading were issued by, say, a German shipowner and contained only a clause choosing English law, the English High Court would have no jurisdiction because Art 4 of the Judgments Regulation would require the defendant to be sued in Germany (assuming that the performance of the contract, or the provision of services or supply of goods, took place outside of the jurisdiction, thereby falling outside of the scope of Art 7). Although the claim would fall within PD 6b 3.1(6)(c), Art 5 of the Judgments Regulation would preclude the English courts from granting permission to serve out in such circumstances, since the defendant is domiciled in a Member State. PD 6b 3.1(7)[97] covers breaches of contract that are committed within the jurisdiction. This would apply to a claim outside para (6), which involved a breach in England, such as a claim involving damage to cargo during discharge at an English port. PD 6b 3.1(8) covers a claim 'for a declaration that no contract exists where, if the contract was found to exist, it would comply with the conditions set out in paragraph (6)'. The doctrine of separability which governs arbitration and proceedings under the Brussels Regulation does not apply to claims under this heading. The claimant must establish a good arguable case that there is a contract and cannot rely on the fact that, if there was a contract, it would be subject to English law or jurisdiction.[98]

---

92 PD 6b 3.1(4) covers an additional claim under Part 20 'and the person to be served is a necessary or proper party to the claim or additional claim'.
93 See, generally, Chapter 19. PD 6b 3.1(2) covers a claim 'for an injunction ordering the defendant to do or refrain from doing an act within the jurisdiction'.
94 Formerly RSC Ord 11(1)(d).
95 A claim for interpleader relief is not a claim in respect of a contract under PD 6b 3.1. See Cool Carriers AB v HSBC Bank USA [2001] 2 Lloyd's Rep 22, QB.
96 Although this would be subject to the applicant satisfying the court that England is the appropriate place to bring the claim, pursuant to PD 6b 3.7.
97 Formerly RSC Ord 11(1)(1)(e).
98 The Jin Man [2009] EWHC 2941 (Comm); [2010] 2 Lloyd's Rep 236.

Tort claims

Practice Direction 6b 3.1(9)[99] applies where the damage was sustained within the jurisdiction or resulted from an act committed within the jurisdiction. Its effect is similar to that of Art 7(3) of the Judgments Regulation as expanded by the decision of the European Court of Justice in *Handelskwekerij GJ Bier BV v Mines de Potasse d'Alsace SA*,[100] which interprets 'the place where the harmful event occurred' as espousing both the place where the damage took place *and* the place where the events giving rise to that damage occurred. Unless the cargo damage can be shown to have occurred at an English port, or within English territorial waters, a cargo claim based on tort will not be able to be brought under this paragraph.

However, a claimant might be able to establish jurisdiction for such a tortious claim if it is able to avail itself of any of the other heads in PD 6b 3.1. Once the English court is satisfied that it has jurisdiction by virtue of one of these heads, the claimant is able to bring any number of claims against the defendant, without reference to the particular rule on which the court's jurisdiction has been assumed.[101]

In personam and *in rem* claims in the Admiralty Court

Jurisdiction

Claims *in rem* may only be brought before the Admiralty Court in the Queen's Bench Division of the High Court. However, not all claims within the jurisdiction of the Admiralty Court can be brought *in rem*. Therefore, in considering whether a particular claim can be brought *in rem*, a claimant will need first to ask whether its claim falls within the general jurisdiction of the Admiralty Court and then, if it does, whether it is the type of claim that may be brought *in rem*. The *res* against which Admiralty claims *in rem* may be brought is wide-ranging in nature. It includes ships, cargo, freight, aircraft and the proceeds of sale of all of the aforementioned.

The Admiralty Court is assigned four heads of jurisdiction by s 20(1) of the **Senior Courts Act 1981**. The first consists of claims listed in s 20(2), the second of proceedings referred to in s 20(1)(b), the third of prior Admiralty jurisdiction and the fourth of future Admiralty jurisdiction. Subject to these provisions, s 20(7) provides that the jurisdiction of the Admiralty Court extends over all ships or aircraft, registered or not, British or not, irrespective of the residence or domicile of their owner.

Claims listed in s 20(2)

The Admiralty Court has jurisdiction over the following list of claims set out in s 20(2) of the **Senior Courts Act 1981**. The most important claims will be those under subheadings (e), (g), (h), (j) and (q). The Act makes no provision for claims under subheadings (d) and (e) to be brought *in rem*.

The full list of claims is as follows:

(a) any claim to the possession or ownership of a ship or to the ownership of any share therein;

(b) any question arising between the co-owners of a ship as to possession, employment or earnings of that ship;

(c) any claim in respect of a mortgage of or charge on a ship or any share therein;

(d) any claim for damage received by a ship;

(e) any claim for damage done by a ship . . .

99 Formerly RSC Ord 11(1)(1)(f).
100 Case 21/76 [1976] ECR 1735.
101 See *Base Metal Trading Ltd v Shamurin* [2004] EWCA Civ 1316; [2004] IL Pr 74, CA; *Matthews v Kuwait Bechtel Corporation* [1959] 2 QB 57, CA.

This covers liability arising out of collisions,[102] alleged negligence of salvors in beaching the salved vessel and exposing her to the hazards of the weather,[103] or economic loss suffered by a vessel when she is deliberately driven off fishing grounds by another vessel.[104] The ship must be the actual instrument by which damage was caused. In *The Rama*,[105] this was held not to be the case when the charterers suffered loss by embarking on a voyage under a charter pursuant to certain fraudulent misrepresentations by the shipowners. The heading also covers shipowners' statutory liability for oil pollution.[106]

(f) any claim for loss of life or personal injury sustained in consequence of any defect in a ship or in her apparel or equipment, or in consequence of the wrongful act, neglect or default of:

(i) the owners, charterers or persons in possession or control of a ship; or

(ii) the master or crew of a ship, or any other person for whose wrongful acts, neglects or defaults the owners, charterers or persons in possession or control of a ship are responsible,

being an act, neglect or default in the navigation or management of the ship, in the loading, carriage or discharge of goods on, in or from the ship, or in the embarkation, carriage or disembarkation of persons on, in or from the ship;

(g) any claim for loss of or damage to goods carried in a ship;

(h) any claim arising out of any agreement relating to the carriage of goods in a ship or to the use or hire of a ship . . .

This covers a claim in respect of damage suffered by a tug under a towage contract,[107] an agreement for salvage services,[108] a claim in tort by a subcharterer against a shipowner,[109] or a claim to enforce an arbitration award under a charterparty.[110] The heading has been held not to cover a claim under a cif contract,[111] nor a contract to carry containers that did not specify carriage on any particular ship or even on a ship owned or chartered by the defendant.[112]

(j) any claim in the nature of salvage:

(i) under the Salvage Convention 1989;

(ii) under any contract for or in relation to salvage services;

(iii) in the nature of salvage not falling within (i) or (ii) above, or any corresponding claim in connection with an aircraft.

This covers claims by salvors for salvage reward, but has been held not to cover claims against salvors in respect of negligent salvage.[113]

(k) any claim in the nature of towage in respect of a ship or an aircraft;

(l) any claim in the nature of pilotage in respect of a ship or an aircraft;

(m) any claim in respect of goods or materials supplied to a ship for her operation or maintenance . . .

---

102 Even if there is no physical contact between the negligent vessel and the property that it damages. See *The Industrie* (1871) LR 3 A & E 303.

103 *The Escherscheim* [1976] 1 WLR 430, HL.

104 *The Dagmara* [1988] 1 Lloyd's Rep 431.

105 [1996] 2 Lloyd's Rep 281.

106 Section 20(5) of the Senior Courts Act 1981.

107 *The Conoco Britannia* [1972] QB 543.

108 *The Escherscheim* [1976] 1 WLR 430, HL.

109 *The Antonis P Lemos* [1985] AC 711.

110 *The Santa Anna* [1983] 1 WLR 895; not followed in *The Bumbesti* [1999] 2 Lloyd's Rep 481, QB.

111 *The Maersk Nimrod* [1991] 3 All ER 161.

112 *The Lloyd Pacifico* [1995] 1 Lloyd's Rep 55.

113 *The Escherscheim* [1976] 1 WLR 430, HL.

This does not cover a claim for damages for conversion of containers under a lease that never specified their use on a *particular* ship.[114] Nor does it cover claims against a shipowner in respect of bunkers ordered by a charterer, as a shipowner is not personally responsible for debts incurred by a charterer.[115]

(n) any claim in respect of the construction, repair or equipment of a ship or in respect of dock charges or dues;

(o) any claim by a master or member of the crew of a ship for wages (including any sum allotted out of wages or adjudged by a superintendent to be due by way of wages)
. . .

This does not cover claims for severance payments,[116] nor for unpaid statutory social security benefits.[117] It does, however, cover crew wages that are paid by a crewing agency to whom the shipowner has remitted funds to be earmarked for that purpose.[118]

(p) any claim by a master, shipper, charterer or agent in respect of disbursements made on account of a ship . . .

This does not cover a claim by an insurance broker in respect of non-payment of premiums.[119]

(q) any claim arising out of an act which is or is claimed to be general average;

(r) any claim arising out of bottomry;

(s) any claim for the forfeiture or condemnation of a ship or of goods which are being or have been carried, in a ship or for the restoration of a ship or any such goods after seizure, or for droits of Admiralty.

Proceedings under s 20(1)(b)

The second head of jurisdiction is to be found in s 20(1)(b) of the **Senior Courts Act 1981**. This refers to s 20(3), which covers, *inter alia*, collision actions and limitation actions brought by shipowners. These proceedings can only be brought *in personam*. However, in relation to collision actions two points need to be made. First, to comply with the provisions of the **Collision Convention 1952**, the *in personam* action of the High Court is restricted by s 22(2) of the **Senior Courts Act 1981** to situations in which the defendant either:

(a) . . . has his habitual residence or a place of business within England and Wales; or

(b) the cause of action arose within inland waters of England or Wales or within the limits of a port in England or Wales; or

(c) an action arising out of the same incident or series of incidents is proceeding in the court or has been heard and determined in the court.

Secondly, most claims arising out of collisions also fall within s 20(2)(e) of the **Senior Courts Act 1981**. They also give rise to a maritime lien.

Prior Admiralty jurisdiction

The third heading, s 20(1)(c), is the 'sweeping up' provision, which covers 'any other Admiralty jurisdiction which it had immediately before the commencement of this Act'. This heading

114 *The River Rima* [1988] 1 WLR 758.
115 *The Yuta Bondurovskaya* [1998] 2 Lloyd's Rep 357, QB.
116 *The Tacoma City* [1991] 1 Lloyd's Rep 330.
117 *The Halcyon Skies* [1977] QB 14.
118 *The Turiddu* [1998] 2 Lloyd's Rep 278, QB.
119 *Bain Clarkson v Owners of The Sea Friends* [1991] 2 Lloyd's Rep 322. Nor do such claims fall under subheading (h). See *Gatoil International Inc v Arkwright-Boston Manufacturers Mutual Insurance Co* [1985] AC 255.
120 [1982] 2 Lloyd's Rep 555.

principally covers maritime liens, but, in *The Despina GK*,[120] was used to justify an arrest in respect of a foreign judgment against the owner of the arrested ship. The only proviso was that the ship must still be owned by the judgment debtor at the time of the arrest. This is in sharp contrast to *The Alletta*,[121] where, following an English judgment concerning a collision, the judgment creditor was unable to arrest the vessel, which had been sold to a third party by the time that the judgment was given. Such a judgment would have to be enforced by the process of execution under the writ of *fieri facias*.[122]

Future Admiralty jurisdiction

The fourth heading, s 20(1)(d), concerns any jurisdiction over ships and aircraft that may, in future, be assigned to the Admiralty Court.

In rem *Admiralty jurisdiction*

Section 21 of the **Senior Courts Act 1981** provides that, subject to the limitations on collision actions imposed by s 22, all of the above categories may proceed by way of an action in *personam*. It also provides three categories of action that may proceed in *rem*.

Ownership disputes

The first category is set out in s 21(2) of the **Senior Courts Act 1981** and covers the matters listed in s 20(2)(a), (b), (c) and (s), and provides that an action in *rem* may be brought against the ship or property in connection with which the claim or question arises. There are no 'sister ship' provisions of the sort available for claims falling under (e) to (r), which are discussed in the subsequent section on 'statutory liens' at pp 364–6.

Maritime liens

The second category is set out in s 21(3) of the **Senior Courts Act 1981** and covers maritime liens or other charges on any ship, aircraft or other property for the amount claimed. The in *rem* action may be brought against the ship, aircraft or other property in question. The provision does not define 'maritime lien', which is defined by pre-existing case law. A claim recognised as a maritime lien in a foreign jurisdiction will not be recognised as such by the English courts unless it falls under one of the categories recognised by English law.[123]

The following claims constitute maritime liens at common law:

(a)   damage caused by a ship – cf s 20(2)(e), although it is doubtful whether the shipowner's statutory liability for oil pollution, mentioned in this heading, constitutes a maritime lien. Cargo claims will not fall under this heading unless they are brought against a vessel that has collided with the vessel on which the cargo was being carried;

(b)   salvage – cf s 20(2)(j);

(c)   seamen's wages – cf s 20(2)(o);

(d)   master's wages and disbursements – cf s 20(2)(o) and (p);

(e)   bottomry and respondentia – cf s 20(2)(r).[124]

---

121 [1974] 1 Lloyd's Rep 40.
122 Execution will be for the full amount of the judgment notwithstanding that security may have been given prior to judgment for a lesser amount. See *The Gemma* [1899] P 285.
123 *The Halcyon Skies* [1977] QB 14.
124 Such claims are now practically obsolete. Bottomry and respondentia bonds were originally given by the master of a ship as security for a loan needed when the ship was in distant parts of the world. Modern methods of communication have made them unnecessary.

The significance of a claim's classification as a maritime lien is that the claim will attach to the *res* from the date of the claim and will be unaffected by subsequent changes in its ownership.[125] Therefore, in *rem* proceedings may be brought against a vessel in respect of a collision notwithstanding that it has been sold to purchasers, without notice of the claim, before the issue of the writ. However, such third parties will not be liable in *personam* and their liability will be limited to the value of the *res*. Further, a maritime lien will be lost if the *res* is sold by an order of the court. A maritime lien may be exercised only against the 'primary' vessel and not against any other vessel in the same ownership. To arrest a 'secondary ship', it will be necessary to rely on a statutory lien. Section 21(8) provides that only one ship may be arrested in respect of the same claim, although a second arrest may be made if the first arrest is discharged without security being provided. Under English law the classification of a claim as a maritime lien is dictated by the law of the place of arrest, rather than the place at which the claim arose.[126]

Statutory liens

An additional category of in *rem* claims is to be found in s 21(4) of the **Senior Courts Act 1981**, which comprises those claims falling within s 20(2)(e)–(r). These claims are commonly referred to as 'statutory liens'. For an in *rem* action to proceed, the claim must arise 'in connection with a ship' where 'the person who would be liable on the claim in an action in *personam* (the relevant person)[127] was, when the cause of action arose, the owner or charterer of, or in possession or in control of the ship'.

There used to be some uncertainty as to whether 'charterer' is limited to demise charterers or covers all types of charterer. The word 'charterer' appeared in the equivalent provision in s 3(4) of the **Administration of Justice Act 1956**. In *The Span Terza*,[128] the majority of the Court of Appeal construed it as including time charterers and not being confined to demise charterers.[129] Lord Donaldson MR, dissenting, was of the view that the Act needed to be read in the light of the **1952 Arrest Convention**, Art 3 of which referred only to ships owned by the owner or demise charterer of the 'primary' ship. He reiterated this view in *The Evpo Agnic*.[130] However, in *The Tychy*,[131] the Court of Appeal adopted a very wide construction of the term 'charterer', encompassing charterers of part of a vessel and slot charterers. Clarke LJ justified this approach on the grounds that the specific reference to demise charterers in s 21(4)(ii)[132] indicates that the word 'charterer' in the 1981 Act should bear its usual meaning and should not be limited to demise charterers. In addition, the Court of Appeal held that an arrest could still be maintained in respect of payments that became due after the end of the slot charter. What was significant was that the payments derived from the slot charter.[133]

If the above two requirements are satisfied, the action in *rem* may be brought against two classes of ship, 'whether or not the claim gives rise to a maritime lien on that ship'. The first, under s 21(4)(i), is against 'that ship, if at the time when the action is brought the relevant person is either the beneficial owner of that ship as respects all the shares in it or the charterer of it under a charter by

---

125 The maritime lien also attaches notwithstanding that at the time of the incident the vessel was on demise charter. *The Father Thames* [1979] 2 Lloyd's Rep 364 (QB).
126 *The Halcyon Isle* [1980] 1 Lloyd's Rep 325.
127 In defining 'the relevant person', s 21(7) directs the court to assume that the person has his habitual residence or a place of business in England. However, this provision does not give the court jurisdiction in *personam* over that person.
128 [1982] 1 Lloyd's Rep 255.
129 Sheen J, in *The Maritime Trader* [1981] 2 Lloyd's Rep 153, had held that the provision did not even extend to other ships in the ownership of the demise charterer of the primary ship.
130 [1988] 1 WLR 1090, 1095–6.
131 [1999] 2 Lloyd's Rep 11, noted (2000) LMCLQ 129, (2000) LQR 36.
132 There was no equivalent provision in the 1956 Act.
133 However, note the more literal approach adopted in *The Faial* [2000] 1 Lloyd's Rep 473, QB, where an arrest was not allowed in respect of an indemnity claim against demise charterers for wreck removal because one of the three conditions precedent to the right of indemnity became satisfied only after termination of the charter.

demise'.[134] Therefore, an in rem action will not lie against a vessel in respect of claims against non-demise charterers of that vessel, although the charterers will be vulnerable to the arrest of any vessel of which they are the beneficial owners. This ship will be referred to as 'the primary ship'. The second, under s 21(4)(ii), is against 'any other ship of which at the time when the action is brought, the relevant person is the beneficial owner as respects all the shares in it'. This ship will be known as 'the secondary ship'.[135] The action will be 'brought' for these purposes when the claim form is issued, and not when it is served.[136]

It is worth noting that the action against the 'primary' ship may be brought if the 'relevant person', at the time that the action is brought, is the demise charterer of that vessel. However, in rem proceedings against a 'secondary' ship may be brought only when the 'relevant person' is the beneficial owner of that vessel.

The distinction can be illustrated by the following example. The defendant is the demise charterer of The Alpha and The Beta. Cargo claims arise during the charter of The Alpha. The claimant cargo owners can arrest The Alpha, as the 'primary' ship, provided that it was still on demise charter to the defendant at the time that they issued their in rem claim form.[137] However, the cargo owners will never be able to proceed against The Beta, the 'secondary' ship, even if it is still on demise charter to the defendant. If, on the other hand, the defendant demise charterer had owned The Beta when the claimant issued its in rem claim form against her, the claimant would be able to arrest The Beta in respect of cargo claims arising under the charter of The Alpha. Moreover, the claimant, in this situation, would still be entitled to arrest The Beta, even if the defendant's charter of The Alpha had not been by way of demise.[138]

Beneficial ownership

In determining 'beneficial ownership' in the context of s 21(4), the courts have been generally reluctant to look beyond the registered owner of that vessel.[139] In The Evpo Agnic,[140] the plaintiffs suffered cargo damage following the sinking of the Skipper 1. They attempted to arrest another vessel that was owned by a different company. Even though they could show that the shareholders and directors of this company were the same as those of the company that had been the registered owner of the Skipper 1, the Court of Appeal ordered the vessel to be released as it was not in the same beneficial ownership as that of the Skipper 1. A similar conclusion was reached in The Mawan,[141] where the alleged sister ship was sold after the issue of the writ. However, even at the time that the writ was issued, prior to the sale of the vessel, the vessel was owned by a different company from that which was the registered owner of the Skipper 1.

Similar problems may arise out of the relationship between fleets of state-owned vessels and their management companies. In The Nazym Khikmet,[142] cargo claims arose following a voyage on a vessel the registered owner of which was the state of Ukraine. This vessel and all of the other vessels

---

134 If the 'relevant person' was the owner or demise charterer of the vessel when the cause of action arose but has ceased to be the owner or demise charterer when the action is brought, in rem proceedings may not be brought against the vessel under s 21(4)(i).

135 This action is commonly referred to as the 'sister ship' action, although the phrase may be something of a misnomer as the 'other ship' need not be in common ownership with 'that ship'. Even Lord Donaldson MR, in The Span Terza [1982] 1 Lloyd's Rep 255, was prepared to accept that the action could lie against a ship owned by the demise charterer of the 'primary ship'.

136 The Monica S [1968] P 741, PD.

137 If the charter was not a demise charter, the claimants would not be able to arrest The Alpha but could arrest any ship of which the charterers were the beneficial owners.

138 Following the decision of the majority of the Court of Appeal in The Span Terza [1982] 1 Lloyd's Rep 255, as applied in The Tychy [1999] 2 Lloyd's Rep 11, CA.

139 This is consistent with their refusal to pierce the 'corporate veil' except in cases of fraud. See Adams v Cape Industries plc [1990] Ch 433, CA, discussed by Baughen, S, 'Multi-nationals and the export of hazard' (1995) 58 MLR, at 57–9.

140 [1980] 1 WLR 1090.

141 [1988] 2 Lloyd's Rep 459. See, also, The Maritime Trader [1981] 2 Lloyd's Rep 153. However, Sheen J, in The Saudi Prince [1982] 2 Lloyd's Rep 255, was prepared, albeit obiter, to overcome the traditional judicial reluctance to pierce the corporate veil.

142 [1996] 2 Lloyd's Rep 362, CA.

owned by the state of Ukraine were managed by BLASCO, to which great commercial authority had been delegated. The plaintiffs arrested another ship owned by the state of Ukraine, which challenged the arrest. It was accepted that BLASCO was the 'relevant person' for the purposes of s 21 and the issue before the Court of Appeal was whether BLASCO was the beneficial owner of the 'secondary ship' so as to justify the arrest under s 21(4)(ii). BLASCO was held not to be the beneficial owner of the vessel. Although the state of Ukraine had made an extensive delegation to BLASCO of commercial authority over vessels in its fleet, it still retained the right and power of ultimate decision over the use and exploitation of the vessel. Therefore, an action *in rem* did not lie under s 21(4)(ii). However, following the decision of the Court of Appeal in *The Giuseppe di Vittorio*,[143] which again involved BLASCO, such management companies are likely to be classified as de facto demise charterers. This will enable the claimant to arrest the 'primary ship' under s 21(4)(i), but not a 'secondary ship' under s 21(4)(ii).

The different effects of statutory and maritime liens

The most important difference between statutory and maritime liens lies in their capacity to affect third parties. This may be illustrated by examining a collision where both colliding ships are sold prior to the issue of a claim form *in rem*. If the claimant is the owner of goods carried on *The Delta*, it will have a maritime lien against the colliding vessel, *The Gamma*, for 'damage done by a ship'. That lien will continue to attach to *The Gamma*, despite its subsequent change of ownership. However, the claimant will also have a contractual claim against the owners of the carrying vessel, *The Delta*. This will only be a statutory lien within s 20(2)(g) and (h) and will not be exercisable against *The Delta* if her ownership changes prior to issue of the writ.

Apart from their lesser capacity to bind third parties, statutory liens differ from maritime liens in the following respects. They are only exercisable against ships, and not against other property of the defendant. However, they are superior to maritime liens in that they may be exercisable against other vessels in the same ownership of the 'relevant person'. Thus, in *The Nazym Khikmet*,[144] the plaintiffs would have been in no better position had they had a maritime lien. Such a lien would have given them a right to proceed *in rem* against the 'primary ship', but to proceed against the 'secondary ship', they would still have had to bring themselves within the provisions of s 21(4)(ii).

The 1999 Arrest Convention

The **Arrest Convention 1999** came into force on 14 September 2011, six months after ratification by the tenth state.[145] It has not been ratified by the UK. Its most important features are as follows.

Claims

Article 1 of the Convention contemplates an expansion of existing categories of arrestable claims under the following headings, some of which – namely, headings (c) and (d) – are already reflected in s 20(2) of the **Senior Courts Act 1981**:

(a) this refers to 'loss or damage caused by the operation of the ship' rather than 'damage done by a ship' and would encompass claims for pure economic loss;

. . .

(c) this extends the category of salvage to include claims arising from salvage agreements or special compensation under Art 14 of the **1989 Salvage Convention;**

(d) this covers damage to environment, including threatened damage;

---

143 [1998] 1 Lloyd's Rep 136, CA, noted (1998) LMCLQ 480.
144 [1996] 2 Lloyd's Rep 362, CA.
145 For a full analysis of the Convention, see Gaskell, N and Shaw, R, 'The Arrest Convention 1999' (1999) LMCLQ 470. The Convention has been ratified by Albania, Algeria, Benin, Bulgaria, Ecuador, Estonia, Latvia, Liberia, Spain, and Syria.

. . .

(l)   this extends the scope of claims in respect of supply of goods and materials to a ship to cover 'provisions, bunkers, equipment (including containers) supplied or services rendered to the ship for its operation, management, preservation or maintenance';

(m)   this extends the scope of claims against ships by shipyards to cover 'construction, reconstruction, repair, converting or equipping of the ship';

. . .

(o)   this extends the scope of claims in respect of port dues, and also in respect of wages, which will now cover repatriation costs and social insurance contributions;

. . .

(u)   this extends the scope of claims in respect of mortgages by removing the reference to a registered or registrable mortgage, thereby encompassing unregistered mortgages.

The Convention also includes the following completely new categories of claims under the headings:

(e)   claims in respect of wreck removal and cargo recovery;

. . .

(q)   claims in respect of insurance premiums, including P&I Club calls;

. . .

(r)   claims in respect of commissions, brokerages, agency fees;

. . .

(v)   claims in respect of disputes arising out of ship sales.

Bottomry claims are, however, excluded from the Convention.

Definition of arrest

Article 1(2) defines 'arrest' so as to cover freezing orders, while Art 2(3) confirms arrest may be used where a state other than the arresting state has jurisdiction over the claim. Article 3(2) provides that national law will decide questions of ownership relating to sister ships, but the explicit rejection of the UK's proposals on 'associated' companies to facilitate piercing the veil at the Convention may preclude national laws from adopting such proposals.[146] Article 3(3) precludes an arrest of a ship where the shipowner is not personally liable unless the law of the arresting state would allow a judicial sale in such circumstances. This is aimed at preventing delays experienced in some jurisdictions where ships are delayed pending provision of security by charterers in respect of claims for which they, and not the shipowner, are personally liable.

    The Convention makes significant changes in connection with the right to re-arrest, which was prohibited by Art 3(3) of the 1952 Convention. Article 5(1) now provides a right to re-arrest when the initial security is inadequate, with Art 5(2) having similar effect in relation to sister ship arrests. Additional security in each case can never exceed the value of the arrested ship.

    As regards wrongful arrests, Art 6(1) gives the court a discretion to require a claimant to provide security for any loss suffered by a shipowner due to the arrest, but does not oblige the court to do so.

Jurisdiction

Article 7(1) gives jurisdiction on the merits to the arresting state *unless* there is an arbitration clause or a jurisdiction clause in favour of another state. These exclusions are not found in the equivalent

---

146 Ibid, at 476–7.

provisions of the 1952 Arrest Convention. Their effect is such that cases like *The Bergen*[147] would, under the provisions of the 1999 Convention, be subject to a mandatory stay rather than a discretionary stay under the doctrine of *forum non conveniens*.

Article 7(2) entitles the arresting state to refuse jurisdiction on the merits while Art 7(5) requires the arresting state to recognise a final decision on the merits by another state by releasing the security.

Other provisions

Article 8 extends the right of arrest to non-seagoing vessels, but states can make reservations against this provision under Art 10(2). Article 13 deals with states with multiple legal systems, as is the case with Hong Kong and China.

Service of proceedings in the Admiralty Court

In personam

A claimant can proceed *in personam* in the Admiralty Court in almost all matters within its jurisdiction. Service on a defendant who is not present within the jurisdiction can be effected in accordance with the provisions of PD 6b 3.1, except for limitation and collision claims. Limitation claims are subject to CPR Pt 61.11(5), which provides:

> A claim form may not be served out of the jurisdiction unless —
>
> (a) the case falls within section 22(2)(a), (b) or (c) of the **Senior Courts Act 1981**; or
> (b) the defendant has submitted to or agreed to submit to the jurisdiction; or
> (c) the Admiralty Court has jurisdiction over the claim under any applicable Convention;[148]
>
> and the court gives permission in accordance with Section IV of Part 6.

Collision claims are governed by CPR Pt 61.4(7), which is in similar terms, save with the omission of subheading (c). The situations referred to in s 22(2) of the **Senior Courts Act 1981** are as follows:

(a) the defendant has his habitual residence or a place of business within England and Wales; or
(b) the cause of action arose within waters of England or Wales or within the limits of a port in England or Wales; or
(c) an action arising out of the same incident or series of incidents is proceeding in the court or has been heard and determined in the court.

Service of in rem proceedings

Civil Procedure Rules Pt 61, Practice Direction 3.6 deals with the methods by which an *in rem* claim form may be served, the most important of which are as follows. First, it may be served on the property against which the claim is brought by fixing a copy of the claim form on the outside of the property in a position where it might reasonably be expected to be seen. Where a claim is made against freight, service is made against either the cargo on which the freight was earned or the ship on which it was carried. Secondly, it may be served on individuals, such as: a solicitor authorised

---

147 [1997] 1 Lloyd's Rep 380, QB.
148 In *The ICL Vikraman* [2003] EWHC 2320 (Comm); [2004] 1 Lloyd's Rep, 21, Colman J held that 'any applicable convention' covered a claim to limit under the 1976 Limitation of Liability Convention. CPR Pt 61.11 provides that, when a limitation decree is granted, the court may order the claimant to establish a fund if one has not been established or make other arrangements for payment of claims against which liability is limited.

to accept service; or the person named in a notice against arrest as having agreed to accept service; or in accordance with any agreement providing for service of proceedings. The filing of an acknowledgment of service does not preclude the defendant from subsequently disputing the jurisdiction of the court under CPR Pt 11.[149] A defendant who puts up security by way of a bail bond will be taken to have acknowledged service.[150] Moreover, by posting the bail bond, the defendant will also be taken to have submitted to the jurisdiction, thereby losing any right to challenge jurisdiction. These are the only possible methods of service.[151] There is no procedure for service out of the jurisdiction equivalent to that provided by PD 6b 3.1 in respect of actions *in personam*.[152] The procedural rules relating to service are unaltered by the Judgments Regulation, unlike their *in personam* counterparts.

The effect of serving in rem proceedings

Once the proceedings have been served, the action will proceed in the same way as an action in *personam*, although they will not entirely lose their *in rem* character.[153] If the defendant contests the proceedings, any ultimate judgment against it will be for the full amount of the claim, even if that exceeds the value of the *res*, provided that the defendant is subject to an *in personam* liability. In *The Dictator*,[154] a salvor arrested a vessel and obtained bail for £5,000. The shipowners defended the action and were liable in respect of the eventual salvage award of £7,500, notwithstanding that it exceeded the amount of the bail bond. However, where the defendant would not be liable *in personam*, the defendant's maximum exposure will be in respect of the *res* itself. An example would be where a vessel is arrested in respect of a maritime lien and has changed ownership since the date of the claim. Where the action is undefended, it used to be the case that any judgment would be limited to the value of the *res* itself. In the light of the reasoning of the House of Lords in *The Indian Grace* (No 2),[155] to the effect that, after service of *in rem* proceedings, the action proceeds as an action *in personam*, this is probably no longer the case. The claimant will be entitled to enforce the full amount of any judgment in respect of the *in personam* liability of the shipowner. Where no such liability has been incurred, however, the judgment will still be limited to the value of the *res*.

If the security obtained following an arrest is inadequate, the English courts may allow the vessel to be re-arrested, notwithstanding the prohibition on re-arrest contained in Art 3(3) of the **1952 Arrest Convention**. In *The Tjaeskemolen* (No 2),[156] the initial arrest in Holland was discharged without security being provided due to the plaintiff's failure to maintain the arrest there. Re-arrest in England was permitted, but the plaintiff was to be put in the same position it would have occupied had it maintained the Dutch arrest – that is, it would have obtained security, but would have been obliged to put up counter-security.[157]

Time limits for commencing proceedings

Whatever the basis on which the English courts may assert jurisdiction over a claim, that claim will fail in limine if proceedings are not commenced within the appropriate limitation period. Under s 5

---

149 For the effect of an acknowledgment of service that is made purely for the purposes of challenging the jurisdiction of the Admiralty Court, see *The Deichland* [1990] 1 QB 361. To avoid the jurisdictional consequences of this decision, the vessel should be arrested. If security is offered before a planned arrest, it should be accepted only if the defendant agrees to submit to the jurisdiction of the Admiralty Court.

150 *The Prinsengracht* [1993] 1 Lloyd's Rep 41. Furthermore, a claimant may proceed with the arrest so as to establish jurisdiction under the 1952 Arrest Convention, even after bail is posted.

151 Although the court has power to order an alternative method of service under PD 61 para 3.6(7), but only if the *res* is situated in England.

152 *Castrique v Imrie* (1870) LR 4 HL 414.

153 Per Lord Brandon in *The August 8* [1983] 2 AC 450, 456.

154 [1892] P 304.

155 [1998] 1 Lloyd's Rep 1.

156 [1997] 2 Lloyd's Rep 476, QB.

157 Under CPR Pt 61.6(2)(b), the court may make an order entitling the claimant to re-arrest the property proceeded against to obtain further security.

of the **Limitation Act 1980**, the general time limit for claims in contract is six years from the date on which the cause of action accrues. Under s 2, a six-year limit also governs claims in tort, save those relating to personal injuries and death, where the limit is three years from the date of the cause of action or the date of knowledge, if later, of the person injured.[158] Collision claims are subject to a two-year time limit.

A lower time limit may be imposed by express terms of the contract. For example, under charterparties on a 'Centrocon' form, the time limit is three months. Certain actions may be subject to a statutory limitation period that is less than that applicable under the **Limitation Act 1980**. An example is the one-year time bar applicable to claims under the Hague-Visby Rules.

Any time limit may be extended by agreement of the parties. However, there is no general judicial discretion to override the applicable time bar where High Court proceedings are commenced out of time.

Where the dispute is subject to arbitration, the court may extend a contractual time bar under s 12 of the **Arbitration Act 1996**, which covers all arbitrations commenced after 1 January 1997, if it is satisfied:

(a)   that the circumstances are such as were outside the reasonable contemplation of the parties when they agreed the provision in question, and that it would be just to extend the time; or

(b)   that the conduct of one party makes it unjust to hold the other party to the strict terms of the provision in question.

These criteria are more stringent than those previously applicable under s 27 of the **Arbitration Act 1950**, where the criterion was the avoidance of 'undue hardship'. Recourse to the courts under this provision can be made only once a claim has arisen and after any available arbitral process for obtaining an extension of time has been exhausted. Time bars imposed by statute, such as the six-year period under the **Limitation Act 1980** or the one-year time limit imposed by the **Carriage of Goods by Sea Act (COGSA) 1971**,[159] are outside the scope of its discretion. This is also the case under s 12 of the 1996 Act.

Arbitration proceedings are commenced, for limitation purposes, when the claimant appoints its arbitrator and notifies the respondent of that appointment at the same time as calling on it to appoint its arbitrator.[160] Where the respondent fails to appoint its arbitrator within seven clear days of this notice being given, s 17 of the **Arbitration Act 1996**[161] allows the claimant to appoint its arbitrator as sole arbitrator subject to the right of the party in default to apply to the court to set aside the appointment.

Time limits for service of proceedings

Once proceedings have been commenced, they must be served on the defendant within the appropriate time limits.

Time limits for service

The time limits for service of an in personam claim form are set out in CPR Pt 7.5 and depend on whether permission is required for service. If the claim form is to be served within the jurisdiction, the claimant must complete the step required for the chosen method of service 'before midnight

---

158   Section 11 of the Limitation Act 1980.
159   *The Antares* [1987] 1 Lloyd's Rep 424, CA. However, the time limit under the Hague or Hague-Visby Rules could be extended where it was incorporated into a contract voluntarily by a 'clause paramount'. See *Nea Agrex SA v Baltic Shipping Co Ltd* [1976] QB 933, CA.
160   *Nea Agrex SA v Baltic Shipping Co Ltd* [1976] QB 933, CA. The position under the 1996 Act was held to be the same in *Vosnoc Ltd v Transglobal Ltd* (1997) The Times, 27 August, QB.
161   An expanded version of s 7 of the Arbitration Act 1950.

on the calendar day four months after the issue of the claim form'.[162] If the claim form is to be served out of the jurisdiction, it must be served within six months of the date of issue. Under CPR Pt 61.3 (5)(b), the time limit for service of an *in rem* claim form is 12 months from the date of its issue. This period may be extended by application to the court in the same manner as applies to *in personam* claim forms.

Extending time for service
Unlike the position with regard to the commencement of proceedings, the court has discretion to extend the time for service under CPR Pt 7.6.

The general rule is that the application to extend time for service must be made either within the period specified for service of the claim form or within the period for service specified by any order made under this provision. If the claimant applies outside these periods, CPR Pt 7.6(3) provides that the court may make an order only if:

(a)   the court has been unable to serve the claim form; or
(b)   the claimant has taken all reasonable steps to comply with CPR Pt 7.5 but has been unable to do so; or
(c)   in either case, the claimant has acted promptly in making the application.

No extension can be granted in respect of a claim form that is issued after the expiry of the relevant limitation period.

Subsequent challenge to jurisdiction by the defendant

Once the claim form has been served, the defendant has an opportunity to challenge the substantive jurisdiction of the English court or to ask the court to stay proceedings. Service of a claim form on a defendant, or its property, is a necessary, but not a sufficient, condition for establishing the jurisdiction of the English courts over the matter. For example, a vessel may be arrested but the claim falls outside the claims scheduled in ss 20 and 21 of the **Senior Courts Act 1981**. Alternatively, the defendant may be properly served in a matter in which the Judgments Regulation allocates jurisdiction to another Convention State. In such circumstances, the defendant can apply to the court under CPR Pt 11 to dismiss the claim for want of jurisdiction. It must do so after giving notice of intention to defend and within the time limit for serving a defence. However, it will lose this right if it submits to the jurisdiction, for example, by serving a defence on the merits, or posting bail without protest.

Even if the court does have jurisdiction, the defendant may apply for a stay of proceedings under CPR Pt 11 on one of four grounds. The first is under the *lis alibi pendens* provisions contained in Arts 29 and 30 of the Judgments Regulation. The second is where the defendant, or its property, has been served by virtue of its presence within the jurisdiction. The defendant may now invite the court to exercise its inherent discretion to stay the proceedings on the general principles of *forum non conveniens*. Where the defendant is served outside the jurisdiction, it may appeal against the granting of permission to serve out of the jurisdiction. The third is where it seeks a mandatory stay of the proceedings under s 9 of the **Arbitration Act 1996** on the grounds that the dispute between the parties is subject to an arbitration agreement. The fourth is where it applies to strike out the action under s 34 of the **Civil Jurisdiction and Judgments Act 1982** on the grounds that a foreign court has given a judgment relating to the same cause of action and the same parties as are before the English court.

---

162 The table in r 7.5 describes the required steps for each method of service. The change also applies to service where permission of the court is required.

Articles 29 and 30 of the Judgments Regulation – *lis alibi pendens*[163]

These Articles are designed to prevent conflicting judgments arising out of the courts of different Member States.[164] The risk of conflicting judgments arises wherever jurisdiction can be established in two or more Member States, as will often be the case with collision actions. The European Court of Justice has given two important rulings on what were then Arts 21 and 22 of the Brussels Convention. The first was in *The Tatry*,[165] where it ruled that the Articles took priority over the provisions of the **1952 Arrest Convention** as that Convention had no equivalent provisions dealing with *lis alibi pendens*.[166]

The second was in *Overseas Union Insurance Ltd v New Hampshire Insurance Co*,[167] where it held that the Articles applied, even when the defendant is domiciled in a non-Convention State. Thus, if the courts of another Member State have already been 'seised' of the matter, the English courts must stay the proceedings before them, whatever the domicile of the defendant and whether or not jurisdiction is based on Regulation or non-Regulation grounds.[168]

The operation of each Article will now be considered in more detail.

Article 29

Article 29 of the Regulation (formerly Art 27) provides that:

> Where proceedings involving the same cause of action and between the same parties are brought in the courts of different Member States, any court other than the court first seised shall of its own motion stay its proceedings until such time as the jurisdiction of the court first seised is established.

If the court first seised establishes jurisdiction over the claim, Art 29(3) directs any other court second seised of the dispute to *decline* jurisdiction in favour of those first seised.

'First seised'

For the purposes of applying both Arts 29 and 30 (formerly Arts 27 and 28), each of the competing courts is the sole arbiter of whether it has, in fact, been 'seised' of the proceedings.[169] The court 'first seised' will cease to be so regarded once proceedings in it have been discontinued.[170] The court 'first seised' is not obliged to accept jurisdiction merely because of that fact. It is a matter entirely for that court to decide whether or not it has jurisdiction. The Articles direct the court or courts that are not 'first seised' as to what they are to do. Thus, the court 'first seised' will be obliged to decline jurisdiction if it takes the view that, under the Judgments Regulation, proceedings should be brought in the courts of another Member State.

In the context of *in rem* proceedings, the Admiralty Court has held that it becomes 'seised' when proceedings are served, not when they are issued.[171] This will be the case even where interim matters, such as applications for freezing orders, have already been heard in the English court prior to commencement of proceedings in the foreign court.[172] The position has been changed by Art 32(1)(a) of the Judgments Regulation, which provides that a court shall be deemed to be seised:

---

163 Formerly Arts 21 and 22 of the Brussels Convention and Arts 27 and 28 of the Brussels Regulation 2001.
164 Conflicts between different courts each with jurisdiction under Art 24 are resolved by Art 31, which also adopts a policy of 'first come, first served'.
165 [1995] 1 Lloyd's Rep 302.
166 Article 3(3) prevents a ship from being arrested more than once in respect of the same claim by the same claimant, but says nothing about the hearing of the substantive claim by different courts.
167 Case C-351/89 [1992] 1 QB 434.
168 This is, however, subject to a tentative exception concerning matters falling within the scope of Art 22 of the Judgments Regulation. See *Speed Investments Ltd v Formula One Holdings Ltd (No 2)* [2004] EWCA Civ 1512; [2005] 1 WLR 1936, CA.
169 Case 129/83 *Zelger v Salinitri (No 2)* [1984] ECR 2397.
170 *Internationale Nederlanden Aviation Lease BV v Civil Aviation Authority* [1997] 1 Lloyd's Rep 80, CA.
171 *The Freccia del Nord* [1989] 1 Lloyd's Rep 388; *The Linda* [1988] 1 Lloyd's Rep 175.
172 *The Sargasso* [1994] 2 Lloyd's Rep 6, CA.

... [a]t the time when the document instituting the proceedings or an equivalent document is lodged with the court, provided that the plaintiff has not subsequently failed to take the steps he was required to take to have service effected on the defendant ...

A difficult issue arises when the proceedings in the court 'first seised' are brought in breach of a jurisdiction clause to which Art 25 (formerly Art 23) applies. Which provision is to prevail: Art 25 or Art 29? The issue came before the Court of Appeal in *Continental Bank NA v Aeakos Compania Naviera SA*,[173] where proceedings were first commenced in the Greek courts in breach of an English jurisdiction clause. The Court of Appeal held that the provisions of Art 17 of the Brussels Convention prevailed over those of Art 21 and refused to stay the English proceedings. It reasoned that, as Art 17 is worded so that it has mandatory effect, the existence of a jurisdiction agreement that satisfies the conditions laid down in Art 17 deprives the courts of any other Contracting States of jurisdiction. This reasoning was, however, difficult to reconcile with the ruling of the European Court of Justice in *Zelger v Salinitri (No 2)*[174] that it is for the court 'first seised' to decide whether it has been validly seised of the matter. This issue was considered by the European Court of Justice in *Erich Gasser GmbH v Misat Srl*.[175] Misat, an Italian company, brought proceedings in the Italian courts against Gasser, a company registered in Austria, for a declaration that the contract between them had been terminated. Seven months later, Gasser brought an action against Misat before the Austrian courts to obtain payment of invoices that were outstanding under the contract. These invoices contained a jurisdiction clause in favour of the Austrian courts, which would satisfy the requirements laid down by Art 23 (now Art 25) of the Judgments Regulation. In these circumstances, the Court of Justice held that the Austrian courts were required, pursuant to Art 27 (now Art 29), to stay their proceedings pending determination of the Italian courts' jurisdiction over the matter. The Court drew upon its earlier decision in *Overseas Union Insurance Ltd v New Hampshire Insurance Co*[176] that the court second seised is never in a better position than the court first seised to determine whether the latter has jurisdiction. The decision has since been begrudgingly followed by the English High Court in *JP Morgan Ltd v Primacom AG*,[177] in spite of the existence of a jurisdiction agreement in favour of the second seised courts that was unambiguously exclusive in effect.

Although the decision of the European Court of Justice in *Erich Gasser* was to be expected, its effect is to be lamented. The decision gives prospective defendants the ability to obstruct and delay good claims against them for lengthy periods of time. In a practical sense, if a party is unsuccessful in ousting the jurisdiction of a court first seised in spite of the existence of a jurisdiction agreement in favour of another court, it will likely fold and settle. Furthermore, even if that party is successful before the court first seised, the costs of this success and the ominous prospects of more litigation in the contractually agreed forum may mean that that party is equally inclined to withdraw. An exception to this unfortunate state of affairs was carved out by the English Court of Appeal for cases in which the court second seised of a dispute is able to establish jurisdiction under the exclusive jurisdiction provisions of Art 24 of the Judgments Regulation.[178] Article 31(2) of the Recast Regulation now provides that where an EU Member State court, in favour of which an exclusive jurisdiction clause exists, is seised, then any other EU Member State court shall stay its proceedings and this is reinforced by Recital 22.

The same claim

For claims to amount to the 'same claim', they must arise between the same parties and involve the same underlying cause of action, although the claims may be expressed in different ways. In *The*

---

173 [1994] 1 WLR 588; applied in *The Kribi* [2001] 1 Lloyd's Rep 76, QB.
174 [1984] ECR 2397.
175 C116/02 [2003] ECR I-14693; [2004] IL Pr 7.
176 Case C-351/90 [1991] ECR I-3317.
177 [2005] EWHC 508 (Comm); [2005] 2 Lloyd's Rep 665.
178 See *Speed Investments Ltd v Formula One Holdings Ltd* (No 2) [2004] EWCA Civ 1512; [2005] 1 WLR 1936, CA.

Tatry,[179] the European Court of Justice ruled on the effect of the equivalent provisions of the Brussels Convention, Arts 21 and 22, in a case involving an allegation of cargo damage following discharge from a Polish vessel at Hamburg and Rotterdam. The vessel's owners promptly commenced proceedings in Rotterdam for a declaration that they were not liable, establishing jurisdiction against the cargo owners under Arts 2 and 6(1) of the Brussels Convention. Some of the cargo claimants then arrested a 'secondary ship' under s 21(4)(ii) of the **Senior Courts Act 1981**.

The European Court of Justice ruled that Art 21 of the Brussels Convention applied to the extent that the English plaintiffs were the same as the Dutch defendants.[180] For the purposes of Art 21, it was immaterial that the English proceedings had been brought in *rem* and the Dutch ones in *personam*.[181] It was also immaterial that the proceedings in the Dutch court involved a claim for a negative declaration.[182] This part of the decision has important implications for 'forum shopping'. It enables a defendant who is quick off the mark to choose the forum in which it is to be sued, provided that the forum has jurisdiction under the Judgments Regulation. If the claimant then commences proceedings in another court that has jurisdiction under the Judgments Regulation, Art 29 will oblige that court to stay the claimant's proceedings, even though it may be a more appropriate forum for the action. Further, the decision adds to the potentially unfortunate effects of the Court of Justice's more recent decision in *Erich Gasser*[183] by allowing prospective defendants to make applications for negative declarations of liability in the courts of their choice, in spite of the existence of a valid jurisdiction agreement in favour of the courts of another Member State.

The European Court of Justice has held that an action in the courts of one Member State involving an insurer and an action in the courts of another Member State involving an insured will be regarded as involving the 'same parties' for the purposes of Art 27 (now Art 29) where there is such a degree of identity between the interests of those parties that a judgment given in one of the sets of proceedings would have the force of *res judicata* in the other.[184] This guidance was recently followed by the English Court of Appeal in *Kolden Holdings Ltd v Rodette Commerce Ltd*[185] in the context of assignment, where it was held that an assignor and an assignee were to be regarded as the 'same parties' where their interests in relation to the claim being advanced were identical and indissociable.

In *The Alexandros T*,[186] however, two sets of proceedings between the insurer and the insured were held not to fall under Art 27 (now Art 29): insurance claims arising out of a vessel's sinking in 2006 which were paid in full in 2007 and final settlement of all future claims under 'Tomlin Orders'.[187] The policies and the settlement agreements were subject to an exclusive jurisdiction clause in favour of the English courts. In 2011, the shipowners sued the insurers in Greece for various breaches of Greek law and damages for loss of opportunity caused by the insurers' late payment of the sum insured. The insurers issued proceedings in England and claimed: (a) damages for breach of an English exclusive jurisdiction agreement; (b) damages for breach of the release in the settlement agreement; (c) a contractual indemnity to be indemnified and held harmless against foreign proceedings; and (d) a declaration that the claim advanced in the foreign proceedings had been settled by the release. The insurers issued proceedings in England to enforce the Tomlin Orders and

---

179 [1995] 1 Lloyd's Rep 302.
180 The English proceedings, as regards those plaintiffs who were not defendants in the Dutch proceedings, were subject to the provisions of the present Art 30, which provide for a discretionary stay of 'related actions'.
181 Thereby overruling *The Nordglimt* [1988] 1 QB 183.
182 Following a previous decision of the European Court of Justice on this point in *Gubisch Maschinenfabrik KG v Giulio Palumbo* [1987] ECR 420.
183 See p 373.
184 Case C-351/91 *Drouot Assurances SA v Consolidated Metallurgical Industries (CMI Industrial Sites)* [1998] ECR I-3075.
185 [2008] EWCA Civ 10; [2008] 1 Lloyd's Rep 434, [91].
186 *Starlight Shipping Co v Allianz Marine & Aviation Versicherungs AG* [2013] UKSC 70; [2014] 1 Lloyd's Rep 223.
187 A Tomlin Order is an order under which a court action is stayed, on terms which have been agreed in advance between the parties and which are included in a schedule to the order.

to seek an indemnity from the shipowner against any costs incurred by themselves in the Greek proceedings. The shipowners applied to stay these proceeding under either Art 27 or 28. The Supreme Court held that Art 27 did not apply to the first three causes of action advanced by the insurers. The 2006 proceedings were contractual and were not mirror images of the claims advanced in the Greek proceedings, the legal basis of which was tortious. The parties were not, therefore, engaged in two sets of legal proceedings in different Member States on the same 'cause of action'. If, however, the insurers chose to maintain the fourth claim, the issue of whether it fell under Art 27 should be referred to the Court of Justice of the EU.[188]

Article 30

Article 30 (formerly Art 28) has similar provisions in relation to 'related actions', save that the court that is not 'first seised' *may* stay the action where the proceedings are pending at first instance. This discretion should be exercised by considering the risk of irreconcilable judgments and should not involve considerations as to the appropriateness of the competing fora.[189] In *The Alexandros T*, the tortious proceedings brought in Greece by the shipowners and the English proceedings brought by their insurers in contract under the settlement agreement were held to fall under Art 28.[190] On the assumption that the English court was not the court 'first seised', the English courts would then have a discretion to stay the proceedings before them.[191] Burton J had refused to stay the actions because the parties had agreed to the exclusive jurisdiction of the English court. The Supreme Court held that it was legitimate to do so. The decision in *Gasser* did not preclude the exercise of discretion in this way as the case related to a stay under Art 27.

The meaning of 'related actions' received the attention of the House of Lords in *Sarrio SA v Kuwait Investment Authority*.[192] The plaintiffs had made a contract of sale with a Spanish company, Grupo Torras SA, in which the defendant, which was domiciled in Kuwait, was the major shareholder. Grupo Torras SA became insolvent and the plaintiffs sued it in Spain for breach of the sale contract, at the same time claiming that the defendant, as its dominant shareholder, should also be liable. A second action was then commenced in England alleging negligent misrepresentation by the defendant in inducing it to enter into the contract of sale with Grupo Torras SA. Their Lordships held that the European Court of Justice's ruling in *The Tatry* required a wide meaning to be given to the equivalent provision of the Brussels Convention (Art 22) and rejected the distinction, applied by the Court of Appeal, between those facts necessary to establish a cause of action and other facts/matters on which conflicting decisions arise and that, therefore, Art 22 covered the two actions in question.

The jurisdiction of the court 'first seised' has to be established under the Judgments Regulation. For related actions, the relevant provisions are contained in Art 6. The jurisdiction of the court 'first seised' is not positively established merely because it is, in fact, 'first seised'. Article 30 has a purely negative effect and creates no new ground for establishing jurisdiction under the Judgments Regulation.[193]

Forum non conveniens

Where Art 6 (formerly Art 4) of the Judgments Regulation provides that the jurisdiction of the English court is to be established in accordance with domestic rules, the defendant may apply to

---

188 As regards Art 28, the two sets of proceedings were held to be 'related'.
189 *The Tatry* [1991] 2 Lloyd's Rep 458, overruled on other grounds by the European Court of Justice. See also *The Happy Fellow* [1998] 1 Lloyd's Rep 13, CA. This case also established that Art 22 (now Art 30) rather than Art 21 (now Art 29) applies where a shipowner is sued in the courts of one Contracting State and commences limitation proceedings in the courts of another Contracting State without admitting liability.
190 [2013] UKSC 70; [2014] 1 Lloyd's Rep 223.
191 The Supreme Court were of the view that the English Court was 'first seised', in that the 2011 English proceedings were not new proceedings but derived from the 2006 proceedings which had been stayed pursuant to Tomlin Orders in 2007. However, if this issue were critical to the decision it would need to be referred to the CJEU.
192 [1998] Lloyd's Rep 129, HL.
193 *Elefanten Schuh GmbH v Jacqmain* [1981] ECR 1671.

stay the proceedings on the grounds of *forum non conveniens*. Section 49 of the **Civil Jurisdiction and Judgments Act 1982** provides that:

> Nothing in this Act shall prevent any court in the United Kingdom from staying, sisting, striking out or dismissing any proceedings before it, on the ground of *forum non conveniens* or other-wise, where to do so is not inconsistent with the 1968 Convention.

This provision applies not only to claims that clearly fall outside the Convention but also to some claims that would appear to fall within it, provided that this leads to no inconsistency with the Convention.

It is presently considered that there can be no such 'inconsistency' if jurisdiction is established on domestic grounds and there is no question of the courts of any other Member State having jurisdiction under the Judgments Regulation. This is illustrated by *The Xin Yang*,[194] where proceedings in a collision action were brought first before the Admiralty Court and then before the courts in Holland. As the defendant was not domiciled in a Brussels Convention State, nor was there any question of any other Convention jurisdiction base applying, the effect of Art 6 was that the English court should apply its own domestic rules of jurisdiction. These rules include the doctrine of *forum non conveniens*, which is specifically preserved by s 49 of the **Civil Jurisdiction and Judgments Act 1982** 'where to do so is not inconsistent with the 1968 Convention'. Accordingly, the court decided to stay the proceedings before it on the grounds that Holland was the appropriate forum. It was immaterial that Holland was a Contracting State and that the Admiralty Court was the 'first seised' under Art 21 (now Art 29).[195]

A potential problem under Art 29 (formerly Art 21) might arise if the claimant, following the stay of the English proceedings, commences fresh proceedings in another Judgments Regulation State only to find that the courts there decline jurisdiction on the grounds that the English courts were 'first seised' notwithstanding the stay. Two observations on this point were made *obiter* by Evans LJ in *Sarrio SA v Kuwait Investment Authority*.[196] First, the difficulty did not arise if the jurisdiction of the English court was regarded as not having been 'established' for the purposes of Art 21 of the Brussels Convention (now Art 29) when a stay was ordered. Secondly, if the alternative foreign forum was likely to decline jurisdiction under Art 21 following a stay of the English proceedings, that would be a factor for the English court to take into account in deciding that there was no 'available' alternative forum, in which case the English proceedings should not be stayed.

Where jurisdiction is based on a Regulation ground, the ambit of the doctrine of *forum non conveniens* has been severely restricted by the European Court of Justice's decision in *Owusu v Jackson*.[197] Prior to this, the English Court of Appeal had been of the view that it retained the discretion to decline to exercise jurisdiction founded upon Art 4 (now Art 6) of the Judgments Regulation on the basis of *forum non conveniens* where it considers the courts of a non-Member State to be a more appropriate forum for the resolution of the dispute.[198] Following the European Court of Justice's decision in *Owusu*, however, such a view is no longer tenable. The claimant, an English domiciliary, was seriously injured while on holiday in Jamaica, when he dived off a cliff and struck his head on a submerged sand bank. He brought an action in the English courts against the owner of the holiday villa that he had rented, another English domiciliary, claiming that it was an implied term of their agreement that the neighbouring private beach would not contain hidden dangers. He also brought

194 [1996] 2 Lloyd's Rep 217. However, the continuing validity of this authority cannot be certain, given that it predates the European Court of Justice's decision in C-281/02 *Owusu v Jackson* [2005] 2 WLR 942, discussed below.
195 The latter consideration would, however, have been relevant to the Dutch court.
196 [1997] 1 Lloyd's Rep 113, CA, 123, overruled on another point in [1998] Lloyd's Rep 129, HL.
197 Case C-281/02 [2005] 2 WLR 942.
198 *Re Harrods (Buenos Aires) Ltd* [1992] Ch 72, CA.

tortious proceedings against a number of Jamaican companies that owned or occupied the beach. The defendant applied to have the action against him stayed in favour of the Jamaican courts, on the footing that the dispute was most connected with Jamaica. On a reference to the European Court of Justice, however, it was held that a court on which jurisdiction is conferred by Art 4 of the Regulation is precluded from declining that jurisdiction on the ground that the court of a non-Member Baer State is a more appropriate forum, even if the jurisdiction of no other Member State is in issue.

Although the Court of Justice's decision in *Owusu* addresses circumstances in which the jurisdiction of the English courts is founded on Art 6, it extends to situations in which jurisdiction is established on the other bases laid down by Chapter II of the Judgments Regulation.[199] The scope of the doctrine of *forum non conveniens* within the Brussels regime has, therefore, been greatly reduced. It is generally considered that only a handful of circumstances remain in which the English courts retain the discretion to decline jurisdiction that is based on a Regulation ground. These concern situations in which the courts would either have discretion to decline jurisdiction under the Regulation, or would be under a duty to do so, had the case involved certain connections with Member States instead of with non-Member States.[200] Article 25 has been held to have 'reflexive effect' where the parties have agreed that the courts of a non-Member State were to have jurisdiction with respect to their disputes,[201] and so too has Art 24(2).[202] In *Ferrexpo AG v Gilson Investments Ltd*,[203] the court stayed English proceedings related to the validity of the decisions of a Ukrainian company. There are divergent first instance decisions as to whether Arts 29 and 30 have reflexive effect.[204]

The recast Regulation, which applies to legal proceedings instituted on or after 10 January 2015, introduces two new provisions relating to proceedings in non-member States. Articles 33 and 34 give EU Member State courts a discretion to stay proceedings brought before them where the same or related matters are already before the courts of a non-EU state, but only where the non-EU proceedings are first in time and where jurisdiction in the EU proceedings is based on Articles 4 (domicile), 7, 8 or 9 (special jurisdiction) of the Recast. The judgment of the non-EU court must also be capable of recognition and enforcement in the EU Member State seized.

General principles

The defendant's application to stay will succeed only if it can establish that another forum is the more appropriate one for the action. The same principles will apply as govern the exercise of the court's discretion to grant permission to serve out under PD 6b 3.1, save that, in applications for stays on the grounds of *forum non conveniens*, the burden of proof will fall partly on the defendant and partly on the claimant. Where the defendant is not present within the jurisdiction and appeals against the grant of permission to serve out of the jurisdiction under PD 6b 3.1, the burden of proof stays with the claimant.

---

199 See, e.g., *Gomez v Gomez-Moncke Vives* [2008] EWHC 259 (Ch); [2008] 1 All ER (Comm) 973, [112].

200 See A-G Léger in Case C-281/02 *Owusu v Jackson* [2005] 2 WLR 942, [70].

201 *Konkola Copper Mines Plc v Coromin* [2005] EWHC 898 (Comm); [2005] 2 Lloyd's Rep 555 and *Winnetka Trading Corp v Julius Baer International Ltd* [2008] EWHC 3146 (Ch); [2009] 2 All ER (Comm) 735.

202 '... in proceedings which have as their object the validity of the constitution, the nullity or the dissolution of companies or other legal persons or associations of natural or legal persons, or of the validity of the decisions of their organs, the courts of the Member State in which the company, legal person or association has its seat'.

203 [2012] EWHC 721 (Comm); [2012] 1 Lloyd's Rep 588.

204 Such that the English courts would be under a duty to stay pursuant to Art 27, where the courts of another Member State were first seised of the dispute. In *Catalyst Investment Group Ltd v Lewinsohn* [2010] EWHC 1964 (Ch), Barling J held that Art 27 could not be applied reflexively, whereas in *JKN v JCN* [2010] EWHC 843 (Fam) it was held that it could. In *Ferrexpo AG v Gilson Investments Ltd* [2012] EWHC 721 (Comm); [2012] 1 Lloyd's Rep. 588, Andrew Smith J expressed the *obiter* view that both articles had reflexive effect. In *Goshawk Dedicated Limited and Kite Dedicated Limited formerly known as Goshawk Dedicated (No 2) Ltd, and Cavell Management Services Ltd, and Cavell Managing Agency Ltd v Life Receivables Ireland Limited* [2009] IESC 7, the Irish Supreme Court referred this issue to the ECJ. However, the reference did not proceed as the case settled.

The principles relevant to this issue were set out in *The Spiliada*,[205] where the House of Lords applied a two-stage test. At the first stage, the burden is on the defendant to establish that there is another forum that is more appropriate for the litigation. If the defendant succeeds at the first stage, the burden of proof shifts to the claimant. At this stage, the claimant can still resist a stay if it can prove that it would suffer injustice if a stay is granted.

Identifying the 'appropriate forum'

In *The Spiliada*, Lord Goff set out the most important factors to be considered by the court as follows:

(a) the convenience of the parties;
(b) the availability of evidence and witnesses;
(c) the law to be applied.

The case involved a claim by Liberian shipowners against Canadian shippers of a cargo of bulk sulphur from Canada to India. The shipowners alleged that the wet condition of the cargo had corroded their vessel and that this amounted to a breach by the shippers of their implied obligation to notify the shipowners of the dangerous characteristics of any cargo to be loaded. The shipowners commenced proceedings in the High Court rather than in British Columbia, where any claim would be barred by a two-year statute of limitation. The shipowners also mounted a parallel claim against the charterers in London arbitration. The contract of sale between charterers and shippers was also subject to a clause providing for London arbitration. The shippers sought to challenge the *ex parte* decision to give the shipowners permission to serve a writ on them under Ord 11, now PD 6b 3.1.

The House of Lords, reversing the decision of the Court of Appeal, upheld the decision of Staughton J that England was the natural forum. The most significant factor that had influenced the judge in reaching this conclusion was the fact that a similar action had been brought against the same shippers in England in respect of damage to another vessel, *The Cambridgeshire*. The factual expertise that would be acquired in that action would be invaluable in the present action. Lord Goff also pointed to two other factors that designated England as being the 'appropriate' forum for the action. First, the *Cambridgeshire* litigation, although it concerned a different shipowner, involved the same solicitors and the same shipowners' insurers. Secondly, he pointed to the applicability of English law to the dispute, given that there were possible differences between English law and Canadian law, both as to the effect of the bill of lading contract and as to the shipper's liability as regards dangerous cargo.[206]

'Appropriate forum' and foreign jurisdiction clauses

The English High Court is generally very reluctant to interfere with the parties' chosen jurisdiction. The circumstances in which the court will do so were set out by Brandon J in *The Eleftheria*.[207] The court will exercise its discretion to stay the English proceedings unless the claimant can show that there is *strong cause* for not staying the action. The same principles apply whether the chosen forum is England or another country,[208] or whether the clause is exclusive or non-exclusive.[209] This will involve the court in considering all of the circumstances of the cases, and, in particular, the following factors:

---

205 [1987] 1 AC 460.
206 In the light of the discussion below where a foreign jurisdiction clause is involved, the relevant law is only likely to be an important factor where it is substantially different from that applied in the appropriate forum as regards the issue between the parties.
207 [1970] P 94.
208 *Akai Pty Ltd v People's Insurance Co Ltd* [1998] 1 Lloyd's Rep 90, 104.
209 *Mercury plc v Communication Telesystems Ltd* [1999] 2 All ER (Comm) 33, 40.

(a)   the country in which the evidence on the issues of fact is situated or more readily available, and the effect of that on the relative convenience and expense of trial as between the English and foreign courts;

(b)   whether the law of the foreign courts applies and, if so, whether it differs from English law in any material respects;

(c)   with what country either party is connected and how closely;

(d)   whether the defendants genuinely desire trial in the foreign country or are only seeking procedural advantages;

(e)   whether the claimants would be prejudiced by having to sue in the foreign court because they would:

- be deprived of security for that claim;
- be unable to enforce any judgment obtained;
- be faced with a time bar not applicable in England; or
- for political, racial, religious or other reasons be unlikely to get a fair trial.

The Eleftheria involved a claim by English cargo receivers against Greek shipowners in respect of the costs of carrying cargo from Rotterdam to London and Hull, the contractual discharge ports under the bill of lading. The shipowners had discharged at Rotterdam, due to a dock strike in London and Hull. Brandon J held that there was a prima facie case in upholding the Greek jurisdiction clause in the bill of lading. Against that was the fact that the bulk of the factual evidence was located in England. However, buttressing the prima facie case was the fact that the bill of lading was subject to Greek law and that the ship was owned by Greek nationals, residing in Greece, whose principal place of business was in Athens. The factors in favour of and against a stay cancelled each other out, so Brandon J gave effect to the prima facie case that the English proceedings should be stayed.

In The Adolf Warski,[210] the same judge was faced with a cargo claim arising out of a carriage, on a Polish-owned vessel, of melons and onions from South American ports to Swansea under bills of lading that contained a clause providing for Polish jurisdiction and Polish law. This time Brandon J refused to order a stay. The balance was tilted away from the jurisdiction clause by the fact that the bulk of the evidence on liability and damages, including expert witnesses, was located in England. Moreover, witnesses from Chile might have had problems in obtaining visas to enter Poland due to political reasons. The Polish law provision, unlike its Greek law equivalent in The Eleftheria, was of little significance as there was no evidence that Polish law differed from English law on the issue between the parties.

Subsequent cases have varied somewhat in the emphasis placed on parties' contractual choice of jurisdiction as against the pull of the 'natural forum' for adjudicating their dispute. In The El Amria,[211] the Court of Appeal held that a strong case needed to be made out before it would disregard the contractual provision for Alexandria jurisdiction. On the facts, however, such a case was made out. The proceedings involved a claim against the defendant shipowners for deterioration that had occurred to the claimant's cargo of potatoes during a voyage from Alexandria to Liverpool. In turn, the defendant alleged that the damage had occurred owing to the unreasonably slow discharge of the cargo by stevedores at Liverpool. Although each of the bills of lading contained exclusive jurisdiction clauses in favour of the Egyptian courts, the English Court of Appeal exercised its discretion to hear the dispute. Expert evidence concerning the issue of deterioration was predominantly available in England, and the participation of the stevedores (who had no connection with

---

210   [1976] 1 Lloyd's Rep 107; aff'd [1976] 2 Lloyd's Rep 241, CA.
211   [1981] 2 Lloyd's Rep 119, CA.

the Egyptian jurisdiction) was necessary to resolve the dispute.[212] In contrast, in *The Nile Rhapsody*,[213] Hirst J was of the view that the effect of an Egyptian jurisdiction clause was merely to shift the burden of proof on *forum non conveniens* in favour of the defendant. On the facts, Egypt was the natural forum and a stay was granted.

Where there is the risk of irreconcilable judgments, due to related proceedings in England, the courts will be inclined to ignore a foreign jurisdiction clause and decline to stay the English proceedings.[214] Similar principles apply in the converse situation in which there are proceedings against multiple defendants, one of whom is being sued under a contract that contains an English jurisdiction clause. In *Caspian v Bouygues Offshore SA*,[215] the Court of Appeal discharged an anti-suit injunction that had been granted by Colman J[216] in respect of multiparty proceedings arising out of the sinking of a vessel where the natural forum was South Africa. The towing contract with the time charterer of the tug was subject to English jurisdiction, as was the time charter itself, but this was not the case as regards the actions the vessel owners had also brought against the tug owners and the South African port authority.[217] However, where the proceedings have been brought against only a single defendant, the courts will almost always uphold the English jurisdiction clause, even though proceedings may have been brought against the same defendant in another jurisdiction in respect of other claims involving similar facts. In *Metro v CSAV*,[218] Gross J stressed that the gravity of the risks of irreconcilable judgments depended on the facts of each case. The claim arose out of alleged misdelivery of cargo in Chile and was subject to a non-exclusive English jurisdiction clause. The claimant had also brought 14 different misdelivery claims against the same defendant in Chile, which applied the two-year Hamburg Rules time bar rather than the one-year period set out in the Hague Rules. Despite the risk of conflicting judgments being given on essentially the same set of facts, Gross J refused to stay the English proceedings.

In *The Hollandia* (sub nom *The Morviken*),[219] the House of Lords made it clear that, in one situation, the courts will definitely refuse to order a stay when a foreign jurisdiction clause is involved. That is where the effect of enforcing the jurisdiction clause will be to allow the defendant to avoid a mandatory rule of English law. A stay was not granted when a cargo claim was pursued in the English courts, notwithstanding a clause in the bill of lading giving jurisdiction to the Amsterdam county court. The cargo had been loaded in the UK and the Hague-Visby Rules thereby applied to the bill of lading 'by force of law' by virtue of **COGSA 1971**. At the time that the action was commenced, the Netherlands applied the Hague Rules and not the Hague-Visby Rules. Had a stay been granted, the effect would have been that a claim that under English law had to be dealt with by the Hague-Visby Rules would, in fact, have been dealt with by the Hague Rules.

Substantial injustice to the claimant

Even if the defendant succeeds in establishing that another forum is the more appropriate forum, the court may still refuse a stay if the claimant is able to establish that litigating in the 'appropriate' forum will involve 'substantial injustice' to the claimant. In his seminal speech in *The Spiliada*,[220] Lord

---

212 Cf *The Kislovodsk* [1980] 1 Lloyd's Rep 183, where Sheen J granted a stay of proceedings brought against a USSR state shipowning company under a bill of lading that provided for Leningrad jurisdiction and USSR law. The claim involved damage to a cargo of coffee due to alleged poor ventilation on the voyage from Mombasa to Rotterdam, and the key witnesses as to the manner of the stowage and the ventilation of the cargo would be Russian.
213 [1992] 2 Lloyd's Rep 399; noted Briggs, A (1993) 109 LQR 382; aff'd [1994] 1 Lloyd's Rep 382, CA.
214 *Standard Chartered Bank v Pakistan National Shipping Corp* [1995] 2 Lloyd's Rep 365. See also *The MC Pearl* [1997] 1 Lloyd's Rep 566, QB.
215 [1998] 2 Lloyd's Rep 461, CA.
216 *Ultisol v Bouygues SA* [1996] 2 Lloyd's Rep 140, QB.
217 See also *Donohue v Armco Inc* [2002] 1 Lloyd's Rep 425, HL, where several co-claimants proceeded against various defendants in respect of an alleged fraud committed in the USA. Proceedings were commenced in New York, which was the natural forum. Although one of the claimants was proceeding under a contract that contained an exclusive English jurisdiction clause, the risk of conflicting judgments entailed that the English proceedings were stayed.
218 [2003] 1 Lloyd's Rep 405, 411.
219 [1983] 1 AC 565.
220 [1987] 1 AC 460.

Goff made it clear that this must involve more than the loss of a procedural or substantive advantage in the suit.

The fact that proceedings in the foreign jurisdiction are time-barred will not necessarily involve 'substantial injustice'. Brandon J in The Adolf Warski declined to express a view on the fact that proceedings in the alternative forum, Poland, had become time-barred.[221] However, in The Spiliada, Lord Goff was of the view that, had British Columbia been the natural forum, a stay would have been granted only on the defendant's undertaking not to take the point in proceedings in that jurisdiction that the plaintiff's claim had become statute-barred. On the facts, the shipowners had not acted unreasonably in failing to commence proceedings in British Columbia within the two-year limitation period applicable there.

In contrast, in The Pioneer Container,[222] proceedings in Hong Kong were stayed on the basis of a Taiwan jurisdiction clause, notwithstanding that proceedings in Taiwan had become time-barred. The plaintiffs were found to have acted unreasonably in not commencing proceedings in Taiwan to avoid the time bar.[223]

'Substantial injustice' may also arise where limitation proceedings are commenced in a jurisdiction that applies a lower limitation figure than that applied by the English courts under the **1976 Limitation Convention**. In Caltex Singapore Pte Ltd v BP Shipping Ltd,[224] a vessel collided with a jetty in Singapore. The shipowners commenced limitation proceedings in Singapore, which was the natural forum for the action. The jetty owners commenced proceedings in the English High Court to obtain the advantage of the higher limitation figure applicable under the 1976 Limitation Convention.[225] It was held that England was the appropriate forum on the grounds of justice and that, if possible, any stay should be temporary only, to allow the Singapore courts to assess the quantum of the claim. If it then appeared that the quantum would fall below the Singapore limitation figure, only then would the stay be made permanent. A different result was reached in The Falstria,[226] where the limitation figure in the alternative foreign jurisdiction, Denmark, exceeded the figure then applicable in England. Notwithstanding this, the limitation proceedings in England were not stayed, despite the risk that the defendants would then seek to stay the Danish proceedings under Arts 21 and 22 of the **1968 Brussels Convention** (now Arts 29 and 30 of the Judgments Regulation). In The Herceg Novi,[227] the Court of Appeal unconditionally stayed in rem proceedings in a collision action where other proceedings had been commenced in Singapore, which was the appropriate forum. The fact that Singapore still applied the 1957 Limitation Convention did not mean that the stay of the English proceedings would result in substantial injustice to the plaintiffs.

However, the position is different where a shipowner commences limitation proceedings in England. Caspian v Bouygues Offshore SA[228] involved multiparty proceedings in respect of the sinking of a vessel under tow. The owners and time charterers of the tug commenced limitation proceedings in England. These would be subject to the provisions of the 1976 Limitation Convention, whereas a limitation action in South Africa, which had the closest connection with the action, would be based on the **1957 Limitation Convention**. Although the limitation figures under the 1976 Limitation Convention are substantially higher, the advantage for the party seeking to limit is that it is much harder for the right to limit to be lost than is the case under the 1957 Limitation

---

221 [1976] 1 Lloyd's Rep 107.
222 [1994] 2 AC 324.
223 Cf a contrary finding in Citi-March Ltd v Neptune Orient Lines Ltd [1996] 2 All ER 545, QB, where the bill of lading holder was held not to have acted unreasonably in letting its claim for short delivery in the Singapore courts become time-barred. Related proceedings were afoot in the English courts against another defendant regarding storage of cargo in England between discharge and delivery to the plaintiff.
224 [1996] 1 Lloyd's Rep 286.
225 The Singapore limitation rule was regarded as procedural and would therefore not be applied in the English proceedings.
226 [1988] 1 Lloyd's Rep 495.
227 [1998] 2 Lloyd's Rep 454.
228 [1998] 2 Lloyd's Rep 461, CA.

Convention, a significant factor when the claim made by the owners of the lost vessel was nearly 100 times greater than the maximum available under the 1976 Limitation Convention. The Court of Appeal refused to stay the limitation actions, notwithstanding its discharge of an anti-suit injunction in relation to the substantive proceedings on the grounds that South Africa was the natural forum in which to hear them. The decision contains no analysis of how the The Spiliada principles should apply to limitation actions and appears to be premised on the assumption that the shipowner should be free to choose where it commences a limitation action.[229]

Where the issue involves the quality of justice available in the alternative forum, the courts are generally reluctant to make adverse comparisons between the trial process in the foreign jurisdiction and that in England. The Court of Appeal shied away from any such comparison in The El Amria[230] and the House of Lords did likewise in The Abidin Daver.[231] However, in The Vishva Ajay,[232] the court did consider the effect of delays in commercial litigation in India and refused to stay the proceedings following evidence that a trial in India would be delayed for many years, making the evidence of witnesses involved less reliable. This was the case notwithstanding that India was the 'appropriate' forum. A more specific factor pointing against a stay may be the practice of the foreign court in awarding costs to a successful litigant. Injustice may arise if costs do not follow the event,[233] or are not awarded on a realistic basis,[234] but will not arise if the successful litigant has to bear some of the costs of the action.[235] However, exceptionally, a stay will not be ordered where the claimant is entitled to legal aid for the English proceedings and would be unable to obtain equivalent funding in the alternative jurisdiction.[236] One interesting element that is recently being pleaded by claimants, and that has been accepted by the courts as amounting to substantial injustice, is the assertion that a judgment in English proceedings would be easier to enforce elsewhere in Europe, pursuant to the provisions contained in Chapter III of the Judgments Regulation, than a judgment obtained in the (more appropriate) foreign forum.[237] Another specific factor is any difference between English rules as to conflict of laws and the equivalent rules in the foreign forum.[238]

The issue of injustice may lead the court to compromise by granting a stay subject to the defendant agreeing to conditions relating to the proceedings in the foreign jurisdiction. In The Kislovodsk,[239] the stay was granted subject to two such conditions. The defendant had to provide satisfactory security to cover any judgment obtained against it in the USSR, and any witnesses that the plaintiff wished to call were to be given visas to attend the court in Leningrad.

Section 34 of the Civil Jurisdiction and Judgments Act 1982

The doctrine of 'merger' means that a claimant's cause of action is extinguished when it obtains a judgment from an English court on that cause of action. Where the judgment is obtained in a foreign court, the position is governed by s 34 of the **Civil Jurisdiction and Judgments Act 1982**, which provides:

---

229 See, too, The Volvox Hollandia [1988] 2 Lloyd's Rep 360, where the court refused an application in the substantive proceedings for a declaration that the shipowners were not entitled to limit.
230 [1981] 2 Lloyd's Rep 119.
231 [1984] AC 398.
232 [1989] 2 Lloyd's Rep 558.
233 Raneleigh Ltd v MII Exports Inc [1989] 1 WLR 619.
234 The Vishva Ajay [1989] 2 Lloyd's Rep 558.
235 The Kislovodsk [1980] 1 Lloyd's Rep 183.
236 Connelly v RTZ Corp plc [1998] AC 854, HL; Lubbe v Cape Industries plc [2000] 2 Lloyd's Rep 383, HL.
237 See International Credit & Investment Co (Overseas) Ltd v Adham (Share Ownership) [1999] IL Pr 302, CA; Inter-Tel Inc v OCIS Plc [2004] EWHC 2269, QB.
238 The Irish Rowan [1989] 3 All ER 853, CA.
239 [1980] 1 Lloyd's Rep 183.

No proceedings may be brought by a person in England and Wales . . . on a cause of action in respect of which judgment has been given in his favour in proceedings between the same parties . . . in the courts of an overseas country.

The House of Lords has considered this provision on two occasions in *The Indian Grace*.[240] The case involved two cargo claims arising from a fire on a vessel. The Indian government proceeded with the smaller claim against the shipowners *in personam* in the courts in Cochin. It then commenced proceedings *in rem* in the Admiralty Court in respect of the larger claim. The courts in Cochin then gave their judgment on the smaller *in personam* claim. Did this judgment bar the *in rem* proceedings from continuing?

To answer this question, two separate issues needed to be addressed. First, did the two sets of proceedings involve the same 'cause of action'? The House of Lords, in the first case, held that they did, because, in both cases, the same facts would have to be proved to establish the liability of the shipowner. Secondly, were the two sets of proceedings between 'the same parties'? In this respect, the matter was complicated by the fact that one set of proceedings was *in personam* and the other *in rem*. Was the defendant in the *in rem* proceedings really the ship, rather than her owners? The House of Lords, in the second case, held that this was not the case. The parties to the *in rem* proceedings were the cargo owners and the shipowners, the same as in the *in personam* proceedings.[241] Furthermore, for the purposes of s 34, proceedings *in rem* were 'brought' not only when they were commenced, but also when they were *continued* following the judgment of the court in Cochin. Their Lordships declined to express a view on what the position would have been had the proceedings *in rem* involved a maritime lien rather than a statutory lien under s 21(4) of the **Senior Courts Act 1981**.

Arbitration

It is common for bills of lading, charterparties, and salvage agreements to provide for the submission of disputes to arbitration, rather than to the jurisdiction of a particular court. The arbitration agreement will also bind parties who obtain derivative rights from a party to the agreement.[242] In England, Wales and Northern Ireland, arbitration is governed by the **Arbitration Act 1996**, which came into force on 31 January 1997. The Act is the latest in a series of Acts governing arbitration – the **Arbitration Act 1950**, the **Arbitration Act 1975**, which gave effect to the provisions of the 1958 New York Convention on the enforcement of arbitral awards, and the **Arbitration Act 1979**, which substantially limited the parties' rights of appeal to the High Court. The 1996 Act applies where the 'seat of arbitration', defined in s 3 as the 'juridical seat', is in England, Wales or Northern Ireland. The Act requires arbitration agreements to be in or evidenced by writing. The Act is based on the principle of party autonomy in the conduct of arbitrations. However, Schedule 1 reserves certain mandatory powers to the High Court – for example, the power to stay legal proceedings, the power to remove an arbitrator, and the power to enforce an award. If court proceedings are commenced the party defending them may apply for a stay, which must be granted unless the court is satisfied that the arbitration agreement is 'null and void, inoperative, or incapable of being performed'.[243]

---

240 [1993] AC 410; [1998] 1 Lloyd's Rep 1, noted (1998) LMCLQ 27. See, also, Teare, N, 'The Admiralty action in *rem* and the House of Lords' (1998) LMCLQ 33.

241 So overruling *The Nordglimt* [1988] 1 QB 183, which had previously been overruled in the context of Art 21 of the 1968 Brussels Convention by the decision of the ECJ in *The Tatry* [1995] 1 Lloyd's Rep 302.

242 Such as where a claimant proceeds directly against a liability insurer pursuant to a direct right of action given by a foreign statute. The claimant will stand in the position of the assured and will be subject to the terms of its contract with the insurer, including a clause submitting disputes under the contract to arbitration. Although the claim arises by virtue of a statute, if it can be characterised as in substance a right to enforce the contract rather than an independent right of recovery, it will fall within the arbitration agreement. *The London Steam-Ship Owners' Mutual Insurance Association Ltd v The Kingdom of Spain, The French State (The Prestige)* [2013] EWHC 3188 (Comm); [2014] 1 Lloyd's Rep 309.

243 Section 9(4).

Where proceedings are brought before the court in breach of the arbitration agreement, s 9 entitles a party to the agreement to apply for a stay of those proceedings. Section 9 of the 1996 Act applies even where the seat of the arbitration is located outside of the English jurisdiction.[244] It is no longer possible to apply to the court for summary judgment under CPR Pt 24 on the grounds that there is no arguable defence to the claim.[245] Section 9(4) requires the court to grant a stay 'unless satisfied that the arbitration agreement is null and void, inoperative, or incapable of being performed'. Where proceedings are brought before a foreign court in breach of the arbitration agreement, the English court will generally issue an anti-suit injunction ordering the party bringing the foreign proceedings not to continue with them. An anti-suit injunction will not be granted where proceedings are brought before the courts of a state that is party to the Brussels Regulation or the Lugano Convention, by reason of the decision of the ECJ in The Front Comor.[246]

Separability of arbitration agreements

Section 7 provides for the separability of arbitration agreements which are regarded as separate agreements from the underlying contract. Accordingly, an arbitration agreement 'shall not be regarded as invalid, non-existent or ineffective because that other agreement is invalid, or did not come into existence or has become ineffective, and it shall for that purpose be treated as a distinct agreement'. This provision was considered by the House of Lords in Fiona Trust & Holding Corp v Privalov.[247] There were eight charters subject to English law and with an English jurisdiction clause for 'any dispute under this charter', with each party having the right to elect to have 'any such dispute' referred to London arbitration. The owners applied for a declaration that the charters had been validly rescinded on the grounds that they had been procured by bribery. The charterers sought to stay proceedings under s 9 of the **Arbitration Act 1996**. The House of Lords held that there was a presumption that all disputes should be submitted to arbitration, including disputes relating to the rescission of a contract for misrepresentation. Lord Hoffmann stated:

> The arbitration agreement must be treated as a 'distinct agreement' and can be void or voidable only on grounds which relate directly to the arbitration agreement. Of course there may be cases in which the ground upon which the main agreement is invalid is identical with the ground upon which the arbitration agreement is invalid. For example, if the main agreement and the arbitration agreement are contained in the same document and one of the parties claims that he never agreed to anything in the document and that his signature was forged, that will be an attack on the validity of the arbitration agreement. But the ground of attack is not that the main agreement was invalid. It is that the signature to the arbitration agreement, as a 'distinct agreement', was forged.

That, however, was not the case in the present case where the allegation was that the agent exceeded his authority by entering into a main agreement in terms which were not authorised or for improper reasons. The arbitration clause was, therefore, a separate contract to the charterparty and its validity was not impeached by any invalidity of the charterparty and the charterers were entitled to a stay of the High Court proceedings brought by the shipowners.

Section 30 provides for the principle of kompetenz-kompetenz whereby the arbitral tribunal has competence to rule on its own jurisdiction. Paragraph (1) provides:

---

244 Section 2(2)(a) of the Arbitration Act 1996.
245 The Halki [1998] 1 Lloyd's Rep 49. This was possible under s 1(1) of the Arbitration Act 1975, which provided that a stay need not be granted if 'there is not in fact any dispute between the parties with regard to the matter referred'. Hayter v Nelson [1990] 2 Lloyd's Rep 265. This change is not as significant as it seems, as it was always open to the tribunal to make an interim award in the reference and the tribunal's powers in this respect have been expanded in the 1996 Act.
246 Case C-185/07; [2009] 1 AC 1138. See discussion in Chapter 19 at pp 409–10.
247 [2007] UKHL 40; [2008] 1 Lloyd's Rep 254.

Unless otherwise agreed by the parties, the arbitral tribunal may rule on its own substantive jurisdiction, that is, as to (a) whether there is a valid arbitration agreement, (b) whether the tribunal is properly constituted, and (c) what matters have been submitted to arbitration in accordance with the arbitration agreement.[248]

Paragraph 2 then provides that 'Any such ruling may be challenged by any available arbitral process of appeal or review or in accordance with the provisions of this Part.' Jurisdiction may be challenged before the courts of the seat of the arbitration (in England this will be under s 67 or s 72, in the case of a party that takes no part in the arbitration proceedings) or when the award comes to be enforced.[249]

Commencement of arbitration

Section 14(1) deals with the commencement of arbitration. The parties are free to make their own agreement as to how arbitration is to be started, but in default it will be commenced when one party serves notice on the other requiring them to appoint their arbitrator. Service is to be by 'any effective means'.[250] Paragraph 4 provides:

> Where the arbitrator or arbitrators are to be appointed by the parties, arbitral proceedings are commenced in respect of a matter when one party serves on the other party or parties notice in writing requiring him or them to appoint an arbitrator or to agree to the appointment of an arbitrator in respect of that matter.

In *The Voc Gallant*,[251] Judge Mackie QC held that the courts had to be flexible in applying s 14(4). The shipowners had sent a message notifying the time charterers that if they did not pay the sum or agree to the appointment of a sole arbitrator, they would appoint their own arbitrator. Over seven days later, the shipowners sent a second message, stating that since the charterers had neither paid nor agreed to appoint a sole arbitrator, they had appointed their own arbitrator to commence arbitration proceedings. The first message was held to be effective in commencing arbitration, which was, therefore, commenced within the one-year time limit specified under the Hague Rules, so allowing the charterers to advance their cargo claims for breach of Art III(2) against the shipowners. What was important was not whether a notice contained a particular form of words but whether it made it clear that the arbitration agreement was being invoked and required a party to take steps accordingly, which was exactly what the first message did. The fact that a subsequent message gave explicit notice of the appointment of an arbitrator did not prevent an earlier communication from complying with s 14(4). Where there is delay in prosecuting claims, s 41(3) gives the tribunal power to dismiss claims where there is inordinate and inexcusable delay by the claimant and the delay creates a substantial risk that it will not be possible to have a fair trial or will result in serious prejudice to the respondent.

The parties are free to specify the number of arbitrators. If no number is specified then s 15(3) provides for the appointment of a sole arbitrator, and if no agreement can be made on the appointment the matter will have to be resolved by an application to the High Court. It is common for it to be agreed that each party will appoint its own arbitrator and the arbitrators will then appoint a third

---

248 Section 32(1) provides that a party to arbitral proceedings may request the court to determine questions relating to the substantive jurisdiction of the tribunal with the agreement of all parties or with the permission of the tribunal.
249 Under s 66(3).
250 Section 76(3).
251 [2009] EWHC 288 (Comm); [2009] 1 Lloyd's Rep 418.

person as a chairman, with the majority decision being binding.[252] It is also possible to provide for the appointment of an umpire in the event that the parties' arbitrators cannot agree, in which case s 21(4) provides for the umpire to make an independent award as if they were a sole arbitrator.

Section 13(1) provides that 'The Limitation Acts apply to arbitral proceedings as they apply to legal proceedings.' Section 12, which replaces s 27 of the **Arbitration Act 1950**, gives the court discretion to extend the time for commencing arbitration. This discretion is not exercisable when the time limit under Art III(6) applies by virtue of statute – for example, **COGSA 1971**[253] – because s 12 is expressed to be without prejudice to any statutory provisions regarding the time for commencing arbitration proceedings. However, *dicta* of the Court of Appeal in *Nea Agrex SA v Baltic Shipping Co Ltd* (*The Agios Lazaros*) relating to s 27 of the **Arbitration Act 1950** suggest that, where the Hague or Hague-Visby Rules apply purely by contractual incorporation, as with a clause paramount in a charterparty, the court will retain its discretion to extend time beyond the one-year limit contained in the Rules.[254] This probably remains the position under s 12.

Applicable law

Arbitration agreements are excluded from the **Rome Convention 1980** and the **Rome I Regulation**. The governing law will be that chosen by the parties. This law will govern the scope of the arbitration agreement itself, as well as issues relating to the validity of the agreement. This law may be different from the law of the contract itself. If none is specified, the law will either be that of the underlying contract or the law of the seat of the forum. Recent decisions favour the latter.[255] As regards the law relating to the substance of the dispute, s 46 provides that the arbitral tribunal shall decide the dispute in accordance with the law chosen by the parties as applicable to the substance.[256] It is worth noting that, unlike the English courts, the arbitral tribunal may legitimately select a law other than the law of a state here, such as a religious law or the *lex mercatoria*.[257] If there is no such law, they must decide 'in accordance with such other considerations as are agreed by them [the parties] or determined by the tribunal'. In the absence of a choice of law, para 3 provides that the tribunal shall apply the law determined by the conflict of laws rules which it considers applicable. The tribunal is given a wide discretion but must apply *a* system of conflict of laws rules. A tribunal will usually apply the conflict of law rules of the seat of the arbitration. The English conflicts of law rules for contracts are contained in either the Rome Convention or the Rome I Regulation, depending on when the contract was made.[258]

Interim relief

Section 38 gives the tribunal power: to make an order for the claimant to provide security for the costs of the arbitration (para 3); to make directions relating to property which is the subject matter of the proceedings (para 4); to order or direct a party or witness to be examined on oath or affirmation (para 5); to give directions to a party for the preservation for the purposes of the

---

252 Section 20(3).
253 As in *The Antares* [1987] 1 Lloyd's Rep 424, in which the Court of Appeal considered the equivalent provision, s 27, in the Arbitration Act 1950.
254 [1976] QB 933, disapproving contrary *dicta* of Kerr J in *The Angeliki* [1973] 2 Lloyd's Rep 226.
255 *XL Insurance Ltd v Owens Corning* [2001] 1 All ER (Comm) 530 and *dicta* in *C v D* [2007] EWCA Civ 1282; [2008] 1 Lloyd's Rep 239, and *Shashoua and others v Sharma* [2009] EWHC 957 (Comm); [2009] 2 Lloyd's Rep 376. The law of the underlying contract was applied in *Sonatrach Petroleum Corporation (BVI) v Ferrell International Ltd* [2001] EWHC 481 (Comm); [2002] 1 All ER (Comm) 627, at para 32, and in *Sulamérica Cia Nacional de Seguros SA v Enesa Engenharia SA* [2012] EWCA Civ 638.
256 The choice of the laws of a country shall be understood to refer to the substantive laws of that country and not its conflict of laws rules.
257 See *Deutsche Schachtbau und Tiefbohrgesellschaft mbH v Shell International Petroleum Co Ltd* [1990] 1 AC 295.
258 Contracts made on or after 17 December 2009 are governed by the Rome I Regulation.

proceedings of any evidence in his custody or control (para 6). Other interim relief, such as freezing orders or anti-suit injunctions, must be obtained by application to the court under s 44.

Appeals

The award must be a reasoned award, unless the parties agree otherwise. This reverses the position that prevailed under the 1979 Act. A party to arbitral proceedings may challenge an award on three grounds.[259] The first two grounds are mandatory and cannot be excluded by agreement of the parties.

Section 67 entitles a party to arbitral proceedings to apply to the court:

> (a) challenging any award of the arbitral tribunal as to its substantive jurisdiction; or (b) for an order declaring an award made by the tribunal on the merits to be of no effect, in whole or in part, because the tribunal did not have substantive jurisdiction.

Whether a tribunal has jurisdiction is something which the court must decide for itself and, accordingly, the court's function is to rehear the case rather than to review the arbitrators' decision.[260]

Section 68 allows a party to apply to the court, 'challenging an award in the proceedings on the ground of serious irregularity affecting the tribunal, the proceedings or the award.' Section 68(2) then goes on to list nine instances of serious irregularity, which the court considers has caused or will cause substantial injustice to the applicant. A party may lose the right to challenge an award under ss 67 and 68 by reason of s 73, paragraph 1 of which provides:

> (1) If a party to arbitral proceedings takes part, or continues to take part, in the proceedings without making, either forthwith or within such time as is allowed by the arbitration agreement or the tribunal or by any provision of this Part, any objection –
>
> (a) that the tribunal lacks substantive jurisdiction,
> (b) that the proceedings have been improperly conducted,
> (c) that there has been a failure to comply with the arbitration agreement or with any provision of this Part, or
> (d) that there has been any other irregularity affecting the tribunal or the proceedings,
>
> he may not raise that objection later, before the tribunal or the court, unless he shows that, at the time he took part or continued to take part in the proceedings, he did not know and could not with reasonable diligence have discovered the grounds for the objection.

Section 69 provides for an appeal on a point of law with the agreement of the parties or with the permission of the court. The right to appeal may be excluded by agreement of the parties and an agreement to dispense with reasons for the tribunal's award shall be considered an agreement to exclude the court's jurisdiction under s 69. However, in *Shell Egypt West Manzala GmbH, Shell Egypt West Qantara GmbH v Dana Gas Egypt Limited* (formerly *Centurion Petroleum Corporation*) Gloster J held that the wording 'final, conclusive and binding' in an arbitration clause did not operate to exclude the right to appeal an arbitral award on a point of law under s 69.[261]

---

259 A party appealing an award should issue an arbitration claim form under Pt 62 CPR.
260 *Azov Shipping Co v Baltic Shipping Co* [1999] 1 Lloyd's Rep 68.
261 [2009] EWHC 2097; [2010] 1 Lloyd's Rep 109.

Permission to appeal shall be given only if the court is satisfied:

(a) that the determination of the question will substantially affect the rights of one or more of
     the parties;

(b) that the question is one which the tribunal was asked to determine;

(c) that, on the basis of the findings of fact in the award

     (i)   the decision of the tribunal on the question is obviously wrong, or

     (ii) the question is one of general public importance and the decision of the tribunal is at
           least open to serious doubt; and

(d) that, despite the agreement of the parties to resolve the matter by arbitration, it is just and
     proper in all the circumstances for the court to determine the question.

The standard practice is for the court not to give reasons when refusing permission to appeal under
s 69. This is not contrary to the right to fair trial under the **Human Rights Act 1998** Sched 1 Pt I
Art 6.[262] In *The Western Triumph*,[263] the Court of Appeal held that Art 6 required the judge refusing
permission to appeal under s 69 to tell the applicant which of the threshold tests in s 69(3) he had
failed, but there was no need to go further and explain in every case why he had failed the relevant
test. The court's function under s 69 is to look exclusively at the award for the purpose of ascer-
taining whether the threshold tests under para 3 have been satisfied. It does not go behind what
appears on the face of the award, nor is it concerned with the circumstances in which the award
came to be made. Section 68 provides an entirely self-contained procedural regime for dealing with
such circumstances.[264]

A party who wishes to challenge an award must do so within 28 days of the issue
of the award.[265] These time limits may be extended by the court. In *Broda Agro Trade (Cyprus) Ltd
v Alfred C Toepfer International GmbH*[266] the application to extend time was made 14 months after that
time limit had expired. During that time the party had consulted only Russian lawyers and had
received a lack of correct advice on the English law of arbitration. The court refused to
extend time because the applicant, a seasoned grain trader with a claim of $5million, had acted
unreasonably.

Challenges by non-participating parties

Section 72(1) allows a party that does not participate in an award to question:

(a) whether there is a valid arbitration agreement;

(b) whether the tribunal is properly constituted; or

(c) what matters have been submitted to arbitration in accordance with the arbitration agree-
     ment, by proceedings in the court for a declaration or injunction or other appropriate
     relief.

Under s 72(2), such a party has the same rights as a participating party to challenge an award under
ss 67 and 68, and s 70(2) (the duty to exhaust arbitral procedures) does not apply in his case.
Where a party challenges an application to enforce an award against it in which it has not participated, inaction following the arbitrator's award, but prior to notice of the application to enforce,

---

262 *Mousaka Inc v Golden Seagull Maritime Inc* [2002] 1 WLR 395; [2001] 2 Lloyd's Rep 657.
263 [2002] EWCA Civ 405; [2002] 1 WLR 2397.
264 Per Colman J, *The Agios Dimitris* [2004] EWHC 2232 (Comm) para 6; [2005] 1 Lloyd's Rep 235.
265 Section 70(3).
266 [2009] EWHC 3318 (Comm); [2010] 1 Lloyd's Rep 533.

will not count against that party when seeking extensions of time.[267] A party will fall outside s 72 when it participates in either a hearing by the tribunal as to whether it has jurisdiction on the merits, or in a hearing on the merits and substance of the claim.[268]

Enforcement of domestic awards

Once a final award of an arbitral tribunal in England, Wales and Northern Ireland has been made it may be enforced, with permission of the court, in the same way as a judgment of the court, pursuant to s 66 of the 1996 Act.[269] Where the award is declaratory it may still, in appropriate circumstances, be enforced as a judgment under s 66. In *West Tankers v Allianz SPA*[270] the shipowners obtained a final arbitration award in England declaring that they were under no liability to insurers in respect of a collision which was the subject of parallel proceedings before a court in Italy. They then sought to convert the award into a judgment against the insurers with a view to blocking any enforcement in England of any potential future judgment against them in the Italian proceedings. Field J held that the declaratory award should be enforced as a judgment under s 66, because the shipowners' objective in doing so was to establish the primacy of a declaratory award over an inconsistent judgment. The court had jurisdiction to make a s 66 order 'because to do so will be to make a positive contribution to the securing of the material benefit of the award'. The decision has been upheld on appeal[271] and has been followed in *The London Steam-Ship Owners' Mutual Insurance Association Ltd v The Kingdom of Spain, The French State (The Prestige)(No 2)*.[272]

Section 66 (3) provides that:

> Permission to enforce an award shall not be given where, or to the extent that, the person against whom it is sought to be enforced shows that the tribunal lacked substantive jurisdiction to make the award. The right to raise such an objection may have been lost (see section 73).[273]

The burden of proof falls on the party resisting enforcement.

Enforcement of foreign awards

Part III of the 1996 Act gives effect to the provisions of the **1958 New York Convention** on the enforcement of arbitration awards. A foreign award made in a New York Convention country will be enforceable on provision of the duly authenticated original award and original arbitration agreement, or certified copies thereof. Section 103 lists various grounds on which the court may refuse to recognise a New York Convention award if the person against whom it is invoked proves:

(a) that a party to the arbitration agreement was (under the law applicable to him) under some incapacity;

---

267 *The London Steam-Ship Owners' Mutual Insurance Association Ltd v The Kingdom of Spain, The French State (The Prestige)* [2013] EWHC 2840 (Comm); [2014] 1 Lloyd's Rep 137. Walker J was also of the view that s 72(1) was not confined to matters before the issue of an award and that s 72(2) was subject to the time limits set out in s 70(3).

268 *Broda Agro Trade (Cyprus) Ltd v Alfred C Toepfer International GmbH* [2009] EWHC 3318 (Comm); [2010] 1 Lloyd's Rep 533.

269 '(1) An Award made by the tribunal pursuant to an arbitration agreement may, by permission of the court, be enforced in the same manner as a judgment or order of the court to the same effect. (2) Where permission is given, judgment may be entered in terms of the award.'

270 [2011] EWHC 829 (Comm); (2011) 161 NLJ 551.

271 [2012] EWCA Civ 27; [2012] 1 Lloyd's Rep 398.

272 [2013] EWHC 3188 (Comm); [2014] 1 Lloyd's Rep 309.

273 In *Sovarex SA v Romero Alvarez SA* [2011] EWHC 1661 (Comm); [2011] 2 Lloyd's Rep 320, the respondent's correspondence with the tribunal did no more than make it clear that the respondent was protesting the jurisdiction of the tribunal and asserting that it should decline jurisdiction and thus had not waived its rights under s 73.

(b) that the arbitration agreement was not valid under the law to which the parties subjected it or, failing any indication thereon, under the law of the country where the award was made;

(c) that he was not given proper notice of the appointment of the arbitrator or of the arbitration proceedings or was otherwise unable to present his case;

(d) that the award deals with a difference not contemplated by or not falling within the terms of the submission to arbitration or contains decisions on matters beyond the scope of the submission to arbitration (but see subsection (4)[274]);

(e) that the composition of the arbitral tribunal or the arbitral procedure was not in accordance with the agreement of the parties or, failing such agreement, with the law of the country in which the arbitration took place;

(f) that the award has not yet become binding on the parties, or has been set aside or suspended by a competent authority of the country in which, or under the law of which, it was made.

In *Dallah Real Estate & Tourism Holding Co v Pakistan*,[275] the Supreme Court held that the wording of s 103(2) required that the party wishing to challenge the recognition and enforcement of a Convention award had to be entitled to ask the court to reconsider all relevant evidence on the facts, including foreign law, rejecting the argument that some more limited review of the arbitrators' decision on their jurisdiction was desirable or necessary. An ICC award was made in France against the Government of Pakistan who had unsuccessfully argued that they were not party to the agreement with the claimant. The claimant then sought to enforce the award in England and the Government of Pakistan challenged enforcement under s 103(2)(b). As the agreement had not specified a choice of law, the law of France, as the seat of the arbitration, would be applied. The evidence showed that under French law the arbitration agreement did not bind the Government of Pakistan. Although the issue raised under s 103(2)(b) had already been considered by the French tribunal, that arbitral tribunal did not constitute a court of competent jurisdiction for the purpose of creating an issue estoppel, and the Government of Pakistan was not required to challenge the award before the French courts. No deference was to be given to the decision of the tribunal, and the English court had to rehear the issue of whether, under French law, there had been a submission to arbitration by the Government of Pakistan.

Applicable law

Arbitration on LMAA terms

It is common for shipping contracts to provide for London arbitration under the rules of the London Maritime Arbitration Association ('LMAA') terms. The 2012 terms came into effect for arbitrations commenced after 1 January 2012 and provide for the appointment of three arbitrators if the number of arbitrators is not specified in the arbitration clause, in contrast to the default position under the 1996 Arbitration Act of appointment of a sole arbitrator. The LMAA Small Claims Procedure can be used where neither the claim nor any counterclaim exceeds the sum of US$50,000 (excluding interest and costs). This provides for arbitration by a sole arbitrator and excludes the right of appeal. Costs recoverable will be assessed at a sum in the arbitrator's discretion not to exceed such sum as may be fixed by the Committee of the LMAA. The procedure is not suitable for complex claims or where there is likely to be examination of witnesses. There is also an intermediate procedure for claims with a value between US$50,000 and US$400,000. This constitutes an

---

274 'An award which contains decisions on matters not submitted to arbitration may be recognised or enforced to the extent that it contains decisions on matters submitted to arbitration which can be separated from those on matters not so submitted.'
275 [2010] UKSC 46; [2010] 2 WLR 805.

advance agreement by the parties to confine appeals to cases (a) where the appeal is alleged to involve a point of law of general interest or (b) where the tribunal certifies that the appeal involves a point of importance to the trade or industry in question. The intermediate procedure puts an upper limit on the parties' costs, calculated by reference to the monetary value of the parties' claims.

Choice of law in contract

The relevant principles will depend on when the contract was made. Where a contract was made after 1 April 1991, the applicable law would be ascertained in accordance with the provisions of the **Rome Convention**. Where a contract is made on or after 17 December 2009, the applicable law is ascertained in accordance with the provisions of **Regulation (EC) No 593/2008** on the law applicable to contractual obligations (the **Rome I Regulation**). However, the principles by which the applicable law was ascertained before these dates will also be examined, as they may still be relevant to arbitrations that are outside the scope of the Convention. Furthermore, it is likely that the English courts will bear these principles in mind in interpreting the Regulation, given the strong similarities between these principles and the provisions of the Regulation.

Pre-1 April 1991 contracts

The law of the contract is determined by applying general principles of private international law. If the contract contains an express choice of law clause, it will be upheld subject to public policy objections, such as those referred to in *dicta* in *The Hollandia*,[276] where the effect of upholding a choice of law clause would be to negate the law of the state that would otherwise apply. However, the courts will not recognise 'floating' choice of law clauses, which give one party to the contract the option to choose between different systems of law.[277] Clauses that merely give the defendant a choice of arbitration venue do not offend against this rule.[278]

The law of the contract may also be implied from a jurisdiction clause, but this presumption will be rebutted if the contract expressly provides for a law other than that of the chosen forum.[279] However, the presumption will not be rebutted merely by reason of the existence of close links between the dispute and another forum. In *The Komninos S*,[280] a cargo claim arose out of a voyage from Greece to Italy involving Greek shippers and a Greek management company of the ship, which was owned by a Cypriot company. Although Greece was the country with the closest connection to the dispute, the Court of Appeal held that this was insufficient to rebut the presumption that English law was to apply that was created by an express reference in the bill of lading to the jurisdiction of the 'British courts'.[281] English law may similarly be implied from the existence of an English arbitration clause.[282]

In the absence of an express or implied choice of law clause, the law with the 'closest and most real' connection with the dispute will be applied.[283] In identifying this law, the courts have taken the following factors into account: the residence and nationality of the parties; the place where the contract was made; the place where it was performed; and with charterparties, the law of the flag.[284]

---

276 [1983] 1 AC 565.
277 *The Iran Vojdan* [1984] 2 Lloyd's Rep 380.
278 *The Star Texas* [1993] 2 Lloyd's Rep 445, CA.
279 *Cie d'Armement Maritime SA v Cie Tunisienne de Navigation SA* [1971] AC 572.
280 [1991] 1 Lloyd's Rep 371.
281 Although, in the absence of the presumption, these factors would have led to the courts applying Greek law.
282 *Cie d'Armement Maritime SA v Cie Tunisienne de Navigation SA* [1971] AC 572.
283 *Bonython v Commonwealth of Australia* [1951] AC 201.
284 Bills of lading incorporating the provisions of the charter will be subject to the law chosen in the charterparty. See *The Njegos* [1936] P 90.

Contracts made between 1 April 1991 and 16 December 2009

The **Contracts (Applicable Law) Act 1990** applied the provisions of the Rome Convention to contracts made after this date, even if the parties or the contract had no connection with a Contracting State.[285] In most cases, the law applicable under the Act will be the same as that which would have been applicable before the Act.

The Rome I Regulation

The Rome Convention has now been replaced by **Regulation (EC) No 593/2008** on the law applicable to contractual obligations (Rome I). This came into force in the EU (except for Denmark) for all contracts concluded on or after 17 December 2009. The **Rome I Regulation** essentially replicates the Rome Convention as an EC Regulation. Article 1 provides that 'This Regulation shall apply, in situations involving a conflict of laws, to contractual obligations in civil and commercial matters.' It is possible that the term 'contractual obligations' is wide enough to encompass non-contractual claims in bailment.[286] If this is not the case, such claims would fall under the **Rome II Regulation**. The rules in the Regulation are of universal application and apply irrespective of whether the applicable law is that of a Member State.[287]

Article 1 is subject to various exceptions, two of which are relevant to the shipping lawyer. The first is to be found in Art 1(2)(d), 'obligations arising under bills of exchange, cheques and promissory notes and other negotiable instruments to the extent that the obligations under such other negotiable instruments arise out of their negotiable character'. This has to be read in conjunction with para (9) in the Preamble, 'Obligations under bills of exchange, cheques and promissory notes and other negotiable instruments should also cover bills of lading to the extent that the obligations under the bill of lading arise out of its negotiable character.' The reference to obligations under a bill of lading would seem to exclude the contractual rights of a lawful holder of bill of lading holder which are conferred by s 2(1) of **COGSA 1992** as these could be said to arise out of the negotiable character of the bill of lading.[288] Although the rights are created by statute, the statutory scheme is tied to the transferability of the bill of lading.[289] The common law rules would, therefore, apply, which would lead back to the law governing the original contract between the carrier and the consignor; which would be determined in accordance with the Regulation. The second is to be found in Art 1(2)(e) which excludes: '(e) arbitration agreements and agreements on the choice of court'.

The basic choice of law rule is to be found in Art 3(1), which now provides that 'The choice shall be made expressly or clearly demonstrated by the terms of the contract or the circumstances of the case', in contrast to the equivalent provision in the Rome Convention, which provided: 'The choice must be expressed or demonstrated with reasonable certainty by the terms of the contract or the circumstances of the case.'[290]

---

285 Article 2 of the Rome Convention.
286 Paragraph (7) of the Preamble mandates that the substantive scope of Rome I should be consistent with the Brussels Regulation EC 44/2001. In *Engler v Janus Versand GmbH* (Case C-27/02); [2005] ECR I-481, the ECJ construed 'relating to a contract' in Art 5(1) of the Brussels Convention as extending to a relationship between the parties which created close links of the same kind as those created by contract; there did not have to be a concluded contract between the parties. As against this, there is *Dresser UK Ltd v Falcongate Freight Management Ltd*, 'The Duke of Yare' [1992] QB 502, where the Court of Appeal held that a sub-bailment did not constitute an 'agreement' and so fell outside Art 17 of the Brussels Convention.
287 Article 2.
288 Strictly speaking, a bill of lading has no 'negotiable' character as its holder cannot obtain a better title to the goods than that possessed by the transferor.
289 Excluding the statutory vesting of rights, the only obligations that could be said to derive from the negotiable character of the bill of lading would be the carrier's obligation to deliver against surrender of an original bill of lading, which would mean that only misdelivery claims were excluded under para 1.
290 In *Egon Oldendorff v Libera Corp* [1996] 1 Lloyd's Rep 380, QB, the presence of an English arbitration clause was held to indicate that a choice of English law had been *demonstrated with reasonable certainty* under this provision of the Convention. The provisions of the Convention would not apply to the arbitration itself but were relevant when the plaintiff sought leave to serve proceedings on the defendant under Ord 11(1)(1)(d)(iii) (now PD 6b 3.1(5)) in respect of interlocutory relief.

Article 3(3) provides: 'Where all other elements relevant to the situation at the time of the choice are located in a country other than the country whose law has been chosen, the choice of the parties shall not prejudice the application of provisions of the law of that other country which cannot be derogated from by agreement.' Thus, if the English courts were faced with a contract where *all* of the relevant factors pointed to the law of Germany then, notwithstanding the parties' express choice of French law, they would give effect to mandatory provisions of German law, which were the equivalent, say, of the **Unfair Contract Terms Act 1977**, although in all other respects they would continue to apply French law. The provision is unlikely to be relevant in actions arising out of contracts of carriage, as these, by their nature, will generally involve performance in different jurisdictions. It would therefore be impossible to say that 'all the other elements relevant to the situation' were connected with either the country of loading or of discharge. Article 3(4) contains a similar provision with respect to the parties' choice of law not prejudicing the application of non-derogable provisions of Community law.

If no law is chosen under Art 3, Art 4(1) then states the law that will govern various specific types of contract, listed in headings (a) to (h).[291] For example, contracts for the sale of goods or for services are governed by the law of the habitual residence of the seller and service provider respectively. If the contract does not fall within this list, or falls under more than one of the headings, then para 2 applies 'the law of the country where the party required to effect the characteristic performance of the contract has his habitual residence'.

The law specified in these two paragraphs will not, however, necessarily govern the contract. Paragraph 3 provides that 'Where it is clear from all the circumstances of the case that the contract is manifestly more closely connected with a country other than that indicated in paragraphs 1 or 2, the law of that other country shall apply.' Where the applicable law cannot be determined under paras 1 and 2, para 4 applies the law of the country with which the contract is most closely connected. With respect to the equivalent provision in the Convention, Art 4(5), the approach of the English courts would appear to be to allow the displacement of the Art 4 presumptions in circumstances that clearly demonstrate the existence of connecting factors justifying the disregarding of the presumptions.[292] Any weaker legal threshold for the application of Art 4(5) would inevitably call into question the value of these legal presumptions. Articles 4(3) and (4) of the Regulation are likely to be applied in similar fashion.[293]

Specific provisions relating to the law applicable to contracts for the carriage of goods, which previously appeared in Art 4 of the Rome Convention, now appear in Art 5(1) as follows:

> To the extent that the law applicable to a contract for the carriage of goods has not been chosen in accordance with Article 3, the law applicable shall be the law of the country of habitual residence of the carrier, provided that the place of receipt or the place of delivery or the habitual residence of the consignor is also situated in that country. If those requirements are not met, the law of the country where the place of delivery as agreed by the parties is situated shall apply.

Unlike Art 4 of the Rome Convention, this article refers to the 'habitual residence' of the carrier and the consignor, rather than to their 'principal place of business', and to the place of 'receipt' and

---

291 Article 4 has a different structure to its equivalent in the Rome Convention but is likely to have a similar effect.

292 See *Samcrete Egypt Engineers and Contractors SAE v Land Rover Exports Ltd* [2001] EWCA Civ 2019; [2002] CLC 533, [45]; *Ennstone Building Products Ltd v Stanger Ltd* [2002] EWCA Civ 916; [2002] 1 WLR 3059, [41]; *Iran Continental Shelf Oil Company v IRI International Corporation* [2002] EWCA Civ 1024; [2004] 2 CLC 696, [82].

293 *Commercial Marine Piling Ltd v Pierse Contracting Ltd* [2009] EWHC 2241 (TCC); [2009] 2 Lloyd's Rep 659, is an example of the presumption being rebutted under the Convention. A claim was made against an Irish guarantor that had guaranteed the obligations of a party performing works in Northern Ireland. Under Art 4(2) the presumption was that the guarantee was governed by Irish law because the obligation to pay money was the performance which characterised the contract and that obligation was imposed upon the Irish guarantor. However, that presumption was ousted by Art 4(5) because the guarantee was more closely connected with England in that the place of payment under the guarantee was England.

'delivery' rather than to the place of 'loading' and 'discharge'. The second sentence of Art 5(1) is new. Recital 22 provides that, no change in substance is intended with respect to Article 4(4), third sentence, of the Rome Convention whereby single-voyage charterparties and other contracts the main purpose of which is the carriage of goods should be treated as contracts for the carriage of goods.[294] For the purposes of the Regulation, 'consignor' means to any person who enters into a contract of carriage with the carrier and 'the carrier' means the party to the contract who undertakes to carry the goods, whether or not he performs the carriage himself.

Article 9 deals with mandatory provisions of domestic law. Article 9(2) provides: 'Nothing in this Regulation shall restrict the application of the overriding mandatory provisions of the law of the forum'.[295] Thus, in a case like *The Hollandia*,[296] the English courts would be able to apply the provisions of **COGSA 1971**, notwithstanding that the **1990 Rome Convention** required them to apply the law of a country that was not a signatory to the Hague-Visby Rules. Article 9(3) of the Regulation, provides:

> Effect may be given to the overriding mandatory provisions of the law of the country where the obligations arising out of the contract have to be or have been performed, in so far as those overriding mandatory provisions render the performance of the contract unlawful. In considering whether to give effect to those provisions, regard shall be had to their nature and purpose and to the consequences of their application or non-application.

The reference to overriding mandatory provisions which 'render the performance of the contract unlawful' is considerably narrower than the previous reference in Art 7(1) of the Rome Convention to 'the mandatory rules of the law of another country with which the situation has a close connection, if and in so far as, under the law of the latter country, those rules must be applied whatever the law applicable to the contract'. Without this amendment the UK would have been unable to opt in to the Regulation, as the required uniform application of Council Regulations would not have been subject to any reservation by a Member State. Article 25, 'Relationship with existing international conventions', provides:

> 1. This Regulation shall not prejudice the application of international conventions to which one or more Member States are parties at the time when this Regulation is adopted and which lay down conflict-of-law rules relating to contractual obligations.

Accordingly, mandatory provisions as to the scope of application in existing conventions such as the Hague-Visby Rules will continue to have effect as regards conventions that were in force as at 17 December 2009 when the Regulation came into force.

Choice of law in tort

Torts committed before 1 November 1996

These were subject to the conflicts of law rules developed at common law. A tort that took place within the jurisdiction would be governed by English law.[297] Where there was a claim before the

---

294 In *Intercontainer Interfrigo SC (ICF) v Balkenende Oosthuizen BV* (C-133/08) [2010] QB 411, the ECJ held that these words in Art 4(4) of the 1980 Rome Convention can apply to a charterparty, other than a single voyage charterparty, but only when the main purpose of the contract was not merely to make available a means of transport, but the actual carriage of goods.
295 Article 7(2) of the Convention provided: 'Nothing in this Convention shall restrict the application of the rules of the law of the forum in a situation where they are mandatory irrespective of the law otherwise applicable to the contract.'
296 [1983] 1 AC 565.
297 *Metall und Rohstoff v Donaldson Lufkin & Jentrette Inc* [1990] 1 QB 391.

English courts involving a tort that took place outside the jurisdiction, the requirement of 'double actionability' had to be satisfied,[298] meaning that it must be actionable as a tort according to English law, and actionable (but not necessarily in tort) according to the law of the foreign country where it was done. In *Boys v Chaplin*,[299] the House of Lords held that, in certain situations, the tort need not be actionable under the law of the *lex loci delicti*. Although the precise *ratio* of the case is elusive, Lord Wilberforce's views that the courts should apply the law of the country that had the 'most significant connection' with the tort has been followed in subsequent cases.[300] In *Red Sea Insurance Co Ltd v Bouygues SA*,[301] the Privy Council went further and applied Lord Wilberforce's test, applying the law of the *lex loci delicti*, which was most closely connected with the tort, even though the tort would not have been actionable under the *lex loci fori*.

Where a tort took place on the high seas, the law of the vessel's flag would be the governing law. If, as with collisions, more than one vessel was involved, and the vessels were under different flags, the law maritime, in effect English law, would be applied. Where a tort took place within the territorial waters of a state, it would be governed by the law of that state.

Torts committed after 1 November 1996

From 1 November 1996 until the implementation of the **Rome II Regulation** on 11 January 2009, the law governing torts committed abroad is to be found in the **Private International Law (Miscellaneous Provisions) Act 1995**. Part III of the 1995 Act contains the rules for choosing the law to be used for determining issues relating to tort or (for the law of Scotland) delict. Section 9(2) provides that 'the characterisation for the purposes of private international law of issues arising in a claim as issues relating to tort or delict is a matter for the courts of the forum'. Section 10 abolishes the double actionability rule and the exception in *Boys v Chaplin*. Section 11(1) then sets out a general rule that 'the applicable law is the law of the country in which the events constituting the tort or delict in question occur'. Where elements of those events occur in different countries, s 11(2) provides that the applicable law under the general rule is as follows:

(a) for a cause of action in respect of personal injury caused to an individual or death resulting from personal injury,[302] the law of the country where the individual was when he sustained the injury;

(b) for a cause of action in respect of damage to property, the law of the country where the property was when it was damaged; and

(c) in any other case, the law of the country in which the most significant element or elements of those events occurred.

Section 12(1) then provides for the general rule to be displaced if the law of another country is substantially more appropriate as the applicable law. In determining this, s 12(2) requires account to be taken of 'factors relating to the parties, to any of the events which constitute the tort or delict in question or to any of the circumstances or consequences of those events'.[303] The Act does not

---

298 See *Phillips v Eyre* [1870] LR 6 QB 1.

299 [1971] AC 356.

300 For example, *Coupland v Arabian Gulf Petroleum Co* [1983] 3 All ER 226, CA.

301 [1994] 3 All ER 749.

302 Section 11(3) provides that 'personal injury' includes disease or any impairment of physical or mental condition.

303 In *Roerig v Valiant Trawlers Ltd* [2002] EWCA Civ 21; [2002] 1 All ER 961, CA, the Court of Appeal held that the wording 'substantially' meant that the law determined by s 11 should not be easily displaced. The claim was brought by the widow of a Dutch employee who was killed in an accident on a trawler that was registered in England and owned by the English defendant company. The court refused to displace the application of English law under s 11, in spite of the case's significant connections with the Netherlands. In contrast, in *Trafigura Behave BV v Kookmin Bank* [2006] EWHC 1450 (Comm); [2006] 2 Lloyd's Rep 455, s 11 was held to be displaced by s 12 in an action arising out of the seller issuing new bills of lading in Singapore after the buyer, who had taken delivery of the goods without production of bills of lading, noticed discrepancies in the bills of lading. Section 11 indicated the application of Singaporean law as this was where the seller had arranged for the issue of new bills of lading, but the close nexus between the alleged tort and the web of contracts such as the letter of credit, the bill of lading and the charterparty, all of which were subject to English law, meant that s 12 displaced s 11.

apply to torts committed on the high seas which are not subject to the rules in ss 11 and 12 which refer to the law of a 'country', or to torts committed in England. These continued to be governed by the common law rules outlined above.[304]

There are two situations in which the courts will not apply a foreign law, notwithstanding that this is indicated by the application of the analysis undertaken under ss 11 and 12. First, s 14(3)(a) provides that a foreign law will not be applied if to do so would involve a 'conflict with principles of public policy'. Secondly, s 14(3)(b) provides that nothing in Part III of the Act shall affect 'any rules of evidence, pleading or practice' or authorise 'questions of procedure in any proceedings to be determined otherwise than in accordance with the law of the forum'.

The Rome II Regulation

Tort proceedings now fall under **Regulation (EC) No 864/2007** on the law applicable to non-contractual obligations (Rome II). The Regulation applies only to events giving rise to damage which occurred on, or after, 11 January 2009.[305]

Article 3 provides for the universal application of any law specified by the Regulation, whether or not it is the law of a Member State.[306] The general rule is to be found in Art 4.1, as follows:

> Unless otherwise provided for in this Regulation, the law applicable to a non-contractual obligation arising out of a tort/delict shall be the law of the country in which the damage occurs irrespective of the country in which the event giving rise to the damage occurred and irrespective of the country or countries in which the indirect consequences of that event occur.

The reference to 'the law of the country in which the damage occurs' means that the existing common law conflicts rules, as modified by the 1995 Act, will continue to apply to torts committed on the high seas. Where the claimant and the defendant both have their habitual residence in the same country at the time the damage occurs, Art 4.2 then applies the law of that country. An 'escape route' from these rules is provided in Art 4.3 which provides:

> Where it is clear from all the circumstances of the case that the tort/delict is manifestly more closely connected with a country other than that indicated in paragraphs 1 or 2, the law of that other country shall apply. A manifestly closer connection with another country might be based in particular on a pre-existing relationship between the parties, such as a contract, that is closely connected with the tort/delict in question.

Where a claim is made in respect of environmental damage, Art 7 provides for the application of Art 4.1 but gives the claimant the option of basing the claim on the law of the country in which the event giving rise to the damage occurred.

The conditions for displacement of the general rule are similar to those in s 12(1) of the 1996 Act. Article 15(c) provides that questions of damages are covered by the applicable law under the Regulation. This reverses the previous position under English law where such issues were dealt with under the law of the forum. Article 16 preserves the application of the mandatory rules of the law of the forum. Article 26 preserves the application of the public policy of the forum.

---

304 Section 14(2).
305 *Homawoo v GMF Assurances SA* (C-412/10) ECJ (Fourth Chamber) [2011] E.C.R. I-11603; [2012] I.L.Pr. 2.
306 Article 25(2) provided that Member States are not obliged to apply the Regulation to cases that give rise to conflicts solely between separate territorial units located within them. The UK has, however, decided to apply the Regulation to such internal conflicts by SI No 2986, Private International Law – The Law Applicable to Non-Contractual Obligations (England and Wales and Northern Ireland) Regulations 2008; and SI No 404, Private International Law – The Law Applicable to Non-Contractual Obligations (Scotland) Regulations 2008.

Chapter 19

Security and Interim Relief

A claimant who has obtained a final judgment from the English High Court or a final English arbitration award will be able to enforce it against assets of the defendant within the jurisdiction in accordance with the provisions of Rules of the Supreme Court (RSC) Orders 45 and 46, which are retained in Sched 1 to the Civil Procedure Rules (CPR).[1] Enforcement in foreign jurisdictions will depend upon the existence of reciprocal arrangements between that country and the UK, relating to the mutual recognition of and enforcement of judgments. Where enforcement is sought before the courts of another Member State under the Judgments Regulation, the matter is governed by Chapter III thereof. Where enforcement is sought in a state that is not a Member State under the Judgments Regulation, the matter is governed either by the **Administration of Justice Act 1920** or the **Foreign Judgments (Reciprocal Enforcement) Act 1933**.[2] Where the claimant seeks to enforce an English arbitration award abroad, the matter is governed by the **New York Convention 1958**, the provisions of which are implemented by the **Arbitration Act 1996**.[3]

However, the above provisions will be of no use to a claimant if the defendant no longer has any assets by the time at which a judgment or arbitration award comes to be enforced. To avoid ending up with such a 'pyrrhic' victory, a claimant will need to invoke the jurisdiction of the English courts for the purposes of securing its claim prior to the substantive hearing of that claim. It can do this in one of two ways. It can invoke the in rem jurisdiction of the Admiralty court to arrest the defendant's vessel or cargo within the territorial waters of England and Wales. Alternatively, it can invoke the in personam jurisdiction of the Commercial Court to obtain a freezing order (formerly known as a Mareva injunction), restricting the defendant from disposing of its assets pending a final judgment or arbitration award in the matter. Both procedures are available to a claimant, even when the substantive dispute is referred to arbitration or should be heard by a foreign court.

This chapter will now consider these interim (formerly 'interlocutory') remedies in turn. It will conclude by examining three other forms of relief: inspection of property; security for costs; and applications by the claimant for an anti-suit injunction to prevent the defendant from bringing or continuing proceedings in a foreign forum.

Arrest

A warrant of arrest is available as of right when an in rem writ is issued. It is no longer conditional, as used to be the case, upon the claimant making full and frank disclosure of material facts at the time that it applies for the arrest.[4] All that the claimant needs to do is to swear an affidavit setting out the matters listed in CPR Pt 61, PD 5.3.[5] Where the claimant seeks to use the English courts merely to secure its claim, it may do so before it commences its substantive proceedings elsewhere.[6] However, it must still commence its proceedings before the English courts within the applicable time limit. A claimant who successfully uses the in rem procedure to secure its claim is not thereby obliged to have the substantive claim heard by the Admiralty Court. It may apply to stay the substantive proceedings, in the same manner as is open to the defendant.[7] Where a stay is ordered,

---

1   CPR Pt 62.18 deals with the enforcement of arbitration awards.
2   Recognition and enforcement in the English courts of judgments obtained in countries that are not covered by either of these statutes depend on common law principles. In very general terms, enforcement will depend upon whether the defendant was present in the foreign state in question or submitted to the jurisdiction of its courts.
3   A wider range of countries is covered by the Convention than under the statutory provisions relating to reciprocal recognition of judgments. This is one reason why many in the shipping industry still prefer to arbitrate, despite the fact that the costs of doing so invariably exceed the costs of litigating in the High Court.
4   Such as the fact that other proceedings in the same matter have been commenced in another jurisdiction. See *The Andria now renamed The Vasso* [1984] QB 477.
5   *The Varna* [1993] 2 Lloyd's Rep 253.
6   The value of the res is limited to the amount that the vessel would fetch in a forced sale at the port of arrest. See *The Bumbesti* [1999] 2 Lloyd's Rep 481, 489.
7   *Attorney General v Anderson* (1988) The Independent, 31 March, although Sheen J expressed disapproval of such a course of action in *The Sylt* [1991] 1 Lloyd's Rep 240. See, also, Jackson, *Enforcement of Maritime Claims*, 2nd edn, 1996, London: LLP, 303.

CPR Pt 61.12 provides for the continuance of any arrest or the maintenance of any security, unless the court orders otherwise. A shipowner who wishes to prevent its ship from being arrested can do so by entering a caution against arrest under CPR Pt 61.7 against its undertaking to file an acknowledgment of service and to give sufficient security to satisfy the claim with interest and with costs.

The property to be arrested will usually be a ship within the territorial waters of the UK. However, other forms of property may also be arrested. For example, a salvor will be able to arrest cargo to secure its claim for salvage services against cargo interests. Service of in rem proceedings serves the dual function of enabling the claimant to obtain security from the defendant by the arrest procedure. Arrest may only be effected by the Admiralty Marshal or his substitute, after the claimant has obtained a warrant of arrest from the court.[8] The res will be detained until the defendant gives security to the claimant for its claim, up to the value of the res. Failing this, the Admiralty Marshal can order the res to be sold and its proceeds distributed among the defendant's creditors. An order for sale may be made pendente lite before judgment even if opposed by the shipowner, but such an order will not be made except for good reason.[9] Sale will usually be by way of auction, although in exceptional circumstances the sale can be made direct by the court.[10] The purchaser of the vessel in a court sale will take free of all prior claims.[11] The claimant who has effected the arrest will be treated as a secured creditor in this distribution. Where the res is a state-owned ship, s 10 of the **State Immunity Act 1978** removes the general rules of sovereign immunity if the ship under arrest was, at the time that the cause of action arose, in use for 'commercial' purposes.[12]

A question arises as to whether a party arresting a vessel owes any duty towards either the owner of that vessel or the owners of the cargo on board the vessel at the time of the arrest. These issues arose in the litigation arising out of a mortgagee bank's arrest of the Tropical Reefer in Panama at a time when the vessel was carrying a cargo of bananas to Germany. The owners, who were heavily in default under the mortgage, were unable to put up security and the court in Panama ordered the sale of the vessel. This necessitated the dumping at sea of the cargo of bananas. In The Tropical Reefer, the Court of Appeal held that the bank, as mortgagor, was entitled to decide when to sell the mortgaged property, without regard to the interests of the shipowner.[13] Panama was not an inappropriate place for selling ships. To have released the vessel and allowed her to complete her voyage to Germany would have been fraught with peril, as the vessel's P&I cover had been withdrawn. Nor could the shipowner rely on the fact that the sale in Panama might have rendered the mortgagee liable to the bill of lading holders. This issue was to come before the court in the next round of the litigation in Anton Durbeck GmbH v Den Norske Bank ASA.[14] Christopher Clarke J held that the applicable law was that of Panama, under which a bill of lading holder could sue a party that had legitimately arrested a vessel if the arrest was carried out in bad faith or with the intention of harming the bill of lading holder. However, it was not enough that an arrest would be likely to cause damage to cargo. There was, therefore, no liability under Panamanian law. Nor would there have been any liability under English law, as the mortgagee's security would have been impaired had the vessel been released from arrest and allowed to sail to Hamburg without P&I cover.

---

8 CPR Pt 61.5(8).
9 The Myrto (No 1) [1977] 2 Lloyd's Rep 243, 260 (QB), where Brandon J gave as an example '[u]nless a sale is ordered, heavy and continuing costs of maintaining the arrest will be incurred over a long period, with consequent substantial diminution in the value of the plaintiffs' security for their claim'.
10 In The Union Gold [2013] EWHC 1696 (Admlty); [2014] 1 Lloyd's Rep 53, Teare J held that special circumstances would be needed to justify a sale to a direct buyer. An example would be where a particularly valuable charter would be lost if sale were delayed.
11 The Acrux [1962] 1 Lloyd's Rep 405, QB.
12 Where a 'sister ship' is arrested, both ships must satisfy this requirement.
13 [2003] EWCA Civ 1559; [2004] 1 Lloyd's Rep 1.
14 [2005] EWHC 2497; [2006] 1 Lloyd's Rep 93.

Priorities

CPR Pt 61.10 provides that any party to an action in rem may, at any stage, apply for an order for the survey, appraisement or sale of a ship.[15] If an arrested vessel has to be sold by the Admiralty Marshal because no bail is put up for her release, the proceeds of sale will be distributed in the following order:

(a) Admiralty Marshal's costs;
(b) statutory claims of harbour authorities;
(c) maritime liens in the following order:

- damage liens, except where a salvage lien is subsequently created[16] (inter se damage liens rank equally);
- salvage liens (priority is in inverse order of attachment – that is, priority to later salvors);
- wages and master's disbursements lien;[17]
- bottomry and respondentia (priority is in inverse order of attachment. Where there is a conflict with a salvage lien, both types of lien rank equally. However, in The Ruta,[18] Steel J held that there were no fixed rules for assessing priority as between competing holders of maritime liens. Priority depended on the merits of each case. On the facts before him, the wages claimants took priority over the damage claimants because they had no alternative means of redress, and public policy should aim to discourage the disembarkation of crew members when a vessel is arrested);

(d) mortgages:

- registered (in order of registration);
- equitable (in order in which made);

(e) statutory liens.

The balance, if any, is distributed to the judgment creditors of the shipowner[19] and then to the shipowner. A possessory lien[20] is enforceable against any interest subsequently acquired, even against a subsequent maritime lien.[21] Exceptionally, costs incurred after sale of the res may be awarded. Such costs will only be accorded priority, after those of the Admiralty Marshal, if they were incurred for the general benefit of all claimants on the fund and were incurred primarily for the preservation or enhancement of the fund as a whole, rather than for the benefit of the party incurring the costs.[22]

Effect of a stay on provision of security

Where the substantive dispute is to be heard in a foreign court or in arbitration, the claimant will still need to have recourse to the English courts to obtain security for its claim by an action in rem. If that action is stayed or dismissed, that will affect the validity of the arrest. In such a case, the property under arrest will be released. If the stay or dismissal occurs after the provision of bail or

---

15 See, also, CPR PD 61.10.
16 The Inna [1938] P 148.
17 The master's claim ranks equally with that of his crew. See The Royal Wells [1984] 2 Lloyd's Rep 255.
18 [2000] 1 Lloyd's Rep 359, QB.
19 In The James W Elwell [1921] P 351, judgment creditors in in personam proceedings obtained priority over an in rem claim for necessaries that only became secured, by issue of the writ, after the claims of the judgment creditors had become secured.
20 Such as a ship repairer's lien over a ship in respect of repair charges, or a shipowner's lien over cargo in respect of freight or general average contributions.
21 The Tergeste [1903] P 26.
22 The Ocean Glory [2002] 2 Lloyd's Rep 679, QB, where such costs were not awarded.

other security, then the court will order that such security be surrendered. Where the stay is discretionary, as in cases involving the principles of *forum non conveniens*, the court can make the stay conditional on the retention or provision of security.

However, where a mandatory stay is involved, as with cases subject to arbitration or cases falling under Art 29 of the **Judgments Regulation**, this option is not available to the courts. *A fortiori* it will not be available when the court dismisses the proceedings on the grounds that another Member State has jurisdiction under the Judgments Regulation or that the claim falls outside the *in rem* jurisdiction of the Admiralty Court, as defined by ss 20–21 of the **Senior Courts Act 1981**.

A way around the problem, as it related to disputes subject to arbitration, was found by Brandon J in *The Rena K*,[23] which was subsequently endorsed by the Court of Appeal in *The Tuyuti*.[24] Although the stay of proceedings would be unconditional, the stay of the warrant of arrest could be made conditional if the claimant could establish that there was a likelihood that the *in rem* proceedings would be revived after an award was eventually obtained. This would involve showing that the defendant was unlikely to be able to satisfy the award.

A more direct solution was provided by s 26 of the **Civil Jurisdiction and Judgments Act 1982**, which allowed the court to do one of two things when it stayed or dismissed Admiralty proceedings 'on the ground that the dispute in question should be submitted to arbitration or to the determination of the courts of another part of the UK or of an overseas country' if, in those proceedings, 'property has been arrested or bail or other security has been given to prevent or to obtain the release from arrest'.

The discretion given to the court operates in two ways. Under s 26(1)(a), it can order the retention of the arrested property as security. If it does this, s 26(2) empowers it to attach 'such conditions to the order as it thinks fit, in particular conditions with respect to the institution or prosecution of the relevant arbitration of legal proceedings'. This proviso conflicts with the provisions of the **1958 New York Convention** and has been omitted from s 11 of the **Arbitration Act 1996**, which otherwise re-enacts the provisions of s 26.

Alternatively, under s 26(1)(b), the court can make the stay conditional on 'the provision of equivalent security for the satisfaction of any such award or judgment'. This option is not available to the court when the defendant is entitled to a mandatory stay or to have the proceedings dismissed. A potential weakness in s 26 is that it takes effect only if the claimant has already arrested the defendant's property or obtained security. There is nothing in the section to allow the court, when staying proceedings, to order provision of security when none has hitherto been provided. The solution to this lacuna is to allow a temporary lifting of the stay to allow a claimant to effect an arrest.[25]

The discretion does not cover cases in which the court never had jurisdiction because the claim fell outside the provisions of ss 20–21 of the **Senior Courts Act 1981**. However, the reference to proceedings being 'stayed or *dismissed*' indicates that the statutory discretion does cover cases where the claim falls within ss 20–21 of the **Senior Courts Act 1981**, but the Admiralty Court is deprived of jurisdiction by reason of the provisions of the **Judgments Regulation**.[26] This conclusion is supported by Art 33 of the Judgments Regulation itself, which provides:

---

23 [1979] QB 377.
24 [1984] QB 838. Both decisions rejected the idea that the court's powers under s 12(6)(h) of the Arbitration Act 1950 gave it any jurisdiction to issue a warrant of arrest in connection with arbitration proceedings.
25 *The Silver Athens (No 2)* [1986] 2 Lloyd's Rep 583, where the plaintiff was allowed to re-arrest after it had to return security from a previous arrest after the defendant had stayed the Admiralty proceedings at a time shortly before the coming into force of s 26.
26 In cases such as *The Deichland* [1990] 1 QB 361 and *The Po* [1991] 2 Lloyd's Rep 206, where the substantive jurisdiction of the Admiralty Court was challenged on Brussels Convention grounds, no attempt was made to ask the court to order that the security provided for the claim be returned.

Application may be made to the courts of a Member State for such provisional, including protective, measures as may be available under the law of that State, even if, under this Regulation, the courts of another Member State have jurisdiction as to the substance of the matter.[27]

Although arrest, under the domestic rules on jurisdiction, is intimately bound up with the process of establishing substantive jurisdiction, it has no role in establishing jurisdiction under the Judgments Regulation.[28] Therefore, it is fair to categorise it as a 'provisional' or 'protective' measure for the purposes of Art 33.[29]

It must be stressed that s 26 merely confers a discretion on the court and gives the claimant no entitlement to the retention of security obtained in in rem proceedings. The discretion will be exercised against the claimant where its claim is likely to fail, as where the substantive claim in the foreign jurisdiction turns out to be time-barred.[30] It will not be exercised against the claimant merely by reason of the fact that the res is heavily mortgaged, making it unlikely that the claimant will recover anything from its value.[31]

If the court does exercise its discretion in favour of the claimant, it will not generally require the claimant to give a cross-undertaking in damages,[32] but it may do so where the arrest is maintained as a holding operation pending provision of evidence as to the merits of the substantive claim in the foreign jurisdiction.[33]

The freezing order

In The Mareva,[34] the Court of Appeal invoked the court's inherent jurisdiction to grant an injunction ordering a foreign defendant not to transfer out of the jurisdiction any assets that it might have there up to the amount of the plaintiff's claim. The injunction would not be given as of right, but only where the court was satisfied that there was a real risk that, but for its intervention, any judgment that the plaintiff might ultimately receive would prove unsatisfied.

The Mareva injunction (now the freezing order) was given statutory recognition by s 37(3) of the **Senior Courts Act 1981**, and its scope has subsequently been expanded by the courts. The injunction is now available, whatever the nationality of the defendant,[35] and can cover the risk that the defendant's assets may be dissipated within the jurisdiction.[36] Although primarily used as an interim remedy, a freezing order can also be used in connection with the enforcement of a final judgment or arbitration award.

It was previously the case that if it was not possible to bring the substantive proceedings within the English jurisdiction, the courts lacked jurisdiction to grant injunctive relief.[37] This unfortunate position was, however, reversed by s 25 of the **Civil Jurisdiction and Judgments Act 1982**, which empowers the English courts to grant interim relief (for example, in the form of freezing orders)

---

27 Formerly Art 24 of the Brussels Convention.
28 Especially given the provisions of Art 3 of the Judgments Regulation and the ruling of the European Court of Justice in The Maciej Rataj (sub nom The Tatry) [1995] 1 Lloyd's Rep 302 that, for the purposes of Art 21 (now Art 27), it is immaterial that one action is brought in personam and another action in rem.
29 See Jackson, op cit fn 7, 306–8.
30 The Havhelt [1993] 1 Lloyd's Rep 523.
31 Ibid.
32 The Bazias 3 [1993] QB 673.
33 The Havhelt [1993] 1 Lloyd's Rep 523, where the defendant argued that the plaintiff's claim would be time-barred under the Hague Rules as construed by Norwegian law.
34 [1975] 2 Lloyd's Rep 509. The injunction falls under CPR Pt 25.1(f).
35 Rahman v Abu-Taha [1980] 1 WLR 1268, CA.
36 Z Ltd v A-Z and AA-LL [1982] QB 558, QB.
37 The Siskina [1979] AC 210.

in circumstances in which proceedings have been commenced or are to be commenced in a foreign jurisdiction. In exceptional circumstances, the injunction may be granted, even in respect of assets outside the jurisdiction, the so-called 'worldwide freezing order'.[38]

The order is usually made *ex parte* with only the claimant appearing before the judge. Where appropriate, the claimant's application will be combined with any application for leave from the court to serve a defendant out of the jurisdiction under CPR Pt 6.36. The claimant may also combine the application with a request that the court order the defendant to make disclosure as to its assets within the jurisdiction.

The claimant must provide an affidavit that sets out the matters on which it bases its claim to the injunction and a draft of the order it seeks from the court. It must make full disclosure of all matters within its knowledge that might be relevant to the court. If the court decides to grant the freezing order, the claimant must notify the defendant and any third party, such as a bank, which holds assets of the defendant.[39] After notification, any defendant or third party that fails to comply with the terms of the order will be liable for contempt of court. It is important to stress the *personal* nature of the remedy. A claimant who has obtained a freezing order over assets of the defendant obtains no security interest in those assets. Its status remains that of an unsecured creditor.[40] The defendant may subsequently apply to have the freezing order varied or discharged at an *inter partes* hearing.

The elements of a domestic freezing order

For a domestic freezing order to be granted, the following conditions must be established:

(a) The claimant must establish that it has an existing cause of action against the defendant, in the sense of an actual or threatened invasion of legal or equitable rights.[41] Accordingly, a freezing order may not be granted when the claimant fears that the defendant is going to break a contractual obligation in the future. In this context, Staughton LJ in *Zucker v Tyndall Holdings*[42] distinguished between a threat to break a contractual obligation that is presently performable and a threat to break a contractual obligation that is not presently performable. Only in the former situation does the court have power to grant a freezing order.

(b) The claimant must establish that it has a good arguable case against the defendant. Mustill J in *The Niedersachsen*[43] defined this as 'a case that is more than barely capable of serious argument and yet not necessarily one that the judge believes to have a better than 50 per cent chance of success'. Further, it is insufficient for an applicant merely to point to a potential cause of action; the court must be assured of the applicant's intention to institute proceedings for substantive relief. A freezing order that does not contain directions regarding the institution of primary proceedings will accordingly be liable to be set aside on application by the respondent.[44]

(c) The claimant must establish a real risk that any ultimate judgment against the defendant will prove unenforceable unless a freezing order is granted. In *The Niedersachsen*, Mustill J[45] set out in broad terms what the claimant needs to show:

---

38 *Babanaft International v Bassatne* [1990] Ch 13, CA.
39 A third party can also be directly enjoined by the injunction if it has been joined to the action against the defendant by a third-party notice. See Devonshire, P, 'Third parties holding assets subject to a Mareva' (1996) LMCLQ 268.
40 *Cretanor Maritime Co Ltd v Irish Marine Management Ltd* [1978] 1 WLR 966.
41 *The Veracruz 1* [1992] 1 Lloyd's Rep 353, CA.
42 [1992] 1 WLR 1127, 1136.
43 [1983] 2 Lloyd's Rep 600, 605; aff'd [1983] 1 WLR 1412, CA.
44 *Fourie v Le Roux* [2007] UKHL 1; [2007] 1 WLR 320, HL.
45 [1983] 2 Lloyd's Rep 600, 606–7.

It is not enough for the plaintiff to assert a risk that the assets will be dissipated. He must demonstrate this by solid evidence. This evidence may take a number of forms. It may consist of direct evidence that the defendant has previously acted in a way which shows his probity is not to be relied on. Or the plaintiff may show what type of company the defendant is (where it is incorporated, what are its corporate structure and assets, and so on) so as to raise an inference that the company is not to be relied upon. Or, again, the plaintiff may be able to found his case on the fact that inquiries about the characteristics of the defendant have led to a blank wall. Precisely what form the evidence may take will depend upon the particular circumstances of the case. But the evidence must always be there. Mere proof that the company is incorporated abroad, accompanied by the allegation that there are no reachable assets in the United Kingdom apart from those which it is sought to enjoin, will not be enough.

On the facts of the case, at an inter partes hearing, the claimant had failed to show the necessary risk. Although the defendant, a West German corporation, had not given adequate evidence as to its financial set-up, it was under no obligation to do so. What was more significant was that the corporate group to which the defendant belonged was of a good reputation and had never defaulted on its debts. In contrast, the requirement was satisfied in Barclay-Johnson v Yuill,[46] where the English defendant had left the country and was living on a yacht in the Mediterranean. There was no information available as to when he might return, but there was evidence that he had gone to the USA when in previous financial difficulties.

The claimant must identify, in its affidavit, its grounds for believing that the defendant has assets within the jurisdiction.[47] However, any freezing order will cover all of the defendant's assets within the jurisdiction up to the amount of the claimant's claim and will not be limited to the specific assets identified in the affidavit. 'Assets' includes money, shares, securities, bills of exchange, ships, vehicles and stock in trade. In this regard, proof of the existence of an overdrawn bank account has been held to be sufficient.[48]

(d) A fair balance between the interests of the claimant and those of the defendant and third parties must be maintained. The granting of a freezing order will have a draconian effect on the defendant's business. It is vital, therefore, particularly at an ex parte hearing, that due consideration is given to the interests of the defendant and any third party that will be affected by the injunction. For this reason, the claimant is always required to undertake to pay damages to the defendant if it is later established that the injunction should not have been granted and to indemnify third parties in respect of any costs incurred in complying with the injunction. As 'costs' do not cover consequential losses, the Practice Direction on Mareva injunctions (now freezing orders) issued in 1994[49] adds the following proviso to the standard undertaking regarding third-party costs: '. . . if the court later finds that this Order has caused such a person loss, and decides that the person should be compensated for the loss, the plaintiff will comply with any Order the court may make.' In an appropriate case, the claimant may be required to back up these undertakings with suitable security. However, notwithstanding the provision of an undertaking by the claimant, compliance with the terms of a freezing order may cause problems for third parties such as banks, particularly if compliance will involve a breach of the law of another country. In Bank of China v NBM LLC,[50] the Court of Appeal recognised that the claimant's standard undertaking to such a third party would not

46 [1980] 1 WLR 1259.
47 The Genie [1979] 2 Lloyd's Rep 184.
48 Third Chandris Shipping Corporation v Unimarine SA [1979] QB 645.
49 [1994] 1 WLR 1233, Annex 2.
50 [2001] EWCA Civ 1916; [2002] 1 Lloyd's Rep 506, CA.

adequately compensate it in respect of damage to its reputation and regulatory consequences abroad. Accordingly, it allowed the standard order to be varied to allow the third-party bank 'to comply with what it reasonably believed to be its obligations, contracted or otherwise, under the laws and obligations of the country or State where the assets were situated or under the proper law of any bank account in question and [with] any orders of the courts of that country or State, provided reasonable notice of any application for such an order by [the bank] or any of its subsidiaries . . . is given to the claimant's solicitors'.

Defendants will be allowed to draw on their assets to cover their reasonable living expenses not exceeding a specified sum. They will also be allowed to continue to meet their ordinary trade debts provided that this is not in conflict with the underlying policy of the freezing order.[51] However, once a claimant has obtained judgment in its favour, it would appear that the defendant is no longer free to dispose of its assets in the ordinary course of business.[52]

Where a freezing order is directed at assets other than funds in a bank account, the resultant prejudice to the defendant and third parties may be such as to make a court refuse an order altogether. Thus, in The Eleftherios,[53] a Mareva injunction was discharged against a ship belonging to the defendant that was in a UK port at the time of the ex parte proceedings because of the prejudice to the business of the third parties involved, such as the owners of the cargo on board at the time.

Freezing orders in support of arbitration or foreign proceedings

A freezing order may be granted where the substantive proceedings will not be heard by the English courts in two situations. The first is in support of arbitration, whether in England or abroad, by virtue of s 44 of the **Arbitration Act 1996**. The second is in support of proceedings in another state, whether or not that state is a Member State under the Judgments Regulation. This jurisdiction initially derived from Art 24 of the **1968 Brussels Convention** (now Art 31 of the **Judgments Regulation**), as implemented by s 25 of the **Civil Jurisdiction and Judgments Act 1982**. As of 1 April 1997, Art 24 was extended to proceedings in all states through the **1997 Civil Jurisdiction and Judgments Act Order**.[54] It is likely that this provision can be used to justify the grant of a freezing order in connection with a judgment obtained in another Convention State, despite the potential conflict with the provisions of Art 22(5).[55]

Following the decision of the European Court of Justice in Van Uden Maritime BV v Kommanditgesellschaft in Firma Deco-Line,[56] the courts are empowered to grant interim relief under Art 33 of the Judgments Regulation in circumstances in which parties have agreed to refer their substantive disputes to arbitration. Such applications fall outside the general exception of the application of the Regulation to arbitration in Art 1(2)(d), since provisional measures do not concern arbitration as such, but rather the protection of a wide variety of rights.[57]

'Worldwide' freezing orders

To obtain a freezing order over assets outside the jurisdiction, the claimant must satisfy all of the requirements necessary to obtain a domestic freezing order, and must furthermore convince the

---

51 Iraqi Ministry of Defence v Arcepey [1981] QB 65.
52 Camdex International Ltd v Bank of Zambia (No 2) [1997] 1 WLR 632, CA.
53 [1982] 1 Lloyd's Rep 351.
54 SI 1997/1302.
55 See dicta of Kerr LJ to this effect in Babanaft International v Bassatne [1990] Ch 13, 35, which dealt with the equivalent provision of Art 16(5) of the 1968 Brussels Convention.
56 Case C-391/95 [1998] ECR I-7091.
57 As long as the nature of these rights is regarded as falling within the material scope of the Regulation by the national court.

court that theirs is a special case, such as to justify the court in exercising what is, in effect, an extra-territorial jurisdiction. The courts have proved more ready to grant these injunctions when propri-etary claims are involved[58] or in support of judgments for a limited duration to enable the claimant time within which to obtain interim relief in the courts having jurisdiction over the defendant's assets. In appropriate situations, the court has gone beyond ordering the defendant not to remove assets from a foreign jurisdiction to ordering it to transfer assets from one foreign jurisdiction to another.[59]

A worldwide freezing order may be granted in support of substantive proceedings in another jurisdiction. From 1 April 1997, the courts have possessed the discretion, where 'expedient', to make such an order in respect of proceedings in *any* foreign jurisdiction under the amended version of s 25 of the **Civil Jurisdiction and Judgments Act 1982**. In *Credit Suisse Fides Trust v Cuoghi*,[60] the Court of Appeal reviewed its discretion under the unamended s 25.[61] It concluded that exceptional circumstances did not need to exist before the courts could exercise their discretion. On the facts before it, the discretion was correctly used to order an extra-territorial freezing order, even when the Swiss courts, which were to hear the substantive dispute, did not themselves possess the juris-diction to grant such extra-territorial relief. But where the claimant chooses not to apply to the courts that will hear the substantive dispute for freezing order-type relief against assets within the jurisdiction of those courts, the English courts have not been inclined to grant a worldwide freezing order.[62]

More recently, further guidance on the application of the test of 'expediency' laid down by s 25 of the **Civil Jurisdiction and Judgments Act 1982** was given by the Court of Appeal in *Motorola Credit Corporation v Uzan (No 6)*.[63] There, Potter LJ was of the view that, when considering whether it was inexpedient to grant interim relief in support of foreign proceedings, the court exercising its discretion should bear in mind:

(a)   whether the making of the order would interfere with the management of the case in the primary court;

(b)   whether it was the policy in the primary jurisdiction not itself to grant the relief sought;

(c)   whether there was a danger that the orders made would give rise to disharmony or confusion and/or the risk of conflicting, inconsistent or overlapping orders in other jurisdictions;

(d)   whether, at the time that the order was sought, there was likely to be a potential conflict as to jurisdiction; and

(e)   whether, in a case in which jurisdiction was resisted and disobedience to be expected, the court would be making an order that it could not enforce.[64]

Another important factor that will influence the courts in the exercise of their discretion is the extent to which sanctions can be brought to bear on the defendant in the event of non-compliance with the order. A defendant within the jurisdiction will be amenable to the judicial sanctions for contempt of court, but not a defendant who is outside the jurisdiction and has no future plans to come within it. In such a case, it becomes relevant to consider whether any injunction will be

---

58 *Republic of Haiti v Duvalier* [1990] QB 202.

59 *Derby & Co Ltd v Weldon (No 6)* [1990] 1 WLR 1139.

60 [1997] 3 All ER 725, CA.

61 The decision of the Court of Appeal in *Rosseel NV v Oriental Commercial Shipping (UK) Ltd* [1990] 1 WLR 1387, where such relief was refused in connection with the enforcement of a New York arbitration award, must now be confined to extraterritorial freezing orders, which do not fall within s 25. After 1 April 1997, when the amended s 25 took effect, there can no longer be any such cases.

62 *The Xin Su Hai* [1995] 2 Lloyd's Rep 15.

63 [2003] EWCA Civ 752; [2004] 1 WLR 113.

64 For a recent example of the application of these principles, see *Banco Nacional de Comercio Exterior SNC v Empresa de Telecomunicationes de Cuba SA* [2007] EWCA Civ 662; [2007] 2 Lloyd's Rep 484 CA.

enforceable by the courts of the foreign jurisdiction in which the defendant's assets are located. In *Derby & Co Ltd v Weldon (No 1)*,[65] Kerr LJ suggested that the injunction should not be granted unless the court was satisfied that the foreign courts were bound by international treaty obligations to give effect to any worldwide freezing order. However, Lord Donaldson in *Derby & Co Ltd v Weldon (Nos 3 and 4)* was of the view that the courts should assume that the foreign courts would enforce the order, unless there was evidence to the contrary. The threat of debarring the defendant from defending the action in England should be sufficient sanction to ensure the defendant's compliance with the order. However, whether or not an English judgment that has been given in circumstances in which a defendant was denied the right to defend itself is readily exportable is questionable.

The terms of the order will differ as regards third parties when a worldwide freezing order is granted. The basic format for such an order was set out by the Court of Appeal in *Derby & Co Ltd v Weldon (Nos 3 and 4)*[66] as follows. Third parties outside the jurisdiction will be affected only if, and to the extent that, the order will be enforced by the state in which the defendant has its assets. An exception to this rule applies when three conditions are satisfied. First, the third party must be subject to English jurisdiction. Secondly, it must be given written notice of the order in England. Thirdly, it must be 'able to prevent acts or omissions outside the jurisdiction of this court which assist in the breach of the terms of this order'.

The third of these conditions was considered in *Baltic Shipping Co v Translink Shipping Ltd*,[67] where the order was varied to allow the foreign subsidiary of a third-party bank in England to comply with the defendant's instructions regarding transfer of funds in the foreign jurisdiction. Without the variation, the third-party bank would have been placed in a dilemma. Compliance with the order would expose its foreign subsidiary to an action for breach of contract in that jurisdiction, while non-compliance would expose the bank in England to the sanctions applicable to the contempt of court.

The terms of the order will also differ as regards the imposition of discovery obligations on the defendant relating to its assets outside the jurisdiction. Generally, the order for discovery will extend only so far as is necessary for the purposes of the freezing order application before the court. However, the discovery order may have a wider ambit where a freezing order is sought in connection with the enforcement of a court judgment.[68] With a worldwide freezing order, the claimant must also undertake, if so required by the defendant, not to use such information without its consent or without the leave of the court.[69]

Other interim relief

Security for the defendant's costs

Under CPR Pt 25.12, the defendant may apply to the court for an order that a claimant provides security for the defendant's costs of the action. The order gives the court a discretion to make such an order when, 'having regard to all the circumstances of the case, the court thinks it just to do so'. Under s 38(3) of the **Arbitration Act 1996**, arbitrators are empowered to make an order for security for costs.

Where the claimant is resident in another EC state, the defendant will generally have no right to demand security from it under CPR Pt 25.13(2)(a)(ii).[70]

---

65 [1990] Ch 48.
66 [1990] Ch 65, 84.
67 [1995] 1 Lloyd's Rep 673.
68 *Gidrxslme Shipping Co Ltd v Tantomar-Transportes Maritimos Lda* [1995] 1 WLR 299.
69 See *Dadourian Group International Inc v Simms* [2006] EWCA Civ 399; [2006] 1 WLR 2499 for the principles on seeking such leave.
70 *Fitzgerald v Williams* [1996] 2 All ER 171, CA.

However, the position is somewhat different where the claimant is a company. A claimant that is an English company can be required to provide security for the defendant's costs under s 726 of the **Companies Act 1985**, which applies similar principles to those in CPR Pt 25.12. It follows that there can be no discrimination against a defendant company resident in another EC state if it is required to give security under CPR Pt 25.12, as it will be treated in exactly the same way as a company resident in England.[71] A foreign company that is ordinarily resident in England will be subject to neither provision.

Inspection of property

CPR Pt 61 contains no equivalent to RSC Ord 75(28), under which the Admiralty Court was given specific powers to order inspection. Accordingly, an order for inspection in an Admiralty claim must proceed by way of the general powers of the court contained in CPR Pt 25. An order for inspection of 'relevant property' may be obtained under CPR Pt 25.1(c)(ii). Section 33 of the **Supreme Court Act 1981** provides for when such an order may be made before a claim is made, while s 34 of the Act provides for when an order for inspection may be made against a non-party.[72]

Anti-suit injunctions

In certain circumstances, the English courts have the power to grant orders restraining persons from commencing or continuing proceedings in a foreign forum. The court's jurisdiction to grant such orders is to be found in s 37 of the **Senior Courts Act 1981**, although a narrower jurisdiction also exists in relation to arbitration proceedings under s 44 of the **Arbitration Act 1996**. If the case is one of urgency, s 44(3) entitles the court to make such an order for the purpose of preserving evidence or assets. Section 44(5) also provides that, in any case, the court may make such an order 'if or to the extent that the arbitral tribunal, and any arbitral or other institution or person vested by the parties with power in that regard, has no power or is unable for the time being to act effectively'. In *The Alexandros T*,[73] Cooke J held that both of these conditions were satisfied when it was clear that the arbitrators would be unable to issue a final award before the court in China had issued a final judgment on the cargo claim. This factor, however, was not decisive as regards the court's jurisdiction under s 37 of the **Senior Courts Act 1981**. A defendant who had commenced proceedings in China and who maintained that the arbitration clause in the bill of lading was ineffective could not argue that the court should refuse to exercise its jurisdiction in favour of allowing the arbitrators to exercise their jurisdiction to make such an order under s 44 of the **Arbitration Act 1996**.

Although these injunctions have undeniable extra-territorial effects, they are granted on the basis of the court's in *personam* jurisdiction over the party enjoined. Anti-suit injunctions are, therefore, directed against the defendant and not against the foreign courts. Their grant has no direct effect on the foreign proceedings, but the defendant will be personally liable for contempt of court if it breaches the terms of the order. It has been confirmed that anti-suit injunctions are not unlawful under s 6 of the **Human Rights Act 1998**.[74]

In order for the court to grant an anti-suit injunction, the claimant must first establish the court's jurisdiction under either the common law rules or the **Judgments Regulation**. An anti-suit

---

71 *Chequepoint SARL v McLelland* [1996] 3 WLR 341, CA.
72 As amended by Civil Procedure (Modification of Enactments) Order 1998, SI 1998/2940, which removes the former restriction in the wording of s 34, which limited its operation to claims relating to death or personal injury. The order may be made in relation to property that is the subject matter of the proceedings or as to which any questions may arise in the proceedings.
73 [2007] EWHC 1893 (Comm); [2008] 1 Lloyd's Rep 230.
74 *The Kribi* [2001] 1 Lloyd's Rep 76, QB.

injunction is not, however, a provisional measure for the purposes of Art 31 of the Judgments Regulation or s 25 of the **Civil Jurisdiction and Judgments Act 1982**.

Although it was previously the case that the courts relied upon the same test for applications for anti-suit injunctions as with applications for a stay of proceedings,[75] this area has seen much change over the last two decades. The present state of the law with respect to anti-suit injunctions was clarified by Lord Hobhouse in *Turner v Grovit*.[76] Anti-suit injunctions will generally be granted in two circumstances. First, they will be granted where one party to an action has behaved, or threatens to behave, in a manner that is unconscionable. 'Unconscionability' in this regard will be found upon proof that England is the *forum conveniens*, and that the foreign proceedings are vexatious or oppressive.[77] It would also appear that in order for an application to succeed on this ground, the party seeking the injunction must be a party to litigation that is presently on foot in the English courts.[78] Secondly, an anti-suit injunction will be granted where one party to an action can show that the other party has either invaded, or threatens to invade, a legal or equitable right of the former.[79] Anti-suit injunctions are frequently granted on this ground where foreign proceedings are brought in breach of a jurisdiction or arbitration agreement. In such a situation, the English court will ordinarily exercise its discretion to restrain the prosecution of the foreign proceedings, unless the party suing in the foreign forum can show strong reasons for proceeding there.[80] It is no answer to the grant of an anti-suit injunction that the foreign court does not recognise the jurisdiction or arbitration agreement.[81] An anti-suit injunction will not be granted where the proceedings before the foreign court are commenced for the purposes of obtaining security for the claim.[82] However, if the intention of the cargo owner and the insurer is to use the arrest as a means of forcing a foreign jurisdiction, if at all possible, the court will issue an anti-suit injunction, as well as awarding damages in contract against the cargo owner for wrongful arrest and in tort against the insurer for procuring a breach of contract.[83]

However, under the Brussels regime, the European Court of Justice in *Turner v Grovit*,[84] has held that national courts are precluded from granting anti-suit injunctions that prevent defendants from bringing claims before the courts of other Member States. It then made a similar finding in relation to the practice of granting anti-suit injunctions that prevent parties from bringing proceedings in the courts of another Member State, on the ground that such proceedings were in breach of an arbitration agreement. The case in question was *The Front Comor*.[85] A vessel collided with the jetty of the charterer's Italian oil refinery. The charterparty was subject to English law and contained a clause providing for arbitration in London. The charterer was paid by its insurers, which initiated proceedings in Italy against the shipowner. The shipowners then sought an anti-suit injunction in England on the grounds that the insurers' claim arose out of the charterparty and they were bound by its arbitration clause. On 4 September 2008, Advocate General Kokott gave an opinion to the effect that

---

75 *Castanho v Brown & Root (UK) Ltd* [1981] AC 557; see p 367.
76 [2001] UKHL 65; [2002] 1 WLR 107, HL.
77 *Société Nationale Industrielle Aérospatiale v Lee Kui Jak* [1987] AC 871.
78 *Turner v Grovit* [2002] 1 WLR 107, [27].
79 See, e.g., *Donohue v Armco Inc* [2002] 1 All ER 749.
80 *The Angelic Grace* [1995] 1 Lloyd's Rep 87. In *OT Africa Line Ltd v Magic Sportswear Corp* [2005] EWCA Civ 710; [2005] 2 Lloyd's Rep 170, the Court of Appeal held that the statutory incorporation of the Hamburg Rules into Canadian law was not a sufficiently exceptional circumstance to justify not holding the parties to the exclusive jurisdiction clause in the bill of lading.
81 *The Ivan Zagubanski* [2002] 1 Lloyd's Rep 106 [52] and [54].
82 See, however, *The Kallang* [2006] EWHC 2825 (Comm); [2007] 1 Lloyd's Rep 160, in which cargo claimants arrested the ship in Dakar and insisted on the provision of a bank guarantee that submitted the claim to the jurisdiction of the courts of Senegal. An anti-suit injunction was issued to prevent the defendant pursuing the substantive claim in Senegal.
83 *The Kallang* [2008] EWHC 2761 (Comm); [2009] 1 Lloyds's Rep 124. *The Duden* [2008] EWHC 2762 (Comm); [2009] 1 Lloyd's Rep 145.
84 Case-C-159/02 [2004] IL Pr 411.
85 *West Tankers Inc v Allianz SpA (formerly Riunione Adriatica di Sicurta SpA)* (C-185/07) [2009] 1 AC 1138. The House of Lords referred the matter to the ECJ, [2007] UKHL 4; [2007] 1 Lloyd's Rep 391, but was of the view that such orders are consistent with the Regulation, since arbitration is excluded from its material scope by virtue of Art 1(2)(d).

a court of a Member State could not grant an injunction in such circumstances. The Italian court had jurisdiction under Art 5 (now Art 7) of the Regulation and it was for that court, as the court first seised, to determine preliminary issues relating to the validity of the arbitration agreement. The **New York Convention** did not require such issues to be determined by a court in the state in which arbitration was to be held. Although the Regulation excluded arbitration, this exclusion related to arbitration of the substantive dispute. Disputes as to the validity of an arbitration agreement were not excluded under Art 1 and could be determined by the court first seised of the claim. On 10 February 2009, the European Court of Justice gave its decision in accordance with the reasoning adopted by the Advocate General.[86] There is now a risk that London will lose its popularity as a seat of commercial arbitration in favour of other venues, such as New York. By selecting London as a seat of arbitration, parties to a contract would be foregoing their right to an anti-suit injunction, should their counterparty litigate somewhere in Europe, in breach of contract.

Since the decision of the European Court of Justice the English courts have had to consider the conflict between English arbitration proceedings and proceedings in the courts of a Member State on several occasions. First, in *The Wadi Sudr*[87] the Court of Appeal declined to grant a declaration that there was a binding arbitration agreement, following the decision of a Spanish court that there was no arbitration agreement. The Spanish court had decided that the arbitration clause was not incorporated and its judgment fell within the Brussels Regulation and had to be recognised by the court of another Member State under Art 33(1) (now Art 35(1)) of the Regulation, which provides that: 'A judgment given in a Member State shall be recognised in the other Member States without any special procedure being required.' If the English court was bound to recognise the Spanish judgment, there was no room for a public policy argument against recognition under Art 34(1) (now Art 36(1)), which provides that: 'A judgment shall not be recognised: 1. if such recognition is manifestly contrary to public policy in the Member State in which recognition is sought.' However, had the English court granted a declaration that there was an arbitration clause *before* the Spanish court had ruled, it would not be necessary to invoke public policy because the arbitration could proceed and the English court would be entitled to enforce any award by virtue of the earlier English judgment under Art 34(3) (now Art 36(3)), which provides that a judgment shall not be recognised 'if it is irreconcilable with a judgment given in a dispute between the same parties in the Member State in which recognition is sought'.

This was the situation in the second case, *West Tankers Inc v Allianz SpA*.[88] In 2008, the shipowners obtained a final arbitration award in England declaring that they were under no liability to the insurers in respect of the collision. They then sought to convert the award into a judgment against the insurers under s 66 of the **Arbitration Act 1996**. In doing so they aimed to prevent recognition in England of any subsequent Italian judgment in favour of the insurers on the grounds that Art 34(3) of the **Brussels Regulation** (now Art 36(3)) provides that a judgment will not be recognised in a Member State if it is irreconcilable with a judgment given in a dispute between the same parties in that Member State and that recognition of such a judgment would be manifestly contrary to public policy in England and Wales. Field J held that the shipowners were entitled to convert the declaratory award into a judgment against the insurers. It was enough for the party seeking to enforce the award 'to show that he has a real prospect of establishing the primacy of the award over an inconsistent judgment'. The decision means that where there are conflicting court and arbitral proceedings in Member States the arbitral proceedings may block the enforcement of the judgment of the court of another Member State provided a final award is converted into an English judgment

86 Case C-185/07; [2009] 1 AC 1138.
87 [2009] EWCA Civ 1397; [2010] 1 Lloyd's Rep 193.
88 [2011] EWHC 829 (Comm); (2011) 161 NLJ 551.

before the foreign court gives its judgment. However, this question has yet to be decided by the English courts and Field J expressly declined to rule on it, stating,

> It is not necessary, nor is it appropriate, for the court finally to decide this hypothetical question – hypothetical because the unsuccessful party to the arbitration will not have obtained an inconsistent judgment in a member state at the time the court is dealing with the s 66 application.

The decision has been upheld on appeal[89] and has been followed in *The London Steam-Ship Owners' Mutual Insurance Association Ltd v The Kingdom of Spain, The French State (The Prestige)* in respect of two awards giving declarations of non-liability in relation to legal proceedings brought in Spain and France against the shipowners' P&I Club in respect of non-CLC pollution claims.[90] It has also been held that an arbitral tribunal has jurisdiction to award damages against a party to an arbitration clause who is in breach by commencing proceedings in a foreign court, irrespective of whether the foreign court is first seised.[91]

However, the judgment of the European Court of Justice has not affected the practice of granting anti-suit injunctions in respect of proceedings commenced outside the EC or EFTA. In *Midgulf International Ltd v Groupe Chimiche Tunisien*,[92] the Court of Appeal granted an anti-suit injunction against the continuation of proceedings in Tunisia in breach of an English arbitration clause. In *AES UST-Kamenogorsk Hydropower Plant LLP v UST-Kamenogorsk Hydropower Plant JSC*,[93] Burton J granted an anti-suit injunction to restrain proceedings in Kazakhstan, notwithstanding that no English arbitration had been commenced. The decision was upheld by the Court of Appeal and the Supreme Court,[94] who held that the court's power to order an injunction under s 37 of the **Senior Courts Act 1981** was not cut back by the power given to order an interim injunction in support of an arbitration under s 44 of **The Arbitration Act 1996**, a power exercisable only in support of an arbitration which was already afoot. A stay under s 37 was not made conditional on arbitration being on foot, proposed or brought.

The English court may also grant an anti-arbitration injunction, although this will only be granted in exceptional circumstances.[95] As a minimum, the applicant's legal or equitable rights must have been infringed or threatened by a continuation of the arbitration. Greater caution is required in the case of arbitrations proceeding outside the jurisdiction. An anti-arbitration injunction was granted in *Claxton Engineering Services Ltd v Tam Olaj-Es Gazkutato KTF*[96] where the English court had already determined that the parties had agreed an English exclusive jurisdiction clause. The defendant subsequently commenced arbitration in Hungary and sought an interim award that the parties were bound by an arbitration agreement. Hamblen J granted the anti-arbitration injunction and held that the ECJ's decision in *West Tankers* had no application to arbitration proceedings because arbitration did not fall within the scope of the **Brussels Regulation**.[97]

The recast Regulation, which applies to legal proceedings instituted on or after 10 January 2015, retains the arbitration exception. Recital 12 emphasises the free-standing nature of the process and states that a court's decision that an arbitration clause is void does not preclude its

---

89 [2012] EWCA Civ 27; [2012] 1 Lloyd's Rep 398.
90 [2013] EWHC 3188 (Comm); [2014] 1 Lloyd's Rep 309. The awards which were converted into judgments had been made before judgments had been given in the proceedings in Spain and France.
91 *The Front Comor* [2012] EWHC 854 (Comm); [2012] 2 Lloyd's Rep 103.
92 [2010] EWCA Civ 66; [2010] 1 CLC 113.
93 [2010] EWHC 722 (Comm); [2010] 1 CLC 519.
94 [2011] EWCA Civ 647; [2012] 1 WLR 920; [2013] UKSC 35; [2013] 1 WLR 1889.
95 *Weissfisch v Julius* [2006] EWCA Civ 218; [2006] 1 Lloyd's Rep 716.
96 [2011] EWHC 345; [2011] 1 Lloyd's Rep 510.
97 Article 1(2)(d).

award on the substance being enforced under the Regulation. This reverses the decision in *The Wadi Sudr*.[98] This is without prejudice to the competence of courts to decide on the enforceability of an arbitral award under the New York Convention on the Recognition and Enforcement of Foreign Arbitral Awards (to which all EU Member States are parties). According to Recital 12 and Art 73(2), the New York Convention takes precedence over the Regulation. However, the recast Regulation does not refer to the issue of anti-suit injunctions in support of arbitral proceedings, and the ECJ's decision in *The Front Comor* will continue to prevent such injunctions being granted.

98 [2009] EWCA Civ 1397; [2010] 1 Lloyd's Rep 193.

Chapter 20

Limitation of Liability

Chapter Contents

In addition to the specific package limitation given by the Hague and Hague-Visby Rules in relation to cargo claims,[1] shipowners may also rely on a global limitation figure based on the vessel's tonnage. This tonnage-based figure provides the maximum financial liability of the shipowner in respect of all claims arising out of any one incident. Tonnage limitation can be invoked in one of two ways. The first is by way of defence to an action brought by a particular claimant. The second is by the shipowner initiating limitation proceedings to set up a limitation fund in a particular jurisdiction. The advantage of this procedure is that the establishment of the fund will cap the shipowner's liability to all claimants and not just the particular claimant who has commenced proceedings against the shipowner. By invoking limitation, the shipowner is not admitting liability in respect of the claims brought against it;[2] it is merely claiming that if it is held liable, its maximum total liability in respect of all claims arising out of the incident will not exceed the amount of the applicable limitation figure.

The two most important international conventions relating to limitation have been the **1957 International Convention Relating to the Limitation of the Liability of Owners of Seagoing Ships**, and the **1976 Convention on Limitation of Liability for Maritime Claims (LLMC)**. From 1 December 1986, UK law has applied the 1976 Convention, which was brought into effect by s 17, Sched 4 to the **Merchant Shipping Act 1979**, now s 185 of the **Merchant Shipping Act 1995**. This provides that the 1976 LLMC Convention shall have the force of law in the UK. The Convention's provisions are set out in Sched 7 of the Act. Prior to that date, UK law applied the 1957 Convention, itself based on the structure of the limitation provisions contained in s 503 of the **Merchant Shipping Act 1894**. The principal difference between the two conventions is that the 1976 Convention calculates limitation in a different manner from that adopted by the 1957 Convention and produces higher limitation figures. However, as a quid pro quo for shipowning interests, it has now become almost impossible for a shipowner to lose the right to limit on the basis of its misconduct. The 1957 Convention still applies in a great number of states.

Who can limit?

Article 1 of the 1976 Convention provides that 'shipowners and salvors' may limit[3] and that invoking limitation shall not constitute an admission of liability.[4] 'Shipowner' includes the 'owner, charterer, manager or operator of a seagoing ship'.[5] However, in *The Aegean Sea*,[6] Thomas J held that the reference to 'charterer' in the definition of 'shipowner' did not entitle a charterer to limit in respect of claims brought against it under the charterparty by the shipowner. This was because a single fund was constituted in respect of any particular incident and therefore to allow charterers to limit their liability in respect of such claims would diminish the amount of the fund available to other claimants. The reference to 'charterer' was intended to allow the charterer to limit in respect of claims made against it by holders of charterers' bills of lading. In *The CMA Djakarta*,[7] the Court of Appeal held that Art 1(2) did not require the charterer to have been undertaking activities associated with ownership. In *The MSC Napoli*,[8] Teare J held that slot charterers fell within the definition of 'charterer' in Art 1(2) and were entitled to limit their liability. Although a literal reading of the

1   And by the 1974 Athens Convention in relation to claims by individual passengers.
2   See *Caspian Basin Specialised Emergency Salvage Administration v Bouygues* [1997] 2 Lloyd's Rep 507, where Rix J confirmed that a limitation action can be commenced without a prior admission of liability by the party seeking to limit.
3   Article 1(1).
4   Article 1(7).
5   Article 1(2).
6   [1998] 2 Lloyd's Rep 39.
7   [2004] EWCA Civ 114; [2004] 1 Lloyd's Rep 460, CA.
8   [2008] EWHC 3002 (Admlty); [2009] 1 Lloyd's Rep 246.

phrase 'charterer of a . . . ship' might suggest that the definition did not include the charterer of a part of a ship, a purposive construction of the phrase had to be adopted. In The Tychy,[9] the Court of Appeal had held that a slot charterer was within the phrase 'charterer of . . . the ship' in s 21(4)(b) of the **Senior Courts Act 1981** relating to the arrest of ships.

'Salvor' includes 'any person rendering services in direct connection with salvage operations'.[10] This provision fills the gap in the 1957 Convention that was revealed in The Tojo Maru.[11] There, the salvor was unable to limit in respect of a claim arising out of the negligence of one of its divers, brought against it by the owners of the salved vessel.

The right to limit is extended to 'any persons for whose act, neglect or default the shipowner or salvor is responsible'.[12] The purpose of this provision is to prevent claimants from avoiding the limitation regime by proceeding against the servants or agents of the shipowner or salvor. Limitation is also possible in respect of undefended in rem claims[13] and in respect of direct action claims against insurers.[14]

Which claims are subject to limitation?

Article 2(1) provides the following six headings of claim in respect of which limitation can be claimed:

(a)   claims in respect of loss of life or personal injury or loss or damage to property (including damage to harbour works, basins and waterways and aids to navigation), occurring on board or in direct connection with the operation of the ship or with salvage operations, and consequential loss resulting therefrom;

(b)   claims in respect of loss resulting from delay in the carriage by sea of cargo, passengers or their luggage;

(c)   claims in respect of other loss resulting from infringement of rights other than contractual rights, occurring in direct connection with the operation of the ship or salvage operations;

(d)   claims in respect of the raising, removal, destruction or the rendering harmless of a ship that is sunk, wrecked, stranded or abandoned, including anything that is or has been on board such ship;

(e)   claims in respect of the removal, destruction or the rendering harmless of the cargo of the ship;

(f)   claims of a person other than the person liable in respect of measures taken in order to avert or minimise loss for which the person liable may limit his liability in accordance with this Convention, and further loss caused by such measures.

The ambit of Art 2(1)(a) received clarification in The CMA Djakarta.[15] A container ship was damaged by an explosion that was caused by bleaching powder shipped in containers in breach of the terms of the time charter. The main part of the owners' claim against the charterers was in respect of the cost of repair of the ship and salvage services rendered. The owners also claimed an indemnity in respect of their liability to contribute to general average and their liability to cargo owners. The time charterers established a limitation fund in France. As against the cargo claimants, the charterer had

---

9 [1999] 2 Lloyd's Rep 11, CA.
10 Article 1(3) also includes the operations referred to in Art 2(1)(d)–(f).
11 [1972] AC 242, HL.
12 Article 1(4).
13 Article 1(5) provides that: '. . . the liability of a shipowner shall include liability in an action brought against the vessel herself.' Under English law, once a shipowner defends an in rem action, it proceeds mainly as an action in personam.
14 Article 1(6).
15 [2004] EWCA Civ 114; [2004] 1 Lloyd's Rep 460, CA.

the same right to limit as the shipowner. However, the charterer could not limit in respect of the shipowners' claims for an indemnity in respect of their liability in general average and for salvage costs as these fell outside Art 2(1)(a). This provision did not extend the right to limit to a claim for damage to the vessel by reference to the tonnage of which limitation was to be calculated. A similar finding was made in The Darfur[16] in respect of time charterers' claims against the shipowner for extra insurance, stevedoring and trans-shipment costs that they had incurred following a collision.

The claims listed in Art 2(1) are subject to limitation, even if brought 'by way of recourse or for indemnity under a contract or otherwise'.[17] Thus, in The Kirknes,[18] a tug collided with a tow, which claimed an indemnity against it under the provisions of the towing contract. The tow was able to invoke limitation, as the claim was one for physical damage to the tug and therefore fell within the permitted category of claims, albeit that the mechanism used for making the claim was by way of contractual indemnity. The claims are also subject to limitation if they are brought by way of an action for misrepresentation.[19]

Claims (d) to (f) are not subject to limitation 'to the extent that they relate to remuneration under a contract with the person liable'.[20] Therefore, it remains possible to fix a charge for the service in excess of the relevant limitation figure. The wreck-raising provision, claim (d), will not be brought into effect until a fund is set up to compensate harbour authorities.[21] Under the current law, a statutory claim by a harbour authority is not limitable. It is not a claim by way of damages against the shipowner, but is a claim to recover expenses in debt.[22]

Which claims are not subject to limitation?

Article 3 of the 1976 Convention excludes from limitation the following claims: claims for salvage[23] – that is, claims by salvors and not claims against them;[24] claims for contribution in general average;[25] claims arising under a shipowner's statutory liability for oil pollution damage;[26] and claims in respect of nuclear damage.[27] It also excludes crew claims against the shipowner or salvor if the law governing their contract of service excludes such claims from limitation or provides for a higher limit than that specified under the 1976 Convention.[28] Where the claimant is an employee whose contract of service is governed by UK law, s 185 of the **Merchant Shipping Act 1995** applies this exclusion in relation to his claims for loss of life or personal injury or for loss of or damage to property.

How can the right to limit be lost?

Under the 1957 Convention, the shipowner or salvor would lose the right to limit unless it could prove that the occurrence giving rise to liability took place without 'their actual fault or

---

16 [2004] EWHC 1506; [2004] 2 Lloyd's Rep 469.
17 Article 2(2).
18 [1957] P 51.
19 Caspian Basin Specialised Emergency Salvage Administration v Bouygues [1997] 2 Lloyd's Rep 507.
20 Article 2(2).
21 An owner faced with such a claim may seek to establish a fund in a jurisdiction, such as the Isle of Man, which has not excluded Art 2(1)(d).
22 The Stonedale (No 1) (Owners) v Manchester Ship Canal Co [1955] 2 All ER 689.
23 By Sched VII, Pt II, para 4(1) of the Merchant Shipping Act 1995, this provision is extended to claims under Art 14 of the 1989 Salvage Convention, which are not salvage claims stricto sensu.
24 See, also, The Breydon Merchant [1992] 1 Lloyd's Rep 373, where cargo's claim against shipowners in respect of their share of a salvage award following an engine room fire was held not to fall within the 'salvage' exception.
25 Article 3(a).
26 Article 3(b). These claims are subject to their own limitation regime, which is dealt with in Chapter 17.
27 Article 3(c) and (d).
28 Article 3(e).

privity'.[29] In *The Lady Gwendolen*,[30] a collision occurred due to a vessel being sailed at full speed in thick fog. The radar was switched on, but the master only glanced at it intermittently. The ship-owners' marine superintendent had failed to examine the ship's log, whereby he could have found out about the master's propensity for excessive speed. He had also failed to draw the master's attention to a Ministry of Transport notice urging vessels, even those equipped with radar, to reduce their speed in conditions of poor visibility. The fault of the marine superintendent on its own would not have been sufficient to amount to that of the shipowners, as he was too far down the corporate hierarchy for his acts to be identified with those of the owning company. However, the fault of the marine superintendent had become that of the company because of the failure of its managing director and traffic manager to take any interest in navigational matters. The shipowners therefore lost their right to limit. A similar result was reached in *The Marion*,[31] where a vessel fouled a pipeline following the master's use of an uncorrected chart. The 'fault or privity' of the shipowners was in their failure to establish a system to check on the master's correction of charts.

The 1976 Convention provides a new test and transfers the burden of proof onto the claimant. Article 4 provides that:

> . . . a person liable shall not be entitled to limit his liability if it is proved that the loss resulted from his personal act or omission, committed with the intent to cause such loss, or recklessly and with knowledge that such loss would probably result.

Under this new test, the right to limit would almost certainly not have been lost in either *The Lady Gwendolen* or *The Marion*. In neither case was there either intentional or reckless wrongdoing by any employee with a status sufficient for his acts to be attributed to the owning company. Although the master of *The Lady Gwendolen* acted recklessly, not only would he have been insufficiently senior in the corporate hierarchy for his recklessness to be attributed to the owning company, but Art 4 also requires that there must be 'knowledge that such loss would probably result'. This element, together with the transfer of the burden of proof to the claimant, makes it almost impossible to break limitation under the 1976 Convention. However, in *The Saint Jacques II and The Gudermes*,[32] the unusual step was taken of denying an application for summary judgment in a limitation action on the ground that there was a real possibility that the right to limit might be lost. This was due to the fact that a contributing factor to the collision had been the reckless navigation of the vessel across the Traffic Separation Scheme in flagrant breach of the Collision Regulations, directed personally by the claimants for their own commercial reasons.

The right to limit may also be lost by an express contractual provision to that effect. In *The Satanita*,[33] a yacht was entered into the Mudhook Yacht Regatta. The rules of the club required each entrant to give an undertaking to the secretary to pay 'all damages' caused by fouling. The terms of the undertaking were construed as excluding the right to limit. However, similar words in *The Kirknes*,[34] where a clause in the contract made the hirer liable for 'all loss or damage', failed to achieve such a result. *The Satanita* was distinguished on the grounds that, in context, the wording used there could only refer to the quantum of any claim against the shipowner. The wording in *The Kirknes*, in contrast, followed a long passage enumerating a number of types of loss or damage. 'All', therefore, could refer to kinds of loss or damage, rather than quantum.[35]

---

29 The burden of proof lies with the defendant.
30 [1965] P 294.
31 [1984] AC 563.
32 [2003] 1 Lloyd's Rep 203, QB.
33 [1897] AC 59.
34 [1957] P 51.
35 A similar construction was reached in *Mason v Uxbridge Boat Centre and Wright* [1980] 2 Lloyd's Rep 592.

How is the limitation figure calculated?

Under the 1957 Convention, the relevant tonnage, based on net registered tonnage plus engine room space, is multiplied by 206.67 SDRs (Special Drawing Rights) to give the limitation figure claims arising out of death and personal injury, and by 66.67 SDRs to give the limitation figure for property damage claims.[36]

Under the 1976 Convention, the relevant tonnage is gross tonnage as measured under the 1969 Tonnage Convention. Under Art 6, a more complex calculation is required to find the limitation funds.

The limitation figures in the 1976 Convention are to be found in Art 6 (general limitation) and Art 7 (limitation for claims by passengers). The 1996 Protocol to the 1976 Limitation Convention substantially increased the limitation figures and entered into force on 13 May 2004.[37] In the UK, the Merchant Shipping (Convention on Limitation of Liability for Maritime Claims) (Amendment) Order 1998 implemented the 1996 Protocols by amending the relevant provisions of the Merchant Shipping Act 1995.

Article 6

Article 6 provides for the establishment of two funds, one for claims arising out of death and injury and one for all other claims. These will be referred to as 'Fund A' and 'Fund B' respectively. The two funds govern the aggregate of all claims arising out of 'any distinct occasion'. The Federal Court of Australia has recently considered this wording in *The APL Sydney*.[38] A pipeline was fouled by a container vessel and was then further destroyed by the vessel's subsequent movements. The shipowners began proceedings in Australia under the 1976 Convention as amended by the 1996 Protocol. The issue arose as to how many 'occasions' there had been, which would determine whether the shipowner would have to establish additional limitation funds. This depended upon whether the causes of the claims that arise from each act, neglect or default were sufficiently discrete that, as a matter of common sense, they could be said to be distinct from one another. The claims here had arisen on two distinct occasions – the anchor fouling the pipeline, and the rupture of the pipeline about 35 minutes later – so that two limitation funds would have to be established by the shipowner.

Where the shipowner brings a counterclaim, the balance of the claim after deduction of the counterclaim is subject to limitation. If the amount of claims exceeds the fund, all claimants share *pro rata* in the fund. If claims for death and personal injury exceed the amount available under Fund A, the unsatisfied balance may be claimed against Fund B, although these claimants obtain no priority over the ordinary Fund B claimants.

Salvors not operating from their own ship are given a deemed limit of 1,500 tons; otherwise, the actual tonnage of the salving vessel is taken. Where limitation is claimed in relation to an incident arising out of a vessel under tow, the relevant tonnage for limitation purposes is that of the vessel liable for the damage. Where the tow is completely innocent, the relevant tonnage is that of the tug, whether or not the tug and tow are in the same or in different ownerships.[39] Where tug and tow are both at fault, the relevant figure will be that of the tow, even if tug and tow are in the same ownership.[40]

---

36 This sum was substituted for the Gold franc in 1984. However, a number of 1957 Convention States still use the Gold franc.
37 There are currently 47 Contracting States, including Australia, Belgium, Canada, Croatia, Denmark, Finland, France, Germany, Hungary, India, Japan, Liberia, Malaysia, Malta, Netherlands, Norway, Sierra Leone, Spain, Sweden and Tonga.
38 [2010] FCA 240, Federal Court of Australia, Rares J, 18 March 2010.
39 *The Bramley Moore* [1964] P 200. As regards third-party claims, any indemnity provisions in the towage contract are irrelevant.
40 *The Smjeli* [1982] 2 Lloyd's Rep 74.

The 1996 Protocol amended Art 3 of the **1976 Limitation Convention** so as to exclude the right to limit in respect of any claim for 'special compensation' under Art 14 of the **1989 Salvage Convention**, and Art 18 of the **1976 Limitation Convention** so as to allow a State Party to exclude from the ambit of the 1996 Protocol any claims covered by the **1996 HNS Convention**.[41]

The 1996 Protocol permits any State Party to make its own provisions for vessels intended for navigation on inland waterways, for ships less than 300 tons. In the UK this has been effected through the **Merchant Shipping (Convention on Limitation of Liability for Maritime Claims) (Amendment) Order 1998**, which applies the 1996 Protocol to any ship, whether sea-going or not, and provides that the Art 6 limits for ships of less than 300 tons will be 1 miillion SDRs under Fund A and 500,000 SDRs under Fund B.

The limitation figures under the 1996 Protocol are as follows:[42]

Fund A – claims arising out of death and personal injury

Tonnage not exceeding 2,000 tons: flat rate figure of 2 million SDRs.[43]
Tonnage in excess of 2,001 tons: 2 million SDRs plus additional amounts on the following sliding scale:

2,001–30,000 tons:	an extra 800 SDRs per ton
30,001–70,000 tons:	an extra 600 SDRs per ton
70,001 tons and above:	an extra 400 SDRs per ton

Fund B – all other claims

Tonnage not exceeding 2,000 tons: flat rate figure of 1 million SDRs.
Tonnage in excess of 2,001 tons: 1 million SDRs plus additional amounts on the following sliding scale:

2,001–30,000 tons:	an extra 400 SDRs per ton
30,001–70,000 tons:	an extra 300 SDRs per ton
70,001 tons and above:	an extra 200 SDRs per ton

The 1996 Protocol has been amended to increase the limits under Art 6 and is scheduled to enter into force on 8 June 2015. The new limits are:

Fund A – claims arising out of death and personal injury

Tonnage not exceeding 2,000 gross tonnage: flat rate figure 3.02 million SDRs,
Tonnage exceeding 2,001 gross tonnage: 3.02 million SDRs plus additional amounts on the following sliding scale:

- For each ton from 2,001 to 30,000 tons, 1,208 SDRs.
- For each ton from 30,001 to 70,000 tons, 906 SDRs.
- For each ton in excess of 70,000 tons, 604 SDRs.

Fund B – all other claims

Tonnage not exceeding 2,000 gross tonnage: flat rate figure 1.51 million SDRs.
Tonnage exceeding 2,001 gross tonnage: flat rate figure 1.51 million SDRs plus additional amounts on the following sliding scale:

---

41 But see fn 23 above.
42 States which are parties to the 1976 Limitation Convention but not parties to the 1996 Protocol continue to use the lower limitation figures in the original Convention.
43 It is unclear whether the 1,500 tons deemed tonnage accorded to salvors by Art 6(4) of the 1976 Limitation Convention continues under the 1996 Protocol.

- For each ton from 2,001 to 30,000 tons, 604 SDRs
- For each ton from 30,001 to 70,000 tons, 453 SDRs
- For each ton in excess of 70,000 tons, 302 SDRs.

Article 7

Article 7 provides for calculation of the limitation fund for loss of life or personal injury to passengers of a ship. The global limits for passenger claims under Art 7 are to be calculated by multiplying 175,000 SDRs by the number of passengers that the ship is authorised to carry. The 1996 Protocol permits any State Party to make its own provisions for passenger claims (provided the figures are not lower than the 1996 Protocol figures). In the UK, this has been effected through the **Merchant Shipping (Convention on Limitation of Liability for Maritime Claims) (Amendment) Order 1998**. This disapplies Art 7 in relation to passenger claims on sea-going ships. These claims will be subject to limitation under the **1974 Athens Convention relating to the Carriage of Passengers and their Luggage by Sea** and, as from 28 May 2014, the **2002 Athens Convention**.[44] For passenger claims on non-sea-going ships, an amended Art 7 applies whereby the limitation figure is 175,000 SDRs per passenger, with no global limitation.

The **Merchant Shipping (Convention on Limitation of Liability for Maritime Claims) (Amendment) Order 2004** removed para 2A from Part II set out in Schedule 7 to the **Merchant Shipping Act 1995**, so as to avoid the possibility that the owner of a non-passenger-carrying vessel would lose the right to limit for personal injury or death claims in the event of a collision with a passenger vessel subject to the 1974 Athens Convention.

Establishing the Fund

Article 11(1) provides that: 'Any person alleged to be liable may constitute a fund with the Court or other competent authority in any State Party in which legal proceedings are instituted in respect of claims subject to limitation.' The words 'legal proceedings' have been held to include a reference to arbitration.[45] Article 11.2 provides: 'a fund may be constituted, either by depositing the sum, or by producing a guarantee acceptable under the legislation of the State Party where the fund is constituted and considered to be adequate by the Court or other competent authority.' A problem arose under English law in that CPR Part 61 and PD61 only expressly contemplate the provision of a limitation fund by means of a payment into court. The position was considered in *The Atlantik Confidence*.[46] The Court of Appeal held that as a matter of law, a limitation fund could be constituted by the production of a guarantee acceptable to the court as an alternative to a payment into court. There was no additional requirement that there should be specific legislation expressly defining what is 'acceptable' for the purposes of the **Merchant Shipping 1995 Act**, which incorporated the Convention into UK law. There was nothing in either the rules or the Practice Direction which precluded the constitution of a limitation fund by means of the production of a guarantee. Although CPR 61.11 (18) provided 'The claimant may constitute a limitation fund by making a payment into court . . .', the use of the word 'may' did not exclude the guarantee method. Article 14 provides that

---

44 The maximum limitation under the 1974 Convention is 46,666 SDRs per passenger on each distinct occasion. For carriers whose ordinary place of business is in the UK, a higher limit of 300,000 SDRs has been applied from 1 January 1999 under SI 1998/2917 Carriage of Passengers and their Luggage by Sea (United Kingdom Carriers) Order 1998. Under the 2002 Convention the limit is 400,000 SDRs per passenger on each distinct occasion. As from 31 December 2012, EU Regulation 392/2009 has applied the 2002 Convention to incidents within the EU.
45 *The ICL Vikraman* [2003] EWHC 2320 (Comm); [2004] 1 Lloyd's Rep 21.
46 [2014] EWCA Civ 217; [2014] 1 Lloyd's Rep 586.

the constitution and distribution of the fund, together with any rules of procedure, are to be governed by the law of the State Party in which the fund is constituted.[47]

The constitution of a limitation fund in accordance with Art 11 has two important consequences on the subsequent proceedings. First, Art 13(1) provides that 'any person having made a claim against the fund shall be barred from exercising any right in respect of such a claim against any other assets' of the person constituting the fund. Secondly, Art 13(2) provides that any arrested property of the defendant within the jurisdiction of a State Party may be released by court order of 'such state'. Release, however, is mandatory where the fund has been constituted: (a) at the port where the occurrence took place, or if it took place out of port, at the first port of call thereafter; or (b) at the port of disembarkation in respect of claims for loss of life or personal injury; or (c) at the port of discharge in respect of damage to cargo; or (d) in the State where the arrest is made. However, in The ICL Vikraman,[48] Colman J held that Art 13(2) applies only as regards arrested property located in a State Party. A limitation fund had been established in England and the shipowner's P&I Club had given security in Singapore, following an arrest, for an amount exceeding that to which the claimants would be entitled under the 1976 Convention. Colman J held that Art 13(2) did not provide the basis for ordering the cargo claimants not to make a claim under the security in Singapore. Article 13(3) provides that the rules of paras 1 and 2 apply only 'if the claimant may bring a claim against the limitation fund before the court administering that fund and the fund is actually available and freely transferable in respect of that claim'.[49]

Article 9 provides for the limits of liability under Arts 6 and 7 to apply to the aggregation of claims that may arise on any distinct occasion. Article 12 provides for the fund to be distributed among the claimants in proportion to their established claims against the fund, subject to Art 6(1)–(3) and Art 7. A fund established by one of the persons mentioned in para 1(a), (b) or (c) or para 2 of Art 9 or his insurer shall be deemed constituted by all persons mentioned in para 1(a), (b) or (c) or para 2, respectively.[50] These are: the person or persons mentioned in Art 1(2) and any person for whose act, neglect or default he or they are responsible; the shipowner of a ship rendering salvage services from that ship and the salvor or salvors operating from such ship and any person for whose act, neglect or default he or they are responsible; the salvor or salvors who are not operating from a ship or who are operating solely on the ship to, or in respect of which, the salvage services are rendered and any person for whose act, neglect or default he or they are responsible.[51] Article 12(2) gives a right of subrogation to the person liable or their insurer where before the fund is distributed they have settled a claim against the fund. They will acquire by subrogation the rights which the person so compensated would have enjoyed under the Convention, up to the amount they have paid.

Jurisdiction

The Convention has no jurisdictional provisions governing the commencement of proceedings, either by the claimant or by the defendant, for a declaration that it is entitled to limit. This issue will be governed by other conventions (for example, the **1952 Arrest Convention** or the **1952 Collision**

---

47 This is 'Subject to the Rules of this Chapter', which includes Art 11.2.
48 [2003] EWHC 2320 (Comm); [2004] 1 Lloyd's Rep 21.
49 In The ICL Vikraman, ibid, Colman J expressed the view, obiter, that a limitation fund established in England would be 'actually available' to a given claimant notwithstanding there being no limitation decree at the material time. The availability of that fund would continue unless and until a claimant discharged the burden of proving that the shipowner was not entitled to the decree.
50 Article 11(3).
51 As regards the limits of liability under Art 7, Art 9(2) provides for aggregation of '[a]ll claims subject thereto which may arise on any distinct occasion against the person or persons mentioned in paragraph 2 of Article 1 in respect of the ship referred to in Article 7 and any person for whose act, neglect or default he or they are responsible'.

Jurisdiction Convention). Article 7 of the Brussels Regulation[52] allows a defendant to commence limitation proceedings in the State in which it is domiciled, provided that State is a party to the Convention. This right is not dependent on the claimant having first commenced proceedings in that State. Limitation actions in the English courts are assigned to the Admiralty Court[53] and proceed by way of a claim in *personam*.

Article 10(1) of the **1976 Limitation Convention** provides that 'Limitation of liability may be invoked notwithstanding that a limitation fund as mentioned in Article 11 has not been constituted.' In *The Western Regent*, the Court of Appeal held that the right to proceed in this way is not dependent on limitation proceedings being commenced in a jurisdiction in which a limitation fund may be constituted under Art 11(1).[54] Article 10(3) provides that questions of procedure are to be decided under the law of the forum. Under English law a limitation action could be brought and served on a person within the jurisdiction, with no requirement that there should also be either the constitution of a limitation fund or the ability to constitute a fund.[55] A liable party may, therefore, exercise a pre-emptive strike by commencing limitation proceedings in the English courts even though the substantive claimant (the defendant in the limitation proceedings) has not commenced proceedings in England.[56]

Compulsory insurance

The **Merchant Shipping (Compulsory Insurance of Shipowners for Maritime Claims) Regulations 2012 SI 2012/2267**[57] came into force on 5 October 2012.[58] The Regulations provide that ships may not leave or enter UK ports unless the shipowner has insurance which must cover at least maritime claims subject to limitation under the 1996 Protocol to the 1976 Convention.

Where the Hague-Visby Rules are incorporated into the contract for the carriage of goods, and that contract imposes liability for loss resulting from delay in the carriage by sea of cargo, the insurance must cover maritime claims in respect of loss resulting from delay in the carriage by sea of cargo. The insurance must cover maritime claims in respect of loss resulting from delay in the carriage by sea of passengers or their luggage, but only where the delay is consequent upon: (a) an incident involving a collision, stranding, explosion, fire or other cause affecting the physical condition of the ship so as to render it incapable of safe navigation to the intended destination of the passengers and their luggage; or (b) any other incident involving a threat to the life, health or safety of passengers.

The Regulations apply to sea-going ships of 300 gross tonnes or more but do not apply to warships, auxiliary warships or other State-owned or -operated ships used for a non-commercial public service.

---

52 Article 9 of the Recast Regulation.
53 The relevant procedure is to be found in CPR Pt 61.11.
54 [2005] EWCA Civ 985; [2005] 2 Lloyd's Rep 359.
55 The Supreme Court Act 1981 s 20 and the Civil Procedure Rules 1998 Part 61 r61.11. Where a limitation fund has been constituted in England pursuant to Art 11(1) the limitation proceedings may be served out of the jurisdiction pursuant to CPR 61 r11(5)(c), which provides for this to be done where 'The Admiralty Court has jurisdiction over the claim under any applicable convention.' In *The ICL Vikraman*, Colman J held that 'any claim' referred to the claim to limit and 'any applicable convention' to the 1976 Convention.
56 However, it is still undecided whether such a party would also have the right to constitute a fund in England where the substantive claimant had not commenced proceedings there. In *The Western Regent*, there was only one claimant and the liable party was seeking a decree that it was entitled to limit and was not seeking to establish a limitation fund.
57 Implementing Directive 2009/20/EC of the European Parliament and of the Council of 23 April 2009 on the insurance of shipowners for maritime claims.
58 Except for regulation 3(3)(b), which comes into force on the date of commencement of Part 9A and Schedule 11ZA(1) of the Merchant Shipping Act 1995 which were inserted by the Wreck Removal Convention Act 2011 (cl 8).

Other limitation regimes

Under s 191 of the **Merchant Shipping Act 1995** – formerly, in part, ss 2 and 3 of the **Merchant Shipping (Liability of Shipowners and Others) Act 1900** – owners of docks or canals, or harbour or conservancy authorities, are entitled to limit in respect of damage caused to vessels or their contents. Ship repairers, but not their employees, are within these provisions, provided that the negligence occurred when the vessel was in the dock, even if the damage only took place some time afterwards.[59] The limit is fixed by taking the tonnage of the largest registered British ship that, at the time that the loss or damage took place, is, or has been within the last five years, within the area over which the dock owner or authority has performed any duty or exercised any power. The limitation figure is then produced in the ordinary way for claims under Fund B of the 1976 Convention. The right to limit will be lost in accordance with the provisions of Art 4 of the 1976 Convention.

Pilotage authorities have their own, very low, limitation regime under s 22 of the **Pilotage Act 1987**.[60] There are also separate limitation regimes established in respect of statutory liability for oil pollution and for damage caused by hazardous and noxious substances. These were discussed in more detail in Chapter 17.

---

59 *Mason v Uxbridge Boat Centre and Wright* [1980] 2 Lloyd's Rep 592.
60 £1000 for each authorised pilot employed by it at the date the loss or damage occurred. The limitation figure for claims against a pilot is £1000 and the amount of pilotage charges in respect of the voyage during which the liability arose.

Index

bills of lading 193–5
causation 192
employment v navigational matters
191–2
other charter provisions 192–3
inter-club agreements 197–8
interest conferred by 190
load ports, shipowners' obligations
cancellation clause 209–10
reasonable dispatch 208
vessel's position/expected readiness,
statements 208–9
permitted ports 202–8
breach of warranty 206–8
express warranty of safety 203
implied warranty of safety 203–4
nature of warranty 205–6
nomination, charterer's rights 202–3
unsafety defined 204–5
time charters see time charters
types of cargo 202
voyage charters see voyage charters/
charterparties
CLC (marine pollution convention)
compulsory insurance 329
contamination damage 325
defences 327
geographical ambit 326
imminent threat 326
jurisdiction 329–30
legislative background 324
liability
channelling of 327–8
limitation 328–9
recovery/reinstatement 326
strict liability 324–6
time limits 329
CMR see road carriage
collisions
agony of the moment 274
basic issues 270
causation 274–5
damages 277–9
jurisdiction 280
liability, apportionment 276–7
lost opportunity rule 275
pilots 271–2
standard of care 272–4
statutory liability 279
time bar 279280

tugs and tows 271
vicarious liability 270–2
combined transport
bills of lading 12
competing conventions 169–70
document of title issues 167–9
key issues 165
as multimodal transport 167
network/uniform solutions 170–2
statute issues 168–9
unimodal see unimodal sea carriage
compulsory insurance 422
conservancy authorities, limitation of liability
423
consignment note see under road
carriage
constructive possession, document transferring
6–7
containers
carriage contracts 13–14
due diligence 123–4
Hague Rules 124–5
Hague-Visby Rules 123–4, 125–6
package limitation 124–6
stowage within 124
contracts
carriage see carriage contracts
choice of law
applicable law 391
pre-1 April 1991 391
1 April–16 December 2009 392
Rome I Regulation 392–4
express see express contracts on loading
frustration see frustration
Hamburg Rules 132–3
High Court claims 359
implied contracts see implied contracts on
loading
international sales 4–5
liabilities, transfers see under statutory
transfers
road carriage see under road carriage
contractual salvage 285

D
damages
assessment 16
basic principles 255
cargo claims see under cargo claims
charterparties 260–3